Harvard Studies in East Asian Law

Harvard Studies in East Asian Law, 2

# The Criminal Process in the
# People's Republic of China,
# 1949–1963: An Introduction

The Harvard Law School, in cooperation with Harvard's East Asian Research Center, the Harvard-Yenching Institute, and scholars from other institutions, has initiated a program of training and research designed to further scholarly understanding of the legal systems of China, Japan, Korea, and adjacent areas. Accordingly, Harvard University Press has established a new series to include scholarly works on these subjects. The editorial committee consists of Jerome Alan Cohen (chairman), John K. Fairbank, L. S. Yang, and Donald Shively.

# THE CRIMINAL PROCESS IN THE PEOPLE'S REPUBLIC OF CHINA 1949–1963

## An Introduction

By Jerome Alan Cohen

Harvard University Press · Cambridge, Massachusetts · 1968

TO MY WIFE, JOAN LEBOLD COHEN

# Preface

The revolutionary triumph of communism in China in 1949 made the world's most populous country the subject of a gigantic political, social, and economic experiment. China also has been the subject of a significant legal experiment. Is the People's Republic of China an example of "'lawless unlimited power' expressing itself solely in unpredictable and patternless interventions" [1] in the lives of its people? Has the People's Republic sought to attain Marx's vision of the ultimate withering away of the state and of the law? Has Mao Tse-tung preferred Soviet practice to Marxist preaching? If so, which Soviet model has he chosen to follow — that of Stalin or that of Stalin's heirs? To what extent has it been possible to transplant a foreign legal system into the world's oldest surviving legal tradition? Should today's Chinese legal system be viewed as a unique amalgam of Communist politics and Chinese culture? To what extent has the system demonstrated a capacity for change since 1949? What has been the direction of that change, and what are the prospects for the future?

Western legal scholars are merely beginning to wrestle with such large questions, and at this stage one can only suggest hypotheses and raise problems for future research. This volume represents the fruits of a preliminary inquiry into one aspect of contemporary Chinese law — the criminal process. The emphasis is on the process itself, but a good deal of attention is necessarily devoted to substantive criminal law as well as to the modes of its application.

The volume consists of three parts. The first is an introductory essay that provides an overview of the evolution and operation of the criminal process from 1949 through 1963. The second part, which constitutes the bulk of the book, systematically presents primary source materials that permit more detailed consideration of problems raised in the introduction. These materials include relevant excerpts from legal documents such as the Constitution, statutes, and other rules and regulations of the People's Republic; from official policy statements; from a treatise on criminal law that has been prepared to assist Chinese judicial officials; and from articles in Chinese law reviews, academic and popular journals, and national and local newspapers. In order to shed light on the law in action as well as the law on the books, I have also included many selections from the written and oral accounts of persons who have lived in or visited the People's Republic. Finally, to suggest the historical and comparative perspective essential for further understanding, I have reprinted at the beginning of Part II a brilliant but little-known essay by Professor Benjamin I. Schwartz, and in various places have reprinted other historical and comparative materials. It is my hope that Part II, from which I have taught my classes at Harvard Law School for the past

1. Lon Fuller, *The Morality of Law* (New Haven, 1964), pp. 157–158.

three years, may be useful for purposes of instruction at the many other law schools and universities that have become interested in Communist law in general and Chinese law in particular. It may also constitute a helpful sourcebook for scholars of Chinese affairs and for comparatists in several academic disciplines.

Because existing English translations of Chinese legal materials have been not only limited in quantity but also inadequate in quality,[2] considerable effort has been made in this volume to provide translations that are accurate and yet not unduly clumsy. This has not been a simple job. Franz Schurmann has pointed out that the categories and language of Chinese Communist ideology are precise and carefully used by those who purvey the ideology.[3] Unfortunately, Chinese Communist legal terminology has not attained the same degree of precision, and it is not unusual, especially in local newspapers, for legal terms to be employed loosely or opaquely. Moreover, given the outside observer's limited access to the contemporary Chinese legal system, it would hardly be surprising if he failed to grasp the meaning assigned to certain legal terms, including those that have been invoked by previous regimes but that now have new meanings.

The principal contribution of Part III is an English-Chinese glossary of the major legal and institutional terms translated in Part II. This glossary does not in any sense purport to be a dictionary. It merely indicates the English terms that have been found to suit the meanings of the Chinese terms in the particular contexts in which they appear. Although the English equivalents given are certainly not the only ones that could have been devised, they are, it is hoped, adequate to the extremely difficult task of finding linguistic analogies between the terms used by systems as different as the Anglo-American and the Chinese Communist. To the extent permitted by the Chinese text, these equivalents have been consistently employed throughout. Thus, for example, each time the Chinese term *tiao-chieh wei-yuan-hui* appears, it has been rendered as "mediation committee" rather than as "conciliation committee," "reconcilement commission," or "arbitration council"; on the other hand, the term *shen-p'an* appears sometimes as "adjudication" and at other times as "trial," depending upon the particular context. Part III also contains a bibliography of the sources drawn upon in Parts I and II and a modest number of English language books and articles that are pertinent to an understanding of the criminal process in mainland China.

The extracts in Part II appear without their original footnotes except where I have considered the footnotes to be of particular importance. I have presented the English translations of other students only where the original Chinese text has not been available to me. The titles or positions by which the authors of extracts are sometimes identified are those they held at the time the given extract was published. The Chinese characters in the glossary were inscribed by Mr. Wang Yeh-chien, and the glossary was typed by Mrs. Bertha Ezell.

I am greatly indebted to David Finkelstein for his talented and unflagging assistance in translation. He spent over a year patiently checking, improving, and

---

2. See Jerome Alan Cohen, review of A. P. Blaustein, ed., *Fundamental Legal Documents of Communist China*, in *Yale Law Journal*, 72: 838–843 (March 1963).

3. Franz Schurmann, *Ideology and Organization in Communist China* (Berkeley, Los Angeles, and London, 1966), pp. 59–62.

making uniform the translations in my unpublished classroom edition. Unless otherwise noted, all translations have been done by me and Mr. Finkelstein. In preparing the unpublished classroom edition I was assisted at different times by Gene T. Hsiao, Peter Wang, and Miss Fu-mei Chang. During the past year Mr. Finkelstein and I profited greatly from discussions of difficult terms with many scholars and especially with our research colleagues Yung-fang Chiang and Wejen Chang. My colleagues on the law faculty, especially Harold J. Berman, John T. Dawson, Alan M. Dershowitz, Andrew L. Kaufman, Arthur T. von Mehren, and Lloyd L. Weinreb, have made many helpful suggestions, as have fellow members of Harvard's East Asian Research Center, particularly Ezra Vogel and Edward Chan. The comments of Tao-tai Hsia, Jerome H. Skolnick, and Derk Bodde improved Part I of this volume, and valuable suggestions by Stanley Lubman and Richard Pfeffer are reflected in the organization of Part II. I also owe a general intellectual debt to Joseph R. Levenson and Franz Schurmann, who initiated me into the mysteries of Chinese studies.

I should like to thank Mrs. Julie Perkins, Russell Munk, and Frank Snyder for their capable editorial efforts and for preparation of the Bibliography. I am also grateful to Mrs. Perkins for compiling the index and to Mrs. Sally Littleton and Miss Ellen Tolstuk for skillfully typing the manuscript and handling a variety of related administrative matters.

The Introduction is a slightly modified version of my article in the *Harvard Law Review,* 79.3:469–533 (January 1966). I am grateful to the American Consulate General Press Monitoring Unit, the American Council of Learned Societies, American Philosophical Society, Derk Bodde, Congress for Cultural Freedom, Victor Gollancz, Ltd., L. C. B. Gower, Harvard Law Review Association, William Heinemann Ltd., International Association of Democratic Lawyers' Review, International Commission of Jurists, Joint Committee on Slavic Studies, Librairie Encyclopédique of Brussels, The London School of Economics, Marzani and Munsel, The M.I.T. Press, *New York Times,* Pall Mall Press, Ltd., Frederick A. Praeger, Inc., the President and Fellows of Harvard College, Random House, Allyn and Adele Rickett, Routledge & Kegan Paul, Ltd., Shindoku Shyosha, Peter S. H. Tang, Thames and Hudson, United Press International, and the United States Information Agency, for permission to quote various materials in Parts I and II. Although, for reasons peculiar to the exigencies of conducting research on contemporary China, I cannot thank by name those who gave me the oral accounts reproduced in Part II, I nevertheless owe them a great debt.

Finally, I want to thank the Ford Foundation, the Rockefeller Foundation, the University of California (Berkeley), and Harvard University for supporting the research upon which the volume is based.

Jerome Alan Cohen

Cambridge, Massachusetts
September 20, 1966

# Contents

# ABBREVIATIONS

| | |
|---|---|
| Arrest Act | Arrest and Detention Act of the People's Republic of China |
| "At the Request" | "At the Request of the Reform Through Labor Department of the Public Security Bureau, the Tientsin City High Court Granted Conditional Release or Reduction of Sentence to Criminals Who Demonstrated Their Repentance and Reform," *Hsin wan pao* (New evening news, Tientsin), Aug. 5, 1956 |
| *CB* | *Current Background* (translations by the American Consulate General, Hong Kong) |
| CC | Comrades' court(s) |
| *CDSP* | *Current Digest of the Soviet Press* |
| CCP | Chinese Communist Party |
| CCPCC | Chinese Communist Party Central Committee |
| *CFYC* | *Cheng-fa yen-chiu* (Political-legal research) |
| Const. | Constitution of the People's Republic of China |
| Court Law | Law of the People's Republic of China for the Organization of People's Courts |
| CPPCC | Chinese People's Political Consultative Conference |
| CYL | Communist Youth League |
| Decision Relating to Counterrevolutionaries | Decision of the Standing Committee of the National People's Congress of the People's Republic of China Relating to Control of Counterrevolutionaries in All Cases Being Decided upon by Judgment of a People's Court |
| "Explanation" | Lo Jui-ch'ing, "Explanation of the Draft Security Administration Punishment Act of the People's Republic of China" |
| *FKHP* | *Chung-hua jen-min kung-ho-kuo fa-kuei hui-pien* (Collection of laws and regulations of the People's Republic of China), 13 vols. |
| *FLHP* | *Chung-hua jen-min kung-ho-kuo fa-ling hui-pien* (Collection of laws and decrees of the People's Republic of China), 7 vols. |
| "High People's Court" | "High People's Court of the Province Grants Early Release to a Number of Women Offenders," *Shan-hsi jih-pao* (Shensi daily), Sept. 11, 1956 |
| *JMJP* | *Jen-min jih-pao* (People's daily) |
| *JPRS* | *Joint Publications Research Service* (translations) |
| KMT | *Kuo-min-tang* (Kuomintang or Nationalist Party) |
| Labor Act | Act of the People's Republic of China for Reform Through Labor |
| *Lectures* | Teaching and Research Office for Criminal Law of the Central Political-Legal Cadres' School, ed., *Chung-hua jen-min kung-ho-kuo hsing-fa tsung-tse chiang-yi* (Lectures on the general principles of criminal law of the People's Republic of China) |
| NPC | National People's Congress of the People's Republic of China |

| | |
|---|---|
| OAM | Office of the Antirightist Movement |
| OLA | Office of Legal Advisers |
| *People's Daily* | *Jen-min jih-pao* |
| PLA | People's Liberation Army |
| PLPG | Political-legal Party group |
| *Political-Legal Research* | *Cheng-fa yen-chiu* |
| PRC | People's Republic of China |
| Procuracy Law | Law of the People's Republic of China for the Organization of People's Procuracies |
| PSB | Public security bureau |
| Public Security Station Act | Act of the People's Republic of China for the Organization of Public Security Stations |
| Release Measures | Provisional Measures of the People's Republic of China for Dealing with the Release of Reform Through Labor Criminals at the Expiration of Their Term of Imprisonment and for Placing Them and Getting Them Employment |
| RSFSR | Russian Soviet Federated Socialist Republic |
| SAPA | Security Administration Punishment Act |
| *SCMP* | *Survey of the China Mainland Press* (Translations by the American Consulate General Press Monitoring Unit, Hong Kong) |
| SDC | Security Defense Committee |
| "Several Problems" | Chang Tzu-p'ei, "Several Problems Relating to the Use of Evidence To Determine the Facts of a Case in Criminal Litigation," *Cheng-fa yen-chiu* (Political-legal research), 4:11–18 (1962) |

PART I  INTRODUCTION

# Introduction

Lead the people by regulations, keep them in order by punishments (*hsing*), and they will flee from you and lose all self-respect. But lead them by virtue and keep them in order by established morality (*li*), and they will keep their self-respect and come to you.

Confucius, *Analects*[1]

During the last one hundred years, the existence of the concessions and the foreign garrison areas, together with the feudal partitioning of the country, were the chief causes for the development of a disdain for government by law, and a negligence in its observance in China. Concessions and garrisoned areas could not be reached by Chinese law, and the people there, who were beyond the reach of the laws of their own country, generally became licentious and violated the laws and discipline of the state in words or action. After a long period, they formed the negative habit of irresponsibility and the positive habit of law-breaking. These habits spread to the people as a whole, who not only failed to realize that these habits were wrong, but actually considered them to be right. The feudal partitioning of the country further destroyed the idea of government by law and the custom of law observance. The warlords and politicians, who supported one leader to overthrow another and shifted their allegiances overnight, not only did not comprehend the meaning of government by law, but considered it an honor to break the law and upset discipline. Under such conditions, how could the idea of government of law be instilled? How could the habit of observing the law be formed?

Chiang Kai-shek, *China's Destiny*[2]

[A] revolution is not the same as inviting people to dinner, or writing an essay, or painting a picture, or doing fancy needlework; it cannot be anything so refined, so calm and gentle, or so mild, kind, courteous, restrained and magnanimous. A revolution is an uprising, an act of violence whereby one class overthrows another.

Mao Tse-tung, "Report of an Investigation into the Peasant Movement in Hunan (1927)" [3]

---

1. II, 3; translated in Derk Bodde, "Basic Concepts of Chinese Law: The Genesis and Evolution of Legal Thought in Traditional China," *American Philosophical Society, Proceedings*, 107:384 (October 1963).

2. Philip Jaffe, ed. (New York: Roy Publishers, 1947), p. 212.

3. Translated in *Selected Works of Mao Tse-tung*, I (London: Lawrence and Wishart Ltd., 1954), 27.

[The following Introduction is adapted from Jerome Alan Cohen, "The Criminal Process in the People's Republic of China: An Introduction," *Harvard Law Review*, 79.3:469–533 (January 1966)][4]

"The trouble with you Westerners," the man said, wagging his finger at me before I could sit down, "is that you've never got beyond that primitive stage you call the 'rule of law.' You're all preoccupied with the 'rule of law.' China has always known that law is not enough to govern a society. She knew it twenty-five hundred years ago, and she knows it today." The man, interestingly enough, was a London-educated Chinese barrister who practices in Hong Kong and is known there as a principal, if unofficial, spokesman of the People's Republic of China (PRC). When properly deciphered his cryptic defense of the regime on mainland China suggests much about the attitude of the Communists toward the criminal process. They have been acutely sensitive to criticism that they have failed to adhere to those fundamental principles of fairness that Western — particularly Anglo-American — societies proclaim as ideals.[5] Yet they have rejected those principles as Western and bourgeois, and inapplicable to a Chinese Communist regime.[6] And from time to time this rejection has been defended in part by an appeal to history and to the low regard that the Chinese have traditionally held for law and lawyers.[7]

4. Copyright © 1966 by The Harvard Law Review Association.

5. Their sensitivity to such criticism is revealed not only in direct attempts to rebut it (see note 6) but also in their attacks upon the alleged hypocrisy of justice in the West. See Li Hao-p'ei, "Condemn American Fascist Legislation and Adjudication, Support the Righteous Struggle of the American Communists," *CFYC*, 1:3–11 (1962); Chang Hsin, "American Justice as Depicted in 'the Unjust Court,'" *CFYC*, 4:45–49 (1962).

6. See Chang Tzu-p'ei, "Censure the Bourgeois Principle of 'the Judge's Free Evaluation of the Evidence,'" *CFYC*, 2:42–48 (1958); Ch'en Ho-feng, "Refute Rightist Chuang Hui-ch'en's Reactionary Fallacy Regarding Legal Relations Among the Public Security, Procuratorial and Adjudication Organs," *CFYC*, 2:64–66 (1958); Feng Jo-ch'üan, "Refute Chia Ch'ien's Anti-Party Fallacy of 'Independent Adjudication,'" *CFYC*, 1:18–23 (1958); Wu Yü-su, "Censure the Bourgeois Principle of 'Presumption of Innocence,'" *CFYC*, 2:37–41 (1958).

7. See Kawasaki Mitsunari, "The Attorney System," in *Chūgoku no hō to shakai* (Chinese law and society; Tokyo, 1960), p. 80. The miniscule number of professional lawyers in the People's Republic of China has been attributed by Wu Te-feng, vice-president of the Supreme People's Court, primarily to a historical factor not common to the history of all socialist countries: the extremely bad reputation of lawyers in pre-Communist China. Traditionally, lawyers were thought to be servants of the exploiting classes, who were cynical, mercenary, and dishonest. For this reason, according to Mr. Wu, following the Communist "liberation" of China the people could not bring themselves to consult lawyers, and the development of the bar has been hindered. See also Tadasuke Torio, "Chinese Lawyers," in *Horitsuka no mita Chūgoku* (China as seen by lawyers; Tokyo, 1965), pp. 216–217.

For a number of years Chinese legal scholars have debated the problem of the extent to which China's pre-Communist heritage should be viewed as influencing contemporary legal development. Their recent writings reflect an increased interest in Chinese legal history and a somewhat greater readiness than in earlier years to find traces of continuity with the present. See, e.g., Hsiao Yung-ch'ing, "A Preliminary Approach to the Study of the History of the Chinese Legal System," *CFYC*, 3:25–35 (1963); Fu Weng, "Talk on the History of Adjudication of Cases," *Kuang-ming jih-pao* (Enlightenment daily), March 20, 1962, p. 4.

## A. BACKGROUND

One should note that the barrister's formulation was that "law" is "not enough" to govern Chinese society, and not that it is unimportant or irrelevant in that task. Confucius and his followers had advocated governing in accordance with approved social norms (*li*) through persuasion and moral example, rather than governing in accordance with positive law (*fa*) through coercion and deterrence. But even they had recognized that penal laws were a regrettable necessity, to be applied against those elements of the community who proved to be unresponsive to the *li*. Although the leaders of the Chinese Communist Party (CCP) have made masterful use of persuasion, ideological incentives, social and administrative pressures, and other measures of control, and still at times predict that the state will wither away, they have never had illusions that they could dispense with criminal sanctions. On the eve of assuming power over the mainland of China, Mao Tse-tung exhorted his Party comrades to strengthen the police and the courts, as well as the army, on the ground that these agencies were the state's major institutions for enforcing the people's democratic dictatorship.[8] And much attention has since been lavished on perfecting the criminal process.

But, as the barrister's remark implies, although the Chinese have been unable to dispense with "law," they have not been preoccupied with the "rule of law." To Westerners that clouded phrase suggests among its many meanings not only a respect for state proscriptions, but also an opportunity for an accused to defend himself effectively. In China, the phrase that Westerners sometimes translate as "rule of law" (*fa-chih*) has been well known for over two thousand years,[9] but a more accurate translation would be "rule by law." Traditional Chinese law was mainly an instrument for enforcing status-oriented Confucian social norms and for bending the will of an unruly populace to achieve the purposes of an authoritarian government. To these ends it provided a complex series of punishments and an elaborate hierarchy of institutions for adjudicating guilt and passing sentence. These institutions relied on orderly but highly repressive procedures that allowed the defendant little opportunity to make a defense.

Under the last of the imperial dynasties, the Manchu or Ch'ing (1644–1912), many offenses were never adjudicated by the state apparatus but were dealt with by the unofficial processes of local groups.[10] With the government's acquiescence, leaders of clans, villages, and guilds dispensed a wide range of sanctions that included public censure, fines, ostracism, and corporal punishment. Ordinarily only major crimes were reported to the county magistrate, who was the

8. Mao Tse-tung, "On the People's Democratic Dictatorship" (address in commemoration of the 28th anniversary of the CCP), *JMJP*, July 1, 1949, p. 1.

9. See Benjamin Schwartz, "On Attitudes toward Law in China," in Milton Katz, *Government under Law and the Individual* (Washington, D.C., 1957), p. 35.

10. See K. C. Hsiao, *Rural China* (Seattle, 1960), pp. 290–294, 342–346; Sybille Van der Sprenkel, *Legal Institutions in Manchu China, a Sociological Analysis* (London, 1962), pp. 88–111. Long after the collapse of the Ch'ing, especially in remote areas, many offenses continued to be dealt with by the unofficial processes of local groups.

government's principal administrative officer in the area, and was responsible for a variety of tasks in addition to maintaining public order and the administration of justice. The traditional criminal process operated with particular harshness upon the impecunious, the uninfluential, and the innocent.[11] Agents of the magistrate frequently sought to extort money from criminal suspects in return for not bringing them before the magistrate. False accusations were sometimes made because they created an occasion for extortion, or because the agents would themselves suffer punishment if the culprit were not caught within the legally prescribed period of time. Certain categories of accused persons were required by law to remain in detention pending trial and appellate review. Others were permitted to remain at liberty if they obtained satisfactory guarantors of their appearance. Relatively few eligible persons obtained such releases, however, because the law threatened guarantors with physical punishment if the defendant failed to appear when ordered, and because few reputable people wanted to become responsible for suspected criminals. Most accused persons who lacked funds and official connections waited out the long process of trial and appellate review in dismal prisons where they were kept in chains and had to depend on food sent by relatives or friends. Guards subjected prisoners to unauthorized brutality, frequently in the hope of extortion, and many persons died while their cases were being processed.

Cases were publicly tried before the county magistrate, who was not a law-trained judge but an administrator steeped in Confucian classics. Despite this moral education magistrates were often corrupt, cruel, and arbitrary, and even those who were conscientious were often overworked, inexperienced, harassed by legal deadlines for the apprehension and conviction of criminals, unable to speak the local dialect, and dependent for outside investigation upon a staff whose reputation for venality was legendary. In these circumstances the temptation was irresistible to make fullest use of legal provisions that authorized torture of the defendant in court if he denied his guilt. The tendency to use torture was reinforced by the rule that the defendant could not be convicted unless he confessed. Forced to kneel abjectly before the magistrate's high bench, flanked by guards wielding bamboo staves, whips, and other instruments, precluded from presenting his own witnesses, and denied the services of a lawyer, the defendant was at the magistrate's mercy. Although the best magistrates sought to verify the accuracy of coerced confessions and often discovered them to be unreliable, most took the easy way out.

The substantive criminal law, which was entirely published, increased the magistrate's power over the defendant. In addition to proscribing a broad spectrum of conduct in highly specific terms, the Ch'ing code permitted those proscriptions to be applied by analogy to conduct that was not specifically described. As a catchall, severe beating but not graver punishment was authorized for per-

---

11. The following summary of traditional practice relies heavily on Ch'ü T'ung-tsu, *Local Government in China under the Ch'ing* (Cambridge, Mass., 1962), pp. 68–70, 116–129; Van der Sprenkel, pp. 66–79; Robert van Gulik, *T'ang-yin-pi-shih, Parallel Cases from under the Pear-tree, a 13th-century manual of jurisprudence and detection* (Leiden, 1956), pp. 52–63.

sons who did "things one ought not to have done."[12] Retroactive application of new criminal provisions was also not unusual. Aside from bribery and influence, a defendant could look for safeguards only to the possibly moderating effects of the public scrutiny to which the magistrate's proceedings were subject; to the magistrate's interest in avoiding punishment for abuse of power and in receiving promotion for conscientious performance; and to the thorough review that automatically occurred at higher levels of government in most cases in which a punishment heavier than severe beating was meted out. But these institutional safeguards constituted an inadequate substitute for an independent role of the accused in his own defense. Thus, despite a desperate attempt in the early 1900's to enact law reforms that might save a disintegrating dynasty, when in 1912 the Ch'ing was succeeded by the Republic of China, there was no developed concept of "rights" of the accused as limitations upon the state.

Both of the rival party dictatorships that have subsequently sought to pick up the pieces, to reintegrate the shattered country, and to convert it into a modern industrial power have consciously looked outside the Chinese tradition for legal models. After gaining control of the Republic of China in 1928, Chiang Kai-shek's Nationalist Party (KMT) built upon the efforts of previous republican governments and perfected codes of criminal law and procedure similar to those of the continental European nations that Japan had earlier sought to emulate. Even before officially founding the People's Republic of China in 1949, during its two decades of rule over "liberated areas" in rural China, the Communist Party began to borrow substantially from the Soviet Union, whose institutions for administering criminal justice also reflect important European influences. Yet, as the Stalinist experience proved, it is one thing for the leadership of a dictatorial regime to adopt European legal forms, but it is quite another thing for that leadership to assimilate the values, attitudes, and assumptions that underlie the forms. In practice, both of the rival Chinese governments have accorded low priority to the observance of safeguards for the accused that existed on paper. When one compares the uses of law in traditional China, in the Republic of China (located on Taiwan since 1949), and in the People's Republic of China, significant differences of course appear. Yet one major similarity stands out — law and legal institutions still serve principally as instruments for enhancing the power of the state and for disciplining the people to carry out its policies. In the Chinese value system the interests of the state and the group have always dwarfed those of the individual. Now, as in the past, this value preference is reflected at every stage of the criminal process.

The goals of the imperial dynasties and of the Nationalist Party were far more limited than those of the Communist Party. The Communists have been determined for the first time in Chinese history effectively to extend the power of the central government to the grassroots level and to control virtually every aspect of human activity. Their avowed purpose is to bring about a rapid political, economic, and social transformation, at whatever cost may be necessary. Their proclaimed program contemplates alteration of both the physical environment and of human nature itself. They have begun this Herculean task while continuing

12. Van der Sprenkel, p. 63 and note 2 which appears there.

the civil war against the Nationalists and while undertaking heavy international commitments. In order to maximize the country's capacity to meet these enormous demands, the Communist leaders have sought to subject the people to increasingly rigorous discipline. In these circumstances the burden that has fallen upon the criminal process has been immense.

A few caveats are in order before attempting to describe the ways in which contemporary Chinese law enforcement agencies deal with persons who are suspected of crime. It is not easy to study any aspect of today's Chinese legal system, let alone a subject as intimately related to the exercise of political power as the criminal process. Chinese scholars have been hampered by officialdom in their efforts to study the legal practice of China.[13] Most foreigners have received less cooperation.[14] The People's Republic does not permit American scholars to visit China. Generally, foreign lawyers who have been able to visit the mainland have been given an opportunity to make only superficial observations.

Moreover, the bulk of China's operative legal norms are not published and are available only to those who administer the system. Those legislative and administrative prescriptions that are published are obtainable outside of China, but they offer only an incomplete and idealized image of law enforcement processes. There is no systematic publication of judicial decisions. A handful of relevant treatises and pamphlets appeared in the mid-1950's, but there are questions about the extent to which they are currently authoritative. The scholarly and informational content of available legal journals sharply declined during the past few years, and in mid-1966 the last of these journals suspended publication. Many Chinese newspapers that were once an excellent source concerning law in action are now both hard to obtain and uninformative.

Only the availability, especially in Hong Kong, of significant numbers of former residents of the People's Republic makes it possible to fit together tentatively the disparate pieces of relevant data in order to see the system as a whole. Thus this Introduction relies not only on published materials but also on over eight hundred hours of personal interviews with thirty-eight recent Chinese émigrés.

13. In 1957, for example, one well-known scholar, Han Teh-p'ei, then Dean of the Law Department of Wuhan University, complained that "under the present circumstances, data concerning the actual trials taking place in different grades of court[s] up and down the country are barely accessible to people like us engaged in legal education . . . The result is, theories inevitably become divorced from reality in teaching. It is the same with research." "We Must Create Conditions to [Let a Hundred Schools] Contend in Legal Studies," *Kuang-ming jih-pao* (Enlightenment daily), June 12, 1957, p. 3, translated in Roderick MacFarquhar, ed., *The Hundred Flowers Campaign and the Chinese Intellectuals* (London, 1960), p. 116. Quoted by permission of the Congress for Cultural Freedom, Paris.

14. Until 1959, a few Soviet scholars enjoyed unique access to Chinese legal documentation and personnel, and they produced some informative works. See especially Vladimir E. Chugunov, *Ugolovnoye Sudoproizvodstvo Kitayskoy Narodnoy Respubliki* (Criminal court procedures in the People's Republic of China; Moscow, 1959); translated in *JPRS*, no. 4595 (Washington, D.C., May 8, 1961); L. M. Gudoshnikov, *Sudebnye Organy Kitayskoy Narodnoy Respubliki* (Legal organs of the People's Republic of China; Moscow, 1957), pp. 2–135; translated in *JPRS*, no. 1698N (Washington, D.C., June 30, 1959).

More recently, certain Japanese scholars have been favored by the Peking government. See Kawasaki; Tadasuke; Fukushima Masao, "Some Legal Problems Relating to the People's Commune," *Tōyō bunka* (Oriental culture), 32:1–26 (May 1962).

Six of the persons interviewed had long experience as responsible Communist police officials in southern China. Three others had worked in various regions as judicial assistants, two of them having at other times also served as defense counsel. And many persons who were not professional participants related their own case histories as (in the Chinese vernacular) "objects" of the criminal process. Selections from a number of these interviews are reproduced in Part II of this volume.

Plainly enough, material of this nature is not the ordinary stuff of legal research and must be treated with proper caution. Apart from such dangers as an informant's hostility toward the regime, his desire to say what might be thought to please the interviewer, his interest in putting the best face on his own past conduct, and his fear of possible reprisals for having cooperated with "American imperialism," there are the problems of the informant's perception, recall, and articulation, as well as those relating to the interviewer's mode of eliciting information and to his comprehension and recording. Moreover, when dealing with a country that is as vast and as dynamic as Communist China, the reports of a limited number of persons cannot provide a basis for any definitive generalizations. Yet there was a strikingly high degree of consistency in the interviews concerning the essential attributes of the criminal process, and at many points the outline that emerged is confirmed by published information that is widely accepted as reliable. In short, interviews provide a clearer means of viewing patterns of official activity than does any other resource likely to be available until fundamental changes take place in China. What follows, then, is a synthesis derived from both published sources and interviews. Although some material of both types is available relating to post-1963 activities, this study does not purport to describe developments that have taken place since January 1, 1964.

## B. A BASIC PERIODIZATION

Thus far I have treated the era of Chinese Communist rule as though it were a single period. Actually, the fourteen years under review should be divided into three major stages.

### 1949–1953

From 1949 to 1953 was a period of economic reconstruction and consolidation of political control, roughly comparable to the period of War Communism in the earliest days of the Soviet Union (1917–1921). During this period the criminal process served as a blunt instrument of terror, as the Chinese Communist Party proceeded relentlessly to crush all sources of political opposition and to rid society of apolitical but antisocial elements who plagued public order. The Nationalist legal apparatus, including the bar, was formally abolished at the outset,[15] yet it was not immediately replaced by a well-regulated system of criminal justice. Although the Communist government created a judicial structure, much

15. Common Program of the CPPCC (passed at the 1st plenary session of the CPPCC, Sept. 29, 1949), *FLHP* 1949–1950, 1:19; Gudoshnikov, pp. 22–23.

criminal punishment during these years was administered outside the regular courts; it was not until the "judicial reform" of 1952–1953 that the courts were sufficiently purged of holdovers from the Nationalist government to inspire the confidence of the Communist Party. In many kinds of cases the police had un-fettered power to investigate, detain, prosecute, and convict. The police also conducted large-scale "administrative" roundups of petty thieves, gamblers, opium addicts, whores, pimps, vagrants, and other dregs of the old society, and subjected them to "noncriminal" reform measures during the course of long confinement. Military control commissions continued to function and to ad-minister punishment in large areas of the country. During the regime-sponsored "mass movements" or campaigns that swept the country, such as those instigated to carry out the land reform, to suppress counterrevolution, and to eradicate of-ficial corruption and related illegal activities in the business community (the so-called "three-anti" and "five-anti" movements[16]), ad hoc "people's tribunals," which were thinly veiled kangaroo courts, dispensed their own brand of justice.

Although these various criminal processes usually functioned in secret, in major cases the last phase of the process was often conducted in the form of a "mass trial" convened before a horde of onlookers. Hundreds of thousands of class enemies were sentenced to death in such trials, and many more were sent to long terms of "reform through labor." [17] In short, the army, the police, and the regular and irregular courts implemented the directive of Chairman Mao to serve as instruments for oppressing the hostile classes and for inflicting "legal-ized" violence and lesser sanctions upon all those who were deemed to be "re-actionaries" and "bad elements." The justification for such an unattractive pro-gram had been offered by Mao some twenty years previously in his famous report on a peasant uprising in his native province: "To put it bluntly, it was necessary to bring about a brief reign of terror in every rural area; otherwise one could never suppress the activities of the counterrevolutionaries in the countryside or overthrow the authority of the gentry. To right a wrong it is neces-sary to exceed the proper limits, and the wrong cannot be righted without the proper limits being exceeded." [18]

## 1953–1957

The second stage in the evolution of the contemporary criminal process began

16. The "three-anti" movement was launched to combat corruption, waste, and bureauc-ratism among government and Party personnel. The "five-anti" movement, which proceeded in coordination with the "three-anti" movement, was directed against bribery, tax evasion, fraud, theft of state economic secrets, and theft of other state property. These movements began in late 1951 and ended in mid-1952.

17. According to excerpts from the unofficial version of Mao Tse-tung's major speech of February 27, 1957, "Problems Relating to the Correct Handling of Contradictions Among the People," "the total number of those [enemies of the people] who were liquidated by our security forces numbers 800,000. This is the figure up to 1954." (New York Times, June 13, 1957, p. 8.) Shortly thereafter, an official and admittedly amended Chinese text of the speech was published, and this simply mentions that "some" counterrevolu-tionaries were sentenced to death. See FKHP, 5:13; MacFarquhar, pp. 261–263, 269–271.

18. Mao Tse-tung, "Report of an Investigation into the Peasant Movement in Hunan (1927)," translated in Selected Works of Mao Tse-tung, I (London, 1954), 27. See also the quotation from this report, at the beginning of Part I.

in the spring of 1953, shortly after initiation of the government's First Five-Year Plan for development of the national economy, and ended with the launching of the "antirightist" movement in June 1957. From the Western viewpoint, this period may be called with some exaggeration the "golden age" of law to date in the People's Republic. Having decided to adopt the Soviet economic model, the Chinese Communist leaders decided to develop further a Soviet-style legal system. By the end of 1954 this decision had resulted in the promulgation of a constitution and a series of laws that established the framework of an orderly system for the administration of justice. Apart from a few liberalizing touches, this system was similar to that which was erected along European lines in the Soviet Union during the relatively moderate period of the New Economic Policy (1921–1928), and which coexisted with a parallel structure of extrajudicial coercion.[19]

Citizens were protected against arbitrary detention, arrest, and search.[20] The nationwide procuracy, which had been organized shortly after the Communist assumption of power, was authorized to fulfill those functions that we associate with a prosecutor's office, including review of police recommendations to arrest and prosecute. It was also to exercise general supervision over the legality of the action of all government organs including the police.[21] Implicit in the constitutional grant of judicial power to the courts was the understanding that, contrary to the situation that prevailed in the Soviet Union until after Stalin's death, they were to serve as the exclusive agencies for the adjudication of criminal responsibility.[22] In most trials in courts of first instance, a judge and two people's assessors were jointly to preside as a judicial college to decide all questions of

19. See Constitution of the PRC [hereinafter cited as Const.] (passed at the 1st meeting of the 1st session of the NPC, Sept. 20, 1954; promulgated by the Presidium, Sept. 20, 1954), *FKHP*, 1:4–31; Act of the PRC for the Organization of Public Security Stations [hereinafter cited as Public Security Station Act] (passed at the 4th meeting of the Standing Committee of the NPC, Dec. 31, 1954; promulgated by the Chairman of the PRC, Dec. 31, 1954), *FKHP*, 1:243–244; Arrest and Detention Act of the PRC [hereinafter cited as Arrest Act] (passed at the 3d meeting of the Standing Committee of the NPC, Dec. 20, 1954; promulgated by the Chairman of the PRC, Dec. 20, 1954), *FKHP*, 1:239–242; Law of the PRC for the Organization of People's Courts [hereinafter cited as Court Law] (passed at the 1st meeting of the 1st session of the NPC, Sept. 21, 1954; promulgated by the Chairman of the PRC, Sept. 28, 1954), *FKHP*, 1:123–132; Law of the PRC for the Organization of People's Procuracies [hereinafter cited as Procuracy Law] (passed at the 1st meeting of the 1st session of the NPC, Sept. 21, 1954; promulgated by the Chairman of the PRC, Sept. 28, 1954), *FKHP*, 1:133–138. For a discussion of the legal system in the Soviet Union during the period of the NEP, see generally John N. Hazard, *Settling Disputes in Soviet Society* (New York, 1960).

20. Const., p. 28, arts. 89–90; Arrest Act, pp. 239–241, arts. 1–9, 11.

21. Procuracy Law, pp. 135–136, arts. 9, 11–12. The procuracy was also authorized to initiate the investigation and accusation process, Procuracy Law, pp. 134, 135, arts. 4(2), 9–10, but in practice its primary role has been as a reviewing rather than as an initiating agency.

22. See Const., p. 25, art. 73; Decision of the Standing Committee of the NPC of the PRC Relating to Control of Counterrevolutionaries in All Cases Being Decided Upon by Judgment of a People's Court [hereinafter cited as Decision Relating to Counterrevolutionaries] (passed at the 51st meeting of the Standing Committee of the NPC, Nov. 16, 1956), *FKHP*, 4:246. See also Ku Ang-jan, "Why Must Control of Counterrevolutionaries Be Decided Upon by Judgment of a People's Court?" *Shih-shih shou-ts'e* (Current events handbook), 23:35–36 (Dec. 10, 1956).

fact and law; normally three judges were to hear appeals.[23] Trial was to be public except in specified circumstances, and the defendant was entitled to offer a defense.[24] It was contemplated that this defense would ordinarily be made for him by the new "people's lawyers" who were beginning to receive training at the recently revamped law schools, and who were to practice in Soviet-type collective organizations. Although individual judges were to serve at the pleasure of the legislative or executive organs,[25] in theory the courts were to be independent in administering justice and to "be obedient only to the law."[26]

Plans were made to draft a criminal code that would provide more guidance to the agencies of law enforcement and to the public than had previously been afforded by the miscellany of isolated published proscriptions and by the "resolutions, decisions, orders, instructions, and policies of the Party and the government" from which the agencies were instructed to shape a substantive law of crimes in the absence of specific proscriptions.[27] Rules of criminal procedure were to be devised for experimental use prior to formulation of a procedural code. Scholars were called upon to write texts that were both to guide the administration of justice during the period prior to the completion of the projected legislation and to aid the drafting of the legislation itself. This entire lawmaking effort was to be undertaken with the aid of Soviet legal experts who had come to help the Chinese understand the Soviet codes and the many treatises on Soviet law that were being translated into Chinese. The Party line on law was the same as that for other aspects of the country's development — to adapt the advanced experiences of the Soviet Union to China's conditions.

These were not mere paper reforms. Another wave of terror — the movement to "liquidate counterrevolution" — almost swamped them in the second half of 1955; at that time, in a manner that was reminiscent of, but more successful than, Stalin's collectivization efforts of the late 1920's and early 1930's, the regime sought to prepare the ground for rapidly completing the "socialist reform" of agriculture and industry. But shortly after Khrushchev publicly launched his program of de-Stalinization in early 1956, an emphasis upon legality reappeared in China, and at least in the larger cities implementation of many of the reforms commenced. The powers of the police to detain, interrogate, and arrest began to be exercised according to procedures that provided for more regularized internal checks against arbitrary action by lower level cadres. Moreover, if the

23. Court Law, p. 125, art. 9. Judges were to be "professional" in the sense that they were to devote their full time to judicial duties, while people's assessors were to serve for only limited periods. All citizens who were twenty-three years of age and who had never been deprived of political rights were eligible for selection as judges. (Court Law, p. 131, art. 31.)

24. Const., pp. 25–26, art. 76; Court Law, p. 124, art. 7. Decision of the Standing Committee of the NPC of the PRC Relating to Cases the Hearing of Which Is To Be Conducted Nonpublicly (passed at the 39th meeting of the Standing Committee of the NPC, May 8, 1956), *FKHP*, 3:178.

25. See Const., pp. 13, 14, 22, arts. 28(4), 31(9), 59; Court Law, p. 131, art. 32.

26. Const., p. 26, art. 78; Court Law, p. 124, art. 4. Cf. Constitution (Fundamental Law) of the Union of Soviet Socialist Republics (Moscow, 1960), p. 97, art. 112, which provides that "[J]udges are independent and subject only to the law."

27. *Lectures*, p. 58.

police did not always comply with the requirement of obtaining the procuracy's approval before issuing an arrest warrant, and if general supervision of the legality of police conduct remained merely an aspiration, nevertheless the procuracy was usually able to carry out conscientiously its obligation to review police recommendations to prosecute. Furthermore, although certain relatively severe sanctions not deemed to be "criminal" continued to be meted out by agencies other than courts, such penalties were employed less frequently and less arbitrarily than in the past, and the courts did assume exclusive jurisdiction over the imposition of sanctions regarded as "criminal."

For the most part adjudication continued to take place behind closed doors. The defendant, who was without counsel, was subjected to judicial interrogation in an effort to verify the evidence assembled by the investigating agencies. This procedure was supplemented by ex parte interrogation of witnesses in those cases in which the information in the file and the account of the defendant left important questions unanswered. Yet even such truncated "trials" often provided a significant check upon the adequacy of the cases presented by the police and the procuracy, and increasingly there were experiments with public trials conducted according to tentative rules of procedure that closely resembled those in force in the Soviet Union. The lay assessors, who only sat with the judge in public trials, were a facade designed to display the participation of the masses in the administration of justice. Innocence was not seriously at issue because, if pretrial judicial screening found proof of criminality to be insufficient, the case was not set down for public trial but was either dismissed or returned to the procuracy or police for further investigation. It was not unusual, however, for defense counsel to appear in public trials and to argue with spirit and ability for conviction of a lesser crime or for mitigation, and the defendant often had at least a formal opportunity to confront his accusers. If initially these experiments only constituted morality plays that were carefully staged for the education and edification of the masses, later public trials were often authentic attempts at determining the degree of the defendant's guilt and the appropriate punishment.

The courts, which were preponderantly staffed by members of the Communist Party and its junior affiliate, the Communist Youth League (CYL), were of course entirely dependent on the Party. Ad hoc interference with individual cases by the local Party apparatus was not an unknown phenomenon. Yet generally this was an era when the Party's will was carried out by means of Party control of the formulation of national judicial policies, rather than by means of local Party control of actual decision making. This arrangement allowed professional judicial considerations to begin to influence the disposition of individual cases. The competence of the judiciary, most of whose members had little or no legal education, was gradually nourished by study of the various laws, decrees, regulations, instructions, reports, and model cases that emanated from Peking; by the spate of serious law review articles that were then published on problems of criminal law and procedure; and by the lectures that were originally delivered at the law schools and subsequently distributed. It was anticipated that enactment of the proposed criminal code that was before the National People's Congress (NPC) in the spring of 1957 would provide further substantial impetus to the evolution of the legal system in a direction similar to that being followed by Soviet law reform during the same period.

These were modest beginnings — to Western lawyers they appear almost pitiable. Certainly the pace was exasperatingly slow to a small but articulate group of Chinese intellectuals who were schooled in Western legal values. At the height of the movement to "let a hundred flowers bloom, let a hundred schools contend," in May and early June 1957 when Chairman Mao induced the intellectuals to help "rectify" the Party by offering criticisms, some legal scholars castigated it on a variety of grounds. They accused it, for example, of assuming a "nihilist standpoint towards law," of maintaining an attitude of superiority to the law, of committing grave violations of legality during past mass movements, of overloading the judiciary with ignorant Party members who imposed arbitrary punishments, of obliterating the distinction between Party and government, and of being reluctant to enact the widely heralded criminal code.[28] One critic said of the proposed code, "one hears the sound of footsteps on the stairs without seeing anyone coming down." [29]

Legal specialists were not the only intellectuals who responded to the invitation to help "rectify" the Party. The depth and scope of the criticism apparently exceeded anything Party leaders had expected and made it clear that intellectuals desired democratic reforms, including more drastic reform of the criminal process, that would end the Party's monopoly of political power and fundamentally alter China's political structure. After a brief period of stunned inaction, the response of the Party leaders was to initiate the "antirightist" movement that savagely struck back at critics both inside and outside Party ranks, and that radically transformed China's political climate. This movement ushered in the third period in the development of the criminal process.

## 1957–1963

One of the principal targets and first casualties of the antirightist movement was the evolving system for administering the criminal law along de-Stalinized Soviet lines. The Party leaders had never felt comfortable about the decision to import the formal Soviet judicial model, which to them was essentially a Western product. As a result of the "hundred flowers" debacle they came to fear that full implementation of this system would unduly curb the power of the Party and introduce bourgeois law and values. Therefore, during the second half of 1957 and in 1958, while de-Stalinization was culminating in a series of reforms that brought Soviet criminal law and procedure closer to Western systems,[30]

28. For a collection of representative criticism translated into English, see MacFarquhar, pp. 114–116.

29. Chi Ch'ing-yi, editor of the Legal Publishing House, quoted in MacFarquhar, p. 115.

30. Western scholars have differed in evaluating these reforms. All recognize the importance of such steps as the abolition of Stalin's extrajudicial agencies for imposing severe criminal punishments, the strengthening of the powers of the procuracy and the court vis-à-vis the police, and the regularization of criminal procedure and substantive criminal law. They also recognize the qualifying impact of Khrushchev's virtually contemporaneous development of "social organizations" — principally the antiparasite tribunals, the comrades' courts, and the volunteer people's guards — that impose administrative sanctions

in China principles of Western justice, such as the independence of the judiciary from political interference and the nonretroactivity of the criminal law, were being systematically denounced.[31] Chinese writers increasingly emphasized the inapplicability of the Soviet legal model to China and severely censured cadres who " 'build their wagon behind closed doors' [are impractical], revere their [Soviet] textbooks as 'classics,' swallow [the contents] without chewing and apply them in their original form, and make a set of trivial procedures." [32]

Drastic changes were deemed necessary. During the 1953–1957 period many procurators had refused to approve arrests and prosecutions, and had instead ordered the release of detained persons on a variety of technical grounds, such as that the act in question did not amount to a completed crime, or that it was not committed with the requisite intent, or that it did not result in serious consequences.[33] Procurators were now warned to abandon this one-sided "favor the defendant" mentality that emphasized "trivial legal procedures and the rights and status of the criminal, opening the door of convenience to the criminal." [34] Defense counsel were also admonished to act "in the interests of the state and the people" rather than to "favor the defendant." Thus, for example, if the defendant reveals to his counsel that he has committed crimes that are not yet attributed to him, it is the latter's duty to inform the police, with or without the defendant's consent.[35] Furthermore, no equality can be tolerated between the procurator and the defendant at trial, for the procurator represents the state while most defendants are enemies of the people and should be allowed to defend themselves only insofar as they do not utter reactionary statements or distort the facts or the laws and policies. It was asserted that the only purpose of the constitutional provision granting the defendant the right to make a defense is to assist the law enforcement agencies in assessing the evidence of his crime and the degree of his repentance, and thus to enable them "more fiercely, accurately and firmly to attack the enemy." [36] Nor can the court be permitted to serve as a fair and impartial arbiter between procurator and defendant, because a clear separation between accusation and adjudication is help-

upon a variety of undesirable persons. Most scholars tend to stress the magnitude of the tasks that remain ahead for law reform in a society that is still subject to effective, albeit now muted, totalitarian controls. Others tend to emphasize the significance of what has been accomplished in a short period of time. For representative views, compare Merle Fainsod, *How Russia Is Ruled*, rev. ed. (Cambridge, Mass., 1963), pp. 118–120, 124–125, 447–452, and Leon Lipson, "Hosts and Pests: The Fight Against Parasites," *Problems of Communism*, 14.3:72–82 (March–April 1965), with H. J. Berman, *Justice in the U.S.S.R.*, rev. ed. (New York, 1963), pp. 66–96. See also Leonard Schapiro, "Prospects for the Rule of Law," *Problems of Communism*, 14.3:2–7 (March–April 1965).

31. See Fan Ming, "Some Opinions about *Lectures on the General Principles of Criminal Law of the PRC*," CFYC, 4:72–75 (1958); Wu Te-feng, "Struggle in Order To Defend the Socialist Legal System" (a speech broadcast Jan. 19, 1958, on the Central People's Broadcasting Station), CFYC, 1:10–16 (1958).

32. T'an Cheng-wen, "Absorb Experience and Teaching, Impel a Great Leap Forward in Procuratorial Work," CFYC, 3:34–45 (1958).

33. T'an Cheng-wen, p. 38.

34. T'an Cheng-wen, p. 38.

35. See Su I, "Should a Defender Attack Crime or Protect Crime?" CFYC, 2:77 (1958).

36. Shen Ch'i-szu, "Censure 'the Principle of Debate' in the Criminal Litigation of the Bourgeoisie," CFYC, 1:34 (1960).

ful to defendant and harmful to that harmonious cooperation among police, procuracy, and court that is the hallmark of true socialist legality. Moreover, the principle of an uninterrupted trial was said to be unacceptable, for criminal cases often require a number of court sessions over a considerable period of time before the facts can be cleared up. And the principles of "directness" and "orality" in adjudication were condemned because they require those who decide the case to hear it; they are therefore inconsistent with the policy that the trial judge submit his proposed decision not only to the chief judge of the court's criminal division and the president of the entire court, but also in cases of any importance to the local territorial Party committee.[37]

It is this explicitly articulated, persistently avowed espousal of local Party control over judicial decisions that in recent years has set Chinese justice most sharply apart from Soviet justice. Even under Stalin, whatever the realities of practice, Party control over judicial decisions was not publicly advocated, and in the post-Stalin era the Soviet press has occasionally reprimanded local Party secretaries for attempting to interfere with individual adjudications.[38] In China, since the antirightist movement, the model judge is one who consults the local Party apparatus about any important case.[39]

These sudden changes in "legal philosophy" were accompanied by profound practical changes. Theoretically, no inroads were made upon the principle that only the courts impose criminal sanctions. But the significance of that principle was undermined because the regime perfected a system of severe police-imposed "administrative" sanctions. The actual jurisdiction of the procuracy and the courts was thus importantly circumscribed. Many Party and non-Party persons were declared "rightists" and removed from their jobs in the judiciary and the procuracy for having "indulged criminals" and "opposed Party leadership." This group included the chief judge and two associate chief judges of the Criminal Division of the Supreme Court, and the director of research for the Supreme Court, as well as major figures at the provincial level.[40] Virtually all the remaining non-Party members of the procuracy and courts were reassigned to less sensitive work in other branches of government. The proposed code of criminal law was never promulgated, and because "judicial work has made new progress along the mass line" the Supreme Court directed the lower courts "to revise, enrich, and improve" the existing rules of criminal procedure in order "to meet the demands of the progress of our work."[41] A number of changes

---

37. See Chang Hui et al., "These Are Not the Basic Principles of Our Country's Criminal Litigation," *CFYC*, 4:77–78 (1958).

38. Raymond H. Anderson, "Courts' Freedom Urged in Soviet," *New York Times*, July 3, 1966, p. 14. It would be rash to assume, of course, that even today in major political cases in the Soviet Union the Party remains merely a disinterested spectator. See Max Hayward, ed., *On Trial: The Soviet State versus "Abram Tertz" and "Nikolai Arzhak"* (New York, Evanston, and London, 1966).

39. See Liu Tse-chün, "Realizations from My Adjudication Work," *CFYC*, 1:48–51 (1959).

40. "High Court's Antirightist Struggle Gains Great Victory," *JMJP*, Dec. 12, 1957, p. 4; Wu Te-feng, p. 10.

41. Kao K'o-lin, "Crimes of Treason by Reactionary Groups in Tibet Are Something the Law of the State Does Not Tolerate" (address to the 1st meeting of the 2d session

were immediately made to "simplify" the system of mutual restraints that the constitution and organizational laws had contemplated would exist among the police, the procuracy, and the courts. The public trial system that had begun to evolve virtually came to an end, except in minor cases, such as bigamy and adultery, that were closely related to civil litigation, and except in the relatively rare instances when a public trial was deemed to have unusual educational significance or was desired in order to accede to a foreign delegation's request to witness a trial. Defense counsel became a rarity, and the recently organized lawyers' collectives soon were operating with skeleton staffs. Control by the local territorial Party apparatus over the decision-making processes of the police, procuracy, and courts was strengthened so that "the three departments have become one fist, attacking the enemy even more forcefully." [42]

During the "great leap forward" that began in the spring of 1958, law enforcement agencies, like all other agencies of government, were called upon to make their own "great leap." Law review essays, newspaper articles, and the work reports of provincial high courts of that era were replete with boasts of extraordinary numbers of arrests, prosecutions, and convictions achieved in remarkably short spans of time. These accomplishments were usually attributed to the observance of the newly re-emphasized "mass line," which had been formulated in the pre-1949 "liberated areas" of China and required legal workers to leave their offices, go down to the people, and dispose of cases "on the spot." A typical description depicted a "work group" composed of several police officers, a procurator, and a judge leaving the county seat to swoop down on a village shortly after receiving a report of a crime. By shrewd and assiduous questioning of local Party and government officials and the masses, the work group quickly ferreted out the identity of the offender and detained him. After jointly interrogating him in order to verify the accuracy of the suspicion, the group promptly filled out legal forms such as the arrest warrant and the bill of prosecution, consulted the local officials about what the sentence should be, and during a rest period in the production day took the defendant before a large assembly of peasants in the fields. There, "under face-to-face exposure by the masses," even the most impenitent offender "could not but bow his head and admit his guilt" and receive his sentence. These procedures were carried out in jig time. Such techniques of "smashing permanent rules" and "having the courage to innovate" "not only reduced the time wasted in traveling [of witnesses to the city] and greatly increased the speed of handling the case, they also punished the criminal promptly and forcefully, made propaganda for the legal

---

of the NPC, April 24, 1959), *Hsin-hua pan-yüeh-k'an* (New China semimonthly), 9:65 (1959).

42. Chang Wu-yün, "Smash Permanent Rules, Go 1,000 *Li* in One Day," *CFYC*, 5:60 (1958). In an interview one former police official has even reported that in 1958 in his rural area of Fukien province there was actually a secret merger of the three departments at the basic level. Subsequently this experiment was abandoned and the three departments returned to their previous administrative identities, but under continuing close Party control. This experiment apparently occurred in some other areas as well. See Jen Chen-to and Ho En-t'ao, "How to Establish China's New System of Criminal Litigation," *Chi-lin ta-hsüeh jen-wen k'o-hsüeh hsüeh-pao* (Kirin University journal of humanistic sciences), 2:123 (1959).

system, and educated the masses." In addition, it was emphasized that these methods elicited more reliable evidence, and brought judicial officials into contact with the masses, who did not like cases to be tried in distant city court-houses. All this was hailed as both "a new creative experience" and "a traditional method of handling cases that has a national style." [43]

Interviews with former police officials indicate that these published accounts of the "great leap" era have to be treated with caution. Although they appear to represent the manner in which the criminal process often functioned in cases of relatively minor crimes, seldom in important cases were law enforcement cadres allowed to act with such dispatch and unreviewed abandon. Certainly the activities described in these accounts cannot be considered typical of the authorized procedures that prevailed after the national paroxysm subsided in 1960; however, the problem of persuading lower-level cadres to adhere to author-ized procedures continued to be troublesome and persistent particularly in rural areas.

Although this third stage in the development of the criminal process brought an end to what may be called the constitutional era of 1953–1957, it did not represent a return to the rather unregulated reign of terror of 1949–1953. The antirightist movement spurred the Party to produce a more integrated and well-ordered system of imposing sanctions than had previously been developed. Be-cause this system neatly meshes "administrative" and "criminal" sanctions, and because many of the "administrative" sanctions and the acts that they punish would be deemed "criminal" in many other countries, it is necessary to treat the sanctioning system as a whole. Details concerning many aspects of the sys-tem will be presented in Part II of this volume. In this part there will only be a sketch of the major components of the system: the actors in the sanctioning apparatus, the sanctions they apply, the substantive standards that guide them, and the procedures that are used.

## C. SANCTIONING APPARATUS

To identify all the participants in the sanctioning apparatus, one would have to describe diverse patterns of organization within the work and residential units of the cities and within the rural communes which since 1958 have integrated the work and residential units in the countryside. Here I will merely take as an illustration a standard residential unit of a large city.

China is a national state that is subdivided into provinces, two major cities, and a number of autonomous regions that are treated as the equivalent of provinces. Other large cities are directly under provincial governments. Large cities are ordinarily subdivided into districts, each of which in turn has several suboffices called street offices, which are the lowest-level government units in the city. In each district there is (a) a basic-level people's court (hereafter referred to as the basic court), (b) a basic-level people's procuracy (hereafter

43. Chang Wu-yün, pp. 58–59.

referred to as the basic procuracy), and often (c) a public security subbureau.[44] The basic court is under the intermediate-level people's court (hereafter called the intermediate court), the basic procuracy is under the intermediate-level people's procuracy (hereafter called the intermediate procuracy), and the public security subbureau is under the public security bureau; these higher-level institutions serve the entire city. Only the public security structure has an organized unit — the public security station — at the street office level. A dozen or so patrolmen work out of the public security station, each treading a specific beat within the area.[45]

Less conventional is the semiofficial substructure that not only feeds information into the official apparatus but also participates in the administration of relatively minor sanctions. The area under the jurisdiction of each street office and public security station is organized into numerous residents' committees, "autonomous mass organizations" which are primarily staffed by elected, unpaid volunteers. According to the authorizing legislation, a residents' committee may be responsible for the activities of one hundred to six hundred households; a committee is subdivided into residents' groups, each of which is responsible for about fifteen to forty households.[46] In many areas the residents' committees act through specialized committees, two of which — the mediation committee and the security defense committee, especially the latter — are of principal assistance in the criminal process.[47] There are usually one or more members of the security defense committee in each residents' group; their major job is to keep abreast of, and to report to the police, all suspicious activities in the neighborhood. The patrolman assigned to the area of the residents' committee works closely with the chairman and other responsible members of that committee, the security defense committee, and the mediation committee; if there are Communist Party or Communist Youth League units within the residents' committee, he also cooperates with their leaders. Together with the patrolman this

44. In the People's Republic of China the "people's police," who are uniformed law enforcement officers, and the plainclothes or secret police are integrated under the administration of the Ministry of Public Security. For convenience the term "police" is generally used in this Part to include all personnel of the Ministry of Public Security and its subdivisions.

45. The legislative basis for the government apparatus may be found in Public Security Station Act; Court Law; Procuracy Law; Act of the PRC for the Organization of City Street Offices (passed at the 4th meeting of the Standing Committee of the NPC, Dec. 31, 1954; promulgated by the Chairman of the PRC, Dec. 31, 1954), FKHP, 1:171–172.

46. Act of the PRC for the Organization of City Residents' Committees (passed at the 4th meeting of the Standing Committee of the NPC, Dec. 31, 1954; promulgated by the Chairman of the PRC, Dec. 31, 1954), FKHP, 1:173–175.

47. For their authorizing prescriptions, see Provisional Act of the PRC for the Organization of Security Defense Committees (approved by the Government Administration Council, June 27, 1952; promulgated by the Ministry of Public Security, Aug. 11, 1952), FLHP 1952, pp. 56–58; Provisional General Rules of the PRC for the Organization of People's Mediation Committees (passed at the 206th meeting on government administration by the Government Administration Council, Feb. 25, 1954; promulgated by the Government Administration Council, March 22, 1954), FLHP 1954, pp. 47–48. In some cities the mediation committee is now called the "adjustment committee" and has somewhat enlarged its functions. Sometimes it has been merged into the security defense committee. See Part II, Chapter II.

group forms the local power elite and brings surveillance of the teeming urban masses down to the level of the individual household, a task that the police alone could not perform.


## D. SANCTIONS

The sanctions imposed by the official and semiofficial apparatus range from private "criticism-education" to the death penalty. I have already emphasized that there are "administrative" as well as "criminal" sanctions. The former embrace "informal" as well as "formal" sanctions. The hierarchy of "informal administrative" sanctions generally includes, in ascending order of severity, the following: (1) private criticism-education by members of the local power elite; (2) private warnings and threats by such persons to impose sanctions; (3) criticism before a small group of one's peers, for example, his residents' group; (4) similar criticism before a larger body, such as a meeting of all residents within the jurisdiction of one's residents' committee; (5) "censure," which is a harsher degree of criticism before such groups and which requires a correspondingly greater degree of positive response from the individual — such as thorough oral or written statements of "self-denunciation," "self-examination," and "repentance," with written statements often posted at prominent places in the vicinity; (6) "speak reason struggle," which seeks to "help" the individual by exposing him to intense vituperation from those in attendance, amid shaking fists, shouts, and accusing fingers; and (7) ordinary "struggle," which reaches an even higher emotional pitch, subjecting the individual to yet graver degrees of public humiliation and physical intimidation, with people often rushing at him, forcing him to kneel and to bow his head, and even hitting or kicking him.

The principal "administrative" sanctions of a "formal" nature, which are all imposed by the police, are[48] (1) the formal warning, modest fine, and short period of detention (up to a maximum of fifteen days) that are prescribed by the Security Administration Punishment Act (SAPA)[49] for a variety of minor offenses roughly comparable to our misdemeanors; also the act's supplementary provisions requiring compensation for victims of offenses and confiscation of

48. In addition to being subject to police-imposed administrative sanctions, extremely important but relatively small groups of persons are subject to disciplinary sanctions imposed by organizations from which their special status derives. These disciplinary measures range from criticism-education to expulsion from the organization. See Provisional Regulations of the State Council of the PRC Relating to Rewards and Punishments for Personnel of State Administrative Organs (approved at the 82d meeting of the Standing Committee of the NPC, Oct. 23, 1957; promulgated by the State Council, Oct. 26, 1957), *FKHP*, 6:199, par. 6; Constitution of the CCP (adopted by the 8th National Congress of the CCP, Sept. 26, 1956), *Jen-min shou-ts'e, 1957* (People's handbook, 1957), pp. 51–52, art. 13; Constitution of the CYL of the PRC (passed at the 9th National Congress of the CYL, June 29, 1964), *JMJP*, July 8, 1964, p. 3, art. 8.

49. Security Administration Punishment Act of the PRC [hereinafter cited as SAPA] (passed at the 81st meeting of the Standing Committee of the NPC, Oct. 22, 1957; promulgated by the Chairman of the PRC, Oct. 22, 1957), *FKHP*, 6:245–254.

instruments used to commit offenses and of illegally obtained property;[50] (2) "supervised labor," which is also known as "controlled production" or "supervised production"; the offender is permitted to remain in society, but is subjected for a long, indefinite period to a severe stigma and required to engage in appropriate labor and special indoctrination programs, to report periodically on his activities to the police and semiofficial "mass organizations," to obtain the permission of the police before traveling, and to abide by other humiliating and burdensome restraints and obligations; and (3) "rehabilitation through labor," which also imposes a severe stigma, but which separates the offender from society and resettles him in the harsh conditions of a labor camp, for what until 1962 was a lengthy, indefinite period;[51] according to several former police officials, this period may have been limited after 1962 to three years.

The major "criminal" sanctions are[52] (1) "control," which in substance is the same as "supervised labor" and is sometimes confused with it, but which is deemed to be a different and more severe sanction because it is imposed by a court for the commission of a crime;[53] (2) imprisonment for a fixed term; (3) imprisonment for life; (4) the death sentence, but with execution suspended for a period of two years in order to observe whether the condemned person earns commutation through self-reform; and (5) death. Imprisonment is also known as "reform through labor" and is actually served either in a prison or in a labor camp whose regimen is somewhat harsher than that of a rehabilitation camp.[54] Ordinarily, confiscation of property and deprivation of political rights are supplementary criminal punishments. Formal reprimand, fine, short-term detention, conditional suspension of a prison sentence, and, in the case of foreigners, deportation, are also criminal punishments. In recent years, however, these sanctions have been imposed less frequently, because cases that warrant such mild punishments are often disposed of by "administrative" or "informal" means.

## E. GUIDING STANDARDS

Some of the standards that guide the application of these sanctions are pub-

50. The term "offenses" is used here, as the Chinese generally use it, to describe not only unlawful acts serious enough to constitute crimes but also other unlawful acts, such as violations of SAPA, deemed less socially dangerous and therefore not criminally punishable.

51. See Decision of the State Council of the PRC Relating to Problems of Rehabilitation Through Labor (approved at the 78th meeting of the Standing Committee of the NPC, Aug. 1, 1957; promulgated by the State Council, Aug. 3, 1957), *FKHP*, 6:243–244.

52. See *Lectures,* pp. 191–214, 239–250.

53. See Provisional Measures of the PRC for Control of Counterrevolutionaries (approved by the Government Administration Council, June 27, 1952; promulgated by the Ministry of Public Security, July 17, 1952), *FLHP* 1952, pp. 53–55; Decision Relating to Counterrevolutionaries.

54. Act of the PRC for Reform Through Labor [hereinafter cited as Labor Act] (passed at the 222d meeting of the Government Administration Council, Aug. 26, 1954; promulgated by the Government Administration Council, Sept. 7, 1954), *FLHP* 1954, p. 33, art. 3.

lished and are therefore available both to the Chinese public and to us. Many others, although printed, are distributed only for the confidential use of officials. The failure to enact a criminal code and the absence of any systematic publication of judicial decisions have already been mentioned. Apart from the broad provisions of the Act for Punishment of Counterrevolution,[55] "criminal" conduct is publicly defined only by a miscellany of specialized regulatory statutes and decrees that vary greatly in the degree of specificity with which they define conduct that is criminal and the punishment that shall attach to a particular crime.[56] Particularly striking is the absence of any published legislation relating to the major common crimes, such as murder, rape, and robbery.

Official doctrine states that in the absence of express proscriptions, the "relevant resolutions, decisions, orders, instructions and policies of the Party and the government are . . . the basis for determining whether or not a crime has been committed." [57] Not surprisingly, to the extent that they have been published, such generalized "sources of law" have been so vague as to provide inadequate guidance for law enforcement agencies and public alike. Chairman Mao's speeches, for example, a catechism for every cadre, refer to the importance of using punishments to suppress counterrevolutionaries and others who seriously disrupt the social order, to reform those who can be saved, to deter potential offenders, and to educate the masses. Mao has even acknowledged the role of punishment in satisfying society's sense of just retribution and in freeing the masses from psychological bondage.[58] Yet apart from admonitions that law enforcement officers are to focus their energies on helping to attain the Party's central programs of the moment, neither the speeches of Chairman Mao nor other published formulations tell how to proceed in cases when the various goals suggest contradictory courses of action with respect to whether criminal punishment should be applied and, if so, to what extent. Similarly, though no distinction is more fundamental to the criminal process than the one Mao elaborately draws between cases that involve "contradictions between the enemy and us," and cases that involve "contradictions among the people,"

55. Act of the PRC for Punishment of Counterrevolution (approved at the 11th meeting of the Central People's Government Council, Feb. 20, 1951; promulgated by the Chairman of the PRC, Feb. 21, 1951), *FLHP* 1951, 1:3–5

56. Compare Marriage Law of the PRC (passed at the 7th meeting of the Central People's Government Council, April 13, 1950; promulgated by the Chairman of the PRC, May 1, 1950), *FLHP* 1949–1950, 1:32–36 (vague description of conduct punished and of penalty) with Circulating Order of the Government Administration Council of the PRC Relating to the Strict Prohibition of Opium (passed at the 21st meeting of the Government Administration Council, Feb. 24, 1950; issued, Feb. 24, 1950), *FLHP* 1949–1950, 1:173–174 (specific description of conduct, vague as to penalty), and Act of the PRC for Punishment of Corruption (approved at the 14th session of the Central People's Government Council, April 18, 1952; promulgated by the Chairman of the PRC, April 21, 1952), *FLHP* 1952, pp. 25–28 (relatively precise as to both crime and punishment).

57. *Lectures,* p. 58. See also Instructions of the CCPCC Relating to Abolishing the Complete Six Laws of the Kuomintang and Establishing Judicial Principles for the Liberated Areas (February 1949); quoted in the *Lectures,* pp. 20–21.

58. See, e.g., Mao Tse-tung, "Problems Relating to the Correct Handling of Contradictions Among the People" (address at the 11th enlarged meeting of the Supreme State Conference, Feb. 27, 1957), *FKHP,* 5:13 (1957).

the attempt to extrapolate concrete rules from his statements has led to considerable confusion both in theory and in practice.[59]

Interviews with former legal officials have established that the law enforcement agencies' need for guidance is met by a vast body of unpublished regulations, rules, orders, instructions, policies, reports, interpretations, and syntheses of judicial decisions that attempt systematically to define both political and nonpolitical crimes, and to set forth applicable ranges of punishments and criteria for their imposition. There are also unpublished handbooks that contain judicial decisions selected as models to illustrate how the standards are to be applied. These materials are subject to continuing revision in the light of experience and China's evolving needs. When the process of revision fails to keep pace with political, economic, and social changes, criminal proscriptions may be applied both analogically[60] and retroactively[61] in order to ensure that legal standards do not lag behind the policy demands of the day, and to prevent previously unproscribed but socially dangerous acts from going unpunished.

The public is not considered to require the guidance of legal standards to the same extent as those who administer the system. Nor is it thought desirable to facilitate public access to written rules and thereby to limit the flexibility with which they can be administered. Yet the public is not entirely neglected, for its compliance is, after all, what is sought. Customary notions of right and wrong, as supplemented by accumulated post-1949 experience, are thought to be a satisfactory substitute for published definitions of the major common crimes. With respect to new crimes that reflect values that the Communist government is seeking to impose upon the community, apart from published proscriptions and experience with their enforcement, the regime relies upon informal, especially oral, communication of relevant norms. Thus, when a new policy is initiated and the use of criminal sanctions is contemplated to assure its enforcement, the requisite rules of behavior are in large part communicated and reiterated in the frequent small group meetings that virtually every Chinese is supposed to attend, either at work or in his residential area. Related techniques are also used, such as stimulating the masses "democratically" to adopt "patriotic pacts" that embody "norms for the conduct of the masses," telling

59. See, e.g., "Are All Crimes To Be Counted as Contradictions Between the Enemy and Us? Are They All To Be Regarded as Objects of Dictatorship?" *CFYC*, 3:73–76 (1958). In his speech "Problems Relating to the Correct Handling of Contradictions Among the People," Mao conceded that "many people do not distinguish clearly between these two types of contradictions which are different in nature — those between the enemy and us and those among the people — and confuse the two. We admit that it is sometimes easy to confuse them. We had instances of such confusion in our past work. In the work of liquidating counterrevolutionaries, good people were mistaken for bad. Such things have happened before, and still happen today" (p. 8).

60. See, e.g., Act for Punishment of Counterrevolution, p. 5, art. 16; *Lectures*, pp. 69–70; Fan Ming, pp. 72–73, criticizing the *Lectures'* suggestion that future conditions may permit abandoning the principle of analogy.

61. See, e.g., Act for Punishment of Counterrevolution, p. 5, art. 18; *Lectures*, p. 44; Fan Ming, p. 72, criticizing the *Lectures'* effort to limit the retroactive application of criminal law.

them "what to advocate and what to praise, what to oppose and what to prohibit." [62] Newspaper editorials, ubiquitous posters, radio broadcasts, large rallies and other media of mass communication all disseminate the substance of official norms that have not been published in formal legal documents. Even those substantive criminal standards that have been formally published have tended to appear at or toward the end of a mass movement in order "to consolidate . . . victories already won," rather than to initiate a program of action.[63]

A similar picture can be drawn of the guidelines for the application of "administrative" sanctions. Although frequent reference is made to the need to subject people who engage in certain kinds of antisocial behavior to sanctions such as "criticism-education" and "struggle," published sources do not systematically articulate the full hierarchy of these "informal" sanctions and the circumstances in which they are to be applied. Published documents do purport, however, to regulate the application of the "administrative" sanctions that are of a "formal" nature. The Security Administration Punishment Act is the nearest thing to a criminal code that China has produced. It sets forth with considerable specificity many types of violations of public order which are closely akin to our misdemeanors, but which the Chinese do not consider "crimes." Assault, petty theft, gambling, infliction of minor property damage, violation of health or safety regulations, and improper advances to women are illustrative of the conduct proscribed. For each type of violation the act sets out a range of sanctions and criteria for their imposition. It also deals with problems that are usually covered by the general part of a continental criminal code, such as the responsibility of the mentally ill, the young, and the intoxicated, mitigation and aggravation of punishment, and time limitations upon accusation and punishment.

Published rules that provide for the most severe "administrative" sanctions are far more sketchy. The documents that govern the imposition of "supervised labor" provide that it shall be applicable to unregenerate former landlords, rich peasants, and counterrevolutionaries, and to certain "bad elements," such as persons who persistently refuse to take part in production.[64] Through unpublished directives the category of "bad elements" has been extended to include such diverse types as hooligans, recidivist petty offenders, "unlawful

62. "A New Form of Self-Government by the Masses" (a report of an inspection team of the political-legal department of the Shensi provincial government), *Shan-hsi jih-pao* (Shensi daily), May 8, 1958, in *Chung-kuo kuo-fang ts'ung-shu* (Collection of reprinted articles concerning China's national defense; Peking, 1958), 2:81.

63. The quotation is from P'eng Chen, "Explanation of the Draft Act of the PRC for Punishment of Corruption," *Hsin-hua yüeh-pao* (New China monthly), 31:24 (May 1952). After a visit to the People's Republic during its early years, Frank Moraes, then editor of the *Times of India*, wrote: "In India, as in other democratic countries, the government passes a law when it wants something done. In China it starts a movement." Frank Moraes, *Report on Mao's China* (New York, 1953), p. 36.

64. See National Agricultural Development Outline of the PRC for 1956–1967 (revised draft, Oct. 25, 1957), *FKHP*, 6:57–58; Instructions of the CCPCC and the State Council of the PRC Relating to Checking the Blind Outflow of People from Rural Villages (Dec. 18, 1957), *FKHP*, 6:229–232.

bourgeois elements," and others who resist the commune movement.[65] For a few years the more serious "rightists" represented a fifth category to which this sanction could be applied. The Decision of the State Council that established "rehabilitation through labor" embraces similar types of "bad elements" as well as minor counterrevolutionaries and reactionaries and those who persistently violate labor discipline and work assignments.[66]

## F. THE PROCESS

The hierarchical structure of the sanctioning apparatus and the formulation of standards to guide those who administer the sanctions suggest the central government's interest in curbing arbitrary law enforcement by cadres at the working level. Yet plainly enough, the applicable standards permit those cadres a considerable amount of discretion. Moreover, the central government frequently emphasizes the importance of applying rules flexibly and sensibly in the light of local conditions. By illustrating the process of imposing sanctions it is possible to provide some insight into the scope of the discretion that is exercised, the factors that condition its exercise, and the procedures for reviewing it.

If we continue to take a residential area of a large city as our example, we note that very minor cases are often disposed of below the level of the official police organization by the semiofficial, grassroots elite. Members of the mediation committee are explicitly authorized to settle both disputes that involve minor criminal infractions and civil matters. In performing this function they engage in a good deal of persuasion, criticism-education, and warning of one or more of the parties either in private or, when necessary, before small or large groups. Members of the security defense committee and the residents' committee and officials of any Party and Youth League units in the area perform similar functions, and such informal sanctioning is a staple in the routine of the policeman on the beat. This informal processing of large numbers of petty violations relieves the formal apparatus of an enormous burden and thereby strengthens its resources for dealing with important cases. It also does much to supplement generalized modes of informing the public about what conduct is prohibited.

When sanctions of greater magnitude are contemplated, the problem usually ceases to be one that can be disposed of by the lower level elite. The police organization identifies at least preliminarily conduct that warrants sanctions of any consequence. It determines whether that conduct should be deemed noncriminal or criminal, that is, whether the police organization will decide the offender's fate or whether it will invoke the participation of the procuracy

---

65. See, e.g., Teng Hsiao-p'ing, "Report Relating to the Rectification Movement" (at the 3d enlarged plenary meeting of the 8th session of the CCPCC, Sept. 23, 1957), *FKHP*, 6:18; Ts'ui Ch'eng-hsüan, "How We Defended the Safety of Hsing-fu People's Commune," *CFYC*, 6:61–63 (1958).

66. Decision of the State Council of the PRC Relating to Problems of Rehabilitation Through Labor,

and the courts. The actual process of imposing the more severe sanctions varies somewhat from city to city and even within a given city. Variations may also depend upon the offense involved, with the difference between counterrevolutionary and other offenses being fundamental. Yet, the essential features of the process can be presented by describing typical methods of handling a series of examples — cases involving theft by laborers who are temporarily unemployed because of urban economic dislocations.

CASE NO. I

A is caught in the act of stealing a small amount of rice from the local government storehouse. He is searched and taken to the neighborhood public security station. The station chief (or his deputy) informally questions A, any witnesses, and the patrolman who apprehended him, and it becomes clear that A stole out of hunger, had never previously run afoul of the law, is duly repentant, and that there is no reason to suspect him of other misconduct. The station chief therefore decides to lecture A severely and to release him on condition that he write out, for posting in public places, several copies of a "guarantee" not to repeat the offense, and that he make an oral "self-examination" before his residents' group. Although Article 11 of SAPA authorizes the issuance of a formal warning, a fine of up to twenty yuan,[67] and detention of up to ten days, the first two sanctions are applied relatively rarely, and in the circumstances of this case detention is deemed to be too harsh. But even in these circumstances, if A were of bourgeois origin, his act of stealing public property would take on a sinister aspect and would usually be classified as a "contradiction between the enemy and us." A would then be treated as an "object of dictatorship," subject not to mere detention but to criminal punishment. Because A belongs to the proletariat, however, his act is viewed as a "contradiction among the people," and therefore relatively innocuous.

CASE NO. 2

B is caught committing the same petty offense as A in similar circumstances, except that this is his third such minor brush with the law. Because previous resort to "guarantee" and "self-examination" does not appear to have stimulated B to reform, the station chief believes that B deserves seven days of SAPA detention. However, since this is a relatively severe punishment, the station chief cannot impose it without approval from the chief of the public security subbureau's security section, which handles ordinary violations of public order. If there is no reason to suspect B of misconduct more serious than petty theft, he remains at the station while the station chief either telephones the security section and discusses his recommendation with the section chief (or his deputy), or sends a policeman to the subbureau to submit the detention application papers for the section chief's perusal. In either event, if the recommendation is approved, as it normally is, B is informed of this decision and is asked whether he has "any opinion" about it, that is, whether he wishes to have the decision

67. According to the Chinese official exchange rate, the value of the yuan is now equal to approximately U.S. $0.42.

reviewed by the city public security bureau under procedures authorized by Article 18 of SAPA. *B* rarely seeks review, and even more seldom obtains relief thereby. He usually accepts the decision and serves his term in the station's detention quarters, either because he cannot comprehend a right to obtain review, or because he is aware that he might well have received heavier sanctions and that a petition for review might be taken as a sign of an unrepentant attitude.

CASE NO. 3

*C* is caught committing the same petty theft as *A* and *B* in similar circumstances, but unlike them he has thrice previously been subjected to SAPA detention for offenses of this type. Thus, short-term detention has failed to educate him and more extensive exposure to reform seems necessary. Yet the offense is too minor to warrant criminal punishment, and *C* is not suspected of any graver misconduct. In these circumstances the station chief recommends to the subbureau's security section not only that *C* receive the maximum detention authorized by SAPA for this offense, but also that on completion of this term he be subjected either to supervised labor or to rehabilitation through labor as a "bad element." While *C* is serving his term of detention at the station house, the section chief reviews his entire record to consider whether it justifies imposing either of these severe administrative sanctions. Although from the point of view of the individual, remaining in society under a strict and stigmatizing regimen is less of a deprivation than being confined in a rehabilitation camp, from the point of view of the regime the two are of comparable magnitude. Whether one or the other is meted out is ordinarily a matter of administrative convenience to be determined by factors such as whether the "bad element" is a family man or a floater, and whether the need for his labor is greater locally or at a rehabilitation camp. Because of the severity of these two sanctions, if the chief of the security section decides that *C* requires either of them, he cannot make the final determination himself, but must submit a recommendation to the chief of the subbureau.

Although "struggle meetings" are not as readily convened against ordinary urban residents as they are against government or factory personnel or rural people, if the case has particular educational significance the station chief and the section chief may also recommend that imposition of the major sanction of supervised labor or rehabilitation through labor be preceded by a "speak reason struggle." If these recommendations are approved, at the end of the period of SAPA detention *C* is "struggled" before a meeting of his neighbors or of residents of the area in which he committed the theft, and the major sanction is announced at the climax. The simplicity of these procedures explains why, as one former police official put it, the regime finds them to be "very convenient."

CASE NO. 4

A policeman catches *D* sneaking out of the local government rationing office with hundreds of new grain ration booklets. Because these circumstances suggest that he has committed a major crime, he is taken to the subbureau rather than to the neighborhood public security station.

*Detention.* At the subbureau *D* is booked on suspicion of the crime of theft. His case is turned over to the subbureau's trial preparation section, and he is detained at the subbureau's detention house. This detention for purposes of criminal investigation is different from the detention that is authorized by SAPA as an administrative punishment for offenses not amounting to crimes (as in Cases 1, 2, and 3). It is also different from another method of apprehending and confining persons who are suspected of crimes: arrest. Detention is the emergency apprehension and confinement of a suspect without an arrest warrant for the purpose of investigating whether there is sufficient evidence to justify his arrest. Arrest, on the other hand, is the apprehension and confinement, or the continuing confinement, of a suspect on the basis of an arrest warrant for the purpose of investigating whether there is sufficient evidence to justify prosecution. Articles 7 and 11 of the Arrest Act[68] require the police, within twenty-four hours after a suspect is detained under the broad "emergency measures" of Article 5,[69] to question him and either release him unconditionally or request the procuracy's authorization of an arrest. The procuracy must within forty-eight hours after receiving such a request either authorize arrest or disapprove it and order the suspect's release.

Frequently, these statutory requirements are not observed by the police, and the procuracy does not become aware of the case until a later stage. Several former police officials have reported that because Article 13 of the Arrest Act explicitly exempts from the provisions of that act "detentions that are administrative punishments for citizens who violate security administration rules," police units sometimes detain criminal suspects under the SAPA in order to circumvent the requirements of the Arrest Act. Others have reported that most police officials are concerned only with "breaking the case," see no need to trouble themselves about the legality of lengthy detention prior to arrest, and simply detain the suspect until they are able to determine whether arrest is appropriate. At least in some cities, in order to permit higher-level police officials to check periodically upon the processing of detained suspects, the trial preparation section must apply to the subbureau chief for an approved ten-day extension once it has held a suspect for ten days. A series of such extensions may be obtained. This procedure is prescribed by internal police regulations

68. Pp. 240, 241.

69. Art. 5 (p. 240) provides as follows: In any one of the following situations, a public security organ may adopt emergency measures to detain immediately [without obtaining a warrant] an offender whom it is necessary to investigate:

    (1) He is preparing to commit a crime, is in the process of committing a crime, or is discovered immediately after committing a crime;

    (2) He is identified as a criminal by the victim or by an eyewitness;

    (3) He has evidence that he has committed a crime discovered on his person or at his residence;

    (4) He attempts to escape or is [in the act of] escaping;

    (5) He may destroy or fabricate evidence or may collude with others regarding statements to be made;

    (6) His status is unclear, or he has no definite residence.

rather than by legislation, and is far less demanding of police investigators than is the procedure required by the Arrest Act.

The legislative provisions theoretically available to implement the Arrest Act's twenty-four hour limit upon police detention are all ineffective. Article 42 of the Labor Act provides:

> When investigation and adjudication have not yet been concluded and the commitment to custody of an offender whose case has not been adjudged exceeds the time limit fixed by law, the detention house shall immediately notify the organ that sent him into custody to deal with the case quickly.[70]

Since in *D*'s case, as in most, the "organ that sent him into custody" is a subdivision of the public security subbureau, and since the detention house is administered by another subdivision of the subbureau, notification by the detention house authorities is regarded as hardly more than a gentle reminder.

One of the procuracy's contemplated duties of "general supervision" of government operations was to see "whether or not the investigatory activities of investigation organs are legal." [71] As already noted, however, after the antirightist movement it was determined that general supervision would not be an important part of the procuracy's functions, but would be used only to assist, not to interfere with, the fight against the enemy.[72] Similarly, although deputies to the national and local legislative bodies — the people's congresses — occasionally inspect detention facilities in accordance with their prescribed obligations,[73] the police are notified of their plans to visit and easily shield from view those individuals whose detention might be deemed unduly long. Finally, even if *D* is sufficiently educated to act in his own behalf, exercise of his constitutional right to complain to the police about their refusal to comply with statutory detention procedures[74] would brand him as a recalcitrant and probably worsen his plight.[75] *D* is thus entirely dependent upon the police to determine the length of his detention.

Because *D* is neither physically or mentally ill nor an expectant or recent mother, and because he is suspected of a major rather than a minor crime, he cannot benefit from the limited legislative authorization for the police to release a suspect pending adjudication under guarantee or surveillance procedures.[76] In any event, these procedures are rarely invoked. Furthermore, although both the police and the trial court have discretion to permit *D* to receive

70. P. 38.
71. Procuracy Law, p. 134, art. 4(3).
72. T'an Cheng-wen, p. 42.
73. See Decision of the Standing Committee of the NPC of the PRC Relating to Inspection of Work by Deputies of the NPC and Deputies of People's Congresses of Provinces, Autonomous Regions and Cities Directly Under the Central Authority (passed at the 20th meeting of the Standing Committee of the NPC, Aug. 6, 1955), *FKHP*, 2:66–67.
74. Const., p. 29, art. 97, provides: "Citizens of the People's Republic of China shall have the right to present written or oral complaints to state organs of the various levels with respect to any violation of law or dereliction of duty by personnel of state organs."
75. Cf. MacFarquhar, p. 229.
76. See Arrest Act, pp. 239, 241, arts. 2, 11; Labor Act, p. 37, art. 37.

visits from his family, and although the police can permit him to send and receive correspondence,[77] in practice no visits or correspondence are generally allowed before the close of the police investigation. Until that time D's family and friends often do not know where he is detained or even whether he is detained. Indeed, in recent years efforts have also been made to insulate D from all contact within the detention house, except with his jailers. If he is confined with others, usually conversation is strictly forbidden. D is left to ponder his past and his future and to study the official exhortations to confess and repent that are often posted on the walls of the cell.

*Interrogation.* A staff member of the trial preparation section is assigned to D's case. After studying the file, he orders D to a small interview room in the detention house. There, often with a clerk present to record D's statements, the staff member subjects D to the first of a number of intensive interrogations. These sessions are founded on the assumption that, although "the probability that . . . [D] will intentionally make a false statement is relatively great," he nevertheless "knows better than anyone else whether he committed the crime of which he is accused and how he committed it," and "it is often not possible to think of clearing up the facts of the case without listening to . . . [his] statement." [78] Chinese Communist law rejects any principle that resembles a privilege against self-incrimination, and relies upon D as a major source of evidence. For this reason the "rightists" were denounced for purportedly maintaining "that the defendant has the right to lie and is free to remain silent." [79] Thus, instead of cautioning D about the pitfalls of loquacity, the interrogator seeks to overcome his reticence.

Most prominent among the techniques that the interrogator has been instructed to apply is persistent reiteration of the much-publicized official policy of "leniency for those who confess, severity for those who resist." [80] Other standard tactics also have a familiar ring to a student of criminal law. The interrogator alternates between a harsh, threatening, impatient manner and a kind, helpful, and understanding one. He ignores D for long periods in order to increase the tension in the interview room. He attempts to mix D up, ordering him, for example, to recite his life history backwards and then by alternate years. Holding up a stack of papers for D to see at a distance, he resorts to the "we've got the goods, so you might as well come clean" approach. And if others are thought to be implicated, D may be told: "Your companions have talked — you're the one who's going to be the fall guy." Seldom is D informed of the specific charges against him, the identity of the witnesses, or the character of the evidence. In part this is to prevent the possibility that upon release D might seek revenge against his accusers. More importantly, this procedure seeks to avoid D's con-

77. Labor Act, pp. 39, 40, arts. 56, 58, 59.
78. Chang Tzu-p'ei, "Several Problems Relating to the Use of Evidence To Determine the Facts of a Case in Criminal Litigation" [hereinafter cited as "Several Problems"], *CFYC,* 4:13–14 (1962).
79. T'an Cheng-wen, p. 38.
80. Wu Lei, "We Must Thoroughly Clean Out Old Legal Concepts and Rightwing Thinking in Our Teaching of 'Criminal Litigation,' " *Chiao-hsüeh yü yen-chiu* (Teaching and research), 4:2 (1958).

fessing only what the authorities already know. Often the interrogator's opening gambit is to ask: "Why are you here? What crimes have you committed? Are you going to resist or be honest?"

The interrogator is trained to view his work as "a battle of wits" and "the sharpest face-to-face class struggle." He is taught to choose his tactics on the basis of an evaluation of $D$'s weaknesses. Since 1954 physical coercion has played only a minor part in the interrogation process. Official policy has long prohibited it,[81] although in practice a certain amount of coercion is winked at as "necessary." For example, handcuffs and leg irons, which are authorized only in emergency situations threatening the security of the detention house,[82] are nevertheless frequently placed on suspects who stubbornly refuse to cooperate in the face of what is deemed to be convincing evidence.

A record is made of the substance of $D$'s statements, and he is asked to sign it as verification of its authenticity. While $D$ waits in his cell, the interrogator and others seek to check this information from other sources. Their investigation provides material for further interrogation, which in turn leads to further investigation. This time-consuming process often requires weeks and sometimes months.

*Search.* The provisions of the Arrest Act relating to search are less rigorous than those dealing with detention, and therefore are usually obeyed. Article 9 states in part:

> In order to find evidence of a crime, when arresting or detaining an offender, the organ executing the arrest or detention may search his person, his articles, his residence or other relevant places; if it believes that another person concerned may be harboring an offender or concealing evidence of the crime, it may also search his person, his articles, his residence or other relevant places. At the time of the search, except in emergency situations, they [those who search] shall have a search warrant from the organ that executes the arrest or detention.[83]

In practice, this ambiguous formulation is interpreted as authorizing the search without a warrant that was made of $D$'s person and of things in his possession at the time of his emergency detention.[84] But $D$, it will be recalled, was apprehended at a government rationing office, rather than at home, so that, absent special circumstances making it unreasonable to apply for a search warrant, Article 9 is interpreted as not authorizing search without a warrant of "his [other] articles, his residence or other relevant places." Yet this limitation does not present any significant obstacle to investigation. Since the required warrant is that of the detaining organ, which in most cases is the police, that organ in effect issues a search warrant to itself when it is satisfied that the standards of Article 9 have been met. Thus, even without an emergency to

81. Chang Tzu-p'ei, "Several Problems," p. 13.
82. Labor Act, p. 38, art. 46.
83. P. 241.
84. Art. 40 of the Labor Act (p. 37) provides for a thorough search of all suspects when they are brought to the detention house, and for forwarding materials that are relevant to investigation and adjudication to the appropriate agencies.

justify search without a warrant, the police can search without seeking approval from either the procuracy or the court.[85]

This does not mean that a patrolman or an investigator has unfettered power to search whenever, wherever, and for whatever he pleases. Internal police regulations require that issuance of a search warrant be approved by a responsible superior. If, for example, during D's detention his interrogator believes that a search of his residence would turn up relevant evidence, the interrogator applies to the chief of the trial preparation section for a warrant. The section chief, if he agrees, passes the application on for scrutiny by the chief of the subbureau, unless the latter has authorized the section chief to act in his behalf in such cases. When executing a search, the police comply whenever possible with the requirements of Article 9 that a neighbor or other bystander and the suspect or a member of his family be present, and that these witnesses sign the record that is made of the items seized.

*Evidence.* There are virtually no restrictions upon the kinds of evidence that may be used to determine D's guilt. In addition to D's statements and those of witnesses, demonstrative evidence, documentary evidence, reports of scientific experts, and investigators' descriptions of the scene of the crime all may go into D's file. Opinions and hearsay may both be received. There appear to be no rules rendering persons incompetent to testify. Nor are there rules of privilege that exclude relevant evidence.

This hospitable attitude toward the reception of evidence does not, however, signify a carefree attitude toward its reliability, at least on the part of the system's higher-level administrators. Mindful of past abuses, Chinese writers have recently emphasized the need for sophistication and discrimination in evaluating the many varieties of evidence.[86] Although officials at the operating level are urged to make full use of scientific assistance, they are also cautioned that its value depends on the skill of the expert and on his equipment, and that scientific reports must be evaluated in light of all the other evidence.[87] Similarly, if a charge is to rest upon a mosaic of circumstantial evidence, the tesserae must be relevant, trustworthy, consistent, and sufficiently convincing to exclude the possibilities that someone else committed the crime or that no crime occurred.[88] Law enforcement cadres are reminded that personal interest, enmity, and other moral weaknesses may affect statements of a witness, and that the most objective witness may perceive, recall, or relate events inaccurately.[89] They are also told that the value of testimony depends, for example, upon whether the information obtained is based on personal observation, on the

85. Chung Yu, "My View [on the Legality of a Search]," *Hsin Chung-kuo jih-pao* (New China daily, Nanking), Oct. 28, 1956.

86. This subject is one of the few current legal problems that has been discussed in recent years. In addition to Chang Tzu-p'ei, "Several Problems," see Ho Shuang-lu, "Several Problems Relating to Evidence in Criminal Litigation," *CFYC*, 2:31–37 (1963); Wu Lei et al., "A Few Realizations from the Study of Our Country's Guiding Principles of Evidence in Litigation," *CFYC*, 1:21–25 (1963).

87. Ho Shuang-lu, p. 33.

88. Chang Tzu-p'ei, "Several Problems," pp. 16–17.

89. "Several Problems," p. 15; Ho Shuang-lu, p. 32.

account of another person, or on common gossip.[90] Moreover, the cadres are warned against assuming their own infallibility in gathering, assembling and analyzing the evidence, and in evaluating $D$'s behavior during interrogation.[91] Above all, they are admonished to doubt $D$'s statements, even when he confesses and it is convenient to believe him, and always to verify his statements through conscientious outside investigation.[92]

*Arrest.* When there appears to be reliable evidence that $D$ has committed one or more crimes,[93] even though interrogation and investigation may not yet have been completed, the interrogator will draw up a "recommendation to arrest," which is an application for a warrant for $D$'s arrest. It states briefly the crimes for which arrest is recommended, the evidence collected relating to each alleged crime, the harm that resulted, and $D$'s class status, family background, past record, and various identifying facts. If both the chief of the trial preparation section and the chief of the subbureau agree that there is reliable evidence that $D$ has committed a crime, an arrest warrant is issued by the subbureau, often without seeking the legally required approval of the procuracy. However, in some cities, especially when the suspect is an important person or the crime is a grave one, unpublished regulations require that this application for an arrest warrant actually be approved not only by the chief of the basic procuracy, but also by the president of the basic court. They, personally or through representatives, meet with the subbureau chief or his representative to work out a joint decision. In some cases the "three chiefs," as they are called, deliberate upon the arrest question with the deputy secretary of the local Party committee who specializes in law enforcement matters, with whom they form the "political-legal Party group" (PLPG) for the district.[94] If an arrest warrant is issued, $D$ and often his family are so informed.

Arrest is a feather in the cap of the interrogator, for, in the idiom that the Chinese share with us, it is taken to mean that he has "broken" the case. It also relieves him of the annoyance of having to ask his superiors for repeated extensions of $D$'s term of confinement, as is often necessary prior to arrest. Neither legislation nor internal police regulations appear to limit the duration of a person's confinement after arrest and prior to adjudication of his case.[95]

90. Ho Shuang-lu, p. 32.

91. Chang Tzu-p'ei, in "Several Problems," writes: "[W]hat are frequently called abnormal emotions, panic and bad facial expressions and red eyes, etc., cannot serve as indirect evidence. Actually, when persons who have not committed crimes are suspected or are confronted by investigators and judges, it is also possible for all kinds of abnormal phenomena to occur; and it is possible for some true criminals in the same circumstances to behave in a normal way as if there were nothing wrong" (p. 17).

92. "Several Problems," p. 13.

93. This standard for assessing the sufficiency of the evidence for purposes of arrest differs from both the standard applicable to detention (see note 69 above), and the standard applicable to conviction (see text at notes 96 and 97, below).

94. Serious disagreements are rare among the "three chiefs" and even rarer among the political-legal Party group. Those that occur are resolved according to procedures similar to those described at pp. 36–37.

95. None of the former police officials interviewed could recall any internal police regulation that limited the duration of postarrest confinement or required periodic review

Arrest also facilitates the remainder of the interrogation process. By indicating to $D$ the increased likelihood of prosecution and conviction, it reinforces the suggestion that he "cooperate" in order to obtain leniency. And by ensuring that $D$ is unlikely to be released soon and thus put in a position to complain about mistreatment, it gives the interrogator more leeway to expose $D$ to pressures, including possible physical coercion.

*Recommendation to Prosecute.* Police investigation usually ends when $D$ has been exhaustively questioned about each of the crimes of which he is suspected, his statements have been checked, outside investigation has ceased to turn up new evidence, and the interrogator believes that he has correctly reconstructed the facts. Sometimes, for reasons unrelated to the case, investigation is prematurely terminated. During a mass movement, the requirement that a large volume of cases be swiftly handled may preclude painstaking investigation. If $D$ is well known, or if the crime for which he is being investigated has otherwise attracted public attention or the Party's interest, cadres at the operating level often labor under intense pressure to announce that the case has been "broken." Their thoroughness may also be influenced by whether the detention house is overcrowded, whether the investigation staff is undermanned, and whether $D$'s family or important friends are clamoring to know what has become of him.

In assessing the evidence in order to decide whether to recommend that $D$ be prosecuted, the police employ a more stringent standard than that applied for arrest. Often this higher standard, which is also applied by the procuracy and the court at later stages of the process, is cryptically expressed as requiring "sufficient" and "reliable" evidence that $D$ has committed the crime in question. Evidence is said to be "reliable" when it is not subject to doubt.[96] Since there must also be a certain quantum of reliable evidence to justify arrest, the distinction between the arrest standard and the prosecution and conviction standard turns upon the meaning of "sufficient." A leading authority seems to suggest that evidence is "sufficient" when it is "comprehensive," that is, when it deals with all the problems in the case that must be resolved.[97] Although each case presents its own evidentiary needs, cadres are urged to find evidence that will show

whether a crime occurred and what crime; the [identity of the] criminal and his origin, history, previous behavior, and attitude after committing the crime; the time, place, method, device, purpose, motive, surroundings, and dangerous consequences of commission of the crime; whether it was committed intentionally or negligently; whether it involves a contradiction between the enemy and us or a contradiction among the people; and whether all evidentiary materials relating to the facts are reliable; etc.[98]

---

of such confinement by higher police officials. Future interviews may reveal such a regulation, for it would seem curious for the Chinese to review prearrest confinement but not postarrest confinement.

96. See Chang Tzu-p'ei, "Several Problems," p. 17.
97. "Several Problems," pp. 17–18.
98. "Several Problems," p. 16.

One important question relating to the legal sufficiency of evidence concerns the significance that may be attached to *D*'s confession. Contrary to the traditional Chinese view, *D* may be convicted even if he steadfastly refuses to confess, when there is reliable, comprehensive evidence of his guilt.[99] If *D* does confess, he cannot be convicted unless there is reliable evidence to corroborate the confession.[100] However, it is not clear whether *D* may be convicted when there is some reliable evidence to corroborate his confession but that independent evidence falls short of being comprehensive. Interviews indicate that in these circumstances conviction has been commonplace. Yet ambiguous statements in recent publications suggest that a higher standard of corroboration" may now be current or at least under consideration.[101]

If the interrogator believes that the materials in *D*'s file meet the requisite standard for proving that *D* committed one or more crimes, he draws up a "recommendation to prosecute," which is a summary of all the information thought necessary for a comprehensive analysis of each charge. This document is submitted to the chief of the trial preparation section for review. If he approves, the "recommendation to prosecute" and the entire file are sent, sometimes without further review by the subbureau chief, to the basic procuracy.

*Decision to Prosecute.* The case is there assigned to an individual procurator, who studies the file and then interviews *D* at the detention house, often in the presence of the interrogator who handled the matter for the police. The procurator questions *D* closely about each charge of the "recommendation to prosecute," and then returns to his office to study the case further. If no evidence seems to be lacking and there is nothing suspicious about *D*'s answers, the procurator usually does not make an independent investigation of those charges to which *D* has confessed. If, however, *D* has denied any of the charges or significant facts relating to them, or if the evidence appears incomplete or open to doubt, the procurator interviews the principal witnesses in an effort to reconcile the contradictions and to fill the gaps. He may also question *D* again and discuss any problems with the police interrogator. For example, he may attempt to persuade the interrogator to undertake further investigation in order to obtain evidence necessary to sustain the charges. Or he may ask that the charges be revised in order to correct their failure to state a crime or to accord with the evidence. If existing evidence is insufficient and further investigation promises to be fruitless, he may suggest that the police dispose of the case through noncriminal processes, or, more rarely, drop the case entirely.

If there are serious problems and the procurator and police interrogator cannot agree informally upon disposition of the case, the procurator may recommend that his chief not approve prosecution. Should his chief agree, the case

99. "Several Problems," p. 14.
100. "Several Problems," p. 14.
101. Chang Tzu-p'ei in "Several Problems," writes: "[W]e should not convict [the defendant] of a crime if we do not obtain other accurate and thorough evidentiary material and should not rely on a statement admitting guilt" (p. 15). "Only when the statement [of the defendant] is checked and found to be in complete agreement with the facts of the crime can it be proved factual and serve as a basis for deciding the case" (p. 17). See also Wu Lei et al., p. 24.

is returned to the police, who may acquiesce and release *D,* or substitute administrative measures for criminal punishment, or continue the investigation and interrogation in order to gather the necessary evidence. The police may also challenge the adverse determination of the basic procuracy in a variety of ways. For example, the chief of the subbureau or the chief of its trial preparation section may enter into direct negotiations with the chief of the basic procuracy in order to obtain reconsideration. Or police officials may take the problem before the "three chiefs," the political-legal Party group, or the secretary of the district Party committee.[102] Or they may complain to their superiors in the city public security bureau (PSB), who can raise the matter with officials in the intermediate procuracy.[103] Several of these procedures may be invoked in the same case before a solution is reached either through consultation and compromise, or through a decision of the Party apparatus or the intermediate procuracy. Disputes reaching this level are relatively unusual of late, and those that do arise tend to be resolved in favor of the police. Procurators do not want to be criticized for professional incompetence or overzealousness that allows improperly prepared cases to reach the courts, but they know that it is far more serious to be accused of "rightist" errors that frustrate the police. Moreover, several other factors tend to minimize friction between police and procuracy. Cadres of the two organizations are in day-to-day contact and depend on each other's cooperation in a variety of ways for the smooth conduct of their respective duties. Police and prosecutors come from roughly the same social and educational backgrounds, receive similar ideological indoctrination and on-the-job legal training, are subject to identical bureaucratic pressures and incentives, and sometimes even belong to the same Party unit. Also, many procurators are former police officials.

If the procurator finds the case appropriate for prosecution, he draws up a bill of prosecution, which is a revised version of the "recommendation to prosecute," and submits it to the chief procurator. With the approval of the latter, the bill of prosecution and the file are transferred to the district's basic court.

*Adjudication.* The procedures of the court are similar to those of the procuracy. The case is assigned to a judge who studies the materials and then, usually in the company of his clerk, goes to question *D* at the detention house. If the evidence in the file appears comprehensive and reliable, and if the essential elements of a charge are admitted in detail, the judge usually considers it to be confirmed. If *D* does not admit all the essential elements and the evidence appears incomplete or unconvincing, the judge or his clerk may interview witnesses and investigate any points of importance that require clarification. When the limited investigation permitted by judicial resources fails to reveal comprehensive and reliable evidence to support the major charges of the bill of prosecution, the judge usually discusses the case with the procurator and police interrogator who handled it, and suggests that they take the case back and either continue the investigation or dispose of the case through administrative sanctions. They often

102. Recall text at note 94 and see T'an Cheng-wen, p. 41,
103. See Procuracy Law, p. 136, art. 13.

acquiesce. When they do not, an informal compromise may be achieved, with the judge, for example, agreeing to recommend to his superiors within the court that *D* be convicted of a lesser crime and sentenced to "control" rather than imprisonment. If no such solution is reached, one of the judge's superiors, either the president of the court or the chief judge of the court's criminal division, may discuss the case with the chief procurator and the chief of the subbureau or their representatives, in an effort to work out a mutually acceptable solution. The secretary of the district Party committee may ultimately have to settle the matter. Such serious disagreements between judges and other law enforcement cadres are relatively rare. As their experience during the antirightist movement demonstrated, judges have no more reason than procurators to feel secure about frustrating the police. Although according to Communist slogans judges are supposed to be "expert" as well as "red," they realize that professional legal considerations cannot take precedence over current needs of the revolution. Both because judges share with procurators and police a similar background, training, occupational status, and outlook, and because many judges have previously served in the police and procuracy, one should not exaggerate the extent to which they may be more sensitive than other law enforcement officials to professional legal considerations.

When the major charges of the bill of prosecution are adequately supported by reliable evidence and present no other difficulties, the judge next decides what sentence to propose. In most cases he recommends that *D* be given a milder sentence than life imprisonment; typically, he suggests that *D* be sentenced to a fixed number of years at reform through labor (imprisonment). The court is neither required to impose the same sentence on everyone who commits the same crime, nor is it free to sentence *D* without regard to existing guidelines. If, for example, *D* is guilty of robbery, the judge knows on the basis of experience and unpublished regulations and other materials that the range of punishment is ordinarily from two to five years of reform through labor. If *D* is guilty of theft by stealth rather than by force, the ordinary range is from six months to three years. In determining the precise sentence for *D*, the judge weighs a number of factors that often conflict. If *D* has a criminal record, or has refused to confess and repent the present crime, or has falsely accused another person of committing it, or by his crime has caused serious damage to state property, or is a member of a disfavored class, or is sentenced during a movement to suppress crimes such as his, the judge will tend to recommend a sentence at the top of the ordinary range of punishment.[104] If several of these factors are present, the recommended sentence may substantially exceed the usual maximum.[105] On the other hand, if any of a number of mitigating factors is present, or if *D* is sentenced at a time when the Party line emphasizes leniency in dealing with crimes such as his, the judge will

104. Published legislation sets forth a variety of aggravating circumstances. See Act for Punishment of Corruption, pp. 25–26, arts. 3–4; cf. SAPA, p. 252, art. 21.

105. See, e.g., "Criminal Judgment of the Nanchang City People's Court," *Chiang-hsi jih-pao* (Kiangsi daily), June 29, 1955, in which a habitual and unrepentant petty swindler whose activities had led two of his victims to attempt suicide was sentenced to death.

be inclined to propose a light sentence.[106] If there are several mitigating circumstances, the proposed sentence may be milder than the usual minimum.[107]

After deciding upon the sentence to recommend, the judge writes a draft
judgment identifying D and reciting his past record, the facts of the case, the
crime or crimes committed, the aggravating and mitigating circumstances, and
the proposed sentence.[108] The draft judgment is submitted for the scrutiny of
the chief judge of the criminal division, who may approve it, modify it, or
disapprove it and either send the case back to the procuracy and police, or set
in motion the previously described interagency consultation and negotiation
process. If D's sentence is to be a substantial one, for example, three years or
more of reform through labor, the proposed judgment will be cleared with the
court president. Generally, in all "important cases" approval of the political-
legal Party group or of the district Party secretary is also necessary. In this
context "important cases" have been described by one writer as "cases of an
important policy nature and of far-reaching implications." [109] And in disclosing
the secret of his success, a model judge from a rural area, who appears more
cautious than his urban counterparts, has boasted of asking instructions from
the Party whenever he intends to sentence a defendant to reform through
labor, as well as whenever a case poses important questions of policy or involves village or commune cadres.[110]

Once approved, the judgment is put into final form and made public, perhaps
by posting copies in prominent places in the district, or perhaps by announcing it
to D at a public meeting convened in the area where he resides or where he
committed the crime. People's assessors are usually selected to participate in
such public meetings, and defense lawyers occasionally appear as part of the
trappings. Whatever the manner in which disposition of the case is made public,
D receives a copy of the judgment, which states that he has a right to appeal
within a certain period, usually ten days or less; often he is also told of this
right informally.

*Appeal.* D seldom appeals. He is usually too uneducated to comprehend the
meaning of his right, or too skeptical that the higher court will be any more
sympathetic to him than the lower court was, or too afraid that appeal will be
construed as a manifestation of an unrepentant attitude warranting heavier
sentence or harsher prison treatment. Yet, at least at certain times, appeals have
helped accused persons.[111] Appellate review may be obtained not only by D

106. For representative mitigating circumstances, see Act for Punishment of Counterrevolution, p. 5, art. 14; Act for Punishment of Corruption, pp. 26–27, art. 5; cf. SAPA,
p. 252, art. 20.
107. See, e.g., "Hearing of the Szu-ming-t'ang Case Concluded," *Chieh-fang jih-pao*
(Liberation daily, Shanghai), Aug. 31, 1957.
108. For a typical judgment, see "Criminal Judgment of the Nanchang City People's
Court."
109. Li Mu-an, "Censure Independent Adjudication That Proceeds from Concepts of the
Old Law," *CFYC*, 1:26 (1958).
110. See Liu Tse-chün, p. 48.
111. In reviewing appeals and protests arising out of convictions for counterrevolutionary crimes by high and intermediate people's courts during the first quarter of
1956, appellate courts remanded no less than 40 percent of the cases for a new trial, imposed reduced sentences in over 20 percent of the cases, and granted outright acquittals

or with his consent by others in his behalf, but also by the procuracy by means of a "protest," and even by a dissatisfied complainant.[112] Appeal may be based on any ground, including error in ascertaining the facts, in applying the law, or in imposing the sentence. Should *D* wish to appeal, he may simply indicate his dissatisfaction orally when sentence is pronounced. Or, back in his cell or at the prison or labor camp to which he may be dispatched before the period for appeal expires, he or someone acting at his behest may write an informal letter requesting appellate review. Taking an appeal is a wholly nontechnical matter.[113] Since lawyers are generally no more available on appeal than at adjudication in the first instance, *D* is untroubled by lawyers' fees.[114] Nor are there court costs or filing fees.

Upon receipt of *D*'s request for review, the city intermediate court assigns the case to one of its judges, who, after a study of the file that is not limited to issues raised by *D*'s request, will reject the appeal without further inquiry if it appears frivolous. If the appeal is not rejected, the assigned judge will discuss it with members of the lower court, and, if he is satisfied with their views, the investigation may go no further. If unsatisfied, he may talk to the relevant procurators, police officers, Party officials, witnesses, and to *D* himself, in an effort to clear up doubtful points. At the conclusion of this investigation the assigned judge submits his recommendation to the chief judge of the intermediate court's criminal division, and frequently the case is discussed with the court president and perhaps the relevant secretary of the city Party committee before a decision is reached.

Thus, appellate review, like adjudication in the first instance, is ordinarily a nonpublic, informal, ex parte administrative inquiry. And since, at least in theory, appeal is not merely a review of the original decision but also potentially a complete readjudication, the court of second instance can be as uninhibited as the lower court. It normally takes one of four steps: (1) it may void the judgment of conviction and order retrial below, which usually means that reinvestigation by the police will be necessary; (2) more rarely, it may void the conviction and dismiss the case; (3) it may affirm both the conviction and the sentence; or (4) it may affirm the conviction but modify the sentence to

---

in about 3 percent. See Tung Pi-wu, "Adjudication Work of the People's Courts in the Preceding Year," *Hsin-hua pan-yüeh-k'an* (New China semimonthly), 15:10 (1956). More recently, Edgar Snow was told that "only about 5 percent of the [criminal] verdicts are appealed and 'not over 20 percent' are reversed." *The Other Side of the River, Red China Today* (New York, 1962), p. 355. See also Allyn and Adele Rickett, *Prisoners of Liberation* (New York, 1957), p. 215.

112. See Court Law, pp. 125–126, art. 11; Wang Chao-sheng, "Refute the Principle of 'Not Making the Position of the Defendant Unfavorable in a Criminal Appeal,'" *Hsi-pei ta-hsüeh hsüeh-pao (jen-wen k'o-hsüeh)* (Northwestern University Journal [humanistic sciences]), 1:65–70 (July 1958).

113. Wang Chao-sheng, p. 69.

114. During the brief era when lawyers were available to help the defendant appeal, the law provided for such assistance to be rendered free of charge in "[c]ases in which it is proved that the party is really in economic difficulties and is unable to pay." Provisional Measures of the PRC for Receipt of Fees by Lawyers (approved at the 29th plenary meeting of the State Council, May 25, 1956; promulgated by the Ministry of Justice, July 20, 1956), *FKHP*, 4:236, art. 6(5).

make it more lenient or more harsh.[115] Since 1958, a sentence can be increased even though the defendant rather than the procuracy or a complaining witness initiated the appeal.[116] According to the prevailing view, appeals should go beyond protecting the interests of the defendant:

The purpose of an appellate instance in the people's courts is correctly to complete the tasks of criminal adjudication, not only by correcting mistaken judgments that result in "miscarriage of justice" (such as finding an innocent person guilty or convicting one who has committed a minor crime of a major crime) but also by correcting mistaken judgments that result in "escape from justice" (such as acquitting the guilty or convicting one who has committed a major crime of a minor crime).[117]

If the appellate judgment has special educational significance, it is announced at a public meeting, normally with *D* present. Otherwise, copies of the judgment may be posted in prominent places, and *D* is given a copy.

*Postconviction Review.* Chinese law allows only one appeal. The judgment of the court of second instance is legally effective. If no appeal is taken, the judgment of the court of first instance becomes effective after the period for appeal has expired.[118] In either event, *D* may still resort to other modes of securing reappraisal of his conviction. In death sentence cases special procedures provide for automatic review by both the high people's court of the province and the Supreme People's Court in Peking.[119] In all other cases *D* or someone acting in his behalf may request the sentencing court or an appellate court to subject the case to "adjudication supervision," a postconviction review proceeding that permits consideration of all substantial questions. The procuracy or local Party officials may be asked to suggest such review to the courts.[120] If while *D* is undergoing reform through labor new evidence is discovered that may materially alter the outcome of his case, it must be transmitted to the sentencing court or to the court that serves the region of the labor camp or prison.[121]

---

115. Wang Chao-sheng, p. 67.

116. Wang Chao-sheng, p. 67. Prior to 1958 lawyers had allegedly encouraged their clients to appeal by telling them that "appeal has only good points and no bad points, and that in appealed cases the higher level courts can only reduce the sentence" (T'an Cheng-wen, p. 42).

During the antirightist movement lawyers were severely attacked for having groundlessly encouraged the defendant to appeal instead of educating "the defendant through persuasion to accept his punishment, observe the law, and through reform through labor become a new person" (Wang Chao-sheng, p. 66).

117. Wang Chao-sheng, p. 66.

118. Court Law, pp. 125–126, art. 11.

119. Court Law, pp. 125–126, art. 11; Reply of the Standing Committee of the NPC of the PRC to the Supreme People's Court Relating to Problems of How To Execute the Resolution that Death Penalty Cases Shall Be Decided by Judgment of or Approved by the Supreme People's Court (Sept. 26, 1957), *FKHP,* 6:297.

120. See Court Law, p. 126, art. 12. As in earlier stages of judicial participation in the criminal process, decisions relating to supervision of adjudication are made by a few important court and Party officials. Wang Hsin et al., "Several Problems Relating to the Procedure of Adjudication Supervision," *CFYC,* 2:72–75 (1958), indicate that there is a good deal of uncertainty among Chinese writers about the nature of this method of postconviction review and that theory and practice diverge in many respects.

121. Labor Act, p. 38, art. 43.

A court reviewing a legally effective judgment often consults representatives of the police and procuracy. If extensive further investigation is necessary, a joint work group of officials from the three departments may be formed. Besides reviewing single cases, sometimes the departments jointly reconsider entire classes of cases, especially in conjunction with shifts in policy calling for harsher or more lenient handling of certain categories of criminals. In 1957, for example, in response to widespread discontent over the severe and often unjust punishments meted out during earlier mass movements, Mao Tse-tung proposed "that the work of liquidating counterrevolution be completely examined." [122] Predictably, this "proposal" was promptly implemented, with the result that in many cases mere "criticism-education" was substituted for the original sentence to imprisonment.[123] It should be emphasized, however, that the low value that the Chinese attach to the finality of criminal judgments is not an unmixed blessing for *D,* since postconviction review, like appeal, can be used to impose a harsher sentence as well as a lighter one. Newspapers contain numerous accounts of how, months after disposition of a case, angry letters and oral petitions from the dissatisfied masses stimulate the sentencing court to reconsider and to double the original punishment.[124]

*Vindication of the Accused.* At each of the major postdetention stages of the process thus far described — arrest, recommendation to prosecute, decision to prosecute, adjudication, appeal, and postconviction review — there is a possibility that the case may be dropped and *D* released. A significant proportion of cases are dropped after postdetention, prearrest, police investigation. But the chance of release declines sharply once the arrest hurdle is cleared. If, however, the process is initiated by arrest rather than by detention, many cases are screened out during the postarrest police investigation.[125]

Whatever the stage at which a case is dropped, such action is regarded as a sensitive matter by a totalitarian regime that seeks to preserve the criminal law's deterrent power, and at the same time to minimize popular resentment and maximize faith in the infallibility of its system. If *D* is a member of a disfavored class, or has a bad record, or if there is some, albeit insufficient, evidence of criminal behavior, he is told that he is being released because of the state's desire to be lenient, rather than because the requisites of a criminal conviction are lacking. He is admonished to keep out of trouble in the future on pain of more substantial deprivations, and sometimes the administrative sanction of supervised

122. Mao Tse-tung, "Problems Relating to the Correct Handling of Contradictions Among the People," p. 13.

123. See, e.g., "Anhwei [Province] Corrects Erroneously Decided Cases in Accordance with the Spirit of Chairman Mao's Speech," *Wen-hui pao* (Literary news, Shanghai), May 13, 1957, p. 1.

124. See, e.g., "The Ku-lou Court of Foochow Accepts the Opinion of the Masses, Corrects the Situation of Too Lenient Sentences and Resentences Two Criminals Who Had Sexual Relations with Young Girls," *Fu-chien jih-pao* (Fukien daily), Nov. 29, 1957; "In Response to the Demands of the People, the Canton Intermediate People's Court in Accordance with Law Resentences Hooligan Chief Ch'en Fu-pi to Four Years of Imprisonment," *Nan-fang jih-pao* (Southern daily), March 13, 1955.

125. One former police officer has informed me that statistics issued exclusively for the use of the police stated that 20 percent of the arrests made in the city of Canton in 1955 proved to be erroneous after postarrest interrogation and investigation.

labor is imposed upon him as a reminder. If, however, *D* is a member of the masses with a pure history, and is clearly innocent, usually a responsible law enforcement official apologizes privately for the inconvenience caused him and attempts to explain why it had been reasonable to suspect him. If, as sometimes happens, *D* has been languishing in jail for months or even years, the lengthy processing of the case is said to demonstrate the state's unremitting efforts never to convict the innocent. In cases of severe hardship *D* may be granted a "living allowance," a euphemistic expression of the state's regret that compensates him for earnings lost during confinement.[126] Necessary medical care is also provided, and if *D* has been fired from his job as a result of his difficulties with the law, steps are taken to reinstate him or to find him equivalent employment.[127]

The regime's most delicate problem in handling cases of blatant wrongs is how to restore *D*'s reputation without "losing face" before the masses. During the years 1952–1957, when efforts were being made to "reform" the judiciary and to educate law enforcement agencies and the masses in the conduct of formal criminal procedures, newspaper accounts of mistakes and abuses were fairly frequent.[128] In early 1957 Mao Tse-tung, in calling for correction of abuses that occurred in the process of liquidating counterrevolution, proclaimed that corrective measures should be publicized to the same extent as the original wrongs.[129] But the antirightist movement magnified the regime's sensitivity to such matters. No published confessions of error have been found in recent years, although in some instances Mao's directive is still carried out through local, informal media. In one case, for example, postconviction review established the innocence of a peasant youth convicted of putting up counterrevolutionary slogans. When the youth was freed, the public security bureau ordered his production brigade to announce his exoneration at a public meeting and to instruct everyone to treat him as an ordinary citizen rather than as a released criminal. In making this announcement the brigade's Party secretary emphasized the state's determination to protect good people, and he sought to avoid any suggestion of inefficiency or unfairness in the system.

*Sanctions against Officials.* Some of the mistakes found in the operation of the criminal process are, of course, unavoidable. Others are the product of intentional or negligent violation of prescribed rules. The regime recognizes the

126. Const., art. 97, provides in part that "[p]ersons shall have the right to obtain compensation for losses received through infringement of their rights as citizens by personnel of state organs" (p. 29). It has been reported that no legislation prescribes procedures for the implementation of this right; that this right may be invoked by either the aggrieved person or the procuracy in his behalf; and that compensation has been awarded in only very few cases. See summary of the remarks of Wu Te-feng by Fukushima Masao, "Chinese Legal Affairs (Second Discussion)," in *Chūgoku no hō to shakai* (Chinese law and society; Tokyo, 1960), p. 47. Interviews suggest that most released suspects are too ignorant, fearful, or skeptical to apply for compensation, but that, while not a frequent phenomenon, compensation is in fact granted on the initiative of the state more often than the state cares to indicate. Classification of the award as a "living allowance" apparently avoids the necessity of reporting the incident as an infringement of rights.

127. Fukushima, "Chinese Legal Affairs (Second Discussion)," p. 47.

128. See, e.g., Yang P'eng and Lin Ch'ih-chung, "Investigate Deeply, Handle Cases Conscientiously," *Fu-chien jih-pao* (Fukien daily), Aug. 14, 1956.

129. Mao Tse-tung, "Problems Relating to the Correct Handling of Contradictions Among the People," p. 13.

need to punish and correct law enforcement officers who fail to observe its rules and to educate them and their colleagues. But it strives to do so without diminishing the efficiency of the criminal process. Therefore, if procedural violations are discovered that do not cast doubt on the question of whether *D* actually is guilty, though sanctions are imposed on the law enforcement officer or his unit, *D* will not benefit. To exclude evidence from consideration because it was illegally seized or to dismiss charges against a known criminal because of some other procedural irregularity would, according to current Chinese thinking, be the most misguided sentimentality. In the Chinese view, violations of pre-scribed rules should be dealt with exclusively by sanctions that are extrinsic to the processing of *D*'s case.

Except when criminal charges are warranted, the power to impose sanctions upon a law enforcement official is confined to the agency for which he works and to his Party or Youth League branch. When punishing law enforcement cadres, the regime tries to avoid dulling their enthusiasm for their task. When Mao issued his call to re-examine the work of liquidating counterrevolution, he was careful to state that "we should not pour cold water on the vast [number of] cadres and activists but rather we should help them." [130] In *D*'s case, for example, if a policeman had made a mistake that could not reasonably have been avoided, even though it led to *D*'s confinement for several months, the policeman's su-periors would not ordinarily impose sanctions upon him. If the policeman had intentionally or negligently violated the rules, he would receive one or more government disciplinary sanctions ranging from criticism to loss of his job,[131] as well as one or more of a similar range of sanctions relating to his Party or Youth League membership.[132] Yet, if the violation is attributable to an excess of zeal, did not have serious consequences, or is the policeman's first transgression, he is usually required only to undergo criticism and make a self-examination before his governmental unit. Criminal sanctions are usually reserved for, but not always applied against, those whose unlawful acts "arose from malicious, retaliatory, corrupt or other personal motives." [133]

*Reform through Labor and Release.* If *D* is not vindicated at any stage of the screening and review process and is sentenced to reform through labor for a fixed number of years, or for life, or under a temporarily suspended death penalty,[134] his sentence may subsequently be modified for reasons unrelated to its original validity or propriety. Favorable modification depends upon whether,

130. Mao Tse-tung, "Problems Relating to the Correct Handling of Contradictions Among the People," p. 13.

131. For the spectrum of sanctions applicable to policemen, see People's Police Act of the PRC (passed at the 76th meeting of the Standing Committee of the NPC, June 25, 1957; promulgated by the Chairman of the PRC, June 25, 1957), *FKHP*, 5:116, art. 10. Similar provisions apply to other law enforcement officials. See Provisional Regulations of the State Council Relating to Rewards and Punishments for Personnel of State Ad-ministrative Organs, p. 199, par. 6.

132. For the spectrum of sanctions applicable to Party and Youth League members, see, respectively, the Constitution of the CCP, pp. 51–52, art. 13, and the Constitution of the CYL, p. 3, col. 3, art. 8.

133. Arrest Act, p. 242, art. 12.

134. See last paragraph of section D, on Sanctions, above.

in the rigorous daily routine of long hours of labor followed by intensive "thought reform" sessions, he consistently demonstrates the qualities of a thoroughly reformed offender. If he fully confesses his crimes, sincerely repents, enthusiastically labors, actively stimulates his fellow prisoners to reform, and reliably informs on many other persons, he may in addition to receiving more modest rewards be selected as one of the relatively small number of prisoners who are held out as models for the others, and are granted reduction of sentence, early unconditional release, or conditional release.[135] If sentenced to a fixed number of years, $D$ is not normally eligible for release until he has served at least one third, and in political cases at least one half, of his original sentence.[136] $D$ does not apply for such consideration and, indeed, does not directly participate in the process by which discretion is exercised. The initiative lies rather with the subdivision of the police organization that administers $D$'s reform through labor, which must recommend favorable action to its police superior. The formal power to order reduction of sentence and release rests with the judiciary, usually the high people's court of the province, which reviews and virtually always accepts police recommendations.[137]

If $D$ receives an unconditional release, he is by definition free of formal supervision when he returns to society. If conditionally released, he is usually placed under the jurisdiction of the neighborhood public security station or security defense committee for surveillance similar to that employed for persons subject to supervised labor or control. The period of conditional release is generally the portion of his sentence that has not been served.[138] If during this period $D$ behaves properly, at its conclusion his sentence is deemed to have been served. There appears to be uncertainty, however, as to what constitutes "proper behavior." Although several other standards have been proposed, published sources from the 1956–1957 era tend to support the position that conditional release will be revoked only if $D$ commits another crime during this period.[139] Yet interviews relating to practice since 1957 indicate that it is not unusual for revocation to follow the commission of undesirable though not necessarily criminal conduct. Interviews also suggest that conditional release is sometimes revoked not by the courts but by the police alone, and that in any event revocation is a summary process in which $D$ has little or no opportunity to participate.

If, while serving his sentence, instead of transforming himself into the model of "a new person," $D$ proves "backward" in his thinking, or lazy or negligent

135. Labor Act, p. 41, art. 68; see "At the Request of the Reform Through Labor Department of the Public Security Bureau, the Tientsin City High Court Granted Conditional Release or Reduction of Sentence to Criminals Who Demonstrated Their Repentance and Reform" [hereinafter cited as "At the Request"], *Hsin wan pao* (New evening news, Tientsin), Aug. 5, 1956; Snow, pp. 369–370.

136. See, e.g., "At the Request"; Special Amnesty Order of the Chairman of the PRC (promulgated, Sept. 17, 1959), *FKHP*, 10:60–61.

137. Labor Act, p. 42, art. 70; see "High People's Court of the Province Grants Early Release to a Number of Women Offenders" [hereinafter cited as "High People's Court"], *Shan-hsi jih-pao* (Shensi daily), Sept. 11, 1956; "At the Request."

138. See "At the Request"; *Lectures*, p. 258, suggest a ten-year period of conditional release in the rare case when a prisoner is conditionally released while serving a life sentence.

139. *Lectures*, p. 258; "At the Request"; "High People's Court."

in labor, or if he violates applicable regulations or actually engages in further antisocial behavior, he runs the risk of being selected to serve as a negative example.[140] The reform through labor unit may itself impose sanctions such as a demerit on his record, a formal warning in front of a meeting of prisoners, overtime work, loss of holidays, transfer from a labor camp to the more stringent regime of a prison, handcuffs, leg irons, or solitary confinement.[141] "Struggle" often accompanies these sanctions. If *D*'s misconduct is serious enough, his unit may file charges with the local people's court, and he may be convicted of and sentenced for a new crime.[142] The local people's court is also authorized to extend the sentence of an unreformed criminal beyond the term originally fixed "[w]hen . . . there really is a possibility that . . . [he] will continue to endanger the security of society after [his scheduled] release." [143] Thus, even if *D* does not commit a new crime, penal authorities may ask their police superiors to recommend judicial extension of his sentence. After an investigation that often proceeds without giving *D* notice or an opportunity to be heard, the court ordinarily approves the police recommendation and *D*'s confinement is usually extended by a year or two. Although only a relatively small number of prisoners have their sentences extended, all are aware of the possibility. To maximize incentives for reform, prison authorities give wide publicity to all modifications of sentences.

Expiration of the sentence does not ensure *D*'s return to the society from which he was removed. It is not unusual for a prisoner who is about to be released to volunteer to remain permanently at his reform through labor factory or camp as a civilian worker.[144] He often does not wish to return to his previous environment because he fears that he might once again go astray, or anticipates a hostile reception from the community, or simply feels unable to make another readjustment. Moreover, incessant persuasion and criticism prior to release, as well as knowledge that the sentence of a recalcitrant can be extended, may be used to induce a prisoner who possesses special skills that are urgently needed at his place of confinement to "volunteer" to remain after release. But an ex-prisoner may be kept at a reform through labor facility without volunteering, either genuinely or euphemistically. If *D* has no family and no job to which to return, or if he has undergone reform through labor in a sparsely inhabited area and is needed for its continuing development, he may upon release be "retained" and "employed" as a civilian without regard to his consent.[145]

Presumably as a precaution against abuse of authority, *D*'s reform through

140. See Labor Act, pp. 41–42, art. 69.
141. For a partial list of the applicable sanctions, see Labor Act, pp. 41–42, art. 69. See also Snow, p. 370.
142. Labor Act, p. 42, art. 71.
143. Labor Act, p. 42, art. 72; see Snow, p. 370.
144. Labor Act, p. 40, art. 62; the Provisional Measures of the PRC for Dealing with the Release of Reform Through Labor Criminals at the Expiration of Their Term of Imprisonment and For Placing Them and Getting Them Employment [hereinafter cited as Release Measures] (approved at the 222d meeting of the Government Administration Council, Aug. 26, 1954; promulgated by the Government Administration Council, Sept. 7, 1954), *FLHP* 1954, p. 44, art. 2(1), authorize reform through labor units to retain volunteers. See also Snow, pp. 367–368; "High People's Court."
145. Labor Act, p. 40, art. 62; Release Measures, p. 44, art. 2(2)–(3).

labor unit cannot retain him involuntarily without the approval of the competent public security organ, usually the unit that recommended his prosecution.[146] But judicial approval need not be obtained as it must when modification of the sentence is sought. If, following the expiration of his sentence, D is retained as a civilian worker, he is not treated as a prisoner. He lives apart from his former colleagues, receives regular wages for his labor, and during nonworking hours his activities are relatively unrestricted.[147] To facilitate what is regarded as his permanent resettlement, the government will help his family to join him.[148]

If D does manage to return to society after his unconditional release, life is difficult for him. Although official policy periodically calls for improvement of the situation, in practice the stigma of being a "released prisoner," the Chinese equivalent of our "ex-convict," is a continuing and severe one. Ordinarily D is placed under no formal regulation, but he may be secretly under the surveillance of the local police apparatus. In daily life he is discriminated against in many ways by both officials and the masses. Unless he has unusual skills, it is hard for him to find a job except in rural labor or other menial work. Socially he is shunned, especially if he has been convicted of a political crime. He is also a likely target the next time that a mass movement occurs and the police have difficulty in rounding up the prescribed quota of suspects. And in quieter times he also enjoys less leeway than ordinary citizens. Interviews reveal numerous instances in which, for identical behavior, former convicts were singled out for criminal punishment while others with clear histories merely drew criticism-education. Thus, contrary to the image created by Chinese publications, even if reform through labor actually succeeds in transforming D into a "new person," his subsequent reintegration into society is far from complete.

### G. CONCLUSION

By concentrating on a few representative cases I have, of course, simplified the Chinese criminal process, omitting all the differences that result from diverse factual situations and varying geographic locations, as well as from the Chinese Communist penchant for almost ceaseless experimentation and tinkering. I have also omitted discussion of procedural modifications adopted for particularly important cases, such as those involving major counterrevolutionary offenders or government or Party officials, and for cases arising during mass movements. By focusing on an urban setting, this Introduction has inevitably underemphasized the problem of assuring adherence to authorized procedures in China's vast rural areas, where cadres tend to be less educated and less supervised than in the cities. However, despite these drawbacks, which are partially remedied by the materials provided in Part II, I believe that enough has been said here to permit answers to some of the questions raised in the Preface.

146. Release Measures, p. 44, art. 3.
147. See Release Measures, pp. 44–45, art. 5; Snow, pp. 367–368.
148. Release Measures, p. 45, art. 7.

At the outset, it should be realized that responses to some of these questions have varied during the fourteen years under review. Although this period represents but a flyspeck in a recorded legal history that goes back over 2,500 years, it has witnessed swift and significant changes in the administration of justice. As a major instrument of the Communists, the criminal process has faithfully reflected the twists and turns that have occurred in the Party's "general line." Until 1957, changes seemed to follow at an accelerated pace the course of development previously traced by Soviet law. During the terror of 1949–1953, when the Chinese Communists were seeking to consolidate their political power, they resorted freely to extrajudicial processes for imposing major sanctions, as their Soviet counterparts had during the comparable era of War Communism (1917–1921). In 1953–1954, when they set about the task of long-term building of the economy, the Chinese de-emphasized extrajudicial punitive processes much as Soviet leadership had done during the New Economic Policy (1921–1928). They established the framework for a formal judicial system similar to that which the Soviet Union had erected along European lines during the NEP. Mid-1955, when the regime prepared to complete the socialization of agriculture, industry, and commerce, was another period of extrajudicial terror, calling to mind Stalin's efforts to force collectivization during the late 1920's and early 1930's.

When in 1956–1957 the Chinese actually began to curb the power of the police and other nonjudicial agencies, and to flesh out the skeleton of the formal judicial system, they were following the very recent example of Stalin's heirs. But in 1957–1958, while Soviet de-Stalinization was continuing to produce reforms that provided greater protection to individuals charged with crime, the antirightist movement abruptly launched China on a new course. Without returning China to the 1949–1953 level of terror, it put an end to efforts that had seemed to be leading the country toward some degree of judicial autonomy, with safeguards for those suspected of antisocial conduct; the movement spurred the creation of a police-dominated, highly integrated system of judicial and extrajudicial sanctions. China has subsequently maintained this course, while the fate of the criminal process under Soviet de-Stalinization has been more complex.[149]

*Izvestia,* the official newspaper of the Soviet government, has heaped scorn upon the post-1957 Chinese system of administering justice as a mockery of socialist legality.[150] American cold war rhetoric has long proclaimed the lawlessness of Chinese Communist rule. What conclusion should be reached by a detached evaluation? From the state's point of view, it can be argued that the contemporary criminal process is not arbitrary in conception. The values and goals of the Chinese Communist regime are protected by a vast body of rules

149. See note 30 above.
150. "Revolutionary Theory Is Guide to Action: On the Dictatorship of the Proletariat," *Izvestia,* May 17, 1964; translated in *CDSP,* 16.21:3–8 (June 17, 1964). Translation from the *Current Digest of the Soviet Press,* published weekly at Columbia University by the Joint Committee on Slavic Studies, appointed by the American Council of Learned Societies and the Social Science Research Council. Copyright 1964, vol. XVI, no. 21, the Joint Committee on Slavic Studies.

that proscribe a broad spectrum of behavior considered by the regime to be antisocial. A refined series of administrative and criminal sanctions stimulates compliance with these rules. A comprehensive network of official and semiofficial institutions, acting in accordance with prescribed procedures, identifies, apprehends, investigates, and judges those who are suspected of violating rules, and imposes sanctions upon offenders. These institutions act not only to suppress and punish offenders but also to reform them, to deter others, to educate the populace, and to satisfy society's sense of just retribution. Because the goals of the criminal law go unrealized to the extent that the innocent are punished and the guilty remain free, these institutions strive to reach reliable results. But, without placing an undue premium upon speed, they also seek to operate efficiently in the sense of wisely utilizing their limited resources to process within a reasonable period of time a large number of suspected offenders.

As thus defined, reliability and efficiency are competing interests.[151] The Chinese have attempted to achieve an optimum accommodation between them by resorting to informal, secret, and inquisitorial factfinding. Their view is that in such a setting the truth is more likely to emerge and the case will be processed more quickly than it would be in formal, public, and adversary hearings in which they believe hairsplitting lawyers would frustrate and delay substantial justice. The Chinese recognize that inquisitorial procedure elicits false confessions in a certain proportion of cases, and they rely on careful investigation and review to correct such errors. Because all offenses and offenders are not of equal concern to the state, institutional resources are husbanded by allocating factfinding and decision-making functions, and by varying procedures according to the gravity of the case. Thus, minor cases are handled by low-ranking police personnel and their semiofficial assistants in very informal ways. Serious cases are processed by more expert and responsible police officials who are expected to act with greater care. Because most criminal sanctions are deemed more severe than administrative sanctions, in criminal cases the conclusions of the police are reviewed by the procuracy and the courts. Although the constitutional separation of powers among the three law enforcement agencies is more apparent than real and they in fact serve as constituent units of a single administrative structure, the separation of functions that does exist provides a significant check upon reliability despite the fact that all three agencies operate in an informal, secret, and inquisitorial manner. The reviewing role of the court is not vitiated by its use of an administrative rather than a judicial decision-making pattern, with the trial judge merely recommending a decision; for institutional decision making facilitates uniform adjudication and sentencing in large numbers of similar cases.

Obviously the system lodges broad discretion in law enforcement personnel and in the Party officials who approve important or difficult decisions; but none of these authoritative persons is free to act without regard to a variety of principles that have been established to guide his discretion, and an appellate court is always available to review the exercise of that discretion. As further

151. See Herbert L. Packer, "Two Models of the Criminal Process," *University of Pennsylvania Law Review*, 113:9–10, 14–15 (1964).

evidence of its interest in preventing the abuse of discretion, the regime can point to the low value that it attaches to finality of decision, permitting error to be challenged at any time. Moreover, when persons have been erroneously confined, the government seeks to minimize the adverse consequences by means of apology and, in cases of the gravest hardship, through compensation or public status-restoration ceremonies. In addition, officials who violate prescribed procedures are disciplined.

Those aspects of the criminal process relating to reform of convicted persons can also be said to reflect rationality and a concern for preventing abuse of official power. Correctional authorities use a system of graded positive and negative incentives to stimulate those who undergo productive labor and thought remolding to conform their behavior to articulated standards. In order to avoid any abuse of discretion, these authorities must obtain the approval of both the competent public security unit and the local court before a prisoner's sentence can be modified. Similarly, before prisoners who are about to be released can be assigned to involuntary service in remote geographic areas, labor camp authorities must have their conclusions approved by the competent public security unit.

On the other hand, a close look at this regulatory edifice reveals a system that leaves a great deal of room for arbitrary action. The rules defining antisocial conduct are often so vague that it is difficult for the citizen, if not the official, to say with any degree of certainty what acts fall within their ambit. Moreover, many important substantive rules are not published and, while informal modes of norm communication may actually provide fair warning, complaints voiced during the brief "hundred flowers" period suggest the contrary. Furthermore, some rules are only enforced at certain times and others are frequently altered, as the Chinese leaders manipulate the population, alternating periods of great tension with periods of relaxation. The regime has also not been reluctant to apply proscriptions both analogically and retroactively. There is thus little that an individual can do to defend himself against a charge of having violated the substantive rules.[152]

Chinese procedural rules also deny a suspect a meaningful opportunity to defend himself. Held incommunicado by the police, not informed of any specific charge, precluded from confronting the witnesses against him or even knowing their identity, denied the services of a defender, wholly dependent upon the police to search for witnesses and evidence that might support him, a suspected offender is severely limited in his ability to rebut the charge against him. Moreover, intensive interrogations in an inquisitorial setting, long periods of detention between interrogations, constant repetition of the theme of leniency for those who confess, and application of other psychological techniques to break the suspect's resistance create an inherently coercive environment that elicits many confessions. Although police investigation and review procedures attempt to separate the authentic from the spurious, the fact that false confessions sometimes go undetected by the police is a subject of continuing concern. In cases in which the police seek criminal rather than administrative punishment, the safe-

152. See generally Fuller, pp. 33–94.

guard of review by the procuracy and the courts appears to detect only some of these false confessions. At the time of such review the defendant is usually acquainted with the accusation, but otherwise his ability to defend himself is no greater than during the period of police investigation. Similarly, although he can initiate appeal and postconviction review, he is not permitted to play an active part in those proceedings; nor does he participate significantly in the processes for commuting or extending his sentence, or for revoking his conditional release.

At every stage of the criminal process the fate of the defendant depends entirely on the degree of conscientiousness and ability of government and Party officials, and he seldom has an opportunity to see and persuade the most authoritative of these officials. The process has no place for independent actors who might defend the accused against abuses committed by those who administer it. Even certain aspects of the system that in theory provide checks against abuses, in practice add to its arbitrariness. Too often, for example, the fact that the system places no premium upon speed means that an innocent person remains in jail for months before his release. And, as we have seen, the flexibility that permits an erroneous decision to be challenged at any time can be utilized by the state, long after original disposition of the case, to reopen it and to increase a prisoner's sentence. Finally, perhaps most importantly, the environment within which the criminal process functions discourages the defendant from utilizing even the limited opportunities to defend himself that do exist. For example, if the defendant chooses not to confess to the police, he knows that he runs the risk of suffering increased punishment as one who "resists" recognizing his guilt and beginning his self-reform. If he confesses and later regrets it, he may recant when interviewed by a procurator or a judge; yet he knows that if he does so and is disbelieved, this will be regarded as a severe aggravating circumstance. And initiation of appeal or postconviction review poses a similar threat.

Both in basic assumptions and in institutions and practices, there are some obvious parallels between the traditional and the Chinese Communist sanctioning systems. Many of these parallels derive from the great extent to which interests of the Chinese state have always prevailed over those of the individual. Thus, it has been assumed that justice in Chinese courts is the exclusive preserve of the state; that no independent actors such as lawyers should be permitted to intrude; that the accused is generally a bad person and would not make proper use of a meaningful opportunity to defend himself; that he is the best source of evidence and should be interrogated according to inquisitorial procedures likely to elicit his confession; and that confessions, if not legally required, are at least eminently desirable. A substantive criminal law that is of uncertain application, that is status-oriented and discriminates against certain classes of people, and that permits proscriptions to be applied both by analogy and retroactively has deep roots in China. The same can be said of a system staffed by adjudicators who have not received significant legal education, are ideologically orthodox administrative officials, and are subject to sanctions that include immediate removal from office for seriously mistaken decisions. Indeed, Max Weber's appraisal of the traditional system as "a type of patriarchal obliteration of the line between justice and administration" [153] would appear to apply to the Communist system.

To be sure, there are important differences between the traditional and contemporary systems. Because the Communist government and its semiofficial substructure extend to every corner of society, relatively autonomous local groups no longer impose sanctions for many kinds of offenses. (But contemporary informal sanctions ranging from criticism to struggle resemble some of those formerly meted out by clan, village, and guild.) Although we do not know to what extent a defendant who has connections with China's new elite can favorably influence the handling of his case, wealth no longer appears to constitute a major advantage. Extortion and other forms of corruption by law enforcement officials have been largely eradicated and, given the passive role of the defendant, there is little on which he can legitimately spend money for his defense. The Communist failures to publish many important rules and to conduct most trials in public represent other noteworthy changes. Yet, on the whole, the similarities with tradition seem more striking and more significant than the differences.

To suggest that the past does not conflict with, but rather reinforces, the Chinese Communist attitude toward the criminal process is not to say that the past holds the only key to understanding the contemporary process. Although since 1957 the Chinese system has departed from the Khrushchev model and even from the Stalinist model, it still bears many marks of Soviet influence.[154] Its ideology remains explicitly Marxist-Leninist-Stalinist, viewing the criminal law as a prime instrument for conducting the struggle against class enemies. Like Soviet law until 1936 and Soviet practice for a period thereafter, Chinese law emphasizes the class status of the defendant. Many of the norms that continue to be enforced, such as those that proscribe counterrevolutionary acts, are of obvious Soviet origin. The vagueness of some of these norms, the failure to publish many, their frequent revision, and their selective enforcement according to periods of tension and relaxation, all call to mind Stalinist justice. Moreover, the analogical application of the criminal law can be said to rest on pre-1958 Soviet principles as well as upon Chinese tradition, and there are Soviet precedents for retroactively imposing criminal punishment. The procuracy and the court structure, along with China's extrajudicial institutions, also reflect Soviet experience. The police-imposed sanction of rehabilitation through labor resembles labor camp sentences meted out by Stalin's Special Board of the Ministry of Internal Affairs; it also has some similarities to the compulsory resettlement and labor imposed by contemporary Soviet antiparasite legislation. Informal administrative sanctions ranging from criticism to struggle, though similar to some of the sanctions imposed by local groups in traditional China, also resemble some of

153. *Law in Economy and Society,* trans. E.A. Shils and M. Rheinstein, IV (Cambridge, Mass., 1954), 264–265; quoted in Van der Sprenkel, p. 128.

Scholarship has yet to explore thoroughly the republican system of administering justice during Chiang Kai-shek's rule of the mainland and its impact upon the Communist system that developed first in the "liberated areas" and subsequently throughout the mainland.

154. This paragraph's discussion of the Soviet experience draws especially upon Berman, pp. 66–96.

those dispensed by Soviet comrades' courts.[155] The security defense committee shares some of the characteristics of the voluntary organizations for the protection of public order that the Soviet Union has employed in various forms.[156] And contemporary Chinese processing of criminal cases suggests the secret, inquisitorial, and summary judicial procedures sometimes used under Stalin for counterrevolutionary offenders who were not sentenced by the Special Board. Finally, the Chinese emphasis upon confession by the defendant has Soviet as well as traditional antecedents, while Party control of judicial decisions is firmly grounded in Stalinist practice, if not theory.

Yet to label the criminal process in contemporary China as "quasi-Stalinist" would be to obscure important differences between it and the Stalinist model. For example, since the 1949–1953 period the use of the criminal process as an instrument of terror has not been so prominent under Mao as it generally was under Stalin. The Chinese Communists have sought to apply criminal punishments less readily and to make greater use of persuasion, ideological incentives, and social and administrative pressures to make people conform. On the other hand, when the criminal process is invoked, in ordinary cases as well as in counterrevolutionary cases, Chinese procedures provide the defendant less protection than he received from Stalinist methods of handling ordinary crimes. Even in the darkest days of Stalinism, nonpolitical trials were often public, with defense counsel playing a role and the defendant having an opportunity to confront his accusers and to benefit from other procedural protections.[157]

Perhaps, at least at this early stage of scholarship on Chinese law, including the obviously significant but relatively unexplored law of the Nationalist era, one can best view the contemporary criminal process as an adaptation of traditional, Nationalist, and Soviet elements. When pondering the possibilities of future change in the Chinese system it may be useful to bear in mind recent Soviet experience.[158] By the time of Stalin's death the transformation of the Soviet Union from a largely agrarian to a highly industrialized society had set in motion in every area of endeavor new forces that led to greater emphasis on specialization, professionalization, and scientific thought. Decades of terror and privation had intensified popular desires, shared even by Stalin's principal lieutenants, to achieve human dignity, security, self-fulfillment, and comfort. His death released these aspirations, and Khrushchev, a more self-confident leader, sought to cope with them in what was perceived to be a vastly improved international and domestic situation for the Soviet Union. It was Khrushchev's belief that, given the advanced level of Soviet development and the broad popular support of the

155. Beginning in 1953 in a number of major factories, the Chinese experimented with the use of Soviet comrades' courts. See "Introducing the Soviet Union's Comrades' Courts for Enterprises," *JMJP*, Oct. 17, 1953, p. 3. By 1957, however, these institutions seem to have been generally superseded by methods of imposing administrative sanctions that are less clearly Soviet in origin.

156. See generally Dennis O'Connor, "Soviet People's Guards: An Experiment with Civic Police," *New York University Law Review*, 39:579–614 (1964).

157. See Berman, pp. 58–63.

158. This paragraph is based on Fainsod, pp. 109, 116–121, 124–125, 439–452, 461–462, 577–598.

regime, terror had become unnecessary and unwise. He acted on the assumption that enlistment of creative energies and individual initiative is essential to the functioning of a highly industrialized society, and that this requires a legal system that will minimize popular feelings of fear and resentment and will instill a sense of security in the social order. His response was a program of de-Stalinization, which had as a major feature the reform of criminal procedure and criminal law. The result has been termed an "enlightened" totalitarianism that has taken important steps toward regularizing the administration of justice and strengthening the protections of the defendant without yielding the regime's ultimate power to sweep aside any restrictions should that be necessary to maintain itself.

There are far too many variables and unknowns to the problem to permit responsible prediction about whether China may begin to evolve in this direction to a more enduring extent than it did during the mid-1950's. Certainly no inexorable rule of social development requires China, with its distinctive characteristics, conditions, and history, to follow the Soviet path in this respect.[159] It has been apparent that pressures to increase specialization, professionalism, and functional autonomy are being suppressed by an aging but still zealous first generation of revolutionary leaders who are obsessed with maintaining Party domination of all aspects of life. Also, "socialist education" campaigns that call for the sacrifice of personal interests to those of the community continue to stifle aspirations for individual self-fulfillment and greater material comforts. Yet it should take a substantial period of time before pressures such as these become as great as those that were released by Stalin's death. China is still a largely agricultural, industrially backward country, whose development is several decades behind that of the Soviet Union of 1953. Furthermore, although an atmosphere of suspicion and insecurity pervades contemporary Chinese society, and although at this writing the implications of the "Red Guard" movement in mid-1966 are unclear, the level of terror has not yet returned to the Stalinist proportions of the regime's earliest years. Thus, when Mao passes from the scene, the pent-up aspirations with which his heirs will have to deal may not have the same degree of force as those that led to de-Stalinization; and efforts to reform the criminal process in order to create a climate of greater security for the individual may be correspondingly less. Much may depend upon factors such as how a new generation of Chinese leaders perceives its country's international position. If the civil war with the Nationalists persists and the leaders of the People's Republic feel surrounded by hostile powers, the prospect for liberalization of the criminal process will be dimmer than otherwise. The same is likely to be true if they lack confidence in their ability to maintain popular support at home. Perhaps the least hazardous prediction one can make about the criminal process at this juncture is that, as long as Mao remains in power, we are unlikely to witness any substantial improvement in the plight of the individual in relation to the state.

159. Chinese writers appear to be moving toward this view as they seek to explain China's departure from the Soviet model. They reject any suggestion that this departure is revisionist, and argue that slavish application of Soviet criminal procedure would constitute dogmatism. See Jen Chen-to and Ho En-t'ao, p. 121.

# PART II  MATERIALS

# Materials

Our country's penal system should be founded on the basis of the principle of the people's democratic legal system. Our state is a people's democratic state. Both state organs and the masses of people must strictly observe the state's legal system. Only by having a strong legal system can we more effectively develop the functions of the state and safeguard the people's rights. Therefore, the principle of a legal system is a basic guide to state organs, especially judicial organs, for conducting their activities. One of the important aspects of guaranteeing that activities of judicial organs conform to the demands of the legal system is that when judicial organs apply punishment to criminals, they must handle matters in accordance with law. Judicial organs can only impose punishment on the basis of the law and in accordance with the seriousness and size of the crimes and the attitude and behavior of the criminal. It is not permissible to handle matters not in accordance with the law.

*Lectures* (September 1957)[1]

The violation of socialist legality has become a practice in the state life of China. Distorting the Marxist-Leninist teaching about the Party's role in the system of the dictatorship of the proletariat, the Chinese leaders assign the Party agencies not the role of organizers and educators of the masses but that of a "command force," which defines and regulates all the activity of local agencies of authority, the courts and the prosecutors. The persistently repeated postulates that "policy is the power of command" and that the Party worker is the 'commander of production' are a sort of theoretical justification for this kind of practice. Things have come to a strange pass when the secretary of a district Party committee ousts the judge, sits at the bench himself and starts to decide cases. And such instances are presented in the press as positive experience.

"Revolutionary Theory Is Guide to Action: On the Dictatorship of the Proletariat," *Izvestia* (May 17, 1964)[2]

## A Note on the Materials

Part II could, of course, be organized in a number of ways. A word about the particular form of organization used here may be appropriate. Chapter I is designed to provide a brief introduction to past and present Chinese thought about the role of the criminal law. Chapters II–V deal with procedures for imposing the variety of sanctions which the Chinese regard as "noncriminal" but which actually constitute

1. P. 189.
2. Translated in *CDSP*, 16.21:5 (June 17, 1964). Translation from the *Current Digest of the Soviet Press*, published weekly at Columbia University by the Joint Committee on Slavic Studies, appointed by the American Council of Learned Societies and the Social Science Research Council. Copyright 1964, vol. XVI, no. 21, the Joint Committee on Slavic Studies. Reprinted by permission.

an integral and important part of the criminal process, broadly conceived. Generally these sanctions are considered in order of increasing severity. However, rehabilitation through labor (Chapter IV) is treated before supervised labor (Chapter V) because the materials that discuss the evolution of supervised labor from the criminal sanction of control illustrate Chinese efforts to distinguish between criminal and noncriminal sanctions. These materials relate closely to Chapter VI, which deals with Chinese efforts to distinguish between criminal and noncriminal conduct. The remainder of Part II traces the successive stages of the formal criminal process from detection and detention to reform through labor and release.

In addition to official documents and pronouncements and articles from various Chinese newspapers, most of Part II is derived from three sources: the treatise *Chung-hua jen-min kung-ho-kuo hsing-fa tsung-tse chiang-i* (Lectures on the general principles of criminal law of the People's Republic of China); the law review *Cheng-fa yen-chiu* (Political-legal research); and interviews with former residents of the PRC. Each of these sources merits some preliminary comment.

The *Lectures* constitute the principal Chinese Communist treatise on criminal law or procedure available in the non-Communist world. They were written by four scholars — Li Meng, Chu Yü-huang, Ch'en Tse-chieh, and Li Chieh — of the Teaching and Research Office for Criminal Law of the Central Political-Legal Cadres' School in Peking "on the basis of collective discussions within the [teaching and research] office." [3] The *Lectures* were prepared not only for officials who were temporarily relieved of their duties and assigned to formal legal training but also for officials who were required to engage in study while continuing in active service. This treatise did not purport to be so scholarly and comprehensive as the treatises said to be in use at regular institutions of higher learning. Rather, its aim was to provide "a necessary theoretical foundation for the solution of certain important problems in practical work." [4]

The *Lectures* were a product of the 1956–1957 era of liberalization and rationalization of criminal law and procedure described in Part I and were completed in the spring of 1957, just before the climax of the movement to "let a hundred flowers bloom." Thus, although the authors were careful to employ conventional techniques of argumentation and to phrase their analysis and recommendations in cautious language, their treatise was essentially a law reform manifesto. It sought, in the words of its preface, dated April 20, 1957, "to re-evaluate [outmoded legislation] and to make it more concrete on the basis of the new situation and experience." [5]

Unfortunately for the authors, the antirightist movement occurred between the time the manuscript was completed and the time it was published in September 1957. In an attempt to adapt to the radically new situation, the authors appended a "brief statement prior to printing," dated August 20, which apologized for their inability to reflect the significance of "this hectic struggle" in their book and "to make it more concrete and to enrich and revise it according to the new spirit . . ." [6] Plainly enough, the *Lectures* had to some extent become obsolete before publication. This creates a problem concerning use of the *Lectures* in this work. I have drawn upon this treatise in two ways. I have frequently quoted passages from it that, even since the antirightist movement, continue to represent prevailing Chinese attitudes toward the criminal process. I have chosen other excerpts, even though their con-

3. *Lectures,* Publication Explanation, p. 3.
4. *Lectures,* Publication Explanation, p. 1.
5. *Lectures,* Publication Explanation, p. 3.
6. *Lectures,* Brief Statement Prior to Printing, p. 1.

tinuing authoritativeness has been undermined, to document the evolution of Chinese doctrine and to illustrate Chinese awareness of alternatives to views that have been in vogue since the great upheaval of mid-1957. In reproducing selections of the second type I have directed the reader's attention to the fact of their obsolescence if the context does not suggest it.

From 1959, when the periodical *Fa-hsüeh* (*Legal Science*) ceased publication, until mid-1966, when it too ceased publication, at least temporarily, *Political-Legal Research* was the only law review in mainland China. *Political-Legal Research* was founded, as a bimonthly, in 1954. Its sponsor was the Chinese Political Science and Law Association, which had been established the preceding year. Among the magazine's assigned tasks was "the introduction of the Soviet Union's jurisprudential theory and advanced experiences in political-legal work." [7] Beginning with the first issue of 1959 it was published jointly by the Chinese Political Science and Law Association and the Institute of Legal Research of the Chinese Academy of Sciences. In 1960 it became a quarterly. As the selections in Part II indicate, after the antirightist movement its contents were designed in large part to refute "bourgeois" views on law, and these often bore substantial resemblance to the Soviet views that the magazine was originally created to propagate. Except for an occasional policy pronouncement by a major official, the articles from *Political-Legal Research* purported to express only the views of their authors. Nevertheless, even when a debate was conducted in the pages of this periodical, it always reflected the accepted limits of the particular period and the then current Party line. After 1959 *Political-Legal Research* published few detailed discussions of contemporary legal subjects. Thus, many of the selections that appear below are from the 1958–1959 era.

The presentation of recorded interviews represents the most novel contribution of Part II. Despite the availability of thousands of knowledgeable former residents of the People's Republic, few social scientists and no lawyers took significant advantage of this opportunity to conduct extensive interviews concerning contemporary Chinese life until very recently, and virtually no interview data have been published. Only Robert Jay Lifton's pioneering work *Thought Reform and the Psychology of Totalism,*[8] which presents and analyzes data from interviews with twenty-five Westerners who had been imprisoned in China and fifteen Chinese refugees, stands as an exception. Yet, for the reasons stated in Part I, interviewing is an indispensable tool for the understanding of contemporary Chinese legal processes. At an early period of my research a man who had served as a trial court judge in mainland China from 1950 to 1954 wrote me:

The following are some of my suggestions on the correct study of Communist Chinese law for your reference:

. . . . .

Of course, you should collect the legal documents promulgated by the Communist Party as the main source of your research. However, I am convinced that this method will never enable you completely to understand the nature of Chinese Communist law. In addition, it will have a seriously dangerous influence on the thought of your students.

7. Tung Pi-wu, "Congratulations on the Founding of the Periodical *Political-Legal Research,*" *CFYC*, 1:1 (1954).
8. *Thought Reform and the Psychology of Totalism, A Study of "Brainwashing" in China* (New York, 1961).

I recall that before the fall of the Chinese mainland young students with curiosity tried to understand the nature of the Communist Party from its documents. As a result, many young people went over to the Communist side. In the early period of the Communist occupation of the mainland, capitalists, former political officials, landlords, and many other people of various strata were taken in by the Communist policies and decrees, such as New Democracy, the Common Program, the Land Reform Law, the Counterrevolutionary Act, and so forth. They returned to the mainland from various places where they had sought refuge, only to lose their property and their lives. Even to date, many young overseas Chinese are attracted by the brilliant documents published by the Communist Party. They do not realize that the published document is one thing, and practice is another.

This is especially true for those legal scholars who live under social systems that are different from Communist China's and whose methods of research are entirely different. In free countries the judiciary is independent, and everyone is required strictly to observe the express rules of law. This, however, is not the case in Communist China. When I was receiving my special judicial training, I was repeatedly told that in the execution of law, the interest of the various political movements is imperative. Law is flexible. Any mechanical application of legal provisions will result in the error of dogmatism. After all, law is an instrument of political class struggle. Therefore, during each political movement secret instructions constantly came down from superiors. These instructions were the criteria on which court decisions were based, and they were by no means open to the public. Thus, in doing your research work, you should never accept at face value the published policies and statutory documents. Instead, you ought to try to understand the essence of Communist law from living examples while studying the statutes and decrees published in each period. If you depart from this, it will not be possible to achieve anything.

All the interviews that are interspersed in the following materials describe personal experiences of the informants. In many of these interviews professional participants in the administration of justice, such as public security officers, relate the details of cases that they handled. In many others, objects of the system, such as defendants, describe their own histories. Other interviews are the accounts of ordinary citizens who witnessed the events in question. Stories that informants were told by others, gossip, rumors, and similar matter are excluded. Most of the accounts presented below, which are a portion of those I have recorded, have been selected because they appear to be fairly representative of the ways in which Chinese law enforcement processes operate. In order not to reveal the identity of informants, in these accounts I have resorted to pseudonyms and have occasionally omitted identifying details. In other respects the information is presented virtually as I recorded it in the course of each interview.[9]

9. For a more extended discussion of my methods and experiences interviewing in Hong Kong, see "Interviewing Chinese Refugees: Indispensable Aid to Legal Research on China," *Journal of Legal Education*, 20.1:33 (October 1967).

# Chapter 1　The Ideology of the Criminal Law

A. Traditional Conceptions

B. Communist Ideology

> In hearing cases I am as good as anyone else, but what is really needed is
> to bring about that there are no cases!
>
> Confucius, Analects[1]

Although the criminal law of the People's Republic of China is a necessary measure for the state's regulation of activities and for the struggle against crime, it is not a fundamental measure but only a supplementary one. During the period of our country's transition to socialism the role of the criminal law in guaranteeing this transition is of major significance. We need a revolutionary legal system; we are not utopians. But in the construction of socialism in our country the criminal law only plays a supplementary role. The undertakings of our country's socialist economic and cultural construction are themselves the foundation and the guarantee for the prevention and elimination of crime in our country. But in the countries of the exploiters, the system of exploitation which a small number of rulers strive to preserve is itself something that ceaselessly creates and produces crime. The contradictions between the ruling class of a small number of exploiter groups and the vast class of laboring masses who are ruled are irreconcilable and develop more sharply every day. In order to protect the interests of the minority exploiting class the rulers resort to violence. And the criminal law has become one of their principal measures for putting into effect this kind of violent rule.

Lectures (September 1957)[2]

What are the goals of the criminal law in contemporary China? How does the government of the People's Republic of China seek to rationalize, legitimize, and limit the application of punishment? What do Chinese scholars mean when they say criminal law is a less "fundamental" method of social control in the PRC than in bourgeois countries? How do they explain the continuing need for punishment after the substantial completion in 1956 of "socialist reform" of the economy? Does the Chinese Communist leadership endorse Marx's prediction of the eventual withering away of the state, including the criminal law? The excerpts that appear in this chapter suggest answers to these questions and provide some insight into the ideological setting of the criminal process.

1. XII, 13; translated in Bodde, p. 384.
2. P. 34.

## A. TRADITIONAL CONCEPTIONS

Before undertaking to survey the contemporary scene, we should know something about traditional Chinese conceptions of law.

### ITEM 1

The following article, written by Professor Schwartz just prior to the advent of the antirightist movement, is an invaluable aid to consideration of problems of continuity and change in the unfolding of the world's oldest existing legal system.[3]

[Benjamin Schwartz, "On Attitudes toward Law in China," in Milton Katz, *Government under Law and the Individual* (Washington, D.C., 1957), pp. 27–39]

No attempt will be made in this paper to account for all attitudes toward law which can be met in the millennial history of China. Our attention will rather be focused on what might be called the main line of Confucian development. While the attitudes discussed are typical they are by no means universal and do not even represent the views of all those in Chinese history who have called themselves Confucianist. The same holds true of our brief survey of the modern scene.

What might be called the typical Confucian attitude revolves about a basic dichotomy — the dichotomy between the concept of *li* and the concept of *fa*. The importance of this dichotomy can hardly be exaggerated. Not only does it have extremely ancient roots but it is linked with certain central events in Chinese history. This historic association lends the antithesis a resonance it would not have if it were merely based on a conceptual distinction derived in abstracto. *Li* is associated with the great figure of Confucius himself while *fa* is associated with the harshly despotic Ch'in dynasty which united the Chinese world under the control of a centralized bureaucratic empire in the third century B.C.

Now we have available certain conventional English equivalents of these two terms. *Li* has been translated as "propriety" while *fa* has been translated as "law." On the basis of these translations, one might assume that any discussion of law in China would revolve about the concept of *fa*.

Unfortunately the actual situation is much more complex. The term *li* embraces a far richer range of meanings than anything encompassed by the pale word "propriety." On the other hand, Western words such as "law," "droit," and "Recht" are freighted with enormous accumulations of meanings. Finally, the word *fa* is probably much narrower in its scope of reference than many Western conceptions of the meaning of law. We thus find that while some meanings of the word *li* may overlap with some meanings of "law," the meaning of the word *fa* is hardly coextensive with all the meanings attributed to the word "law."

Thus, instead of attempting to find single-word definitions of these terms, it

3. For other stimulating studies, see Bodde, p. 375, and the works cited there in note 1.

would perhaps be better to attempt to describe in as brief a compass as possible (with all the risks of error involved) some of the major associations with them.

In the background of the concept *li* there lurk certain assumptions which resemble some of the assumptions underlying Western conceptions of natural law. One is the assumption of the existence of an eternal "natural" order underlying both the human and the nonhuman world (*tao*). As far as human society is concerned, this *tao* is normative — it tells us what human society ought to be or what it "really" is in a Platonic sense. As in Western conceptions of natural law, we are constantly confronted with the problem of how actuality is related to the normative order. In the view of Confucius, his own period was marked by a tragic falling away of actuality from the *tao*. In the past — particularly during the early Chou dynasty — the *tao* had actually been realized in actuality. Thus in studying the institutions of the historic past one was, in effect, recovering the pattern of the *tao*.

So far, we are strongly reminded of some of the basic assumptions underlying concepts of natural law in the West. However, when we come to examine more closely the concrete vision of this "natural" order, we immediately note a marked difference of focus. The basic units of this order in the Confucian case are human beings enacting *certain fundamental social roles*. As in some modern schools of sociology, social role is the key term in the Confucian definition of social structure: the structure of society is basically a network of relations of persons enacting certain social roles. Social roles do not merely place individuals in certain social locations but also bear within themselves normative prescriptions of how people ought to act within these roles. The notion "father" does not refer to a social status but prescribes a certain pattern of right behavior. It is this, of course, which has led many to speak of the importance of personal relations in China. Actually, there is something very impersonal about these personal relations since they are always relations of persons acting according to norms prescribed by social roles. Later Confucianism reduces these relations to the "five relations" — relations between father and child, husband and wife, elder and younger brother, ruler and subject, friend and friend (the latter being the most "personal"). These categories are presumed to embrace all fundamental relationships. Actually the "ruler-subject" relationship involved a tremendous variety of patterns of behavior based on one's position in an elaborate hierarchy.

Now within this structure *li* refers to the rules of conduct involved in these basic relationships. They are the rules governing the behavior of the individual in his own social role and governing his behavior toward others in their social roles. Actually *li* has a wider range of meaning. The character is derived from the name of an ancient sacrificial vessel and many of the prescriptions of *li* involving sacrifices to ancestors and gods' festive rites, etc. belong to the category of religious ritual. This, indeed, may have been the original sense of the term. *Li* are thus rules of conduct governing the relations between men (in their proper social roles) and the gods and ancestors, as well as relations between men and men. However, leaving aside the much debated question of Confucius' religious attitude, there can be no doubt that the purely human aspect of *li* has become of central importance with him even though the religious rites continue to form an integral part of the whole order of *tao*.

Another basic aspect of *li* is its association with moral force rather than with the sanction of physical force. Confucian thought is marked by an extremely strong feeling for the antithesis between moral force or spiritual force and physical coercion. So strong is this feeling, that moral force is practically equated with the good while anything associated with the sanction of physical coercion is tainted with evil. Granet has gone so far as to maintain that moral force was regarded as a magical potency by the Chinese. A man in whom moral force has won the ascendancy will naturally live up to the ethical demands of his social role. He will submit to *li* without hesitancy. Furthermore, the moral force which the noble man manifests in his behavior and in his attitudes acts as a radiating force, as it were, bringing others into its field of radiation. Hence the tremendous emphasis on the power of example as well as on proper education. Furthermore, while the prevalence of *li* depends on the prevalence of this moral force, moral perfection of the individual can only manifest itself in outward behavior as *li*. There are, to be sure, many schools of thought within Confucianism concerning the actual relationship between moral perfection in the individual and *li*. Some maintain that *li* is merely a manifestation of the moral perfection of individuals. Others maintain that it is *li* itself which, through education, brings about the moral improvement of men. Others maintain that only the ancient sages possessed moral perfection innately, while mankind as a whole must acquire it through the training in *li*. In all cases, however, the moral force which works within men and the *li* which manifests itself in external conduct are inseparable.

Within the *ideal* Confucian order, the institution of government would play a peculiarly restricted role. The good ruler and his ministers would, on the one hand, provide the people with an example of proper behavior according to *li* (it should be noted that many of the duties of *li* are confined to the ruling classes), and on the other hand would educate the people in *li*. Within the ideal system, the ruling class becomes a sort of focal point of this moral force. Presumably the foundation of such a state would rest wholly on moral force rather than on physical coercion.

When we come to examine some of the concrete prescriptions which come under the heading of *li,* we find that many of them concern matters of proper ritual, etiquette, manners, gestures, and mien. There are points at which rules of *li* impinge upon matters which would come under the heading of civil or private law in the West — marriage, divorce, support of parents, burial responsibilities, disposition of property within the family, the status of concubines, etc. Taken as a whole, however, *li* as a body of rules, does not touch vast areas of experience which fall within the scope of Western law.

It is important to remember here that *li* is not a body of rules designed to take care of every circumstance. *Li* is an instrument for training character, and nourishing moral force. In a society where *li* prevails, unbridled self-interest is placed under effective control from within, as it were. Men may continue to have individual interests, and these interests are legitimate up to a point; but in a society where men are governed by *li,* conflicts of interest can be easily resolved. Both sides will be ready to make concessions, to yield (*jang*), and the necessity for litigation will be avoided. In such a society any highly explicit system of civil law would be unnecessary.

It is at this point, by the way, that the Confucian conception of *li* becomes linked to the Confucian attitude toward the whole realm of what we call "individual rights." Individuals have legitimate interests, to be sure, and in the good society these interests will be taken care of (in accordance with requirements of the individual's social status). To surround these interests with an aura of sanctity and to call them "rights," to elevate the defense of these individual interests to the plane of a moral virtue, to "insist on one's rights" — is to run entirely counter to the spirit of *li.* The proper predisposition with regard to one's interests is the predisposition to yield rather than the predisposition to insist. A man who has led a life conforming to *li* will know how to behave properly when his interests are involved.

These, it seems to me, are some of the main characteristics of *li* and the question remains — are we here dealing with a variety of law? According to some Western definitions of law, the roles of *li* would definitely fall under the category of law. Stammler maintains that law includes any rule of conduct considered to be inviolable, universal, and independent of the wishes of the individual, whether such rule is supported by political sanction or not. However, if *li* is law, it is law within a restricted framework. Presumably, in most Western conceptions of law the primary focus is on human behavior in various given circumstances. The subjects of law are only of interest to the extent that they are involved in the legal action. In *li* the primary focus is on the relations of social roles, and the rules of conduct are significant because they are concerned with these relations.

Now in discussing *li* so far we have been describing the ideal social order. Both Confucius and his followers were only too acutely aware that actuality falls short of the ideal. Confucianism recognizes that there are elements in human society impervious to the influence of *li,* and that there are whole periods when *li* cannot be made to prevail. There is even the notion that in periods of deep economic distress the masses cannot be led by *li.* The economic distress itself, of course, is generally attributed to the ruling class's failure to conform to the demands of *li.* In all areas where *li* cannot be made to apply, *fa* must be employed to maintain order. *Fa* is enacted law designed to keep order by the appeal to the fear of punishment. It is thus based directly on the sanction of force. So closely is *fa* associated with punishment, that the word has become a synonym of the word punishment. *Fa* thus represents the sanction of force in a very direct and literal sense and its first and primary meaning is penal law. Where *li* is ineffective in maintaining public order, *fa* must take over. Where the ruling class must place heavy reliance on *fa,* it is a symptom of its own inability to rule by *li.*

However, since Confucianism recognizes that there are always elements in human society which must be controlled by *fa* — that human reality almost inevitably embodies this element of defect — *fa* still occupies a legitimate, albeit regrettable, place in the general nature of things. It is recognized as a necessity but deprecated. "If the people be led by laws," states Confucius, "and uniformity sought to be given them by punishments, they will try to avoid punishments but have no sense of shame. If they be led by virtue and uniformity sought to be given them by *li,* they will have a sense of shame and, moreover, will become good." *Li* and *fa* produce as it were their own corresponding psychologies. Where government does not rely on *li, li* cannot exercise its educative effect — it cannot become a transmission belt for transmitting virtue to the people and the people will not be curbed by an inner moral force. *Fa* makes its appeal to the bare interest in avoiding pain. It works with a simple hedonistic pleasure-pain psychology. Not only does it lead men to think in terms of self-interest in avoiding punishment but makes them litigious — makes them skilled in the ways of manipulating laws to suit their own interests. In a society dominated by *fa,* the people as a whole will all develop the peculiar talents of the shyster lawyer and the sense of shame will suffer.

In one of the Confucian classics we find a fierce diatribe against a minister who has publicized a penal code (by having it engraved on bronze vessels). There is a double offense here — the heavy reliance on *fa* and its publicization. This act, it is contended, will inevitably lead to a litigious spirit on the part of the people. They will no longer look to their superiors for an example of moral behavior but "appeal to the letter of the text hoping that, by chance, they may succeed in their argumentation. . . . They will reject *li* and appeal to your text." Here we note that the psychology which underlies the litigious spirit has nothing to do with the psychology which underlies *li.* There is another significant point made in this passage which reflects an important facet of the whole Confucian attitude toward law. "The ancient kings," states our author, "deliberated on circumstances in deciding (concerning the punishment of crime)." The Confucian view that where men are guided by *li,* conflicts are easily resolved, has made it possible for Confucianists to develop an acute feeling for the uniqueness of every human situation — for the fact that "no two cases are alike" and a corresponding skepticism toward all attempts to subsume all possible circumstances under certain generalized legal categories. As a result, the judge — whom we may presume to be a man guided by *li* — will (within limits) simply think of the legal code as providing certain guidelines but in his judgment will rely very heavily on the unique features of the circumstances of the case. He may even base his judgment on some situation described in the classics rather than on the provisions of the code. Hence, as one Chinese author states, "it is the judgment and not the law which makes justice."

These, it seems to me, are some of the major characteristics of the Confucian concept of *fa,* as it developed in the centuries immediately following the Master's death. However, as we know, the Confucian gospel by no means found immediate acceptance in the stormy period which followed his death. It is interesting to note, however, that many of the basic antitheses established by Confucianism (which undoubtedly rested on a much older substratum of thought) furnish the frame of reference within which later thought operates. Thus in the fourth and third centuries B.C. we have the emergence of a group of political philosophers known as the "school of *fa*" or "legalists" in current Western literature. Their view of the nature of *fa* is strikingly similar to that of Confucius. *Fa* is penal law — directly based on the sanction by force. It presupposes that the people can be led only by an appeal to the pleasure-pain principle. However, not only do the legalists accept these definitions, but they frankly and boldly assert that social order can be maintained only by *fa*. Contemporary events led them to a radical disbelief in *li* and moral force as ordering principles of society.

However, their thought is not only characterized by a revaluation of *fa* but by what might be called its heavily statist orientation. Living in an environment where great powers were contending for domination of the Chinese world, they offered themselves to the rulers of this world as experts in the science of power. By relying on *fa*, the ruler would be able to establish a Draconian order within his borders. However, this was not the final end. By making the people a pliable instrument of his will, the ruler would be able to use them in increasing the economic, political, and military power potential of the state and thus make possible ultimate victory in the international struggles of this period of "contending states." Beyond their addiction to harsh penal law, the legalists thus became the advocates of what Max Weber would call the "rationalization" (within the limits of the period) of the social order from the point of view of enhancing the power of the state. They were advocates of the bureaucratic principle, of something like a conscript army, of sweeping economic reforms, etc. Thus, *fa* became with them not only penal law but all forms of state-initiated institutional change.

We know, of course, that the Ch'in dynasty, which finally united the Chinese world during the third century B.C. into a centralized bureaucratic empire, actually operated within the framework of a legalist philosophy. It not only established a harsh and detailed system of penal law but, by the very nature of bureaucratic government, brought about an enormous extension in what might be called administrative law. It also initiated all sorts of institutional changes by government enactment.

While the dynasty was short-lived, this historic experience strongly conditioned the whole subsequent orthodox Confucian attitude toward *fa chih* (which, ironically, must be translated as "rule of law"). Harsh despotism, heavy reliance on brute force, oppressive demands on the people by an interventionist state — all these are the orthodox associations with *fa chih*. Furthermore, all attempts to improve society by heavy reliance on institutional change initiated by state enactment has also been associated with *fa* as a result of this experience. Presumably, the common denominator between this meaning of *fa* and its meaning as "penal law" are the facts that (1) the sanction of force lies behind both, (2) they both try to reform men "externally" by using incentives of reward and fear, (3) in both, the reliance on *li* is neglected.

While the Ch'in dynasty disappeared, while Confucianism subsequently became the official state philosophy, the basic structure of the centralized bureaucratic state created by the Ch'in remained. To the extent that the Chinese state has had to rely on the machinery of compulsion and rules based on the sanction of force (and it has probably had to do so to the same extent as any other state) it has relied on a machinery whose basic skeletal structure was created by the Ch'in legalists.

Now, if we survey the immense period from the second century B.C. until the 1911 revolution, we find a considerable — albeit extremely slow — growth in the area of law. More and more detailed criminal codes make their appearance, culminating in the imposing Criminal Code of the late Ch'ing dynasty. There is a steady accumulation of rules governing government administration coinciding with the growing complexity of government. There is a slow evolution in the complexity of the specialized judicial organs of government, and we also have the emergence of certain recognized traditions of legal interpretation. Furthermore, while the official codes are thought of as criminal codes, they actually contain some categories which would fall under the heading of civil law in the West. Finally, we even find the emergence of a class of legal specialists (not lawyers). Almost invariably, however, such specialists occupy a lowly position in government both in rank and in prestige.

In spite of this modest growth of law, however, the Confucianized environment plays a decisive role both in shaping the direction of legal development and in inhibiting this development. We have what Professor Ch'ü T'ung-tsu calls the Confucianization of law. That is, matters of law which impinge on the area of *li* receive particular attention in this code; heinous crimes against the "five relations" receive particularly severe punishment so that the realm of *li* which is supposed to rest on the sanction of moral force comes to receive strong support from the criminal law itself. Furthermore, much of what can be called civil law in these codes involves matters which impinge closely on the realm of *li* — laws of inheritance, marriage, disposition of property, etc. While such laws appear in the law books, the general assumption is that respectable people will be able to settle such matters outside of court. In other civil matters local custom plays a much more important role than enacted law. While custom does not enjoy the high moral standing of *li*, it is superior to *fa*. It is not enacted; it does not rest on the sanction of political force; and it is generally permeated with the spirit of *li*. On the whole, however, the main effect of Confucianism has been to inhibit the growth of an all-inclusive legal system and of an elaborate system of legal interpretation. It has inhibited the emergence of a class of lawyers and has, in general, kept alive the unfavorable attitude toward the whole realm of *fa*.

When we turn to the modern scene, we find that the politically articulate classes in China are often extremely hostile to the typically Confucian attitudes on these matters. It is remarkable that both the Nationalist Government and the present Communist regime have both been committed to a reversal of the Confucian attitude toward *fa chih* (rule of law). The Nationalist Government not only proclaimed its devotion to *fa chih* but made great efforts with the help of foreign advisors to frame a modern legal code. Here, as elsewhere, it was unable to implement its professed intentions to any great degree before 1949, but its professed intentions are undeniable. Contrary to the impressions of many, the present Communist regime is also extremely devoted to *fa chih, as it conceives of this term.*

In spite of this transvaluation of values in connection with the "rule of law," however, it would be extremely dangerous to assume any automatic connection between the modern enthusiasm for *fa chih* and commitment to Western types of liberalism. Actually some of the modern attitudes are more akin to the old legalist conception of the function of law rather than to the whole series of associations linked with the phrase "rule of law" in the Anglo-Saxon West. There have been many sincere liberals in China both in and outside of government who have indeed thought of *fa chih* in the sense of the Western "rule of law." When one reads Chiang Kai-shek's *China's Destiny,* however, one finds that his primary association with *fa chih* is with the "respect for law" as a method of inculcating discipline in the undisciplined Chinese masses — with law as a necessity in a modern industrialized and bureaucratized state. In order to bring China to the rank of a first-class power, China must become a modern state with a modern military, industrial, and administrative system. Such a system is inconceivable without *fa chih* — the rule of law. It is noteworthy that in the same chapter in which Chiang speaks of the "rule of law," he — like Sun Yat-sen before him — deprecates the exaggerated insistence on the freedom of the individual. There is, to be sure, an entirely novel element here — the notion of the sovereignty of the people. Since the state derives its sovereignty from the people, the law, even though it rests on sanction of force, is nevertheless an expression of the will of the people. Hence *fa* now has a more respectable moral basis than it has ever enjoyed in the past. However, in such a book as *China's Destiny,* the primary association with "rule of law" is the notion of law as a means of increasing the power of the state.

When we turn to the Communists, we must, of course, distinguish between the ultimate utopia and the Soviet Stalinist model of state. In the original conception of the ultimate Communist utopia, law, of course, would play as negligible a role as in the ideal Confucian society. The social origins of crime would have disappeared and conflicts of interest would not arise. In the Stalinist model, however, contrary to popular impression, law must play a central role. The interest in law is not a post-Stalin phenomenon in the Soviet Union. Stalin himself stated in 1936 that "we need the stability of law more than ever." Here again, as with our Chinese legalists, law disciplines the people and makes them a pliable instrument for attaining the objectives of the state. Again, the machinery of modern industry, political administration, and military administration presupposes the existence of an elaborate network of rules governing the people's behavior. The timid talk about legality in the post-Stalin period in the Soviet Union actually involves the hope that the respect for legality will be extended from those areas where it already enjoys enthusiastic state support to the realm of personal rights.

The Communist Chinese attitude toward law is very similar here to the Soviet attitude. The regime is extremely interested in fostering respect for law in certain well-defined areas. In certain narrowly prescribed areas — rights of women, freedom of marriage — it even impinges on the realm of personal rights. On the whole, however, law is associated with the necessities of a modern industrial, administrative, and military system. While the ultimate professed aim is social welfare, there is still a strong kinship (probably not conscious) to the legalist conception of the function of law. It should be noted that some of the ancient legalists also maintained that social welfare was the ultimate goal.

All of this should lead us to a fresh look at some of our own unexamined assumptions concerning the "rule of law." The experience of Western Europe, particularly of the Anglo-Saxon West, has tended to establish an immediate mental association between reverence for the sanctity of law, freedom of the individual, and legal limits on the power of government. Yet even in the West it is well to remind ourselves that the growth of Roman law in the late Middle Ages coincided with the emergence of the absolute states. It is also extremely interesting to note that Max Weber — a man formed in a German rather than an Anglo-Saxon environment — tended to link the growth in the "rationality" of law in the modern world with the necessities of the absolutist bureaucratic state on the one hand and with capitalism on the other. It should be immediately added that Weber does not associate capitalism with the freedom of the individual but with the growing bureaucratization of human society.

It is undoubtedly true that a reverence for the sanctity of law is a necessary prerequisite for the emergence of a democratic state — that no such state is conceivable where such a reverence does not exist. It is probably also true that an absolute state which attempts to inculcate respect for legality within cerain prescribed limits is not creating a very firm basis for such a respect. On the other hand, it is important to note that something akin to the old Chinese legalist conception of the role of the law has not only existed in various times and places, but has actually found concrete implementation.

When we turn to China, we find that there is very little in her past traditions of thought, historic experience, or even in her contemporary experience which would tend to establish a close association between the notion of "rule of law" and the notion of the freedom of the individual. There are those who optimistically maintain that if the present Communist regime is able to establish a respect for legality in the areas where legality concerns the state, there will be a growing clamor for the extension of legality to other areas. Actually one might also argue the very opposite case. At the present time, there is a close association between the emphasis on legality and the attempt to control every aspect of individual life. It is possible that a revulsion against this control might carry with it a reversion to early antinomian attitudes. At any rate, it would be extremely foolhardy to assume that, in China, the growing emphasis on the role of legality in the Communist sense must inevitably lead to the freedom of the individual under law. Certainly other factors must also intervene if this end is ever to be achieved.

## B. COMMUNIST IDEOLOGY

Before embarking on an excursion into the ideology of Chinese Communist criminal law, a preliminary word might be said about the importance of ideology.[4] Although in legal affairs, as in other spheres of Chinese Communist activity, one may not be certain of the degree to which ideology influences the actual operation of the system, it seems clear that it has some substantial effect. Available documentation and extensive interviews indicate that the results reached by the legal system are certainly expressed in idcological terms. Indeed, this ideology provides legal cadres with the only vocabulary, concepts, and method of analysis that they know. It would be surprising if their daily study and repeated rationalization of conduct in terms of ideology did not have an impact upon their future conduct. Moreover, administrators of the system of criminal justice have emphasized the practical importance of ideological clarification (see Item 8). The student of Chinese criminal law therefore ignores Chinese political-legal theory at his peril.

## ITEM 2

The following excerpts are from a speech made by Mao Tse-tung on the eve of Communist assumption of power over the entire mainland of China on October 1, 1949. These brief remarks provided a theoretical framework for the application of criminal punishment during the early years of Communist rule and continue to have major doctrinal significance.

[Mao Tse-tung, "On the People's Democratic Dictatorship" (address in commemoration of the 28th anniversary of the CCP), *JMJP,* July 1, 1949]

[T]he Western bourgeois civilization, the bourgeois democracy, and the plan for a bourgeois republic all went bankrupt in the minds of the Chinese people. Bourgeois democracy has given way to a people's democracy under the leadership of the proletariat, and a bourgeois republic has given way to a people's republic. A possibility has thus been created of attaining socialism and communism through the people's republic, of attaining the elimination of classes and of attaining a harmonious world . . . The bourgeois republic has existed in foreign countries but it cannot exist in China because China is a country oppressed by imperialism. The only road [for China] is through a people's republic under the leadership of the proletariat.

[U]nder the leadership of the Chinese Communist Party, Chinese revolutionary theory and practice have made great forward strides, fundamentally changing the face of China. Up to now, the Chinese people have had these two major and basic [lessons of] experience: (1) Domestically the masses must be aroused. This is to solidify the worker class, the peasant class, the petty bourgeoisie, and

4. For recent studies of Chinese Communist ideology, see Franz Schurmann, *Ideology and Organization in Communist China* (Berkeley, Los Angeles, and London, 1966); Stuart R. Schram, *The Political Thought of Mao Tse-tung* (New York, Washington, D.C., and London, 1963); A. A. Cohen, *The Communism of Mao Tse-tung* (Chicago and London, 1964). For the pre-1949 development of Maoist thought, see the landmark works: Benjamin Schwartz, *Chinese Communism and the Rise of Mao* (Cambridge, Mass., 1951); Conrad Brandt et al., *A Documentary History of Chinese Communism* (Cambridge, Mass., 1959).

the national bourgeoisie and to unite them into a national unified front under the leadership of the worker class, and develop it into a state of the people's democratic dictatorship led by the worker class with the alliance of workers and peasants as its basis . . .

"You are too provocative." We are talking of dealing with domestic and foreign reactionaries, that is, imperialists and their running dogs, and not of dealing with any other people. With respect to these people [foreign and domestic reactionaries], the question of whether we are provocative does not arise. Because they are reactionaries, it is the same whether we are provocative or not. Only by drawing a clear line between reactionaries and revolutionaries, by exposing the conspiracies and plots of the reactionaries, by arousing vigilance and attention among the revolutionaries and by raising our own morale while eliminating the awesomeness of the enemy — can the reactionaries be isolated, conquered, or replaced. In front of a wild beast you cannot show the slightest cowardice. We must learn from Wu Sung [one of the 108 heroes in the famous Chinese novel, *All Men Are Brothers,* who killed a tiger with his bare hands] on the Ching-yang ridge. To Wu Sung, the tiger on the Ching-yang ridge would eat people all the same whether they provoked it or not. You either kill the tiger or are eaten by it; it is one or the other.

．　　．　　．　　．　　．

"You are dictatorial." Dear sirs, you are right; that is just what we are. The experience of several decades, amassed by the Chinese people, tells us to put the people's democratic dictatorship into effect. That is, it tells us to deprive reactionaries of the right to speak out and only to allow the people to have the right to speak out.

Who are the people? At the present stage in China, they are the worker class, the peasant class, the petty bourgeoisie, and the national bourgeoisie. Under the leadership of the worker class and the Communist Party, these classes solidify to form their own state and elect their own government so as to put into effect a dictatorship over the running dogs of imperialism — the landlord class, the bureaucratic capitalist class, and the Kuomintang reactionaries and their henchmen representing these classes — to suppress them, permitting them only to behave properly and not to talk and act wildly. If they want to talk and act wildly they will be immediately repressed and will be given punitive restraints. The democratic system is to be put into effect among the people, giving them such rights as freedom of speech, assembly and association. The right to vote is given only to the people and not to the reactionaries. These two aspects, democracy among the people and dictatorship over the reactionaries, combine to form the people's democratic dictatorship.

Why should it be done this way? Everybody clearly knows that if it were not this way, the revolution would fail, the people would meet with disaster, and the state would perish.

"Don't you want to eliminate state authority?" We want to, but we do not want to at present; we cannot want to at present. Why? Because imperialism still exists, domestic reactionaries still exist, and classes within the country still exist.

Our present task is to strengthen the apparatus of the people's state, which refers mainly to the people's army, people's police and people's courts, for the country's defense and the protection of the people's interests, and with this as a condition, to give China the possibility of advancing steadily, under the leadership of the working class and the Communist Party, from an agricultural to an industrial country and from a new democratic society to a socialist and communist society, of eliminating classes and of realizing [a state of] harmony. The state apparatus such as the army, police, and courts consists of instruments by which classes oppress classes. To the hostile classes the state apparatus is the instrument of oppression. It is violent, and not "benevolent." "You are not benevolent." Just so. We decidedly will not apply a policy of benevolence to the reactionary acts of the reactionaries and reactionary classes. We only apply a policy of benevolence among the people, and not to the reactionary acts of the reactionaries and reactionary classes outside the people.

[The function of] the people's state is to protect the people. Only when there is the people's state is it possible for the people to use democratic methods on a nationwide and all-round scale to educate and reform themselves, to free themselves from the influence of domestic and foreign reactionaries (this influence is at present still very great and will exist for a long time and cannot be eliminated quickly), to reform their own bad habits and ideologies acquired from the old society and not to let themselves walk the erroneous road pointed out by the reactionaries, but to continue to advance and develop toward a socialist and communist society.

The methods we use in this field are democratic, that is, are methods of persuasion and not coercion. When the people break the law they should be punished [*other than by imprisonment or death*], imprisoned, or given the death penalty. But these are individual situations, and they differ in principle from dictatorship over the reactionary class as a class.

Obviously, Mao's speech offered convenient justification for the organized terror that was to sweep the country as the regime destroyed the old order, consolidated its power, and began to reshape society by means of the land reform, suppression of counterrevolution, "three-anti" and "five-anti," liquidation of counterrevolution, and other mass movements.[5] Since the principal targets of these movements were "reactionaries" rather than "people," according to Mao's doctrine there were no barriers to the application of violence to them. Note that Mao, who at that time had already had some twenty years of experience in governing "liberated areas," gives short shrift to the ultimate Communist goal of the "withering away of the state" and emphasizes the need to strengthen the legal organs for the exercise of dictatorship over the reactionaries.

1. What factors might have shaped this attitude?
   a. Is Mao's "legalist" heritage showing?
   b. Is he simply adhering to the Stalinist orthodoxy of the day?
   c. Did the situation confronting him allow any practical alternative?

5. For valuable accounts of the first period of nationwide Communist rule, see A. Doak Barnett, *Communist China: The Early Years, 1949–55* (New York, Washington, D.C., and London, 1964); Richard L. Walker, *China Under Communism: The First Five Years* (New Haven, 1955).

2. Why would a Communist revolutionary government want to use courts as well as police and army for the elimination of its opponents?

3. What does Mao mean in the last paragraph?

a. "When the people . . . [are] punished [other than by imprisonment or death], imprisoned, or given the death penalty" — is this "persuasion and not coercion"?

b. Does he mean that methods of persuasion will be applied to the people as a class but not to the reactionaries as a class?

c. What implications might this have for the conduct of the criminal process?

d. Is the persuasion-coercion dichotomy Confucian or Communist?

e. Should the theory of one law for the reactionaries and another for the people be deemed Confucian or Communist?

4. Does American criminal justice have an ideology? What are its sources?

## ITEM 3

This initial selection from the *Lectures* suggests that the Chinese have adopted the standard Marxist explanation of the causes of crime. At the time the *Lectures* were first published, in September 1957, socialist reform of agriculture, industry, and commerce had been substantially completed only a short time. In subsequent years the Chinese have been sorely troubled by the intractability of the problem of crime, especially during the period of severe economic hardship in 1959–1961. Yet there is no evidence that the persistence of the problem has spurred them to discard orthodox formulas and to undertake serious inquiry into the causes of crime. It is interesting to note that, after almost half a century of struggling with crime, the Soviet Union has recently begun to recognize the need for research in criminology.[6]

Also of interest in this item is the Chinese resort to the Soviet technique of dealing only in selected, relative percentages and not providing aggregated legal statistics.

[*Lectures* (September 1957), pp. 49–55]

[C]rime is a product of class society, a class phenomenon.

In his book, *The German Ideology,* Marx explained the essence of crime. He pointed out: "Just as with law, crime is also the struggle of the isolated individual against the relationship of domination. It, too, does not derive from the individual's pure whimsy. Just the contrary, the conditions that give rise to crime are the same as the conditions that give rise to the current domination."[7] This explains that crime is conduct that opposes and undermines the interests of the ruling class. Crime did not exist before human society created the relationship of dominance between ruler and ruled.

The primitive commune system was the first form developed by human society and also was the first stage in the development of human society. In this stage there were neither exploiters nor exploited, neither rulers nor ruled: ". . . all disputes and misunderstandings were settled collectively by the entire group of those who were concerned — the clan or tribe — or were settled between the various clans; . . . in most instances, time-honored custom adjusted

6. See, e.g., V. Kudryavtsev, "Pressing Problems of Soviet Criminology," *Sovetskaya Yustitsia,* 20:6–9 (October 1965), translated in *CDSP,* 17.48:12–13 (Dec. 22, 1965).

7. *Complete Collection of Marx and Engels,* first Russian edition, Book Four, p. 312 (quoted in Vyshinsky, *Questions on Theory of State and Law,* Law Publishing House, 1955, p. 25 [as in original text].

everything." [8] Crime as "the struggle of the isolated individual against the relationship of dominance" did not exist. The concept of crime was created only after the emergence of private property, the split of society into classes, and the formation of the state. This has already been thoroughly proved by the classic writings of Marxism-Leninism.

Since the emergence of private property, the split of society into classes and the formation of the state, the slave system, the feudal system, and the capitalist ownership system have all been systems of exploitation built upon the basis of private property. Under these systems of exploitation the laboring masses became the exploited. Their lives sank into a state of extreme poverty. They were in this way stimulated to commit crimes. Just as Lenin said in his book, *State and Revolution*: the exploitation of the masses and the extreme poverty into which their lives have sunk are the basic social causes of the excesses which violate the rules of common living.[9]

It can be seen from this that the various systems of exploitation that are built upon the basis of private property are the social sources of crime. This explains why the phenomenon of crime has always existed throughout the long historical period of the various exploiting class societies.

In modern capitalist countries the phenomenon of crime is increasing even more widely. This is something that is directly determined by the essence of the capitalist system, the nature of the capitalist economic base, and the system of class inequality. The basic law of modern capitalist development is [the means for] the cruel exploitation of the laboring people and the bankruptcy and poverty of the great majority of residents. Unemployment and poverty compel a portion of the laboring people who still do not understand their own class interests to commit crimes. Thus this also is determining the wide increase in crime in the various modern capitalist countries.

Besides the decisive role played by economic causes in the ceaseless increase in crime, in modern capitalist countries, especially in America, the decadent morality of the ruling class, which is reflected in art, culture, and movies, is also involved. This kind of rottenness in the spirit of the people also plays a definite role in the ceaseless increase in crime.

We can use the figures of crime occurring in America as an example of the wide increase in crime in the various modern capitalist countries. There were 1,517,026 felony cases in America in 1940; 1,790,030 in 1950; and 2,036,510 in 1952. In 1955, such cases increased to 2,264,450.

It is just because the capitalist social system is the social source of crime that bourgeois criminal law scholars always think of every possible method to cover up this fact when they discuss the causes of crime. They attempt to use various methods to prove that the causes of crime have no relation to the social and economic system. For example, one school attempts to prove that the commission of crime is an act of absolute free will not influenced by any outside

8. Engels, *Origin of the Family, Private Property and the State,* People's Publishing House, 1954, p. 92 [as in original text].

9. See Lenin, *State and Revolution,* Liberation House, 1949, pp. 114–115 [as in original text].

phenomenon. One school attempts to prove that some people are seemingly born criminals, and therefore crime has absolutely nothing to do with the social and economic system. Another school attempts to prove that crime does not arise from contradictions of the class society as a whole, but is created by individually isolated social factors (such as the high price of food, and bad housing conditions). Very obviously, all these attempts themselves serve the purpose of bourgeois class interests; their aim is to make the masses of people abandon the class struggle; they vainly hope to make the capitalist system into a permanent, unchanging social system and to obstruct the development of society.

It is only socialist legal theory guided by Marxism-Leninism that for the first time revealed the truth that the existence of the exploiting system is the source of crime.

The facts of the more than seven years since the founding of the People's Republic of China show that under the people's democratic system, the fundamental cause of crime — the system of private ownership of the instruments of production and the means of production — is gradually being eliminated. Our country's cultural and educational undertakings have played a role in helping the people of our country establish the correct world outlook of dialectic materialism and in propagating lofty Communist ideology and morality. Thus, our country is not only eliminating, from the standpoint of economic factors, the fundamental cause of the occurrence of the phenomenon of crime, but it is also ceaselessly conducting a firm struggle on the ideological front with the remnants of capitalist and feudal ideologies which are one cause of the occurrence of that phenomenon in our country. This explains that our country's social system itself is not a cause of crime. The existence of the phenomenon of crime in our country is left over from the old society. It is a historical phenomenon that cannot be completely eliminated for a fairly long period of time. Specifically, there are the following five causes:

First, the existence of imperialism and of the remnants of the overthrown reactionary classes. Imperialism will certainly never idly watch the undertakings of socialist construction in our country. Domestically, the remnants of the overthrown exploiting classes will certainly never desire their own death. Those exploiting classes that are about to be eliminated will certainly never stop resisting.

This objective situation shows that, since the founding of our country, we have dealt with an extremely complex and sharp class struggle. The aggressive group headed by America has never desired to give up its aggressive designs upon our country. Also, American imperialism is at present still illegally occupying our territory, Taiwan, and supporting the reactionary group of Chiang Kai-shek in a vain attempt to conduct a restoration [movement]. For this reason, they have continually used conspiratorial and contemptible methods to send their secret agents and spies to infiltrate the mainland and also to support the remnant counterrevolutionary force in the conduct of counterrevolutionary sabotage activity.

Second, the dregs of the old society, such as hooligans, swindlers, habitual robbers, and the enemy's counterfeit [KMT] military, government, police and military-police personnel who served [as such] for a long period and who have not gone through reform or are difficult to reform. They are still attempting to live a decadent, rotten, exploiting, and parasitic life, and continue to do evil and to conduct various kinds of criminal activities. In recent years our country has conducted a series of social reform movements. A great number of these dregs left over from the old society have, through education, reformed into new persons and now engage in labor and production. But we still have not attained the thorough reform and liquidation of this group. This is a problem that certainly cannot be completely resolved within a short period of time. These dregs of society who have not been reformed or are difficult to reform, not only do wrong by sexually violating [women], swindling, stealing, and engaging in other such criminal acts, but they also entice some youths and juveniles into organizing groups of hooligans or thieves. Some of them even collaborate with counterrevolutionaries in the conduct of counterrevolutionary sabotage activity.

Third, in the period of transition to a socialist society, the bourgeoisie still exists in our country. We know that "[a]s long as exploiting classes and exploited classes exist in society, class struggle will continue to exist. But our country was originally a country oppressed by foreign imperialism. Because of this special historical condition of our country not only is there a struggle between the working class and the national bourgeoisie, but there also has been and still exists a relationship of alliance between them." [10]

As for [separate] elements of the Chinese bourgeoisie, their ideology is both progressive and backward. But the class itself has a common character, and this reflects the capitalist ideology of exploitation of hired labor. This ideology is manifested in sole pursuit of profit, speculation, and cunning; damaging public interests to benefit private interests; rottenness and decadence. This ideology is extraordinarily dangerous to the masses of people. In his *Capital,* Marx has a very vivid section describing the nature of the bourgeoisie. He said [quoted], "Like nature which abhors a vacuum, capital abhors making no profit or little profit. With proper profit, capital can be fearless. Ten percent [profit] can safeguard the use of capital at any place; twenty percent can make it active; fifty percent can lead to positive audacity; 100 percent can make men disregard all men's law; and 300 percent can make men disregard crime, even to the point of not caring about the risk of being hanged." [11] Therefore, in recent years, although the bourgeoisie of our country is in the midst of being reformed and of being eliminated, the unlawful bourgeois elements still inherit and support the poisonous principal social class foundation left over by all the exploiters and reactionary rulers of the old society. In the past some unlawful elements among the bourgeoisie carried out the "five poisons" [the objects of the "five-anti" movement]. Later they also engaged in criminal acts of resisting socialist reform. Even after the elimination of the bourgeoisie, individual bourgeois elements will still carry out definite criminal acts.

10. Liu Shao-ch'i, "Report on the Draft Constitution of the People's Republic of China" [as in original text].
11. Marx, *Das Capital,* People's Publishing House, 1953, Book One, p. 961 [as in original text].

As for the entire nation there still exists a certain number of producers of small commodities. Although they are in the midst of being reformed, they still accept the corrosive social foundation of the exploiting class ideology.

Fourth, the remaining feudal and bourgeois ideologies still exist in the people's consciousness. Their source is [to be found in the fact] that social consciousness lags behind existing development and is influenced by the foreign capitalist world. Thus this causes a few irresolute laboring people to behave in a way that undermines the people's democratic legal order on certain problems. For example, the criminal acts of compelling arranged marriages and mistreating children and women are engaged in under the controlling influence of feudal ideology. The bourgeois ideology remaining in the people's consciousness, such as selfishness and self-interest, may be manifested in theft, corruption, hooligan[like] acts, and criminal acts that are destructive of social order and public property. Because these bad ideologies and habits inherited from the old society cannot be liquidated within a short period of time, these criminal acts which originate from the feudal and bourgeois ideologies remaining in the people's consciousness not only exist at present, but will be impossible to eliminate for a fairly long period.

Fifth, old China suffered a long period of imperialistic, feudalistic, and bureaucratic exploitation and enslavement, and its economy and culture were both very backward. In the several years since the founding of the People's Republic of China, although there has been great change and rapid improvement, the level of productive force at our country's present stage still cannot completely satisfy the needs of the people's life. Therefore, this phenomenon of backwardness and poverty cannot be completely changed within a short period of time. Because of the economic poverty and cultural backwardness left over from the old society, some people will oppose the interests of society with their individual interests, their motives being accumulation of wealth and egoism. Thus, this has made some people commit criminal acts, manifested mainly in crimes against property.

The reasons [stated] above show that the occurrence of the phenomenon of crime is not a product of the people's democratic system of our country but is left over from the old social system. And it is just for this reason that it will be gradually eliminated. Actually, because of the superiority of the people's democratic system of our country, and following the socialist undertakings of construction and socialist reform which have been victoriously conducted, certain crimes have been greatly reduced. "On the basis of statistical materials of people's courts in the great majority of districts of the entire country, criminal and civil cases of first instance heard in local people's courts of the various levels in 1955 decreased four to five percent as compared to 1954." "The cases of economic crimes of unlawful capitalists decreased more than sixty percent." [12] Again, for example, criminal cases in Peking in 1956 decreased fifty-two percent in comparison with 1955. It can be expected that following the development of socialist construction and socialist reform in our country, the number of

12. Tung Pi-wu, President of the [Supreme] Court, Speech given at the Third Meeting of the First Session of the National People's Congress [as in original text].

criminal cases will tend to be further reduced in the future. But this certainly does not mean that in a certain period and in a certain district, the phenomenon of an increase in some kinds of cases will not emerge. But such increase will be a temporary or a limited phenomenon. In view of the general tendency, the number of criminal cases will decrease.

## ITEM 4

One cannot hope to understand any legal phenomenon in contemporary China without first ascertaining the precise period in which it occurred. In every country the resources of law enforcement are limited and must be largely allocated to the principal policy objectives of the society. However, in a country that proceeds rapidly through different stages of development, policy objectives change frequently, requiring commensurate reallocation of law enforcement resources. Item 4 elaborates the regime's view of the criminal law as an instrument for implementing those objectives that enjoy highest priority during a given period.

[*Lectures* (September 1957), p. 28]

. . . . .

The criminal law of our country mainly attacks counterrevolutionary criminals and criminals who murder, commit arson, steal, swindle, rape, and commit other crimes that seriously undermine social order and socialist construction. We must make it clear that the sharp point of our criminal law is mainly directed at the enemies of socialism.

In order to realize this task, the form and the important points of the struggle adopted by our criminal law change and develop on the basis of the requirements of the different stages of the state's development and on the basis of the change and development in the political and economic situation. During the period of restoration of the national economy, the central tasks of the state were sternly to suppress counterrevolutionary activity, to consolidate the revolutionary order, and to restore the national economy. At that time, our country's criminal law also met the needs of the movement to reform the land system, the resist America and aid Korea movement, the movement to suppress counterrevolution, the "three-anti" and "five-anti" movements, the movement to reorganize the security of society, and all other social democratic reform movements, and it punished counterrevolutionary criminals and all other criminals in order to safeguard the smooth conduct of the work of restoring the national economy. Since 1953, when our country entered the period of planned economic construction, the general task of the state has been to realize socialist industrialization and socialist reform and to establish socialism. Criminal law also closely evolves around and serves the task of this great struggle. Because a good social order and the full development of the activism of the citizenry are necessary conditions for guaranteeing the victory of our country's economic construction, it therefore appears more important every day to strengthen the struggle against habitual robbers, habitual thieves, hooligans, and all other criminals who endanger the social order, and strengthen the struggle against criminals who encroach upon the lawful interests of citizens. Since 1953, the judicial organs of the various levels have paid attention to strengthening the struggle against these criminals. On the eve of the great social revolutionary high tide in 1955, the class struggle was extremely intense. Counterrevolutionary and other hostile elements took advantage of that opportunity to engage in wild sabotage activity. The struggle to liquidate counterrevolutionaries thus became one of the central tasks of the people throughout the country. Because of the correct leadership of the Party, this struggle won a decisive victory and safeguarded the rapid development of the high socialist revolutionary tide. At present, a fundamental change in our country's internal political situation has already occurred. The main task of the Party and of the people of the entire country at present is to concentrate our strength to transform the nation as quickly as possible from a backward agricultural country into an advanced industrial country. "The main task of the state has changed from liberating productive forces to protecting and developing productive forces. We must further strengthen the people's democratic legal system and consolidate the order of socialist construction. The state must, on the basis of its needs, gradually and systematically adopt a complete [set of] laws. All state organs and state personnel must strictly observe the law of the state so that the people's democratic rights will receive the full protection of the state." [13]

From this it can be seen that because the state's task of struggle changes, the central task and the form of struggle of the criminal law change accordingly.

1. What are the implications of this view of the criminal law?

a. Does it mean that, for identical conduct, a counterrevolutionary convicted in 1955 might receive a severe sentence and one convicted in 1956 a milder sentence?

b. Does it mean that a defendant might enjoy a greater degree of procedural protection in a 1956 prosecution than in a 1955 prosecution?

c. Might he be convicted in 1955 and not in 1956?

d. Bearing in mind that in our country we have campaigns such as those against vandalism, theft, and jay-walking, how should similar questions be answered about our own system?

2. Item 4 is also interesting because it reflects the Party line for the 1956–1957 period that, to be successful, the criminal law must not only punish but must do so according to "a complete [set of] laws" that is "strictly observe[d]" in order to guarantee "the people's democratic rights" and thereby reinforce their sense of security in the social order and their "activism" in production. By "the people," do the authors mean everyone or only the nonreactionaries?

### ITEM 5

The following excerpt attempts to spell out the goals for which the Chinese strive in the application of punishment.

[*Lectures* (September 1957), pp. 177, 180]

We know that criminal punishment is only one coercive measure of the state, is only one instrument. In itself, it certainly has no "goals." Therefore, the so-called goals of criminal punishment actually refer to the goals of people's

13. Resolution by the Eighth National Party Congress of the Chinese Communist Party on the Political Report [as in original text].

courts in applying punishment to criminals (called for simplicity the goals of punishment).

On the basis of the above-mentioned tasks of people's courts of our country, we believe that the goals of people's courts in applying punishment to criminals may be expressed [as follows]: they are not only to punish and to reform criminals but they are also to educate the citizenry and to prevent crime. Stating them separately, these are:

(1) To punish and reform criminals so that they will not commit crimes again;

(2) Through punishment of criminals, to warn unstable elements in society so that they do not walk the road of crime;

(3) Through punishment of criminals, to educate the citizenry and also to inspire them to rise and to struggle against the various kinds of criminals.

.     .     .     .     .

The above is an explanation relating to the three aspects comprising the goals of punishment in our country. From the standpoint of the theory of criminal law, the first aspect is called "special prevention," and the second and third aspects are called "general prevention."

In our country's punishments, general prevention and special prevention are intimately associated. When punishment is applied to criminals by people's courts, both general and special prevention emerge simultaneously. Because of one-sidedness in their methods of thinking, some judicial cadres take into account only special prevention and ignore the goal of general prevention. Thus, they cannot understand why a counterrevolutionary who committed a serious crime in 1951 had to be sentenced to death, while in 1956 another counterrevolutionary who committed the same serious crime could be sentenced to fifteen years of imprisonment; why, in a factory where production order was good and where few incidents occurred, a worker who on [one] occasion violated labor discipline and thereby caused the death of another worker, was given a suspended sentence of two years of imprisonment, while in another factory where incidents happened quite often and the same criminal act occurred, he should be sentenced to three years of imprisonment. The reasoning for this is that, when people's courts apply punishment, besides the goal of special prevention, they also have [in mind] the goal of general prevention.

1. The authors recognize that the stated goals may often be inconsistent with one another. What weight do they attach to each?

a. Do their examples suggest that the aims of deterrence and education are always to be preferred to the aim of reform?

b. Do these examples have nothing to do with reform but suggest the balancing of deterrence and education against a fourth, unstated goal — that of satisfying the society's sense of just retribution?

In this respect consider the following comment on traditional Chinese law: "The mere existence of the law was intended to deter the commission of such [antisocial] acts, but once they occurred, the restoration of social harmony required that the law be used to exact retribution from their doer." [14]

14. Bodde, p. 375.

2. What other goals might be embraced within the ambiguously articulated first goal stated in Item 5? What about the often voiced call to "suppress" counterrevolutionaries and other major criminals?

a. Is this designed to achieve merely what we commonly term "disablement," that is, taking dangerous persons out of circulation in society?

b. Is it designed to prevent recidivism through the imposition of harsh punishment?

The material in subsequent chapters reveals a good deal about the priorities that are accorded to these goals in practice.

## ITEM 6

This makes clear the need that was felt by 1957 for a rational, sophisticated system of punishment that could achieve the goals of the criminal law. We will see in later chapters that the authors' plea did not go unheeded, although they undoubtedly neither anticipated nor desired the manner in which the regime responded.

[*Lectures* (September 1957), pp. 187–188]

The main kinds of criminal punishment applied by people's courts are uniform. But it has to be pointed out that, because our country's criminal code has not yet been promulgated, the various methods of punishment and problems of their application are not covered by uniform provisions of law. Thus, there still exists certain confusion in practice. For example: some punishments are the same in nature but differ in name (the death penalty is sometimes called capital punishment); some punishments are the same in name but differ in nature (the term of reform through labor service is sometimes as high as eight years, and actually is imprisonment for a fixed term; and sometimes reform through labor service is a punishment of a reformatory nature that does not deprive [the offender] of freedom). Also, the scope of application and the principles of application of the various punishments are not completely consistent. This, of course, is a phenomenon in the process of the development of our revolutionary legal system that is difficult to avoid. But in order to meet the requirements of the state's continual, daily strengthening of the people's democratic legal system, on the basis of a summary of our past experience, we should change this situation and correctly establish our country's penal system.

What kind of penal system should be established in the criminal code of our country? What punishments should be prescribed? How should these punishments be applied? And what should be the relations among the various methods of punishments? In this lecture, we will study these problems.

The penal system adopted by each country reflects the essence of that country. States that differ in nature thus have penal systems that differ in nature. We believe that when we are establishing our country's penal system, we must start out from the nature of our country and grasp the following principles:

(1) On the basis of the situation of the class struggle of our country and the requirements of the struggle against crime, we should establish a penal system that fits the different crimes and that is coordinated, but one which has no duplications or contradictions. During the period of transition in our country the class struggle manifested very complex circumstances. At present,

although there is generally a downward trend in the number of crimes committed, the phenomenon of crime is still extraordinarily complex. Crimes differ in the degree to which they endanger society. There exist not only counterrevolutionary crimes that greatly endanger society and other serious crimes that endanger the interests of the state and people, but also very minor crimes such as minor bodily injuries that occur as a result of the disputes of daily life. In order to meet this situation our country's methods of punishment cannot but be of comparatively many kinds. Even though we need relatively severe punishments, we also need the various relatively light punishments. Of course, the various methods of punishment, from the lightest to the most severe, should have their own content and role so that they are connected and constitute a scientific system and also clearly divide into principal punishments and secondary punishments (supplementary punishments). Any punishment we establish should not be one that we can do without; it should not overlap other punishments and its boundaries should not be confusing.

## ITEM 7

This is a long excerpt from a famous speech delivered by Chairman Mao February 27, 1957. It provides the most up-to-date formulation of the theoretical framework for the application of punishment in China. This speech was originally delivered to a closed session of the Supreme State Conference at a time when the Party was attempting to stimulate a genuine "blooming and contending" among intellectuals. It was not made public, however, until June 18, 1957, shortly after the "antirightist" movement had been launched, that is, when the Party had initiated a new era of rigorous control and repression. The published version of the speech is widely held to have altered the oral version substantially, not only by having "made certain additions," as is conceded, but also by having made significant deletions.

It is difficult to overestimate the continuing impact of this speech, even though, as Mao indicates, it represents largely a restatement of a theme that he had been elaborating for a number of years. Because of Mao's godlike status and the importance that the Chinese Communists attach to ideology, his chef d'œuvre has affected every aspect of the criminal process.

[Mao Tse-tung, "Problems Relating to the Correct Handling of Contradictions Among the People" (address at the 11th enlarged meeting of the Supreme State Conference, Feb. 27, 1957), *FKHP*, 5:1–4, 5–7, 8–9]

### 1. Two Types of Contradictions Which Are Different in Nature

Never has our country been so united as it is today. The victories of the democratic revolution of the bourgeosie and of the socialist revolution, coupled with our accomplishments in socialist construction, have rapidly changed the face of old China. Now we see before us an even more beautiful future for the mother country. The days of national disunity and turmoil which the people detested have gone forever. Led by the worker class and the Communist Party, and united as one, our 600 million people are engaged in the great work of building socialism. Unification of the country, unity of the people and of the various nationality groups within the country — these are the basic guarantees for the certain victory of our undertakings. But this does not mean that there are no longer any contradictions in our society. To think that there were no more contradictions would be naive and would not accord with objective reality. We are confronted with two types of contradictions in society — contradictions between the enemy and us and contradictions among the people. These two types of contradictions are completely different in nature.

In order to understand correctly these two different types of contradictions, we should first clarify what is meant by the people and what is meant by the enemy. The concept of the people has different meanings in different countries, and in different historical periods in each country. Take our country for example. During the Anti-Japanese War, all those classes, strata, and social groups which resisted Japan belonged to the category of the people, while the Japanese imperialists, Chinese traitors, and the pro-Japanese parties were enemies of the people. During the War of Liberation, the United States imperialists and their running dogs — the bureaucratic bourgeoisie and the landlord class — and the Kuomintang reactionaries who represented these two classes, were the enemies of the people, while all other classes, strata, and social groups which opposed these enemies belonged to the category of the people. At this stage of building socialism, all classes, strata, and social groups which approve, support, and participate in the undertakings of socialist construction belong to the category of the people, while all those social forces and groups which resist the socialist revolution and are hostile to and try to undermine socialist construction, are enemies of the people.

The contradictions between the enemy and us are antagonistic ones. As for contradictions among the people, those among the laboring people are nonantagonistic, while those between the exploited class and the exploiter class also have, apart from their antagonistic aspect, a nonantagonistic aspect. Contradictions among the people have always existed. But their content differs in each period of the revolution and of the building of socialism. In the conditions existing in China today, what are called contradictions among the people include: contradictions among the worker class; contradictions among the peasant class; contradictions among the intellectuals; contradictions between the worker class and the peasant class; contradictions between the worker class and the peasant class on the one hand and the intellectuals on the other; contradictions between the worker class and other laboring people on the one hand and the national bourgeoisie on the other; contradictions among the national bourgeoisie; etc. Our people's government is a government that truly represents the interests of the people and serves the people, yet there are certain contradictions between the government and the masses. These include contradictions between the interests of the state and collective interests on the one hand and individual interests on the other; contradictions between democracy and centralism; contradictions between the leaders and the led; and contradictions between certain state personnel, with their bureaucratic demeanor, and the masses. These kinds of contradictions are also contradictions among the people. In general, although there are contradictions among the people, beneath these contradictions there is a foundation of fundamental unity of the people's interests.

In our country, the contradictions between the worker class and the national bourgeoisie belong to [the category of] contradictions among the people. The class struggle between the two belongs, generally, to [the category of] class struggle among the people. This is because of the dual nature of the national bourgeoisie in our country. During the period of the democratic revolution of the bourgeoisie, it had a revolutionary nature on the one side, and it also had a compromising nature on the other. During the period of the socialist revolution, it exploited the worker class for the acquisition of profits on the one side, while it supported the Constitution and was willing to accept socialist reform on the other. The national bourgeoisie differs from the imperialists, the landlord class, and the bureaucratic bourgeoisie. Contradictions between exploiter and exploited, which exist between the national bourgeoisie and the worker class, are antagonistic ones. But, in the concrete conditions in our country, antagonistic contradictions between these two classes, if properly handled, can be transformed into nonantagonistic ones and resolved in a peaceful way. But if they are not properly handled, if the policy of uniting, criticizing, and educating the national bourgeoisie is not adopted or if the national bourgeoisie does not accept this policy of ours, then contradictions between the worker class and the national bourgeoisie can turn into contradictions between the enemy and us.

Since contradictions between the enemy and us and those among the people differ in nature, they are resolved in different ways. To put it simply, the former is a problem of distinguishing clearly between the enemy and us, while the latter is a problem of distinguishing clearly between right and wrong. Naturally, a problem between the enemy and us is also a kind of problem of right and wrong. For example, the problem as to who, ultimately, is right and who is wrong between domestic and foreign reactionaries — imperialism, feudalism, and bureaucratic capitalism — and us is also a problem of right and wrong, but it is different in nature from a problem of right and wrong among the people.

Our country is a people's democratic dictatorship, led by the worker class and based on the worker-peasant alliance. What is this dictatorship for? Its first function is to suppress the country's reactionary classes and parties and the exploiters who resist the socialist revolution, to suppress all those who undermine socialist construction; that is to say, to resolve contradictions between the domestic enemy and us. For instance, to arrest certain counterrevolutionaries and convict them of crime, and for a period of time not to give the landlord class and the bureaucratic bourgeoisie the right to vote or the right to speak out freely — all this comes within the scope of dictatorship. In order to protect the social order and the interests of the vast [number of] people, it is also necessary to put dictatorship into effect over robbers, swindlers, murderer-arsonists, hooligan groups, and all kinds of bad elements who seriously undermine social order. The second function of this dictatorship is to defend our country against subversive activity and possible aggression by the foreign enemy. When this kind of situation occurs, it is the task of this dictatorship to resolve the external contradictions between the enemy and us. The aim of this dictatorship is to protect all the people so that they can labor in peace and build our country into a socialist country that has modern industry, modern agriculture, and modern science and culture. Who is to exercise the dictatorship? Naturally, it must be the worker class and the people led by it. The system of dictatorship does not apply among the people. The people cannot exercise dictatorship over themselves; nor can a part of the people oppress another part. Lawbreaking elements among the people should also be subjected to punitive legal restraints, but this is different in principle from using dictatorship to suppress the enemies of the people. Democratic centralism is in effect among the people. Our Constitution prescribes that citizens of the People's Republic of China have freedom of speech, of the press, of assembly, of association, of procession, of demonstration, of religious belief, and so on. Our Constitution also prescribes that state organs put democratic centralism into effect and must rely on the masses of people and that the personnel of state organs must serve the people. Our socialist democracy is the broadest of democracies and cannot be found in any bourgeois country. Our dictatorship is known as the people's democratic dictatorship, led by the worker class and based on the worker-peasant alliance. This indicates that the democratic system is in effect among the people, while the worker class, uniting with all people who have the rights of citizens, pre-eminently the peasants, puts dictatorship into effect over the reactionary classes and parties and those who resist socialist reform and socialist construction. Having the rights of citizens means having freedom and democratic rights in a political sense.

But this freedom is freedom under leadership and this democracy is democracy under centralized guidance, not anarchy. Anarchy does not conform to the interests or wishes of the people.

.    .    .    .    .

We advocate freedom under leadership and democracy under centralized guidance, but in no sense do we mean that coercive methods may be used to resolve ideological problems and problems involving differentiation between right and wrong among the people. Any attempt to use administrative orders or coercive methods to resolve ideological problems or problems involving right and wrong will not only be ineffective, it will also be harmful. We cannot eliminate religion by administrative orders; we cannot compel people not to believe in religion. We cannot compel people to give up idealism, and we cannot compel them to believe in Marxism. In resolving all problems of an ideological nature or problems involving disputes among the people, we can only use democratic methods, we can only use methods of discussion, criticism, and persuasion-education, and we cannot use coercive, oppressive methods. In order effectively to engage in production and study and in order to live ordered lives, the people request their government and the leaders of production and of cultural and educational organs to issue various kinds of appropriate administrative orders of a coercive nature. It is common sense knowledge that there is no way of maintaining social order without administrative orders of this kind. This [the method of using administrative orders] and the method of using persuasion-education to resolve contradictions among the people complement each other. Administrative orders issued for the purpose of maintaining social order should also be accompanied by persuasion-education; reliance on administrative orders alone will not work in many situations.

In 1942, we worked out the formula "unity-criticism-unity" to describe this democratic method of resolving contradictions among the people. To elaborate, this means to start off with a desire for unity and to resolve contradictions through criticism or struggle so as to achieve a new unity on a new basis. According to our experience this is a proper method of resolving contradictions among the people. In 1942 we used this method to resolve contradictions within the Communist Party, namely, contradictions between the dogmatists and the rank-and-file Party members, between dogmatist ideology and Marxist ideology. Previously, in intra-Party struggles, the "left" dogmatists used the method of "ruthless struggle and merciless attack." This method was wrong. In criticizing "left" dogmatism, we did not adopt this old method, but rather we adopted a new one which started out from a desire for unity, distinguished clearly between right and wrong through criticism or struggle, and achieved a new unity on a new basis. This was the method used in the "rectification [movement]" of 1942. After a few years, in 1945, when the Chinese Communist Party convened its Seventh National Congress, unity was really achieved throughout the Party, and a great victory of the people's revolution was won. It is first necessary to start out from a desire for unity. Without this subjective desire for unity, once the struggle starts, it will inevitably get out of hand. Would not this then be the same as "ruthless struggle and merciless attack"? Would there be any Party unity left? It was in this experience that we found the formula: "unity-criticism-unity," that is, punishment of the past in order to have caution in the future, and treatment of the illness in order to save the patient. We extended this method beyond our Party. It was used very successfully in the various bases of Japanese resistance to deal with relations between the leadership and the masses, between the army and civilians, between officers and [ordinary] soldiers, between different units of the army, and between different groups of cadres. It can be traced back to still earlier times in the history of our Party. We began to build our revolutionary army and bases in the south in 1927 and ever since then we have used this method to deal with relations between the Party and the masses, between the army and civilians, between officers and [ordinary] soldiers, and to deal with other relations among the people. But, during the period of resistance to Japan, we established this method on a foundation of even greater awareness. After the liberation of the entire country, we used this method — "unity-criticism-unity" — in our relations with other democratic parties and with industrial and commercial circles. Now, our task is to continue to extend and make still better use of this method among all the people; we request all our factories, cooperatives, stores, schools, [government] organs, organizations, in a word, all the 600 million of our people, to use it in resolving contradictions among themselves.

. . . We have already spoken on this problem of using democratic methods to resolve contradictions among the people many times in the past, and in our work we have, fundamentally, acted in this way. Many cadres and many people have a practical understanding of the problem. Why then do some people now feel that this is a new problem? The reason is that, in the past, the struggle between domestic and foreign enemies and us was very sharp, and there was not so much attention paid to contradictions among the people as there is now.

Many people do not distinguish clearly between these two types of contradictions which are different in nature — those between the enemy and us and those among the people — and confuse the two. We admit that it is sometimes easy to confuse them. We had instances of such confusion in our past work. In the work of liquidating counterrevolutionaries, good people were mistaken for bad. Such things have happened before, and still happen today. We have been able to keep our mistakes within bounds because it has been our policy to prescribe that there must be a clear distinction between the enemy and us and to prescribe that mistakes should be rectified.

Marxist philosophy holds that the law of the unity of opposites is a fundamental law of the universe. This law exists everywhere, in the natural world, in human society, and in people's thinking. Opposites in contradiction unite as well as struggle with each other, and thus impel things to move and change. Contradictions exist everywhere, but as things differ in nature, so do contradictions. In any given thing, the unity of opposites is conditional, temporary, and transitory, and hence relative; struggle between opposites is on the other hand, absolute. Lenin gave a very clear exposition of this law. In our country, the number of people who understand it is gradually increasing. But for many people recognition of this law is one thing, and its application in observing and dealing with problems is quite another. Many people do not dare to admit publicly that contradictions still exist among the people in our country. But these contradictions are just what impel our society's forward development. Many people refuse to admit that contradictions still exist in a socialist society, with the result that when confronted with contradictions in society they withdraw and take a passive position. They do not understand that socialist society grows more united and consolidated precisely through the ceaseless process of correctly handling and resolving contradictions. For this reason, we need to explain things to our people, first of all to our cadres, to help them understand contradictions in a socialist society and what methods to adopt to handle such contradictions correctly.

1. Does the above elucidation of the concept of "the people" and "the enemy" clarify its meaning?

a. What if A is a poor peasant who out of hunger steals a day's rice ration from the public granary — is this a contradiction among the people?

b. What if A is a former rich peasant?

c. What if B is a worker who picks a fight with and kills C, a coworker, over C's attentions to B's wife — is dictatorship likely to be exercised over him on the ground that he is a murderer?

d. Or is he one of the "[l]awbreaking elements among the people [who] will also be subjected to punitive legal restraints"?

e. What if C is not a worker but a "bureaucratic capitalist"?

f. What if B is a "bureaucrat-capitalist" and C a worker?

2. What difference is the classification likely to make anyhow? Might it determine:

a. Whether or not a prosecution will be initiated?

b. What procedure might be applied?

c. What punishment might be assessed?

3. According to Mao, who should make the classification and at what point?

## ITEM 8

The essay that follows suggests that questions such as those raised at the end of Item 7 are not merely the preoccupation of a foreign academic observer. This essay was the first of a series that appeared in *Political-Legal Research* in the latter part of 1958 on the problem of how to apply Mao's version of the theory of contradictions to concrete cases. The series is of interest not only because of the content and the understandable diversity of the views expressed, but also because the authors are practical men of affairs who served as judges and professional administrators of the legal system prior to undertaking study and research at the principal school for training government cadres in law.

["Are All Crimes To Be Counted as Contradictions Between the Enemy and Us? Are They All To Be Regarded as Objects of Dictatorship?" *CFYC*, 3:73–76 (1958)]

Editor's Note: Are all crimes to be counted as contradictions between the enemy and us; are they all to be regarded as objects of dictatorship? This is at present still a debated question among some comrades in political-legal circles.

On the basis of our understanding of the circumstances, when the students of the research class of the Central Political-Legal Cadres' School debated this question there were generally three different opinions among them. One believed that if it [an act] constitutes a crime and if a sentence has been imposed, then it is always a contradiction between the enemy and us and an object of dictatorship. Another believed that a crime for which a sentence has been imposed is not necessarily a contradiction between the enemy and us and an object of dictatorship, but may be a crime that in nature belongs to [the category of] contradictions among the people. Still another believed that one who commits a crime and is sentenced is always an object of dictatorship, but such a case does not necessarily involve a contradiction between the enemy and us.

As a beginning for the discussion of this question we are publishing the speeches made at the debate meeting by three comrades, Teng P'ing, Yü T'iehmin, and Kao Ming-yü. Naturally, these are not their final opinions, and even less are they the conclusions of the school's research class. We hope that the comrades will link them to actual political-legal work and examine and study them on the basis of the principles in which Chairman Mao instructed us in the essay, "Problems Relating to the Correct Handling of Contradictions Among the People."

*Lawbreaking Elements Among the People Definitely Cannot All Be Treated as Objects of Dictatorship, by Teng P'ing* (formerly deputy director of the department of justice, Hopei province)

When the people break the law and are placed under punitive legal restraints, do they all become objects of dictatorship, and are all such cases in the nature of contradictions between the enemy and us? Comrades engaged in the people's judicial work have different understandings with respect to this question. I believe that of those lawbreaking elements among the people who are sentenced, some are involved in problems concerning the enemy and us and should be objects of dictatorship. But the majority belong to [the category of] those who commit ordinary crimes among the people, and sentencing them is punitively restraining them according to law, and not [imposing] dictatorship. These [crimes] are not contradictions between the enemy and us. Chairman Mao, in his article "On the People's Democratic Dictatorship" has said it this way: "When the people break the law, they should be punished [other than by imprisonment or death], imprisoned, or given the death penalty. But these are individual situations, and they differ in principle from dictatorship over the reactionary class as a class." In his article "Problems Relating to the Correct Handling of Contradictions Among the People," Chairman Mao again said, "Lawbreaking elements among the people should also be subjected to punitive legal restraints, but this is different in principle from using dictatorship to suppress the enemies of the people." On the basis of the principles in Chairman Mao's instructions, we should specifically study why punitive restraint according to law of lawbreaking elements among the people is different from [imposition of] dictatorship over the enemy.

First, we should clarify the question of who exercises the dictatorship and over whom it is exercised. In the present stage of revolution in our country, we have put into effect the people's democratic dictatorship. It is in substance a proletarian dictatorship, and the organs of state power (such as the army, the public security organs, the courts, and the procuracy) are instruments of the dictatorship. Class enemies and counterrevolutionaries are the main objects of the dictatorship. In order to maintain order in socialist construction so that the laboring people may peacefully labor, dictatorship must also be enforced against all kinds of bad elements. They are also our enemies. As for the people, "[t]he system of dictatorship does not apply among the people. The people cannot exercise dictatorship over themselves; nor can a part of the people oppress another part." [15] This is a premise which cannot be forgotten in the consideration of whether someone is to be treated as an object of dictatorship. This being so, it is necessary to distinguish who are the people and who are the enemies. This is a question of demarcation between our enemies and us. Who are the people, and who are the enemies? "In the present stage, during the period of building socialism, all classes, strata and social groups which approve, support and participate in the undertaking of socialist construction belong to the

15. Mao Tse-tung, "Problems Relating to the Correct Handling of Contradictions Among the People" [as in original text].

category of the people. All social forces and groups which resist the socialist revolution, and are hostile to and undermine socialist construction, are enemies of the people." [16] Who are the bad elements? They are hooligans, hoodlums, thieves, murderers, rapists, swindlers, and those who commit crimes of corruption, seriously threatening and undermining social order in the cities and in the country, and [other] criminals who undermine public order and seriously violate the law and disrupt discipline. Some comrades do not oppose this concept. But they believe that when the people break the law and are sentenced, they become bad elements and are no longer people. According to their view, the people do not break the law. Such an understanding and view are, of course, not correct. When Chairman Mao and other leaders of our Party refer to bad elements, they always list a number of criminals under this concept, and though some leaders list more [categories] on the basis of given circumstances in given districts, nobody has ever stated that all those who commit crimes are bad elements. What does this mean? It means that there is a difference between ordinary criminals among the people and bad elements. Therefore, it would be a serious error if, in adjudication work, we did not recognize ordinary criminals among the people but indiscriminately called them bad elements and treated them as objects of dictatorship.

In the second place, let us again study the questions why enemies and bad elements who commit crimes must be objects of dictatorship (of course, these elements are also objects of dictatorship when they [commit acts which] do not amount to crimes), and why ordinary criminals among the people are not objects of dictatorship. This is mainly because their crimes are different in nature. How are they different and of what do the differences consist?

Let us first talk of the situation in which the enemy commits crimes. They commit counterrevolutionary crimes, such acts as subversion of the state regime, armed rioting, murder of people involved in the revolution, and state personnel, organization of secret agents and spies, theft of state military and political secrets and intelligence, spreading poison, arson, and [setting off] explosions. Those who commit these types of crimes all come from the enemy classes, or they are insurrectionists who have been bought over by enemy classes or foreign imperialists. Their crimes are organized, planned, and have a goal. Once the criminal act of a counterrevolutionary is realized, it will cause a certain degree of loss to the undertakings of socialist construction in one place or in one section. Whether the results of the sabotage are great or small, the goal is always the attempt to overthrow the state regime led by the worker class, the futile attempt to restore the rule of the landlords and the bourgeoisie. It is very apparent that these types of crimes are in conflict with the basic interests of the working class and the whole people and involve the question of life or death. Therefore, we must put dictatorship into effect against those who commit these types of crimes. To do otherwise would be to commit an error of principle.

Let us next talk of the situation in which bad elements commit crimes. The crimes they commit seriously undermine the order of socialist construction or

16. Mao Tse-tung, "Problems Relating to the Correct Handling of Contradictions Among the People" [as in original text].

infringe the socialist system of ownership. For example, some make a profession of stealing and regularly steal the property of the state and the people. Some masquerade as state personnel and swindle people everywhere. Some regularly gather together to fight, destroying public order and creating havoc. Some are full-fledged hooligans and rape women. Some openly rob and commit deadly acts of robbery on the roads and other such crimes. Some of these bad eggs are elements of enemy classes. Others are the dregs remaining from the old society. Their crimes are also planned and have a goal; moreover, they are committed regularly and consistently. The crimes of these bad elements often upset the social order in a given place for a given period and create uneasiness in the people. These crimes play the role of coordinating directly with counterrevolutionary sabotage, and are often utilized by counterrevolutionaries. In order to consolidate the social order, to protect the interests of the public, and to enable the people to labor peacefully, dictatorship over elements that commit this type of crime must be put into effect.

What, then, are the situations in which crimes are committed by ordinary criminals from among the people? They [the criminals] commit mostly crimes involving dereliction of duty. For example, a nurse who was looking after a child was derelict in her duty, and the child fell in the water and drowned. A cadre who was leading civilian workers in the maintenance of a dike left his position without authority, and as a result the dike was breached, and a large area of cropland was inundated. For another example, there is the crime of inflicting bodily injury, such as when one party was injured as a result of being beaten up in a fight occasioned by a quarrel. There are also the crimes of bigamy, mistreatment, interfering with the freedom of marriage of others, drowning babies, and crimes arising from traffic and transportation incidents that cause serious consequences, and so forth. Most of the consequences arising from these crimes infringe individual interests or violate the morality of society or certain policies, laws, or decrees of the state. Although these constitute a definite danger to society and the people, they are only limited and temporary in nature. Especially from the point of view of the lawbreaker himself, he does not come into conflict with the basic interests of the working class, and there is no question of life or death. Moreover, most of these crimes are individual situations which occur on [one] occasion, and many are of a negligent nature. Obviously, such crimes among the people are completely different in nature from the crimes of the enemies and bad elements. Having made clear the nature of the problem, we may study further the task and goal of the proletarian dictatorship. Chairman Mao said that the task of dictatorship is to resolve contradictions between the enemy and us both inside and outside the country, and that the goal of dictatorship is to defend the peaceful labor of all the people so as to build our country into a socialist state with modern industry, modern agriculture, and modern science and culture. Since life or death contradictions between the enemy and us do not exist between lawbreaking elements among the people and the worker class, and since lawbreaking elements among the people are not the principal underminers of the order of socialist construction, when they have broken the law, it will do just to restrain them punitively according to law. Why is it necessary to treat them as objects of dictatorship? Is this not extending the scope [of the definition] of the enemy? What is the purpose of forcefully putting dictatorship into effect over them? Obviously there is no reason for it. The purpose of our differentiating between the nature of crimes here is to distinguish between the enemy and us in the adjudication of cases, and it is not to impose punitive restraints on people who commit crimes.

In order to make the nature of the problem somewhat clearer, let us list a few cases as examples:

(1) A certain girl, A, had been at loggerheads with another girl, a neighbor, B. One day, A could not find her stool (it was actually not lost) and suspected that B had stolen it. She cursed B indirectly. B came to her house and questioned her about whom she was cursing. This made A even more suspicious, and she cursed B by name. B cursed back, and the two began to fight. A knocked B over with one butt of her head. B, being weak, could not get up, and A continued to hit and kick her. B was injured as a result of the beating. After B made a complaint, the court sentenced A to imprisonment for several months.

[In another case] in a certain city there was a gang of persons without proper employment. They regularly went to public amusement places, acted indecently with women, and insulted and cursed the masses. When they met resistance, they joined together to beat up those who resisted and then dispersed. As a result, women did not dare to go to public amusement places. When this gang went to see movies, they did not buy tickets. When the ticket seller refused them [admission], they beat him up and smashed the tables, chairs, and stools. The leaders were sentenced to criminal punishment after they were arrested by the city.

Both these cases appear to be cases of the unlawful beating up of others. But if we analyze the facts of the cases in detail and compare them, it is not difficult to see that they are completely different in nature. The former was a case of breaking the law on [one] occasion as a result of a quarrel; the latter was a case of habitual conduct. The former only caused damage to an individual; the latter endangered social order and resulted in unrest among the masses. Thus we may come to the following conclusion: the former involved a lawbreaker from among the people for whom punitive restraint according to law is necessary but who cannot be regarded as an object of dictatorship. The latter involved hooligans, and they are objects of dictatorship.

(2) Some civilian workers who were repairing a dike were eating. A and B, seated opposite each other, were jesting with each other. A stood up, grabbed some dirt and put it into B's rice bowl. B then gave A a kick and accidentally kicked him in the testicles, which led to the latter's death. This was accidental homicide for which there must be conviction. But this negligent causing of a crime on [one] occasion is completely different from the counterrevolutionary murders and rape-murders which we often see. So the case of B can only be treated as that of a crime committed by [one of] the people. B absolutely cannot be handled as a bad element and treated as an object of dictatorship.

Does this mean that so long as one is from among the people, no matter what crime he commits, he cannot be made an object of dictatorship? Of course not.

To distinguish whether or not one is an object of dictatorship at least two aspects should be looked at: first, the nature of the crime; and second, the circumstances of the origin and history of the criminal. Even if one is a laboring person, if because he has been bought over and utilized by the enemy or for other reasons he commits a crime of sabotage with a counterrevolutionary purpose, or if he has been corroded by bourgeois ideology and has degenerated into a person who habitually steals and robs, then such a person has changed in nature, betrayed the people, and become a counterrevolutionary or bad element, and naturally he is an object of dictatorship. When handling cases, if the question of whether or not he [the criminal] is an object of dictatorship is considered only from the aspect of origin and [class] status, and the nature of the facts of the case is not investigated, then this is the theory of [taking into account class] status alone and is equally wrong.

When the people break the law they are subjected to punitive legal restraints. When the objects of dictatorship commit a crime, they also are punished. What, then, is the difference between dictatorship and nondictatorship? Of course, there is a difference. The crimes of the people and those of the enemy and the bad elements are different, and this has determined our different treatment, a difference which is expressed in several ways. For example, in cases in which the consequences of a crime committed by a counterrevolutionary and a crime committed by a laboring person are approximately the same, it is because the crimes are different in nature that the counterrevolutionary is more severely punished than the laboring person. As for a landlord class element, even if he has not violated the state's criminal law, he does not have the right to vote for a given period. As for counterrevolutionary and bad elements, even if the circumstances of their lawbreaking are minor and it is not necessary to sentence them to imprisonment, they may still be sentenced to deprivation of their political rights for a number of years. If their crimes are sufficient to sentence them to imprisonment, when they are so sentenced they may in addition be deprived of their political rights for a number of years. Sentencing these elements plays a role in suppressing them. As for the people, if their lawbreaking acts do not constitute acts for which they can be sentenced, they can only be given criticism-education or other sanctions that are prescribed by administrative laws, but they definitely cannot be given the punishment of deprivation of political rights. If their acts constitute crimes, but not counterrevolutionary crimes or the type of crime committed by bad elements, when they are sentenced they cannot in addition be deprived of their political rights. Punitively restraining lawbreaking elements among the people, in accordance with law, is "punishment for the past in order to have caution in the future" and is not suppression. Therefore, such punitive restraint has positive significance for the people and plays an educational role. The handling according to law of lawbreaking elements among the people emerged as a supplementary educational measure. All of these [the above] are legal differences and political differences.

Some comrades classify cases as follows: those in which there is a sentence are cases of contradictions between the enemy and us; and those in which there is a violation of the Security Administration Punishment Act are cases of contradictions among the people. This method of understanding the problem is terribly mistaken, because contradictions are things that exist objectively and have their own concrete conditions and characteristics, and these concrete conditions and characteristics determine their nature. In the process of resolving contradictions, a person can only make a concrete analysis of their concrete circumstances and thereby find out their characteristics and understand their nature. Then he can decide what kind of measures to adopt to resolve contradictions on the basis of their nature. He definitely cannot decide the nature of the contradictions through [looking at] the measures and methods for resolving them. It is also this way in handling cases. If we want to ascertain what the nature of a case is, we must, in the process of handling it, make a concrete analysis of the entire process of the case, the various elements of which it is composed, the motive, purpose, and methods of the criminal, the circumstances of his origin and history, the consequences of the crime and the other concrete circumstances, and from the analysis find the special characteristics of the case in order to distinguish what the nature of the case is. In order to prevent bias we should also listen attentively to the opinions of the masses. Only in this way can we reach a relatively correct conclusion about the nature of a case. Some people say that when the people break the law, cases in which they are sentenced to death are cases of contradictions between the enemy and us. Not discussing for the moment how many lawbreaking elements among the people should be sentenced to death, but just from the point of view of the method of understanding the problem, this view is equally mistaken, because what determines the nature of a case is its own concrete facts and not our written judgment. On the contrary, the judgment as to what kind of punitive legal restraint and what kind of sentence to give a lawbreaking element is made, according to the law of the state and the policy of the Party in a certain period, on the basis of the nature of the facts of a case, the degree [of seriousness] of the crime, the degree of responsibility, the criminal's demonstration of repentance and reform, and other concrete circumstances. Therefore, that method which does not start out from a concrete analysis of the facts of a case but rather uses the criterion of whether or not there is a sentence to classify the nature of the case, is a kind of unconsciously idealistic or subjectivistic method. As for the enemy's subjective desire, he wants to do as much as possible to destroy us. But because of a high degree of vigilance and all kinds of work on the part of special organs and the vast [number of] people, the enemy's sabotage has been limited to the smallest degree. Some of the enemy are discovered before they have attained their goal of sabotage. If they have radically reformed their previous wrongs, some of them may be exempted from criminal sanctions. But it cannot be said that the nature of the problem is not a problem between the enemy and us. As for persons who violate the Security Administration Punishment Act, "[s]ome of the persons . . . are various kinds of originally [thoroughly] bad elements. They steal and swindle property, act indecently and obscenely with women, disrupt public order, interfere with public safety, spread rumors and make trouble, and engage in other such unlawful activities. These bad elements are the objects of our dictatorship. Against their unlawful activities dictatorship must be put into effect and punishment imposed. It is only because the circumstances of their violation of the law are relatively minor, do not constitute crimes, and are insufficient for giving criminal sanctions, that they are given definite administrative punishments. For these reasons, in this sense the Security Administration Punishment Act is a weapon by means of which the people put dictatorship into effect against various kinds of bad elements." [17] In summary, of those who receive criminal punishments, some are counter-revolutionary elements, some are bad elements, and some also are lawbreaking elements among the people. Of those who are punished under the Security Administration Punishment Act, some are ordinary lawbreakers among the people, and some also are various kinds of bad elements. If we do not concretely analyze involved and complex cases but rather, for the purpose of determining whether a defendant should be the object of dictatorship and whether there is a contradiction between the enemy and us, invariably use the criterion of whether or not the defendant has been sentenced, the result inevitably will be to blur the line between the enemy and us in the adjudication of cases, and both "left" and right deviations may emerge.

1. Does the concept of "bad elements" complicate or clarify the application of the theory of contradictions? What types of persons are "bad elements"?

2. Does Teng P'ing take the position that the distinction between the two kinds of contradictions is significant only for purposes of determining punishment? If so, in what respects is it significant for determining punishment?

a. Does he mean that punishment of a counterrevolutionary or a bad element will be heavier than that of a member of the people who commits the same crime?

b. Or that the punishment will be different, the former, for example, being deprived of political rights and the latter not?

c. Or that different goals may be sought in punishing the former (for example, "suppression") and the latter (for example, "punishment for the past in order to have caution in the future")?

3. Also of importance in Teng's essay is his discussion of the concept of "law-breaking acts" that "do not constitute acts for which . . . [people] can be sentenced" and that warrant only "sanctions that are prescribed by administrative laws." The Chinese usually attach a different meaning to the term "crime" than they do to the term "lawbreaking acts." Does our own system recognize an intermediate category between criminal and noncriminal conduct?

17. Lo Jui-ch'ing, "Explanation of the Draft Security Administration Punishment Act of the PRC" [as in original text].

# Chapter II    Informal Adjustment and Sanctioning

The village or district forms one whole, and each individual in it is but a cog-wheel in the social machine. He must work with the rest, or the whole machine will get out of gear. Personality disappears, and ostracism of a complete and oppressive kind is the fate of those who venture to oppose themselves to the public opinion of those about them. Armed with the authority derived from this condition of popular sentiment, the village elders adjust disputes of a civil nature. They settle questions of trespass, they arrange money disputes, and they grant divorces to husbands impatient of the failings of their wives. It is seldom that in such cases their decisions are not final. Frequently, however, they overstep the limits which surround civil causes, and usurp to themselves the functions of criminal judges. In this way a large proportion of criminal business never reaches the courts of the mandarins, but is adjudicated upon by the village elders, with the consent and approval of the inhabitants. Occasionally appeals are carried to public functionaries against the judgments thus given, and the magistrates, as in duty bound, express their surprise and horror that such an irregular procedure should have been followed. But this is only one of pretty Fanny's ways. It is perfectly well known to every mandarin in the empire that a vast amount of business which should fall on his shoulders is borne by his unofficial colleagues, and he is quite content that it should be so. He only bargains that, in case of necessity, he may be free to disown them and all their works.

Sir Robert K. Douglas,
*Society in China* (1895)[1]

1. London, pp. 112–113.

After the masses have been aroused, not only can criminals be vigorously subdued, the confidence of the masses in on-the-spot reform of criminals can also be strengthened. Originally, the masses demanded the arrest of some criminals for handling according to law, but after they themselves had struggled against and had subdued those criminals, the masses believed that local reform was more beneficial. Thus they no longer demand that contradictions be "passed on to a higher level."

> Chang Ting-ch'eng, "Work Report of the Supreme People's Procuracy" (Jan. 1, 1965)[2]

## A. THE NEIGHBORHOOD APPARATUS

### 1. Precommunist Institutions[3]

How to strike a balance between persuasion and coercion and how to allocate the persuading and coercing functions among governmental and nongovernmental institutions are difficult problems in the maintenance of every social order. The first quotation that introduces this chapter recalls the fact, already mentioned in Part I, that during the Ch'ing dynasty elders and village gentry, clan leaders, and guild members dealt with a great many instances of antisocial conduct and that in doing so they did not confine themselves to persuasion. Respected friends, relatives, neighbors, and middlemen also played a role, especially in helping to adjust minor frictions. As Sybille Van der Sprenkel has described the processes of these unofficial local groups:

"The form of intervention ranged from completely private mediation at one end of the scale to public adjudication at the other, the one shading into the other almost imperceptibly as public opinion was felt to be more strongly involved. There was rarely any question of contestants agreeing in advance to accept the decision of an impartial umpire: the process was rather a struggle to exert and resist pressure, *either* between the parties, through an intermediary, *or* between authority backed by growing public opinion and the individual subject to that authority." [4]

Moreover, minor criminal cases that did reach the magistrate's yamen (office) were sometimes referred back to the relevant local group for informal handling. Despite the fact that this appears to have violated the laws of the Ch'ing dynasty, which required the magistrate personally to hear such cases, the government acquiesced in the practice.[5]

This system of unofficial adjustment and sanctioning freed the energies of officialdom for more important tasks and saved the government a considerable amount of expense. Nor could the government overlook the political desirability of permitting

---

2. *JMJP*, p. 3.

3. The summary in subsection 1 is based largely on: Van der Sprenkel; Ch'ü T'ung-tsu, *Local Government in China Under the Ch'ing*, pp. 116–129; K. C. Hsiao, pp. 290–294, 342–348.

4. P. 117.

5. See Jerome Alan Cohen, "Chinese Mediation on the Eve of Modernization," *California Law Review*, 54:1201–1226 (August 1966).

local people to dispose of relatively unimportant violations in accord with local customs and procedures. This system also fostered social cohesion within the local group, not only because it effectively punished offenders, but also because the process of doing so often constituted an effective instrument for educating the group in community values. In addition, permitting the group to handle most violations with which it was intimately concerned had the more than incidental virtue of enabling it to avoid the loss of prestige that would have been suffered from revealing its internal troubles to outsiders. Finally, because the Ch'ing courts, far from being guardians of individual liberty and procedural fairness, inspired dread among the people, extra-governmental sanctioning also seems to have been relatively more attractive to offenders, complainants, and witnesses.

Nevertheless, despite the fact that in practice sanctioning by unofficial persons disposed of many controversies involving antisocial conduct, the Ch'ing government did make a series of efforts to extend its control over the criminal process beyond the county seat and into the villages, which contained the overwhelming majority of China's population. The methods adopted by the government differed in detail from time to time and place to place, but the most prominent of them generally represented some variant of what has for centuries been known as the *pao-chia* system.[6]

## ITEM 9

The following excerpt from C. K. Yang describes this system as it was revived by the Nationalist government and indicates some of the reasons for its failure to displace the unofficial sanctioning process both during the imperial regime and during the Republican era. Unlike C. K. Yang, some authorities on twentieth-century China state that ten families formed a *chia* and ten *chia* formed a *pao*.[7]

Item 9 also suggests the limited extent to which the legal system that was shaped by the Nationalists as an instrument of modernization actually succeeded in breaking tradition's hold upon rural China.

[C. K. Yang, *A Chinese Village in Early Communist Transition* (Cambridge, Mass., 1959), pp. 102–104, 105–108]

The Republican formal political structure consisted of the central government, the provincial government, the county government, and the subdistrict (*ch'ü*) offices which were the operational agencies of the county government. It can be said that in practice the system of formal government stopped at the county level, a county in China having on the average about 200,000 to 300,000 population and 200 to 500 villages, and that, traditionally, the village community was not a formal unit in the central government system. To increase the effectiveness of governing such a large population with a scantily staffed county government, there had developed the system of collective responsibility, or *pao chia*, rooted far back in Chinese history, especially in the "new policy" of the Sung prime minister Wang An-shih (1021–1086). Since Wang An-shih's time, for eight centuries the system had been alternately practiced and abandoned in response to the demands of historical situations.

6. For a comprehensive discussion of the *pao-chia* under the Ch'ing, see K. C. Hsiao, *Rural China*, Ch. 3.
7. See Martin C. Yang, *A Chinese Village* (London, 1947), pp. 244–245.

In the Republican period, political order within the county functioned mainly through the informal local community leadership, with the county government as the supervising agent; and the village stood as a highly autonomous self-governing unit. In 1932 the Nationalist government revived the collective responsibility system. The ostensible purpose was to use it to tutor the population in self-government in preparation for democratic constitutional rule, but the actual objective was to use the system to combat the spreading of the Communist movement in the countryside.

The system was based on the family as the primary unit of collective responsibility for the proper and law-abiding conduct of all its members. Ten families formed a *pao,* and ten *pao* formed a *chia.* In this particular locality, several *chia* formed a *hsiang,* sometimes called an administrative village, a unit usually composed of several villages, and the *hsiang* was subordinated to the subdistrict (*ch'ü*) office of either the county or municipal government. The subdistrict office was usually a part of the county government, but since the vicinity of Nanching belonged to the Greater Canton metropolitan administrative area, the subdistrict office was under the municipal government. From the municipal government the line of political authority traced upward to the central government. It was through these levels of organization that political authority reached down from the national capital to the individual families in the village.

In Nanching there were twenty-three *pao* and two *chia,* both of which formed a part of a *hsiang* of five villages with headquarters in a village about two miles away. The subdistrict office was located in Pingan Chen. In terms of population, the *pao* unit here was composed of about 50 persons, the *chia* of slightly over 500, and the *hsiang* of about 6,000.

Organizationally, each family sent a representative to elect the head of a *pao,* and the heads of the *chia* and *hsiang* were each elected by the respective constituting representatives. The headship of these units of collective responsibility was thus set up by indirect election which became official only after the government had added its formal appointment. The chief of the subdistrict office was directly appointed by the municipal government (by the county government for territories beyond the municipal area) without even the formality of indirect election. Under this system, the line of authority was from the top down, the head of each unit being responsible not to the constituents below but to the superior chiefs above. *Pao chia* therefore took on the nature of being an extension of the centralized bureaucratic system.

Being such, its main function was to assist the government in the administration of law and the execution of policies, and it did little or nothing to develop local welfare or to foster decision-making by the people through the democratic process. Concretely speaking, the head of each unit was held responsible to the superior chiefs for the good conduct of all constituents and for transmitting government orders to them. He and the entire constituent membership were held collectively responsible for anything that went wrong, and especially for harboring any illegal elements in the locality, the crime of one individual theoretically bringing punishment to all. As a part of routine function, the head of each *pao* unit reported regularly to the superior chief on births, deaths, marriages, movements of his constituents, and any unlawful activities found among them. He helped the tax collector to collect taxes, and in wartime, with population records in hand, he aided in conscription.

Facts show that, from its revival by the Nationalist government in 1932 to its termination by the Communist conquest in 1949, the system accomplished little in the Nanching area with respect to either its ostensible or real functions. With the family as the basic collective unit responsible to the superiors for law and order, the individual member had no direct role or active interest in the operation of the system. Devised essentially for facilitating the flow of central authority down to the village and family level, there was no genuine popular participation in the functioning of the units. After seventeen years of its existence (1932–1949) in this village, the villagers had gained little knowledge of democracy and the democratic process of self-government, the declared purpose of the revival of the system.

.    .    .    .    .

The control of criminal and disorderly elements was a major traditional function of the collective responsibility system, but its usefulness in this respect was also negligible. The general prevalence of peace and law in this village and its vicinity was due to social control by the kinship system and the local informal power structure, not to the operation of any formalized system of collective responsibility. During the Republican period, open gambling and opium smoking were alternately permitted and suppressed in the big city. During the periods of suppression, gambling houses and opium dens would mushroom in the suburban villages, including Nanching. The system of collective responsibility did nothing to suppress them. Corruption of the officials was of course one factor in the situation, but since this factor operated in the city also, a further explanation must be sought to explain the fact that the favorite hiding place for bandits and illegal traffic was not the big city, where the impersonal social milieu provided an easy cover for lawless elements, but the intimate rural community where primary group pressure was strong. One explanation is that the system of collective responsibility, the only agent of formal government in the village, was not effectively integrated with the local agents of social control. Another is that the informal power structure was not averse to occasional gambling, limited illegal traffic, or even harboring bad elements among kinsmen so long as they did not disturb the local peace.

Our conclusion is that the national government failed to substantially alter the traditional decentralized pattern of local government in which the village political life operated largely by its own local power structure and was but weakly integrated into the system of central authority. One reason for the failure was the variance between formal law and local mores. Lack of interest and knowledge in formal government on the part of the responsible personnel was another; the heads of *pao* and *chia* units were generally untrained in government affairs, and they received no remuneration for their services; many heads of *pao* units were illiterate peasants, and the others barely literate, incapable of reading any elaborate government documents, the essential communication links in the operation of an extensive system of central authority. We were told by the villagers that one *chia* chief, having over 500 people under his charge, had been an illiterate — obviously the kind of man who in an uncompensated position commanded little respect from the community and could not make the power of his office felt; and during the period of our investigation, only one *chia* chief was a man of influence in the village. Generally, men of wealth and power in the community shunned such posts.

Then there was the factor of structural incompatibility in grafting the family as a basic unit to the formal system of central authority. As a part of the kinship system, the family was of a particularistic nature, while formal law and government operated on the universalistic principle in order to produce a national political order out of heterogeneous groups. Conflict between the particularistic and universalistic systems was seen in many instances of defective operation of the *pao chia* organization. On the *pao* level, the leaders representing families had not risen above family interests and identified their position with the interests of the state, a condition plainly evident in the lack of sincere interest in helping with tax collection, conscription, and other official duties. On the higher *chia* level, where the unit comprised 100-odd families often distributed across the clan boundary, inter-clan conflict made smooth operation of the organization difficult. One *chia* leader in Nanching, Lee Feng, always had trouble in getting co-operation from the member families under him because many of them belonged to the Wong clan, which had traditional conflicts with his own clan.

The particularistic nature of the village as a localistic communal structure contributed similar difficulties to the functioning of the *hsiang* unit. Nanching always had had conflicts with a neighboring village some two miles away, but the two villages were lumped together in the same *hsiang*. It was clear that co-operation between the two villages could not be expected so long as vital interests based on the village communal units remained unaltered, and that if, for instance, one village insisted upon the suppression of gambling in another village, the action might well end in a feud. (The difficulty in the operation of the collective responsibility system across family, clan, and village boundaries was common to other parts of China, Fei noting the same phenomenon in his Yunnan study.)

For the peasants, the village was a self-contained little world in which most of them were born, lived, and died; and only what happened in this little world aroused their intimate interest. They had a sound knowledge of such happenings and the ways in which they were handled organizationally, but since contacts between leaders and the members were close, any elaborate hierarchy of authority was unnecessary. In fact, the homogeneous nature of the agrarian community and the relatively simple and tradition-bound character of agrarian life rendered formalized laws and regulations both superfluous and uncomprehensible to the peasants.

.    .    .    .    .

It should be noted that ignorance of national affairs did not necessarily mean unawareness of the existence of a higher political entity than the village and its immediate vicinity. The Nanching peasants knew concretely that there was a class of people called officials or rulers who had little contact with them and whose power was not derived from playing a role in the local community life. They knew concretely that the power of these officials was traditionally used to maintain peace, order, and justice; that when robbers plundered their homes, it was the officials' duty to apprehend the criminals; that in case of gross mistreatment by other fellowmen beyond the limit of the local mores one way to redress the wrong was to go to the subdistrict government in the neighborhood, where judicial and administrative powers were not differentiated. They knew that above the subdistrict officers were higher authorities to whom they could appeal their case — although the average individual did not know where the municipal or county government was located, and did not know the procedure of appeal. In other words, the common peasants were fully aware of the existence of officials as a ruling group, but they had very little precise knowledge of the organization and operational procedure of formal political power. In fact, the peasants' vocabulary contained the word "official" but not the term "government"; they spoke of government merely as *kuan fu,* or the house of the officials.

It would seem that the *pao chia* system of collective responsibility might well have brought the greater political world nearer to the peasants, but its structure and functions were such that apparently the peasants had no more understanding of it than they had of the system of central government as a whole.

### 2. A Preliminary Note on Relevant Soviet Institutions

As further background for considering the problems raised in this chapter, one should also refer to Soviet experience.

### ITEM 10

In the late 1950's the Soviet Union began to place renewed emphasis upon the progressive transfer to "social organizations" of the responsibility for imposing sanctions for minor violations of law and morality. These social organizations had flourished during the first two decades of Soviet rule but had subsequently faded into relative obscurity. Item 10 reproduces the pertinent portion of a speech by Premier Khrushchev that did much to stimulate the growth of these institutions.

[N. S. Khrushchev, "Problems of Theory" (report to the 21st extraordinary congress of the Communist Party of the Soviet Union, Jan. 27, 1959), *Pravda,* Jan. 28, 1959, translated in John N. Hazard and Isaac Shapiro, *The Soviet Legal System* (Dobbs Ferry, N.Y., 1962), p. 15]

Matters are approaching a situation in which public organizations, alongside and parallel with such state agencies as the militia and the courts, will perform the functions of safeguarding public order and security. This process is now under way. The size of the militia has been sharply reduced; the state security agencies in particular have been considerably reduced.

Socialist society forms such voluntary organizations for safeguarding public order as the people's militia, comrades' courts and the like. They all employ new methods and find new ways of performing public functions. The voluntary detachments of people's militia should undertake to keep public order in their respective communities and to see that the rights and interests of all citizens are respected and protected.

The time has come when more attention should be paid to the comrades' courts, which should seek chiefly to prevent assorted kinds of law violations. They should hear not only cases concerning behavior on the job but also cases of everyday deportment and morality, cases of improper conduct by members of the group who disregard the standards of social behavior . . .

Of course, definite functions will remain with the courts, the militia and the Prosecutor's office. These agencies will continue to function in order to exert influence on persons who maliciously refuse to submit to socialist society's standards of behavior and are not amenable to persuasion.

Like Confucianists, contemporary Soviet political theorists regard law as an instrument of coercion. They hold that in the current period of "expanded construction of communism" there will be less and less need to resort to governmental coercion and that organizations such as the people's militia (volunteer police) and the comrades' courts will play an increasing role in the regulation of antisocial conduct.[8] These voluntary organizations are regarded as informal instruments of persuasion and are said to represent the first tentative steps towards the Communist goal of the withering away of the state. Yet they obviously can and do employ coercive measures, as when the comrades' courts impose fines, require damage payments, or recommend an offender's eviction from his residence, demotion in his job, or outright dismissal from employment. We will want to inquire about the extent to which knowledge of the Soviet volunteer police and comrades' courts helps us to understand the variety of means for informally coping with relatively minor infractions of the social order in contemporary China.

### 3. Chinese Communist Institutions

The following excerpt, taken from the longer quotation from Mao Tse-tung that appeared as Item 7, bears repetition here:

"We advocate freedom under leadership and democracy under centralized guidance, but in no sense do we mean that coercive methods may be used to resolve ideological problems and problems involving differentiation between right and wrong among the people . . . In resolving all problems of an ideological nature or problems involving disputes among the people, we can only use democratic methods, we can only use methods of discussion, criticism, and persuasion-education, and we cannot use coercive, oppressive methods. In order effectively to engage in production and study and in order to live ordered lives, the people request their government and the leaders of production and of cultural and educational organs to issue various kinds of appropriate administrative orders of a coercive nature. It is common sense knowledge that there is no way of maintaining social order without administrative orders of this kind. This [the method of using administrative orders] and the method of using persuasion-education to resolve contradictions among the people complement each other.

8. For authoritative discussions of these organizations see Dennis O'Connor; and H. J. Berman and J. W. Spindler, "Soviet Comrades' Courts," *Washington Law Review* 38:842–910 (1963).

Administrative orders issued for the purpose of maintaining social order should also be accompanied by persuasion-education; reliance on administrative orders alone will not work in many situations." [9]

1. Does Mao clearly draw the line here between those situations in which only persuasion may be applied and those in which coercion may be applied? What does Mao mean when he says that coercive methods may not be used to resolve "problems involving differentiation between right and wrong among the people" but that they may be used to enable the people "effectively to engage in production and study and . . . to live ordered lives"?

2. If prevailing theory does not help us to determine in what circumstances coercion may be applied, can it at least enable us to determine who may apply coercion? Recall Mao's 1949 statement (Item 2) that "the army, police and courts are instruments by which classes oppress classes." But note that above Mao speaks of "various kinds of appropriate administrative orders of a coercive nature" being issued not only by those agencies, but also by "leaders of production and of cultural and educational organs." In reading the following material, consider:

a. If persons other than government officials may apply coercion, who might they be?

b. Who are the successors to village, clan, and guild adjusters and adjudicators? To what extent are their functions comparable to those of their predecessors?

c. Does China have counterparts to Soviet volunteer police and comrades' courts?

## ITEMS 11A–11B. THE NEIGHBORHOOD POLICE

Before describing the contemporary semiofficial, local elite, we should introduce the neighborhood police organization that presides over this elite. An official police force is essentially a twentieth-century phenomenon in China. By the end of the nineteenth century the complete breakdown of the Ch'ing dynasty's *pao-chia* system and the flagrant abuses of the magistrate's staff stimulated a search for more reliable methods of detecting and apprehending criminals. The police system adopted by the Communist regime is similar in structure to that which was inherited from the Republican era and which is still in operation on Taiwan.

Item 11A is part of a statutory complex enacted at the end of 1954 (see Items 12A and 12B) in order to consolidate and make uniform the urban organizational system. A key unit in the system is the public security station. It is the lowest unit in the formal police structure and usually is responsible for the same area that is served by a city street office (Item 12A).

The public security station has a chief, one or several deputy chiefs, and a small number of office staff who divide administrative burdens. Some staff members are occupied with keeping accurate records on the number and identity of all persons in every household in the area. Others are responsible for the special files regarding residents who have had other than trivial brushes with the police. A staff member, called the security secretary, is normally on duty at all hours to expedite the process of handling whatever public order problems may arise. In addition to the office personnel, every public security station has a number of patrolmen, each of whom patrols a particular beat. The number of patrolmen varies with the size and population of the place and might range from seven to

9. Mao Tse-tung, "Problems Relating to the Correct Handling of Contradictions Among the People," pp. 5, 6.

eighteen per station, with an average of perhaps eleven. Often there is one patrolman for the area under the jurisdiction of each residents' committee (Item 12B). The patrolman is the lowest government link in the urban political-legal network.

Items 11A and 11B provide a comprehensive description of the duties and general powers of the police, indicating their broad authority over the populace.

## ITEM 11A

[ACT OF THE PRC FOR THE ORGANIZATION OF PUBLIC SECURITY STATIONS (passed at the 4th meeting of the Standing Committee of the NPC, Dec. 31, 1954; promulgated by the Chairman of the PRC, Dec. 31, 1954), *FKHP,* 1:243–244]

Article 1. In order to strengthen the security of society, to preserve public order, to protect public property, and to safeguard the rights of citizens, city and county public security bureaus may establish public security stations in districts under their jurisdiction.

Public security stations are subagencies through which city and county public security bureaus administer the work of security.

Article 2. The powers of public security stations shall be as follows:

(1) To safeguard the enforcement of laws relating to public order and the security of society;

(2) To suppress current sabotage activity of counterrevolutionary elements;

(3) To prevent and to check sabotage activity of bandits and other criminal elements;

(4) To control counterrevolutionary and other criminal elements according to law;

(5) To regulate household registration;

(6) To regulate theaters, cinemas, hotels, engraving, radio equipment, and other such trades and also explosives, inflammables, and other dangerous articles;

(7) To protect the scene of major crimes and to assist the relevant departments in solving the cases involved;

(8) To guide the work of security defense committees;

(9) To conduct among residents propaganda work relating to heightening revolutionary vigilance, observance of law and public order, and respect for social morality;

(10) Actively to participate and to assist in the conduct of work relating to the welfare of residents.

Article 3. Public security stations shall be established on the basis of the size of districts, the size of their population, social conditions, and work requirements.

Article 4. Public security stations shall each have a chief, one or two deputy chiefs, and a number of people's policemen.

Public security stations shall conduct their work under the direct leadership of city or county public security bureaus or subbureaus.

Article 5. Public security stations must be intimately linked with the masses. They must conscientiously deal with letters sent in by the people and receive visits from the people. Moreover, they must report on their work at meetings of residents or of residents' committees and listen to criticisms and suggestions of the people.

Article 6. Personnel of public security stations must faithfully observe the law and observe work discipline. They may not violate the law or disrupt discipline, and they may not infringe the rights of citizens.

Article 7. Railroad and water public security stations shall be managed with reference to the provisions of this Act.

## ITEM 11B

[PEOPLE'S POLICE ACT OF THE PRC (passed at the 76th meeting of the Standing Committee of the NPC, June 25, 1957; promulgated by the Chairman of the PRC, June 25, 1957), *FKHP*, 5:113–116]

Article 1. The people's police of the People's Republic of China belongs to the people. It is one of the important instruments of the people's democratic dictatorship and is an armed administrative force of state security.

Article 2. The tasks of the people's police shall be, in accordance with law, to suppress counterrevolutionary elements, to prevent and to check the destructive activity of other criminal elements, to preserve public order and the security of society, to protect public property, and to protect the rights and lawful interests of citizens, in order to defend the people's democratic system and to safeguard the smooth conduct of the socialist construction of the state.

Article 3. The people's police must rely on the masses of people, always maintain intimate links with them, attentively listen to their opinions and accept their supervision, and must strictly observe the Constitution and the law and strive to serve the people.

Article 4. The people's police is led by the Ministry of Public Security of the People's Republic of China and local public security organs of the various levels. The organizational and administrative structure of the people's police shall be [covered] by provisions separately issued by the State Council.

Article 5. The responsibilities of the people's police shall be as follows:

(1) To prevent, to check, and to investigate the sabotage activity of counterrevolutionary and other criminal elements, and to apprehend offenders who evade investigation, adjudication, or execution of sentence;

(2) To control counterrevolutionary and other criminal elements in accordance with law;

(3) To guide the work of security defense committees, and to lead the masses in conducting the work of preventing [the activities of] secret agents, and preventing banditry, robbery, and arson;

(4) To guard courts, to escort offenders who are in custody, and to guard prisons, detention houses, and places for reform through labor;

(5) To regulate explosives, virulent poisons, guns and ammunition, radio equipment, the printing and casting trades, and the engraving trade in accordance with law;

(6) To regulate household registration;

(7) To regulate the residence, travel, and other affairs of aliens and stateless persons in accordance with law;

(8) To regulate city traffic, vehicles, and drivers;

(9) To preserve order and safety at public places and mass meetings;

(10) To preserve order at railway stations, piers, airports, and on trains and vessels, and to protect the safety of passengers and transport;

(11) To protect the safety of foreign embassies and consulates in China;

(12) To guard the safety of major organs, factories, mines, enterprises, and other such departments;

(13) To supervise public health and the cleaning up of the appearance of cities;

(14) To conduct fire prevention work;

(15) To trace property taken by robbery or theft, to look for missing children and persons whose whereabouts are unknown, to help injured persons and those who suddenly fall ill and are in an isolated and helpless state;

(16) To transmit forecasts of natural disasters to residents and actively to assist the relevant departments in mobilizing the masses to adopt measures to prevent and to eliminate disasters;

(17) Actively to participate and to assist in the conduct of other work relating to the welfare of the masses;

(18) To conduct propaganda work among the masses for heightening revolutionary vigilance, devotedly protecting public property, observing the law, observing public order, and respecting social morality;

(19) [To deal with] all other matters within the scope of the responsibilities of the people's police.

Article 6. The jurisdiction of the people's police shall be as follows:

(1) They may arrest, detain, and search counterrevolutionary and other criminal elements in accordance with law.

(2) When investigating criminal cases, they may summon and interrogate criminal suspects and witnesses in accordance with law.

(3) With respect to acts which endanger public order and the security of society but which do not constitute a crime, they may repress them or impose security administration punishment in accordance with law.

(4) If, in the performance of their duties, the people's police encounter an emergency situation, such as resistance to arrest, rioting, attack, forcible seizure of firearms, or any other use of violence to destroy the security of society, which persists despite efforts to check it, they may use their weapons when necessary.

(5) The people's police, for the purpose of urgently pursuing an offender or quickly saving a citizen whose life is in danger, may borrow any instrument of transportation or communication belonging to [state] organs, organizations, enterprises, or individual citizens.

(6) [They may exercise] other [powers within the] jurisdiction of the people's police as prescribed by law.

## ITEMS 12A–12C. STREET OFFICES AND RESIDENTS' COMMITTEES

Together with the public security stations, city street offices and city residents' committees were established on a nationwide basis at the end of 1954. These institutions were designed to assist the city district government apparatus in carrying on the manifold activities of running urban society. They are still functioning today, although in some cities their names may be different as a residual effect of the largely unsuccessful 1960 movement to establish urban communes.[10] For example, in certain large cities the street office is called the "commune" and the residents' committee is called the "brigade."

## ITEM 12A

[ACT OF THE PRC FOR THE ORGANIZATION OF CITY STREET OFFICES (passed at the 4th meeting of the Standing Committee of the NPC, Dec. 31, 1954; promulgated by the Chairman of the PRC, Dec. 31, 1954), *FKHP*, 1:171–172]

Article 1. In order to strengthen the work of city residents and to make more intimate the links between residents and their government, the people's councils of city-administered districts and undistricted cities may, in accordance with work requirements, establish street offices to serve as their subagencies.

Article 2. City-administered districts or undistricted cities with a population of more than 100,000 shall establish street offices; city-administered districts or undistricted cities with a population of less than 100,000 but more than 50,000, if their work actually requires, also may establish street offices; city-administered districts or undistricted cities with a population of less than 50,000 shall generally not establish street offices.

The establishment of street offices must be approved by the people's council of the next higher level.

Article 3. Generally, the area of jurisdiction of street offices shall be the same as that of public security stations.

Article 4. The tasks of street offices shall be as follows:

(1) To manage those affairs relating to the work of residents that are turned over to them by the people's councils of cities and city-administered districts;

(2) To guide the work of residents' committees;

(3) To report opinions and requests of residents.

Article 5. Street offices shall each have a director and, according to the complexity of their work and the size of the area of their jurisdiction, a number of staff members. When necessary, street offices may each have a deputy director.

Street offices shall each have three to seven full-time cadres, one of whom will be concerned with women's work.

The director, the deputy director, and the staff of each street office shall be delegated by the people's councils of city-administered districts and undistricted cities.

---

10. See generally Henry J. Lethbridge, *China's Urban Communes* (Hong Kong, 1961).

Article 6. The various work departments of the people's councils of cities and city-administered districts may not directly allocate tasks to street offices without the approval of the relevant people's council.

Article 7. Office expenses of street offices and salaries of their personnel shall be provided exclusively by the people's council of the province or of the city directly under the central authority.

Is the street office a "mass organization"? Does it make any difference?

## ITEM 12B

The Act of the PRC for the Organization of City Residents' Committees allocates the tasks of security defense and of mediating disputes to certain personnel or work committees of each residents' committee. However, the chairman and other members of the residents' committee also tend to play a considerable role in handling the various kinds of disturbances that arise. For example, when a fight occurs, a member of the residents' committee may be on the scene or nearby, or he may be notified of its occurrence by a bystander, or one or both disputants may go to committee headquarters to report the matter. If the patrolman or a person who specializes in security defense or mediation work is available, he will normally attempt to dispose of the matter. But often such persons are occupied elsewhere, and the member of the residents' committee who is on the spot will deal with the problem. The recommendations of the committee member are often heeded by the disputants, in part because, in view of the large scope of the residents' committee's activities, it is important to maintain good relations with its members.

[ACT OF THE PRC FOR THE ORGANIZATION OF CITY RESIDENTS' COMMITTEES (passed at the 4th meeting of the Standing Committee of the NPC, Dec. 31, 1954; promulgated by the Chairman of the PRC, Dec. 31, 1954), *FKHP*, 1:173–175]

Article 1. In order to strengthen the organization and work of residents of city streets and to promote their public welfare, residents' committees may be established according to residential districts under the guidance of the people's councils, or their subagencies, of city-administered districts, and undistricted cities.

Residents' committees are mass, autonomous residents' organizations.

Article 2. The tasks of residents' committees shall be as follows:

(1) To manage affairs relating to the public welfare of residents;

(2) To report opinions and requests of residents to local people's councils or their subagencies;

(3) To mobilize residents to respond to calls of the government as well as to observe the law;

(4) To lead security defense work of the masses;

(5) To mediate disputes among residents.

Article 3. The organization of residents' committees shall be as follows:

(1) Residents' committees shall be established in accordance with the living conditions of residents and with reference to the area of jurisdiction of public security household list sections. The extent of this area is generally from one hundred to six hundred households of residents.

Residents' groups shall be established directly under the residents' committee. Residents' groups generally shall be composed of from fifteen to forty households. No residents' committee may have more than seventeen residents' groups.

(2) Residents' committees shall have seven to seventeen committee members. Each residents' group shall elect one member to the residents' committee. Moreover, a chairman and one to three vice-chairmen shall be selected by and from among the committee members; one of them shall be designated to take charge of women's work.

Residents' groups shall each have a chief. Generally, the member of the residents' committee shall concurrently serve as chief. When necessary, one or two deputy chiefs may be elected by the group. When a committee member is selected as chairman or vice-chairman of a residents' committee, the group that elected him may elect another chief.

(3) Residents' committees [in areas] where the number of residents is relatively small shall generally not establish work committees but the committee members shall divide responsibility for the various items of work [among themselves]. Residents' committees [in areas] where the number of residents is relatively large, if their work actually requires it and if the people's council of the city approves, may establish permanent or temporary work committees which shall conduct their work under the unifying direction of [their respective] residents' committees. Permanent work committees may be set up according to social welfare (including special compensatory allowances), security defense, culture-education-health, mediation, women's [activities], and other work [categories], with five being the maximum number of permanent committees allowed. The dissolution of temporary work committees shall be announced upon conclusion of their work.

Work committees shall absorb the activists among residents to participate in committee work, but they shall as much as possible assign only one function to each person so that no individual's work burdens are excessive.

(4) Residents who are controlled elements and other elements who have been deprived of their political rights shall [be allowed to] join residents' groups, but they may not serve as members of residents' committees, group chiefs, or members of work committees. When necessary, a group chief has the right to prevent such residents from taking part in certain meetings of the group.

Article 4. Every term of office for residents' committees shall be one year.

When a committee member is for some reason unable to serve in this capacity, he may be replaced at any time in a regular election or a special election.

Article 5. Organs, schools, relatively large enterprises, and other such units generally shall not participate in residents' committees; however, they must send representatives to attend meetings relating to them which are convened by residents' committees. Moreover, they must observe residents' committees' decisions and pacts relating to the public interest of residents.

In staff and worker dwelling districts and in relatively large collective dormitories where staff and workers reside in concentrated groups, residents' committees shall be established under the unifying guidance of the people's councils, or their subagencies, of city-administered districts and undistricted cities; or committees organized by labor unions and composed of members of the families of staff and workers shall concurrently perform the work of residents' committees.

Article 6. In city districts where minority nationality groups reside together, these minority nationality groups may separately set up residents' committees; where the number of minority households is relatively small, they may separately set up residents' groups.

Article 7. If work departments and other organs of the people's council of a city or a city-administered district find it necessary to allocate tasks to a residents' committee or to any of its work committees, they shall, with the approval of the people's council of the city or the city-administered district, do so in accordance with a centralized plan. These work departments may exercise professional guidance over the relevant work committees of residents' committees.

Article 8. Residents shall observe residents' committees' resolutions and pacts relating to the public interest. When conducting their work, residents' committees, following the principles of democratic centralism and voluntarism of the masses, shall fully develop democracy and may not coercively command the masses.

Article 9. Miscellaneous public expenses of residents' committees and subsistence allowances given to their members shall be provided exclusively by the people's council of the province or of the city directly under the central authority, in accordance with standards the provisions for which shall be separately issued by the Ministry of Interior.

Article 10. In order to meet expenses of managing affairs relating to the common welfare, residents' committees, with the consent of the residents concerned and with the approval of the people's council of the city-administered district or of the undistricted city, may solicit contributions among residents in accordance with the principle of voluntarism. Apart from this, residents' committees may not conduct any other solicitations or fund-raising among residents.

The amount of funds solicited for the common welfare and an itemized account of their expenditure shall promptly be made public after the matter has been concluded.

## ITEM 12C

[Tu Chi-yüan, "Report on Improving the Work of Residents' Committees in Shanghai" (speech at the 75th administrative meeting of the Shanghai Municipal People's Government), *Chieh-fang jih-pao* (Liberation daily, Shanghai), Dec. 17, 1954]

The formation of residents' committees in Shanghai started in April 1951, at the request of residents and on the foundation of lane organizations set up by residents during the early days of liberation. [Shanghai's residential areas are largely composed of long narrow lanes that lead into larger streets.] In the course of employment registration in the city, these committees were reorganized and their respective areas redemarcated in September 1952. At the same time, additional committees were formed in all parts of the city where none had existed. By the end of the first half of this year, the city had 1,852 residents' committees, 109 committees composed of members of the families of staff and workers, and over 36,000 residents' groups. More than 95,000 persons served on work committees or higher bodies.

Under the leadership of the Chinese Communist Party and the people's government and the people's government and in co-operation with women's lane organizations, residents' committees did a great deal of work in the three years from April 1951 to the first half of this year. They succeeded not only in making more intimate the links between the masses of residents and the government but also in attracting ever-increasing numbers of residents to participate in the conduct of state and public affairs. They played an active role in economic rehabilitation and construction as well as in various democratic reforms in Shanghai.

First, residents' committees organized the masses of residents to sponsor welfare enterprises for their common benefit. For instance, they have set up or organized 106 nurseries, 4,632 literacy classes and over 9,000 newspaper reading groups. Records show that in 1953 alone they mediated no less than 75,000 disputes among the residents. Sanitation campaigns have been universally launched, garbage bins have been provided, and urinals constructed. At the same time, according to the residents' requirements, the committees have undertaken road repairs, sewer clearing, protection of public equipment, precautions against fire and natural calamities, and maintenance of peace and order. These services have solved the problem of satisfying the demand for political and cultural studies on the part of residents who do not belong to any production organizations, of improving the surroundings of residents, of strengthening the unity among residents, and of safeguarding social order so that the laboring people may set their minds at rest while engaging in production.

Second, residents' committees transmitted the opinions and requests of residents to the authorities, further cemented the relations between the government and the masses, and thus improved the work of state organs.

· · · · ·

Third, residents' committees responded to the calls of the government, mobilized the masses of residents to observe government policies and decrees, educated them, and raised their political consciousness.

· · · · ·

Judging from residents' committees which have undergone readjustment, notable results have been achieved. The vast masses of residents have gained a better understanding of the relationship between lane work on the one hand and socialist construction, socialist reforms, and the consolidation of the people's democratic dictatorship on the other hand. They have strengthened the unity among householders of various strata. They have denounced and exposed certain remnant counterrevolutionaries. When readjusting their organizations, they promoted democracy, launched criticism and self-criticism, commended good people and good deeds, and dealt with violators of law and discipline.

## ITEMS 13A–13B. SECURITY DEFENSE COMMITTEES

Even today, public security stations do not appear to exist in most of the Chinese countryside and in some of the city suburbs. In the countryside, the county public security bureau, situated at the county seat, is generally the lowest unit in the police hierarchy. The bureau generally assigns one of its staff to supervise public security work in a cluster of two or three rural communes, and this "special agent" constitutes the lowest official rung in the rural police ladder. But, since each rural commune is composed of numerous far-flung production brigades and has a population of many thousands, this policeman cannot keep in touch with the situation throughout his jurisdiction. Even a city patrolman will ordinarily be responsible for an area that contains several thousand people, and, with factories, enterprises, schools, and other sizable units in his area, it is impossible for him to maintain the omniscience that the regime requires of its public security system.

It was to fill this gap that "mass security defense organizations" were organized in 1952. These units continue to play a crucial role in the political-legal network not only in the countryside, where their relative freedom from continuing police supervision allows them broad scope, but also in the cities, where the official public security apparatus subjects them to closer scrutiny. It is largely because these security defense committees "penetrate into every corner," as is said in Item 13 B, that the Chinese Communist regime has been so successful in developing what is widely regarded as the most thorough nationwide security system the world has known.

## ITEM 13A

The Provisional Act of the PRC for the Organization of Security Defense Committees (Item 13A), although promulgated in 1952, continues to provide the principles that govern the tasks, powers, and organization of these committees. Some of the Act's provisions, of course, have never been implemented. In the city, for example, in practice the public security station or patrolman "guides" the masses in "electing" the committee. Even so, new elections are seldom held; several public security officers have reported that only three such elections were held in ten years in their areas. Other "democratic" provisions, such as the requirements that committees periodically report to the masses and that awards and sanctions for committee members be decided upon by the masses, also do not seem to have been widely carried out.

Certain organizational accommodations have had to be made in the light of post-1952 developments. Since the urban reorganization achieved by the legislation of December 31, 1954, where a residents' committee is responsible for a relatively small number of people, security defense problems are assigned to a residents' committee member called the "security defense member" rather than to a special security defense committee. Where a residents' committee is responsible for a large number of people, a security defense committee is utilized. In either situation, although the 1952 Act places security defense work under the dual leadership of the public security station and the residents' committee, in practice effective leadership appears to be exercised exclusively by the station and its patrolmen.

In the countryside, since the absorption of the administrative villages into the then newly established rural communes in the latter part of 1958, each commune has assigned one or more members of the commune management committee to handle public security problems. These security personnel, who are among the commune's most powerful executives, normally devote full time to their duties and are paid from commune funds. With the aid of the county public security bureau's special agent in the area, they supervise the activities of the security defense committees usually set up in each of the commune's constituent production brigades. Although post-1958 readjustments have reduced the size of many rural communes, this has not significantly altered the organization of security defense work.

[PROVISIONAL ACT OF THE PRC FOR THE ORGANIZATION OF SECURITY DEFENSE COMMITTEES (approved by the Government Administration Council, June 27, 1952; promulgated by the Ministry of Public Security, Aug. 11, 1952), *FLHP* 1952, pp. 56–58]

Article 1. In order to rouse the masses and to assist the people's government in preventing treason, espionage, theft, and arson, in liquidating counterrevolutionary activity, and in defending state and public security, it is specially prescribed that security defense committees be universally established throughout the country, in every city after development of the movement for the suppression of counterrevolution and in every rural village after completion of the land reform.

Article 2. Security defense committees are mass security defense organizations. They are responsible for conducting their work under the leadership of the basic level government and public security defense organs.

Article 3. When establishing security defense committees, organs, factories, enterprises, schools, and streets shall generally be taken as units in cities, while in rural villages the administrative village shall be the unit. The committees shall be composed of three to eleven members, depending on the number of persons in a unit and the complexity of its situation. There shall be one committee chairman, and there may also be one or two vice-chairmen.

After the establishment of security defense committees, in accordance with the needs of the situation and with the approval of city or county public security bureaus, security defense groups may be established. They shall be composed of three to five activists elected by the masses; and they shall each have a chief and shall conduct their work under the leadership of security defense committees.

Article 4. The election of members of security defense committees:

(1) All those who are among the people, who have clear histories and proper demeanor, who excel in linking themselves with the masses, and who are enthusiastic about security defense work may be elected committee members.

(2) When electing members of security defense committees, there shall be thorough advance preparation. A roster of candidates shall be presented by the masses, and shall be introduced, examined, and evaluated. After this [the evaluative process] is completed, the election shall be carried out. A new election shall be held every six months. Those who are re-elected may continue to serve. However, if during the term of office a majority of the masses consider it necessary, they may replace members in a regular election.

Article 5. The concrete tasks of security defense committees [shall be]:

(1) To link themselves intimately with the masses and to conduct among the masses regular propaganda-education about preventing treason, espionage, arson, and theft and suppressing counterrevolutionary activity, in order to heighten the political vigilance of the masses;

(2) To organize and to lead the masses in assisting the government and public security organs in denouncing, supervising, and controlling counterrevolutionaries, in order strictly to prevent counterrevolutionary sabotage activity;

(3) To organize and to lead the masses in assisting the government and public security organs in conducting the work of education and thought reform among members of the families of counterrevolutionaries, striving to obtain their support for policies and measures of the government;

(4) To rouse the masses collectively to adopt antitreason patriotic pacts and also to organize the masses conscientiously to execute them, in order to preserve the security of society.

Article 6. The powers of security defense committees:

(1) They shall be responsible for arresting and taking to the government or to public security organs current counterrevolutionaries and criminals who are fugitives; but they have no power to interrogate or to hold such criminals in custody or to handle their cases.

(2) They shall be responsible for investigating, watching, denouncing, and reporting noncurrent counterrevolutionaries but they have no power to arrest, to take into custody, to search, or to repress them.

(3) With respect to the security of society and the work of control, they shall be responsible for educating the masses to preserve revolutionary order and for supervising the labor and production of those under control, for not permitting them to say or do whatever they please, and for promptly reporting the state of their behavior to public security organs; but they have no power to detain, to punish, or to drive them away [from the area].

(4) They shall assist public security personnel in maintaining order at places where counterrevolutionary sabotage has occurred and in protecting the scene of such sabotage, thereby facilitating on-the-spot investigation by public security organs; but they may not alter and deal with that scene.

Article 7. Members of security defense committees must strictly observe all the following kinds of discipline:

(1) Observe the laws and decrees of the government.

(2) Keep work secrets and not divulge them.

(3) Hold firmly to the principles of the people's revolution, not conceal counterrevolutionaries, not harbor resentment and make maliciously false accusations, and not corruptly accept bribes.

(4) Unify and help the masses, and not coercively command them or rely on power to take advantage of them.

Article 8. The leadership relationships of security defense committees [shall be as follows]:

(1) Security defense committees in organs, factories, enterprises, and schools shall be under the leadership of the administrative organs and public security defense departments of their respective units.

(2) Security defense committees of city streets shall be under the leadership of public security stations. Where there are residents' committees, security defense committees shall be under the dual leadership of public security stations and residents' committees. In outlying areas where there are no public security

stations, they shall be under the leadership of public security subbureaus and district public security assistants.

(3) Security defense committees in rural administrative villages shall be under the leadership of village governments and village public security representatives.

(4) Security defense committees in coastal villages shall be under the leadership of coastal defense public security stations and coastal defense public security representatives.

Article 9. Basic level governments and public security organs in the various places shall strengthen the leadership of the work of security defense committees and also establish necessary systems:

(1) They shall require all security defense committees periodically to report on their work to the local masses, to invite the opinions of the masses, and to accept the criticism of the masses.

(2) Those who are active and have conspicuous accomplishments in their work shall promptly be given commendations and rewards. Those who separate themselves from the masses and violate discipline shall promptly be given criticism and penalties. Before rewards or penalties are given they must be discussed and decided upon by the local masses and approved by the leadership organs.

Article 10. Provincial and city public security departments and bureaus may, on the basis of the spirit of this Act, formulate concrete measures for executing the Act and report them to the [authorities of] large administrative areas and to the Central Ministry of Public Security for the record.

Article 11. After approval by the Government Administration Council of the Central People's Government, this Act shall be promulgated and put into effect by the Central Ministry of Public Security.

## ITEM 13B

To facilitate understanding of Item 13B (and some of the other material in this volume), a word should be said about rural organization prior to the advent of the people's communes in the latter part of 1958. From 1949 to 1958 the Chinese Communists did a good deal of experimenting with rural organization. Yet, despite their elimination of the *pao-chia* system and their establishment of formal government at the level of the administrative village, the basic pattern of rural government was still a familiar one to those who recalled the Nationalist regime (see Item 9). A cluster of families continued to form a natural village, although its affairs were now administered by leaders selected by Party and government officials from among politically reliable, enthusiastic village residents. As before, a group of natural villages in the same neighborhood formed the administrative village, which now had an elected people's congress and a people's council that constituted the lowest level of formal government in the countryside. At the level of the district (referred to by C. K. Yang in Item 9, as "subdistrict") there continued to be a branch office of the county government that supervised the activities of the group of administrative villages within its jurisdiction.

The pattern of agricultural organization, however, had been markedly altered by 1958. The land reform of 1949–1953, which distributed land to individual peasant families, was merely the first step on the road to "socialist reform" of agriculture. That road subsequently led China's peasants from family farming through "mutual aid teams" and lower level cooperatives to collectives called "advanced agricultural producers' cooperatives." Although the details varied greatly, a typical administrative village governed an area that comprised two or three such cooperatives, and each cooperative had a number of production brigades. The people's communes were formed from the merger of the government of one or more administrative villages with the agricultural cooperatives in the area. Thus, the commune combined governmental and production functions.

[Shang Yin-pin, "Fully Develop the Militant Role of the Basic Level Security Defense Organizations," *CFYC,* 5:71 (1958)]

The basic level security defense committees of Hopei province, like those of other regions throughout the country, were created during [mass] movements and also grew up and became powerful during those movements. They were first established in rural villages and [at the level of] city streets. Later, they were established in factories, mines, enterprises, and cultural and health departments. Following the three large-scale struggles to suppress counterrevolution, the 1956 changes in the ownership system, and some revisions in the work of basic level organizations, the security defense organizations also went through several relatively great changes. Each change enabled them to go further down the road toward even greater strength and perfection. Security defense committees that previously took the village as their unit have now changed into security defense committees that take the administrative village as their unit. Their chairmen are for the most part freed from having to take part in production. Some members of the security defense committees also concurrently serve as deputy secretaries of Party branches or as deputy chiefs of the cooperatives. Besides this, in cooperatives and in production teams, security defense groups and security defense personnel have also been established. In the cities, in addition to the security defense organizations established in the suburbs and [at the level of] the streets, workshop or trade security defense organizations, or [crime] prevention organizations have also been established in factories, mines, enterprises, organs, and schools. This has enabled the basic level security defense organizations — mass organizations — to penetrate into every corner. Their membership is also of a broadly representative nature. The great majority of members are members of the Party or of the Youth League and are activists. There also are neutral members of the masses. There are workers, peasants, students, and also technical personnel, engineers, professors, etc., who manifest the broad mass nature of this organization. It was last year's national rectification and socialist education movements that particularly enabled the security defense committees . . . to make even greater progress in organization and in the ideological demeanor of the cadres. Now the SDC is no longer an organization of a small number of activists nor only a band that links the public security organs with the masses. Rather, it is a militant unit that unifies, educates and leads the masses in the struggle against the enemy and in conducting social reform.

1. Compare the security defense committee to the *pao-chia* as described in Item 9. What are the major similarities and differences? One crucial difference in fact, of course, is that the contemporary system appears to work rather well, as subsequent materials demonstrate. In evaluating the security defense committee, bear in mind the following analysis of the theory of the *pao-chia* as adopted by the Ch'ing emperors.

"Another distinctive feature of the *pao-chia* that deserves notice is that local inhabitants themselves were made to operate it, while local officials supervised its operation without taking any direct part in it. Such an arrangement had its advantages. By enlisting the help of the local inhabitants, the government extended its control to the remotest hamlets without multiplying the number of government officials; by putting the *pao-chia* under the supervision of local officials, it prevented the *pao-chia* heads from acquiring undue power or influence. Under this system the people became potential informers against wrongdoers or lawbreakers among their own neighbors — in other words they were made to spy upon themselves. Such mutual fear and suspicion were instilled in their minds that few of them dared to venture into seditious schemes with their fellow villagers. Thus even if individual criminals could not be completely eliminated, the opportunity for instigating concerted uprisings was greatly reduced. The usefulness of the *pao-chia* as an instrument of control lay as much in its deterrent effects on the people as in whatever actual assistance it might render the government in suppression of crimes. A nineteenth-century Western writer correctly said of the Ch'ing dynasty that 'what is ostensibly a paternal government ruling its subjects through their filial affection is in reality a tyrannical administration that maintains its power by *fear and distrust*.' The *pao-chia* was one of the instruments employed by the emperors for this very purpose. To regard it as 'an organization for census taking,' 'the self-government of old China,' or 'a system of local government,' as some writers do, is to misinterpret not only the function of the *pao-chia* but also the nature of the imperial system." [11]

2. On the basis of the following passage from Berman, *Justice in the U.S.S.R.*, compare the security defense committee to the volunteer police, below called "People's Patrols," that have come back into prominence in the Soviet Union in recent years.

## "THE PEOPLE'S PATROLS

The People's Patrols are a sort of auxiliary police. The Russian term for them, *druzhiny*, is an old Slavic word referring to the band of comrades (*druzhinniki*) who advised the princes of Kievan Rus and at the same time formed the nucleus of their armies. Various organizations performing auxiliary police functions existed during the 1920's. They were often known as 'Commissions of Social Order.' By 1930, these were reformed into 'Voluntary Societies for Aiding the Police.' In January 1930 there were 2500 such societies in the Russian Republic alone. In May 1930, through a charter issued by the Council of People's Com-

11. K. C. Hsiao, pp. 45–46.

missars, the societies were given a legal basis for the police functions they had been exercising. In the later 1930's, the Voluntary Societies were reorganized into Brigades and placed under strict central control. During World War II, 'Groups for the Protection of Social Order' were formed to provide protection against spies, saboteurs, and line-crossers. After the war, the Brigades were reformed and placed under the direction of local detachments of the police, and they devoted themselves largely to the enforcement of traffic regulations and automobile inspection.

"Beginning in 1958, People's Patrols, with some millions of members, were formed throughout the country. The 1960 R.S.F.S.R. Statute on Voluntary People's Patrols grants them broader functions than those exercised by the earlier organizations. The statute lists the following tasks:

1. To maintain public order on streets, in stadiums, parks, and other public places, at meetings, demonstrations, sports events, etc.;

2. Together with police, court, and Procuracy agencies, to combat petty crime ('hooliganism'), drunkenness, theft, violations of trade regulations, speculation, moonshining, and other offenses;

3. To enforce traffic regulations;

4. To combat neglect of children;

5. To make suggestions to state and social organizations for taking measures of influence against persons who violate public order;

6. To send materials concerning offenders to Comrades' Courts or administrative agencies, to send *druzhinniki* as social prosecutors where necessary, and to report offenses in the press, wall newspapers, posters, window displays, and bulletins;

7. To participate in educational work among the population concerning the observance of the rules of socialist community life and the prevention of anti-social offenses.

"The *druzhinnik* has the right to demand that a citizen stop violating public order and to demand that he produce identification papers or a driver's license; to take an offender to the headquarters of the Patrol, to the police, or to the local soviet; to obtain transportation for the victim of an accident or a crime; freely to enter clubs, stadiums, cinemas, and other public places, in order to maintain order.

"The Patrols are not subordinate to any ministry or to any government agency, but are independent local (city or district) units. The 1960 statute expressly places them under the direction of Communist Party agencies.

"It is evident that in addition to powers normally exercised by regular police in all countries, the Patrols also have specific educational functions. They are concerned with anti-social activities not amounting to crimes — for example, neglect of children. They sometimes ridicule offenders in the press or on public display boards ('Billboards of Shame'). They speak to general meetings of workers and employees in enterprises and institutions. They roam the city in pairs, taking issue with conduct of which they do not approve, such as boisterous parties, drunkenness, wearing of 'Western' clothes, or dancing of 'Western' dance steps.

"Lacking the training of the regular police, they are apt to be rough and discourteous and to exceed their powers. Some have been indicted for brutal crimes. At the same time, disobeying a lawful order of a *druzhinnik,* insulting him, or resisting him, have been made criminal offenses, and an attempt on his life (if accompanied by circumstances which aggravate the offense) has been made punishable by death.

"The aim of the People's Patrols is to establish an educational agency for law-enforcement whose members will be an integral part of the society itself, who will, in the words of the 1960 statute, 'be an example in work and in everyday life.' The aim is a characteristic one. Whether the Soviets can overcome the difficulties inherent in a reliance on amateurs to perform police functions — remains to be seen." [12]

## ITEM 14. PEOPLE'S MILITIA

The PRC has also developed its own volunteer people's militia. Although the primary goal of this militia has been to provide a mass reserve as auxiliary support for the People's Liberation Army, in the countryside the militia has also provided substantial assistance to the police and security defense organizations in the maintenance of public order. Its participation in the criminal process is much more limited in the cities.

Theoretically, in the countryside all able bodied citizens of both sexes between the ages of 16 and 50 belong to the militia. Actually, except in times of crisis, the only meaningful militia is the "basic militia." This is composed of reliable citizens, mostly men and usually CYL members or activists, who in addition to their usual occupations, devote their spare time to military training, local patrolling, and performing tasks assigned by rural security personnel. Whenever needed, members of the basic militia have access to firearms that are stored at units of the commune. To assure the militia's integration into the system of local public security control it is not uncommon, for example, for the chief of a commune production brigade's security defense committee to be deputy chief of the brigade militia unit and for the militia chief to be deputy chief of the security defense committee.

Although the role of the militia in law enforcement has yet to be studied, some of the material in this volume illustrates its scope. Background information on the evolution of the militia can be found in John Gittings, "China's Militia." [13]

Item 14 is a recent, official assessment of the militia.

["The Militia Plays an Enormous Role in Consolidating National Defense and Defending Socialist Construction," *Hsin-hua t'ung-hsün-she* (New China news agency, Peking), Sept. 26, 1964; translated in *SCMP,* 3314:8–9 (Oct. 8, 1964)]

Guided by Chairman Mao's thinking on the people's war, militia organizations all over the country form [a] powerful armed force of the people. These armed organizations of the people are playing an enormous role in the cause of consolidating the national defense and defending socialist construction, proving themselves to be an able assistant and a powerful reserve force of the People's Liberation Army [PLA].

Now, in the vast territories of our country from the cities to the countryside,

12. Rev. ed. (New York, 1963), pp. 286–288.
13. *China Quarterly,* 18:100–117 (April–June 1964).

and from coastal islands to the remote grassland and pastureland, we can often see spirited militiamen and militiawomen, making positive use of odd moments spared from production, study and work, arduously practicing the skills of killing the enemy with their rifles and grenades. In coastal areas in Fukien, Chekiang, and Kwangtung, the broad masses of militiamen are very enthusiastic in carrying out military training. They can shoot accurately and throw grenades to a great distance, and some of them can also operate artillery pieces, anti-aircraft weapons, and signalling equipment. They carry out patrol and do sentry duty shoulder to shoulder with PLA soldiers at ordinary times, and fight by their side in battle. In border regions, many militiamen can fight on horseback on the grassland. Some of them are sharp shooters and expert grenade throwers and are skilled in fighting on horseback. These coastal and frontier militia units have formed a joint defense system among villages, that is, when an incident occurs in a certain place, the militia forces in nearby villages and townships will come to its aid. Some militia organizations and local PLA forces have together set up a network of joint defense, so that, as soon as an order is issued, the soldiers and the people will set out together to exterminate an invading enemy. These ever ready, combat worthy, and invincible militia organizations, in co-operation with the People's Liberation Army, have cast the motherland's long coastal line and frontiers into a wall of steel.

This powerful armed organization of the people has developed in prolonged revolutionary struggle and has a long history and a glorious tradition. In the past revolutionary wars, thousands upon thousands of militiamen joined the armed forces in striking blows at the enemy and defending their hometowns and the revolutionary bases. Since the establishment of the new China, the people have inherited the glorious traditions of revolutionary struggle, held the weapons firmly in their hands, and consolidated and improved the militia organizations unceasingly. After Chairman Mao called for vigorous formation and training of militia divisions in 1958, the militia organization in our country has developed on an unprecedentedly large scale. In places all over the country, ranging from rural people's communes to urban factories, mining enterprises, public offices, and schools, militia divisions and regiments have been set up universally, forming a powerful armed force participated in by hundreds of millions of people. Particularly in rural people's communes, the militia organization has further strengthened the combination of labor with military training and carried out military and political training in close conjunction with production and in accordance with time and regional factors. As a result, the political and ideological consciousness of the broad masses of militiamen have increased, and their level of military techniques has been heightened day after day, and the organization and discipline among them is being strengthened unceasingly.

This nationwide militia force plays an important role in cooperating with the PLA for defending the coast and frontiers, in maintaining law and order in society, and in protecting factories, mining enterprises, warehouses, railways, bridges, and forests. The militiamen not only cooperate with the People's Liberation Army and public security organs in exterminating remnant bandits and arresting reactionary criminals, but coastal militiamen have constantly carried out patrol, stood on sentry, and fought battles shoulder to shoulder with the local PLA forces.

How does the Chinese militia appear to differ from the Soviet volunteer police?

## ITEMS 15A–15B. MEDIATION COMMITTEES

Almost immediately upon capturing the major cities of China in 1949, the Communists established out-of-court mediation committees there. In doing so, they were consciously building upon the traditional Chinese preference for coping with disputes and antisocial conduct by means of persuasion and informal pressures. All of the major areas that had been "liberated" by the Communists prior to 1949 had established such mediation committees, which were basically similar to those that had been organized by the Nationalist government in its areas beginning in 1930. The Communist government was therefore experienced in mediation work by the time it came to national power.

Item 15A, the Provisional General Rules for the Organization of People's Mediation Committees, represents the regime's distillation of the first five years of nationwide experience with mediation. It constituted an effort to curb the abuses that had been revealed and to impose a regularized system. Item 15B in effect provides the "legislative history" of the Provisional General Rules. As it indicates, the theory that underlay the establishment of mediation committees was that Party officials, government cadres, courts, police, and those who staffed residents' committees and other mass organizations would be unable to perform their major tasks if they were required to spend a great deal of time, patience, and energy disposing of unimportant disputes. By providing special mediation personnel, it was hoped to relieve those institutions of a substantial burden.

## ITEM 15A

These Provisional General Rules may be regarded as still basically operative. Promulgation of the Act for the Organization of City Residents' Committees at the end of 1954 required some minor organizational adjustments in cities in order to integrate mediation into the residents' committee structure. A residents' committee either may have one or more of its members take charge of mediation work or it may organize its own mediation committee. In the former situation, the persons charged by the residents' committee with responsibility for mediation work usually serve as members of a higher level mediation committee whose jurisdiction is the entire area covered by the public security station and the street office. Following the promulgation of the legislation that formalized their existence, the street office and the residents' committee appear to have taken over the role of leading mediation work which Article 2 of the Provisional General Rules had assigned to the basic level government.

In the countryside, since the 1958 absorption of administrative villages into communes, mediation work in each commune has been led by a member of the commune management committee. He in turn supervises the activities of the mediation committees that are ordinarily established in each production brigade. As in the case of security defense work, subsequent reductions in the size of many communes have not significantly affected the organization of mediation work.

Since 1958, in certain rural and urban areas the mediation committees have merged into the security defense committees and, in some places, the functions of merged and unmerged mediation committees alike have been enlarged to go beyond mediation (see Chapter II, section C, subsection 2).

[PROVISIONAL GENERAL RULES OF THE PRC FOR THE ORGANIZATION OF PEOPLE'S MEDIATION COMMITTEES (passed at the 206th meeting on government administration by the Government Administration Council, Feb. 25, 1954; promulgated by the Government Administration Council, March 22, 1954), *FLHP* 1954, pp. 47–48]

Article 1. These General Rules are adopted specifically in order to establish people's mediation committees (hereafter simply called mediation committees) for promptly resolving disputes among the people, strengthening the people's education in patriotic observance of the law, and promoting the internal unity of the people in order to benefit production by the people and construction by the state.

Article 2. Mediation committees are mass mediation organizations which conduct their work under the guidance of basic level people's governments and courts.

Article 3. The tasks of mediation committees shall be to mediate ordinary civil disputes among the people and minor criminal cases and also, through mediation, to conduct propaganda-education concerning policies, laws, and decrees.

Article 4. Generally, in establishing mediation committees, the area under the jurisdiction of a public security station or the street shall be the unit in cities, and the administrative village shall be the unit in the countryside. Mediation committees shall be composed of from three to eleven members.

Article 5. Generally, in cities members of mediation committees shall be elected by representatives of the residents, under the direction of the basic level people's government. In the countryside, they shall be elected by the people's congress of the administrative village. Mediation committees shall each have one chairman and also may have one or two vice-chairmen, all of whom shall be elected by and from among the committee members. There shall be one election each year. Those members who are re-elected may continue to serve.

All those among the people whose political appearance is clear and who are impartial, linked with the masses, and enthusiastic about mediation work may be elected to membership on mediation committees. If during their term of office there are instances when committee members violate the law, are derelict in their duty, or are unfit to discharge their duty, the institution that elected them may at any time recall them and replace them at a regular election.

Article 6. Principles which must be observed in mediation work:

(1) Mediation must be conducted in compliance with the policies, laws, and decrees of the people's government.

(2) Agreement of both parties must be obtained and mediation may not be coerced.

(3) It must be understood that mediation is not a procedure to which resort is necessary in order to bring suit. The parties may not be prevented from

bringing suit in the people's court on the ground that they did not resort to mediation or that mediation was unsuccessful.

Article 7. Discipline which must be observed by mediation committees:

(1) Corruptly accepting bribes or practicing favoritism and other abuses shall be prohibited.

(2) Punishing the parties or taking them into custody shall be prohibited.

(3) Engaging in any oppressive or retaliatory conduct against the parties shall be prohibited.

Article 8. When mediating cases, mediation committees shall conduct their work during periods of production leisure, and they shall attentively listen to the opinions of the parties and penetratingly investigate, study, and clarify the circumstances of the case. They shall conduct mediation with a friendly and patient attitude and in a reasoning manner. Successful mediation of a case may be registered, and, when necessary, the parties may be given a certificate of mediation.

Article 9. If, in mediating cases, mediation committees violate policies, laws, or decrees, the people's court shall correct or annul the action.

Article 10. Basic level people's governments and courts shall strengthen their guidance and supervision over mediation committees and also help them in their work.

Article 11. These General Rules shall go into effect on the day they are promulgated by the Government Administration Council of the Central People's Government.

## ITEM 15B

[Editorial, "Do People's Mediation Work Well, Strengthen the Unity of the People, Impel Production and Construction," *JMJP*, March 23, 1954, p. 1]

Unity is strength. Unity is the strength to impel the masses of people to carry on construction for production. Under the leadership and education of Party committees and of the people's governments of the various levels, and especially after undergoing various social reform movements, the political consciousness of the people of our country has been greatly enhanced. The majority of the masses of people consciously observe the laws, decrees, and policies of the state. Therefore, the number of disputes among the masses has been reduced in comparison with preliberation days, and the internal unity of the people has been strengthened as never before. But the number of cases received by basic level people's governments and courts has risen year by year. That is because, during the period of the Kuomintang's reactionary rule, the courts were institutions of the reactionary government for suppressing the people. Not only was their troublesome system of litigation inconvenient for the people, but in all sorts of ways they were a form of extortion which arbitrarily oppressed and encroached upon the people. Because of this, when people were involved in a dispute, they generally were unwilling to bring suit. Since the liberation of the entire country, when the masses are involved in a dispute, they generally all want to ask the people's government to resolve it or to go to the people's court to bring suit, because the government and the court belong to the people themselves. These disputes among the people in the great majority of cases concern land, housing, timberland, water utilization, marriage, debts, and other questions. If these disputes cannot be promptly and correctly resolved, it will affect the unity of the masses, interfere with their production and work, and at times may even be the cause of armed fighting, murder, and other bad results, which obviously is disadvantageous to developing production. For this reason, the people's government and the people's court are responsible for finding a satisfactory resolution for these disputes among the people, and absolutely must not consider them trifles unworthy of attention. But, it is impossible for the basic level people's government and court in the district or administrative village to resolve all disputes among the people. It is necessary to adopt an effective organizational form and work method to resolve them. The people's mediation committee created by the masses is an excellent organizational form which is convenient not only for resolving disputes among the people but also for carrying out the mass line in judicial work. It is a mass organization for the people's self-education.

According to the experiences of those areas which established mediation committees relatively early with relatively good results, there are the following advantages to pursuing this method: First, since the mediation organization is in the administrative village or district, mediation personnel are familiar with the situation and it is easy for them to absorb the opinions of the masses; therefore, they can handle problems relatively promptly and there is a great saving in the masses' time compared to their seeking relief from the government or court. According to the incomplete statistics of people's courts in Szechuan province alone, from January to September 1953, more than 40,000 cases of disputes among the people were resolved by people's mediation committees in 117 counties. If these disputes among the people had to be resolved by the people's court or the people's government, not only would they not be resolved promptly but an incalculable loss in money and production time would be incurred by the masses travelling between their villages and the county seats. Second, through mediation, the mediation committee can conduct propaganda-education for the masses about policies, laws, and decrees; make them familiar with policies, laws, and decrees; raise their political consciousness and concept of observing the law; strengthen the unity of the people; and prevent and reduce disputes among the people and the occurrence of criminal acts. This is of benefit to production and construction. In Ping-shun county of Shansi province, because mediation among the people was done well, and because attention was given to propaganda-education, the reaction of the people was: "Disputes are fewer year by year, and food grains are more abundant year by year." In the administrative village of Chai-hsi in Chekiang province's T'ung-lu county, the people's mediation committee settled a dispute about water utilization during the drought of July 1953 and simultaneously publicized the policy of the people's government for fighting the drought and protecting the harvest and explained why the masses should unite for mutual assistance. As a result, the masses themselves conceived a rational water utilization system and resolved their problem at its root. Because of the development in every area of the mutual aid and cooperation movements, some areas have now already begun to send people's mediation personnel to mutual aid groups and agricultural producers' cooperatives to assist in resolving disputes between members of the groups and cooperatives, and through mediation to conduct socialist education. This has impelled the development of the mutual aid and cooperation movements. Third, doing people's mediation work well is also of great use in improving the work of basic level governments and courts. If the disputes among the people must all be resolved by basic level governments or courts, the cadres from many districts and administrative villages will be unable to concentrate their strength on leading the people in the various kinds of production and construction, and basic level courts will be unable to concentrate their strength on dealing with major cases. Moreover, not only will it [cadres' handling of mediation] keep these cadres busy all day mediating disputes among the people, but it will also pile up cases as before and thus cause the masses to be dissatisfied. Doing people's mediation work well can greatly reduce the time spent by the district and village cadres in mediating disputes among the people, and can permit them to concentrate their strength on guiding the masses in production and construction. Therefore, all people's mediation organizations that are really useful universally receive the welcome and respect of the cadres of the districts and administrative villages. As far as basic level people's courts are concerned, they obviously receive a reduced number of cases and can concentrate their strength on dealing with serious violations of state policies, laws, and decrees and major cases of damaging economic construction.

It was precisely because people's mediation work is so important that, in April of last year, the Second National Judicial Conference decided that from now on, the establishment and strengthening of the people's mediation committee in a guided and planned way in the cities and administrative villages throughout the country must be one of the important tasks in the people's judicial construction and must also be an important task of the Party and government organizations in districts and administrative villages in the course of their rousing the masses to increase their participation in the important work of building the government. Now, the Provisional General Rules for the Organization of People's Mediation Committees promulgated by the Government Administration Council of the Central People's Government have more concretely defined the nature, tasks, scope of jurisdiction, and the organizational and operating principles of people's mediation committees, thus providing the committees with a clear and definite basis for conducting their work.

In order to facilitate the development of people's mediation work, it is first necessary to correct the erroneous view that some cadres take towards this work. Last year, when we opposed the "five too many" in the rural villages, some areas regarded people's mediation committees as superfluous and, ignoring actual conditions, uniformly abolished them or merged them into other organizations. The occurrence of this sort of phenomenon is chiefly explained by the fact that some cadres did not understand the role of the people's mediation committee and also distorted the meaning of our opposition to the "five too many."

The "five too many" is a product of subjectivism and commandism, and is a burden to the masses and the basic level cadres. It affects their production and work, and of course must be opposed with determination. Really useful people's mediation committees, however, not only do not increase the burdens of the masses and the cadres, but are organizations that are urgently needed by the masses and by basic level governments and courts and that are beneficial to production and work. Some people's mediation committees were not effective, mainly because local people's courts and governments were deficient in providing them with leadership. One certainly cannot, because of this, completely deny the role of the people's mediation committees. Since last year, although some areas have abolished people's mediation committees, they go on among the masses, "existing after the name has perished." Some areas accepted the requests of the masses by restoring them.

The people's mediation committee is under the direction of the basic level people's government and court of the district or administrative village. It is a mass organization which resolves disputes among the people by means of criticism and self-criticism by the people themselves; and is not a judicial organ. Its task is to mediate ordinary civil disputes and minor criminal cases and, through daily mediation work, to conduct propaganda-education among the masses about policies, laws, and decrees in order to prevent and reduce the occurrence of criminal acts and disputes among the people. Because of this, when the people's mediation committee conducts its work, it must resolutely adhere to the three principles laid down by the Provisional General Rules for the Organization of People's Mediation Committees: matters must be handled in accordance with governmental policies, laws, and decrees, and no unprincipled mediation may be conducted; mediation must be voluntarily entered into by both parties and may not be coerced, nor may parties be coerced into carrying out the reconciliation "agreement"; mediation is not a necessary procedural prerequisite to litigation, and the parties may not be prevented from bringing suit in the people's court because they have not resorted to mediation or because mediation was unsuccessful. In the past, when people's mediation committees of many areas correctly carried out these principles, mediation work had conspicuous accomplishments and received the welcome and support of the local masses. But, in some areas, people's mediation committees violated these principles. They applied pressure to the parties or resorted to "holding a struggle meeting," "passing by a show of hands," and other rough methods to coerce the parties into accepting and carrying out the reconciliation "agreement." Or else, they did not dare to use appropriate criticism-education against the erroneous views of the parties and adopted a compromising attitude. As a consequence, mediation failed or the reconciliation agreement did not accord with policies, laws, and decrees, or it injured the interests of the other party. Some other mediation personnel mistakenly thought that the people's mediation committee was a judicial organization of the first level with powers equal to those of the people's court. Consequently, there arose forbidden phenomena such as "no suit may be brought unless mediation has been tried," "restrict the bringing of suits," "cases cannot leave the village," "if you want to bring suit, you must be introduced by the district or village," and treating the reconciliation agreement as a judgment and forcing the parties to carry it out. Only if we resolutely correct these errors can we develop the role of people's mediation work and help resolve disputes among the people while not damaging the interests of the masses and causing dissatisfaction with the government on the part of the people. Besides promptly correcting the cases which should not be mediated or which were mediated incorrectly, people's courts of the various areas must also organize the mediation personnel to study the Provisional General Rules for the Organization of People's Mediation Committees, using model examples to educate the mediation personnel, thereby raising their policy and ideological levels and work ability and preventing the occurrence of errors.

1. For purposes of applying Article 3 of the Provisional General Rules, what are "minor criminal cases"? Would this category include a fist fight? What if one of the disputants got a bloody nose? Would it include petty theft? Defamation? Adultery? Negligent homicide?

a. Consider this quotation from K. C. Hsiao, *Rural China*:

"Arbitration, however, was not always efficacious. Generally it could not be resorted to in very grave incidents. Cases involving *jen-ming* (human death) were seldom settled out of court, even where no crime (manslaughter or murder) was committed. Villagers thus implicated seldom escaped the blackmail and extortion of yamen underlings or rural bullies. The suicide of a daughter-in-law in a southern village in the nineteenth century reduced a well-to-do family to ruin. Moreover, so long as lawsuits were a source of income for *sung-kun* (litigation sticks, that is, pettifoggers) and for those who connived with them, arbitration could never supplant yamen justice." [14]

b. Also consider the following account of the work of a mediation committee in an administrative village of Szechuan province in 1948 under the Nationalist regime:

"The Mediation Committee in the *Hsiang* Government is a five-man board (according to the regulations, there should be seven) responsible for administering justice. There is no court of law in the *Hsiang*. All disputes that can be handled locally are settled by this committee on the basis of equity. For example, if a man is accused of robbery, his neighbors escort him to the Mediation Committee, which hears both sides of the case, decides whether or not the man is guilty, and then proposes some sort of settlement that is accepted by all concerned. Crime is not a serious local problem, however. In the rare cases where a serious crime is committed, the man is sent to the Chungking Local Court for trial. Normally, he would be sent to the *Hsien* Local Court, but Pahsien has no court of its own and uses the one nearby in Chungking.

"The Mediation Committee holds its sessions on market days, and at each session a minimum of three committee members must meet to handle the cases brought before them (they average two to six cases each market day). Decisions must have the concurrence of at least two committee members and

14. P. 292.

the committee's chairman. If the disputes are trivial and informal, the meeting is held in a teahouse. If they are more serious and a formal written report is presented, then the session is held in the *Hsiang* Office. All the current committee members are old men who have the respect, and command the deference, of the entire community. Four of the five belong to the group of twenty-one gentlemen [leaders] already mentioned. None of them receives any salary for serving on the committee.

"The cases brought before the Mediation Committee in Hsieh-mahsiang include petty criminal cases such as stealing, commercial disputes, personal arguments, debt trouble, and landlord-tenant disputes." [15]

c. Article 2 of the Act for Mediating Civil and Criminal Cases in the Border Regions in [the provinces of] Shensi, Kansu, and Ninghsia, which was promulgated by the Communist regime at Yenan in 1943, provided:

"Mediation shall be undertaken in all civil disputes. Mediation may be undertaken in all criminal cases, with the exception of the following crimes:

(1) A crime against the internal security of the state; (2) A crime against the security of the state committed in conjunction with a foreign power; (3) Treason; (4) Murder; (5) Banditry; (6) Kidnapping for ransom; (7) Violating government laws and decrees; (8) Undermining social order; (9) Corruption and misconduct in office; (10) Interfering with public affairs; (11) Interfering with elections; (12) Escaping from custody; (13) Concealing offenders or destroying evidence; (14) Undermining the currency or valuable securities; (15) Forging official documents or seals; (16) Creating public danger; (17) Perjury; (18) Interfering with water utilization; (19) Sabotaging transportation and communication facilities; (20) Falsifying weights or measures; (21) Interfering with agricultural or industrial policy; (22) Opium crimes; (23) Other crimes of a habitual nature." [16]

Under the Shen-Kan-Ning Act, can a rape case be mediated?

d. What crimes are subject to mediation in our country? How should a proper line be drawn?

2. What legal effect should be accorded to a reconciliation agreement? The editorial from the *People's Daily* (Item 15B) tells us that it is forbidden to treat that agreement as a judgment and force the parties to carry it out. Should it be treated as a contract? Or as not binding?

3. Article 17, paragraph 1 of the Marriage Law, which was promulgated in 1950, provides:

"Divorce shall be granted when both the [married] man and woman themselves desire it. Also, when either the man or the woman firmly requests it, divorce shall be granted if mediation by the district people's government and judicial organs proves ineffective." [17]

15. A. Doak Barnett, *China on the Eve of Communist Takeover* (New York and London, 1963), pp. 131–132.
16. This act may be found in Office of the Shen-Kan-Ning Border Region Government, ed., *Shan Kan Ning pien-ch'ü cheng-ts'e t'iao-li hui-pien* (Collection of policies and acts for the border regions in Shensi, Kansu, and Ninghsia, second series; n. p., 1944), p. 266.
17. *FLHP* 1949–1950 (1), p. 34.

The above-cited provision is relevant to the criminal process, because many minor disturbances of public order arise out of matrimonial discord and are handled together with the fundamental marital problem. It is one of several provisions which, prior to the promulgation of the Provisional General Rules for the People's Mediation Committees, made mediation compulsory in certain areas of activity. Is there a conflict between the Marriage Law and the General Rules in this respect? How should it be resolved?

## ITEM 16. COMMUNIST PARTY
## AND COMMUNIST YOUTH LEAGUE

A description of the neighborhood political-legal apparatus that did not refer to the Communist Party would be incomplete. As Part I suggests, at least since 1957 the local territorial Party committee has generally had the ultimate authority over law enforcement processes. In a city district, for example, although the secretary of the district Party committee will be consulted on only the most important questions, usually one of his deputy secretaries closely supervises legal affairs. He often meets with the district's principal law enforcement officials — the chief of the public security subbureau, the chief of the basic level procuracy, and the president of the basic level court. These "three chiefs" are, of course, all Party members. Together with the deputy Party secretary, they form the local "political-legal Party group" and frequently consider cases that are too difficult or significant for the law enforcement agencies to dispose of on their own.

The district public security subbureau, procuracy, and court have their own Party units; whether the unit is a group, branch, general branch, or basic level committee depends on the number of Party members within each institution, a factor that in turn reflects local circumstances. Many of the leading members of the semiofficial law enforcement elite are also Party members. In a production brigade of a rural commune, for example, often the chairmen of the security defense and mediation committees and the chief of the militia unit are all Party members who serve not only as members of the brigade management committee but also as members of the brigade Party branch committee. A certain amount of confusion derives from this wearing of both Party and non-Party hats, and the confusion is compounded when Party members have two or more non-Party responsibilities. Therefore, when members of the local elite settle disputes and impose sanctions, it is sometimes difficult to know in which capacity they are acting.

It has been estimated that as of 1962 there were approximately 17 million Party members. Yet at that time China was thought to have a population of almost 700 million. Thus, Party members are not found in all rural production teams, factory work groups, and city residents' committees. To keep in close touch with the daily life of the masses, in addition to other mass organizations, the Party relies upon its subsidiary, the Communist Youth League. It has been estimated that as of 1962 there were 25 million members of the CYL, which is composed of especially energetic supporters of the regime whose ages generally range from fourteen to twenty-five years.[18] Apart from propagandizing and mobilizing the masses, CYL members not only provide valuable reporting services on the activities and attitudes (including antisocial activities and attitudes) of the masses, but they also engage in settling minor disputes and imposing lighter sanctions. Younger members of the local elite

18. In certain circumstances persons may continue to be CYL members after they reach the age of 25. See Const. of the CYL, p. 3, art. 1.

who are not in the Party are usually in the League. Many police patrolmen, for example, are League members.

The following excerpts from the Party Constitution suggest the basic principles and patterns of Party organization at the local level. The Constitution of the CYL (for an English translation see *CB,* 738:23–30 [July 30, 1964]) prescribes a similar type of organization.

[CONSTITUTION OF THE CCP (adopted by the 8th National Congress of the CCP, Sept. 26, 1956), *Jen-min shou-ts'e, 1957* (People's handbook, 1957), pp. 51, 52, 53–54, 55]

．　　　．　　　．　　　．　　　．

Article 1. Any Chinese citizen who engages in labor and does not exploit the labor of others, who recognizes the Party program and Constitution, who participates and works in one of the Party organizations, who executes Party resolutions, and who pays Party dues as prescribed may become a member of the Party.

Article 2. Party members have the following obligations:

(1) To strive to study Marxism-Leninism and unceasingly raise the level of their understanding;

(2) To protect the Party's solidarity and consolidate its unity;

(3) Conscientiously to implement Party policy and resolutions and actively fulfill the tasks assigned them by the Party;

(4) Strictly to observe the Party Constitution, the laws of the state, and communist morality, no exception being made for any Party member, whatever his services or his position;

(5) To place the interests of the Party and the state, that is, the interests of the masses of people, above their personal interests, and when there is a conflict between the two, resolutely to follow the interests of the Party and the state, that is, the interests of the masses of people;

(6) To serve the masses of people with heart and soul, to make more intimate their links with them, to learn from them, to listen with an open mind to their requests and opinions and report these promptly to the Party, and to explain Party policy and resolutions to them;

(7) To set a good example in their work and unceasingly raise their production skill and professional ability;

(8) To carry out criticism and self-criticism; to expose shortcomings and errors in work and strive to overcome and correct them; to report shortcomings and errors in work to the leadership organs of the Party, up to and including the Central Committee; and to struggle against everything, inside and outside the Party, that endangers the interests of the Party and the people;

(9) To be loyal to and honest with the Party and not to conceal or distort the truth;

(10) To be constantly vigilant with respect to the conspiratorial activity of the enemy, and to guard the secrets of the Party and the state.

If a Party member does not observe any one of the above-mentioned responsibilities, he shall be given criticism-education. If a Party member seriously violates these responsibilities, undermines Party unity, violates the laws of the state, violates Party resolutions, endangers Party interests, or deceives the Party, it shall be [considered] a violation of Party discipline, and he shall be given disciplinary sanctions.

Article 3. Party members shall have the following rights:

(1) To participate in free and truthful discussion at Party meetings or in the Party press of theoretical or practical questions relating to Party policy;

(2) To make proposals regarding the work of the Party and in their work to develop their creativity fully;

(3) To vote and to be elected within the Party;

(4) To criticize any Party organization or personnel at Party meetings;

(5) To request to participate personally [in the meeting] when a Party organization makes a resolution of a disciplinary or an evaluative nature;

(6) If they disagree with any Party resolution, to retain [the right to] their own opinions and to submit their opinions to the leadership organs though they must execute the resolution unconditionally;

(7) To submit any statement, petition, or accusation to any Party organization, up to and including the Central Committee.

If Party members and responsible members of Party organizations do not respect these rights of a Party member, they shall be given criticism-education. If they infringe these rights, they shall be given disciplinary sanctions for violating Party discipline.

Article 4. Only those who have reached the age of eighteen can be accepted as Party members.

Persons who apply for admission to the Party must carry out admission procedure individually.

Acceptance of Party members must be through a Party branch. Persons who apply for admission to the Party must have the recommendation of two full Party members, and their admission must be approved by the Party branch at a general membership meeting and by the Party committee of the next higher level. Moreover, only after a one year period of preparation can they become full Party members.

Article 19. The Party shall be organized in accordance with [the principle of] democratic centralism.

Democratic centralism means centralism on a foundation of democracy and democracy under centralized guidance. Its basic conditions shall be as follows:

(1) The Party's leadership organs of the various levels shall be elected.

(2) The highest leadership organ of the Party shall be the National Party Congress and the highest leadership organ of the Party at the local level shall be the local Party congresses of the various levels. The National Party Congress shall elect the Central Committee and the local Party congresses of the various levels shall elect their respective local Party committees. These committees are responsible to their respective Party congresses and report their work to them.

(3) The Party's leadership organs must regularly listen to the opinions of lower level organizations and the rank-and-file Party members, study their experiences and promptly resolve their problems.

(4) Lower level Party organizations must periodically report their work to higher level organizations. When lower level organizations have problems in their work that should be decided by higher level organizations, they must promptly ask for instructions.

(5) Party organizations of the various levels shall put into effect the principle of combining collective leadership and individual responsibility. Any important problem shall be decided upon collectively, and at the same time the individual shall be enabled fully to develop the role he ought to have.

(6) Party resolutions must be executed unconditionally. Individual Party members must obey Party organizations, the minority must obey the majority, lower level organizations must obey higher level organizations, and all [Party] organizations throughout the country must uniformly obey the National Party Congress and the Central Committee.

Article 20. Party organizations shall be established according to district and production.

Within a given district, the organization that administers Party work throughout the district shall be the higher level organization as far as all constituent Party organizations in that district are concerned.

Within a given production or work unit, the organization that administers Party work throughout the unit shall be the higher level organization as far as all constituent Party organizations in that unit are concerned.

Article 21. The Party's highest leadership organ at the various levels shall be as follows:

(1) For the entire country, it shall be the National Party Congress. During periods when the Party Congress is not in session, it shall be the Central Committee elected by the Party Congress.

(2) For the province, autonomous region, or city directly under the central authority, it shall be the Party congress of the province, autonomous region, or city directly under the central authority. During periods when the Party congress is not in session, it shall be the committee of the province, autonomous region or city directly under the central authority elected by the Party congress.

For the autonomous *chou,* it shall be the Party congress of the autonomous *chou.* During periods when the Party congress is not in session, it shall be the committee of the autonomous *chou* elected by the Party congress.

(3) For the county, autonomous county, or city, it shall be the Party congress of the county, autonomous county, or city. During periods when the Party congress is not in session, it shall be the committee of the county, autonomous county, or city elected by the Party congress.

(4) For basic level units (factories, mines, and other enterprises, rural administrative villages, administrative villages of nationality groups, towns, and agricultural producers' cooperatives, organs, schools, streets, companies of the People's Liberation Army and other basic level units), it shall be the basic level Party congress or the general membership meeting. During periods when the basic level Party congress or the general membership meeting is not in session, it shall be the basic level Party committee, the committee of the general Party

branch, or the committee of a Party branch elected by the basic level congress or by the general membership at its meeting.

Article 43. Every Party congress of a county, autonomous county, or city shall be [elected] for a term of two years. The number of representatives and the measures governing their election and their replacement in a regular or a special election shall be decided upon by the [Party] committee of the county, autonomous county, or city.

A meeting of the Party congress of a county, autonomous county, or city shall be convened once each year by the [Party] committee of the county, autonomous county, or city.

Article 44. The Party congress of a county, autonomous county, or city shall hear and examine the reports of the [Party] committee and other organs of the county, autonomous county, or city and shall discuss and decide upon questions relating to the policy and work of the county or city which are of a local nature. It shall elect the committee of the county, autonomous county, or city and the representatives who attend the Party congress of the province or autonomous region.

The Party congress of a county, autonomous county, or city that is under the jurisdiction of an autonomous *chou* shall only elect representatives to attend the Party congress of the autonomous *chou*.

Article 45. The term of office for the Party committee of a county, autonomous county, or city shall be two years. The number of members and candidate members of the committee of the county, autonomous county, or city shall be decided by the committee of the province or autonomous region. Vacancies on the committee of the county, autonomous county, or city shall be filled by candidate members in order of precedence.

During periods when the Party congress of the county, autonomous county, or city are not in session, the committee of the county, autonomous county, or city shall, within that county or city, execute the Party's resolutions and instructions, lead the various kinds of local work, establish various organs of the Party, and lead their activities, regulate and assign work to Party cadres on the basis of the system prescribed by the Central Committee, lead the work of Party groups in local state organs and people's organizations, and systematically report on its work to higher level Party committees.

Article 46. The Party committee of a county, autonomous county, or city shall convene a plenary meeting at least four times each year.

At a plenary meeting the committee of the county, autonomous county, or city shall elect a standing committee and a secretary. When necessary, it may elect a secretariat. During periods when the plenary meeting of the county or city committee is not in session, the standing committee shall discharge the duties of the committee. Under the leadership of the standing committee, the secretary and the secretariat shall handle daily work.

The election of persons to the secretariat and to the standing committee must be approved by the [Party] committee of the province or autonomous district. But in a city with a population of over 500,000 or in an important industrial city, the election must be approved by the Central Committee. A secretary of a committee of a county, autonomous county or city must have been in the Party no less than two years. In a city with a population of over 500,000 or in an important industrial city, a secretary must have been with the Party no less than five years.

.    .    .    .    .

Article 47. Basic level Party organizations shall be established in every factory, mine, and other enterprise, administrative village and administrative village of a nationality group, town, agricultural producers' cooperative, organ, school, and street, company of the People's Liberation Army and other basic level units that have three or more full Party members. If a basic level unit has less than three full Party members, it can not establish a basic level organization but it may establish a group of full Party members and preparatory Party members or it may join a basic level Party organization in the vicinity.

Article 48. The organizational form of basic level Party organizations shall be as follows:

(1) All basic level Party organizations with over one hundred members, by decision of the committee of the next higher level, may hold a congress or a general membership meeting to elect a basic level Party committee. Under the basic level Party committee a number of general branches or branches may be established according to production, work, and residence units. Under a general branch a number of individual branches may be established. The general branch committee shall be elected by the general membership at its meeting or by the congress. The branch committee shall be elected by the general membership at its meeting. The basic level Party committee and the general branch committee shall have the authority to approve resolutions of the branch relating to accepting and disciplining members.

In special situations an individual basic level organization with less than one hundred members, by decision of the committee of the next higher level, may also establish a basic level Party committee.

(2) All basic level Party organizations with over fifty members, by decision of the committee of the next higher level, may hold a general membership meeting or a congress to elect a general branch committee. Under the general branch committee, a number of branches may be established according to production, work, and residence units. The general branch committee shall have the authority to approve resolutions of the branch relating to accepting and disciplining members.

In special circumstances, a basic level Party organization with less than fifty members but with work that requires a general branch committee or a basic level Party organization with more than one hundred members which does not need to establish a basic level Party committee may, by decision of the committee of the next higher level, also establish a general branch committee.

(3) All basic level Party organizations with less than fifty members, by decision of the committee of the next higher level, may hold a general member-

ship meeting to elect a branch committee, and they shall have the authority to make resolutions relating to accepting and disciplining members.

(4) Groups may be formed under the general branch and the branch.

Article 49. The congress of a basic level organization that has established a basic level Party committee shall convene at least once each year. A general branch shall convene a general membership meeting or a congress at least twice each year. A branch shall convene a general membership meeting at least once every three months.

The congress or general membership meeting of a basic level organization shall hear and examine the reports of the basic level Party committee and the general branch committees, discuss and decide questions relating to the work of the unit, elect the basic level Party committee, the general branch committees, and the branch committees, and elect representatives to attend the higher level [Party] congress.

The term of office for the basic level Party committee, the general branch committee, and the branch committee shall be one year. The number of members of these committees shall be decided by the committee of the next higher level.

The basic level Party committee shall elect a secretary and from one to four deputy secretaries. When necessary, it may elect a standing committee. The general branch committee and the branch committee shall each elect a secretary and, when necessary, may also elect from one to three deputy secretaries.

A Party branch with less than ten members shall only elect a secretary or a secretary and a deputy secretary, but it shall not establish a branch committee.

A Party group shall elect a leader and, when necessary, it may also elect a deputy leader.

Article 50. Basic level Party organizations must make more intimate the links between workers, peasants, intellectuals, and other patriotic people and the Party and its leadership organs. The general tasks of the basic level organizations shall be as follows:

(1) To conduct propaganda and organizational work among the masses and to carry out the suggestions of the Party and the various resolutions of higher level organizations;

(2) To pay constant attention to the sentiments and requests of the masses and report them to higher level organizations and to be concerned about the material and cultural life of the masses and strive to improve it;

(3) To accept Party members, to collect Party dues, to examine and evaluate Party members, and to carry out Party discipline among Party members;

(4) To organize Party members to study Marxism-Leninism, Party experience, and Party policy and raise their ideological and political level;

(5) To lead the masses in active participation in the political life of the country;

(6) To lead the masses in developing their activism and creativity and to consolidate labor discipline and guarantee the fulfillment of production and work plans;

(7) To develop criticism and self-criticism, to expose and eliminate shortcomings and errors in work, and to struggle against all violations of law, disruption of discipline, corruption, waste, and bureaucracy;

(8) To educate Party members and the masses to heighten their vigilance and to pay constant attention to the struggle against the sabotage activity of the class enemy.

Article 51. Basic level Party organizations in enterprises, rural villages, schools, and military units shall lead and supervise administrative departments and mass organizations within their units in the active realization of the resolutions of higher level Party organizations and higher level state organs and in the ceaseless improvement of the work of their unit.

Because of special conditions in the work of [state] organs, basic level Party organizations within those organs cannot lead and supervise their work. But they shall supervise every Party member (including persons responsible for administration) within those organs, ideologically and politically, and they shall be constantly concerned about improving the work of those organs, shall strengthen work discipline, struggle against bureaucracy, and promptly notify the persons responsible for administration within those organs of shortcomings in the latter's work and report such shortcomings to higher level Party organizations.

Article 55. The Chinese Communist Youth League shall conduct its own work under the leadership of the Chinese Communist Party. The Central Committee of the Youth League shall be subject to the leadership of the Party Central Committee. Local Youth League organizations of the various levels shall simultaneously be subject to the leadership of Party organizations of the same level and higher level Youth League organizations.

Article 56. The Communist Youth League shall be the Party's assistant. All Youth League organizations shall be active propagandists of and shall implement the Party's policy and resolutions with respect to all socialist undertakings. In the struggle to develop production, to improve work, and to expose and eliminate shortcomings and errors in work, all Youth League organizations shall give the Party energetic assistance and shall also have the responsibility of making proposals to the Party organizations concerned.

Article 57. Party organizations of the various levels shall take a deep interest in the Youth League's ideological and organizational work, lead the Youth League in using the communist spirit and Marxist-Leninist theory to educate all League members, pay attention to maintaining the intimate links between the Youth League and the vast masses of youth, and pay constant attention to the selection of a leadership core for the Youth League.

Article 58. Members of the Communist Youth League who have been accepted into the Party and who have become full Party members shall, if they do not have responsibility for leadership work or hold special office within Youth League organizations, withdraw from the Communist Youth League.

Article 59. A Party group shall be established in all leadership organs within state organs and people's organizations that have three or more Party members who are in positions of responsibility. The tasks of the Party group in these organizations shall be: to assume responsibility for the realization of the Party's policies and resolutions; to strengthen unity with non-Party cadres; to make more intimate the links with the masses; to consolidate Party and state discipline; and to struggle against bureaucracy.

Article 60. Members of the Party group shall be assigned by the competent Party committee. The Party group shall have a secretary and, when necessary, a deputy secretary.

The Party group must accept the leadership of the competent Party committee on all questions.

## ITEM 17. ORGANIZATIONAL OUTLINES: CHARTS IA–IB, IIA–IIB

Charts IA and IB are designed to provide a schematic overview of the official law enforcement organs and their relation to the central state organs in Peking. Charts IIA and IIB relate the official law enforcement organs of the basic level to the semiofficial mass organizations that participate in the sanctioning process and to the local Party organization that presides over it.

The charts are simplified in a number of ways. They do not purport to show either the entire structure of government or all of the mass organizations that comprise the local socio-political environment. Nor do they show the Party and CYL affiliations of the various participants in the political-legal apparatus. Although charts IIA and IIB outline typical patterns of organization for districts in large cities and for county governments, the actual patterns often vary in detail from those represented on the charts. By way of illustration, in some cities mediation committees are organized at the residents' committee level but not at the street office level. Moreover, as previously noted, security defense and mediation personnel are sometimes merged into a single organization. Also the names attached to certain institutions vary from place to place. Nevertheless, the charts do represent widespread patterns of organization.

Details on the organization of the procuracy and the courts will be presented

Chart IA. Simplified outline relating the official law enforcement organs of a large city to the central state organs (1963)

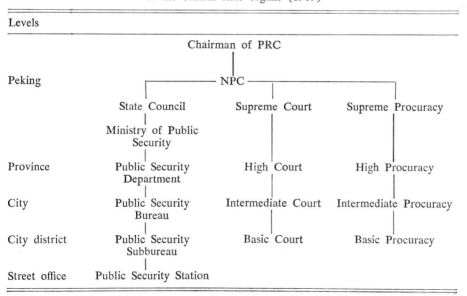

| Levels | | | |
|---|---|---|---|
| | Chairman of PRC | | |
| Peking | NPC | | |
| | State Council | Supreme Court | Supreme Procuracy |
| | Ministry of Public Security | | |
| Province | Public Security Department | High Court | High Procuracy |
| City | Public Security Bureau | Intermediate Court | Intermediate Procuracy |
| City district | Public Security Subbureau | Basic Court | Basic Procuracy |
| Street office | Public Security Station | | |

Chart IB. Simplified outline relating official law enforcement organs in the countryside to the central state organs (1963)

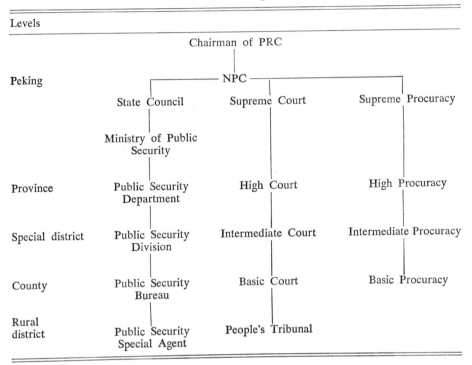

Chart IIA. Simplified outline relating the official law enforcement organs of a large city district to the semiofficial mass organizations and to the district Party organization (1963)

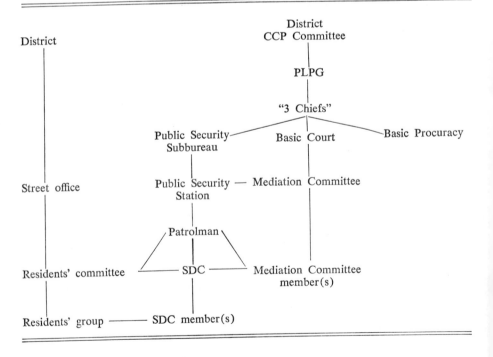

Chart IIB. Simplified outline relating the official law enforcement organs of a county government to the semiofficial mass organizations and to the county Party organization (1963)

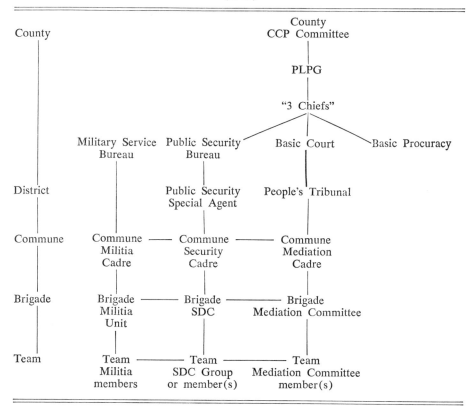

in Chapters VII and VIII. It should be noted here, however, that the "people's tribunal" referred to in Charts IB and IIB is a constitutionally authorized branch of the basic level court and should not be confused with the temporary kangaroo court of 1949–1953 that bore the same name.

## B. THE NEIGHBORHOOD APPARATUS IN ACTION

### 1. Mediation

### ITEM 18

[Chiang Shih-min et al., "Correctly Handling Disputes Among the People," *CFYC*, 4:29, 30 (1959)]

·    ·    ·    ·    ·

Our firm and unchanging policy for handling disputes among the people is to use persuasion-education and mediation. The basic method is energetically conducting socialist and communist education of the vast masses of people and propagandizing socialist law and discipline, thereby heightening the political awareness of the masses of people and their concept of law and discipline and preventing or reducing the occurrence of disputes. When we say that in resolving disputes one should persist in persuasion-education and in mediation, we certainly do not mean to reject the use of appropriate coercive sanctions when they are necessary. Persuasion-education and mediation have principles and a standpoint. Their principles are the benefiting of unity among the people and the benefiting of production and construction; their standpoint is the use of proletarian concepts to analyze affairs and to resolve problems. They are not vulgar mediation methods that rely on some abstract, supra-class "fairness" and "humanitarianism" or that in an unprincipled way make big matters into small matters and small matters into nothing. If we do not censure those who ought to be censured and if we do not give sanctions to those who must be sanctioned, then we cannot effectively educate the parties and the vast masses of people.

When handling disputes among the people in various places we have also created many advanced experiences and new methods and forms. Disputes among the people are manifested in many forms. There are many kinds and types, all different in nature. Therefore, when resolving the various kinds of disputes, we must adopt methods and forms that correspond to the different form and nature of the dispute [in question].

.    .    .    .    .

Family meetings resolve family disputes. Since family disputes are problems within the same family, a meeting of the family members living within the same household may be held so that they can take the initiative in discussing problems and resolving them. When necessary, they may invite relatives, friends, or neighbors to participate in the discussion in order to clarify right and wrong so as to arrive at a resolution of the dispute. It is their own affair, and this is a method whereby they themselves analyze and resolve it.

.    .    .    .    .

In addition, there are also other effective measures for resolving disputes among the people, such as persuasion by intimate friends, persuasion by relatives and friends, mobilization [of others] to persuade [the parties] individually, negotiations between the two parties, and collective mediation. These measures may be used flexibly in accordance with different circumstances and concrete problems.

Are the admonitions of the authors of Item 18 consistent with the prohibition against coercion laid down in the Provisional General Rules for the Organization of People's Mediation Committees (Items 15)? Whom are the authors addressing?

## ITEM 19

[Yang Kuang-teh, "Neighbourhood Committee," *China Reconstructs,* July 1955, pp. 23–24]

"Our mediation committee is very good at sorting out difficulties."
This question of mediation interested me very much. After I had said goodbye

to Mrs. Liu, I went to see the outstanding mediator of the area, a retired actor, who now devotes all his time to the committee work.

His name is Hung Tseh-pu, and I found him at home with his daughter-in-law and grandchildren. He was being shaved by an itinerant barber. As soon as the barber had finished, Mr. Hung put on his horn-rimmed glasses, smoothed his long gown, and took out his notebook.

"We try to help people resolve their differences and quarrels by agreement instead of by going to law," he said, "so we save the courts a lot of work — and the police too. We also settle quarrels which don't involve the law but are a source of friction."

"Are there rules for your work?" I asked.

"We have a manual printed by the District People's Court which sets down the basic principles for mediation, and last winter all the voluntary mediators in this district attended a series of lectures given by a legal expert. But it's mostly common sense that is needed. Our settlements are based on mutual agreement, and of course we cannot compel the parties to abide by them. Still, we manage to conciliate a lot of cases and keep them out of court."

I tried to get Mr. Hung to talk about his personal successes, but he was too modest to do so. Later on, at the local suboffice of the district council [the street office], I was told about the skillful way in which he had helped to reconcile two families, the Lis and the Lius, who were estranged by an old feud. They were close neighbours, and the original cause of the quarrel was almost forgotten, but all their members were by now [then] involved, the elders even encouraging the children to fight. Each family was constantly going to the police station to lay complaints about the other. Finally, after a bad quarrel, Mr. Hung tried his hand at reconciling them.

He gathered the facts, and then invited some of the residents in the same courtyard to come to a meeting with the heads of the two families. The neighbours began to speak their minds. One said, addressing both Mr. Li and Mr. Liu, "You not only disturb our rest with your noise, but you are making yourselves the laughing stock of the whole street!" Other neighbours also gave their views. After a long discussion, during which Mr. Hung put in a few words of sound advice every so often, the rivals agreed that both had been in the wrong at one time or another, and shook hands. The Li and Liu children now play together and the grown-ups are on speaking terms again.

Experiences like this are published in a monthly bulletin, issued by the law courts so that the various mediation committees can learn from them.

1. In evaluating Mr. Hung's technique of inviting the disputants' neighbors "to speak their minds" at a residents' meeting, it is useful to bear in mind the following background information:

"This is not to imply, however, that the Communists do not apply force in more subtle forms. Social pressure and intimidation are used with great effectiveness and are probably felt by ordinary Chinese to a degree they have never experienced before, because the Communists not only control the instruments of power — the army, Party, bureaucracy, and police — but have also developed propaganda techniques and methods of social manipulation as powerful political weapons.

"Many things the Communist authorities require people to do are 'voluntary' in theory but are brought about by pressures of various sorts. Direct pressure is applied by political workers who make house-to-house visitations. If individuals are uncooperative, political workers may devote hours or days to questioning, persuading, indoctrinating, and 'reforming' the persons involved. These political workers are generally polite, but they have the backing of the regime, they can produce stock answers to most evasions and objections, and they usually get results. Through them, Communist influence reaches far deeper into the lives of ordinary people than has that of any past regime. People who do not cooperate are often ostracized by public criticism that marks them as politically contaminated and dangerous elements.

"The pressure of propaganda is tremendous. Some propaganda contains direct or implied threats; some of it is persuasive. Verbal vitriol in the form of constant propaganda attacks against 'enemy agents' and 'reactionaries' contains implied threats for everyone, because these are loose terms and tend to be applied to opposition and obstruction of any kind. Such attacks run as a constant theme throughout Communist propaganda and create an atmosphere in which people fear that any disagreement with, or criticism of, the Communist line is dangerous. For the Communists there is only one 'correct' line on any important question." [19]

2. In these circumstances is "mediation" an appropriate term for Mr. Hung's technique?

## ITEM 20

Item 20 illustrates the relationship between mediation and social control.

[Interview]

The Li and Chou families shared a crowded apartment in Canton. A series of minor frictions arose, and relations between the two families deteriorated. On several occasions, they invoked the aid of a member of the neighborhood mediation committee, a woman named Chang, who lived in their building. Chang was a good friend of the Chou family, however, and the Lis felt that, in hearing their disputes, she always sided with the Chous. Finally, Mr. Li refused to take any problems to her. Failing to find a satisfactory outlet for his grievances, he plotted revenge on Mr. Chou, and one day poisoned what he thought would be Chou's food. One of the young Chou children ate part of the poisoned portion and died shortly thereafter, while Mr. Chou only became ill from the portion that he ate.

Public security cadres quickly discovered the culprit, and Li was sentenced to five years of imprisonment. Because their investigation led the cadres to share Li's belief that Chang had been unfair in her mediation, they severely criticized her and told her that the incident might not have occurred had it not been for her biased conduct. Although she wanted to continue to serve on the

19. Barnett, *Communist China: The Early Years, 1949–55,* pp. 18–19.

mediation committee, the chief of the public security station refused to permit her to do so.

1. In discussing the disadvantages of informal mediation in the Ch'ing period, Mrs. Van der Sprenkel writes:

"[A]nxiety to put an end to a dispute, and so remove the appearance of conflict which was embarrassing to all, sometimes prevented parties from reaching a real settlement of the differences that divided them. The disagreement was merely driven below the surface and went on simmering, and the situation was ripe for explosion on provocation. The emphasis on finding a compromise which the parties could be persuaded to accept rather than one which was based on the claims of justice gave power to the party able to bring most strength to bear." [20]

2. Item 20 also suggests another of the dangers of allowing a member of the "face to face" community in which the disputants reside to play an authoritative role in settling disputes. In this connection, consider the following quotation from K. C. Hsiao's *Rural China*:

"Perhaps the greatest misfortune was that village arbitration did not always insure equity or impartiality. The following description of conditions in a village in South China [in the early twentieth century] is revealing:
'Justice is not always rendered in an even-handed manner in Phenix Village. There have been cases where the leaders have been under the influence of large branch-families or sib moieties [*fang*] that have been able to pervert or miscarry justice. If the offended party belongs to a decadent line of the sib [clan], if his immediate relatives are few and *his financial resources and his learning limited*, he hardly dares to demand absolute justice from the offender who may have the support of a powerful familist group. Should he insist upon absolute justice, the leaders may grant it, but members of the strong familist group may subject the plaintiff to unending persecution in all sorts of indirect ways.' Justice therefore proved powerless against the dominant influences of clan, wealth, and 'learning' in this modern village. It is reasonable to suppose that this held true in some of the rural communities of earlier times." [21]

What should Mr. Li have done about the felt unfairness of the mediator? What reasons might he have had for not following such a course?

## ITEM 21

[Interview]

Liu was a landlord's daughter who lived in Shanghai. In 1957, when she was eighteen, her mother, eager to improve her daughter's class status, married her off to P'an, a member of the People's Liberation Army. He was considerably her senior and of a much lower educational level. Shortly after the marriage, P'an was demobilized and went to work in a factory in Shanghai. Because of the

20. Pp. 119–120.
21. P. 292.

differences in their ages and education, there was no affection between the newlyweds, and Liu was extremely unhappy. Desperate to improve her lot, without telling her husband, Liu volunteered to go to Kansu province to join the large numbers of young people who had been mobilized to take part in the building of China's northwest. When P'an learned of her plan, he too volunteered, and together they were sent to work in a factory in the city of Lanchow. They lived on the factory premises in a one-room apartment of a building that housed workers like themselves.

In Lanchow, Liu and P'an got along even worse than they had in Shanghai. They quarreled constantly and frequently engaged in violence. P'an beat Liu severely on several occasions. These outbursts were often overheard by neighbors or the leader of their residents' group, who would report them to the mediation committee at their street office. A member of that committee, which was composed entirely of women, would call upon the couple and lecture them, telling them that the law prohibited violence, that their fighting prevented their neighbors from sleeping, and that they should seek the help of the mediation committee to work out their problems in true socialist fashion. On two occasions, when the committee member saw that Liu was rather bruised, she asked P'an to go back to the street office with her. (Because there was no public security station on the factory grounds, the street office handled public order problems in its stead.) There P'an received further criticism-education, and he had to guarantee not to strike Liu again. Otherwise, he was warned, his case would have to be "handled."

After P'an's second visit, the street office reported the matter to the secretary of the Communist Youth League branch in P'an's workshop in the factory. He severely criticized P'an in several private talks, stressing that P'an was not behaving like a "soldier of the revolution." Any further incidents would lead to sanctions, he threatened. Liu went to the CYL secretary in her workshop and then to the secretary of the Party branch in the factory branch to persuade them to permit her to file an application for divorce in the local court. After they gave their approval, her divorce was granted and harmony in the neighborhood was restored.

Does the practice described in Item 21 violate the Provisional General Rules for the Organization of People's Mediation Committees (Item 15)? In what respects? What remedy might P'an have sought?

## ITEM 22

The mediators in Items 20 and 21 were women. Housewives tend to staff the mediation committees in China's cities, while men predominate in the countryside. The prestige of these designated mediators is often considerably lower than that of other members of the local elite. This may be attributed to a variety of reasons, such as their lack of power to force acceptance of their proposals, their low "cultural level," and their failure to inspire confidence in their ability to analyze problems accurately and fairly. Thus, many disputants refuse to heed members of mediation committees. The only power that such members hold over disputants is the threat to turn the matter over to those who can subject them to certain deprivations. The chairman of the residents' committee, for example, can assign residents to some unpleasant "voluntary labor" such as sweeping the streets or cleaning public lavatories, or, however unauthorized the practice might be, he can cut down on a recalcitrant's food rations. Similarly, at one's place of employment, Party and CYL leaders, shop chiefs, work group heads, and union officials have considerable leverage over him through their ability to impose a variety of disciplinary sanctions including dismissal. In the cities it is standard practice, as in Item 21, for authoritative persons in one's residential unit to notify his work unit of any repeated failure to respond to persuasion. And in both urban and rural areas a commonly invoked technique for settling disputes involving alleged offenses is for a member of the mediation committee to threaten to refer the matter to the local public security station or security defense committee for the possible initiation of formal sanctioning processes.

The fact that a dispute or infraction has been referred to the chairman of the residents' committee, to a work unit leader, to a public security officer, or to some other person endowed with prestige or coercive power does not, of course, mean that coercion will be applied. Such persons usually attempt to adjust the problem and to induce conforming behavior by means of further persuasion. Because of their prestige and power, their words carry considerably more weight than those of the member of a mediation committee, and this often results in ending the matter. Indeed, it is precisely because their proposals will carry more weight that disputants frequently bypass the mediation member and go directly to these persons in order to obtain an authoritative solution. Item 22 suggests the role of a commune's principal cadres in settling disputes.

["At Yangtan Commune Headquarters," *Peking Review,* 11:19–20 (March 11, 1966)]

·      ·      ·      ·      ·

The Yangtan C.M.C. [Commune Management Committee] has a secretary in charge of civil affairs and one, two, or three members to look after each one of the following tasks: (a) production and construction, (b) public security, (c) militia and conscription, (d) finance and trade, and (e) culture, education, and public health. Production brigade leaders and others who are not members of the C.M.C. may be called to meetings for discussions.

·      ·      ·      ·      ·

During the days we were at the commune offices, we saw its staff at work. Informality was the keynote. Leading comrades from the co-op store would come in for advice on how to distribute the commune's quota of chemical fertilizer or what sort of insecticide to order and how much. Credit co-op cadres came to discuss how to allocate the state loan for farm production among the different brigades. Medical workers dropped in to settle the date for the next phase of the patriotic health movement. A visiting group of agronomists came to arrange consultations about cotton growing. Several young couples came to the office to register their marriages. When they came out with their marriage certificates and saw us, these bold young girls of Yangtan who can shoot a rifle with the best in the militia, would lower their eyes and blush, smiling. Visitors like us came and were as warmly welcomed. The office was sometimes like an extempore judge's chambers. Two or three persons would come to lay complaints or get a quarrel or dispute settled. The commune cadres mediated, calmed the excited, and soon everyone departed satisfied. There are no policemen in Yangtan.

## ITEMS 23A–23C

In many situations the parties to a dispute need not take the initiative in seeking its settlement, because mediation committee members or more authoritative persons seek them out. Items 23B and 23C provide typical illustrations of the role played by cadres of the major mass organizations that embrace every sphere of Chinese life.

Before reading Item 23B, the reader should be aware of the provisions of the Marriage Law that appear in Item 23A.

## ITEM 23A

[MARRIAGE LAW OF THE PRC (passed at the 7th meeting of the Central People's Government Council,[22] April 13, 1950; promulgated by the Chairman of the PRC, May 1, 1950), *FLHP* 1949–1950, 1:32–33, 36]

Article 1. The feudalistic marriage system, with its arranged marriages and compulsion, its [concept of the] nobility of man and the baseness of woman, and its indifference to the interests of children, shall be abolished.

The new democratic marriage system, with its freedom of marriage for both sexes, its monogamy, its equal rights for both sexes, and its protection of the lawful interests of women and children, shall be put into effect.

Article 2. Bigamy and concubinage shall be prohibited. Child betrothal shall be prohibited. Interference with the freedom of widows' marriage shall be prohibited. The use by anyone of problems in another's marriage relationship to extort property shall be prohibited.

Article 8. Husband and wife shall have the obligation to love, respect, help and support each other, to live together in harmony, to labor for production, to care for their children, and to struggle jointly for the prosperity of the family and for the construction of the new society.

Article 26. Persons who violate this law shall be punitively restrained in accordance with law.

In all cases where interference with the freedom of marriage leads to the death or injury of the person whose freedom of marriage has been interfered with, the interfering person shall be held criminally responsible.

---

22. "The Central People's Government Council (CPGC) was the supreme organ of the government of the Chinese People's Republic (CPR) from its founding on October 1, 1949, to the adoption of the Constitution on September 20, 1954. Under the terms of the Organic Law of the Central People's Government of September, 1949, it exercised during its existence both legislative and executive powers. Composed of a Chairman (Mao), six Vice Chairmen, and a total of fifty-six members, all elected by the plenary session of the CPPCC, the Council formulated general policy, approved basic laws and regulations, and made appointments and dismissals of senior officials from the national down to the municipal level." Peter S. H. Tang, *Communist China Today*, I, 2d ed. (Washington, D.C., 1961), 211.

## ITEM 23B

[Ch'en Mei-ying, "How I Fight for Freedom of Marriage," *Chung-kuo fu-nü* (Women of China), 10:18–19 (Oct. 1, 1963)]

I am a worker of the first turbine workshop of Foochow Ship Buildings Factory. I am now twenty-one years old . . .

In the course of production and work I became acquainted with the chairman of the factory workers' trade union, Ch'en Huan. He was twenty-eight years old. He first started as a teacher in the factory's spare-time school. He helped me with cultural studies enthusiastically. When I encountered difficulties during working in the messhall, he helped me patiently. When I worked in the workshop and was using arithmetic for calculations, I constantly asked him for help. I saw that he was progressive in thinking and active in work. Though crippled, he was in no way affected in serving the workers wholeheartedly. All the workers reflected: "If we have trouble, go to Ch'en Huan, for he is ready to show concern for us and will resolve problems for us" . . . His behavior impressed me very deeply. I thought to myself: "It is important for a person to be good in his thinking; otherwise it would be useless no matter how good-looking he was." Ch'en Huan, seeing that I labored actively and took the initiative in working, also had a good impression of me. It was in this way, through daily work, study, and living, that Ch'en Huan and I were frequently together. As we understood each other better and better, mutual affection developed between us. However, our love met with strong opposition from my family. Some people in the factory, knowing that I was in love with a disabled person, were also surprised. They said: "How is it that Mei-ying sets her eyes on Ch'en Huan? It is really like a beautiful flower thrown on cow dung."

My parents wanted me to marry someone who had a bigger income. My mother said to me: "Since he has money, he can give you all the food you want to eat, all the clothes you want to wear. Whatever you want, he can give you". This I turned down firmly. As my mother was very superstitious, she went to a temple to draw [fortune telling] sticks. It was only because she drew an unlucky stick that she did not persist in the matter.

My father, learning that I was in love with Ch'en Huan, said to others: "If my daughter were not beautiful, I would not mind if she married Ch'en Huan. How could a healthy girl marry a cripple? Besides, his salary is so low." My parents were very obstinate and my father had a very hot temper. In order to avoid trouble, Ch'en Huan and I, after discussing the matter, decided last October to complete the marriage registration procedure. When the news reached my family, my father became angry and told me to come back from the factory (I was living in the factory's dormitory). He scolded me: "You're pretty bold to dare to do this on your own." He wanted me to cancel my engagement immediately. I said: "I did not violate the law, and I do not wrongfully love anyone. Let us go to the district government and let it judge whether I ought to cancel my engagement." My father would not allow me to go to work. I said: "Your disagreement on my marriage has nothing to do with my going to work, and I must go to work." Mother advised me: "Try to compromise. If your father dies of anger, what shall we, a family of eight or nine members, do?" Cheng Chin-mei, a member of the Women's Federation, who lived in the same quarters, after seeing this, asked me to sleep in her room. I begged her to report the matter to the chairman of the Women's Federation and to ask the Federation to help me resolve the problem. In order to obstruct my marriage, my father made complaints at various places, including the district procuracy, the court, and the CYL district committee, accusing Ch'en Huan of having deceived me. My mother also said Ch'en Huan had deceived me. But I responded courageously: "My relationship with Ch'en Huan is legitimate. I covet neither property nor profit and he has not used money or goods to tempt me." Lin Mei-hen, Chairman of Ling-hsia Women's Federation, and comrades from the district Women's Federation came to our home to persuade my parents: "To look for a husband for your daughter, the most important thing is to see whether or not the man's thinking is good. If only his looks are good but his heart is not, later on your daughter cannot have happiness. A man like Ch'en Huan, progressive in thinking and honest, will not only treat Mei-ying well but will also respect you." Thus did they repeatedly persuade and enlighten my parents.

. . . [F]inally, my parents changed their minds and they were not antagonistic to Huan . . .

I feel very thankful to the Party and Women's Federation for their support of and concern for our marriage.

## ITEM 23C

[Wang Yü-feng, "Realizations from My Experience as a Secretary of a CYL Branch," *Chung-kuo ch'ing-nien* (China youth), 22:2, 3, 4 (Nov. 16, 1963)]

I began to serve as a secretary of a Communist Youth League branch in 1958. In the past five years, I have encountered many difficulties, gone through all sorts of troubles, become disheartened, and sometimes even shed tears. Of course, I have also had the joy of conquering difficulties. Let me talk about some of the realizations from my work:

. . . [W]ith respect to youths, we should have the class analysis viewpoint and should show class feelings to the vast [number of] youth who originate from families of poor and lower-middle peasants. I am now able to remember the names, tempers, and characters of the more than 240 young men and young women in our brigade. With the help of the Party branch, I have also tried gradually to study and understand their family conditions and social relations. This provides a very important reference for our work of ideological education among the youths . . .

Finally, I feel that there is another very important point in our uniting with and educating the youths, namely, we should show concern for the individual lives of the youths, especially their marriage and family problems. In my opinion, this is a very effective method for uniting with and making friends with the youths. This can also be said to be a "key." Cases like this were numerous:

Some frequently were little concerned with politics and they seldom talked with us. However, after we had helped them in handling their matrimonial and family problems, the situation changed. They began to keep in touch with us and to participate in CYL activities, and they could generally accomplish the tasks assigned to them. Some youths were even prejudiced against me. But, after I had helped them in handling their family and marriage problems properly, they were no longer prejudiced against me. What really was the reason for this? I think the answer may be that some youths regard their family, marriage, and livelihood problems as problems relating to their personal welfare, in which, according to traditional practices, only their fathers, brothers, and most intimate friends cared to become involved. Now that we show concern and become involved, they feel that we are concerned about them and that the CYL is really a bosom friend of theirs. Certainly, this is not all that is important in our efforts to help the youths in resolving their problems. What is more important are the problems concerning their upbringing and education. Ideological struggle also exists in this respect. If we do not teach the youths to use the ideology of the proletariat in handling these problems, they might use nonproletarian ideology to handle them. In the past several years, I have helped six or seven young couples correctly handle their marriage problems and have helped still more youths resolve their family disputes. Some people say: "Even a wise judge cannot settle a family dispute." I feel that this is not true. With Marxism-Leninism and the standard of communist morality, if only we do not listen to or believe anything one-sidedly, we will be able to handle family disputes properly.

## ITEMS 24A–24B

These items illustrate instances of police mediation of potential criminal cases.

## ITEM 24A

[Interview]

Brigade A of a rural commune in the western suburbs of Canton had for several years been sending its men into the city each week to collect night soil from a certain public lavatory. Because fertilizer was in short supply, in the early months of 1962 brigade B of a commune in the northern suburbs began to send its men to avail itself of the resources of the same lavatory. Although brigade B tried to time its activities to avoid the notice of brigade A, on several occasions A's agents discovered the "poaching" and bitter arguments ensued. Finally, in April 1962 a group of A's men caught B's agents in the act and a fight involving over twenty persons broke out. Both sides used their heavy bamboo poles as clubs, and many men were hurt before police from the local public security station came on the scene. One of B's men was so seriously injured that he had to have the lower part of one leg amputated shortly after the incident. After breaking up the fight and sending the men home, the officers from the public security station notified the public security subbureaus in whose respective jurisdictions the two communes were located, and each sent its investigators down to the brigade with which it was concerned. No one in either of the groups that had been involved in the fight confessed his responsibility or informed on any of his cohorts. Each group steadfastly laid the blame on the other and was supported by the Party secretary of its brigade. Inquiry into the backgrounds of those involved satisfied the investigators that the dispute had not been provoked by bad elements and that all of the men were good peasants striving zealously to meet their production quotas.

Upon completing their investigations the representatives of the respective subbureaus summoned the Party secretaries of the two brigades and the Party secretaries of the two communes to a meeting. After each side presented the reasons for its actions, the investigators successfully urged them to accept a proposal for resolving the dispute, which was as follows: No sanctions were to be applied to any of the individuals involved; brigade A would compensate B for the medical expenses incurred by the man whose leg had had to be amputated, but otherwise each side was to sustain its own losses; brigade B would not again use night soil from the lavatory in question, and the Party secretary of each brigade would lecture his men on the importance of avoiding outbursts of violence.

## ITEM 24B

[Interview]

Some workers who were building a road through a rural suburb of the city of Canton in late 1955 became involved in a persistent dispute with local peasants, who accused them of causing unnecessary damage to their crops. This culminated in a violent clash in which over forty persons participated. Some of the peasants who were members of the people's militia used their guns to beat the workers and threatened to shoot them. The workers retaliated by wielding a variety of construction tools. By the time the local public security station obtained reinforcements from a public security subbureau in Canton, injuries had been inflicted on a number of people from both sides.

After putting an end to the fighting, the police sent the participants home to cool off and ordered the leader of the peasants and leader of the construction team to come to the public security station to discuss the case. Each leader then stated the grievances of his group and gave his version of how the fight had started. The cadres criticized them for permitting violence and urged them to settle the matter amicably in order to prevent a recurrence. The workers' leader said that there could be no settlement unless the peasants compensated his men for the injuries they had suffered. The peasants' leader replied that his men would do so only if the workers paid compensation for the damage that they had done to the crops. After a great deal of talk the public security cadres persuaded them that the best way to end the matter would be for each side to assume its own losses and to forget questions of compensation. When the leaders finally agreed, the cadres instructed each of them to chasten and to educate his group in order to prevent further outbursts.

[After successfully mediating this dispute, the public security cadres undertook an investigation to discover whether it had been fomented by counterrevolutionary elements without the knowledge of the group leaders. For this aspect of the case, see Item 230, below.]

Mediation by police officers appears to be a universal phenomenon but may be especially prominent in authoritarian or totalitarian societies. The following comment on the role of the police in Japan is of interest:

"In addition to chōtei [mediation by a committee of laymen and a judge], there is a long tradition of police intervention in disputes between citizens. Officers act as mediators on the basis of their authority, particularly when another man with sufficient prestige and authority is not available. Chōtei, as legalized by the series of mediation statutes, may in a sense be a modified, perhaps rationalized, form of the type of mediation performed by police officers. But even after chōtei was legalized, mediation by the police did not lessen. With their authority and psychological dominance, particularly under the authoritarian regime of the old Constitution, police mediators were by and large effective and efficient." [23]

### 2. Nonmediation Sanctioning

Although members of the local elite engage in a good deal of informal sanctioning in the course of mediating disputes, informal sanctioning is certainly not confined to mediation situations. When one of the parties to a dispute is plainly in the wrong and "persuasion-education," warning, or harsher informal sanctions are applied only to him, we seldom think of this process of disposing of the matter as mediation. Moreover, mediation has no applicability in the case of "victimless crimes," where the harm is suffered by society at large rather than by an individual. The materials in this subsection illustrate informal sanctioning that does not involve mediation.

### ITEM 25

[Ch'en Huai-ning, "People's Policewomen Who Closely Rely on the Masses," *JMJP*, March 4, 1959, p. 6]

In the city of Nan-ning in Kwangsi, the Lin-chiang public security station is entirely staffed by young people's policewomen. Within a very short period after its establishment in September of last year, because the policewomen closely relied on the masses, the unsolved cases accumulated during the previous few years were completely solved and the station became the red star of public security work in the city of Nan-ning.

Within the district regulated by this public security station there are over 2000 families and eighty [state] organs. A part of the district is situated at the boundary between the city and the administrative village. It is a vast and far-flung area in which the situation is complex. But these disadvantageous conditions had absolutely no effect upon their work, and these policewomen had

---

23. Kawashima Takeyoshi, "Dispute Resolution in Contemporary Japan," in A. T. von Mehren, *Law in Japan* (Cambridge, Mass., 1963), p. 55.

outstanding accomplishments. Because they are all members of the Communist Party, they all know how to bring out the wisdom and strength of the masses so that work can be done quickly and well.

.    .    .    .    .

Because they understand the importance of relying on the masses, they are always concerned with the interests of the masses. If it is something of benefit to the masses, then no matter how big or small it is, they do their utmost to do it. They regularly call meetings of the children on the street and patiently educate them to pay attention to fire prevention, to obey traffic regulations, and devotedly to protect public property. When they find lost children, even if it is late at night, if they can find out to which family they belong, they always think of a way to get them home. They also pay special attention to educating the small number of persons among the masses whose thinking is backward. When they run into a dispute among the residents of the street, they strive to find a way to mediate and to make everyone united and friendly. There was a middle-aged woman named Huang Te-ai who lived on East Chung-shan road, section two and who was always quarreling with others. None of her neighbors wanted to have anything to do with her. In recent years many people's police have mediated disputes between her and others, but none of these disputes has been thoroughly resolved. After establishment of this public security station staffed by people's policewomen, one policewoman determined to educate Huang to be good. Through private talks with Huang she found out that before liberation Huang's life was very poor and bitter and that, while things had improved after liberation, she had to go to work every day. She had four children and had many household tasks, so that she did not want to take part in the social life of that street. Moreover, she felt harassed, and thus she easily got into quarrels with others. This people's policewoman patiently gave her class education and explained that after liberation, under the leadership of the Party, her life had improved; that politically her situation had also changed for the better and that in today's society everyone had to be united and friendly and there had to be mutual respect and mutual assistance. She also regularly helped her with the household chores and took an interest in her life and her production. Hunag Te-ai, being deeply grateful for the concern and help of this policewoman, underwent an obvious change. Now, not only does she actively participate in all kinds of social activity but she also no longer quarrels with her neighbors.

## ITEM 26

["The Good Eighth Company of the Public Security Front," *JMJP,* Jan. 25, 1964, p. 1]

The cadres and people's police of the public security station of Hai-ch'eng station in Liaoning province have inherited the glorious tradition of the old Eighth Route [army] and in their security defense work and in their daily life they have everywhere manifested the noble character and superior demeanor of the people's police. The people have named them "the good Eighth Company of the public security front." The public security department of Liaoning province, the Shen-yang [Mukden] Railroad Bureau and the political department of the Shen-yang Railroad Bureau recently awarded this station the honorable title of "the public security station of the four goods."

This public security station has twelve cadres and people's policemen. It is responsible for the task of defending the security of 128 *li*,[24] eight railroad stations, and three small way stations. Here each day, on an average, several thousand passengers get on and off trains, and goods are shipped and loaded on or unloaded from a number of trains. In order to defend the safety of railroad transportation, they [the police] have roused the masses to undertake concrete work in regular [crime] prevention. The moment that something occurs that requires their action, they never give a thought to fatigue, and they do not avoid hardship or danger but persist in promptly completing the task . . . When they discover that a peddler is not observing order within a railroad station, they alway patiently persuade him and never lose their temper. Sometimes they have to use persuasion-education on an individual peddler more than ten times, but the final result is that order is preserved within the station.

## ITEM 27

[Felix Greene, *Awakened China* (New York, 1961), p. 117]

.      .      .      .      .

Today, near the covered market on Wang Fu Ching, a pedicab, loaded with bolts of cotton from the textile factory, went through a red light. These Peking pedicab drivers are humorously contemptuous of the traffic police — like the cockneys in London. The police carry small megaphones and yell through them, but pedicab drivers seem to make a point of never paying the slightest attention and usually get away with it. But today the policeman ran after the driver and made him pull over and stop. We were standing nearby, so I waited to see what would happen. The policeman talked and talked while the pedicab driver, an old hand at this, said nothing but kept mopping his sweaty face. I asked my guide what the policeman was saying. Apparently he was delivering the man a lecture on what socialism means, **the responsibility all** have for the safety of everyone, and what would happen if everyone disobeyed the lights, and that if China was to become great, her people must be socially conscious. It went on and on — a long lecture, nothing more. No ticket. This is an example of what the Chinese call *shuo fu* (to convince by talk) [persuasion]. The idea that explanation, talk, discussion will eventually convince, runs through Chinese society today.

24. A *li* is approximately one-third of a mile.

## ITEM 28

[Mu Fu-sheng (pseud.) *The Wilting of the Hundred Flowers; The Chinese Intelligentsia under Mao* (New York, 1963), pp. 180–182]

.    .    .    .    .

In China foreigners, and even natives who could not speak the particular local dialect, used to be overcharged in almost everything. When one considered the starvation level of income of the pedlars and the rickshaw men one would hardly call that a crime if one could afford it. This type of abuse was for obvious reasons difficult to deal with, but the Communists could eliminate it. A train pulled into Tsinan in Shantung one autumn morning with a woman ill on it. Her relative helped her to a rickshaw and went with her to a hospital. The fare asked was five dollars, but on arrival the relative thought the distance was too small for that amount. He paid the fare but took down the number of the rickshaw and later reported it to the police. Rickshaws in China are now organized into co-operatives with Party members to direct indoctrination or "education" in them. The police in this case agreed that the fare was exorbitant and telephoned the rickshaw co-operative. Since the cadre[s] there could be and probably were accused of not educating the rickshaw men properly, they got hold of the guilty man and sent him to the police station within minutes. There, after identification, he was simply asked to "confess any incorrect behaviour" that day. The man said he could not remember any. The police sergeant then took him to a bench at the other end of the room and asked him to sit down to think. After a few minutes he realised the futility of denial and came to the police sergeant to confess that he overcharged a man and a sick woman going to a hospital. Then he was given a long lecture on the correct behaviour in the socialist society, the importance of voluntary consideration for other members of the society, the meaning of labour and wages, and so on, and was asked if he understood now. The man said yes. The police sergeant then asked him some questions on the lesson by way of examination and the man did not answer entirely correctly. Off went the lecture from the beginning: the correct behaviour in the socialist society, the importance of voluntary consideration for other members of the society, till the man was "corrected". Only then was he asked to fix the correct fare himself, hand over the difference, apologise and leave.

Some edification probably does come from the long lectures used for correcting minor abuses, such as carving park benches, writing on walls and throwing paper in the street, but the main effect is likely to be the prolonged mental torment suffered, a combination of embarrassment and compunction, not so much for having done something wrong as for causing so much trouble to the ever-patient commissar or policeman. When rickshaw men violated traffic regulations the policemen used to strike them with their truncheon, but now one often sees in Chinese cities a man standing at the side of the street, rickshaw or bicycle in hand, facing with a sorry look the interminably lecturing policemen and a cluster of silent onlookers, the guilty man nodding once in a while to the questions: "We should all obey regulations voluntarily, shouldn't we?" — nod — "We need not wait till comrade policeman interferes, need we?" — shake — "What would happen if comrade policeman were not around? People might get hurt, might they not?" — nod. One can almost hear the victims speaking out of their eyes, "Please, give me three strokes with the truncheon and let me go."

## ITEM 29

We have previously noted that because of the small number of policemen in the countryside, security defense committees play a larger role there than in the city. Item 29, written before the establishment of communes, illustrates a typical rural case in which security defense cadres decide to forego formal sanctioning, and through informal means make the offenders return the stolen property and suffer loss of respect before their group.

[Shang Yin-pin, "Fully Develop the Militant Role of the Basic Level Security Defense Organizations" (1958), p. 72]

.     .     .     .     .

In this series of activities the basic level security defense organizations and the vast masses of people have already established inseparable flesh and blood links. Whenever the masses come up against problems, they take the initiative in seeking out the security defense cadres in order to report them, and when the security defense cadres meet some problems that must be resolved by the masses, they dare to discuss them boldly with the masses, and together they think of methods for resolution. This not only continually raises the prestige of the security defense committees among the masses but it also greatly steels security defense cadres in their actual work. Among the problems which they handle every day there are contradictions between the enemy and us, and there are also problems among the people. Thus, they are quite naturally involved in many problems concerning Party guidelines and policies. An examination of the actual circumstances shows that they generally work relatively well and that their methods for handling problems are also very flexible. This is the result of their being intimately linked with the masses under the leadership of the Party, and their understanding the feelings and demands of the masses. We can take this occasion to cite an example. In the administrative village of Ch'en-kuan-t'un in Ching-hai county, seven backward members of the masses stole over seventy bundles of millet stalks belonging to the cooperative. After the security defense cadres discovered this matter, they felt that it involved problems of the relations between the individual and the collective and that if dealt with inappropriately it could [adversely] affect the consolidation of the cooperative. As a result of consultation with the masses, they did not adopt inflexible methods of punishment for the seven backward members of the masses but allowed them to return the millet stalks and to admit their wrongdoing before the masses. The cooperative also helped those of the group whose households were really in difficulty to resolve those difficulties. This educated the people who stole the millet stalks and also the masses of cooperative members.

1. What difference is it likely to make that informal sanctions are administered by members of a security defense committee instead of by the police? Consider the following:

"Legal research has primarily been occupied with individual freedom and law enforcement in those situations of police-citizen encounter where liberty is curtailed, and with the criminal process; it has focused on apprehension, search and seizure, interrogation, and certain methods of surveillance. Less attention has been given to the comparative methods to achieve parallel objectives. Sanctioning may be defined as inducing value changes through deprivation and reward to produce behavior conforming to norms, and general studies of the sanctioning potential of policing agents would appear both possible and useful. Since broad experimentation with policing functions is not possible in free societies, comparative studies, particularly of Soviet use of citizens for policing, will illuminate peculiar features of differing social orders and should contribute to our knowledge of the effects of employing citizens as policing agents in local communities." [25]

2. What factors appear to have been determinative in the decision to forego formal sanctioning? Could it be that the thieves had stolen out of hunger and that prosecuting them would have aroused popular hostility?

3. Should one expect Chinese law enforcement personnel to have more discretion not to prosecute than their Western counterparts?

4. What procedures did the security defense cadres observe in exercising their discretion in the case reported in Item 29? Note that the decision not to prosecute was made "[a]s a result of consultation with the masses." Is this evidence of the democratic nature of the administration of justice? How do you suppose the masses were consulted? The following quotation suggests a likely answer:

"Party leadership and thorough cooperation with relevant departments is the fundamental guarantee for our handling disputes correctly. The Party committee has a comprehensive grasp of production, living, and ideological conditions and has very high prestige among the masses. Only under the unifying leadership of the Party committee can we resolve disputes correctly and smoothly. Similarly, since the people's commune is the organizer of production and life, many disputes directly concern the work of the relevant departments. Therefore, to strengthen the links with the relevant departments or to strive to have them participate in handling the disputes has very great significance in the resolution of disputes." [26]

## ITEM 30

Item 29 illustrated the use of the self-examination meeting as a substitute for the imposition of criminal sanctions in the case of a crime that involved a contradiction among the people. Such meetings, and the milder sanction of criticism and self-criticism before a meeting of a group of one's neighbors or coworkers, are common means of dealing with minor antisocial infractions, either in the first instance, as in Item 29, or after private persuasion and admonition have failed.

25. O'Connor, p. 580.
26. Chiang Shih-min et al., p. 30.

Item 30 further illustrates the fact that, after repeated exposure to this process of "education," most deviants tend to conform.

[Wang Yü-feng, "Realizations from My Experience as a Secretary of a CYL Branch" (Nov. 16, 1963), p. 3]

A CYL member named Chang Chi-hsin originated from a poor peasant family but he did not take part in labor for some time last year. The CYL branch educated him on several occasions, but without effect. Later, we studied the reasons why a son of a poor peasant could have changed in this way. We studied his situation in conjunction with his family conditions and social relations, and finally clarified the problem. Originally, his mother's father was a broken landlord. His mother was seriously affected by exploiter [class] ideology, and she loved to eat but was too lazy to work. Chang Chi-hsin was influenced by her. Grasping this root, we specifically educated Chang Chi-hsin to draw a clear ideological boundary between himself and his mother, letting him know the miseries his father had suffered in the old society and at the same time letting him clearly see the nature of exploitation of the landlord class. Educated by us on several occasions, Chang Chi-hsin finally changed and actively participated in collective labor.

## ITEM 31

The following excerpt reflects the renewed emphasis that has been placed on forms of group pressure since the antirightist movement in mid-1957.

[Chiang Shih-min et al., "Correctly Handling Disputes Among the People" (1959), p. 30]

.     .     .     .     .

The great debate is a democratic debate and is a democratic form for using the wisdom and strength of the masses to discuss, study, analyze, and resolve problems. Since disputes among the people all arise from among the masses of people and, under present circumstances, all directly or indirectly affect production and life, the masses are the clearest about the circumstances and are also concerned about the handling of the disputes. Thus, we have the condition for using the masses' own wisdom and strength to handle disputes among the people. Based upon experience in various places, the debate meeting that is convened generally should be a small-scale one. The large-scale debate meeting is only applicable to handling problems of a mass nature in which all the masses are concerned. The use of the debate form to resolve disputes among the masses generally should be limited to those disputes in which right and wrong are still unclear and in which both parties have their supporters and sympathizers and to those disputes in which right and wrong are very clear but in which one party persists in his error and which are [therefore] difficult to resolve and are rich in educational significance. In the debate meeting over these kinds of disputes, everyone should dispassionately present the facts, speak reasonably, distinguish between right and wrong, resolve his thoughts, and resolve the dispute. The democratic debate is certainly not applicable to all disputes. There should be a definite limit to its role.

The democratic debate meetings, whether large scale or small scale, all have a common characteristic. This is that through debate, both parties to the dispute resolve the dispute under circumstances in which they are in a cheerful state of mind because they not only say they are convinced, in their hearts they are convinced. Moreover, the process of debate, which in reality is the process whereby the masses engage in self-education by participation, can make all the masses who attend the meeting clearly know what is right and what is wrong and what to oppose and what to support. Their understanding is thereby heightened and thus it is possible to prevent the recurrence of the same type of problem.

Democratic debate is a new development of socialist democracy. We must strictly differentiate debate meetings for resolving disputes among the people from struggle meetings for resolving contradictions between the enemy and us. The struggle meeting against the enemy is a form of dictatorship against the enemy. Having their offenses thoroughly exposed by the masses makes the enemy lower their heads, admit their guilt, and honestly accept reform. But the debate meeting for resolving disputes among the people, by presenting the facts and speaking reasonably, induces the people to resolve problems with self-awareness on the basis of their heightened understanding. Therefore, during the debate not only do we make the masses who are at the meeting express all kinds of different opinions, we also give the parties themselves an opportunity fully to express their own opinions, which can be freely aired and mutually debated whether they are pro or con. Only in this way can we clarify the facts, distinguish between right and wrong, heighten understanding, resolve disputes, and attain the goal of unity.

## ITEM 32

Item 32 offers an insight into the nature of criticism and self-criticism.

[Kuan Feng, "Cannot the Criticized Comrades Have a Chance To Explain?" *Hsüeh-hsi* (Study), 102:6–7 (Dec. 2, 1956)]

The Criticized: ". . . That is not quite accurate — I have to explain . . ."

The Critic: "Comrade! Be humble. When you are being criticized, you should not explain."

The Criticized: "At that time I certainly did not think like that . . ."

The Critic: "Look. You are trying to explain again. This is a matter of attitude toward criticism."

We not infrequently witness this kind of situation at our criticism meetings. It seems that in the minds of certain comrades there is an unwritten law: the criticized can only "accept" criticism, he cannot give an explanation; if he does try to explain, he is not humble and his attitude toward criticism is questionable. Is this correct? Does it conform to the spirit of "treating the illness in order to save the patient"? No. It is incorrect and contrary to that spirit.

Generally there are three kinds of explanations given by criticized comrades:

one kind is an arbitrary defense by persons who "insist on arguing without any good reasons" and whose attitude is questionable; another kind is an explanation given when the person's thinking is clouded, there are some "knots" that he is unable to untie and there are some things that he has to get off his chest; still another kind is an explanation given when the criticism (or a part of it) is basically incorrect, does not fit the thinking of the criticized person or even the specific situation, and therefore it is the duty of the criticized to give an explanation. The first kind of explanation is rather rare, while the latter two situations occur fairly frequently. In fact, it is often even more complicated, for the explanations of some comrades involve both the second and third situations, and sometimes the first and second are combined. But no matter what the explanation, we must not rudely prohibit it. To explain is the right of the criticized comrade. Of course, the effectiveness of criticism is of even greater importance, but from the point of view of making criticism effective, we must also let the criticized air his views.

Needless to say, we must listen to the third kind of explanation since it is correct. We must also humbly listen to the second kind, for if you do not know the location of the ideological "knot" that the criticized cannot untie, how is your criticism to be effective? You must even listen to the first kind of "explanation" (naturally, this kind is very bad). If you do not let the criticized speak up, how will you know the errors in his attitude toward criticism and thus know how to help him correct them? Moreover, when he begins to explain, how can you tell that his explanation is arbitrary? Even if the first half of what he says is arbitrary, perhaps the second half is not. Also, even if you think what he is saying is arbitrary, it may still be worth studying whether it actually is or not. Thus, no matter what the explanation, we must not bully the criticized comrade into silence but must let him "fully explain what he has on his mind" and speak up without the least hesitation. And the critic must listen humbly and study these explanations.

The reason for this is obvious. When examining his patients a doctor of Chinese medicine must "look, hear, ask and feel." To "ask" is a major factor because what the patient says is very important in diagnosing the illness. Even in the case of a person suffering from mental illness, the nonsense that he speaks may contain something that is useful to the examination. The most difficult thing is for a doctor to diagnose the illness of a little child because the little child cannot talk and cannot respond to the doctor's inquiries. I think that it is extremely difficult when, whether you say "black" or "white," the person being criticized "does not speak" but only nods his head. When a doctor treats a patient he stresses "cooperation between doctor and patient." Since criticism is treatment of an ideological illness and requires even more dedication and also even more voluntary participation on the part of the "patient," why not cooperate with the criticized? Furthermore, relations between the criticized and the critic are not entirely the same as relations between the doctor and the patient — the critic himself may have an ideological illness and thus misapprehend "ideological illness" in others.

Why will some comrades not let comrades who are being criticized make an explanation? I think that their manner of thinking is incorrect. There are essentially two reasons for this: (1) They feel that their own criticism or that of other critics is completely, 100 percent correct. Since this is the case, if you still want to make an explanation, you are not being humble. I think that this "feeling" is itself not so humble. A "completely correct" "100 percent correct" attitude cannot always be relied on. Even if the mistake committed by the criticized has already been proved, your analysis is not necessarily correct. The process of criticism is also a process of study, study of the nature of the mistake of the mistaken comrade, the reason for the mistake, the method of correcting it, etc. This requires humble discussion with everyone, including the comrade who has made the mistake. (2) They have oversimplified ideological work to such an extent that we may term it a remnant of a crude attitude toward criticism. It is no simple, easy matter for a comrade to change from a mistaken way of thinking to the correct way. We must patiently talk with him and concretely help him to untangle one "knot" after another. If our criticism is the type which "cuts entangled threads with a sharp knife" and jumps to "conclusions," and if we insist that the person accept it and say that any attempt at explanation shows lack of humility, then our attitude toward criticism is questionable. If this is not oversimplification of ideological work, what is it? If this is not a crude attitude, what is it?

We frequently speak of "straightening out thinking." If we are going to help others straighten out their thinking, we need very great patience and have to undertake the arduous work of persuasion, and this also often includes revising our own view of things. If we only let the criticized accept and do not let him explain, that is the same as I will "dish it out" and you will "take it" and have no choice about it. What would be the result of "dishing it out"? Where would "taking it" lead to? Obviously, this is contrary to the policy that by criticism "not only must we clarify thinking but we must also unite the comrades."

In giving his explanation, the attitude of the criticized comrade may be questionable, but it also may not be. If the critic does not permit the criticized to explain, the attitude of the critic is undoubtedly questionable.

Of course, the criticized comrade must humbly consider the criticism of others and must not seize upon isolated inaccuracies in criticism to explain everything away. It would be best if he first humbly accepted the correct parts of the criticism. If he feels that the criticism is incorrect he must not immediately reject it but should humbly think it over and then explain the inaccurate parts. But if, instead, he first explains the inaccurate part of the criticism, the critic must not be dissatisfied and must certainly not prevent it. If the explanation is reasonable, that part of the criticism must be retracted. Is not this the way to stimulate a criticized comrade to reflect upon his mistakes calmly?

An American who was taken prisoner of war by the Chinese in Korea and who remained in China until 1965 recently described the impact of a criticism meeting:

"You go into a criticism meeting shaking inside. There is no escape. You sit there, and every one of your best friends blasts you. Your first reaction is you feel very, very small. You **really crawl**. They can't all be wrong. It is your fault. Then, after a day or so, you get angry. At the next session, they have to attack you stronger. They beat this anger right down into you. You become sort of a whipped dog. You can't look at anyone. That's how you are supposed to feel. That is repentance. Finally, the party member will say you realize your mistakes now and will improve yourself. It's over for you, thank goodness. Sort of a sense of exhilaration comes over you. You get a sense of determination. You will strive, you will do better. You walk out feeling you have cleansed yourself. You really feel closer to them. You have repented. You won't dirty yourself again. This is a powerful system." [27]

## ITEMS 33A–33B

Another popular technique of informal sanctioning is to put on public display "large character posters" that expose the undesirable conduct of petty offenders and nonconformists. These posters may be written out by denouncers or self-denouncers. In the former case, they may appear without prior notice to the person whose conduct is in question or they may appear following a criticism or accusation meeting. The long-lasting publicity which they give to undesirable conduct seems to constitute an effective method of preventing its repetition. Item 33A suggests the regime's enthusiasm for this technique, and Item 33B, which calls the poster a "wall newspaper," gives an insider's view of the diverse uses to which it is put.

## ITEM 33A

[Chiang Shih-min et al., "Correctly Handling Disputes Among the People" (1959) pp. 29–30]

The vivid and lively democratic forms of great blooming and contending, large character posters and great debates, which were created during the rectification movement among the entire people are good methods of resolving disputes among the people.

The large character poster is a new form of rousing the masses to conduct a blooming-contending debate and to display socialist democracy. Its contents are simple and conspicuous; its form is fresh; it exposes problems profoundly and sharply, promptly and forcefully, and, in particular, it resolves problems of relations between the advanced and the backward, the individual and the collective, etc.; it restrains and criticizes parochialism, individualism, and delinquent conduct, etc. The use of the form of the large character poster develops debate of a mass nature, criticism, and self-criticism; its effectiveness is conspicuous and its role great. In his essay, "Introducing a Cooperative," Chairman Mao rated the large character poster very highly. He said: "The large character poster is an extremely useful weapon of a new form. It can be used in cities, the countryside, factories, cooperatives, shops, organs, schools, military units, streets, and, in short, in all places frequented by the masses. It is already universally used and it should always be used."

27. Morris R. Wills (as told to J. Robert Moskin), "Why I Chose China," *Look Magazine*, Feb. 8, 1966, pp. 75, 84.

## ITEM 33B

[Mu Fu-sheng, *The Wilting of the Hundred Flowers* (1963), pp. 158–159]

·    ·    ·    ·    ·

Besides these meetings criticisms and self-criticisms are also voiced in the form of the "wall newspaper". A piece of "wall newspaper" is a large sheet of cheap paper, sometimes ordinary used newspaper, with words more than an inch high written on it and pasted on the walls of an office building and sometimes on bamboo mats specially erected for the purpose. Anyone may write a "wall newspaper". It may be signed, by a person or by a group, or it may be unsigned; it may be addressed to a particular person, or to "the Leadership" or to the whole organisation, the writer or writers included. Since everybody is supposed in campaigns of mutual criticism to write a "wall newspaper" it is usually an amusing exhibition of strange syntax and improvised rhetoric. The meaning of the writings may not be always clear, but the enthusiasm is always evident. After a "wall newspaper" is prepared it is normally handed to the committee of Party members, who put it up according to the order in which it is received. This procedure is presumably a safeguard against unsigned "reactionary" writings. There is no limit to the scope of the criticisms apart from the political limit of support for socialism; all private and public matters may be exposed, discussed, or criticised. In fact the "wall newspaper" is often a reliable directory of the romances among the staff of the organisation, called "peach-coloured affairs". Those criticised, "the Leadership" in particular, must collect the questions and criticisms directed to them and answer them one by one in the meetings. They can dispel doubts, clear up misunderstandings, explain difficulties, offer alternatives, or confess mistakes and promise improvements. Expiated political sins are marked in the "wall newspaper" with confessions and "guarantees" for "sincere efforts" to make good. In private matters, no one may say, "This is none of your business", because in the socialist society the business of a person is the business of everyone else. In particular cases the "wall newspaper" is posted on the office door of the person criticised. When the writers feel that words cannot do their feelings justice they add amateurish cartoons, caricatures, and allegorical drawings.

## ITEM 34

Another distinctive method of informal sanctioning is the "statement of repentance" or "statement of guarantee" which many offenders are required to write and to make public as the price of avoiding more serious sanctions. Item 34 is typical of such statements. It was written out by a former public security officer as a hypothetical example.

[Statement of Repentance]

I, Chang Te-cheng, male, 34 years old, have a
bad temper, and, because of it, I beat and injured          [Picture of Penitent]
Li Ming on June 21, 1962.

Now, after receiving education and lenient handling by the comrades of the public security station, I admit my error and I recognize that it is unlawful to hit people. Now, I not only apologize to Li Ming, but I especially assure everyone that I will never dare to commit the same act again. Here I express my repentance.

Chang Te-cheng, Penitent

341 Hsin-kang road, Ho-man district, Canton

## ITEM 35

The authors of Item 31 took care to distinguish "debate meetings for resolving disputes among the people from struggle meetings for resolving contradictions between the enemy and us." As indicated in Part I, there are varieties of "struggle meetings." At the "speak reason struggle," although the atmosphere is more intense and hostile than at a criticism or denunciation meeting, some pretense is nevertheless made at reasoning with the offender and allowing him to respond. No such effort is made at the ordinary struggle meeting. Physical violence is sometimes inflicted at the most extreme variety of struggle, despite periodic efforts on the part of higher level Party and public security officials to curb such excesses.

Struggle may precede the imposition of formal administrative or criminal sanctions or may be the only sanction received by an offender. It may be imposed after persuasion, admonition and group criticism, and denunciation have failed to reform him or, in the case of a relatively serious offense, it may be applied in the first instance. In form, struggle is usually carried out by "the masses," but it is actually led by cadres from the Party, the residential organization or the work unit. The following account of what its author terms an "investigation meeting" describes what is in effect an ordinary struggle meeting.

[Mu Fu-sheng, *The Wilting of the Hundred Flowers,* pp. 157–158]

.     .     .     .     .

Those who have done "wrong things" in the past and are likely to do more "wrong things" in the future are "helped and corrected" in the "investigation" meetings. In these the life of those found guilty by "the Leadership" becomes a political case for study by the amateur and for expert diagnosis and prognosis by the cadre and the laymen who attend the meetings. "The Leadership" makes a report on the case, giving in outline the political crimes the culprit has committed and the political heresies he has spoken or written. Exposure is invited from the audience and exposures follow. Since everybody acquainted with him is expected to contribute to the proceedings — and everybody concerned is eager to stay uninfected by the political indisposition — irrelevancies and personal grievances are dug out and aired, and they all pass as evidence. One physicist, required to speak against his research superintendent and former professor, accused the erring man of his crimes as reported and pointed out that his erroneous ideas were all interrelated and came from his worship of American imperialism. Those without the "political sense of smell" would think this was progressiveness. The physicist was, however, criticised in his turn: "That is not enough. We are here to destroy the political errors still subsisting among us by carrying out an ideological struggle and not to explain his errors for him." This showed what irrelevant charges one might indulge in, so long as they constituted a "struggle" against the guilty. Of course, the physicist was "free" to speak in the way he chose: "no one in a socialist society could be forced to do anything". The culprit under investigation is not normally given a chance to answer the charges, and when he is, unless he confesses forthwith, he faces shaking fists, shouts, pointing fingers, and even people rushing toward him. The "investigation" meetings do not end with confessions but with "sincere" confessions. Insincerity can always be detected "by the crystal-clear discernment of the people." The end of the confession usually reads, "I truly realise now what a shameless ungrateful scoundrel I have been; I wish to thank you all, especially our dear Party members, for the help you have given me to see myself as what I really am and I ask the people to give me another chance to reform myself, if they can be so moved by my sincere guarantee, which I hereby solemnly give, that I will henceforth serve only their interests under the leadership of the Chinese Communist Party . . ." Monotonous examples of this style can be found by the hundreds in the Chinese Press.

That the Chinese leaders are highly sensitive to the distinctions between "struggle meetings" and milder sanctions, and to the consequences that the various forms of informal sanctioning are likely to have, is amply documented in the twenty-nine 1961 issues of the secret "Bulletin of Activities" of the People's Liberation Army that have been made available by the United States Department of State. In January 1961, for example, at a time when the leadership was striving to improve badly deteriorating military morale, Marshal Lin Piao, Minister of National Defense, issued a directive that included the following instruction:

"In dealing with the soldiers' problems, it is best for the cadres of various levels not to conduct 'struggle meetings' at will. In fact, it should not be permitted to criticize an erring soldier openly without grave cause, nor is it wise to force them to 'wear hats' [to be stigmatized]. It is also not permitted to mention the names of wrongdoers and criticize them in public. I wish now to emphasize the method of separately and individually talking with those who are incorrect in their thinking, giving them the help and support of the small group to which each belongs, and slowly and patiently proceed with the education that leads to true conviction. At any rate we must be careful first to give clear reasons, such as, why is it not good to do it this way and good to do it that way? We must realize that to put a man before a crowd and 'have his picture taken,' that is, during a meeting to have everyone take a good look at the mistaken one, is a very wrong way of handling the matter." [28]

In a February 1961 report that criticized military cadres' methods of handling problems among their soldiers, Lo Jui-ch'ing, then Chief of Staff of the army, stated:

"The greatest weakness is that the form of their supervision is simple and entirely lacking in skill. They do not know how to make skillful use of persuasive education. With respect to the so-called individual backward soldiers, they are

28. Canton Military Region Committee of the CCP, "Regulations for Improving the Methods of Supervisory Education in Army Units," *Kung-tso t'ung-hsün* (Bulletin of activities), 7:27 (Feb. 1, 1961).

very apt to adopt erroneous attitudes. Some comrades in the Army Unit 8559 considered that during last year eleven soldiers of this unit committed suicide, and only two of them took their own lives because they were afraid of being prosecuted on political charges. The other nine persons took their own lives because of slight offenses, such as petty thievery, and the improper handling of their offenses by the cadres. One political director, in order to ask a soldier whether he had stolen another person's trousers, mobilized all the cadres at the platoon level and above in the entire company to 'talk' by rotation continously with him for eighteen hours. Finally, this soldier was forced to commit suicide." [29]

Shortly thereafter, in summarizing the results of his investigation into the thoughts of soldiers and cadres, Hsien Heng-han, Political Commissar of the Lanchow Military Region, noted:

"The form and method of investigation had to be carefully studied and carried out in a very delicate and gentle way. The soldiers were in favor of putting up high requirements. They liked very much to live an active and intensive life and were much dissatisfied with those who failed to supervise [them] or who were afraid of supervising them, as well as with the laxity of morale and discipline in the companies. They were not afraid of being criticized when they showed defects or made mistakes. What they demanded was that in the face of criticism their self-respect should not be hurt. Their concrete demands are as follows: (a) When they have defects or mistakes, they hope that the cadres will in the beginning talk with them individually, point out the place wherein their defects and mistakes lay, and tell them how to correct these defects and mistakes; (b) they oppose direct public denunciation and suggest that those who had mistakes and defects should be allowed to develop their own thoughts in order to recognize their defects and mistakes and self-consciously to examine themselves in their respective squads or platoons; (c) they oppose unjustified criticism, struggle, and 'analysis' in the assembly of their platoon or company; (d) with respect to those who have made serious mistakes, they are in favor of 'name-calling' before the assembly if it has any generally educative significance, but they oppose frequent and repeated 'name-calling,' especially when the defects and mistakes have already been corrected; (e) they do not like the practice of 'total liquidation,' the digging into their old background, and the exposure of 'shortcomings.' Wang Sheng-lung, a soldier of the First Company, had committed petty thievery. The company struggled against him a number of times. Afterwards, he could have changed himself. But the squad leader kept on exposing his 'defects' from time to time, calling him a 'thief.' This made it impossible for him to stand up like a man again. He thus became depressed in thought and negative in work. Later the squad leader was replaced. The new leader changed the method of leadership by treating him equally, and managed to discover and praise his merits. Now this soldier is a model of the entire platoon." [30]

29. "Comrade Lo Jui-ch'ing's Inspection Report on the Conditions of Army Units in Several Areas," *Kung-tso t'ung-hsün* (Bulletin of activities), 11:6 (March 2, 1961).

30. Hsien Heng-han, "How Successfully to Conduct Supervisory Education in Army Units," *Kung-tso t'ung-hsün* (Bulletin of activities), 18:13–14 (April 30, 1961).

## ITEM 36

In recent years in the Chinese press references to informal sanctioning generally have been less detailed than in the regime's first decade. This item is a typical recent account.

["Poor Peasant Girl, T'ang Yu-lien, Bravely Struggles Against Theft of Collective Property," *Chung-kuo ch'ing-nien pao* (China youth news, Peking), Nov. 24, 1964, p. 1]

According to a *Hupeh Daily* report, T'ang Yu-lien, a nineteen-year-old peasant girl attached to production team No. 5 of Ch'ün-kuang production brigade of Shih-tzu-lu commune, Hsien-feng county, courageously exposed the theft of collective property by her uncle, T'ang Chiu-chiang, who was a deputy leader of the production team, and thereby protected the collective interests. For this, she has been praised by the vast masses of commune members and commended by the brigade Party branch and the [management] committee of the production team.

Well-to-do middle peasant T'ang Chiu-chiang was a man seriously affected by bourgeois ideology. Last winter, he pretended to be an active worker and was elected a deputy leader of the production team. He then obtained work in the brewery. After he got into the brewery, his behavior aroused the suspicion of the poor peasant girl T'ang Yu-lien who, working in a flour mill next to the brewery, discovered that T'ang Chiu-chiang drank wine three times a day during his meals, that after he returned from the market he would always bring back a piece of meat, and that some dubious characters often visited his house. When she went home, she told all this to her father, T'ang Yüan-hsiang, and put to him a string of questions: In the past one hundred catties [a catty is one and one-third pounds] of wine were produced in a year, but why were only seventy to eighty catties produced this year? Why did T'ang Chiu-chiang always have visitors? From what Yu-lien told him, T'ang Yuan-hsiang also became suspicious of T'ang Chiu-chiang's behavior . . . He then asked Yu-lien to watch more closely T'ang Chiu-chiang's movements, and courageously struggle against his wrongful acts. Thereupon, T'ang Yu-lien paid more attention to T'ang Chiu-chiang's movements.

At noon one day, male commune members of the team went out carrying coal to make lime, while most of the female commune members were cutting grass on the slope. Only T'ang Yu-lien worked as usual at the grinder in the flour mill. Suddenly she was assailed by a strong smell of wine, and turning her head, she saw that T'ang Chiu-chiang was walking out of the brewery carrying two buckets. Yu-lien dashed into the brewery, where she found an enamel vessel hung on the wall, with drops of wine still dripping from it. Obviously, the vessel had been used for ladling wine. Her suspicion aroused, she wondered if her uncle had stolen wine from the collective. "Papa says that I am a poor peasant's daughter and should act like a poor peasant who must be honest even in small things and who must dare to expose and struggle against those who violate the collective interest." With this thought, she closely followed T'ang Chiu-chiang, determined to get to the bottom of the matter.

With the guilty conscience of a thief, T'ang Chiu-chiang knew that something was wrong when he saw his niece coming toward him. His face paled. When Yu-lien saw this, she knew what was going on. So she asked him directly: "What is inside your buckets?" T'ang Chiu-chiang muttered: "It is waste water from the brewery." "But waste water is turbid. How is it that the water in your buckets is so clear?" Knowing his trick had failed, T'ang Chiu-chiang changed the subject quickly and said: "Oh, the water had been boiled to heat the wine." Seeing that he was trying to deceive her, Yu-lien became indignant and asked him to put down the buckets for her to inspect the contents. It was wine, and good wine at that. Then Yu-lien criticized him angrily: "Uncle, you are a deputy leader. Why do you do such a thing?"

T'ang Chiu-chiang never expected that his niece would talk to him like this. At first, he tried to sweet talk her into covering up for him. When he found that this would not work, he opened his eyes wide and swore at her: "Whether or not there is wine in the bucket is none of your business." Then, he said threateningly: "If you dare spoil my reputation, I'll break your jaw and tear your mouth wide open." Yu-lien was not afraid. Taking a step forward, she grasped the bucket with one hand and caught hold of T'ang Chiu-chiang with the other. She said loudly: "If you dare to damage the collective, then I dare to mind your business. You have stolen wine and evaded taxes so I can mind your business." T'ang Chiu-chiang wanted to pour the wine into a well so as to destroy any evidence. But Yu-lien held the bucket until other commune members, attracted by the noise, came over, and T'ang Chiu-chiang dared not use violence.

Because in the past T'ang Chiu-chiang had committed the illegal act of obtaining unreasonably large profits and now he had also stolen collective property, the production brigade and the management committee of the production team dealt with him severely. They also commended T'ang Yu-lien for her exemplary act of honesty and for furthering justice. This gave great satisfaction to the vast masses of poor and lower-middle peasant commune members, many of whom expressed their determination to learn from T'ang Yu-lien.

1. Although Item 36 fails to specify the nature of the "severe" punishment imposed, it seems probable that formal criminal punishment was not meted out, since only brigade and team cadres took part in the decision making. In the light of Item 36 and the preceding materials, how should one evaluate claims such as the following, made by Hsieh Chüeh-ts'ai, then President of the Supreme People's Court, in his 1964 report on the work of the Supreme People's Court?

"During this [1959–1964] period the security situation in our country was very good, and generally there was a downward trend in the number of criminal cases. This year the number of criminal cases received by the various levels of people's courts throughout the country will be much smaller than in any other preceding year. This shows that the degree of political awareness and the degree of organization of the people of our country have been further heightened and that the system of the people's democratic dictatorship has become more consolidated." [31]

31. *JMJP*, Jan. 1, 1965, p. 3.

2. "The criminal process, from arrest through release, is comprised of a series of 'status degradation ceremonies.' A status degradation ceremony is 'any communicative work between persons whereby the public entity of an actor is transformed into something looked on as lower in the social scheme of social types.' Garfinkle, 'Conditions of Successful Degradation Ceremonies,' 61 *Am. J. Sociology* 420 (1956)." [32]

Is it fair to say that China has devised a series of prearrest status degradation ceremonies that often make resort to the criminal process unnecessary?

3. How would you modify Mrs. Van der Sprenkel's summary of informal adjustment and sanctioning in Manchu China (quoted above, section A, subsection 1) in order to make it applicable to contemporary China?

## C. SELECTED SANCTIONING PROCEDURES

Sections A and B of this chapter dealt with institutions for informal adjustment and sanctioning that affect the populace at large. Section C is concerned with institutions that have only affected a segment of the Chinese people, either because they have represented experiments in certain places and periods or because, although fixtures on the Chinese scene, they are applicable only to certain groups within the population.

### 1. Comrades' Courts

Among the problems discussed in Part I was the question of the extent to which the Chinese have chosen to import Soviet legal institutions and the degree of success that such efforts have enjoyed. Following the decision to industrialize along Soviet lines and the concomitant decision to develop a Soviet-style legal system, the Second National Judicial Conference that was held in Peking in April 1953 called for the establishment, on an experimental basis, of "comrades' courts" at a number of large-scale industrial enterprises. These comrades' courts were to be set up primarily in order to instill labor discipline in the masses, many of whom had only recently been introduced to factory work and to the demands of a government that was bent on rapid industrialization. Problems such as tardiness. absenteeism, poor quality work, and serious and costly accidents had become a subject of great concern by 1953, and the comrades' courts were devised as part of an effort to combat them.

The Chinese openly adopted as their model the comrades' courts that had been established in Soviet enterprises and institutions in 1951 after a checkered history of Soviet experimentation going back as far as 1919. The cadres who undertook the experiment with this institution studied the relevant Soviet legal documents as well as the "advanced experiences" of the Soviet Union and were told that in the Soviet Union the comrades' court "occupies a major place in the entire process of social reform." [33]

### ITEM 37

By July 1955 comrades' courts had been established in 170 major state-operated factory and mining enterprises. They were the subject of a good deal of favorable

32. Joseph Goldstein, "Police Discretion Not to Invoke the Criminal Process: Low Visibility Decisions in the Administration of Justice," *Yale Law Journal*, 69:590 (1960).
33. "Introducing the Soviet Union's Comrades' Courts for Enterprises," p. 3.

attention in the press, of which the following article is typical. It presents a comprehensive discussion of one Chinese experiment with comrades' courts and also provides more than a glimpse into the methods by which the PRC carries out political and legal innovations.

[Wang Ju-ch'i, "How the Enterprise Comrades' Courts Were Established in K'ai-luan Coal Mine," *JMJP,* April 19, 1954, p. 3]

In order to gain experience in establishing tribunals for the protection of economic construction and enterprise comrades' courts (hereafter simply called comrades' courts [CC]) in city industrial and mining areas, the central legal organs sent a judicial work group to K'ai-luan coal mine in the city of T'ang-shan in Hopei province to conduct a model experiment. We report below the circumstances of the establishment of the CC at K'ai-luan mine by the judicial work group and some preliminary experiences.

## 1. Coordinate with What Is Central, Acquire General Knowledge About Production, and Establish Judicial Business

After the judicial work group went down to the mine, the first problem encountered was the difficulty of hearing cases relating to production without common knowledge about production. Most of the staff and workers were also not very clear about whether the work which the judicial work group was going to do would in fact benefit production. After lengthy consideration the judicial work group decided, in order to serve the central work of the mine, to acquire general knowledge about production and establish judicial business. Therefore they asked the mine's leadership to assign them to some work: helping to write large character posters in the mine, arranging the safety inspection records, and helping three model small groups summarize their model activity. Afterwards they further participated in mass movements such as those for increasing production, for austerity, for labor competitions, for wage reforms, and for major safety inspections.

Having done the above work, the judicial work group began to gain a general knowledge of production — for example, the production process, the circumstances of labor organizations, the production management system, the responsibility system, and the factors promoting or impeding production. At the same time it also gained the support of the masses and the confidence of the cadres and created conditions favorable for the establishment of the CC. No matter whether the workers were faced with problems relating to production or to their personal lives, they always reported them to the judicial work group or sought to discuss them with the judicial work group. The judicial work group also promptly mediated and resolved family or worker disputes. It also resolved production difficulties as much as possible.

## 2. Propagandize on the Significance of the CC, Find and Train Activists

Because of the fact that the CC is a new kind of organizational form and is quite unknown both to the masses of staff and workers and to the cadres, when the judicial work group began to establish the CC, it immediately coordinated with the mine's central work and broadly and deeply propagandized on the nature of the CC, the scope of its jurisdiction, its relationship to the leadership, etc. The propaganda emphatically explained: the CC is a mass organization for the self-education of the masses of staff and workers; its task is to deal with cases such as those involving labor discipline, responsibility for minor incidents, petty thefts, and minor bodily injuries which occur in factories and mines. If a staff member or worker commits one of the above-mentioned wrongs and does not change after criticism at a small group meeting, and the degree of his wrong has not reached the point of requiring punitive legal restraints, the administrative leadership may turn him over to the CC for disposition. The CC is not a court. It has no power to convict people for crime. It can only give the person tried criticism-education or order him to make a public self-examination. If the wrong committed by the person tried is relatively serious, it can also suggest that the administrative leadership give him sanctions such as warning, demerit, a demotion in office, or even expulsion. But the CC also differs from criticism by the small group in that its judgments are compulsory and must be obeyed. Therefore, the CC is an excellent organizational form by means of which the masses of staff and workers make use of the Communist spirit to carry out self-education. It can raise the political and ideological consciousness of the masses of staff and workers, strengthen their concept of the legal system and reduce and prevent cases of violation of labor discipline and other criminal acts. The chairman and members of the CC are elected by a meeting of all the staff and workers of the factory, mine, or enterprise or by a meeting of their representatives.

The method of propaganda was first to explain and elucidate the various problems of the CC to the responsible cadres of the Party, government, union, and Youth League in meetings called by the Party committee at K'ai-luan, the Party committee at T'ang-shan mine, the Party general branch of mining district number 72, the Party general branch of the mechanical-electric departments and other levels of Party organizations, or to make use of the opportunity of individual conversations. This provided the key to successful development of the work by enabling them to understand that that organization [the CC] is in fact beneficial to production. Next was the training of activists from the masses to form the backbone for conducting propaganda among the vast masses of staff and workers and at the same time training them to serve as candidates for the CC. The judicial work group talked with these activists during their leisure time, after they came up from the mine shafts, before meetings, or at the workers' quarters, and during their regular rest time so that they understood the content of the propaganda. It then allowed them freely to propagandize vast [numbers of] staff and workers. The facts proved this method to be very effective. Because these activists engaged in production alongside the workers, they were familiar with the workers' ideological situation and could make use of all leisure time. For instance, while the workers were going up or down the mine shaft, eating their meals, or sometimes even at the scene of production, the activists repeatedly propagandized them.

After the propaganda concerning the CC had made a preliminary impact upon the masses of workers, the judicial work group, with the permission of the leading cadres from the Party, the government, and the workers' union organizations of the mine, also used the activity periods preceding or following work. The secretary of the Party general branch, the district chief, and the chairman of the union all combined to make extensive propaganda containing vivid examples. Simultaneously this was coordinated with the use of large character posters, blackboard announcements, announcements accompanied by percussion instruments, broadcasts, and other methods. After this repeated propaganda the great majority of workers realized that the CC was beneficial both to production and to the individual, and they welcomed it. The general reaction of the workers of coal-mining district number 72 was: "It is good to establish the CC's — in the future people like foolhardy Chao should be taken care of." (Chao An is the name of a foreman who on June 13 of last year lost his life in an accident because he violated operating rules.) "From now on we have to keep an eye on that kind of person. In the past an incident was forgotten as soon as it occurred; it will not be like that in the future." After this propaganda the percentage of workers reporting for duty at the number 7532 work site increased from 85.8 percent in September to 89 percent in October and to more than 90 percent in November. This shows that propagandizing the staff and workers on the CC has played a role in their education about law.

## 3. Election of the Members of the CC

The qualifications of candidates for the CC are: a clear history, a firm standpoint, impartiality in handling matters, proper demeanor, activism in production, observance of labor discipline, prestige among the masses, and not having too many concurrent positions. In accordance with these qualifications and while coordinating with the various kinds of central work of the mine, the judicial work group found and trained a group of activists and, after repeated discussion and consideration by the cadres and masses, the activists were decided upon as candidates for membership in the CC. Then with the responsible cadres of the Party, government, and union personally presiding, an election was conducted. Because thorough preparatory work was done prior to the election, at the time of the election full play was given to democracy, and the staff and workers were allowed to evaluate the qualifications of the candidates in detail. Therefore, all the elected members were qualified. As a result of the election, work site number 7532 elected a CC of five members of whom one was a member of the basic level organization of the union and four were workers. Work sites number 7811 and number 7643 together elected eleven people of whom one was a squad foreman, five were members of the basic level of the union, and five were workers. The mechanical-electrical departments of the latter two sites elected ten people of whom four were members of the union's basic level, two were members of the Party branch, and four were workers. They did various kinds of work in different squads and in the mechanical-electrical department at the sites. According to the experience of the judicial work group, in order to facilitate the handling of cadres' problems, it is best to have cadres from the unit in which the CC is located participate as members of the CC. Furthermore, since a coal-mining site is usually mined out in a few months, and the staff and workers may then be dispersed among several other sites, to take the site as the unit for establishing the CC will prove fruitless. Therefore, the entire mining district should be taken as the unit for establishing the CC. Then, if the members of the CC are elected from each squad of every site, when they are confronted with a problem, they may resolve the problem at a meeting of the staff and workers of their respective squads. In that way, although a small number of coal-mining sites are closed down, the basic organization still remains, and it is only necessary to hold a supplementary election at the new sites. In regard to voting units [for individual CC members] the squad is the voting unit in the mine, while in the mechanical-electrical department it is the congress of the basic level of the union.

## 4. How the CC Is Convened

Before convening the CC, the judicial work group cooperated with the union and with the newly elected CC to do some preparatory work. They first studied the materials concerning workers who violated operating rules or who presented serious cases of absenteeism. From these they selected one or several of the most conspicuous persons, whom repeated education had failed to change. Then, they investigated the history, the seriousness, and the ideological source of the person's wrongdoing with the person himself, his family, his relatives, his neighbors, and his coworkers. Then, they patiently undertook persuasion-education of the person and mobilized his family and neighbors jointly to persuade him. Only after all this did they decide to select him as a target for trial. In other words, for a person to be chosen as a target for trial, four conditions must exist:

(1) The wrong committed is a problem within the worker class and is not a problem of a violation of law requiring criminal punishment.

(2) The wrong committed is typical and is also one which repeated education has failed to change.

(3) The material has been verified and the ideological source of the wrong found.

(4) After undergoing persuasion-education the worker who has committed the wrong has manifested a determination to change.

These conditions guarantee that the CC will attain good results and also guarantee that its judgments can be executed. Therefore, this must be done not only in our experimental work but also in regular work. For example, one trial target selected by the judicial work group was Liu Tung-hsing, a worker from site number 7643. He was of poor peasant origin and had worked in K'ai-luan for fifteen years. In the past he had led a completely degenerate life. There was nothing that he had not done. After liberation, he continued to be habitually absent from work without cause. What with the accompanying difficulty in earning a livelihood, at forty-five he was still unable to find a wife. From July of last year, when he was transferred to site number 7643, until the end of

September he worked only twelve days out of eighty-four. He was absent without cause sixty-six days, and he frequently did not take part in meetings of the workers' small group. The union viewed him as "deadwood" whom repeated education had failed to change, and the workers looked upon him as an example of one who loved to eat but was too lazy to work. His own view was that, since he had no family, it made no difference whether he went to work or not. Once he remarked: "If I got married, I would not be absent from work." But nobody was willing to marry this person "without any future." After the judicial work group, the union, and the CC understood this situation, they held a discussion meeting with his older brother and his neighbors to study the reason for his absenteeism and ways of helping him. Afterwards they also talked with him several times, using the facts to explain repeatedly the different positions of the worker class in the new and the old societies and the harm that laziness does to the state and to the individual. They also pointed out to him the brilliant road that he could take. His brother and his neighbors also helped to persuade him. He was deeply moved and despised what he had done in the past. He resolved to be a conscientious worker for production. In order effectively to consolidate his resolution, the judicial work group mobilized him to prepare to make a self-examination before the CC and to make out a plan for his repentance and reform. During this mobilization, they explained that he would not be subject to the kind of struggle with which reactionaries are treated; nor would he be sent to court. They only demanded that he conscientiously correct his wrongdoing.

After having properly selected a trial target, the judicial work group submitted his [Liu's] materials and its recommendation regarding sanctions for the approval of the Party and government leadership organs of the mine and the city. It also helped the CC to formulate a written judgment and completed other preparatory work.

In November and December of last year the T'ang-shan mine held full meetings of the CC on three occasions, always using the activity period preceding or following the work of the unit's staff and workers. Besides trying Liu Tung-hsing, these three meetings also tried worker Yang Ch'ing-yin of mine site number 7532, who was a habitual absentee, worker Sun Kuo-t'ang of the same site who violated labor discipline and did not respect the leadership, and an apprentice of the mechanical-electrical department, T'ien Hui-lin, who consistently committed serious violations of operating rules. Participating in these full meetings were all of the staff and workers of the unit in which the CC was located, and from other units there were cadres from the unions, some of the activists among the staff and workers, and backward elements. When the first meeting of the CC was held, the following people were also invited to participate: responsible comrades from the mine's Party, government, union, and Youth League organizations, and responsible comrades from the city people's court, the city labor bureau, the city procuracy, and other organs. Afterwards, when the mechanical-electrical department held the same sort of meeting, they also invited the family of the worker on trial and families of some other workers to attend. The procedure of the meeting was: the union chairman gave a report about the significance of establishing the CC; the chairman of the CC made known the facts about the wrongdoing of the worker on trial; the worker on trial made a self-examination; the masses of staff and workers at the meeting voiced their objections to the worker on trial; the worker on trial expressed his willingness to accept education and formulated a plan for his correction; the order or judgment of the CC was announced; the official responsible for administration of the mine accepted the proposal of the CC regarding sanctions for the worker on trial (of the four people tried, one made a self-examination, two received demerits, and one was removed from his position); the responsible people from the Party and the union made speeches; and the workers who attended the meeting spoke up freely.

All of the three meetings of the CC were conducted in a solemn and earnest atmosphere. Consequently, the person on trial submitted wholeheartedly. This showed the great strength of correctional education of a mass nature. For example, one of the persons on trial, Sun Kuo-t'ang, used to bear a heavy burden — he was afraid of a large struggle meeting or of being sent to court. But when he participated in the first meeting, at which Yang Ch'ing-yin was tried, he saw the sincere attitude of all the staff and workers, and, therefore, he relaxed. Right then and there he wanted to go up on the platform and make a self-examination. He later said: "That meeting was really well-conducted. People are all a little careless. If I could often be educated in this way, it could help me to correct my wrongdoing." Pai Pao-huai, a worker from coal-mining district number 91 said: "This meeting was very helpful to us. In the past we went to political classes and carried out the system for managing mine workers. Although this had a certain effectiveness, there were still some people who passively or openly resisted. Now that we have the CC, we can resolve this problem." Many family dependents said they would tell their husbands and sons to work conscientiously and not to violate labor discipline. The convening of the CC also made a deep impression upon the cadres.

### 5. Consolidating the Results of Adjudication Work

Consolidating labor discipline is a long-term job. It is unrealistic to think that after one meeting of the CC there will be no violation of labor discipline or that backward workers who are tried by the court will have changed completely. Therefore, the CC must frequently conduct propaganda-education among the staff and workers and consolidate the accomplishments already achieved. This is just as important as the session of ideological work to which workers are exposed prior to their trial by the CC. The work group has helped the members of the CC clearly to understand that their future duties are:

(1) To prepare the convening of meetings of the CC, and after the meetings to continue to educate the persons tried;

(2) Constantly to propagandize the staff and workers about the general line, production plans, safety rules, operating rules, labor discipline, and other policies, laws, and decrees concerning production;

(3) To educate those staff members and workers who are habitually ab-

sent from work, who arrive late, leave early, and who become involved in disputes;

(4) To prevent fights and corruption, theft and other criminal acts among the staff and workers and promptly give them persuasion-education. According to the report of the two CC's of mining district number 72, in the thirty-four days from November 21 to December 24 of last year, in addition to their job of consolidating the accomplishments of adjudication, they also discovered fifty-two problems. Among them there were seventeen cases of absenteeism without cause, five cases of violation of safety rules, nine cases of violation of operating rules, eleven cases of lack of activism in production, and nine cases of stirring up disputes. All but five or six of these cases have already been resolved.

In consolidating the results of adjudication, the two CC's assigned special persons to continue educating the targets who had already been tried, to encourage their progress, to resolve their difficulties, and severely to criticize repetition of their wrongs. The results have all been very good. Liu Tung-hsing in the past three months actually had a record of 100 percent attendance at work, regularly participated in meetings of his small group, and his attitude toward production and study has been very good. Others of the handful of workers who have been tried have also made excellent progress. In addition, the CC is also conducting propaganda about implementing safety and operating rules and, in order to consolidate the percentage of workers reporting for work, using persuasion-education on those who were absent without cause.

1. Is the comrades' court confined to considering cases of labor discipline and industrial accidents?

2. Do the critical procedures of the comrades' court take place during the hearing or during the preparatory stages? What purposes are served by the hearing?

3. How does a meeting of the comrades' court differ from criticism by the small group? What does the author mean when he says that the comrades' court's judgments are compulsory and must be obeyed"?

4. How does a meeting of the comrades' court differ from "the kind of struggle with which reactionaries are treated"?

5. Is the comrades' court persuasive or coercive? Note that in the Soviet Union a comrades' court may "impose a fine of up to ten rubles if the offense is not connected with a violation of labor discipline," [34] "and a fine up to 30 rubles in cases of petty stealing, [and] up to 50 rubles for repeated petty stealing." [35]

6. Need the comrades' court have been Soviet-inspired? Is it consistent with Chinese tradition?

7. Should the comrades' court be viewed as a useful means of gradually accustoming the masses to legal forms and of permitting the masses to participate in the administration of justice? Or should it be deemed a dangerous distortion of legal forms that causes the masses to associate "law" with an institution that lacks the safeguards of due process procedures?

8. To what may the comrades' court be analogized in our own system?

34. 1961 RSFSR Statute on Comrades' Courts, art. 15(5), *Vedomosti Verkhovnovo Soveta RSFSR* (Gazette of the Supreme Soviet of the RSFSR), 26:401; translated in *CDSP*, 13.33:9 (Sept. 13, 1961).

35. 1965 Amendment to RSFSR Statute on Comrades' Courts, art. 15(5), *Vedomosti Verkhovnovo Soveta RSFSR* (Gazette of the Supreme Soviet of the RSFSR), 4:81. [The editor is grateful to Prof. H. J. Berman for this translation.]

## ITEM 38

Despite the extraordinary accomplishments that were claimed for the experiments with comrades' courts, which all took place in north China, they do not appear to have been put into use on a widespread basis. Virtually no mention has been made of them in the press since the end of 1955, although Soviet publications suggest that they were still in use as of 1957. Most interviews failed to yield evidence of their continued existence, although it should be noted that a majority of the persons interviewed came from south China. However, a former Party official who, prior to his departure from the mainland, had been assigned to an important Tientsin factory was familiar with the term "comrades' court," although he emphasized that it was seldom heard in recent years. He gave the following account of a session that he had witnessed in January 1961.

[Interview]

Just as they were coming off their shift, the workers of a workshop in a large underwear factory in Tientsin were called to a meeting that was convened in the factory auditorium. An overhead banner revealed that this was to be a meeting of a comrades' court [CC]. Seated at one half of a long table on the stage were the chairman, vice-chairman, and five members of the comrades' court. A few of them were members of the Party or Youth League; the others were activists, "old workers," or labor models. They had been elected by the factory workers' congress for a one-year term. Seated next to them as "observers" at the other half of the table were a member of the factory Party committee, the head of the factory union, a staff member of the factory security defense section, and a representative of the basic level people's court. A clerk sat next to the end of the table at which the CC was seated. A secretary was seated near the front of the stage but to one side. The "target," a worker named Li, stood in front of the table.

The CC chairman opened the meeting by introducing the purpose of a CC, which, he explained, was an experiment to help backward elements reform their thinking and become good persons. He then recited Li's background and history and his bad conduct. Li, he said, was a historical counterrevolutionary who had belonged to a secret society prior to liberation. After liberation he had been sentenced to a three-year term of "control" [see Chapter V], which the government had terminated out of leniency at the end of two years. Yet in the past few years Li had not behaved well. He did poor work and often turned out goods that were too inferior to be acceptable. There had been a number of incidents involving damage to machines on which he had worked. Recently his cotton spinning machine had caught fire because he had left it running at high speed while he took a nap in the men's room. All of this showed how damaging his conduct was to production. Therefore, the chairman urged, all of Li's co-workers should subject him to severe criticism, adopt the attitude of the workers being master, and help him to reform.

Li then read a prepared statement of "self-examination" in which he detailed his earlier crimes, the Party's leniency, his failure to reform, and his recent misconduct. He emphasized that he needed the help of his comrades and would seriously consider all the criticism that they offered, because he was now determined to reform.

The clerk then rose and invited "the first representative of Li's work group" to come up to the stage and state his views. He was the leader of the group, and the speech that he read itemized the losses that Li's misconduct had caused production. Four or five other members of Li's group then followed in succession with similar statements. Several of them said that Li's self-examination had not been profound or complete and that he should confess more fully, and they all criticized him severely.

At this point the vice-chairman of the CC rose and read a document that summarized Li's misconduct and that concluded with the CC's decision. It consisted of a recommendation that the factory administration give Li a large demerit and a recommendation that the basic level people's court sentence him to "control." The meeting then adjourned.

Under the enthusiastic patronage of Premier Khrushchev, comrades' courts enjoyed a great vogue in the Soviet Union during the 1959–1964 period. What reasons might there be for their failure to play an important role in China? One possible explanation of the fate of the Chinese comrades' courts is that they have generally disappeared in name, but have actually been merged into the self-examination meetings that prevail throughout the country.

### 2. Adjustment Committees and the Socialist Patriotic Pact

More recent and widespread experiments have been conducted with the "socialist patriotic pact" and "adjustment committees."

The socialist patriotic pact is said to have first appeared in the Communist guerrilla bases during the Anti-Japanese War. It came to prominence in 1950–1951 as part of the "resist America and aid Korea" movement. The contents of the slogans of these pacts, which were signed by individuals, families, residential units, and work units, reflected the needs of that era for political, economic, and social mobilization. The pact was regarded as a technique of mass exhortation rather than as an enforceable legal instrument. Press reports suggest that it fell into disuse in 1952 following a series of unsuccessful efforts to devise some method of making the masses treat it as more than a document to be signed and forgotten.

The socialist patriotic pact was revived in the course of the antirightist movement in the latter half of 1957, when the Party was moving to reorganize and perfect the sanctioning system. This time, however, in some areas adjustment committees were created to assure its enforcement. The adjustment committee is said to be the successor to the mediation committee. It is supposed to play a broader role than its predecessor institution, being able not only to mediate disputes that involve minor criminal offenses, but also to "deal with" or "handle," that is, to decide, such cases and other instances of relatively minor antisocial conduct.

The extent to which the pact and the adjustment committee have actually been put into effect is unclear. Law review articles, speeches by officials, and annual court reports indicate that experiments with them have taken place throughout China and that, at least during the period 1957–1961, they were widely used in many provinces and cities. On the other hand, most interviews suggested that this recent patriotic pact movement was taken no more seriously than the earlier one and that, while the mediation committee had changed its name in certain areas, it had not actually enlarged its functions. Yet a public security officer from a southeastern province described the adjustment committee in his county as an effective and important instrument of social control. In the absence of a larger interviewing sample, one can do no better than to conclude, tentatively, that the impact of the adjustment committee has probably been greater than that of the comrades' court but less than that of those institutions, like the mediation committee, that are plainly operating on a nationwide basis.

## ITEM 39

This excerpt from the famous report by Teng Hsiao-p'ing, General Secretary of the Chinese Communist Party Central Committee, appears to have spawned the adjustment committee and the revival of the patriotic pact.

[Teng Hsiao-p'ing (General Secretary of the CCPCC), "Report Relating to the Rectification Movement" (at the 3d enlarged plenary meeting of the 8th session of the CCPCC, Sept. 23, 1957), *FKHP*, 6:17–18]

.    .    .    .    .

In rural villages in all places there are some delinquent elements who "do not break major laws but who often break minor laws." It is too much trouble for these people to be dealt with by the local courts, but if they are not dealt with, there is a great deal of interference with production order and social order. Consideration may be given to restraining these people by means of genuinely enforceable pacts concluded by congresses of members of cooperatives or by people's congresses of administrative villages, with the approval of the government of the next higher level, and also to establishing adjustment committees to be responsible for the execution of the pacts. Cooperatives or administrative village governments may be authorized to give appropriate punishment to those who violate these pacts. This is a measure for mass self-education, self-supervision, and self-restraint. It is an important method by which socialist society limits individualism and changes old customs and habits and forms new ones. It may be put into effect on an experimental basis not only in rural villages but also in cities, factories, mines, organs, and schools.

## ITEM 40

The following account, published in the first stage of the "great leap forward," describes one of the early experiments in implementing the proposal of Teng Hsiao-p'ing.

["A New Form of Self-Government by the Masses" (a report of an inspection team of the political-legal department of the Shensi provincial government), *Shan-hsi jih-pao* (Shensi daily), May 8, 1958, in *Chung-kuo kuo-fang ts'ung-shu* (Collection of reprinted articles concerning China's national defense; Peking, 1958), 2:80–85]

After the administrative village of Kuan-ti in P'ing-yao county underwent the national rectification movement, concluded "the pact of three loves," and established an adjustment committee, the enthusiasm of the cadres and the masses grew great and they came to love the Party and socialism more than ever. Politically, the entire administrative village took on a brand new appearance. "The pact of three loves" has already become the norm for the conduct of the masses of the entire administrative village. It has put into concrete form what we should advocate and what we should oppose. Owing to the fact that the members of the cooperative have consciously linked together the interests of the state, the collective, and the individual, we hear everywhere the sounds of a great army leaping forward in production. This is a vivid and concrete legal and political education for every person who comes to inspect this place.

### It is the Continuation and Development of the Rectification Movement

In February of this year the chief procurator of the people's procuracy of P'ing-yao county, Sun Pang-chin, with the active support of the county Party committee, led a four-man work group to the administrative village of Kuan-ti. At that time, just as the national rectification movement entered its final stage, they had already begun the period of education for rectifying the Party, the Youth League, and the cooperatives, for conducting the election of the cadres of the cooperatives, and for summarizing and evaluating experiences. The political and ideological consciousness of the masses had been raised to a new high; the energy of the cadres had also increased. The work group unanimously held that this was a good opportunity to establish on an experimental basis "the pact of three loves" and the adjustment committees. So, first of all, in inquiring about the [local] situation, they repeatedly explained the purpose of their visit to the Party and government leaders in the administrative village. Then, under the leadership of the administrative village Party general branch, they called a meeting of the cadres of the administrative village and the cooperatives and the members of the work group. They set forth and explained the goals, the significance, and the methods of concluding the socialist "pact of three loves" and establishing the adjustment committee. At the same time, they questioned the comrades who were at the meeting about the [local] situation. They discovered that in the entire administrative village there were forty-eight persons engaged in minor speculating activities, thirty-two petty thieves, twenty-four persons who were lazy, who were loafers, or who would not engage in labor and production, four persons who mistreated others, thirty-six persons who gambled, fifteen persons who were constantly fighting, and forty-seven persons who did not respect public property and who damaged the public interest in order to benefit themselves. In all there were 206 such persons, representing 3.29 percent of the entire population of the administrative village. The masses were very much dissatisfied with them and called them troublemakers, shirkers, and stumbling blocks to the great leap forward in production. After going through preparation and discussion, the cadres of the administrative village and the cooperatives unanimously agreed to conclude "the pact of three loves" and to establish adjustment committees. The deputy chief of the administrative village, Sung Huai-chieh, said: "In the past, those who did not break major laws but who often broke minor laws simply turned the administrative village upside down. Even though the administrative village secretary devoted full time to dealing with the problems they created, he could not deal with them all. With 'the pact of three loves,' they no longer dare to create havoc."

### Propagandizing, Educating, and Rousing the Masses

There were a number of mass meetings of the cadres of the administrative village and the cooperatives with the working group; these emphasized propagandizing the masses for a situation where there would be a dramatic, comprehensive leap forward. Yet there still existed some delinquent elements who did not break major laws but who often broke minor laws. They did not labor for production and they did not observe the policies, laws, or decrees of the state; they interfered with public order and undermined labor discipline. Thus, if we were to build socialism, we had to have the masses consciously adopt "the pact of three loves" in order to supervise and to restrain these people. After the propaganda, the masses understood that adoption of "the pact of three loves" was a continuation and development of the national rectification movement and was a good means of consolidating the results of the rectification movement. Some people said: "The pact is the concentrated expression of the will of the masses. It tells us what to advocate and what to praise, what to oppose and what to prohibit." Amidst a great deal of propaganda, we also organized 210 high school and elementary school students to write eighty-five essays on blackboards and to do fifty-six radio broadcasts, and we very quickly carried out propaganda by striking the gong and beating the drum in the streets and lanes. We also carried our explanation to the masses on a door-to-door basis. We really acted so that everyone would understand and know about "the pact of three loves." Thus, adoption of the pact became an urgent demand of the masses.

### Adopting "the Pact of Three Loves" and
### Establishing the Adjustment Committees

The process of concretely preparing the contents of "the pact of three loves" came after the process of propagandizing, educating, and rousing the masses. After the masses finished their basic preparation, they then elected a committee to draft "the pact of three loves." The main contents of the pact as put forth by the masses were: love the nation, the cooperative and the home, advocate fervent love of socialism and of labor, respect for public property, observance of public order and of labor discipline, respect for socialist morality, etc. After completion of the draft, a mass meeting was convened in order to permit the masses fully to discuss the contents of "the pact of three loves," to present their opinions for completing and amending it, and to say whether or not they would be able to observe and execute it. During discussion by the masses of the village of West Wang-chin they made a proposal about that part of the draft pact that read, "In production, guarantee that tasks will be completed in terms of quantity and quality and on time, and oppose people who only care about how many labor points they earn and who do not care about quality." They said that this alone would not do, that the following had to be added: "When the quality is not high, we must do the job over; when crops are damaged, we must pay compensation for the damage." This made the pact even better and more enforceable. After the masses adopted "the pact of three loves," they sent it to the people's council of the administrative village for approval and for formal promulgation and execution. After adoption of "the pact of three loves," they began to set up the adjustment committees. The requirements for committee membership were: (1) political reliability and a pure record; (2) activism in work and conscientiousness in handling business; (3) impartiality, unselfishness, and freedom from corruption; (4) a correct demeanor and support by the masses. After the masses finished their discussion and the list of nominees for the committees was presented, a vote was conducted by a show of hands. Three, five, or seven members, depending on the size of the population of the natural village, were elected to the adjustment committees. An adjustment committee was also established for the administrative village at the same time. It was composed of the chiefs of the committees of the various cooperatives. The deputy chief of the administrative village assumed the responsibility of serving as chairman of this adjustment committee. This committee is under the direct leadership of the administrative village Party general branch and of the administrative village people's council, and the county political-legal departments are responsible for guiding it. Moreover, things are arranged so that the adjustment committee is in constant contact with the people's court of the county. After the creation of the adjustment committees of the administrative village and cooperatives, the system of meetings and of comprehensive reporting was promptly adopted; the tasks of the committees and the scope of their powers were determined; and the five provisions of labor discipline, the three provisions of the reward and punishment system, and the six provisions relating to those matters to which attention should be given were expressly prescribed. At the same time it was also prescribed that, with respect to those delinquent elements who had already been dealt with, files must be established in preparation for future examination.

## Restrain Delinquent Elements;
## Adjust Disputes Among the Masses

With respect to those delinquent elements who did not break major laws but who often broke minor ones, "the pact of three loves" actually played a supervising and restraining role. After establishment of the adjustment committee, based on the requests of the masses, every cooperative individually selected some typical cases to deal with. Depending on the differing problems and the degree of seriousness of the circumstances, in dealing with cases they adopted such methods as the large self-examination meeting, the written statement of repentance and the written guarantee, the giving of a warning or, in serious cases, the imposition of punishment that does not exceed one labor day or one yuan. The results of these methods were good, and their role was very great. For example, in the village of North Kuan-ti, two women, Chang Kuei-hua and Chao Pen-hua, were constantly mistreating their mothers-in-law, and the masses could no longer tolerate it. Based on the requests of the masses the adjustment committee called a women's meeting, tried to reason with the two women concerned, and exposed the facts of their mistreatment of their mothers-in-law. Finally, these two women admitted their error, and the adjustment committee let them write statements of repentance. Since then, relations between the mothers-in-law and their daughters-in-law have improved. There was a couple who did not get along with the wife's aunt and constantly quarreled and never called her "aunt." Recently, they took the initiative in self-examination and said to the aunt: "Let's resolve our family problems by ourselves and not wait for the adjustment committee to resolve them." Now relations are much better. The prosperous middle peasant, Sung Kuo-wu, also underwent self-examination and said: "When I joined the cooperative in 1956 I hid a wagon somewhere outside the cooperative. At that time I still thought of walking the capitalist road. Now I have come to recognize my error." The next day he brought the wagon in and gave it to the cooperative. Hou Sheng-cheng, a speculator, only put in about ten days of work in 1957. Since adoption of "the pact of three loves," he has already earned over 400 labor points.

The situation in the administrative village of Kuan-ti used to be confused. The sabotage activity of counterrevolutionary and other criminal elements occurred ceaselessly. Since the rectification movement, the adoption of "the pact of three loves," and the establishment of the adjustment committees, there has not been a single criminal case in the entire administrative village. Production conditions in the cooperatives have also been good. The public order situation has also been more peaceful than ever. The cadres of this administrative village say: "The rectification movement is the main cord of the net, the pact is the net. Now that we have this cord and this net, we can do all kinds of good things."

### Constantly Promote Production

Because "the pact of three loves" plays the role of educating the masses and of raising their socialist ideology, it has powerfully promoted the great leap forward in agricultural production. In the past, sparks used to fly from disturbances in the administrative village, in the cooperatives, and among the cadres; now the situation has been changed so that sparks fly from stimulating fertilizer production, water utilization, and land use. In the past, in production there were three "don't works" (don't work until the formal time of work arrives, don't work if all your coworkers have not shown up, don't work if you do not get many labor points for it). Now this situation has completely changed. Everyone is truly happy and smiling . . .

The facts of the situation at the administrative village of Kuan-ti prove that adoption of "the pact of three loves" and establishment of the adjustment committees have not only consolidated the results of rectification but have also prevented violations of law, reduced the number of disputes, and played an even more important role in guaranteeing a great leap forward in agricultural production.

1. How does the role of the Kuan-ti adjustment committee differ from that of the comrades' court? From that of the mediation committee? From that of the security defense committee? From that of the criticism or struggle meeting?

2. One of the devices designed to assure implementation of the patriotic pact is periodic inspection and evaluation by the adjustment committee. Note, for example, the following quotation from Hsieh Chia-lin et al.:

"The commune members say: 'The patriotic pact is our little Constitution. It's like a ruler. Once a month we measure ourselves against it and thus can see who is long and who is short, who good and who bad. Patriotic pact day is like a little rectification [movement]. It is like a public bath. If we bathe in it once a month, our bodies will not be dirty.' " [36]

3. To what extent should the patriotic pact be regarded as local legislation?

4. The claim has repeatedly been made that "[t]he people's adjustment work is the concrete application of Chairman Mao's theory [of how correctly to handle contradictions among the people]." [37]

To what extent might this concrete application reflect traditional Chinese practices? Together with the material from section A, subsection 1, consider the following:

a. "Each community [under the Ming dynasty, 1368–1644 A.D.] functioned in accordance with the so-called community agreement, a sort of constitution for local self-government prepared by the members in a pattern prescribed by imperial edict. This provided for the communal management of all local affairs and especially for the settling of disputes by the community chief; for the magistrates chastened communities that could not resolve their own intra-community litigations. The community agreement also included an exhortation to all citizens, first promulgated by the emperor T'ai-tsu, to be filial and obedient to their parents, to be respectful to their superiors, to be harmonious within the community, to educate their sons and brothers, to be content each in his lot, and not to do evil. The entire text of the agreement was read aloud at monthly community assemblies, and participants in the assemblies also recited an oath that they would preserve propriety and the law, would not permit coercion of the weak, would deal with lawlessness themselves within the community, would care for the poor, and would assist one another to bear the burdensome expenses of weddings and funerals." [38]

b. "Village order [during the nineteenth century] was maintained in a more positive way by formulating and enforcing *hsiang-kuei* (village regulations). According to the compiler of a modern gazetteer, the earlier editions of this gazetteer contained a section which recorded the rules and prohibitions calculated

36. "The Role of the Socialist Patriotic Pact," *CFYC*, 1:53 (1959).

37. Wang Min, "The Great Significance of People's Adjustment Work in Resolving Contradictions Among the People," *CFYC*, 2:27 (1960).

38. Charles O. Hucker, *The Traditional Chinese State in Ming Times (1368–1644)* (Tucson, 1961), p. 26.

to promote the welfare of the community. These rules were formulated by the gentry and commoners of the rural areas and approved by the local official. Another local historian recorded a case in which a wealthy merchant of Tu-hsing village (in Hua Hsien, Kwangtung, population about 1,200 persons), who had purchased a fifth-rank official title, 'brought together a number of rural gentry and drew up a set of *Hsiang-kuei* for the guidance of all.'

"The effectiveness of village regulations depended much upon the quality of the persons who enforced them. It was said that when Hung Hsiu-ch'üan, the Taiping leader, lived in his home village in the 1830's, he set up five rules for his fellow villagers to follow. He promised flogging to anyone who committed adultery, seduced women, proved himself undutiful to parents, indulged in gambling, or loafed and 'did evil.' He wrote these rules on wooden tablets and distributed copies of them to heads of families. His commandments were so greatly respected by the villagers that two persons who committed adultery fled from the village for fear of his punishment. In another rural community in South China, a *chü-jen* scholar (a contemporary of Hung Hsiu-ch'üan) succeeded in 'purifying the morals' of his community by forbidding all wrongdoing. He enforced the prohibition against gambling so thoroughly that 'no gamester dared to gratify his desires.' " [39]

## ITEM 41

In those areas in which adjustment committees have functioned there appears to have been some uncertainty over their relationship to the security defense committees. In some of these areas the two committees have merged into "security adjustment committees." In others, *de facto* working relations have developed, as is suggested below.

[Wang Kuang-li (President of the High Court of Honan), "How Judicial Work in Honan Province Serves the Central Work," *CFYC*, 6:46, 49–50, 51 (1958)]

The adjustment work which intimately links judicial work with the masses has been considerably strengthened in recent years. According to incomplete statistics, in the entire province there are 8,081 adjustment committees, the members of which are all chosen by election. Their prestige among the masses is very high, and they are trusted by the masses.

Adjustment work has been broadly developed with respect to civil disputes and minor unlawful acts that occur among the people. The personnel of the [people's] tribunals principally assist the adjustment committees in penetrating the masses and investigating things in detail; grasping the thinking of the parties; transmitting policies, laws, and decrees; smashing anxieties; separately conducting, depending on the different targets, collectivist education, education on the glory of labor and the superiority of the commune system; further convening informal discussion meetings of relevant personnel; adopting the method of one key to open one lock; and resolving contradictions through precise calculation of accounts, separation of right from wrong, and clearing up thinking. The concluding of patriotic pacts and the presenting of guarantees by both parties

39. K. C. Hsiao, pp. 292–293.

strengthen unity and mutual help and attain the goal of thoroughly eliminating differences of opinions and disputes. Some cases of unlawful acts reach resolution through joint study and handling by members of the adjustment committee and security defense personnel.

. . . Contradictions among the people differ in content and undergo changes over time. In order correctly to handle contradictions there must be self-education by the masses. Internal causes play a decisive role in changes in all things. Thus, we must work through the forms of great blooming and contending and great debate to heighten the awareness of the masses, to use the advanced to bring along the backward, and to censure words and deeds that are not advantageous to unity or to production. In handling disputes among the people, minor unlawful acts and acts that violate commune regulations or patriotic pacts, we must make full use of the organizational function of the adjustment and security defense committees.

## ITEM 42

Although revival of the patriotic pact antedated both the "great leap forward" of early 1958 and the nationwide movement to establish people's communes that was launched in August of that year, its development was intimately related to these phenomena. Mid-1958 was a time of frenzied enthusiasm, when China's leaders prophesied the imminence of the country's "transition to communism." As an article from the *People's Daily* stated:

"[W]e are living in beautiful surroundings in a countryside where buds of communism are sprouting everywhere . . . China is moving forward at the speed of space flight. Not long ago, peasants in their fifties were worried that they might not last long enough to see the good days of communism. Now even octogenarians and nonagenarians firmly believe that they will enjoy the happiness of communism." [40]

This item indicates that in the legal field the patriotic pact, as enforced by the adjustment committee, was cited as a major basis for this euphoria.

[Hsieh Chia-lin et al., "The Role of the Socialist Patriotic Pact" *CFYC*, 1:53 (1959)]

·    ·    ·    ·    ·

Under the direct leadership of the local Party committee and under the leadership and guidance of the basic level government, the patriotic pact is, through mass organizations, directly adopted by the people in accordance with their own will. Persuasion-education, moral condemnation, and the coercive power of public opinion and the mass organizations of the people are used to guarantee that it is executed, to resolve contradictions among the people and to adjust the rules of conduct for relations between people. Some of the characteristics of the adoption and execution of the patriotic pact are the same as those of the rules of Communist behavior. This is because the rules of Communist

40. *JMJP*, Aug. 6, 1958; translated in Robert R. Bowie and John K. Fairbank, ed., *Communist China 1955–1959, Policy Documents with Analysis* (Cambridge, Mass., 1962), p. 23.

behavior are the concentrated manifestation of the will of all the people in Communist society; are directly adopted by the masses of people themselves, using democratic methods and organizations for the administration of society and production; and are established on the basis of self-awareness and voluntarism, using persuasion-education, Communist moral condemnation, and the coercive power of public opinion and of the organizations for the administration of society and production to guarantee their execution. It is precisely because of these characteristics that we have decided that the patriotic pact is the bud of the rules of Communist behavior.

1. Are the sanctions for enforcing the pact that are referred to in Item 42 the same as those mentioned in Items 39 and 40? What might account for the difference?

2. Recall Premier Khrushchev's proposal of January 28, 1959, for the progressive transfer to social organizations of the responsibility for imposing sanctions for minor violations of law and morality (Item 10). Might there be a connection between it and the extravagant claims and apocalyptic visions emanating from Peking during the six preceding months?

3. A more sober appraisal by the Chinese leadership in 1959 of the time required for the country to reach the stage of the transition to communism did not dampen the ardor of legal workers for "adjustment work of a mass nature." For example, in 1960 a report on the work of the high court of Honan province called it "the fundamental path toward rule by the people," [41] and an article in *Political-Legal Research* predicted that it would be needed "for a long period in the future" and "even in Communist society." [42]

### 3. Party and Youth League Disciplinary Procedures

We have seen that the Party and the Youth League permeate every sphere of Chinese life and play an important role in informal adjustment and sanctioning among the masses, both through the direct action of their members and through their leadership of other participants in the political-legal apparatus. In this subsection we shall briefly consider the role of the Party and Youth League in adjusting disputes that arise among their members and in disciplining their members.

The more than 17 million members of the Party and 25 million members of the League obviously constitute an elite that exercises effective power over a society of over 700 million people. In recent years membership in one of these organizations has generally been indispensable to the ambitious individual's maximization of his career potential. His expulsion from the Party or CYL is thus a severe sanction, and even lesser disciplinary measures may permanently halt his upward rise. Thus, Party and CYL members often regard the sanctions imposed by their organizations as harsher than some types of criminal punishment.

The following items, which because of space limitations deal only with the Party (similar material exists concerning the CYL), suggest the range of such sanctions, the kinds of conduct for which they can be imposed, and the methods of imposing

41. Wang Kuang-li, "Report on High Level Court Work in Honan Province, Communist China," *Hou-nan jih-pao* (Honan daily), March 1, 1960; translated in *JPRS*, 6082:1 (Oct. 13, 1960).
42. Wang Min, p. 29.

them. The materials beginning with Chapter III will provide a considerable amount of additional information.

## ITEM 43

Recall Item 16, especially Articles 2 and 3 of the Party Constitution, which should be read in conjunction with the following provisions of that Constitution.

[CONSTITUTION OF THE CCP (Sept. 26, 1956), pp. 50–52, 54–55]

*General Program*

. . . . .

No political party or person can be free from shortcomings and errors in its activities. The Chinese Communist Party and its members must constantly practice criticism and self-criticism to expose and eliminate their shortcomings and errors so as to educate themselves and the people. In view of the fact that the Party plays the leading role in the life of the state and society, it is even more necessary that the Party should make stringent demands on every Party organization and member and promote criticism and self-criticism; and, in particular, it should encourage and support criticism from the bottom up inside the Party as well as criticism of the Party by the masses of people, and should prohibit any suppression of criticism. The Party must prevent and resist corrosion by the ideological demeanor of the bourgeoisie and petty bourgeoisie and guard against and defeat any rightist or "leftist" opportunist deviation inside the Party. As for Party members who commit errors, the Party should adopt the guideline of "treating the illness in order to save the patient" and allow them to remain in the Party and be given education to help them to correct their errors, provided such errors can be corrected within the Party and the erring Party member himself is prepared to correct his errors. As for those who persist in their errors and engage in activities that endanger the Party, a determined struggle must be waged against them even to the point of expelling them from the Party.

Article 13. Party organizations of the various levels may, according to concrete circumstances, individually give any Party member who violates Party discipline such sanctions as warning, serious warning, removal from Party office, probation within the Party, or expulsion from the Party.

The period for which a Party member is placed on probation shall not exceed two years. During this period, the rights and responsibilities of the Party member concerned shall be the same as those of a candidate member. If, after a Party member has been placed on probation, the facts prove that he has corrected his errors, his rights as a Party member shall be restored, and the period in which he was placed on probation shall be included in [totaling] the years he has been with the Party. If he is considered to be unfit to be a Party member, he shall be expelled from the Party.

Article 14. Disciplinary sanctions given to Party members must be decided upon by the Party branch to which they belong at a general membership meeting and then must be approved by a higher level Party supervision commission or by a higher level Party committee.

In special situations, a Party branch committee or a higher level Party committee has the authority to give disciplinary sanctions to Party members, but such sanctions must first be approved by a higher level Party supervision commission or by a higher level Party committee.

Article 17. Expulsion from the Party is the most severe sanction within the Party. In deciding upon or approving the expulsion of a Party member from the Party, Party organizations of the various levels shall maintain the utmost care, shall conscientiously examine and study the relevant facts and material and shall listen carefully to the petition for review of the member concerned.

Article 18. When a Party organization discusses or decides upon a sanction against a Party member, it shall, except in special situations, notify the member concerned to attend the meeting to conduct his defense. After passing a resolution to discipline, the member concerned shall be notified of the reasons for it. If the Party member does not accept the sanction, he may request reconsideration and may petition higher level Party committees and Party supervision commissions, up to and including the Central Committee, for review. Party organizations of the various levels shall be responsible for handling the written petition for review of any Party member or for forwarding it promptly; no suppression shall be permitted.

Article 52. The Party's Central Committee; the Party committees of the provinces, autonomous regions, cities directly under the central authority, and autonomous *chou;* and the committees of the counties, autonomous counties, and cities shall establish supervision commissions. The central supervision commission shall be elected by the Central Committee of the Party at a plenary meeting. Local supervision commissions shall be elected by Party committees of the corresponding levels at plenary meetings, subject to approval by the next higher Party committees.

Article 53. The tasks of the central and local supervision commissions shall be as follows: regularly to examine and handle cases of violation by Party members of the Party Constitution, Party discipline, Communist morality, and state laws and decrees; to decide upon or annul disciplinary sanctions against Party members; and to handle accusations and petitions of Party members.

Article 54. The supervision commissions of the various levels shall conduct their work under the leadership of the Party committees at corresponding levels.

Higher level supervision commissions shall have the authority to examine the work of lower level supervision commissions and to approve or modify their decisions on any case. Lower level supervision commissions shall report on their work to higher level supervision commissions and shall present accurate reports on the violation of discipline by Party members.

## ITEM 44

The disciplinary measures listed in Article 13 of the Party Constitution are not the only sanctions imposed upon transgressing Party members. "Criticism-education," authorized by the General Program and the last paragraph of Article 2 (Item 16), is, of course, the most common and mildest sanction. Recall Item 32, which is as applicable to Party criticism meetings as to others. Being required to make a "self-examination" or "self-denunciation" before one's Party unit is a more severe sanction than ordinary self-criticism, since it involves a greater degree of self-humiliation before one's peers and more intensive criticism by them. It is frequently imposed in situations in which ordinary criticism has proved to be ineffective. The following account suggests such a typical situation.

["He Should Be Punitively Restrained by Law," *JMJP,* July 18, 1956, p. 4]

Comrade Editor:

I am a soldier on active duty. I now want to make an accusation to you about the unlawful conduct of Hu Ching-chou, an officer of the public security department of Chekiang province, who undermined the marriage of a revolutionary soldier.

In October 1954 my wife, Tuan Cheng, was transferred from her job in the armed forces to work in the public relations office of the city of Shen-yang [Mukden]. At that time Hu Ching-chou, who was a cadre in the International Travel Agency in Peking, was also transferred to the same office. During the time that the two worked together, although Hu clearly knew that my wife was married, he nevertheless illicitly fell in "love" with her. Later Hu was transferred to the public security department of Chekiang province, but he still continued to write letters to my wife. In October 1955, even more shamelessly than ever, he proposed a love affair to my wife. In November I completed my studies at a military school, was assigned to work in Shen-yang, and discovered their illicit relationship. I reported the matter to the organization, and through the organization they were separately given persuasion-education. According to reason, Hu Ching-chou should have thoroughly reformed and severed his relations with my wife. Yet, on the contrary, he intensified his advances toward my wife and even tried to coerce her to divorce me. Even more intolerable was the fact that on the Chinese New Year of 1956, after I had returned from the public relations office to my military unit, Hu Ching-chou took a plane from Hangchow to Shen-yang and lived with my wife in a hotel for two days. It was only when the organization discovered them on the third day that he was compelled to return to Chekiang. After this the Party organization within the public relations office undertook to educate and deal with my wife (she was a member of the Communist Party). She also had to make a self-examination before a meeting of all the members of the [Party] branch, and she indicated that she was determined to improve relations with me. Nevertheless, Hu Ching-chou continued his involvement with her and would not let her alone. He secretly incited her to divorce me.

Hu Ching-chou is a cadre of a state organ. Yet he knowingly broke the law. He should be punitively restrained by law.

Hsü Yüan-i

## ITEM 45

This item illustrates one type of situation in which the Party imposes severe sanctions upon its members. It should be noted that expulsion from the Party may or may not be accompanied by the application of criminal sanctions but that the application of criminal sanctions must always be preceded by expulsion from the Party, as we shall subsequently see in some detail.

["Party's Supervision Organs Dispose of Cases of Party Members Violating Party Discipline in Grain Collection," *Chi-lin jih-pao* (Kirin daily, Changchun), Feb. 28, 1958]

Supervision commissions of the Party in the various areas have disposed of cases involving members violating Party discipline in the grain collection and have, by means of the facts brought out, given the Party membership a vivid education in discipline.

In the course of the collection, the majority of Party members have set good examples in mobilizing the masses to overcome difficulties, implementing the collection policy, and consummating the grain mission. But there have been a number of Party members who have failed to observe Party discipline and violated the grain policy. For example, secretary Li Fen-hsien of the Party branch for the thirty-third production team in the administrative village of Li-hsia in Pai-cheng county did not participate in the branch's meeting on the grain work but went to call on a rich peasant to study methods to conceal production. When a work team went among the masses to urge sales of grains, he went there later to deceive them. When it called on the families of several of the cooperative members to suggest sales of grains, he went there later to criticize the idea. Candidate Party member Chi Wan-chi obtained by fraud the grain tickets of three peasant households and made a profit of fifty-five yuan on transactions in 4000 catties of grains, seriously obstructing smooth progress of the collection policy. The Party branches concerned have dealt with cases of this nature, and some of the members involved have been expelled.

In dealing with such cases, the various areas have exercised strict care and have made different decisions appropriate to the cases at hand. These decisions have not only educated Party members and strengthened the fighting power of the Party organs but have also raised the political consciousness of the masses and have attacked spontaneous capitalism in rural areas and the activities of unlawful elements, thereby consolidating cooperativization, making more intimate the links between the Party and the masses, and strengthening supervision over Party members.

From some of the cases, we can see that the struggle between the capitalist and socialist roads in the countryside is bound to reflect itself within the Party. For this reason, we must strengthen the supervision of the Party and the masses over its members and step up education in political ideology and Party discipline. Dealing with cases involving Party members who violate the grain policy is one of the effective measures to strengthen political education.

### 4. Disciplinary Procedures for Government and Factory Employees

The reader will recall that the shameless lovers of Item 44 worked together in the Mukden public relations office and that, when the cuckolded husband discovered their affair, he "reported the matter to . . . [their] organization, and through the organization they were separately given persuasion-education." Informal intervention by this government unit failed to end their illicit relationship and, since the offending wife was a Party member, the Party organization within the government unit dealt with her. We are not told whether or what action was taken against her lover. But it is clear that, in addition to being subject to the "punitive restraints" for which the husband called, as a government officer he was also subject to a variety of disciplinary sanctions that were more severe than the informal criticism that had proved to be ineffective. To the millions of government cadres (their number is uncertain) the harshest of these sanctions — expulsion, that is, being "fired" from the government — is far more severe than some types of criminal punishment, for it is tantamount to being relegated permanently to the status of the ordinary laborer, peasant, or peddler. One has to understand not only Chinese economic conditions but also Chinese society to appreciate the extent to which many government officials are appalled at the prospect of a lifetime of manual labor.

The materials that follow indicate the range of government disciplinary sanctions, the kinds of conduct for which they can be imposed, and the procedures for imposing them. Technically, most of these sanctions are not "informal." They are neither applied informally, nor are they administered by a nongovernmental agency. Yet, like other sanctions discussed in this chapter, they are often applied in lieu of, or together with, the sanctions that will be studied in subsequent chapters.

It should also be noted, as the materials on comrades' courts (section C, subsection 1) suggest, that factory workers are subject to a similar set of disciplinary sanctions, which are imposed by factory administration.

## ITEM 46

[PROVISIONAL REGULATIONS OF THE STATE COUNCIL OF THE PRC RELATING TO REWARDS AND PUNISHMENTS FOR PERSONNEL OF STATE ADMINISTRATIVE ORGANS (approved at the 82d meeting of the Standing Committee of the NPC, Oct. 23, 1957; promulgated by the State Council, Oct. 26, 1957), *FKHP*, 6:198–202]

5. Personnel of state administrative organs who violate the law and are derelict in their duties by [committing] the following acts that do not constitute crimes, shall be given disciplinary sanctions. If the circumstances of the case are minor, after undergoing criticism-education, they may also be exempted from sanctions.

(1) Violating policies, laws, or decrees of the state and resolutions, orders, rules, or systems of the government;

(2) Making light of their duties and causing delay in their work;

(3) Violating democratic centralism, disobeying resolutions and orders of higher levels, suppressing criticism, or attacking in retaliation;

(4) Being deceitful and cheating their organization;

(5) Stirring up dissension and destroying unity;

(6) Losing their standpoint and concealing bad persons;

(7) Corruptly stealing state property;

(8) Wasting state assets and damaging public property;

(9) Misusing their powers, infringing the interests of the masses of people, and damaging relations between state organs and the masses of people;

(10) Divulging state secrets;

(11)  Being rotten and decadent, and damaging the prestige of state organs;

(12)  [Engaging in] other acts that violate state discipline.

6. Disciplinary sanctions shall be divided into eight categories: warning, demerit, large demerit, demotion in grade, demotion in office, removal from office, probationary expulsion, and expulsion.

7. When pursuing personnel for their violation of state discipline and when giving them disciplinary sanctions, state administrative organs must follow the guideline of seriousness and care and give appropriate disciplinary sanctions or exemption from sanctions on an individual basis in accordance with the nature of the wrong committed and the seriousness of the circumstances of the case and with reference to the person's usual behavior and the degree to which he admits his wrong.

Personnel who violate state discipline and cause the interests of the state and the people to suffer definite loss, but who may continue to serve in their currently held office, may on an individual basis be given the sanctions of warning, demerit, large demerit, or demotion in grade.

Personnel who seriously violate state discipline and create great loss to the interests of the state and the people and [therefore] who cannot continue to serve in their currently held office may be given the sanctions of demotion in office or removal from office. If there is no office from which they can be demoted or removed, they may be given the sanction of demotion in grade.

Those elements who seriously violate the law, are derelict in their duty and whom repeated education fails to change, and those elements who shed their skin and change in nature, who cannot be saved by any medicine and who are not suited to continue to work in state administrative organs may be given the sanction of expulsion. In order to give some of these personnel a final opportunity to repent and reform, on the basis of concrete circumstances they may also be dealt with leniently and given the sanction of probationary expulsion.

Counterrevolutionary and other bad elements who sneak into state administrative organs to conduct their sabotage activity must be firmly expelled from state organs and dealt with according to law.

8. When personnel of state administrative organs violate criminal law, if the circumstances of the case are minor and they are not pursued for criminal responsibility, they may be given appropriate disciplinary sanctions or, after undergoing criticism-education, may be exempted from sanctions.

When a people's court sentences personnel of state administrative organs to control or to imprisonment or deprives them of their political rights, they shall automatically be removed from office. Personnel who are sentenced to imprisonment but whose sentences are pronounced suspended shall also automatically be removed from office. During the period of suspension they still may remain in the organs and continue to work and [if they so continue] they shall be assigned appropriate work on the basis of concrete circumstances.

9. When state administrative organs discover that their personnel have committed violations of discipline which deserve disciplinary sanctions, they must deal with the matter quickly and may not procrastinate without reason. Generally, sanctions should be given within half a year of the date on which the wrong was

discovered. If the circumstances of the case are complex or there are other special reasons, the time for giving sanctions may not exceed two years at the latest.

11. When state administrative organs give sanctions to any personnel, they shall conscientiously examine and check the evidence with regard to the facts of the wrong committed and, after discussion at a definite meeting, arrive at a conclusion in writing. At the time of discussion, except in special situations, they shall notify the person receiving the sanction to attend the meeting to state his opinions. After the disciplinary sanction has been decided upon or has been approved and gone into effect, written notice shall be given to the person receiving the sanction and recorded in his file.

When personnel of state administrative organs commit serious wrongs, before sanctions have been decided upon or approved, if it is not fitting that they [continue to] serve in their currently held office, higher level organs or their own organs may first suspend them from office.

12. When personnel of state administrative organs do not accept the disciplinary sanctions they have received, they shall, within a month of receipt of notification, request reconsideration by the organ that dealt with their case. Moreover, they have the right directly to petition higher level organs for review. State administrative organs shall conscientiously deal with the petitions for review of persons who have received sanctions. The written petitions for review that persons who receive sanctions give to higher level organs must be quickly forwarded and may not be shelved. The enforcement of sanctions, however, is not suspended during the period of reconsideration or petition for review.

14. These Regulations shall apply to personnel of state administrative organs of the various levels who have been elected by local people's congresses of the various levels to assume state administrative duties, to personnel who are appointed by state administrative organs of the various levels, and to personnel who are appointed by state administrative organs in enterprise and business units.

### ITEM 47

[Wang Yü-nan, "Important Measures For Strengthening State Discipline," *CFYC*, 1:51–53 (1958)]

.    .    .    .    .

It would obviously be insufficient for the purpose of strengthening state discipline if, besides the necessary emphasis upon strengthening the political-ideological education of personnel, we only paid attention to rewards. Although the overwhelming majority of personnel are able consciously to observe state discipline, certainly not all of them are able to do so, and education is not all-powerful. Therefore, discipline is of a coercive nature, and the use of methods of punishment on persons who violate state discipline is an indispensable method for preserving state discipline. If we do not give appropriate sanctions to those who seriously violate the law and are derelict in their duties, to those whom repeated education has failed to change, or to those who intentionally violate the law, discipline will inevitably relax and organization disintegrate. Articles

5–12 of the Provisional Regulations Relating to Rewards and Punishments [for Personnel of State Administrative Organs] make concrete provisions concerning acts of state personnel which violate discipline, the various types of sanctions and their application, the guidelines and policies for executing disciplinary sanctions, the bases for determining sanctions, the authority and the procedures for [giving] sanctions, the right of persons who receive sanctions to petition for review, and other problems. These provisions are all very necessary and at the same time they are appropriate.

The wrongful acts of personnel of state organs who violate discipline may generally be classified into three categories: (1) Wrongful acts related to their office such as acts which violate resolutions, orders, rules, and systems of the government; make light of duties and cause delay in work; violate democratic centralism; and misuse power and infringe the interests of the masses of people. Because the above-mentioned acts cause the interests of the state and the people to suffer loss, they should bear responsibility for violation of discipline. (2) Minor unlawful acts. All acts that violate the laws of the state, such as those which violate the Constitution, the Marriage Law, labor law, and criminal law, are unlawful acts. But violations of law do not all constitute criminal acts. Even though one violates the state's criminal law, if the circumstances of the case are minor and if according to law there is no need to sentence him to criminal punishment he need not be punished as if he had committed a crime. Minor unlawful acts by state personnel are also something that state discipline cannot permit, and it is absolutely necessary to prescribe that disciplinary sanctions be given with consideration to the circumstances. For example, appropriate disciplinary sanctions with consideration to the circumstances should be given for corruption involving, or theft of, small amounts of state property, for divulging state secrets when the circumstances of the case are minor, or for losing standpoint and concealing bad persons when the circumstances of the case are minor. (3) Acts that violate socialist morality. Acts that are rotten and decadent and that damage the prestige of state organs belong to this category. An illicit sexual relationship is an example of an act that generally has no relation to the duties of an office and does not constitute a crime. But this kind of act does not comport well with the holding of state office. It often has a very bad influence on the masses and damages the reputation and prestige of state organs. Therefore, on the basis of concrete circumstances, criticism-education or sanctions should be given for it, also.

When pursuing personnel for their violation of state discipline and when giving them disciplinary sanctions, we must implement the guideline of strictness and care and that of differential treatment. Our Party has continually advocated this, and now clear provisions for this have been made in the Provisional Regulations Relating to Rewards and Punishments. By strictness we mean firmly conducting the struggle against wrongful acts that damage the interests of the state and the people, and opposing indifference and indulgence. By care we mean painstakingly distinguishing between right and wrong and minor and serious, and opposing careless work. Some people believe that strictness means giving sanctions of increased severity to personnel who have committed wrongs.

This is incorrect. Differential treatment means distinguishing the line between the enemy and us and the line between right and wrong, and individually handling a matter on the basis of its different nature and on the circumstances of the case. The evil activities of counterrevolutionary and other bad elements who have sneaked into state organs to conduct sabotage endanger the state and socialism and constitute criminal acts. Therefore, these elements must be expelled from state organs and dealt with by judicial organs in accordance with law. With respect to elements who have seriously violated the law and been derelict in their duty and whom repeated education has failed to change and with respect to elements who have shed their skin and changed in nature and who cannot be saved by any medicine, because they have already lost the qualities that state personnel ought to have, they too should be expelled in order to purify the organization of the state organs. With respect to personnel who have committed ordinary wrongs, we must implement the principles of "punishment in order to have caution in the future," "treatment of the illness in order to save the patient," and "clarification of thinking and of the comrades"; emphasize conducting ideological education; analyze in a truth-seeking manner the nature and origins of the wrongs; help those who have committed wrongs to heighten their ideological consciousness; and, considering the nature and circumstances of the wrong that they have committed and the amount of damage to the interests of the state and the people, and with reference to the individual's normal behavior and the degree to which he admits his wrong, give appropriate disciplinary sanctions. Or, after criticism-education, we may exempt him from sanctions. The Provisional Regulations Relating to Rewards and Punishments for Personnel of State Administrative Organs make principled provisions on guidelines and policies for disciplining, and this is the basis upon which we shall impose disciplinary sanctions in the future.

Giving disciplinary sanctions to any personnel who have committed wrongs is always a very grave matter. Articles 10 and 11 of the Provisional Regulations Relating to Rewards and Punishment prescribe the authority and the procedures for [giving] disciplinary sanctions. Managing things according to these provisions can guarantee correct handling and prevent good people from being wronged. First, the sanctioning of personnel who have committed wrongs must be based on actual facts. We cannot rely on speculation or guesswork, on gossip, or on looking at a person's demeanor and then reaching a conclusion. We should conscientiously examine the facts and check the evidence concerning the wrong that has been committed. When investigating, we must pay close attention to witnesses and evidence, and we must also excel at distinguishing between the truth and falsity of the witnesses and evidence, rejecting the false and accepting the true. Next, we should correctly analyze the nature of the wrong. By the nature of the wrong we mean the essence of the matter. To analyze the nature of the wrong is not an easy thing. We must conduct a comprehensive and objective analysis and study of the facts of the wrong and through the phenomena seek the essence (the internal connection of the matter). If the nature of the wrong is misapprehended, there will be errors in handling it. Next, before sanctioning any personnel, the matter must be brought before a definite meeting where it is discussed and a conclusion is reached. Doing this can develop democracy, collect opinions to broaden benefits, guarantee that the decision reached will be even more comprehensive and objective, and prevent the occurrence of deviations.

The Provisional Regulations Relating to Rewards and Punishments for Personnel of State Administrative Organs also pay full attention to the problems of safeguarding the democratic rights of personnel who receive sanctions. They prescribe that prior to the decision to sanction, at the discussion meeting, a person who is to receive the sanction is, except in special circumstances, allowed to attend and to state his opinions. After the sanction has been decided upon or after it has been approved and has become effective, if the person receiving the sanction does not accept the decision, he may, within a month of receiving notification, request the organ that handled the matter to reconsider it, and he has the right directly to petition higher level organs for review. It is completely appropriate to make this provision in order to safeguard the democratic rights of the person receiving the sanction. If we impose sanctions in accordance with these provisions, not only can we prevent the occurrence of deviations but we also can promptly correct errors that have already occurred.

## ITEM 48

["Answers of the Ministry of Supervision[43] of the PRC to Some Questions of the Provisional Regulations Relating to Rewards and Punishments for Personnel of State Administrative Organs" (June 12, 1958), *FKHP*, 7:219]

.     .     .     .     .

Second, relating to questions of applying the sanctions of demotion in grade, demotion in office, and removal from office. The sanction of demotion in grade is a reduction in salary and in grade. The sanction of removal from office is removal from currently held office. If personnel who receive the sanction of removal from office concurrently hold other offices, they shall generally be removed only from the primary office and not be removed from the concurrent offices. If the circumstances of their wrongs are especially serious, they may also be removed from both primary and concurrent at the same time. The organ in which they are located shall decide how to execute this sanction. The provision of Article 7, Paragraph 3, of the Provisional Regulations on Rewards and Punishments that "[i]f there is no office from which they can be demoted or removed, they may be given the sanction of demotion in grade" applies to personnel who do not have administrative duties, such as interpreters and typists. It also may be applied to personnel who have the lowest administrative duties, such as clerks.

43. The Ministry of Supervision was abolished April 28, 1959. Each state agency was then made responsible for supervising the conduct of its own personnel under the leadership of the Party. See Resolution of the First Meeting of the Second Session of the NPC of the PRC Relating to Abolition of the Ministry of Justice and the Ministry of Supervision (passed, April 4, 1959), *FKHP*, 9:108.

Third, relating to questions of applying the sanction of probationary expulsion. Personnel who receive the sanction of probationary expulsion shall be assigned work the duties of which are of an uninformative nature, shall have their original wages reduced, and shall be strictly examined in order to observe the outcome. There is no need to prescribe a limit to the period of probation for the sanction of probationary expulsion. After undergoing examination and proof, those who have demonstrated repentance and reform may be formally assigned work; as for those who have not demonstrated repentance and reform, it may be decided to expel them.

.    .    .    .    .

Fifth, relating to questions of automatic removal from office. Personnel of state administrative organs who violate the law and are sentenced by people's courts to imprisonment, control, deprivation of political rights, or imprisonment with sentence pronounced suspended, shall all automatically be removed from office and there shall be no need to resort to the procedure for disciplinary sanctions. If these personnel have been appointed to office by a higher level organ, then a report shall be made to the appointing organ for the record.

## ITEM 49

The following excerpt from Mao's famous speech was directed to the problem of how to handle strikes such as those that had occurred among workers and students during 1956. Implicit in Mao's remarks is recognition of the severity of the sanction of expulsion from employment or from school.

[Mao Tse-tung, "Problems Relating to the Correct Handling of Contradictions Among the People" (Feb. 27, 1957), p. 29]

(2) If disturbances occur as a result of bad work on our part, then we should guide those among the masses who are involved in those disturbances along the correct road, make use of those disturbances as a special means of improving our work and educating the cadres and the masses, and resolve the everyday problems which have gone unresolved. In the process of handling disturbances, we should work painstakingly, and should not use [overly] simple methods, nor "halt the troops before the battle is really won." Except for those who violate the criminal law and active counterrevolutionaries, who should be handled according to law, the leading figures in disturbances should not be lightly expelled [from their jobs or from school]. In a big country like ours, it is not worth becoming alarmed if a small number of persons create disturbances; on the contrary we should use such an occurrence to help us overcome bureaucracy.

# Chapter III    The Security Administration Punishment Act

A. Rationale

B. Kinds of SAPA Sanctions
   1. Range of Sanctions
   2. Warning
   3. Order to Make Compensation, a Statement of Repentance, Apology, Etcetera
   4. Fine
   5. Detention
   6. Confiscation

C. Conduct That Violates Security Administration

D. SAPA Procedure

E. SAPA: "The General Part"

F. Applicability of the SAPA to Other Petty Offenses

> When executing correct rules and a correct system, we should also start out from what benefits production, and we should not hinder production. When handling problems among the people, we must persist in the method of persuasion. Punishment and detention can only be a supplementary measure for circumstances in which there is no alternative. With respect to problems among the people, misuse of detention and punishment is completely wrong.
>
> Lo Jui-ch'ing (Minister of Public Security), "Public Security Work Must Further Implement the Mass Line" (1958)[1]

We have seen that informal adjustment and sanctioning dispose of a great many minor infractions of the social order. But the various modes of persuasion, criticism, warning, and censure often fail to prevent the recurrence of minor infractions. In the Chinese view, to impose criminal punishment for such relatively unimportant misconduct would be excessively harsh, and it would also burden the courts with a multitude of petty offenses which traditionally have been disposed of by other means. The PRC has thus recognized the need for intermediate sanctions that are not criminal in nature and yet are sufficiently formal and severe to induce compliance. When in the latter part of 1957 it sought to create a more orderly system for the adminis-

---

1. *CFYC*, 3:26.

tration of the criminal law, it enacted the Security Administration Punishment Act as a major means of meeting this need. The Act was based upon eight years of experiment with police imposition of administrative punishments. Although, of course, the fact is never mentioned, the Act bears strong resemblance to the Law for the Punishment of Police Offenses of the Republic of China, which was originally promulgated in 1928 and which in revised form has continued to play a very important part in the administration of punishment on Taiwan.[2]

## A. RATIONALE

### ITEM 50

[Lo Jui-ch'ing (Minister of Public Security), "Explanation of the Draft Security Administration Punishment Act of the PRC"[3] (hereinafter cited as "Explanation"), *FKHP*, 6:254–259 (Oct. 22, 1957)]

Chairman, Vice-Chairmen, and Members:

I will now explain several questions in connection with the draft Security Administration Punishment Act:

(1) The SAPA is presented under circumstances when our country has gone through five major movements and three major reforms, the socialist revolution has already won a decisive victory, and the people are requesting further consolidation of the order of socialist construction. Our people's democratic regime is consolidated, and the social order is stable. This reveals the incomparable superiority of our socialist system and the great accomplishments of the five major movements and three major reforms conducted by our country. It also demonstrates the political awareness, organization, and discipline of our industrious and brave Chinese people. But much work remains to be done if we are further to consolidate the order of socialist construction and create a better environment for our people in their work, study, and way of life. One aspect of our numerous tasks is to strengthen security administration and to struggle against all acts that do not comport with order and discipline, that damage the people's interests, and that corrupt public morality. It has only been eight years since the founding of the People's Republic of China, and the great socialist reform was basically completed only last year. Many people still feel unaccustomed to the new socialist system. To change this state of affairs, the entire body of people will have to go through a relatively long process of self-education and awareness. Special cases are various kinds of bad elements left over from the old society, and the exploiting class's bad thoughts, bad habits, and bad demeanor of benefiting themselves at the expense of others, obtaining things without labor, and corrupting morality; they are at every moment still influencing certain unaware elements or weak-willed elements of bad character among the people, and are playing a corrosive and destructive role

2. For an English translation of this law, see Law Revision Planning Group, Council on United States Aid, the Executive Yuan, the Republic of China, comp., *Laws of the Republic of China* (First series — major laws; Taipei, December 1961), pp. 997–1025.

3. The exact date of this is not given, but the speech was apparently delivered shortly before the adoption of the SAPA on October 22, 1957.

in the new society. This shows that the phenomena of interference with public order and corruption of the public morality existing in socialist society have their social sources. From the standpoint of ideological sources, although our country has already basically realized socialist reform of the ownership of the means of production, the socialist reform that is going on politically and ideologically in the minds of the people is still far from completion. Some people still maintain the bourgeoisie's evil habits of benefiting themselves at the expense of others, caring nothing for public morality, and not observing public order. Many acts that violate security administration are demonstrations of the clash between this individualist thinking and collectivist thinking. In order to protect further the people's interests and to safeguard the order of socialist construction, we must, at the same time we strengthen the work of ideological education, put into effect necessary, coercive administrative punishments for all acts that violate laws and discipline and corrupt morality by disrupting public order, interfering with public safety, infringing citizens' rights of the person, and damaging public or private property. This is the common desire of the vast masses of people and at present is also one of the urgent demands for further consolidating the work of the security of society. On the basis of these reasons and in keeping with the spirit of Article 49, Paragraph 12, and Article 100 of the Constitution,[4] it is quite necessary for our country today to adopt and to promulgate a security administration punishment act.

(2) The problems treated by the SAPA are those of minor unlawful acts which violate security administration. These minor unlawful acts are not of a degree that offends criminal law and do not warrant criminal sanctions, but they are beyond solution by ordinary criticism-education and require the imposition of definite administrative punishments. Some of the persons to be punished for violation of security administration are various kinds of originally [thoroughly] bad elements. They steal and swindle property, act obscenely and indecently with women, disrupt public order, interfere with public safety, spread rumors and make trouble, and engage in other such unlawful activity. These bad elements are the objects of our dictatorship. Against their unlawful activity dictatorship must be put into effect and punishment imposed. It is only because the unlawful circumstances of their cases are relatively minor, do not constitute crimes, and do not warrant criminal sanctions, that they are given definite administrative punishments. For these reasons, the SAPA is a weapon by means of which the people put dictatorship into effect against various kinds of bad elements.

But there is still another kind of situation. Among the unlawful acts that should be punished there are many minor ones that occur among the people. Or, to say it another way, among the people there are certain acts which violate state discipline and interfere with public order: for example, certain acts that violate traffic regulations or household registration regulations or that interfere with

4. Article 49, paragraph 12 provides: "The State Council shall exercise the . . . power . . . to protect the interests of the state, to preserve public order and to safeguard the rights of citizens . . ."; and Article 100 provides: "Citizens of the People's Republic of China must observe the Constitution and the law, must observe labor discipline and public order, and must respect social morality." (*FKHP*, 1:19, 30).

public health, etc. Some of these acts occur because of errors in ideological consciousness, some because of poor moral demeanor, and some because of faults in their way of life and in their work. Because these persons who violate security administration infringe or interfere with interests of the vast masses of people and public order, they must be punished, and imposition of this punishment carries with it definite coercion. Why must coercive punishment definitely be put into effect against the minority of persons among the people who violate discipline? Is this in contradiction to the principle of using the method of persuasion-education to handle problems among the people correctly? Our answer is: there is no contradiction. This is because, if the people want to organize their own state and to maintain order in their own state, besides the necessity of putting dictatorship into effect against the enemy, they should at the same time establish discipline and public order in the people's state. We cannot tolerate any person's damaging the discipline or public order of the state. Therefore, enforcing state discipline, that is, putting into effect necessary administrative punishment against the minor unlawful acts of a small number of persons, not only does not violate the principle of using the method of persuasion instead of the method of compulsion to handle ideological problems among the people and [problems of] differentiating right from wrong, but rather supplements it. Besides, the discipline of the people's state originally was founded on the basis of self-awareness and voluntarism of the vast [number of] people, and discipline itself is not purely for the purpose of negative punishment but is mainly for the purpose of attaining the goal of positive education. It should be explained repeatedly that thoroughly putting into effect the SAPA adopted by our country, like putting into effect other laws and decrees or government administrative orders, requires passing through [a period of] thorough propaganda-education. If the reasons are not clearly explained to the people to obtain their adherence and support, and if it is not founded on the basis of self-awareness and voluntarism of the vast [number of] people, but rather, coercion is simply understood to mean crude oppression that does not require any educating, it will be completely incorrect, and it will definitely get nowhere . . .

. . . At present, acts that violate security administration are generally dealt with too leniently. The masses of people have already expressed very great dissatisfaction and blame the security administration organs for being unable to maintain order. This clearly reflects the will of the vast [number of] people. Now that the state has adopted the SAPA, we have standard rules for the correct handling of problems, and the vast masses of people also have a weapon with which to struggle against those unlawful acts and acts that do not comport with state discipline. It may be expected that this will play a very important role in our further protecting socialist order, consolidating state discipline, defending socialist construction, defending the interests and rights of the vast [number of] people, and educating the people to establish socialist concepts of morality and of collectivism.

(3) Our country is a large country, and its circumstances are complex. On the whole, the scope of the applicability of the SAPA takes into account the common characteristics of large, medium, and small cities and rural villages,

but it also pays appropriate attention to special characteristics of specific circumstances. The scope of the punishments prescribed in the draft Act can generally be divided into four categories: the first is disrupting public order; the second is interfering with public safety; the third is infringing citizens' rights of the person; and the fourth is damaging public or private property. The above four categories are contained in Articles 5 to 15, eleven articles that have a total of sixty-eight paragraphs. These clauses basically cover acts that at present require security administration punishment. The principal clauses reflect the common characteristics of cities and rural villages and are applicable to both places: for example, stealing, swindling, misappropriating small amounts of property, acting indecently with women, gambling, beating up others, violating household registration regulations, organizing mass assemblies in disregard of safety, etc. Some of them are generally applicable only to rural villages: for example, injuring livestock, spoiling crops, burning hillsides or barren fields without authorization, cutting down trees of another person or of a cooperative, etc.

Is it necessary to put security administration punishment into effect in the vast [number of] rural villages? We believe that this too is necessary. In rural villages, cases of interference with the security of society and of endangering the public interest are far from few. Some already have directly influenced the consolidation and development of the agricultural producers' cooperatives and the production and the way of life of the masses. Because some cases have been inappropriately handled by the government, the masses have had a good many opinions [about the situation]. In some cases, the masses went so far as straightforwardly to take matters into their own hands, and the results led to a certain amount of turmoil. Therefore, in rural villages, appropriate punishment must definitely be given to all those who ought to be punished. Moreover, if we will only do thorough mass work, rely on self-awareness and voluntarism of the vast [number of] peasants, rely on the support of the vast [number of] peasants to regulate bad elements, rely on the support of the majority to restrain the acts of the very small minority who infringe the interests of others and disturb and damage public order, it [the Act] can definitely be carried out smoothly.

There are also a few clauses that are only applicable to cities: for example, disturbing order at stations, wharves, and parks, and arbitrarily making loud noises. These cannot be applied in rural villages. As to punishment for acts that violate traffic regulations, at present this is generally applicable only to large and medium cities. Not only does it not apply to rural villages, it is also inapplicable to small cities that have not yet put traffic regulations into effect. For these reasons, the Act cannot be executed in a mechanical and inflexible way. Naturally, it would be wrong to apply it uniformly and without inquiring into specific circumstances.

## B. KINDS OF SAPA SANCTIONS

### 1. Range of Sanctions

## ITEM 51

[SECURITY ADMINISTRATION PUNISHMENT ACT OF THE PRC (passed at the 81st meeting of the Standing Committee of the NPC, Oct. 22, 1957; promulgated by the Chairman of the PRC, Oct. 22, 1957), *FKHP*, 6:245–246, 253]

Article 1. This Act is adopted in keeping with the spirit of the provisions of Article 49, Paragraph 12, and Article 100 of the Constitution of the People's Republic of China.

Article 2. An act that disrupts public order, interferes with public safety, infringes citizens' rights of the person, or damages public or private property violates security administration if the circumstances of the case are minor, if the act does not warrant criminal sanctions, and if it is punishable according to this Act.

Acts that violate security administration, by citizens of the People's Republic of China or by foreigners within the territory of the People's Republic of China, shall all be dealt with according to this Act.

Article 3. Punishments for violation of security administration shall be divided into the following three categories:

(1) Warning.

(2) Fine: not less than five *chiao*[5] nor more than twenty yuan; punishment of increased severity may not exceed thirty yuan. A fine shall be paid within five days after decision; one who has not paid the fine by the expiration of the period shall instead be punished by detention.

(3) Detention: not less than half a day nor more than ten days; punishment of increased severity may not exceed fifteen days. During detention the detained person shall assume the cost of his own meals; one who cannot pay the cost of his meals shall use labor as a substitute [for payment].

Article 4. Instruments [used] to commit acts that violate security administration and which must be confiscated, shall be confiscated.

Property obtained from acts that violate security administration shall be confiscated.

With the exception of contraband articles, the instruments and property mentioned above shall be returned to the original owner if the original owner is someone other than the person who violated security administration.

Article 29. If a violation of security administration creates loss or injury, the violator shall pay compensation or assume the medical expenses; if the person who causes the loss or injury has not reached eighteen years of age or is mentally ill, the head of his family or his guardian shall be responsible for paying compensation or assuming the medical expenses.

5. A *chiao* is one-tenth of a yuan (see Part I, note 67).

## ITEM 52

["Explanation" (Oct. 22, 1957), p. 259]

(4) In imposing punishments the scope of the SAPA should be understood: first of all, such punishments must be strictly differentiated from criminal sanctions. Some of the types of offenses [enumerated] in the clauses of the SAPA are the same as some of the offenses [enumerated] in provisions of the criminal law — for example, theft and fraud. But they differ from the offenses [enumerated] in the criminal law mainly in that their circumstances are relatively minor, their degree of danger is not so severe, and they do not warrant criminal sanctions. In order to understand this differentiation correctly and to avoid giving SAPA punishment to those who should receive criminal sanctions or erroneously pursuing for criminal responsibility those who should receive SAPA punishment, we must specifically analyze each case and adopt a serious and cautious attitude.

Next, we should differentiate between the scope of the SAPA and the scope of criticism-education. Some of the SAPA's clauses are similar to [those in other acts prescribing] ordinary criticism-education: for example, insulting and cursing others and obstructing traffic by setting up stalls or piling things in the streets. But, there is a difference between these two: conduct which warrants punishment must have produced a definite, bad consequence; have been committed in disregard of an order to stop; or have been committed repeatedly despite repeated warnings. Naturally, wrongful acts that have not reached this degree of seriousness and that involve problems that can be resolved with criticism-education rather than punishment, should not be punished.

Third, three kinds of punishment are prescribed by the Act — warning, fine, and detention. If we want to impose appropriate punishment, we must make an overall analysis on the basis of the specific circumstances of the violation of security administration, the magnitude of the violation's effect, the attitude of the person receiving punishment toward admitting his error, and other such circumstances; and we must guard against handling the case one-sidedly and carelessly. Some people may be punished lightly or be exempted from punishment. Also, some may be punished with increased severity or, after punishment, be sent for rehabilitation through labor. Special clauses of the Act have made provisions for these matters.

## 2. Warning

## ITEM 53

[Interview]

Because of poor management by its team leader, who was named Ling, a production team of commune A in Fukien province had too little seed to meet its 1959 spring planting needs. Ling was afraid to report the shortage, since he knew that he would be criticized for causing it. Yet he also realized that if the team failed to plant enough seed, it would be unable to meet its production quota and he would then be criticized more severely. Having heard that a nearby production team of commune B had an ample supply of seed, Ling told several members of his team to go there under cover of darkness and secretly take seed from it. He promised them extra work points for their cooperation. However, the members of Ling's team were seen taking the seed by a member of the victimized team, who followed them back to their homes. The next morning he reported the theft to his team leader, who told the Party secretary of his production brigade, who telephoned the special agent whom the public security bureau maintained in commune B, who called the bureau. The bureau in turn notified its special agent in commune A, who went down to Ling's production brigade and discussed the case with the brigade leader and the chairman of the security defense committee. The three of them then called in Ling, who quickly confessed when questioned about the theft.

After considering the matter further, the special agent, the brigade leader, and the SDC [Security Defense Committee] chairman agreed on a recommended disposition of the case. The agent telephoned the bureau's security section to obtain its approval, which was granted. They then organized a meeting of the entire brigade to discuss the case. The members of Ling's team who actually did the stealing were criticized at the meeting. Ling was also subjected to criticism, and it was announced that he would receive a formal written warning under the SAPA for having incited the team members to commit the theft. In addition, he was removed from his position as team leader.

## ITEM 54

[*Lectures* (September 1957), p. 191]

·　　·　　·　　·　　·

Reprimand is the lightest method of criminal punishment. It is mainly a punishment of an educational nature, a public condemnation that is given to criminals by people's courts in the name of the state. It is only applied to the most minor crimes.

During the past several years, people's courts in the various places have extensively applied this punishment. But it has been called by many different names. For example, it has been called criticism-education, warning, reproach, condemnation, and an order to repent. The methods of execution have also been different: for example, reprimand in court, repentance before the masses, repentance and self-examination published in the newspaper, or an order to pay compensation. Some individual judges have even applied this sanction to persons whose acts do not constitute crimes but are only ordinary unlawful acts, and thus they have confused the boundary between criminal sanctions and administrative or civil sanctions.

Because of the existence of the above-mentioned confusion and shortcomings in practice, some people have suggested that we do not need the punishment of reprimand or that we need not list it as a kind of punitive sanction. Naturally this suggestion may be studied. At present, since this punishment is still widely applied by the people's court and plays a certain role in very minor crimes, we temporarily must continue to list it as a kind of punishment in order to summarize experience. But it should be pointed out that if reprimand is to be used as a kind of punishment, it can only be applied to criminals and not to persons whose acts do not constitute crimes. We should also be serious in applying this method of punishment. For instance, within a fixed period of time after judgment, the written judgment should be published either in the newspapers or by posting it in other public places (such as the place of the crime or the place where the criminal resides) to make condemnation of the criminal known to the masses, so that the desired educational effect may be achieved.

Item 54 was published just prior to enactment of the SAPA and dealt with the imposition of reprimand or warning as a criminal punishment. Since Article 3(1) of the SAPA made warning an administrative punishment, should reprimand no longer be employed as a criminal punishment? Why do the authors of Item 54 assert that "if reprimand is to be used as a kind of punishment, it can only be applied to criminals"? The SAPA relieves the courts of having to deal with many kinds of minor criminal cases. Yet reprimand has continued to be meted out by the courts in certain cases that do not fall under the SAPA. On the other hand, a formal written warning is seldom imposed by the public security forces under the SAPA. Of course, an informal warning is often given, either alone or in conjunction with other administrative sanctions such as an order to make compensation or to publish a statement of repentance. Item 55 illustrates the latter situation.

### 3. Order to Make Compensation, a Statement of Repentance, Apology, Etcetera

## ITEM 55

[Interview]

During the spring festival of 1960 four sixteen- or seventeen-year-old boys persisted in carrying on horseplay at the door of a state department store in a county seat. They ignored the store sales personnel and the store security man who asked them to go away. Finally, one of them damaged some goods at an adjacent sales counter. The security man told them not to leave and called the nearby public security bureau to report the incident. The bureau sent an agent over to investigate, and he took the boys back to the bureau's security section, where the secretary on duty questioned them. The secretary then went back to the store with the boys to inspect the damage, which amounted to forty yuan.

After calling the deputy chief of the security section to receive his approval, the secretary lectured the boys on the spot and told them that they had violated Article 5(3) of the SAPA (Item 62A, below). He ordered each of them to pay ten yuan compensation to the store so that the total compensation would equal the total damage they had caused. Each was also required to write ten statements of repentance, which were to be posted on the doors of the department store, on the bulletin boards and walls of their school, and at other relevant places. They were not given detention because the secretary did not want to interfere with their schooling or to put a serious black mark on their records.

4. Fine

## ITEM 56

[Interview]

Mu was an overseas Chinese who had returned to China and taken up residence in a county seat. In addition to his normal occupation, in 1959 he covertly sold medicines that were sent to him from overseas relatives and friends. This was held to be unlawful operation of a business in violation of the SAPA, and the public security bureau imposed a 100-yuan fine upon Mu.

He paid the fine but asked the bureau to reconsider the reasonableness of the fine. He pointed out that he had not made large profits on sale of the medicines but had sold them at bargain prices as an accommodation to sick friends and neighbors at a time when medicines were in short supply in China. After inquiry revealed the truth of this claim, the bureau reduced the fine to twenty yuan and refunded the excess payment.

Is a 100-yuan fine authorized by the SAPA? As Item 56 indicates, at least in some rural areas the public security cadres do not strictly observe the Act's limitations upon the amount of the fines that may be imposed.

## ITEM 57

[Interview]

Toward the end of 1960, two peasants, Hsia and Chiao, had a fist fight. Because they were near commune headquarters, they took the dispute directly to the commune security chief. Since Hsia was badly hurt and had required medical treatment, the security chief decided that the case ought to be handled by the public security bureau, which was not far away. After a secretary of the bureau's security section heard both sides and examined the medical certificate, he decided that both parties had violated the SAPA. Hsia merely received an oral warning, however, while Chiao was ordered to pay a compensatory fine of ten yuan to cover his victim's medical expenses. Chiao agreed to pay the fine in a few days. Because it would have been embarrassing for him to pay Hsia directly and because it would have been inconvenient to all concerned for him to pay Hsia through the bureau, it was arranged that Chiao would give the money to the chairman of the security adjustment committee [formed by merger of the security defense and adjustment committees] of their production brigade.

But after three days no payment had been made. Hsia got the committee chairman to prod Chiao, who said he would take care of the matter in another few days. When the same thing happened a few days later, the committee chairman called the bureau's security section, which ordered the parties up to discuss the matter. Chiao again promised to make good in the near future. When he did not, the chairman informed the security section, which gave Chiao seven days of detention for failure to pay the fine. It also ordered his family to take ten yuan that belonged to him and to hand it over to the committee chairman for transmittal to Hsia.

1. The SAPA provides for the sanctions of paying a fine and of making compensation. Does it provide for compensatory fines? Is this a question of practical significance in administering the Act? Interviews suggest that points such as this tend to be ignored by cadres who are stationed at public security bureaus in the countryside.

2. Was Chiao's detention authorized by the Act? Having detained him for nonpayment, was the bureau authorized also to require payment of the fine?

3. Is the provision of Article 3(2) for detention of one who does not promptly pay his fine consistent with socialist precepts of egalitarianism? Consider the following excerpt from the *Lectures*:

"In the criminal punishments of capitalist society, this property punishment, the fine, also has class character. To rich men, it is essentially a method which exempts them from suffering punishment. But to a proletarian, it is a heavy punishment — if he pays the fine, it is depriving the proletarian of all or part of his property. If he does not pay the fine, he will suffer the punishment of deprivation of freedom." [6]

How should fines be imposed and enforced in a socialist country? Note that a 1961 Soviet decree on administrative fines provides that the amount of a fine shall be based upon the seriousness of the offense and the character and economic situation of the offender. Moreover, it prohibits imposition of corrective labor in cases in which the fine is not paid.[7]

### 5. Detention

### ITEM 58

[Interview]

One day in 1958 prior to the advent of the rural commune, Wang and her daughter-in-law Teng had a bitter quarrel that led to blows. By the time neighbors arrived and separated them, Wang was rather badly beaten up. Bitter about the injuries that she had received from her daughter-in-law, after going to the medical station of their administrative village for treatment, Wang reported the incident to the member of the security defense committee who resided in their village. He in turn reported it to the chairman of his committee at the administrative village.

The chairman summoned both Wang and Teng for a joint interview to inquire about the facts of the case. When this confirmed that Teng's enthusiasm for the fray had been excessive and that Wang's injuries appeared to be fairly substantial, the chairman discussed the case with the secretary of the Party branch for the administrative village. The chairman then went to talk with the doctor who had treated Wang and obtained a medical certificate that verified the fact that she had suffered serious bodily injury. Since the Party secretary had agreed with the chairman that the case was more serious than the ordinary

6. September 1957, p. 14.

7. Concerning the Extension of Restrictions in the Application of Fines Levied Administratively (Decree of June 21, 1961), arts. 7, 20, *Vedomosti Verkhovnovo Soveta SSSR* (Gazette of the Supreme Soviet of the USSR), 35:842 (1961).

family fracas, the chairman reported the case by telephone to the special agent of the county public security bureau who was stationed at the district level. The special agent did not go down to the administrative village to check on the case, because at the time his energies were absorbed in educating the fishermen along the Fukien coast in a security campaign. Instead, he directed the chairman to take the materials relating to the case directly to the county public security bureau, which he would notify to expect them.

Having filled out an application for Teng's detention, the chairman took it and the medical certificate up to the bureau and submitted these documents to the bureau's security section. A secretary of the security section studied the application. Although he was authorized to handle the case on his own and merely report the disposition to the section chief, because the case arose out of a family quarrel the secretary deemed it wise to clear the decision with the section chief, who was at a meeting concerning the regulation of returned overseas Chinese. Over the telephone he informed the section chief of the essential facts. When the latter learned that Wang's injuries had been substantial, he told the secretary to give Teng ten days of detention under Article 10(2) of the SAPA. The secretary then made out a detention warrant and gave it to the waiting SDC chairman, who returned to the administrative village and, in the company of a member of the people's militia, went to Teng's home to present it to her. The militiaman escorted her to the public security bureau, where she was detained for the prescribed period.

## ITEM 59

The following excerpt, published prior to the enactment of the SAPA, as part of the authors' attempt to bring greater rationality and order to criminal law, sheds light on the nature and background of the sanction of detention. Since the SAPA, judicially imposed detention seems largely to have fallen into disuse. Police detention may now be the most frequently invoked, as well as the most severe, of the administrative punishments authorized by the SAPA.

[*Lectures* (September 1957), pp. 197–198]

.        .        .        .        .

Detention belongs to [the category of] light criminal punishment that deprives a person of freedom for a short period. Although the current legislation of our country does not expressly prescribe detention as a method of punishment, local people's courts actually have extensively applied this method because in fact some minor crimes exist for which it is necessary to hold offenders in custody for a short period. It is only the names that are not the same. Education during confinement to quarters, and education during confinement in custody, etc., used in the adjudication practice of the various places, are types of detention. Experience proves that in the struggle against minor crime, detention is indispensable.

On the basis of experience in adjudication practice, ordinarily it is proper to set the period of detention at not less than seven days nor more than six months.

If the period is shorter than seven days, it may well create the phenomenon of having to handle release procedures just after sentence. This would not only damage the dignity of the law, it also would not perform the function of punishment and reform. But if the period is longer than six months, it may well be confused with imprisonment for a fixed term and lose its significance as a light punishment. For criminals who are sentenced to detention, reform through labor at the place of detention should be put into effect.

Although detention and imprisonment for a fixed term are both punishments which deprive a person of freedom, they are different not only in the length of the term of imprisonment but also in nature. First, imprisonment for a fixed term is a relatively heavy punishment (in our practice it is known as such). It can be applied only to relatively serious crimes. Detention is a light punishment. It is applicable to relatively minor crimes. For minor crimes which necessitate holding the offenders in custody for a short period it would be obviously inappropriate if they [the offenders] were sentenced to imprisonment for a fixed term or if holding them in custody for ten days or so were called imprisonment for a fixed term. These circumstances not only show the necessity for the existence of the punishment of detention, but also clearly show that detention and imprisonment for a fixed term are different in nature. Next, the term of imprisonment and the place of executing it are naturally also bases for differentiating between them. Furthermore, a criminal sentenced to imprisonment for a fixed term who, within a given period of time after expiration of sentence and release, again commits a crime that is punishable by imprisonment for a fixed term is a recidivist; but a criminal who has served [a period of] detention is not to be treated as a recidivist if he again commits a crime. Thus they [detention and imprisonment for a fixed term] also differ in their legal consequences.

### 6. Confiscation

### ITEM 60

Should confiscation (under Article 4 of the SAPA) of either the instruments used to commit a violation of security administration or the property obtained from such a violation be deemed "punishment"? Consider the following item pertaining to confiscation as a criminal sanction.

[*Lectures* (September 1957), p. 209]

.        .        .        .        .

In addition, we also should talk about problems of confiscating criminal articles. This includes confiscation of instruments of crime, of the fruits of crime, and of contraband articles. These confiscations differ from confiscation of property as a method of criminal punishment. Confiscation of criminal articles cannot be treated as a punishment. Instruments of crime, such as a [printing] machine for making [counterfeit] money, naturally should be confiscated as real evidence for [criminal] litigation. Only when they do not belong to the criminal are they not confiscated. The fruits of crime, such as those obtained through corruption, theft, or robbery, should be returned to their original owner.

This is only a question of restoring state property or citizens' property to its original condition. If they are things that do not belong to the state, to organizations, or to individual citizens, such as unlawful profits obtained through speculation, they may be regarded as part of his [the criminal's] property and confiscated when necessary. With respect to contraband articles, such as opium, it is unlawful to possess them without permission from the relevant organs. Confiscation of contraband articles belongs within the sphere of coercive administrative sanctions. Whether or not the possessor has used them to engage in criminal activity, they all should be confiscated.

## ITEM 61

In Item 6 the authors of the *Lectures* called for reform and rationalization of the system of criminal law. The SAPA was an important part of the regime's response. Do you think the authors of the *Lectures* were pleased by its enactment? Consider the following item.

[*Lectures* (September 1957), 175–176]

.   .   .   .   .

In the criminal law of the People's Republic of China criminal punishment is a coercive measure applied by people's courts as the representative of the state in accordance with law to protect the interests of the state and the people, to punish and reform criminals, and also to educate all the citizenry.

Now we further explain this concept as follows:

First, in the criminal law of the People's Republic of China, criminal punishment is a coercive measure applied to criminals by people's courts. In our country, of the coercive measures applied, besides criminal punishment, there is also coercion of an administrative nature (for example, a fine for violation of tax laws and regulations), coercion of a disciplinary nature (for example, demerit, demotion in office, or removal from office for dereliction of duty by state personnel), civil coercion (for example, an order for a civil defendant to pay compensation for damage and compulsory execution [of a civil judgment]), and coercion in criminal litigation (detention or arrest of criminal suspects, or seizure of a defendant or witness who ignores a summons). Criminal punishment, as one coercive measure of the state, has the following special characteristics as compared to the other above-mentioned coercive measures:

(1) Criminal punishment is one of the most severe coercive measures of the state. It may not only deprive the sentenced person of his property and rights, but may also deprive him of his freedom for a fixed term or for life and may even deprive him of his life. Thus the degree of deprivation or pain suffered under it by one who is coerced is far more serious than that suffered under other coercive measures. We know that an administrative sanction is generally nothing more than a fine. The most serious disciplinary sanction is nothing more than expulsion from certain organs, enterprises, or organizations. The most serious civil sanction is nothing more than an order to pay compensation for damage. And a coercive measure in criminal litigation is nothing

more than a temporary limitation of one's freedom of activity, etc. The difference in the degree of severity of the coercive nature [of the measure] is one of the distinctions between criminal punishment and other coercive measures.

(2) The coercive measure of criminal punishment can only be applied to criminals. To apply criminal punishment to a person who has not committed a crime is a violation of law. In practice, if this error occurs, it must be corrected. Administrative sanctions, disciplinary sanctions, civil coercive sanctions, and coercive sanctions in criminal litigation are all inapplicable to criminals. Such coercive sanctions in criminal litigation as arrest, detention, and [release from confinement upon] obtaining a guarantor are all for the purpose of preventing the defendant from evading investigation and adjudication or from destroying evidence of the crime. But at the time it has not yet been determined whether the act of the defendant constitutes a crime, and it is incorrect to confuse these sanctions with criminal punishment.

(3) [The power] to give criminal punishment can only be lawfully exercised by people's courts, the special adjudication organs that represent the state. Article 73 of the Constitution of our country prescribes: "The Supreme People's Court, local people's courts of the various levels, and special people's courts shall exercise the power of adjudication in the People's Republic of China." This established the principle that the power to adjudicate in our country is exclusively exercised by people's courts. Therefore, only people's courts [acting] in accordance with legally prescribed procedures, can apply criminal punishment to criminals who should be punished. All other state organs, including procuratorial and public security organs, have no authority to apply criminal punishment. For them to do so would be an unlawful act.

Is the SAPA inconsistent with Article 73 of the Constitution? Why? What defense might be made in its behalf?

## C. CONDUCT THAT VIOLATES SECURITY ADMINISTRATION

### ITEMS 62A–62B
### ITEM 62A

[SAPA (Oct. 22, 1957), p. 246]

Article 5. A person who commits any one of the following acts disrupting public order shall be punished by detention of not more than ten days, a fine of not more than twenty yuan, or a warning:

(1) [Participating in] gang fighting;

(2) Disrupting order at stations, wharves, civilian airports, parks, market places, amusement places, exhibitions, athletic fields, or other public places, in disregard of dissuasion;

(3) Disrupting order in offices of state organs, in disregard of dissuasion;

(4) Refusing [to cooperate with] or obstructing state security administration personnel who are performing their duties according to law, but not to such an extent as to constitute violent resistance;

(5) Damaging public notices or seals of state organs that are still in effect;

(6) Defacing scenic or historic places or structures that have commemorative political significance;

(7) Putting up for sale or rent reactionary, obscene, or absurd books, periodicals, picture books, or pictures that have previously been repressed;

(8) Engaging in prostitution or having sexual relations with a woman secretly engaged in prostitution in violation of the government order repressing prostitutes.

## ITEM 62B

[Interview]

On October 1, 1959, P'eng, a student of an upper middle school, tried to leave one of the great mass rallies that was held to celebrate the tenth anniversary of the founding of the People's Republic. Two public security cadres in plain clothes who were stationed at the exit refused to let him leave, and an argument developed. When the cadres revealed that they were public security men, P'eng became angry and still refused to listen to them. They took him to the nearest public security station, where the station secretary talked with the cadres, interviewed P'eng, and told him to write out a statement of the facts. The secretary then filled out a form that summarized the facts of the case and his recommendation for disposing of it. While P'eng waited at the public security station, a policeman took this form and P'eng's statement to the public security bureau.

The secretary of the bureau's security section quickly studied these documents and, after consulting the bureau chief, decided that P'eng's conduct had violated Article 5(4) of the SAPA and that he should receive three days of detention plus criticism upon his return to school. The secretary of the security section then made out a detention warrant and gave it to the waiting policeman, who returned to the public security station with it. There P'eng was informed of the bureau's decision. He was told that he could give his "opinion" of this disposition and that it would be sent to the bureau for consideration, but he declined to do so.

Upon P'eng's release from detention the public security station notified his school to hold a large-scale criticism meeting. P'eng was required to make a self-examination in front of the whole student body and, after receiving the censure of his fellow students, to guarantee that he would not behave in the same way again. After the meeting his statement of self-examination and guarantee was posted at a prominent place in the school.

## ITEMS 63A–63B
## ITEM 63A

[SAPA (Oct. 22, 1957), pp. 246–249]

Article 6. A person who commits any one of the following acts disrupting public order shall be punished by detention of not more than seven days, a fine of not more than fourteen yuan, or a warning:

(1) Gambling for property, having undergone education without changing;

(2) Engaging in drawing lots, establishing lotteries or other methods of disguised gambling, having undergone education without changing;

(3) Spreading rumors and making trouble to obtain by fraud small amounts of property or to affect production [adversely], having undergone education without changing;

(4) Carving official seals without authorization or forging or altering certificates, where the circumstances of the case are minor;

(5) In printing, casting, or carving enterprises, undertaking to make public seals or other certificates, in violation of administrative provisions;

(6) Putting up for sale fake drugs to obtain by fraud small amounts of money or property.

Article 7. A person who commits any one of the following acts disrupting public order shall be punished by detention of not more than three days, a fine of not more than six yuan, or a warning:

(1) Fishing and hunting in districts where fishing and hunting are prohibited, in disregard of dissuasion;

(2) Photographing or surveying and mapping in districts where photographing and surveying and mapping are prohibited, in disregard of dissuasion;

(3) Passing without authority through districts through which passing is prohibited, in disregard of dissuasion;

(4) Damaging or unauthorized moving of temporary surveying markers;

(5) In cities, willfully making loud noises that [adversely] affect the work and rest of surrounding residents, in disregard of an order to stop.

Article 8. A person who commits any one of the following acts interfering with public safety shall be punished by detention of not more than seven days, a fine of not more than fourteen yuan, or a warning:

(1) Digging holes in or placing obstacles on railroads or highways in a way that does not make vehicular operation dangerous;

(2) Throwing stones, lumps of mud, or other similar articles at trains, motor vehicles, or boats;

(3) Damaging traffic signs or other traffic safety equipment;

(4) Damaging street lights;

(5) Making, storing, transporting, or using explosive or inflammable chemical articles in contravention of safety provisions;

(6) Making, purchasing, keeping, or using virulent poisons in contravention of safety provisions;

(7) Violating fire prevention rules, having refused to comply with a request for improvement;

(8) Damaging fire prevention equipment or fire prevention instruments;

(9) Transferring without authority public fire prevention equipment or fire prevention instruments to other uses;

(10) Without permission of the local government, burning hillsides or barren fields in a way that does not create disaster;

(11) Negligently destroying by fire state property, cooperative property, or the property of other persons in a way that does not create serious loss.

Article 9. A person who commits any one of the following acts interfering with public safety shall be punished by detention of not more than five days, a fine of not more than ten yuan, or a warning:

(1) Without government permission, purchasing or possessing firearms or ammunition for use in athletic activities, or keeping or using such firearms or ammunition in contravention of safety provisions;

(2) Without government permission, making, purchasing, or possessing firearms for hunting or opening a workshop for repairing such firearms;

(3) Establishing or using civilian firing ranges in contravention of safety provisions;

(4) Installing or using antennae in contravention of safety provisions;

(5) Creating danger of personal injury or death by organizing mass assemblies without adopting commensurate safety measures, and not improving the situation after it has been pointed out;

(6) Overloading a ferry, or continuing to use a damaged vessel that is in danger of sinking, in disregard of an admonition to repair it;

(7) Forcing ferry service during a storm or flood that creates a danger of capsizing, in disregard of an order to stop;

(8) Struggling to be first to board a ferry, in disregard of an order to stop, or coercing a ferry pilot to overload in the course of providing ferry service;

(9) Creating the possibility of an incident by selling tickets of admission to public amusement places in excess of their capacity, in disregard of dissuasion;

(10) Not keeping clear entrances, exits, and safety exits of public amusement places during the hours that they are open.

Article 10. A person who commits any one of the following acts infringing citizens' rights of the person shall be punished by detention of not more than ten days or a warning:

(1) Using obscene language and acting indecently with women;

(2) Beating up others;

(3) Insulting and cursing others, in disregard of dissuasion;

(4) Intentionally dirtying the body or clothing of others.

Article 11. A person who commits any one of the following acts damaging public property or property of citizens shall be punished by detention of not more than ten days, a fine of not more than twenty yuan, or a warning:

(1) Stealing, swindling, or illegally appropriating small amounts of public property or the property of others;

(2) Taking the lead in raising an uproar and carrying off small amounts of property of an agricultural producers' cooperative.

Article 12. A person who commits any one of the following acts damaging public property or property of citizens shall be punished by detention of not more than five days, a fine of not more than ten yuan, or a warning:

(1) Injuring livestock in a way that does not create serious loss;

(2) Damaging agricultural crops in the fields, melons in melon patches, or fruit in orchards, in disregard of dissuasion;

(3) Damaging agricultural implements, small-scale water utilization facilities, or other production equipment of an agricultural producers' cooperative in a way that does not create serious loss;

(4) Cutting down small amounts of bamboo or trees belonging to the state, to a cooperative, or to another person without authorization;

(5) Damaging tree seedlings in a nursery in a way that does not create serious loss.

## ITEM 63B

[Interview]

The commerce bureau of a city in Fukien province ran a pig farm in the outskirts of the city next to a rural commune. Three cadres from the commerce bureau administered the farm, while sixteen peasant girls actually fed the pigs. One night in 1960 a large number of pigs escaped through the farm gate, which had been in a state of disrepair, and ate up over fifty *mou*[8] of vegetables being grown by the commune. When this substantial damage was discovered the next morning, the commune notified the public security bureau, which assigned some investigators to the case. They quickly discovered the place through which the pigs had passed. When questioned about why they had not had the gate repaired, the cadres could make no response. They were found to have violated Article 12(2) of the SAPA and were each fined one month's wages, the total being well in excess of 100 yuan. The fine was paid over by the public security bureau to the commune as partial compensation for the damage suffered. In addition, the commerce bureau transferred the cadres to other jobs.

On the facts stated above, should the cadres have been found to have violated the Act? Assuming that they had "committed an act," had they done it "in disregard of dissuasion"? The latter phrase, which appears in many provisions of the Act, has been interpreted to mean in disregard of a request to stop by any person. This is in contrast to the phrase "in disregard of an order to stop" which is deemed to refer to an order by an authorized official such as a policeman. In practice, however, as this item indicates, these limitations are not always observed.

## ITEMS 64A–64B
## ITEM 64A

[SAPA (Oct. 22, 1957), pp 249–250]

Article 13. A person who commits any one of the following acts violating traffic regulations shall be punished by detention of not more than ten days, a fine of not more than twenty yuan, or a warning:

(1) Appropriating or lending a vehicle [registration] certificate or a driver's license;

(2) Driving a motor vehicle without a driver's license;

8. A *mou* is one-sixth of an acre.

(3) Driving a vehicle that is in defective condition or, if a defective condition appears while en route, driving in a manner contrary to regulation;

(4) Driving an overloaded motor vehicle, speeding, or violating the instructions of traffic signs or signals, in disregard of dissuasion;

(5) Instructing or coercing personnel who drive vehicles to violate traffic rules;

(6) Violating traffic rules as pedestrians or as persons who drive vehicles other than motor vehicles, in disregard of dissuasion;

(7) Obstructing traffic by setting up stalls, piling things or working in the streets, in disregard of an order to stop.

## ITEM 64B

Although the following news item concerns pre-1957 traffic regulations, the cases described are typical of the experience with traffic cases under the SAPA.

[Chiang I-fan, "Western District Public Security Subbureau Handles a Batch of Traffic Violation and Accident Cases," *Kuang-chou jih-pao* (Canton daily), July 4, 1956]

On the twenty-eighth of last month at the western district people's meeting place, the western district public security subbureau convened a large meeting for the handling of traffic violation and accident cases, and handled a batch of serious violations of traffic rules that led to accidents affecting persons.

Carpenter Wu Hsien-liang drove his brakeless bicycle at an excessive speed, and struck and injured a pedestrian who was walking in a crosswalk. In addition to being made responsible for all the medical expenses, he was punished by three days of detention. Vehicle repairman Huang Chu-sheng drove a motorbike without a license, did not obey traffic directions, and almost caused an auto accident. He was punished by three days of detention.

Without obtaining approval of the public security organ, Ch'eng-feng Wood Shop of En-ming road used the sidewalks to display its wood and failed to heed repeated urging [to desist]. It was fined fifteen yuan.

In addition, on To-pao road, a local spice merchant, Huang Yü-chiao (female), habitually did not observe traffic rules. On May 3 of this year, when crossing To-pao road, once again she did not walk in the crosswalk, and she was struck and injured on the left hand by a bicyclist. Based on the allocation of responsibility for the accident, the medical expenses were assumed by the bicyclist, and the injured person was fined two yuan.

Over six hundred delegates from organs, factories, enterprises, organizations, and schools in this district and from the neighborhood masses attended the large meeting. After they heard the public security organ announce the disposition of the violators' cases they all manifested their support.

## ITEM 65

[SAPA (Oct. 22, 1957), p. 250]

Article 14. A person who commits any one of the following acts violating the regulation of household registration shall be punished by detention of not more than five days, a fine of not more than ten yuan, or a warning:

(1) Not reporting [matters of] household registration as prescribed [by law];

(2) Falsely reporting [matters of] household registration;

(3) Altering, transferring, or putting up for loan or sale household registration certificates;

(4) Impersonating another for purposes of household registration;

(5) As a manager of a hotel, not registering guests as prescribed [by law].

Article 15. A person who commits any one of the following acts interfering with public health or the clean appearance of cities shall be punished by detention of not more than three days, a fine of not more than six yuan, or a warning:

(1) Dirtying well water, spring water, or other sources of water used by the public for drinking;

(2) In cities, willfully piling things up, drying things in the sun, or cooking articles with a foul odor, in disregard of an order to stop;

(3) Dumping rubbish or filth in the street, throwing away the carcasses of animals there, or urinating or defecating anywhere in the street;

(4) Willfully smearing, carving up or painting on structures, or pasting advertisements or items of propaganda at places other than those assigned, in disregard of dissuasion;

(5) Intentionally damaging flowers, grass, or trees in parks or on the sides of streets.

## ITEM 66

Recall the case histories related in Items 55–58. Items 57 and 58 are plainly cases of beating that fell under Article 10(2) of the SAPA. But what provision was violated by the offender in Item 56? Is adultery made unlawful by the SAPA? What about bigamy? Does Article 2 (Item 51) provide any independent justification for the imposition of sanctions? Does the following provision of the Act?

[SAPA (Oct. 22, 1957), p. 254]

Article 31. Acts which violate security administration but which are not enumerated in this Act may, by comparison with the most similar [acts enumerated in the] clauses of Articles 5 to 15 of this Act, be punished by city or county public security bureaus. However, such action shall be subject to the approval of the city or county people's council.

If you were a public security officer or a member of a people's council, how would you determine whether certain undesirable conduct that is not specifically proscribed by the SAPA should or should not be deemed a violation of the Act?

## D. SAPA PROCEDURE

## ITEM 67

[SAPA (Oct. 22, 1957), pp. 250–251]

Article 16. Cases of violation of security administration shall be under the jurisdiction of city and county public security organs.

Article 17. Security administration punishments shall be decided upon by city and county public security bureaus and public security subbureaus; warnings may be decided upon by public security stations.

In rural villages detention of not more than five days may be decided upon by public security stations; in places where there are no public security stations, administrative village (town) people's councils may be entrusted to decide upon warnings and upon detentions of not more than five days. In order to deal with the specific circumstances in rural villages, public security stations and administrative village (town) people's councils may impose labor instead of detention.

Article 18. Procedures for the imposition of security administration punishments:

(1) A summons shall be used to summon persons who have violated security administration; persons who are in the act of violating security administration may be summoned orally on the spot.

(2) A record must be made of acts that violate security administration, and the person who violated security administration must sign it; if there are witnesses, the witnesses shall also sign their names.

(3) A decision to impose security administration punishment must be written and given to the person who violated security administration.

## ITEMS 68A–68B

These two documents, derived from an interview with an experienced public security officer and based on a hypothetical fact situation, are typical of those employed in administration of the SAPA. The first represents an application for detention that is submitted by the security adjustment committee of a production brigade. It is supported by the public security special agent in the area and is approved by the county public security bureau. The second represents a copy of the security detention warrant in the case. The stub of the warrant is retained by the bureau, and the larger portion is given to the violator. This warrant is often used in lieu of the written decision called for by Article 18(3).

## ITEM 68A

Application for Security Detention [derived from interview]

Name: Ho Hsiu-ch'ün         Sex: female         Age: 28

Family Status: middle peasant

Address: 2nd team, agricultural production brigade of the suburban commune of the city of Shan-t'ou, Kwangtung province.

Family circumstances: husband, mother-in-law, two brothers, two sisters, six persons in all.

---

### Principal facts

1. During the initial period of the people's commune in 1958 Ho had a fight with a certain commune member named Ho Chün and received criticism-education.

2. She has had two previous fights with the women in her family in 1960 and received criticism-education but did not change.

3. On August 13, 1960, Ho Hsiu-ch'ün without reason beat up her mother-in-law Ch'en Pin because of a family matter and injured her to a great extent. (Please see the examination record made out by the doctor.)

---

Opinion of the Security Adjustment Committee

Ho Hsiu-ch'ün has had fights with other people on several occasions, but despite criticism-education she has not changed. She has disrupted social order. We request that her case be dealt with

Li Tseng-jen, Chairman
[Date]

---

Examination opinion

Investigation indicates that the circumstances of the case are serious. She should be given security detention

Wang En, Public Security
Special Agent
[Date]

---

Approval opinion

On the basis of the materials in the report, she is given a punishment of 10 days of security detention.

Public Security Bureau
[Chop]
[Date]

### ITEM 68B

Security Detention Warrant [derived from interview]

| Stub | Kwangtung province |
|---|---|
| Ho Hsiu-ch'ün, female, of the 2nd team, agricultural production brigade of the suburban commune, is given 10 days of security detention for violation of Article 10(2) of the Security Administration Punishment Act. | City of Shan-t'ou Security Detention Warrant<br>Because Ho Hsiu-ch'ün, female, 28 years old, of the 2nd team, agricultural production brigade of the suburban commune of the City of Shan-t'ou, beat someone up and the circumstances of the case were serious, she is given 10 days of security detention in accordance with the provisions of Article 10(2) of the Security Administration Punishment Act. |
| Approved by<br>Li Chia-i Chief of the Security Section | Certified<br>Public Security Bureau, City of Shan-t'ou<br>[Date] |

### ITEM 69

For cases that illustrate some typical adjudication procedures, recall Items 55, 57, 58 and 62B. This item reflects a more elaborate hearing because of the relatively serious nature of the case and the participation of another government organization.

[Interview]

In late 1958 a truck driven by a cadre of the county communications bureau was proceeding down a highway within the city limits of the county seat. At one point the highway was partially obstructed because a supply-marketing cooperative had allowed some agricultural equipment that was in its care to remain on the road. As the truck passed the obstructed area it struck a child, who died at the hospital shortly thereafter.

Representatives of the public security bureau and the communications bureau investigated the scene and questioned the driver, the manager of the cooperative, the two cadres who were directly in charge of the agricultural equipment, and witnesses. After studying the materials thus gathered, the public security bureau convened an informal meeting of the parties involved and the witnesses. It was held at the bureau and, although a representative of the communications bureau participated, the deputy chief of the public security bureau's security section presided. The representatives of the respective bureaus questioned the parties and witnesses about matters that had not been clear to them during their study of the investigation materials. All the parties and witnesses were given an opportunity to clarify previous statements, to present their views and to defend themselves. After the meeting the representatives of the bureaus studied the case further and arrived at a tentative decision, which was cleared with the chief of the public security bureau.

Before announcing its decision, because those who were deemed to have violated the SAPA were state cadres, the public security bureau notified their employing units — the communications bureau and the commerce bureau — and the county Party organization department of the facts of the case and its impending action under the Act. It also recommended to them what it considered to be appropriate disciplinary sanctions apart from the administrative punishments to be meted out by it under the SAPA. After a few days the public security bureau was informed that the employing organs had decided to follow its recommendations and to give the truck driver a demotion of one grade and a large demerit for careless driving and, for their carelessness in allowing the road to be obstructed, to criticize the three cadres from the cooperative in a bulletin describing the case that would be circulated to all cadres in the area.

The public security bureau then made public its decision, which was to require each of the four violators of the Act to pay in one month's wages. The total, approximately 200 yuan, was sent by the public security bureau to the county civil affairs section, which contributed an equivalent sum and sent the entire amount to the family of the deceased child as "dependents' supplementary aid money."

1. Does the SAPA provide for a fair hearing prior to imposition of sanctions?
2. Do the interviews suggest that a fair hearing is accorded in practice?

3. What should be the elements of fairness in the context of SAPA adjudication?

4. How and why might the answers of Chinese Communist, non-Communist Chinese, and Soviet lawyers differ from your own and from each other? Consider the following excerpt from the *Lectures*:

"Also, when people's courts apply criminal punishments to criminals, they conduct the proceedings publicly. On the basis of provisions of the Law of the People's Republic of China for the Organization of People's Courts, except in special circumstances, all hearings of cases in people's courts are to be conducted publicly, and all judgments are to be pronounced publicly. Thus criminal punishments differ from administrative sanctions, disciplinary sanctions, and other such coercive measures in that the organs of and procedures for enforcement are different." [9]

## ITEM 70

[SAPA (Oct. 22, 1957), pp. 251–252]

Article 18. Procedures for the execution of security administration punishments:

(4) If a person who has violated security administration does not accept the decision made by a public security subbureau or a public security station, he may file a petition for review within forty-eight hours; the organ that originally decided the case shall, within twenty-four hours, send the petition for review, together with the written decision, to the public security organ of the next higher level; within five days of its receipt of the petition for review the public security organ of the next higher level shall make the final decision. If the decision of the administrative village (town) people's council is not accepted, the county public security bureau shall receive the petition for review.

(5) If a person who has violated security administration does not accept the decision made by a city or county public security bureau, he may file a petition for review within forty-eight hours; within five days of its receipt of the petition for review the city or county public security bureau shall reinvestigate and make the final decision.

(6) In remote mountainous districts, where communications are difficult, when the organ that originally decided the case or the organ that accepted the petition for review actually has no way to send the petition for review or to make the final decision in accordance with the times prescribed by Paragraphs 4 and 5, it need not observe the prescribed time limitations, but it is required to make a notation in the written decision of the time by which the prescribed time was exceeded and the reason therefor.

(7) Execution of the original decision shall be temporarily suspended from the time a person who violates security administration files his petition for review. If a person who has violated security administration has no fixed local residence, execution of the original decision can be temporarily suspended only after he finds a guarantor or pays a given amount of guarantee money.

9. September 1957, p. 176.

## ITEMS 71A–71B

Recall Item 56, which relates one instance in which a petition for review was successful. The interviews that follow provide other accounts. It is important to note here that, while interviews reveal the actual availability of review procedures, at least at certain times and places, they emphasize that for a variety of practical considerations review is rarely sought.

## ITEM 71A

[Interview]

In the summer of 1960 Yang was a member of a production team of a rural commune in Kwangtung province. Despite the fact that he had not been well and had asked for time off from work so that he might receive medical treatment, Yang was ordered to go out to the fields by Liu, the leader of his production team. Yang refused to go. This led to a harsh argument, with a good deal of cursing, and Yang finally struck Liu on the jaw. The blow did not injure Liu, but since Liu was a cadre, this was clearly a serious matter. Liu reported it to the chief of the brigade's security adjustment committee, who thought the matter serious enough to require an immediate report to commune headquarters. Since Liu had not suffered any injury the commune security chief said that there was no need to notify the public security bureau of the case. But he ordered Yang sent up to commune headquarters for questioning, and a militiaman escorted him there. When questioned by the commune security chief, Yang admitted the offense but argued that he had been provoked by the team leader who had unreasonably refused to allow him sick leave. The security chief replied that, no matter what the provocation, to refuse to abide by a work order and to strike a cadre were matters that could not go unpunished. The security chief conferred with the special agent of the public security bureau, and as a result of their consultation it was decided to give Yang five days of detention, with labor substituted for detention. Yang thus stayed at commune headquarters and labored nearby instead of being detained at the public security bureau.

At the conclusion of his first day of labor, Yang left the commune and went to the public security bureau to seek review of his punishment. He was received by a secretary of the security section, who interviewed him about the case and then told him to return to the commune to continue his labor while the bureau sent someone to investigate. The next morning the bureau sent an officer down to the team to check on Yang's story. He reported back that Yang had been ill and that the incident had occurred as Yang had described it. The case was then discussed by the section chief, the deputy section chief, and the three secretaries of the section. They agreed that Yang did not deserve detention, and the bureau's special agent for the commune was notified by telephone that detention was too harsh for Yang and that he should be released and sent home after receiving criticism-education. When the special agent and the commune security chief talked to Yang, they told him that he had to apologize to the team leader. To make certain that the apology was made and that the dispute was smoothed over, the chief of the brigade security adjustment committee escorted Yang back to the team, listened to the apology, and then admonished both men about the importance of having no further incidents between them because of the bad effect such incidents had upon production and upon the public. At the conclusion of the lecture, both men agreed to forget the matter.

## ITEM 71B

[Interview]

Hu was a staff member of a production brigade in a rural commune. His job was to record the work points earned by brigade members each day. On one occasion in 1959 he and one of the members became embroiled in a heated dispute over the accuracy of Hu's figures, and a fight broke out. Hu, who had been losing the fight, picked up a knife and slashed his opponent. Although blood flowed as a result, the wound was not serious. Hu was sentenced by the public security bureau to fifteen days of detention for violating Article 10(2) of the SAPA. He was also required to pay the medical expenses of his victim. Hu had a better than average education and asked a secretary of the security section of the bureau who came from the same administrative village as Hu what he could do about reducing the sentence. The secretary told him to write a letter to the bureau chief, which he did. After reviewing the case, the chief decided that Hu's use of the knife had been an unpremeditated response to provocation and reduced the detention to seven days.

1. If review of SAPA adjudication is available, what factors might account for the fact that it is seldom sought?

2. Should the availability of review be deemed to cure any deficiencies that might exist in the fairness of initial adjudication procedures? What kind of review should be necessary?

3. Can one who is subjected to sanctions under the SAPA obtain review by any other authority? Consider the following excerpts:

a. Lo Jui-ch'ing states in his "Explanation":

"The decision[-making] procedure prescribed by the Act not only reflects the seriousness which the law should have but also safeguards the right of petition for review of the person receiving punishment. At the same time, because the facts of cases involving the violation of security administration generally are relatively simple and easily clarified, they [the cases] can be quickly handled. If they are not handled for a long time, they may lose their educational significance. Therefore, the decision[-making] procedure strives for simplicity to facilitate execution [of the Act]. Apart from this, in cases decided by county or city public security bureaus, after the person receiving punishment presents a petition for review, it is prescribed that the county or city public security bureau review the case. This is because there is no actual need to send these cases of petition for review to the public security organs of the provinces or the special districts for review and also because the matter might well be delayed by going to and fro. Handling this kind of case belongs within the scope of administrative powers, so we believe that it is also unnecessary to turn the petition for review over to the procuracy for it to handle. Naturally, if public security personnel commit unlawful acts in violation of the Act or misuse their powers, procuratorial organs should conduct supervision in accordance with law." [10]

b. Article 81 of the Constitution provides in part:

"The Supreme People's Procuracy of the People's Republic of China shall exercise procuratorial authority over the various departments belonging to the State Council, local state organs of the various levels, personnel of state organs, and citizens to see whether they observe the law. Local people's procuracies of the various levels and special people's procuracies shall exercise procuratorial authority to the extent prescribed by law." [11]

## E. SAPA: "THE GENERAL PART"

### ITEMS 72A–72B
### ITEM 72A

[SAPA (Oct. 22, 1957), p. 252]

Article 19. Persons who commit acts that violate security administration shall be exempt from punishment if after three months they have not been pursued [for responsibility].

The period specified in the previous paragraph shall be calculated from the day on which the acts that violate security administration occur. If acts that violate security administration are of a successive or continuing nature, calculation shall begin with the day on which the acts terminate.

Security administration punishment shall not be executed if, after three months from the day of decision, it has not yet been executed.

Article 20. Persons who commit acts that violate security administration shall be punished lightly or shall be exempted from punishment in any one of the following situations:

(1) Actual lack of understanding of the rules of security administration;

(2) Coercion by another;

(3) Spontaneous confession or sincere admission of error.

### ITEM 72B

[Interview]

In patrolling his beat one night, a city policeman apprehended four men who had just illegally broken into a state warehouse. He took them directly to the public security bureau. There the secretary of the security section who was on duty questioned them after talking with the policeman and with warehouse employees who had also come upon the scene. After getting the facts straight,

10. P. 260.
11. Pp. 26–27.

the secretary went to the bureau dormitory, woke up the section chief, and discussed the case with him. Because none of the men had previous records, it was decided that criminal punishment would not be appropriate. But since breaking into a state warehouse was a serious violation of the SAPA, they determined that detention was justified for those who voluntarily participated in the offense. The ringleader received a fifteen-day sentence and two others were given ten days each. The fourth member of the group, however, merely received a warning, since questioning of the group had made it clear that he had been afraid of being caught, had been unwilling to join in their plan, and had only yielded after considerable moral pressure by the others. This was deemed to constitute coercion as defined in Article 20(2) of the Act.

Did the fourth member of the group violate the Act? Should coercion serve as an exculpating or a mitigating circumstance? Should "moral pressure" constitute "coercion"? How and why might the answers of Chinese differ from our own?

## ITEMS 73A–73C

## ITEM 73A

[SAPA (Oct. 22, 1957), p. 252]

Article 21. Persons who commit acts that violate security administration shall be punished severely or shall be given punishment of increased severity in any one of the following situations:

(1) The consequences are relatively serious;

(2) Repeated punishment fails to change the violator;

(3) The violator shifts the blame to another person;

(4) The violator refuses to respond to a summons for interrogation or evades punishment.

## ITEM 73B

[Interview]

One night in late 1959 Ch'en, a worker who lived adjacent to a state food store in a small city, sneaked into the store and stole some cooking oil, salt, and tobacco to meet the needs of his family. This would ordinarily have been treated as a petty offense, since the amounts involved were modest, the offense had no political implications, Ch'en's class status was good, and he had had no previous difficulties with the law. But Ch'en had failed properly to close the spigot to the barrel in which the oil was kept, and after he left the premises the storeroom became inundated with cooking oil. This not only ruined a large quantity of oil but also a great deal of tobacco and salt. Therefore, instead of merely receiving the customary warning and having to return the stolen goods or pay a small fine, Ch'en was given twenty days of detention by the public security bureau on the ground that his violation of the SAPA had had rather serious consequences.

# ITEM 73C

[Interview]

In late 1959 Chou, a staff member of a production brigade in a rural commune, embezzled a batch of grain ration coupons that were in his charge. He sold some, used the money thus obtained to buy large amounts of grain with other coupons, and retained still others. He informed the county public security bureau that the ration coupons had been stolen from his custody. After a brief investigation, cadres from the bureau came to suspect Lo, who had previously been punished for such thefts under the SAPA and whose family seemed economically better off than most. But there was no evidence linking Lo to this incident.

In these circumstances the bureau's security section decided that it was necessary to detain Lo informally for a few days of "surprise-attack interrogation." Lo was taken to the bureau and subjected to lengthy questioning by two cadres. In rotation one of them questioned Lo while the other listened for contradictions, discrepancies, and loopholes in Lo's answers. Lo confessed to an offense of which the bureau had been previously unaware, theft of some agricultural crops, and for that offense he was held by the bureau to have violated Article 11(1) of the SAPA. Since the consequence of that offense was rather serious and he already had a record of similar offenses, he was given fifteen days of detention [see Article 21(1), (2), Item 73A] instead of the maximum ten days of detention prescribed by Article 11. He steadfastly denied theft of the ration coupons and was absolved of responsibility for it.

This left the theft of the ration coupons still unsolved. The bureau began to suspect Chou, because he had had the coupons in his charge. Two investigators checked with his neighbors and heard that Chou's family had a lot of grain on hand and some extra pigs. On the basis of this information and Chou's position, the security section issued a search warrant authorizing the search of his house. The search revealed a great deal of grain and many extra ration tickets. When unable to explain this situation, Chou broke down and confessed.

The bureau notified the commune of the facts of the case and its intended decision. Chou was suspended from his position pending disposition of the case by the bureau. Since he was a member of the Communist Youth League, the bureau also informed the CYL of its plans. The next day the CYL, after having had a private interview with Chou, sent the bureau a copy of its certificate expelling him from its ranks. In the interim a public security cadre had discussed the case with the secretary of the Party branch of Chou's production brigade, who agreed with the public security's recommendation to remove Chou from his position as a brigade cadre and send him down to labor in a production team. Chou's dismissal was then announced at a meeting of all brigade cadres. The following evening, at a meeting of all brigade members, the first item on the agenda was a speech by the chairman of the brigade security defense committee, who was also the deputy secretary of the Party branch. He related the facts of the case and announced that Chou had been removed from his staff position and that the public security bureau had deemed it necessary to give him fifteen days of detention in view of the fact that Chou had attempted to attribute his violation to another [see Article 21(3), Item 73A]. After this announcement two militiamen took Chou off to the bureau's detention house. Upon his release he became an ordinary peasant laborer.

The detention meted out in Item 73B was ten days beyond the maximum prescribed in Article 11 and that in Item 73C was five days beyond the prescribed maximum. Does the Act place any limit on the extent to which punishment may be increased under Article 21? Recall Article 3(3), Item 51.

## ITEMS 74A–74B
### ITEM 74A

[SAPA (Oct. 22, 1957), pp. 252–253]

Article 22. Where one person commits two or more kinds of acts that violate security administration, the punishments shall be determined separately but shall be combined in one decision. However, the combined [period of] detention may not exceed fifteen days, and the combined fine may not exceed thirty yuan. When detention and a fine are imposed at the same time, they shall be executed at the same time.

When two or more kinds of results arise from one act, punishment shall be [determined] on the basis of the most serious kind of result.

When a person successively commits the same kind of act that violates security administration, he shall be punished severely or shall be given punishment of increased severity.

Article 23. When two or more persons jointly commit acts that violate security administration, they shall be punished separately.

One who incites or coerces another to violate security administration shall be given the punishment prescribed for the acts incited or coerced.

### ITEM 74B

[Interview]

Ho, who had been a malcontent ever since his small business had been subjected to "socialist reform," was a staff member of a supply-marketing co-operative. He was in the habit of venting his spleen on a particular truck driver who frequently came to the cooperative. One day in 1960, after an unpleasant scene with the driver, he gave candy to some eight-year-old children and persuaded them to let the gas out of the gas tank of the driver's truck. The driver reported the incident and his suspicions to the public security bureau. Its investigators questioned the children, who told them about Ho's incitement. After Ho was questioned and admitted responsibility, he was taken to the security section of the bureau, where he was criticized and given a twenty-yuan fine for violation of the SAPA. The children were given a lecture on keeping out of mischief.

## ITEMS 75A–75B

Recall Item 53.

## ITEM 75A

[SAPA (Oct. 22, 1957), p. 253]

Article 24. When acts that violate security administration by an organ, organization, school, enterprise, or cooperative actually arise from orders of that unit's responsible executive administrator, the responsible executive administrator shall be punished.

## ITEM 75B

[Interview]

Leng was the principal of a primary school in a small city. He wanted the school to have an attractive rock garden, so one day in 1960 he told the school children to go out to search for slabs of stone and rocks and to bring back all that they could. He said nothing about the nearby highway that was in a run-down condition, and some enterprising children carried away a good many fragments of the highway without Leng's knowledge. When this was discovered, the public security bureau gave those children a lecture on the importance of not violating the SAPA and on the effect their conduct might have had on safety. Because the principal had instructed the children to gather such materials and because he had failed to caution them against resort to the highway, which was an obvious source, he was deemed to have caused the damage in violation of Article 8(1) of the Act and was given a formal warning.

## ITEMS 76A–76B

## ITEM 76A

[SAPA (Oct. 22, 1957), p. 253]

Article 25. No punishment shall be given to one who violates security administration due to an irresistible cause.

## ITEM 76B

[Interview]

During the iron and steel ("backyard furnace") movement of 1958, many temporary roads were built in China to help meet transportation needs. One day in 1959 in Fukien province a truck belonging to a transportation company of a county communications bureau suddenly swerved off one such road and turned over. The transportation company asked the county public security bureau to investigate the driver's responsibility. Investigation revealed that the road had been built hastily and badly and had suddenly collapsed under pressure of the truck, causing the truck to turn off the road despite the driver's best efforts to master the situation. The bureau concluded that the driver had not been at fault and that the action had occurred as the result of an irresistible cause, and it gave the company a certificate to this effect.

1. The bureau took no action against the driver in this item. Should it have adjudged him to have violated the Act but not imposed punishment?

2. Does any provision of the SAPA purport to punish negligent conduct?

3. Does any provision make negligence a mitigating circumstance?

4. What inference can be drawn from Article 25 concerning the punishability of negligent conduct? Recall Item 63B.

## ITEMS 77A–77B

### ITEM 77A

[SAPA (Oct. 22, 1957), p. 253]

Article 26. No punishment shall be given for acts that violate security administration by persons who have not reached the age of thirteen; acts that violate security administration by persons who have reached the age of thirteen but who have not reached the age of eighteen shall be punished lightly. However, the heads of their families or their guardians shall be ordered to discipline them more strictly. If this kind of act arises from overindulgence by the head of the family or guardian, the head of the family or guardian shall be punished, but punishment shall be limited to a warning or a fine.

### ITEM 77B

[Interview]

An eleven-year-old boy and his father were returning home from a barber shop in the suburbs of a city in Fukien province in 1958. A truck was coming down the road. While his father watched, the boy picked up a rock, waited for the truck to get within range and threw the rock at it. The rock smashed a window in the truck and grazed, but did not hurt, the driver. The driver stopped the truck and began to shout at the boy and his father, and a crowd gathered. The crowd finally prevailed upon father and son to accompany the driver to the nearest public security station in the city. The secretary on duty at the public security station sent them to the public security bureau. There the boy was only given criticism-education, but by virtue of Article 26 of the SAPA his father was fined twenty yuan for a violation of Article 8(2) of the Act.

1. Article 8 provides for a maximum fine of fourteen yuan. Could a twenty-yuan fine be justified?

2. If investigation by the police had revealed that the father had not been present at the time his son threw the rock but that the father had "spoiled" the boy through excessive lenience, would this have been "overindulgence" within the meaning of Article 26?

3. Why do you suppose the Act precludes giving detention to overindulgent parents?

ITEMS 78A–78C

ITEM 78A

[SAPA (Oct. 22, 1957), p. 253]

Article 27. No punishment shall be given to a mentally ill person who violates security administration at a time when he is unable to understand the nature of or to control his own acts; the head of his family or his guardian shall be ordered to watch over him more strictly and to give him medical care. If the family head or guardian actually has the ability to watch over him but does not and he causes a violation of security administration, the family head or guardian shall be punished, but punishment shall be limited to a warning or a fine.

ITEM 78B

[Interview]

Yen lived with his parents and siblings in a commune in the suburbs of a county seat in Fukien province. Until 1959 he had had no history of involvement with the law. At that time, when he was twenty-six, he fell ill as a result of overwork during the "backyard furnace" movement, and during this illness he also developed symptoms of mental illness. He often refused to eat, would laugh without reason, and frequently hit children. On one occasion he severely beat a neighbor's child, but his family managed to smooth the incident over. His parents did not report his unusual conduct to the chairman of the security defense committee of their production brigade or to the secretary of the Party branch, nor did they themselves take measures to help him.

One day Yen set fire to the house of the deputy leader of their production team. When a child saw him do this and told him to stop, Yen hit him. Other people who came on the scene after the fire had started saw Yen laughing nearby. The fire destroyed the house and caused 700-yuan damage. The chairman of the SDC reported the fire to the county public security bureau, which sent out two investigators. They interviewed the child, the other witnesses, and Yen, who merely laughed and acted odd. They sent Yen back to the PSB in the company of two militiamen. The PSB then telephoned the county hospital to notify them to expect Yen, who was escorted there. While he underwent several mental examinations in the hospital, the PSB investigators continued to inquire into his history, since they suspected that he might be feigning mental illness in order to escape punishment. They learned of his physical illness, his subsequent strange and violent actions, and the failure of his parents to control him or to report their inability to do so. They informed the hospital of this background data.

On the basis of the doctors' examinations of Yen and his history, the hospital sent the bureau a certificate which stated that he was suffering from mental illness. From this the bureau inferred that he had been unable to understand the nature of or to control his conduct at the time of the fire and that he should receive mental treatment rather than administrative or criminal punishment. Since Yen's illness was serious and he constituted a danger to the community, the PSB applied to the provincial public security department for authority to send him to the provincial hospital for the mentally ill rather than have him remain at the county general hospital. This authority was granted, and he was still in the mental hospital as of 1961.

Although Yen was thus exempted from punishment, the PSB found that, by virtue of Article 27 of the SAPA, his parents had violated the Act, because they had failed to report his mental illness and violent conduct. This had given him the opportunity to remain at large and to violate the Act by burning down the house of the team's deputy leader. The parents were required to pay a 100-yuan compensatory fine, which was turned over to the deputy leader. Since the fine did not make the victim whole but rather reflected the financial situation of Yen's family, the PSB recommended to the county civil affairs section that it assist the victim. It gave him 200 yuan and this total of 300 yuan was used to buy the materials necessary for building a similar house. The secretary of the Party branch of the production brigade then authorized a group from the victim's production team to build the house free of charge, which they did in a short time.

## ITEM 78C

[Interview]

Li was a young schoolteacher who was unhappily married to the principal of her primary school. Knowing that a divorce would be very difficult to obtain without a substantial reason, she thought that one might be granted if her husband were found to be a counterrevolutionary. Therefore, in late 1957 she reported him as such to the city public security bureau, and then applied for a divorce. The bureau's investigation confirmed what was already known to it — that the husband had served in a minor government post under the Nationalists and therefore had a "history" — but it failed to uncover any evidence of what was deemed to constitute counterrevolutionary activity. Thus no action was taken. Yet Li kept making daily visits to the bureau to make new accusations, and after a few weeks developed an affection for one of the staff members of the bureau's public reception office. When it became clear that the bureau was unimpressed by her accusations, Li began to make similar ones in school and caused repeated scenes there.

The city education bureau was prepared to expel her from her teaching position, but the PSB counseled patience and subjected Li to numerous sessions of criticism-education. But she became more difficult than ever when the local people's court, having learned from the PSB that the latter did not regard Li's husband as a counterrevolutionary, refused to grant her a divorce. When Li began to make anti-Communist statements and to beat on the doors of the PSB, the PSB decided that stronger measures were needed. It detained Li and called in a doctor from the local hospital to give her a mental examination. He reported that Li was not suffering from mental illness or abnormality but was extremely provoked and spiteful. On this basis the PSB decided that she should not be hospitalized for treatment but should be punished. It notified the education bureau to go ahead with Li's expulsion and that it would give her seven days of detention for violation of Article 5(3) of the SAPA.

Following her release from detention, Li continued in the same vein. She was twice more found to have violated the Act, being detained each time, the last for twenty days. On each occasion medical experts reported that she was not mentally ill. When short-term detention seemed ineffective, the PSB placed Li, along with a group of other urban misfits, on a farm in a mountainous area of the county. But in a few days she returned to the PSB to continue her protests. At that point the PSB simply detained her indefinitely without resorting to any legal procedures whatever.

After three months of labor, study, and daily lectures by public security cadres, Li seemed to have improved considerably. When the prospect of release was discussed with her, she asked to be given a factory job in the city rather than work in the countryside, and the PSB agreed to this. Once at the factory, working and living apart from her husband, she behaved reasonably except for continuing to send letters to the PSB receptionist of whom she was fond. The PSB put an end to this by transferring him to another city, and Li ceased to be a problem.

1. Who determines whether an offender is mentally responsible for violation of the SAPA?

2. What weight appears to be attached to the views of medical authorities?

3. Does the Act authorize confining irresponsible offenders in hospitals? For how long?

4. If a friend violated the SAPA and was confined to a hospital on the ground that he was not responsible for his unlawful conduct, what procedure might be invoked to obtain review of that decision?

## ITEMS 79A–79D
### ITEM 79A

[SAPA (Oct. 22, 1957), p. 253]

Article 28. One who violates security administration while in a state of intoxication shall be punished after his state of intoxication has passed.

When, during the state of intoxication, there is danger to the person of the one who is intoxicated or a threat to the safety of the surroundings, the intoxicated person shall be restrained until he recovers sobriety.

### ITEM 79B

[Interview]

Kung was a labor model of his production brigade. One evening in 1959 he and other models were invited to a banquet at the county seat. As a special treat they were served wine. Kung, who was unaccustomed to wine, drank too much. On his way home that night he stopped in a field to rest and smoke a cigarette. The next thing he remembered was being awakened by a fire. It had been caused by his cigarette after he had fallen asleep. The fire destroyed a large area of grazing land. Yet, because of his labor exploits and his previously unblemished record, the county public security bureau gave him no sanction whatsoever.

## ITEM 79C

[Interview]

Ts'ai was a farmer who had too much to drink one evening. En route home, as he was walking in the middle of a small bridge, a truck sounded its horn to warn him to step to the side so that it could cross the bridge. Ts'ai merely laughed and refused to get out of the way. At the last moment the truck swerved to avoid hitting him, went out of control, and plunged over the side of the bridge into a shallow stream. The driver was not seriously hurt, nor was the truck badly damaged. Ts'ai was detained by the militiaman who was on guard at the bridge and was taken to the county public security bureau. After a few hours he sobered up and appreciated what had happened. Because he had been drunk, the security section decided not to recommend that he be prosecuted for a crime, as it otherwise would have, but to give him five days of detention and to make him pay compensation for obstructing bridge traffic in violation of Article 13(6) of the SAPA.

## ITEM 79D

[Interview]

One evening in early 1958 Kuo got drunk. On his way home he opened the door of the house of a neighbor whom he did not know and embraced the lady of the house. She screamed for help, and other neighbors immediately came on the scene and seized Kuo. Thinking that this might have been an attempted rape, these citizens took him to the nearby office of the residents' committee and notified the chairman of the security defense committee and the local patrolman, who soon appeared. After a few questions, it became apparent that Kuo was either intoxicated or was pretending to be. The policeman took Kuo to the public security station, and a doctor was summoned to examine him there. The doctor talked to Kuo, gave him a physical examination, and took a urine sample. He concluded that Kuo had been highly intoxicated. After a few hours in a cell in the public security station Kuo sobered up and sheepishly admitted to the station chief the facts that had been related by the neighbors and the victim.

The station chief then called the public security bureau's security section to ask for approval of his proposed disposition of the case. After the secretary who was on duty gave this approval, the station chief told Kuo that he had violated Article 10(1) of the SAPA and would have to pay a seven-yuan fine and make an apology to his victim. He ordered Kuo to appear at the bureau the next day to pay the fine and to pick up a copy of the bureau's decision in the case.

1. Does drunkenness constitute a violation of the SAPA?
2. Does the Act make drunkenness a mitigating circumstance?
Recall Article 20, Item 72A.


## F. APPLICABILITY OF THE SAPA TO OTHER PETTY OFFENSES

### ITEM 80

[SAPA (Oct. 22, 1957), p. 254]

Article 32. Apart from Articles 5–15, all provisions of this Act shall be applicable to other rules of security administration that prescribe security administration punishments except, however, where laws and decrees have [made] separate provisions.

### ITEM 81

[RULES OF THE PRC FOR REGULATION OF EXPLOSIVE ARTICLES (approved at the 63d plenary meeting of the State Council, Nov. 29, 1957; issued by the Ministry of Public Security, Dec. 9, 1957), *FKHP*, 6:270]

Article 10. A person who violates these Rules, if the circumstances of the case are minor, shall be given security administration punishment by public security organs in accordance with law. If the circumstances of the case are serious and if the violation constitutes a crime, the violator shall be pursued for criminal responsibility by judicial organs in accordance with law.

### ITEM 82

[FIRE PREVENTION SUPERVISION ACT OF THE PRC (approved at the 86th meeting of the Standing Committee of the NPC, Nov. 29, 1957; promulgated by the State Council, Nov. 30, 1957), *FKHP*, 6:263]

Article 11. A person whose violation of fire prevention rules, measures, or technical standards creates loss through fire disaster or a person who, although he does not create loss through fire disaster, refuses to execute fire prevention measures that fire prevention supervisory organs have notified him to adopt, shall, if the circumstances of the case are minor, be given security administration punishment by public security organs. If the violation constitutes a crime, the violator shall be pursued for criminal responsibility by judicial organs in accordance with law.

# Chapter IV    Rehabilitation through Labor

A. Antecedents

B. Rehabilitation through Labor
1. Authorizing Legislation
2. Nature of the Sanction
3. Persons Eligible for the Sanction and Procedures for Imposing It
4. Release
5. Evaluation and Interpretation

Some of the masses have described the transformation of elements who have been rehabilitated through labor and the forceful reform which the people's government has given them as follows:

> "Having dug up the decaying roots, we find a
> different person;
> A bad person becomes a good person, and stone turns
> into gold;
> Both hands are still as of old, but their function is
> very different;
> The old society forced people into becoming ghosts, the
> new changes ghosts into people."
>
> Chang Chien, "The System of
> Rehabilitation Through Labor
> in Our Country" (1959)[1]

The Chinese leaders, distorting Leninism, see the dictatorship of the proletariat primarily and even exclusively as an instrument of violence, keeping silent about the chief and most essential thing, the fact that it is a democracy for the working people, a socialist democracy. In the numerous Chinese articles and official documents there is not even a mention of democracy.

The practice of state construction that has taken shape in China conforms to this interpretation of the essence of the dictatorship of the proletariat. The broadly advertised campaign of struggle against so-called "right-wing elements and right-wing opportunists," accompanied by mass repressions, can serve as an example of this. On August 1, 1957, the C.P.R. [PRC] State Council adopted a resolution on labor re-education [rehabilitation through labor] that gave administrative agencies the right to confine practically any Chinese citizen in a special camp for an indefinite period without trial or investigation. On the basis of this resolution, labor re-education [rehabilitation through labor] was imposed on people, for example, "who refused transfer to other work,"

1. *CFYC,* 6:44 (1959).

"who constantly interfered in the work of others without reason," and so on. Many hundreds of thousands of people were subject to repression. What is this if not a gross violation of the elementary democratic rights and freedoms of citizens!

> "Revolutionary Theory Is Guide to Action: On the Dictatorship of the Proletariat," *Izvestia* (1964)[2]

Not every petty offender responds to informal adjustment and sanctioning or to SAPA punishment, as the case related in Item 78C illustrates. Habitual offenders of various types have proved troublesome to the Chinese government. Moreover, many antisocial acts by first offenders are deemed to be so serious as to warrant sanctions more severe than those described in Chapters II and III. The PRC has sought to deal with some of these situations through imposition of criminal sanctions. In other cases it has applied "noncriminal" sanctions that nevertheless constitute substantial deprivations. Chapter IV is concerned with the most severe of the noncriminal sanctions, "rehabilitation through labor," which was enacted into law as a major part of the reordering of the criminal process that took place during the second half of 1957.

In reading the following materials, one should ask:

1. What is rehabilitation through labor? How does it differ from criminal punishment?

2. For what kinds of conduct is rehabilitation through labor imposed? How does such conduct differ from that for which criminal punishment is imposed?

3. By what procedure is rehabilitation through labor imposed? How does it differ from criminal procedure?

4. What procedures and what standards are applied to determine when an individual's rehabilitation through labor should terminate?

5. Why is rehabilitation through labor useful to the PRC?

## A. ANTECEDENTS

Rehabilitation through labor grew out of a variety of experiments that took place in the years immediately preceding its formal enactment. Beginning with the early 1950's, many government and Party cadres who were suspected of serious political deviations and of perhaps even harboring counterrevolutionary sentiments were sent to "new life schools" in which they were involuntarily confined while undergoing examination and indoctrination. In some places, by 1956 the name of such schools had been changed to "rehabilitation through labor," reflecting the greater relative emphasis that had come to be placed upon physical labor in their "curriculum."

During its earliest years the PRC also resorted to similar measures to meet the serious threat to public order that was posed by the prevalence of prostitutes, petty thieves, black marketeers, opium addicts, vagrants, and other social parasites. Items 83–85 suggest various aspects of these early measures as background for our consideration of the present sanction.

2. May 17, 1964; translated in *CDSP*, 16.21:5 (June 19, 1964). Translation from the *Current Digest of the Soviet Press*, published weekly at Columbia University by the Joint Committee on Slavic Studies, appointed by the American Council of Learned Societies and the Social Science Research Council. Copyright 1964, vol. XVI, no. 21, the Joint Committee on Slavic Studies. Reprinted by permission.

## ITEM 83

[Mu Fu-sheng, *The Wilting of the Hundred Flowers* (1963), pp. 178–180]

.    .    .    .    .

In China one outlet and symptom of the surplus population was the great number of pickpockets in the larger cities. They were those whom circumstances more than moral depravity drove to a mode of income involving only minor danger. They were impossible to eradicate: when a few were arrested their activities subsided but soon after the convicted finished their short prison terms pickpockets throve again. The Communists wanted to wipe them out in one city in south China. First a few pickpockets were arrested and taken to the police station. There they put down their names, ages, addresses, and other particulars and were given a lecture on correct behaviour in a socialist society, the meaning of labour, the importance of public order, and so on, at the end of which they were asked whether they understood and repented. They all said they repented and each was then given a slip with his name on it which said that the holder was a pickpocket but had repented under the magnanimous treatment of the people. With these slips the thieves continued their activity and policemen pretended they were innocent when they were caught and showed the "repentance slips." Picking pockets became a safe and profitable activity; meanwhile the register in the police station grew. When the cadre[s] thought the files were more or less complete they took the second step. The most daring pickpockets, who were likely to be the leaders, were caught in cases which were almost robbery. They all "repented" and co-operated with the police and from them the cadre[s] gathered all the information they wanted about the types, methods, recruits, zoning, amount and histories of the pocketpicking population of the city. Then the third step came: one day these leaders were asked to summon all the pickpockets to a meeting; only those with these "repentance slips," that is, registered pickpockets, were admitted. There were the usual speeches by the Party members, confessions, applause and more speeches, but towards the end an official came to the microphone to announce that the Government, for the benefit of pickpockets, had organised a training course for them and that he was sure they all wanted to join it. Some veterans knew that that meant prison, but noticed only then that the place was surrounded by armed police. When they marched out under guard and passed a river bank some jumped into the water trying to escape, but police opened fire and they had to surrender and swim back. In the end they walked two by two into the prison like children from the orphanage going to Sunday school and their picture appeared the following day in the papers with the caption: "Criminals Voluntarily Joining the Training Course." In prison they were divided into small groups with a leader for each to report on their progress in indoctrination and a few veteran pickpockets who co-operated with the police to supervise them all. Like everyone else in China they had pamphlets read to them, elementary lessons in socialism, songs, speeches, criticisms, confessions, biographies, self-criticisms, discussions and interrogation — the whole Communist treatment. After a few weeks the training was pronounced complete and an official made a final speech telling the "converted" criminals that the Government would find jobs for them as far as possible, but if they offended again the punishment would be severe. Then they were sent home. By now the police knew everything about every pickpocket and the criminals knew each other better than they ever did before. After a while, some of them started nefarious activities again, and these, when convicted, were summarily sent to distant labour camps and never heard of anymore. Without help from the police the news spread speedily among the pickpockets and pickpocketing henceforth stopped.

## ITEM 84

The following excerpt is from an unpublished account by one of a group of Western lawyers who visited China in April 1956.

[L. C. B. Gower, "Looking at Chinese Justice: A Diary of Three Weeks Behind the Iron Curtain" (unpublished manuscript, n.d.), pp. 118–121]

.    .    .    .    .

In the morning . . . [my companions] and I set off with an interpreter to see the Loafers' Camp. We had been interested in it because it, and the Prostitutes' Camp, are two institutions where, admittedly, people are detained without trial. We were received by two officials who were described to us as the joint Directors. Why there should be two bosses of equal authority was not clear to me — it seemed a strange set-up. These two took it in turns to explain the place to us and to answer our questions.

The object of the Camp was to take in, reform, and educate in a trade "loafers," that is to say, thieves, pickpockets, pimps and idlers — anyone who had no work except some anti-social activity. Such people would normally be reported by someone (for example, the Residents' Committee) to the Bureau of Civil Affairs or the Bureau of Public Security and, after investigation, these Bureaux would ask the man or woman concerned to become an inmate in the Camp. Most came willingly because this provided them with food and lodging, and because they realised that in their present state there was no future for them in the New China. Those who refused might be brought in compulsorily. (Since they presumably realised that, it was hardly surprising that most came willingly.) They were retained until (a) they had accomplished an ideological reformation and (b) had learned a trade. The maximum period of detention was 3 years.

Since the Camp was set up in 1951, 4,047 had been taken in and 2,600 discharged. Of the 1,447 remaining, 750 had reached a condition justifying discharge but remained because they had not yet been placed in jobs. I asked if these 750 had been there more than 3 years and was told that some of them had. But all the 750 were paid wages varying from 18–70 yuan a month according to their skill. And if they had families in [nearby] Shanghai they could go home to sleep. Those who were still being reformed were paid no wages but were given rewards in money or kind. We were told that it was planned to do away with the reward system, which smacked too much of a prison, and to pay some sort of wage.

Those who misbehaved were punished by group criticism, warnings, and demerit marks. We tried to get a clear answer about what happened if none of these penalties sufficed. Apparently they nearly always did, but there were a few renegades. We asked about escapes. There had been some (in 1951–53, from 8 to 10 per annum, in 1954–3, and none since) but generally the family or neighbours "persuaded" the truants to return. On their return they were not punished but "educated even more patiently". There was no corporal punishment and no armed guards. Were there many institutions of this type? In Shanghai there had been four, two of this type and two which had merely engaged in ideological re-education without productive work: the latter two had now been closed. They couldn't tell us much about other cities, but there certainly were other camps elsewhere.

At this point . . . [a companion] raised the vital point about how someone brought in could effectively dispute that he was a loafer. "Suppose", he said, "I'm an artist (or musician); the neighbours are jealous of me and report me. What could I do?" The Director admitted very frankly that there had been cases in 1951 where people were brought in mistakenly. There had been no cases since because very careful enquiries were made.

"But what could a man do who thought his detention was wrongful? Could he bring the matter before a Court?"

"Certainly."

"But how? How does he get to a court while he is shut up?"

He was let out on leave during the latter part of his detention. And there was an official of the Camp who was a representative of the People's Reception Office which helped people to bring their cases to Court.

However, in the end they admitted that they didn't know of any cases where the matter had been taken to court. The 1951 mistakes were cleared up after an internal investigation and great care had been taken since and there had been no complaints. Here one of our hosts who had accompanied us, intervened to point out that before Liberation Shanghai had been a den of vice and that this very building was a thieves' kitchen which no decent citizen would dare approach. There had been a general appeal to the Government to clean up the City and one of the methods employed was to convert the thieves' kitchen into a reformatory and place of work. We assured them that we fully appreciated the problem and that no one could help but be impressed by the way in which vice had been suppressed. But we, as lawyers, were concerned with the civil liberties aspect and were trying, by our questions, to see exactly what the position of the individual was.

However, time was pressing so we asked if we could have a rapid glance round the Institution. Most of the inmates are sent out to work on building sites, but some are employed in the factory on carpentry (making medicine chests and the like) and the repair of simple machinery. It was these that we saw and talked to. There could be no complaint about their working conditions, but the sleeping quarters were appallingly over-crowded — worse than in the prisons we had seen — and the Directors frankly acknowledged it.

We questioned a man in the carpentry shop. Of course, we had to do so through an interpreter but, unlike our experience in the prisons and Work [reform through labor] Camps, the officials did not attempt to overhear the conversation. He had been an inmate for just over 3 years, was now 21, and, since the expiration of the 3 years had earned 35 yuan a month. During the latter part of the 3 year term he had been let out on leave once every fortnight. He had formerly been a wanderer. Someone sent him in to the Camp and he was willing to stay. He had now become a skilled carpenter.

We started to question another man but found that he too was one of those whose term had expired and we wanted to question a genuine "detainee". After some difficulty, one was found (it was said that nearly all those in the carpenters' shop were among the 750 whose terms had expired). He had been detained for 2 years and 10 months, and was expecting to be let out at the end of the month. He was 27 years old and had been a thief. He had received rewards nearly every month of about 7 yuan in cash and learned the trade of lathe-turner. He said that there was a regular medical examination once every 3 months.

It need hardly be said that this institution had somewhat disturbed us. Here, admittedly, people, who were not necessarily criminals and who certainly had not been convicted by any court, were compulsorily detained and made to work virtually without pay. To this extent, here we had "forced labour" in a naked and unashamed form. On the other hand, the authorities clearly were faced with an appalling problem of dealing with the riff-raff of a City like Shanghai . . . Reformation through work is at least a positive programme for converting the dregs of society into decent and productive citizens. Nor is it altogether fair to complain about the absence of a "trial". The whole point is that the vagabonds and prostitutes are not being punished for any particular crime. The worst feature, I suppose, is the apparent inadequacy of the remedies available to an individual who is wrongly accused of being an idler, a pickpocket or a prostitute. An administrative body acts both as investigator and as judge of a charge preferred by some unknown informer. If there is any laxity or corruption within that body, the risks are great.

Clearly this device is a ruthless solution of a social problem. But so far as one can see it has proved a pretty effective one. A man, woman, or child could now wander unmolested through the streets of Shanghai at any hour of the day or night. And neither there, nor in any of the other cities, did I see any sign of prostitution. From the viewpoint of sexual morality, Shanghai must now be the cleanest seaport in the world — and perhaps the dullest. This is another illustration of the age-old problem of whether the ends can justify the means. If, as we were assured, these Camps are merely temporary expedients to deal with a declining problem, I personally wouldn't take much exception to them. But although the number of admissions is pretty clearly on the decline, it is disturbing that inmates are not always released when their 3-year term is up. This may be unavoidable while there is still substantial unemployment.

But to express any real opinion on this vexed "forced labour" question one wants to find out how many people are involved. It's these statistics which no one will give us. Well, we'll go on asking.

## ITEM 85

The doubts which the Western lawyer, Mr. Gower, felt about the "loafers' camp" were also shared by Chinese in 1956. This item exemplifies the fruit of their then current zeal for law reform. Note the changes which it makes in the nature of the sanction and in the scope and procedure of its application. And compare Item 85's frank admission that mistakes were being made with the answers given to Mr. Gower in Item 84.

[INSTRUCTIONS OF THE MINISTRY OF INTERIOR OF THE PRC RE-LATING TO THE WORK OF PLACEMENT AND REFORM OF CITY VA-GRANTS (July 11, 1956), *FKHP*, 4:212–217]

Since the National Conference on the Work of Reforming City Vagrants in March of this year, the work of reforming vagrants in the various places has undergone very great development. Whether in resolving problems of the production and livelihood of vagrants themselves, in providing a labor force for industrial and agricultural production, or in preserving city social order, it has begun to play a conspicuous role. Energetically conducting the work of reforming vagrants has proved to be completely in conformity with the correct guideline of mobilizing all forces to serve socialist construction. However, even though the problem of dealing with vagrants by concentrating them in relatively large numbers is still new work in which the various places lack experience, and even though, at the time of our National Conference on the Work of Reforming City Vagrants, we did not sufficiently understand the actual circumstances of vagrants throughout the country in the new situation, we now see that it may not be necessary to provide shelter to some of those whom we then proposed as targets and that we also insufficiently emphasized that providing shelter should be conducted on a voluntary basis. Therefore, quite a few shortcomings and problems have been created in some places in the work of concentration, placement, and reform. This has been manifested mainly in [the following]: (1) during the initial period some places were not clear as to the scope of the classification "vagrant," and investigation work was not thorough enough — this led to some errors in providing shelter; (2) in the work of providing shelter some places did not hold firmly enough to the principle of voluntarism and adopted the erroneous method of coercively providing shelter; (3) in arranging for vagrants to participate in labor and production some places did not sufficiently comprehend and implement the guideline of combining reform with placement and they only concerned themselves with present production problems and did not care about the needs of long-term placement; (4) also, some places executed the work too mechanically in the direction that considered agriculture to be paramount in placement and reform, and they placed on farms vagrants who were not suited to participate in agricultural production; (5) also, some places were not reasonable enough in the work of disciplining vagrants and in compensating them for their labor. Some of the above shortcomings and problems were promptly overcome and resolved after being discovered, but, if we do not pay attention to them, they may recur in the future. Some still need to be overcome and resolved. Therefore, we have specially prepared the following Instructions and hope that the various places will study and execute them.

1. Since the arrival of the socialist high tide, opportunities for getting employment in cities have increased. Under the influence of the new situation, quite a few vagrants have changed. Some of them have already gotten employment, and some are about to get employment. Therefore, the category of vagrants who require placement and reform should be appropriately narrowed. In the future, vagrants who need to be placed and reformed are mainly to be elements who have not engaged in labor and production for a long time, have no proper employment, or have not the conditions for finding employment, to the extent that they have no way of maintaining a livelihood and instead steal, swindle, gamble in groups, beg for food, and use other such improper means in an effort to live.

The following kinds of persons shall not be dealt with as vagrants: (1) employed personnel and temporary workers who on occasion have committed an improper act: their problems shall be resolved by those concerned through the method of education; (2) laid-off personnel, jobless personnel, and peasants and disaster victims who have flowed from rural villages into cities and who have not committed improper acts or who have only committed minor improper acts shall generally be dealt with on an individual basis by adopting social relief [measures], by helping them to get employment, by mobilizing them to return to the country, and by other such measures; (3) if persons who in the past committed improper acts but who have now been corrected are still without fixed employment and have difficulty in earning a livelihood, they too shall be helped to get employment, and they are no longer to be treated as vagrants. Apart from this, elements among vagrants who must be punitively restrained according to law because they have committed crimes shall be dealt with by judicial and public security departments and also shall not be treated as targets of placement and reform.

2. Vagrants generally lack the labor habit and have no proper employment or proper source of livelihood. Therefore, in the work of reforming them we must firmly implement the guideline of combining reform with placement. That is, on the one hand, we should organize them to participate in labor and production so that they gradually change their loafing and lazy habits and have the labor habit inculcated in them. On the other hand, we should make the place of their reform the place of their long-term placement so that from it they obtain proper employment and a reliable source of livelihood and will not wander around, become homeless and again walk down the vagrants' road. Only in this way can the problem of vagrants be resolved from the roots.

Because conditions in various places differ and circumstances of vagrants themselves also vary greatly, the concrete methods of placement and reform of vagrants may be determined on the basis of the principle of doing what is suitable to the places and the persons involved. We need not forcibly demand uniformity. Generally speaking: (1) As for vagrants who have the conditions for participating in agricultural production, in rural villages where there are large pieces of barren but reclaimable land, farms shall be established for more concentrated placement and reform; in places where agricultural producers' cooperatives need a labor force, methods may also be adopted of subjecting these vagrants to supervision and reform by the masses by organizing production teams and planting them in cooperatives in a concentrated way or by dispersing them in cooperatives individually. The minority of vagrants who have homes in rural villages to which they can return shall be sent back to cooperatives of their native rural villages and subjected to supervision and reform by the masses. (2) Those vagrants whose involvement with home tasks or children is relatively great and who have other family members with fixed employment in a city, as well as those vagrants who really are not suited to agricultural production, shall not be compelled to go to rural villages for placement; rather, in cities, the measure of organizing rough work construction teams and other appropriate measures shall be adopted for their on-the-spot placement and reform.

We should not confuse the treatment of ordinary vagrants with the treatment of those disabled or aged vagrants who have basically lost their labor capacity and those children who have loafing and lazy habits and commit improper acts. The rehabilitation of those [of the latter groups] who have homes to which they can return shall be the responsibility of their families; those who do not have homes to which they can return shall be sent on an individual basis to institutions of rehabilitation for the disabled and the aged and to institutions of rehabilitation for children.

3. The work of placement and reform of vagrants is in substance a kind of work that helps vagrants to labor and to get employment, and it is not the enforcement of punitive legal restraints against them. Therefore, when concentrating, providing shelter for, and dealing with vagrants, we must publicize our policy and patiently persuade and mobilize them so that society sympathizes with us, the masses support us, members of vagrants' families are satisfied, and vagrants are willing. In this way, not only can we lay a good ideological basis upon which vagrants can accept placement and reform, but we can also create favorable mass conditions for the future dispersal of placed and reformed vagrants. At the same time we can also avoid the occurrence of errors in providing shelter and methods of placement and reform that are unsuited to the circumstances of the vagrants themselves. Conversely, to adopt the method of coercively providing shelter not only would be a kind of unlawful conduct, but it would also inevitably arouse the vagrants' feelings of resistance and create errors in providing shelter and inappropriate methods of placement and reform. In the future the method of coercively providing shelter must be firmly checked. Naturally, it is quite possible that after going through propaganda and mobilization a minority of vagrants will [still] not want to accept placement and reform. But the correct method for these people can only be to wait awhile and slowly persuade and mobilize them. We should not adopt any method that is coercive or that disguises coercion.

At present we must conduct a clean-up in places that have already concentrated and provided shelter to vagrants. As for vagrants for whom use of the concentration method of placement and reform is unsuited, we should instead use the method of dispersal. We should immediately send back [home] those who were not vagrants but who were erroneously treated as vagrants and were coercively provided shelter, and we should do all necessary work to remedy their situation. In the future, in order strictly to prevent errors in providing shelter, the right to approve providing shelter to vagrants shall be held exclusively by city level civil affairs departments.

4. At present most districts have already made the farms that have been established the main method of placement and reform of vagrants, have invested the greatest financial power in them, and have planned to place in them the largest number of vagrants. Therefore, whether the farms are managed well or badly will play a decisive role in the future effectiveness of the entire work of reforming vagrants. The leadership in the various places must give sufficient attention to this point. At present we believe that in order to manage the farms well the following links must be firmly grasped:

First, we should select the location of the farms well. The quality of the soil must be relatively good, the sources of water ample, the communications relatively convenient, the amount of land sufficient, and the prospects for the development of production good. Only this kind of farm can make vagrants feel that they have a reliable place to settle and an attractive future life, and thereby make them willing to accept reform more than ever. Also, it is only to this kind of farm that members of vagrants' families can gradually be brought for placement, thus attaining the goal of placing vagrants on a long-term basis.

.    .    .    .    .

Fourth, in compensating farm production personnel for their labor, we should treat them the same as ordinary employed personnel and put into effect [the principle] to each according to his labor. The form of compensation should be determined on the basis of the direction of the farm's development. Some may put into effect the salary system in accordance with the practice of ordinary state-operated farms. Also, some may put into effect the bonus system in accordance with the practice of agricultural producers' cooperatives. Raises in the standard of compensation should follow rises in the level of production. In addition, farms still should actively create conditions and strive to attract members of vagrants' families to join the farms as early as possible to contribute to production and to live together with the vagrants. It does not matter whether or not members of vagrants' families have already joined the farms; if they have difficulty in earning a livelihood, they all should be given necessary social relief.

Fifth, we should do good work in administering farm production personnel. Except for an extremely small minority of vagrants who have been deprived of their rights as citizens in accordance with law, vagrants generally enjoy the rights of citizens. Therefore, we must strictly differentiate between the treatment of them and the administration of criminals. We should emphasize principles of democratic administration, gradually increase their ability to administer their own collective labor, their own study, and their own lives, and at all times develop and cultivate their self-awareness and self-respect. It is necessary to fix an appropriate system of rewards and sanctions, but it should be understood that rewards should be given as much as possible and sanctions as little as possible. Putting into effect corporal punishment and disguised corporal punishment are strictly prohibited. Only in this way can we gradually cultivate them so that they become good citizens who, with self-awareness, observe law and public order and possess socialist public morality.

Sixth, we should do good work in educating farm production personnel. The core of education on the farm must be education in production and in the actualities of life. There should be little talk of empty doctrines and much contact with farm realities. We should take the farm's management guideline, long-range plan and production plan, and income distribution plan of every period as teaching material for educating production personnel, so that from these they can see the brilliant future of the farm and, through the actual road of this future, can see the complete congruency of their individual prospects and the prospects of the farm and thereby establish the ideology that considers the cooperative the home and [that induces] active participation in labor and production on the farm. We must develop labor competitions, periodically evaluate production accomplishments, and promptly summarize production experience, thus leading them to know the major significance of labor and to learn all the techniques of labor. In this way we can attain the goal of reforming them.

5. The above-mentioned basic principles for the compensation of farm production personnel for their labor and the administration of their education also apply to the use of construction teams, to the dispersal of vagrants in cooperatives, and to other forms of placement and reform of vagrants. Some institutions of production and rehabilitation that provide shelter to vagrants also should undergo reorganization so that these principles achieve faithful implementation.

6. The placement and reform of vagrants is an aspect of city socialist reform work that cannot be disregarded and at present it is an important task of civil affairs departments. On the basis of these Instructions civil affairs departments of provinces, autonomous regions, and cities should thoroughly examine the arrangement and performance of the local work of placing and reforming vagrants, promptly resolve existing problems, and correct deviations that have occurred, summarize and disseminate good experience, and also closely rely on the leadership of the local Party and government, and strive to obtain energetic coordination with the public security, agriculture, water utilization, labor, supply and marketing, and other such related departments, so that this work can develop actively and with stability. In order to strengthen concrete leadership of the work of placement and reform of vagrants, civil affairs departments in the various places should, on the basis of the magnitude of the task, separately establish more special institutions or [appoint] special cadres for this function. The necessary organizational facilities may be [obtained] through self-adjustment within those units or through submitting a request to the local people's council.

## B. REHABILITATION THROUGH LABOR

### 1. Authorizing Legislation

### ITEM 86

[DECISION OF THE STATE COUNCIL OF THE PRC RELATING TO PROB-
LEMS OF REHABILITATION THROUGH LABOR (approved at the 78th meet-
ing of the Standing Committee of the NPC, Aug. 1, 1957; promulgated by the
State Council, Aug. 3, 1957), *FKHP*, 6:243–244]

On the basis of the provisions of Article 100 of the Constitution of the
People's Republic of China, the following Decision with respect to problems of
rehabilitation through labor is made in order to reform into self-supporting new
persons those persons with the capacity to labor who loaf, who violate law and
discipline, or who do not engage in proper employment, and in order further to
preserve public order and to benefit socialist construction:

1. The following kinds of persons shall be provided shelter and their rehabilitation through labor shall be carried out:

(1) Those who do not engage in proper employment, those who behave
like hooligans, and those who, although they steal, swindle, or engage in other
such acts, are not pursued for criminal responsibility, who violate security administration and whom repeated education fails to change;

(2) Those counterrevolutionaries and antisocialist reactionaries who, because their crimes are minor, are not pursued for criminal responsibility, who
receive the sanction of expulsion from an organ, organization, enterprise, school,
or other such unit and who are without a way of earning a livelihood;

(3) Those persons who have the capacity to labor but who for a long
period refuse to labor or who destroy discipline and interfere with public order,
and who [thus] receive the sanction of expulsion from an organ, organization,
enterprise, school, or other such unit and who have no way of earning a livelihood;

(4) Those who do not obey work assignments or arrangements for getting
them employment or for transferring them to other employment, or those who
do not accept the admonition to engage in labor and production, who ceaselessly and unreasonably make trouble and interfere with public affairs and whom
repeated education fails to change.

2. Rehabilitation through labor is a measure of a coercive nature for carrying
out the education and reform of persons receiving it. It is also a method of
arranging for their getting employment.

Persons who receive rehabilitation through labor shall be paid an appropriate
salary in accordance with the results of their labor. Moreover, in the exercise
of discretion a part of their salary may be deducted in order to provide for the
maintenance expenses of their family members or to serve as a reserve fund
that will enable them to have a family and an occupation.

During the period of rehabilitation through labor, persons who receive it must
observe the discipline prescribed by organs of rehabilitation through labor. Those
who violate this discipline shall receive administrative sanctions. Those who

violate the law and commit crimes shall be dealt with in accordance with law.

As for the aspect of administering education, the guideline of combining labor and production with political education shall be adopted. Moreover, discipline and a system shall be prescribed for them to observe in order to help them establish [in their minds] the concepts of patriotic observance of law and of the glory of labor, learn labor and production skills, and cultivate the habit of loving labor, so that they become self-supporting laborers who participate in socialist construction.

3. If a person must be rehabilitated through labor, the application for rehabilitation through labor must be made by a civil affairs or a public security department; by the organ, organization, enterprise, school, or other such unit in which he is located; or by the head of his family or his guardian. The application shall be submitted to the people's council of the province, autonomous region, or city directly under the central authority, or to an organ that has been authorized by them, for approval.

4. If during the period of rehabilitation through labor a person who receives it behaves well and has the conditions for getting employment, he may, with the approval of the organ of rehabilitation through labor, separately [independently] get employment. If the unit, head of the family, or guardian that originally made the application for the person's rehabilitation through labor asks to take him back so that it can assume responsibility for disciplining him, the organ of rehabilitation through labor may also, giving consideration to the circumstances, approve the request.

5. Organs of rehabilitation through labor shall be established at the level of the province, autonomous region, and city directly under the central authority and shall be established [at lower levels] with the approval of the people's council of the province, autonomous region, or city directly under the central authority. Civil affairs departments and public security departments shall jointly be responsible for leading and administering the work of organs of rehabilitation through labor.

## ITEM 87

[SAPA (Oct. 22, 1957), p. 254]

Article 30. After their [SAPA] punishment has been completed, persons who are habitual loafers, who do not engage in proper employment and who repeatedly violate security administration may be sent to organs of rehabilitation through labor if they require such rehabilitation.

Compare Article 28 of the Law for the Punishment of Police Offenses of the Republic of China, which provides:

"A person who habitually commits police offenses because of vagrancy or idleness may be given a punishment of increased severity and may also, after his punishment has been completed, be sent to a suitable place for correction or be ordered to learn a skill for earning a livelihood." [3]

3. In Chang Chih-pen, ed., *Tsui-hsin liu-fa ch'üan-shu* (Newest book of the complete six laws [of the Republic of China]; Taipei, 1959), p. 355.

## ITEM 88

[INSTRUCTIONS OF THE CCPCC AND THE STATE COUNCIL OF THE PRC RELATING TO CHECKING THE BLIND OUTFLOW OF PEOPLE FROM RURAL VILLAGES (Dec. 18, 1957), *FKHP*, 6:230]

3. Those people from rural villages who have blindly flowed into cities and into industrial and mining districts must be mobilized to return to their native places, and drifting and begging must be strictly prohibited. Public security organs shall strictly conduct the regulation of household registration in accordance with the Rules for the Regulation of City Household Registration. In large cities into which have flowed relatively many people from rural villages, civil affairs departments shall establish places for providing shelter, temporarily provide shelter to these people, concentrate them [into groups], and send them back to their native places. While being provided shelter, they may be organized to labor for production and to strive to earn funds for their trip home. Bad elements who swindle, undermine the legal system, and disrupt security shall be punished according to the circumstances of the case. When the circumstances are serious they shall be given rehabilitation through labor or criminal sanctions in accordance with law. Control over city food supplies shall be strengthened. Being without household registration and the act of making a false report about the number of people [in a household] in order to obtain food wrongfully or in order to buy or sell food ration coupons shall be prohibited and shall be punished in serious cases.

### 2. Nature of the Sanction

What kind of sanction is rehabilitation through labor? What does it entail? One Chinese writer has called it "a kind of administrative system of a coercive nature." [4] Recall the definition given in Article 2 of the authorizing Decision, Item 86. After reading the materials in this subsection, how would you characterize this sanction?

## ITEM 89

Item 89 provides a detailed account of how one county public security bureau set out to implement the rehabilitation through labor Decision on an experimental basis in an agricultural producers' cooperative. The experiment described is only typical of the mildest form of rehabilitation through labor, which does not appear to have been widely used after the first year of the Decision's implementation, probably because of its close resemblance to the sanction of "supervised labor."

["How the Chuangtzup'ing (Kansu) Cooperative Carries Out Experiment in Labor Custody [Rehabilitation Through Labor]," *Kan-su jih-pao* (Kansu daily), July 20, 1958; translated in *SCMP*, 1862:6–8 (Sept. 26, 1958)]

After the Chuangtzup'ing Agricultural Cooperative in Kaolan *hsien* [county] became a higher cooperative, it managed to increase its production year by year, and the enthusiasm of its members for labor became ever higher. But the co-

4. Chang Chien, p. 43.

operative cadres and members felt glum about the presence of several loafers in the cooperatives who had to be fed but did not work. These loafers refused to be led, cursed the cadres, and made trouble for fun. Loafer Yang Yu-wu, for example, contributed not a day of work after he joined the cooperative. He operated on his own in hog and goat trade and in speculative business. Yang Yuan-tung was another loafer. When his mother died in 1953, his neighbors and clansmen donated 90 catties of wheat for funeral expenses. But he stole 40 of the catties of wheat and spent the money recklessly. In the end his wife had to raise funeral expenses from other sources. He would take seven days of rest after he gave the cooperative one day of work. He frequently feigned sickness and claimed the "five guarantee" privilege from the cooperative. In 1956, he borrowed 20 [20 yuan] from the cooperative and 50 from the credit cooperative on the ground of hardship, and he never returned his loans. Because he did not work, his family of five had constantly to starve with him. Because of this his wife was frequently at odds with him and threatened divorce and [or?] separation. There was no tranquility in his family.

Although there were not many members of this kind in the cooperative, they had a very bad effect on the cooperative. The upright men were highly dissatisfied with them. They criticized the cadres by saying: "You know how to make the hard-working people work harder. But why do you not find some ways to deal with these loafers?" However, the cooperative cadres had . . . their difficulties. Those people committed small mistakes frequently but they never committed major mistakes. There was no good way to deal with them.

In August last year, the State Council promulgated its Decision on the question of labor custody [Decision of the State Council of the PRC Relating to Problems of Rehabilitation Through Labor]. The public security bureau of the *hsien* decided to make the Chuangtzup'ing Cooperative . . . an experimental point for carrying out labor custody [rehabilitation through labor]. At the beginning of the experiment, the leadership lined up the people for investigation on the one hand, and gave wide publicity to the spirit of the State Council's decision on the other. The *hsiang* Party branch first called a conference for *hsiang* and cooperative cadres and Party and Young Communist League [Communist Youth League] activists. These people were organized to study the State Council's decision. After that, this decision was announced to the different production teams on blackboards. In the evenings, the masses were organized to study and discuss the decision item by item with the production team as the unit. After giving the matter wide publicity, the broad masses understood the merits of enforcing labor custody and voiced their support.

Following this, the different production teams organized the masses to agitate discussion according to the State Council's decision and in conjunction with the actual conditions of the people in the teams who did not work. According to the results of lining up people for probing and mass discussions carried out within the cooperative, there were 16 loafers, equivalent to 0.7 percent of the aggregate manpower in the cooperative, who had no proper employment. The Party branch made files out of concrete information on these 16 persons and discussed them at an enlarged meeting. After a consensus was reached, the approval of the *hsien* people's council was sought through the *hsiang* people's council. On October 7 last year, with the approval of the *hsien* people's council, labor custody was enforced in the cooperative.

Before labor custody was enforced, some preparatory work was done in the *hsiang* and the cooperative.

First, the people to be placed under labor custody and their family members were called to a conference in which the object of labor custody was explained to them. They were told that it was with the object of making useful men of them that they were placed under labor custody, that "labor custody" was not "reform through labor," and that the people placed under labor custody were paid according to their work like other cooperative members. They were told that they would be given a course of education on the glory of work so that they would make up their minds to work. At the same time, the Party branch also called on the masses to take pains in having these people transformed without discrimination or ridicule.

Next, some practical systems were drawn up. The people placed under labor custody are required to work together in day time and to spend two hours in the evening to record work hours and to study. They eat and sleep in their own homes. When they are unable to turn up for work or in meetings, they have to ask for leave of absence in advance. They have to meet to review their lives once a week, and are appraised quarterly. Subject to the approval of the *hsiang* people's council those who have completed their transformation may leave the labor custody team.

The cooperative specially drafted a Communist Party member, Comrade Wei Yu-ch'u, leader of the 4th production team, to head the labor custody team. Comrade Wei Yu-ch'u is firm in his stand and good at work. He knows production technique and is respected by the masses. The loafers also looked up to him with awe and respect. The cooperative got ready the land and tools for the loafers.

Thus prepared, collective labor custody was enforced. Because the Party branch took great pains to have the ideological and preparatory work well carried out, everything went well with the work. After the loafers were grouped together, they were divided into two sections, and two persons from among the people placed [under] labor custody were elected to head them. Comrade Wei Yu-ch'u, leader of the labor custody team, set . . . an example everywhere in production. His work was of good quality and his efficiency high. He showed concern for the people under labor custody in everything. At the beginning, because these people were not used to labor, knew no production techniques, and varied in physical strength, some difficulties were experienced in production. Comrade Wei Yu-ch'u did his very best to give every person the kind of farm work which he was physically capable of carrying out, and taught them techniques whenever necessary. In this way, these people gradually got used to their work and were able . . . slowly [to] master production technique.

In study, the people placed under labor custody were required to study chiefly the State Council's decision on labor custody and the system of the labor custody team during the first two weeks. Later, they were organized to study the regulations of the cooperative, important state events, and relevant policies and laws and decrees to enable them to remold their thinking. They met once every week to review their lives. Those who put up good performances were commended, and those who failed to abide by the system were criticized.

Wei Hung-yu was in a bad mood after he heard that his thinking had to be remolded. He quit work for two days without asking for leave of absence. Wang Yung-sheng talked nonsense while he worked. The team leader [promptly] called the whole team . . . to a conference, and organized the team members to discuss and criticize their mistaken thought. When these two persons found that other people were at variance with them, they bowed to admit their mistakes.

Apart from this, the cooperative constantly sent people to the families of those who had been placed under labor custody to find out their views and what progress the people in question had made in transformation. Because of this, the families involved were very satisfied.

After seven months of labor custody, these loafers have cultivated the working habit, and some are quite active in work. During the first 210 days, they each put in 209 days of work on the average. One of them, Yang Fu-k'o, put in as many as 301 working days [probably based upon an eight-hour workday].

By way of work and study, these people have witnessed changes not only in thinking and work style but also in financial standing because of their additional income. They have also improved their ties with their families. In the case of Yang Yuan-tung, for example, his wife [in the past] refused to have anything to do with him even when he was sick . . . . Because he works hard now and has straightened up his thought, his wife no longer quarrels with him and takes good care of him. She told the team leader: "Chairman Mao's policy is very good indeed, for he has saved the lives of our whole family. But for the labor custody, we would have nothing to eat." Chang San-hung who went through the process of labor custody said: "In the past, I worked only six days and earned five days of wages in eight months. I have now put in more than 200 working days in seven months. In the past, I did not work and was constantly sick with stomach ache. Having tempered myself in labor, I have cured my illness, and my stomach bothers me no longer." This method was also universally applauded by the masses.

## ITEMS 90A–90C

Chinese publications have been reticent about the harsher and more common form of rehabilitation through labor. Items 90A and 90B present only the limited amount of information the government has desired to make public. But the interview recorded in Item 90C describes in detail one man's experiences in undergoing the rehabilitation process.

## ITEM 90A

[Editorial, "Why Should Rehabilitation Through Labor Be Carried Out?" *JMJP*, Aug. 4, 1957, pp. 1–2]

.    .    .    .    .

The facts prove that with respect to bad elements ordinary methods of persuasion-education are ineffective; nor can simple measures of punishment be adopted. Bad elements certainly cannot continue to remain in organs, organizations, or enterprises; and [even] if they are allowed to get other employment, no one will want to accept them. Therefore, with respect to these people we need a proper method that will not only reform them but will also guarantee them a livelihood and a future. After a long period of study and consideration, the people's government has come to the conclusion that to provide them with shelter and to enforce rehabilitation through labor is the most appropriate and also the best method.

To put it in plain language, this method calls for the state to provide bad elements with shelter, make arrangements for them, and provide them with appropriate conditions for labor. For example, the state invests in establishing some farms and factories, organizes bad elements to produce, and even compels them to produce, using this method to enable them to have food to eat. Thus, rehabilitation through labor involves their supporting themselves through their own labor while at the same time reforming themselves through labor. This indicates the concern and the spirit of responsibility of our socialist state for the life, labor, and future of these people. The state's handling of and arrangements for them are also designed to safeguard against damaging the free, happy, and prosperous lives of the great majority of the laboring people and the socialist order.

The method of rehabilitation through labor embodies the socialist principle that he who does not labor does not eat. In socialist countries labor is an honorable thing for all citizens who have the capacity to labor. Also, to observe labor discipline, to observe public order, and to respect socialist morality are the obligations of every citizen and are all written in our Constitution. Thus, those persons who have the capacity to labor but do not labor and those persons who undermine discipline and order and corrupt social morality not only undermine socialist principles but also violate our country's Constitution. This will not be permitted by the people.

It should be pointed out, however, that rehabilitation through labor differs from reform through labor of criminals. It is also not the same as the institutions for the relief of widowers, widows, orphans, and childless old people. The organs that administer rehabilitation through labor must adopt an administrative system and discipline of a coercive nature, and cannot permit persons who are undergoing rehabilitation through labor to undermine this system or discipline. For example, those persons are not allowed to leave the farm or factory and freely move as they please, nor are they allowed to undermine public order or production. If they do, they will receive sanctions, and if the circumstances of the case are serious, they will also receive punitive legal restraints. But in labor and production the principle of compensating them according to the fruits of their labor is also put into effect. Specifically, this means that the more they labor the more they earn, the less they labor the less they earn, and, if they do not labor, they do not earn. With the exception of that part of their salary which is required to be deducted in order to provide for the maintenance expenses of their families or to serve as a reserve fund that will enable them to have a family and an occupation, they have the right to handle the rest freely.

## ITEM 90B

[Meng Chao-liang, "Preliminary Accomplishments of the Work of Rehabilitation Through Labor," *CFYC,* 3:47, 48–49 (1959)]

·    ·    ·    ·    ·

In accordance with the guideline of "combining labor and production with political education," the organs of rehabilitation through labor in the various places quickly organized persons who had been provided shelter and had been concentrated for rehabilitation through labor to engage in labor and production beneficial to society. The basic method for reforming them, labor and production, is also a measure for arranging to get them employment . . . If we want to reform thoroughly the ideology that led them to commit crimes or wrongs, we must first change their old ways of life and their exploiting class ideology. But the basic means of reaching this goal is through practice in productive labor. In "On Practice" Chairman Mao counseled us: "Marxism believes that mankind's productive activity is its basic activity and is the thing that determines all other activity. Man's understanding derives mainly from material productive activity." If we want to change the reactionary standpoint and exploitative ideological consciousness of those persons who undergo rehabilitation through labor, we must make them go through production practice activity. At the same time, only if they go through labor and production can we make them gradually rely on their own labor to support themselves.

·    ·    ·    ·    ·

Organizing persons undergoing rehabilitation through labor to engage in production labor beneficial to society is the basic method of reforming them. But because of the thickness of their exploiting class ideological consciousness and their deeply rooted reactionary standpoint, we must also educate them in political ideology. We must explain the truth to them and show them the future of reform. We must organize them to conduct self-examination, self-criticism, mutual analysis, and censure, to develop the two-road struggle in politics and ideology, to admit their guilt and their errors, and to wipe out their reactionary ideology. In the practice of productive labor they gradually establish the determination to reform themselves, to walk the socialist road, and to be laborers in socialist society. In order to hasten their political and thought reform, keeping coerced reform as a possible last resort, we also adopt many positive measures to stimulate their awareness for accepting reform. We put into effect relatively lenient measures for regulating their lives. (For example, they may correspond with relatives and friends and are permitted to have relatives and friends visit them. If their units already have the facilities, they are permitted to live with their wives, their family members may join them, and it may be arranged for them to get employment in the rehabilitation through labor units.) They are given thorough reasoning-education. The minority of persistent reactionaries who continue to conduct destructive activity are promptly attacked according to law. While we are educating them in political ideology and in labor and production, we are also wiping out illiteracy among them; educating them in science, culture, and production skills; developing various kinds of cultural, recreational, and sports activities; and regularly conducting cleaning and sanitation work.

Adopting the above-mentioned series of measures and conducting the arduous work of educating them in political ideology make the great majority of persons undergoing rehabilitation through labor feel that the government is concerned with reforming them. They only have to accept reform sincerely, and then they will still have a future in socialist society. Therefore, within a relatively short period, they are able to calm down and are willing to accept reform. Some of the persons undergoing rehabilitation through labor actually attain some preliminary reforms in their political ideology. These are conspicuously reflected in the following ways:

When persons undergoing rehabilitation through labor are initially provided shelter and concentrated, the great majority of them are not willing to labor. After undergoing repeated and thorough education by organs of rehabilitation through labor, they make some progress in understanding their own evil crimes and errors and their danger to the state and to society, and they are willing to go through labor to reform themselves. Many persons also indicate to the government their determination to repent and reform by confessing previously concealed evil crimes and handing over previously concealed guns and ammunition, evidence of crime, and illegally obtained money and goods. Some persons also reveal through denunciations materials involving many counterrevolutionary cases, bad persons, and bad things. These facts signify that the political ideology of persons undergoing rehabilitation through labor is changing; politically they are beginning to bow their heads to the people, and they have preliminarily demarcated the boundary between themselves and bad people and bad things.

## ITEM 90C

[Interview]

Ma was a Shanghai intellectual who was an important figure in one of the "democratic parties" with which the CCP maintains a united front. He also was a successful businessman who managed the Shanghai factory of a major state-private, jointly operated enterprise. In July 1957, as a result of a series of meetings that had been held in his factory during the initial stage of the antirightist movement, he was branded a "rightist." Shortly thereafter, he heard from a relative who worked in one of the ministries in Peking that the government was about to promulgate a regulation that would authorize expelling many rightist cadres from state organs and enterprises and sending them to rehabilitation through labor. The relative urged him to resign from his factory post so that he might become ineligible for rehabilitation through labor. Ma followed this advice and resigned a few days before the promulgation of the Decision of the State Council of the PRC Relating to Problems of Rehabilitation Through Labor. He remained at home studying and writing until the autumn of 1958.

In September 1958 the Party secretary of his factory, with whom he was still quite friendly, warned him to "reform" or risk rehabilitation through labor. Ma replied that he could not receive such a sanction because he had not been expelled from the organ in which he worked. The Party secretary told him that, despite this, he had better be careful. On October 16, 1958, at three o'clock in the afternoon Ma received a telephone call that summoned him to the factory "for a chat." When he arrived there at four that afternoon he was received by the head of the factory defense section, who told him that the government had decided to send him to rehabilitation through labor. Ma protested that they had made a mistake, that he was loyal to the government and had served it well, that he had not been expelled from a state organ, and that he had important friends among the leadership of the Communist Party in Peking. When this fell on deaf ears, he insisted on his right to appeal the decision, but the section chief said that there was no way to do so. Ma's mother was notified to bring some of his clothing and articles of daily use to him. When she arrived, Ma told her to write immediately to one of the Party's best known leaders. The section chief said this would be fruitless. Ma was then taken by jeep to a public security subbureau and put in a cell. He again said he wanted to appeal, but the chief of the sub-bureau told him that this would be impossible. After eating a dinner of very poor quality, Ma spent the night on the cement floor of the cell.

The next morning another jeep took him to the Shanghai rehabilitation through labor center, which he recognized as having been the mortuary that formerly embalmed the bodies of all people from Ningpo who died in Shanghai. The building was vast, since the Ningpo community had been large and prosperous, but it was now equipped as a jail. At the entrance two soldiers with submachine guns stood guard in front of a new iron gate. Inside the center, Ma was searched, identified, processed, and sent to a crowded cell. Again he ate and slept badly.

The following morning he and hundreds of other new arrivals were summoned to a meeting in the courtyard. There they were addressed by the chief of the center. He first told them that their daily routine would consist largely of "study" and that the first document to be studied was the Decision Relating to Problems of Rehabilitation Through Labor. He then said: "Who are you? Why are you here? Are you good people or bad people? If you were good people, you would be out on the streets like ordinary citizens, enjoying all their rights. On the other hand, if you were really bad, you would have been branded criminals, sent to reform through labor, and deprived of the right to vote and all wages. You are people who have 'bad in the good and good in the bad.' " Having made clear their in-between status, the chief urged them to think of the future. He repeatedly directed their attention to the fact that rehabilitation through labor was not the same as reform through labor, and he emphasized that one significant difference was that the latter had a fixed term while the former did not. Thus, their release depended entirely upon their behavior during the rehabilitation process.

For the next two weeks Ma and his companions engaged in eleven hours a day of "study." In addition to the Decision Relating to Problems of Rehabilitation Through Labor, during the first few days they also studied copies of the speech that the center chief had delivered. Then each member of the nine- or ten-man groups into which they were divided had to tell the group why he had been declared a rightist. The first to give this oral report was the leader whom the group members had elected from among themselves. He took several hours to explain why he was there, beginning with his family background, class status, education, work, and social experiences, and ending with an analysis of his "guilt" or "error." Each of the group members then had to ask him questions in order to develop various aspects of his account. The official whose task it was to supervise the group then summarized the discussion, developed the significant points, and concluded by stating those respects in which the group leader needed to reform his thinking. The process of hearing and analyzing each person's report took about a day.

When all members of the group had been heard, each was required to put his report into writing. In order to assure the comprehensiveness of these written reports an outline of the points to be covered was provided. It directed the reporter to describe what changes had occurred in his thinking — the degree of his progress — since entering the center, as well as his pre-center history. It also required him to state a concrete plan for reforming his thinking. In response to this last point, everyone in Ma's group wrote that he wished to be assigned to the most arduous work possible. The members of the group did this because the supervising official had hinted that it would be the best thing to do. The Party, he had stressed, had been good to "nurture" them rather than punish them for their "crimes." In return they should do whatever the Party asked of them.

For a few days after completing these written reports Ma and his companions had little to do but clean the building. Then the chief of the center made another speech. Their progress had not been insubstantial, he said, but if they were genuinely to reform they needed labor as well as talk. The state also needed their labor and, although he did not yet know where they would be assigned, he urged them to prepare to leave the center. At eleven o'clock that night they were awakened to listen to another speech by the chief. Unlike the previous meetings, this time the courtyard was lined with public security officers, and two guards with submachine guns were on the platform with the chief. In a stern voice he announced that they were to leave immediately for Anhwei province. The inmates were actually relieved to hear that their destination was not Sinkiang province or some other distant, dreaded place. Guarded buses took them to Shanghai's military railroad station, which was ringed by policemen. There they were loaded onto cattle cars. Each person was given two rolls of Chinese bread for the trip. It took five days to make the relatively short journey, and they arrived in Anhwei starved and exhausted. Their destination turned out to be a grassy plain in the middle of nowhere. After an evening meal of poor but welcome food and a night's rest on the grass in tents that were to serve as their permanent shelter, they awoke to begin rehabilitation through labor.

The camp had over 1,000 men and was called a battalion. It was broken down into four companies, which in turn were composed of platoons. Each platoon contained four or five groups of approximately fifteen members. The commanders of the battalion and the companies were state officials, who appointed the platoon and group leaders from among the inmates. On their first day at the camp Ma's company commander made a speech which was far harsher than any that they had heard at the center in Shanghai. He told them that they were all criminals who could have received reform through labor but that the government chose to "care for" them rather than punish them. Yet he pointed out that the only significant difference between reform through labor and rehabilitation through labor was that the latter had no time limit. This could be an advantage, he said, since they were free to go as soon as they had reformed. In the interim it would be pointless to try to flee, and those who did so would be shot by the guards. After several hours "studying" the company commander's speech, the groups were assigned to labor, which consisted of crushing rocks.

The work was normally divided into two twelve-hour shifts a day. A group would take the day shift one week and the night shift the next. Ma's group started with the night shift. This meant that they were awakened at ten-thirty at night for "breakfast," left camp for the worksite at eleven that evening, and arrived there after a forty-five-minute hike carrying their own tools. Following a brief rest, they began to break rocks at midnight. At five-thirty in the morning they ate again and relaxed for a few minutes before going back to work at six o'clock. They were replaced by the day shift at noon and returned to the camp for dinner and for two hours of intensive "study" and criticism meetings before being allowed to go to sleep at four in the afternoon. This schedule was only varied on three occasions during Ma's stay. For a month at the height of the frenzy of the "great leap forward" the group was required to work twenty-two hours in succession. It would then return for two hours of study and six of sleep before going out for another twenty-two hours on the rock pile. The camp leaders took no account of the fact that this period also happened to be one of very heavy rains, which made the work more difficult than usual. Twice during Ma's stay the work schedule was reduced for a few weeks in order to allow more time for carrying out thought remolding campaigns that swept the camp. The first was a confession movement in which everyone had to write repeated confessions which were amended in the light of the group's intensive criticism. The second was a "mutual denunciation" movement which was conducted at an even higher pitch than the first and constituted one long struggle meeting.

Each member of the group had to crush a minimum of eight baskets of rocks per twelve-hour day. Some of the workers, hooligans, and petty offenders could do as many as fifteen a day. But many of the capitalists, professors, and university students often could not meet the quota. A graduated series of sanctions was applied to those whose "production" fell behind. The first day of failure to fill eight baskets would result in a warning. If it happened again, the laggard would be criticized during the group's study period. On the third occasion he would be severely criticized by a joint meeting of several groups. After that his food ration would be reduced by as much as a third, thereby making it harder than ever for him to fulfill the quota. Ma's rations were reduced, but he did not care, since his family was wealthy enough to be able to send him food parcels and, unlike reform through labor prisoners, he and his companions were permitted to receive such parcels. Few of the intellectuals were as wealthy as Ma, however, and their plight became intolerable. Some of them remonstrated several times with the company commander, and after a meeting with the battalion commander, their work load was finally reduced to five baskets per day.

On April 22, 1959, over six months after leaving home, Ma's company commander told him that he would be released immediately. He gave no reason. Since during his stay at the camp Ma had not distinguished himself in labor or in ideological reform and since he was the first member of his company to be released, he inferred that in reviewing his case the authorities had decided that a mistake had been made, perhaps because of his status as a leader of one of the democratic parties or because of his friends in Peking or because he had resigned from his post and had not been expelled from a state organ. (After his release he learned that a combination of these factors had worked in his favor.) Ma was taken back to the Shanghai rehabilitation through labor center for two days of rather relaxed study. He noted that the center had only about one third of the number of inmates as on his previous visit. He was then sent home via his local public security station. No restrictions were placed upon his postrelease activities except that he was required to participate once a week in study sessions with a group of high level intellectuals at the office of the Communist Party's United Front Bureau in Shanghai.

Recall Item 61, on the nature of criminal punishment. Can you defend the view that rehabilitation through labor is not criminal punishment? What arguments might you make?

### 3. Persons Eligible for the Sanction and Procedures for Imposing It

Was the protagonist of Item 90C correct in supposing that resignation from his post made him ineligible for rehabilitation through labor? What language in the Decision supports this interpretation? The materials in this subsection provide further examples of the kinds of conduct that have led to imposition of rehabilitation through labor. They also illustrate the variety of procedures employed to impose it.

### ITEM 91

Before receiving the sanction of rehabilitation through labor the protagonist of Item 90C had been declared a rightist. The Decision that established this sanction was in large measure designed to meet the needs of the antirightist movement. Which of its provisions deals with rightists? What is a rightist? Item 91 sheds some light on the answer to this last question and should be of special interest to lawyers.

[Interview]

After graduating from law school in 1956, Chou was assigned to work in an office of legal advisers [OLA] that had just been set up in one of China's major cities. [See Item 200D.] Although he was not a member of the Communist

Party, his work record was excellent and his thinking "progressive" so he quickly established himself as, in his words, "the Party's number one activist" in the office. As such, during the "blooming and contending" movement that reached its peak in May and early June 1957, while many of his colleagues responded to the Party's exhortations frankly to criticize existing practices, he served as administrative assistant to the office for the rectification movement that was temporarily established by the Party within the OLA. His principal duty was to do content analyses of the large character posters that lawyers of the OLA were mobilized to write and of transcripts of their speeches at the daily meetings that were convened by their office, the city lawyers' association, the city bureau of justice, or the city court.

Unlike the criticisms of many lawyers who served at higher levels of the government [see Part I, at notes 28 and 29], those expressed by Chou's colleagues tended to focus upon job conditions rather than upon the operation of the legal system. Some argued that lawyers' salaries were too low and that they should receive a percentage of the fees received by the OLA rather than a regular salary. Others complained that they were discriminated against in their advancement within the office because of their bourgeois backgrounds. Chou would classify and synthesize the various criticisms and present them at the nightly conferences of the office for the rectification movement, which was composed of the chief, deputy chief, and Party secretary of the OLA, Chou, and a clerk. This group, all of whom were Party members except Chou, discussed each class of complaints and suggestions and decided whether changes should be made or recommended to improve the situation. Whenever a change was made, Chou would write out a large character poster to announce it to the OLA.

After the outbreak of the antirightist movement, the office for the rectification movement continued under a new name — the Office for the Antirightist Movement [OAM]. During the first few days of this movement Chou was summoned several times for talks with the chief of the personnel division of the city bureau of justice, who prepared him ideologically for a change in his work as administrative assistant to the OAM. A representative of the city Party committee's OAM spent several hours instructing him about the new techniques his work would require and subsequently made periodic inspections. Chou also had daily consultations about the work with the chief of his OLA and the head of the secretariat of the lawyers' association, which coordinated the several OLA in the city in behalf of the bureau of justice.

Unlike its predecessor, the OAM did not concern itself with rectifying the grievances of the lawyers of the OLA but with rectifying the lawyers themselves. Thus Chou's task shifted from collating and synthesizing the multitude of complaints and suggestions contained in their speeches and posters to classifying and summarizing every opinion that many of his colleagues had expressed during the "blooming and contending" period. He did not have to review these materials for all of his thirty-five colleagues, but only for those whose names were selected by the OAM as possible targets on the basis of previous acquaintance. Yet this number came to twenty. The OAM would give Chou a day or two to assemble and analyze the materials about each of these persons. He would in each case submit a written report listing the various items of "evidence" under categories such as "anti-Communist words and deeds," "thought problems," and "antiunited front remarks." This report would be submitted to the members of the OAM in advance of their conference on the individual in question, and, since they seldom had a chance to study it in detail, Chou would give an oral summary of the report at the conference. The OAM would then discuss whether this lawyer should or should not be deemed a rightist. It usually devoted an evening to each case.

During the first review, the OAM in Chou's OLA failed to find a single rightist among the potential targets. A few of them had "thought problems," because they still retained "bourgeois legal views," but none was found to have made any anticommunist statements. Those with thought problems were severely criticized for their "errors" at the daily meetings which the OLA held while the OAM proceeded with its secret labors. However, no one was yet identified as a rightist, and the atmosphere was still one of comradeship rather than struggle.

Although the OAM had not initially considered it unusual not to have discovered any rightists, the attitude of its leaders suddenly changed. One day the OAM chief said to Chou: "How can it be that there are no rightists here? What about Li? Don't tell me he's not a rightist!" Chou later learned that the chief of the city OAM had paid a visit and had expressed dismay over the failure of the OLA's OAM to make any recommendations for labeling some of its group rightists. "It's not possible that you have none," he had said. So Chou was instructed to take another look at Li's materials. At a second conference on Li's case the OAM found that statements which it had previously deemed to be innocuous were actually hostile to the Party, and it recommended that Li be given the rightist "cap," a figurative expression that symbolizes the stigma imposed. Therefore, the OAM ordered Chou to get Li's personnel file from the OLA office, to cull it for unfavorable information, and to prepare a report for submission to the city OAM. This report consisted of four parts: an analysis of Li's class status and that of his family, a summary of Li's personal history, a detailed scrutiny of his statements during "blooming and contending," and a conclusion embodying the recommendation. Upon completing this report, Chou showed it to the chief of his OAM, who placed his chop on it and sent it on to the joint OAM that handled matters for the bureau of justice and the city court. That organization noted but did not review the report and sent it to the city OAM, which reviewed the case in detail. After approving the recommendation, the city OAM sent this approval back to Li's OAM in the form of a printed report, which was inserted in his file.

Upon receipt of the city organization's approval, the Party secretary of Li's OAM called a meeting of the Party and Youth League members and activists within the OLA to prepare them to "struggle" Li. Each of these "backbone" cadres was assigned a role to play in denouncing Li. At the meeting of the OLA the following day the OLA chief, without any notice to Li, announced that the meeting would be devoted to discussing Li's thoughts, words, and deeds with a view to determining whether or not he was a rightist. The well-prepared backbone cadres then went into action accusing Li of various rightist manifestations.

The tenor of the meeting swiftly shifted from that of severe criticism to that of struggle, although, because intellectuals were involved, this was not a crude, violent type of struggle but one which was conducted solely at the verbal level. At the end of the meeting, when he was required to comment briefly on these charges, Li steadfastly denied having had any anti-Communist intent. The Party secretary announced that this "discussion" would continue at the next meeting, which proved to be similar to the first. Li was required to open the third session with a lengthy statement of "self-examination" which he had been ordered to write out in advance. This provided additional material for the barrage against him.

While the struggle process thus began, the OAM continued its second review of the potential targets. Approvals of other recommendations were soon received until a total of ten targets was achieved, some of whom were Party members. Struggle meetings were organized against these targets and usually proceeded on a rotating basis. While one person was being struggled, the others were busy writing statements of self-examination for the next meeting on their cases. At the outset virtually all of these targets refused to admit the charges against them, for they feared that severe punishment might accompany the rightist label. Generally they argued that they truly supported socialism and the Party and had only carried out the Party's wishes in suggesting certain criticisms of the existing situation. But after a few meetings it became clear to each that he would ultimately be branded a rightist and that continued resistance would only make matters worse. Eventually each of the targets came to admit the accusations. At that point the leader of the meeting would recite that, according to the target's own confession and the facts and views presented by the masses, he had to be deemed a rightist. Before that point was reached, each target had gone through at least five or six sessions, some of them in front of the entire lawyers' association or a joint meeting of the lawyers' association and the staff of the bureau of justice.

The sanctions to be given the rightists were not immediately made known. The only exception made was with respect to a man named Liang, who had been discovered to have engaged in pre-1949 counterrevolutionary activity. This "history" plus his present rightist views were deemed to have converted him into a current counterrevolutionary, and he was taken off by the public security bureau for criminal prosecution. As to the others, shortly after a group of their nonrightist colleagues was "sent down" to help staff a rural cooperative, they followed. It was while they were at the cooperative that their fates were announced. Two of them, who were declared "extreme rightists," were expelled from their positions and sent to rehabilitation through labor camp. Two others were also expelled but were given "supervised labor" [see Chapter V] within the cooperative. Three remained law office officials, but were demoted in office and in grade and were required to labor with the peasants of the cooperative. The remaining two received no sanction other than the "cap" itself and were permitted to serve as cadres within the cooperative. Like all other rightists, however, their freedom of speech and action was much more circumscribed than that of the ordinary cadres who were sent down to the countryside.

## ITEM 92

[Interview]

Lo was a Party member who served as a section chief in the public security bureau of Canton. In his student days during the Anti-Japanese War he had been a member of the Nationalist Party. He revealed this in the many biographical statements that he had submitted since liberation, but he never mentioned having served as an official of a KMT district office. Yet during the movement to liquidate counterrevolution in 1955–1956 his name was discovered on a list of such officials. The disposition of his case was delayed because investigation had not been completed concerning whether he had actively performed the duties of a KMT district official and could, therefore, be deemed a "historical counterrevolutionary" or whether, as Lo claimed, he had merely been given the title.

In 1957 the public security bureau decided to "solve" Lo's case by sending him to rehabilitation through labor. Because Lo was a section chief and Party member, the bureau was required to clear its decision with the city Party committee. Since the antirightist movement was in full swing the bureau, instead of waiting for the committee's approval as it normally did, confidently sent Lo off to rehabilitation through labor with a group of lower level cadres whose fate did not have to be reviewed by the city committee. However, after studying Lo's file, the city committee decided that he did not deserve rehabilitation through labor because the evidence failed to show that he had actually performed the duties of a KMT official. Accordingly, it ordered that Lo be released and restored to his rank and salary. But it approved his expulsion from the Party on the ground that he had wrongfully concealed an important fact about his KMT "history." And, fearing that dissatisfaction over the handling of his case might lead to his disaffection, it transferred him from the public security bureau to less sensitive employment.

## ITEM 93

[Interview]

Kao was an attractive orphan girl who married a traffic policeman in Canton when she was sixteen. A short time later her husband was convicted of corruption and was sentenced to prison. Left alone in the world, Kao was exploited by an older woman who persuaded her to offer her favors to five or six men to whom the older woman introduced her. These men began to contribute regularly to Kao's support, but the older woman appropriated the bulk of their contributions. In 1958 Kao and one of the men, a factory worker named Hsia whose wife lived in the countryside, grew fond of each other about the time that they heard that the police were investigating her activities. They decided to set up housekeeping together and to go to another area so that Kao could break off her undesirable relationships. They moved to a production brigade of a newly established rural commune in the suburbs.

Soon after their arrival at the brigade the public security station in the area was notified by the public security subbureau that had been processing her case that Kao was to be subjected to rehabilitation through labor because she had secretly engaged in prostitution. After an inquiry into Kao's new situation, the station chief recommended that she be allowed to participate in the brigade's rehabilitation through labor unit, whose members lived at home, instead of being sent off to a rehabilitation camp, and the subbureau approved. Hsia, however, was convicted of adultery, and the couple was ordered to separate. [See Item 239 and Item 321.]

## ITEM 94

[Interview]

Shortly after the system of rehabilitation through labor went into effect in the area around Canton in late 1957, Ch'en, a seventeen-year-old boy who had a record of petty thefts and other minor offenses, let the water out of the fishpond of the advanced agricultural producers' cooperative in which he lived and stole many of the fish. The members of the cooperative were furious and insisted that serious action be taken against him. The public security special agent of the administrative village reported the case to the suburban public security station, which sent a cadre out to investigate. After confirming the facts of the case and Ch'en's record of misbehavior, the investigator had a talk with Ch'en's poor peasant parents and told them that their son needed rehabilitation through labor, which, he said, was designed to handle cases like this and could save their son from a life of crime. The investigator persuaded Ch'en's father to write a note to the public security station requesting that his son be given rehabilitation through labor. A few days later Ch'en was summoned to the public security station and sent off to begin his rehabilitation.

When by 1960 Ch'en had not yet been released, his aged grandmother became very upset. She feared that she might soon die without seeing her grandson again, and she scolded the boy's father severely for having heeded the bland words of the public security officer. She began visiting the public security station every day and often persuaded Ch'en's father to join her. They asked for Ch'en's release and promised that they would subject him to strict custody. But the public security station repeatedly informed them that the rehabilitation through labor camp was not yet prepared to release him. For two years the Ch'en family made a fuss about their absent son. Finally he was released and returned home in 1962.

## ITEM 95

[Interview]

Ho was a member of the people's militia of an administrative village in the suburbs of Canton. One night in 1958 he went to the house of a local landlord element named Liu to seduce Liu's attractive daughter. Despite the fact that he had no authority to do so, in order to gain entry into the house he announced that he had come for the purpose of checking household registration. Liu was too frightened not to admit Ho to the house. But when his daughter resisted Ho's advances and Ho began to exert force, Liu intervened, and Ho beat him up rather badly. He left without achieving his goal, however, since the fight had awakened the neighbors.

The next morning Liu went to the suburban public security station and reported the incident. The station chief subsequently summoned Ho for questioning. At first Ho denied the whole affair, even after the chief confronted him with Liu. But after the chief threatened to detain him if he persisted in lying, Ho became frightened and admitted the facts related by Liu. The station chief told Ho that he had better compensate Liu for the injuries that Ho had inflicted upon him, and Ho agreed to do so. No sanction was mentioned at the time.

Shortly afterward, Wang, the leader of the production brigade of the advanced agricultural producers' cooperative in which Ho and Liu both worked, went to the public security station to urge that Ho be punished. Wang and Ho had been unfriendly to one another for some time prior to the incident. Since militiamen often went unpunished for misconduct toward landlord elements and their daughters, Wang knew that unless he made an effort the public security station would probably let the matter drop. In his talk with the station chief he argued that Ho could not go unpunished, because he had unlawfully claimed that he was checking on household registration, had attempted rape, and had severely beaten the girl's father. If the public security forces tolerated behavior like Ho's, he said, everyone would feel free to violate the person of the members of landlord families, and social order would disintegrate.

If Liu had been an ordinary peasant, Ho might have been sentenced to five to seven years in prison. But the station chief did not like the idea of punishing a "good person" such as a militiaman for misconduct toward a "bad person" such as a landlord. Yet he felt that some action had to be taken against Ho in order to settle the matter. He finally decided to recommend that Ho be sent to rehabilitation through labor, and the public security subbureau approved this recommendation.

When a member of the people's police showed Ho a copy of the order to take him to rehabilitation through labor, Ho refused to go. The policeman had to force him to go, and when Ho resisted, the policeman and a few militiamen subdued him after a struggle, handcuffed him, and took him away.

After arriving at the rehabilitation camp, Ho wrote many letters of protest to various government agencies. One letter that he sent to the State Council in Peking claimed that he had not tried to rape Liu's daughter, that the brigade leader had "framed" him out of enmity, and that the policeman who seized him had unlawfully beaten him. The State Council sent this letter to the public security bureau of Canton for investigation. The policeman who seized Ho denied that he had used excessive force, the brigade leader denied that any bias had influenced him, and since Ho was obviously lying about not having attempted to rape Liu's daughter, the bureau rejected all of his charges in its report to the authorities at the rehabilitation camp and suggested that Ho be severely "educated" for dishonesty and refusal to admit his wrongdoing. After the camp authorities conducted a bitter struggle meeting against him, Ho admitted his wrongdoing. He was released in the spring of 1962.

Note the differences in procedure between Items 91 and 92, on the one hand, and Items 93, 94, and 95, on the other. What factors might account for these differences?

### 4. Release

## ITEM 96

The rehabilitation through labor Decision (Item 86) does not prescribe a minimum or maximum duration for this sanction. Does it set forth other criteria to guide the authorities who must decide whether and when to release someone? Recall Items 90C, 92, 94, and 95, each of which touches upon the termination of rehabilitation through labor. What grounds for termination do they suggest? The following document is related to termination problems.

[DECISION OF THE CCPCC AND THE STATE COUNCIL OF THE PRC RELATING TO THE PROBLEM OF DEALING WITH RIGHTISTS WHO REALLY DEMONSTRATE THAT THEY HAVE REFORMED (passed at the 92d plenary meeting of the State Council, Sept. 16, 1959; issued, Sept. 16, 1959), *FKHP*, 10:61–62]

In 1957 the Chinese Communist Party and the people's government led the people of the entire country in smashing the wild attacks of the bourgeois rightists, exposed a group of them, and won a great victory on the political and ideological fronts of our country's socialist revolution. During the past two years, because of the influence of the great victory of the general line of our country's socialist construction, because of the education and reform work of the Party committees and people's government of the various levels, because of the supervision and help of the masses of people who have a high degree of socialist consciousness, and because of the further consolidation of the people's democratic united front that is led by the Communist Party and the efforts of all democratic parties and groups, at present a great many of the rightists have, to differing degrees, demonstrated their repentance and reform. Some persons among them have sincerely admitted their own errors and in words and deeds have demonstrated that they have sincerely reformed. When celebrating the tenth anniversary of the establishment of the great People's Republic of China, in order to enable these persons and other rightists to reform even more, to facilitate even more the transformation of negative factors into positive factors, and to enable them to feel that, under our country's great socialist system, if they only change from evil to good they will have their own brilliant future, we now decide: all rightists who have already changed from evil to good and who in words and deeds have demonstrated that they have really reformed shall henceforth no longer be treated as bourgeois rightists, that is, their rightist caps shall be removed. The units in which they are located shall reach conclusions on the basis of their behavior in work and study and shall announce them to the masses.

It has been reported that removal of the rightist "cap" represented a step toward release for those rightists who received rehabilitation through labor but that it did not automatically result in their release.

## ITEM 97

Several former public security officers who have left China since the spring of 1962 have said that shortly before that time the government issued instructions that limited the term of rehabilitation through labor to three years. They pointed out, however, that local police officials were skilled in finding ways to apply such instructions flexibly. In this connection consider the following item.

[Meng Chao-liang, "Preliminary Accomplishments of the Work of Rehabilitation Through Labor" (1959), p. 49]

.     .     .     .     .

In a little over a year some persons undergoing rehabilitation through labor have already reformed relatively well, and they have been discharged from rehabilitation through labor. Most of these persons have applied to remain in their rehabilitation through labor units and to get employment there, indicating their determination honestly to rely on their own labor for their future livelihood.

What reasons might motivate people genuinely to desire to remain with their rehabilitation through labor units? What techniques might officials use to stimulate people to apply to remain in such units? Recall the discussion in Part I of this volume, at notes 144 and 145 and see Items 314–316.

### 5. Evaluation and Interpretation

## ITEMS 98A–98B

These two excerpts are typical of published Chinese evaluations of rehabilitation through labor.

## ITEM 98A

[Chang Chien, "The System of Rehabilitation Through Labor in Our Country," *CFYC*, 6:43–44 (1959)]

[T]he vast masses of people praise this [rehabilitation through labor] policy as being the "policy of the three goods": "good for the state, good for the members of the families of elements who are rehabilitated through labor, and good for the persons [who are rehabilitated] themselves." They also praise it as "the measure with the four benefits": "benefits for the state, benefits for the people, benefits for the members of the families of elements who are rehabilitated through labor, and benefits for the persons themselves." For example, in Tientsin there was a youth named Wei who in the past committed acts of hooliganism and theft and who was constantly fighting and debauching women. His family had absolutely no way of dealing with him. The local public security station educated him many times, but he repented and reformed very little. But later, after less than a year of rehabilitation through labor, not only was he active in production, he was also able to send home a part of his monthly wages. His mother gratefully said: "The people's government can make a lawless person into someone who can labor and who can afford to support a family. That's not easy . . ."

This is how the masses assess the important accomplishments of our country's system of rehabilitation through labor.

In addition, there are also many elements who have been rehabilitated through labor and who, having undergone education and reform, feel very jubilant and excited; they call the Communist Party and the people's government the "parents of their rebirth." Entire families have written letters of thanks to the Party and the government for the education and reform of some of the elements who have been rehabilitated through labor and who have left the places of rehabilitation which gave them the opportunity to become "new persons" and to study a "skill."

## ITEM 98B

[Meng Chao-ling, "Preliminary Accomplishments of the Work of Rehabilitation Through Labor" (1959), pp. 47–48, 49]

In order to attain these goals [of rehabilitation through labor] the state has appropriated capital, land, and equipment and assigned a group of cadres to establish a number of production units in industry, agriculture, and construction. Moreover, they [the persons undergoing rehabilitation through labor] are organized for labor and production basically in accordance with the principles for managing state-operated enterprises and on the basis of their sex and their physical condition. In the course of production, on the one hand, through coercive and educational methods we force them to labor; on the other, we also adopt various kinds of measures to stimulate their activism in productive labor and, basically in accordance with the principle of to each according to his labor, we give them a salary. During the early period of their labor, when their income from production is still insufficient for their self-support, the state also provides them with something to eat, something to wear and necessary funds for expenses of daily life. This enables them to be guaranteed the material necessities of life and to concentrate on labor and production and thought reform. Over a year of practice has proved that these methods which we have adopted are completely correct and very effective.

Many persons who previously never labored and even detested labor and hated laboring people began to cultivate some laboring habits. Many who in the past did not understand production, or who could not [even] distinguish between the five types of grain, now have learned production skills. The rehabilitation through labor unit in the city of Shen-yang [Mukden], during the first quarter of last year, assigned a group of persons undergoing rehabilitation through labor to study mechanical and electrical skills. In less than a year 30 percent of them had reached the level of second-grade technicians while 70 percent had reached the level of first [initial]-grade technicians. This change is not a simple matter for them. Although this is only a beginning, it signifies that they are in the midst of changing their eating-without-laboring, exploiting, and parasitic ways of life and have taken the first step toward the goal of reform — becoming self-supporting laborers.

Rehabilitation through labor production, in a little over a year of development and construction, has already had preliminary accomplishments and has produced many products that are beneficial to society. For example, in agriculture, there were formerly only 2,000 *mou* of land on Hupei province's rehabilitation through labor farm. Last year 5,000 *mou* of barren land were opened up. They produced over 810,000 catties of raw cotton, an average of 117 catties per *mou*.

Some rehabilitation through labor units also had rather conspicuous accomplishments in industry. The rehabilitation through labor unit in the city of Shih-chia-chuang in only a little over a year set up twelve kinds of industrial production and successfully manufactured on an experimental basis nineteen kinds of important products in succession . . .

A little over a year of reform has already created conspicuous changes in the ideology and feelings of some persons undergoing rehabilitation through labor. There is a unit of rehabilitation through labor where thirty-eight former thieves became honest models who would not [even] keep money they found. Among them was a man named Hu who habitually stole from the time he was thirteen years old. During the early period of being provided shelter he still stole things in the rehabilitation through labor unit. After undergoing education many times he began to repent. Once on the way back from work he found a watch worth over a hundred yuan, but he handed it over to the government to return to the owner who had lost it.

## ITEM 99

This excerpt suggests the author's sensitivity to the fact that many persons both within China and in other countries failed to share his enthusiasm for the program of rehabilitation through labor.

[Chang Chien, "The System of Rehabilitation Through Labor in Our Country" (1959), 44–45]

·     ·     ·     ·     ·

The bourgeois rightists and bourgeois "jurists" attack our country's putting into effect the system of rehabilitation through labor as "a violation of the Constitution." Therefore, they attempt wholly to deny the lawfulness of this creative system. This is a barefaced malicious attack.

As previously stated, the system of rehabilitation through labor has been put into effect on the basis of the State Council's Decision Relating to Problems of Rehabilitation Through Labor. This Decision was approved by the seventy-eighth meeting of the Standing Committee of the National People's Congress on August 1, 1957. Article 31 of our country's Constitution expressly prescribes that the Standing Committee of the National People's Congress has the power to adopt laws and decrees. Therefore, this Decision is in the nature of legislation. There can be no doubt whatever about that. At the same time, Article 100 of the Constitution prescribes: "Citizens of the People's Republic of China must observe the Constitution and the law, observe labor discipline, observe public order and respect social morality." Some of those whom the State Council's Decision Relating to Problems of Rehabilitation Through Labor indicates should be the targets of rehabilitation through labor are precisely some of the persons who undermine the spirit of the provisions of Article 100 of the Constitution.

This is a very obvious fact. By unreasonably maintaining that rehabilitation through labor is "a violation of the Constitution," it is not difficult to see that they [the bourgeois rightists and others] certainly are not genuinely concerned with the Constitution of our country but are trying, by attacking it, to deny the great role of the system of rehabilitation through labor in our country . . .

The bourgeois rightists and bourgeois "jurists" are hostile to socialism and to all the new things that have developed under the socialist system. Primarily, they hope to make society stop in its tracks and to have a restoration of the reactionary rule of the bourgeoisie. Therefore, on legal problems, they still raise reactionary points of view from the old law and a set of so-called "standards" from the reactionary bourgeois laws in order to confuse the masses. They try by these means to bind the hands and feet of the vast masses of laboring people, who are led by the worker class, in their struggle against all bad people and things, and to benefit their conspiracy to conduct a restoration. This is their purpose in tarnishing the innovative Decision Relating to Problems of Rehabilitation Through Labor as "not in conformity to the 'standards' " and a so-called " 'monstrosity' that is not law." Here we must point out that we are unceasing revolutionaries, that our law embodies the spirit of unceasing revolution and has contempt for all the "old rules" of bourgeois law. We want to smash the old unceasingly and establish the new. We do not accept the restraint of any old and crude rules. Whatever forms we adopt and whatever contents we prescribe are determined by whether or not they are beneficial to the dictatorship of the proletariat and to the undertakings of socialist construction.

1. Does the author of Item 99 address himself to all of the arguments that might be made to challenge the constitutionality of rehabilitation through labor?

2. Recall the quotation from *Izvestia* at the beginning of this chapter that professed shock over the PRC's resort to this sanction. What might the editors of *Izvestia* say of the Soviet antiparasite laws? Their origin is discussed in Leon Lipson's "Hosts and Pests: The Fight Against Parasites" as follows:

"The anti-parasite laws began their modern career before the revival and reformation of the comrades' courts and the volunteer people's guard. Draft statutes appeared in party newspapers through the Union in early 1957. Under those drafts, 'able-bodied citizens leading an anti-social, parasitic way of life, deliberately avoiding socially useful labor, and likewise those living on unearned income' could be tried at a public meeting of fellow-residents. In cities, the meeting would be convoked by a street committee or apartment house management's committee for cooperation in maintaining public order; in rural areas, by a village Soviet. Sentence could be passed by a majority of those attending, who in turn had only to be a majority of the adult citizens of the given local unit. Although the meeting could confine its action to a warning for a period of probation, the primary sanction was exile at forced labor for two to five years. The sentence would be subject to no judicial review, but would go into effect on being confirmed by the executive committee of the local Soviet.

"The drafts met opposition, some of which was made public in articles and letters to the newspapers. A number of people asserted that the definition of living on unearned income was vague; that sham-workers should be included beside non-workers; that the requirements for a quorum at the public meeting should be tightened. Someone urged that the government prosecutor (*prokuror*) should be present at the trials to watch over legality; it was suggested that the power of the general meeting should be limited to the uncovering of facts to be brought to the attention of the *prokuror* for further action in the course of regular criminal prosecution; others urged that the public meeting be invested with a wider range of possible sanctions than the choice between a warning and two-to-five-year exile.

"The anti-parasite measures were nonetheless enacted, mostly in a form close to the drafts, in nine "outlying" republics between 1957 and 1960. In the Russian Republic and the Ukraine, no anti-parasite law was enacted until 1961; opposition there may have been even stronger though less visible." [5]

3. An English translation of the Russian Republic's 1961 antiparasite law may be found in *CDSP*, 13.17:8–9 (May 24, 1961). As substantially amended in 1965 that law provides:

"[A]ble-bodied, legally adult citizens who refuse to perform a major Constitutional duty — to work honestly according to their capabilities — and who avoid socially useful work and lead an antisocial, parasitic way of life are subject, upon the order of the executive committee of a district (or city) Soviet of Working People's Deputies, to mandatory enlistment in socially useful work at enterprises (or construction projects) situated in the district where they reside permanently or in other places within the given province, territory or autonomous republic.

"Persons who avoid socially useful work and lead an antisocial, parasitic way of life and who live in the city of Moscow, Moscow Province, or the city of Leningrad are subject, upon the order of the district (or city) people's court, to deportation to specially designated localities for a period of from two to five years with mandatory enlistment in work at the place of deportation.

·     ·     ·     ·     ·

"Persons who have been sent to work by decision of the executive committee of a district (or city) Soviet of Working People's Deputies or who have been deported by order of a district (or city) people's court to specially designated localities and who do not take up work or, having taken jobs, do in fact avoid working may, upon representation of militia agencies or of the management or public organizations of the enterprises (or construction projects), be subjected by the district (or city) people's court to corrective [correctional] labor for up to one year with deduction of 10% of their earnings. In cases of evasion of corrective [correctional] labor the court may, upon representation of the agencies for the safeguarding of public order, substitute for such labor deprivation of freedom under the procedure stipulated in Art. 28 of the Russian Republic

5. *Problems of Communism*, 14.3:73–74 (March–April 1965). Quoted by permission of the United States Information Agency, publisher.

Criminal Code. The term of corrective [correctional] labor or deprivation of freedom is not considered a part of the term of deportation." [6]

Compare these Chinese and Soviet sanctions in terms of (a) deprivations imposed; (b) conduct proscribed; (c) procedures employed.

4. How would you explain the almost simultaneous development of these sanctions in the Soviet Union and the PRC?

6. Decree of the Presidium of the Russian Republic Supreme Soviet, "On Amendments to the May 4, 1961, Decree of the Presidium of the Russian Republic Supreme Soviet 'On Intensifying the Struggle Against Persons Who Avoid Socially Useful Work and Lead an Antisocial, Parasitic Way of Life,'" *Vedomosti Verkhovnovo Soveta RSFSR,* 38 (364): 737–739 (Sept. 13, 1965); translated in *CDSP,* 17.44:13 (Nov. 24, 1965). Translation from the *Current Digest of the Soviet Press,* published weekly at Columbia University by the Joint Committee on Slavic Studies, appointed by the American Council of Learned Societies and the Social Science Research Council. Copyright 1965, vol. 17, no. 44, the Joint Committee on Slavic Studies. Reprinted by permission.

# Chapter V  Supervised Labor versus Control: The Borderline between Administrative and Criminal Sanctions

A. Development of Control and the Administrative-Criminal Distinction

B. Emergence of Supervised Labor

In the course of this [supervised] labor, the thinking of these landlord, rich peasant, counterrevolutionary, and bad elements is in the process of changing. In the past, twenty-six of these persons were regularly violating the law and committing sabotage. Within a month after they joined the team, only three of them were still engaging in minor sabotage activity, and they promptly received disciplinary sanctions. The others behaved honestly and labored actively. All elements whose production is being supervised average at least five, and sometimes as many as eight or nine work points a day. In the past, when the fruit ripened, a loafer, Wu T'ai-pao, would not cook his meals but would steal fruit for his meals. Whenever he went to labor in the fields he had a "stomachache" or was "dizzy." Now he earns five or six work points a day. Every night they [these elements] study politics, culture, and technical skills. There are more than ten illiterates who now know how to read over one hundred characters. The elements whose production is being supervised have already started to realize the glory of labor and have developed an affection for labor. The hooligan, Wu Yü-ying, said: "Participating in the supervised production team makes me truly feel the glory of labor for the first time and feel that the individual has a future and has opportunities." Very recently the twenty-six elements whose production is being supervised took the initiative in applying to stay with the team permanently. The vast masses were very satisfied with this, and the members of the families of those who asked to stay together also supported it. The mother of a habitual thief, Wu Yü-chun, was moved to tears and gratefully said: "If the supervised production team had been organized earlier and had saved my son earlier, he would not have committed a crime and been sentenced to imprisonment."

Hsü Yu-shan, "The Work of Reforming Bad Persons Is Actively Being Done Well" [1]

[O]riginally, the government of Hsi-ho-pai village had approved two years of control for the controlled element, Ho Yung-li. But because he was able

---

1. *Kuang-ming jih-pao* (Enlightenment daily), July 4, 1958, p. 3.

to labor actively during the term of his control and in the course of flood-control work was able to relieve some emergency situations in the interests of the public, and because he was also able to observe strictly the policies, laws, and decrees of the government, the masses proposed that the government be requested to terminate his control in advance of schedule. On the other hand, the term of Fan Lan-ni's control has already expired. But because he did not labor actively and did not observe the policies, laws, and decrees of the government, the masses requested the government to extend the term of his control one year.

"A Majority of Landlord and Rich Peasant Elements in the Administrative Village of Chang-ch'ing Change Their Status" [2]

Rehabilitation through labor separates an individual from society and resettles him in the harsh conditions of a labor camp. According to Soviet sources, hundreds of thousands of people fell victim to this form of oppression. Yet the Chinese leaders recognize the existence of limits upon their ability to subject to this sanction all those who might be deemed eligible for it. Former public security officers have pointed out that the establishment of rehabilitation through labor camps placed a considerable strain upon the government's administrative resources, whatever the ultimate gain in terms of freely exploitable labor. They have also emphasized that the government has been alert to the possibility that too broad an application of so severe a sanction might provoke popular discontent of serious proportions.

In order to meet the need for a sanction that would provide long-term reform without constituting a substantial deprivation of freedom or an undue administrative burden, virtually at the same time that the government established rehabilitation through labor, it also perfected the sanction of "supervised labor." This sanction is often referred to as "controlled production" or "supervised production." Like rehabilitation through labor, it too is deemed to be "administrative" in nature, despite the fact that it closely resembles a criminal sanction. In this case the difficulty of distinguishing between criminal and administrative sanctions is compounded because the criminal sanction that it resembles is known as "control" and is therefore easily confused with "controlled production," particularly by officials to whom legal niceties are still novel.

## A. DEVELOPMENT OF CONTROL AND THE ADMINISTRATIVE-CRIMINAL DISTINCTION

As suggested by Chapter IV, post-1957 political conditions have not permitted Chinese writers to come to grips with the legal problems raised by the imposition of severe noncriminal sanctions. Publications relating to the development of control, on the other hand, deriving from the pre-antirightist era, reflect an effort by some scholars to work out a rational basis for both administrative and criminal sanctions and for distinguishing between them.

2. *Shan-hsi jih-pao* (Shansi daily), Nov. 23, 1956.

## ITEM 100

The Provisional Measures were a product of the intensive nationwide campaign conducted from 1950 to 1952 to suppress counterrevolution (see Chapter VI). In addition to the hundreds of thousands of major offenders who were sentenced to death and the many more who received long terms of reform through labor, the campaign identified large numbers of persons who had provided important support to the Nationalists prior to 1949 but whose post-1949 loyalties were unclear. These "historical counterrevolutionaries" could not be ignored. Yet, to subject them to severe punishment would have been politically and administratively inexpedient. Control was devised as the appropriate response, and these Provisional Measures were promulgated on the basis of a good deal of experience with that sanction.

[PROVISIONAL MEASURES OF THE PRC FOR CONTROL OF COUNTER-REVOLUTIONARIES (approved by the Government Administration Council, June 27, 1952; promulgated by the Ministry of Public Security, July 17, 1952), *FLHP* 1952, pp. 53–55]

Article 1. These Measures have been specially adopted on the basis of the provisions of Article 7 of the Common Program of the Chinese People's Political Consultative Conference [see Item 116] and in keeping with the spirit of the Act for Punishment of Counterrevolution [see Item 118], in order thoroughly to eliminate counterrevolution, consolidate the people's democratic dictatorship, and strengthen control of counterrevolutionaries who should be controlled.

Article 2. The goal of control shall be, under control by the government and supervision by the masses, to give counterrevolutionaries definite punishment and ideological education to enable them to reform into new persons.

Article 3. The following counterrevolutionaries who historically committed evil acts and who, since liberation, have not demonstrated or proved their repentance and reform though they have not engaged in current counterrevolutionary activity, must be given definite punishment; but if the degree [of seriousness] of their evil acts does not require that they be arrested and sentenced, they all shall be controlled in accordance with these Measures:

(1) Counterrevolutionary secret agents;

(2) Backbone elements of reactionary parties and youth leagues;

(3) Heads of reactionary societies;

(4) Landlord elements who persist in their reactionary standpoint;

(5) Chiang [Kai-shek]'s counterfeit military and government officials who persist in their reactionary standpoint;

(6) Other counterrevolutionaries who should be controlled.

Article 4. Controlled elements shall be deprived of the following political rights:

(1) The right to vote and the right to stand for election;

(2) The right to hold administrative office in state organs;

(3) The right to participate in the people's armed forces and in people's organizations;

(4) The rights of freedom of speech, publication, assembly, association, correspondence, [choice of] residence, movement of household, and demonstration and procession;

(5) The right to the people's honors.

Article 5. Controlled elements must observe the following provisions:

(1) Observe the government's control provisions;

(2) Engage in proper employment and actively labor for production;

(3) Upon discovery, immediately report the counterrevolutionary activity of others.

Article 6. The term of control shall be fixed at not more than three years. It may be extended when necessary.

Article 7. If controlled elements violate control provisions or continue to conduct counterrevolutionary activity, on the basis of the seriousness of the circumstances of the case, the term of their control may be extended, or they may be arrested and dealt with according to law.

Article 8. In any one of the following situations the term of control of controlled elements may be reduced, or control may be terminated:

(1) They conscientiously observe the laws and decrees of the government and the provisions of control, and their actions really indicate good behavior;

(2) They accept the supervision of the masses, actively labor for production and really reform;

(3) They establish their merit by denouncing counterrevolutionaries to the people's government;

(4) They establish their merit and atone for their crimes in other ways, or they make special contributions.

Article 9. Control of counterrevolutionaries shall be limited to the individuals themselves; members of their families, relatives, and friends may not be involved.

Article 10. Anyone shall have the right to supervise controlled elements and to denounce their unlawful activity.

Article 11. The right to approve control of counterrevolutionaries shall belong to courts, which decide upon approval by judgment in accordance with law, and to public security organs of the county and city [level] and above. In the countryside the government of the district or the administrative village shall submit its recommendation for control to the county public security bureau for examination and approval. In cities the public security station and the public security subbureau shall submit the recommendation for control to the city public security bureau for examination and approval. The same procedure shall apply to extension and reduction [of the term of control] and to termination [of control].

After approving control of controlled elements, the approving organ shall immediately send down a formal notification and also shall announce the imposition of control at an appropriate mass meeting.

Article 12. All counterrevolutionaries who are sentenced to control by the people's judicial organs shall also be dealt with in accordance with these Measures.

Article 13. Public security organs in the various places shall be responsible for enforcing these Measures.

Article 14. All provinces (cities) may, on the basis of the provisions of these Measures and on the basis of concrete local situations, adopt detailed rules for enforcement [of these Measures] and submit them for approval and execution by the people's governments of large administrative areas (military government committees).

Article 15. After approval by the Government Administration Council of the Central People's Government, these Measures shall be promulgated and put into effect by the Central Ministry of Public Security.

Under the Provisional Measures:
1. Is conduct that subjects one to control deemed to be a crime?
2. Is control a criminal sanction?
3. Who may impose control? According to what kind of procedure?
4. May control be imposed upon those who commit nonpolitical crimes?

## ITEM 101

[DECISION OF THE STANDING COMMITTEE OF THE NPC OF THE PRC RELATING TO CONTROL OF COUNTERREVOLUTIONARIES IN ALL CASES BEING DECIDED UPON BY JUDGMENT OF A PEOPLE'S COURT (passed at the 51st meeting of the Standing Committee of the NPC, Nov. 16, 1956), *FKHP,* 4:246]

The Standing Committee of the National People's Congress at its fifty-first meeting on November 16, 1956, decides:

In the future, control of counterrevolutionaries and other criminals shall in all cases be decided upon by judgment of a people's court in accordance with law, and the judgment shall be transferred to public security organs for execution.

If, during the term of their control, controlled elements are discovered to have committed a new criminal act for which it is necessary to extend that term, or if, because their behavior is good and they have established their merit, it is necessary to reduce the term of their control or to terminate control in advance of schedule, this also must be decided upon by judgment or order of a people's court in accordance with law.

## ITEM 102

[Ku Ang-jan, "Why Must Control of Counterrevolutionaries Be Decided Upon by Judgment of a People's Court?" *Shih-shih shou-ts'e* (Current events handbook), 23:35–36 (Dec. 10, 1956)]

Hereafter, why must control of counterrevolutionaries and other criminals in all cases be decided upon by judgment of a people's court? This is because the Provisional Measures for Control of Counterrevolutionaries were formulated in 1952 in the light of the situation that existed at the time. Under the leadership of the Chinese Communist Party and the people's government, the people of our country had with great fanfare launched the movement to suppress counterrevolution. At that time there was a group of counterrevolutionaries whose acts did not require that they be arrested and sentenced to imprisonment but which did require that they be promptly controlled so that, under control by the government and supervision by the masses, they would reform into new persons. But at that time the institution of people's courts had not been perfected throughout the country, and they could not yet completely assume the task of approving control of counterrevolutionaries. Therefore, the Provisional Measures for Control of Counterrevolutionaries prescribed that the right to approve control of counterrevolutionaries belonged to courts, which decide upon approval by judgment in accordance with law, and to public security organs of the county and city [level] and above. At that time handling things in this fashion was completely correct and necessary.

But at present the situation is different. In the past few years a decisive victory has been won in the struggle to suppress counterrevolution. The organization of the procuratorial organs and the courts is being perfected more and more every day, and the people's democratic legal system of our country is becoming increasingly perfect. The Constitution of our country prescribes that the people's courts have the power to adjudicate cases, and control is one of the state's devices for punishing counterrevolutionaries. It consists mainly of depriving the controlled elements of their political rights and compelling them to observe control provisions. Therefore, it is no longer proper for public security organs to approve control of counterrevolutionaries and other criminals. It was for the purpose of thoroughly implementing the system of mutual restraint and the division of work responsibilities in legal matters among the public security organs, the procuratorial organs, and the courts, thereby further perfecting our country's legal system, that the Standing Committee decided that in the future, the control of counterrevolutionaries and other criminals shall in all cases be decided upon by judgment of a people's court.

Why is it that the term of control can only be extended when controlled elements are discovered to have committed a new criminal act for which it is necessary to extend that term? This is also a provision based on a different situation existing in a different period.

According to the provisions of Article 7 of the Provisional Measures for Control of Counterrevolutionaries, the term of control of those who continue to conduct counterrevolutionary activity and those controlled elements who violate control provisions may, on the basis of the seriousness of the circumstances of the case, be extended. Compared with the decision of the Standing Committee, this is severe. But in the conditions of the past few years, when relatively many counterrevolutionaries still existed and counterrevolutionary activity was still rather rampant, this kind of relatively severe provision was beneficial to the suppression of counterrevolution and to the consolidation of the people's democratic dictatorship.

But now circumstances have changed. Counterrevolutionary strength is more and more reduced and divided. We must further implement a policy of leniency toward counterrevolutionaries in order further to isolate and liquidate the remaining counterrevolutionaries and mobilize all forces that can be mobilized to participate in the socialist construction of the country. Therefore, the Standing

Committee decided that the term of their control can only be extended when controlled elements are discovered to have committed a new criminal act for which it is necessary to extend that term. Naturally, we must strengthen the work of educating and reforming those controlled elements who behave badly but who have not committed any new crimes, but out of consideration for perfecting our country's legal system, we must not extend the term of their control. That is to say, if they have not committed a new crime, when their term has expired their control must be terminated on schedule.

1. Does the above Decision suggest that by 1956 control was being applied to persons other than counterrevolutionaries?

2. Under the above Decision may control be applied to persons who have not been convicted of a crime?

3. How would you summarize the legal reasoning that led to the conclusion (a) that control must in all cases be decided upon by judgment of a court; and (b) that the term of control can only be extended if the controlled element commits a new crime?

## ITEM 103

In the following excerpt, the law-reforming authors of the *Lectures* advocate treating control exclusively as a criminal sanction and spell out what they believe should be its content.

[*Lectures* (September 1957), pp. 194–197]

．　　．　　．　　．　　．

But if we apply control as an ordinary punishment of the criminal law, we still must resolve the problem of the content of control. Originally, control had two elements: one was reform through labor without holding offenders in custody; one was deprivation of political rights. In the past, control was applied mainly to counterrevolutionaries. Therefore, deprivation of their political rights during the term of control was completely necessary. But when control is applied to thieves, swindlers, and other criminals who endanger the security of society, the question of whether or not they should be deprived of their political rights should be resolved on the basis of the concrete circumstances of each case. Next, as mentioned before, deprivation of political rights is a supplementary punishment of the criminal law. If control also includes deprivation of political rights, it duplicates that punishment. But the punishments themselves demand that they not duplicate each other but rather that each have its own different, specially prescribed content and function. In order to resolve this contradiction we advocate that control be limited to reform through labor, without deprivation of freedom or political rights. Naturally, when counterrevolutionaries are sentenced to control, they should be sentenced to deprivation of their political rights at the same time.

Since control is limited to reform through labor without holding offenders in custody, what then is its content? On the basis of the provisions of Article 5 of the Provisional Measures for Control of Counterrevolutionaries, controlled elements must: (1) observe the government's control provisions, (2) engage in proper employment and actively labor for production, (3) upon discovery, immediately report the counterrevolutionary activity of others. In practice, controlled elements periodically report to the controlling organ and [if they want] to travel, they must obtain approval. In Several Regulations Relating to Dealing with Corruption, Waste and Overcoming Bureaucratic Errors, it is prescribed that corrupt elements who are subjected to control by their organs ". . . shall remain in the same organs while bearing their guilt and working, but that during the term of control they shall have no title . . . but they shall be given an opportunity to learn and their necessities of life shall be guaranteed." We believe that since control is a light punishment applied to various criminals without holding them in custody, too many and too strict limitations would not be fitting. In keeping with the spirit of the above-mentioned Regulations and also with reference to our practical experience, the following provisions may be made with respect to the content of control: (1) controlled elements must observe the laws of the state, accept the supervision of the government and the masses and actively labor for production; (2) once a month they must report on the circumstances of their activities to the people's council of the administrative village, the public security station, or the department for which they have originally been working, whichever body has the power of supervision; (3) when changing residence or traveling, they must get the approval of the people's council of the administrative village, the public security station, or the department for which they originally have been working, whichever body has the power of supervision. Aside from these, we should not establish other limitations. As for controlled elements who have employment in society [that is, nongovernmental], not having a title and not having this period of employment count toward work seniority are natural consequences of control.

·　　·　　·　　·　　·

With respect to the term of control, Article 6 of the Provisional Measures for Control of Counterrevolutionaries prescribes that it shall be fixed at not more than three years. Article 3 of the Act for Punishment of Corruption prescribes that it shall be fixed at not more than one year. As for the minimum term of control, there are no express provisions in the law. In practice, terms imposed by control and labor service [outside prison] sentences have sometimes been longer than three years, but they have also been as short as one month or even fifteen days. In view of the fact that control is a light punishment for certain minor crimes that does not involve holding offenders in custody, too long or too short a term is not consistent with the nature of the punishment. We believe that it would be more appropriate to fix the limits at six months and three years.

The term of the punishment of control is calculated from the day on which the judgment is rendered, and the period in which he [the offender] has been confined in custody prior to the day on which the judgment is rendered should be deducted from the term of the punishment. The standard for [making such] deduction has not yet been expressly prescribed by law. On February 22, 1957, in a reply to the high people's courts of Anhwei, Chekiang, and Kiangsu provinces, the Supreme People's Court pointed out: "Temporarily, before the promulgation of our criminal code, the deduction problem relating to the period in which a counterrevolutionary criminal has been confined in custody before he is sentenced to control may be handled in this manner: one day of confinement in custody reduces the term of control one day." But in view of the fact that control is a punishment that does not involve deprivation of freedom and in nature is different from such punishments as imprisonment for a fixed term and detention that do involve such deprivation, the standard for [making] the deduction should also be different. We believe that it would be appropriate if each day of the period of confinement in custody reduced the term of control two or three days.

During the term of control, if controlled elements behave well and really demonstrate repentance or if they establish their merit, the organ responsible for executing the sentence may recommend to the people's court that it approve, by judgment or order, reduction of the term of control or discharge from control in advance of schedule. If during the term of control controlled elements violate control provisions, the term of control may be extended if necessary. If during the term of control controlled elements commit a new crime, or if a previously undiscovered crime of theirs is discovered, they should be tried and dealt with in another case. For this there are clear provisions . . . We believe that extension of the term of control generally should not exceed one half of the term of the original sentence.

1. Are the recommendations of the authors entirely consistent with the 1956 Decision on control (Item 101)?

2. Compare control with (a) rehabilitation through labor; and (b) the sanctions applied under Soviet antiparasite legislation.

3. Recall that under Soviet legislation (see p. 273) parasites who refuse to work in their new environment are in the first instance given "corrective labor." The Criminal Code of the RSFSR defines that sanction, below translated as "correctional labor," as follows:

"Article 27. *Correctional labor tasks without deprivation of freedom.* Correctional labor tasks without deprivation of freedom shall be assigned for a term of one month to one year and shall be served, in accordance with the judgment of the court, either at the place of work of the convicted person or in any other place determined by the agencies in charge of application of correctional labor tasks, but in the convicted person's district of residence.

"Deductions from the wages of a person condemned to correctional labor tasks without deprivation of freedom shall be made at a rate established by the judgment of the court within the limits of five to twenty per cent of the wages, and transferred to the state." [3]

How does control differ from the Soviet corrective labor?

3. Translated in H. J. Berman and J. W. Spindler, *Soviet Criminal Law and Procedure, The RSFSR Codes* (Cambridge, Mass., 1966), pp. 156–157.

## ITEM 104

This item, which, like the *Lectures,* was written in early 1957, summarizes the development of control up to the time of the antirightist movement and presents a justification for the existence of both the administrative and criminal varieties of control.

[Hsiao Ch'ang-lun, "A Preliminary Approach to Problems of Control," *CFYC,* 2:9–10 (1957)]

.    .    .    .    .

1. The Nature of Control. This is a problem about which there has been great debate in the past. Correct understanding of the nature of control is a prerequisite for correct evaluation of the role of control and for the resolution of problems relating to control.

What is control? Controlled elements must earnestly observe the following provisions from the Provisional Measures for Control of Counterrevolutionaries, from local provisional measures for controlling counterrevolutionaries (for example, the city of Shanghai's), and from the methods [used] in practice with respect to the control of other criminals: (1) [observe] the policies, laws, and decrees of the state and certain provisions and orders of the organs that execute control (public security organs); (2) engage in proper employment and actively labor for production; (3) accept the supervision of local people's organizations or the masses of people; (4) upon discovery immediately report the counterrevolutionary activity or other criminal activity of others.

These Measures show that control is a coercive sanction. It strengthens the legal responsibilities and obligations which the controlled elements must assume, strengthens their education and supervision, controls their activities, and attains the goals of punishment.

In the past, when a people's court determined after adjudication to apply the coercive sanction of control, it was a criminal sanction, that is, a criminal punishment. Criminal punishment is a coercive measure which people's courts apply to criminals in accordance with law. When a public security organ approves and decides to apply control it is, on the other hand, an administrative sanction. An administrative sanction is a coercive measure which is applied in accordance with law by administrative organs in the exercise of their administrative powers against those who have violated administrative laws.

But some comrades have exaggerated and made absolute one of the two kinds of control reflected in the two different situations, to the extent that some believe that control is not an administrative sanction but only a criminal punishment while others believe that control is not a criminal punishment but only an administrative sanction. The latter also believe that control must not be included among the categories of punishment in the criminal code being drafted by our country. This was the generally prevailing view of an early period. The above two views are both one-sided.

Actually, although some criminal punishments and some administrative sanctions are the same in form, they are different in nature since the organs that decide upon adopting them, the procedures for adopting them, and the legal consequences of adopting them are different. This is not a unique situation. For example, in some separate criminal laws and regulations there are provisions for detention, fine, and other criminal punishments. But the City Traffic Rules prescribe that public security organs have the authority to detain those who violate the Rules, according to the circumstances of the case; the Provisional Customs Law prescribes that customs has the authority to impose on violators fines of different amounts according to the circumstances of the case; various kinds of special tax statutes and the detailed rules for their implementation all prescribe that the tax organs have the authority to impose on violators fines of different amounts according to the circumstances of the case. This detention and these fines are the same in form, that is, the contents and the methods for imposing them are the same in form, as the detention and fines that serve as criminal punishment. Sometimes even the periods of detention and the amounts of the fines are the same. But we should differentiate between the following situations: if a state administrative organ decides to apply these sanctions as administrative sanctions, the sanctioned person does not have a criminal record; if a people's court by judgment applies these sanctions as punishments, the sentenced person has a criminal record. Expunging this record requires a certain period of time. Very obviously, the two have different legal consequences, and the nature of the two is also not completely the same.

A recently promulgated regulation prescribes: "In the future, control of counterrevolutionaries and other criminals shall in all cases be decided upon by judgment of a people's court . . ." Thus, in the future, control shall only be a criminal punishment. Therefore, when it is necessary to propose adoption of the criminal code, provision should be made for control as a criminal punishment.

1. The author of Item 104 states that:

"Actually, although some criminal punishments and some administrative sanctions are the same in form, they are different in nature since the organs that decide upon adopting them, the procedures for adopting them, and the legal consequences of adopting them are different." Do you agree?

2. Does the author's position receive any support from the following quotations?

a. "A crime is an act capable of being followed by criminal proceedings having a criminal outcome, and a proceeding or its outcome is criminal if it has certain characteristics which mark it as criminal . . . I do not think that a definition of crime in terms of criminal procedure, jurisdiction, and sanctions, is necessarily circular, even though it may superficially appear to be so." [4]

b. "What distinguishes a criminal from a civil sanction and all that distinguishes it . . . is the judgment of community condemnation which accompanies and justifies its imposition." [5]

4. G. Williams, "The Definition of Crime," in George W. Keeton and Georg Schwarzenberger, ed., *Current Legal Problems,* VIII (London, 1955), 125, 130.
5. H. M. Hart, Jr., "The Aims of the Criminal Law," *Law and Contemporary Problems,* 23:404 (1958).

## B. EMERGENCE OF SUPERVISED LABOR

At the time of its publication, the thesis concerning control that was advanced by the author of Item 104 was of only academic significance, since, as the last paragraph notes, control no longer existed as an administrative sanction. But shortly thereafter, following the start of the antirightist movement, the substantial equivalent of control reappeared as an administrative sanction, but this sanction was distinguished from control by the labels of supervised labor, controlled production, or supervised production. No detailed analyses of this "new" sanction have been found in the journals or the press, although brief references to its existence are common.

## ITEM 105

This item, although only a legislative draft, actually was employed to authorize the application of this sanction, here called supervised production, to landlord, rich peasant, counterrevolutionary, and other bad elements in the countryside.

[NATIONAL AGRICULTURAL DEVELOPMENT OUTLINE OF THE PRC FOR 1956–1967 (revised draft, Oct. 25, 1957), FKHP, 6:37, 57–58]

*(This draft Outline was presented by the Chinese Communist Party Central Committee in January 1956 and has already played an active role in actual life. Now, based upon some factual changes and work experiences of the past two years, some necessary revisions and supplements have been made. They were presented to the peasants and to the entire body of the people to develop discussion and again to make [further] revisions. They are being prepared for presentation to the National Congress of the Chinese Communist Party for passage. Afterward they will be presented to the State Council for discussion and passage. Finally, after being presented to the National People's Congress for discussion and passage, they will serve as a formal document for promulgation. It is contemplated that during the next ten years many new situations will definitely emerge, and revisions will again have to be made.* Note of the Chinese Communist Party Central Committee, October 25, 1957)

．　　．　　．　　．　　．

(39) Reform Landlord, Rich Peasant, Counterrevolutionary, and Other Bad Elements in Rural Villages, Protect Socialist Order in Rural Villages.

According to the provisions of the Model Regulations for Advanced Agricultural Producers' Cooperatives, an agricultural cooperative may on an individual basis and on the basis of their actual behavior, absorb into the cooperative as members of the cooperative or as candidate members of the cooperative former landlord and rich peasant elements who have abandoned exploitation, and former counterrevolutionaries in rural villages. Those whose conditions are insufficient to join the cooperative may be turned over to the cooperative by the people's council of an administrative village for supervised production. The cooperative should strengthen the education and administration of these persons on the basis of individual circumstances. Moreover, it should regularly educate members of the cooperative and peasants who are outside the cooperative to heighten their vigilance to prevent the possibility of sabotage activity occurring among them. If the behavior of former landlord, rich peasant, and counterrevolutionary elements who have already become members or candidate members of the cooperative is not good and repeated education fails to change them, those who are members may on an individual basis be demoted to candidate members or to supervised production [status]; those who are candidate members may be demoted to supervised production [status]. If they commit acts of sabotage, they shall also be given punitive legal restraints.

Gambling shall be strictly prohibited, and the activities of societies shall be repressed. Thieves, swindlers, hooligans, secret agents, and all kinds of bad elements who seriously undermine social order must all be punished according to law.

## ITEM 106

The cartoon on the next page appeared in a pamphlet that illustrated the application of the various provisions of the revised draft of the national agricultural development outline (Item 105). The English translations have been added.

[Cheng Wen-chung, cartoon; in *Ch'üan-kuo nung-yeh fa-chan kang-yao (ts'ao-an) t'u-chieh* (National agricultural development outline (draft) illustrated; Peking, 1957), p. 9]

## ITEM 107

This item provides legal authority for imposing the sanction upon another special class of the rural population.

[INSTRUCTIONS OF THE CCPCC AND THE STATE COUNCIL OF THE PRC RELATING TO CHECKING THE BLIND OUTFLOW OF PEOPLE FROM RURAL VILLAGES (Dec. 18, 1957), pp. 229–230]

.    .    .    .    .

1. In rural villages ideological education of the masses shall be strengthened . . . Agricultural producers' cooperatives and people's councils of administrative villages shall earnestly dissuade those people who attempt to flow out of rural villages, and may not freely issue certificates permitting them to do so. Those who do not engage in production, who loaf, who like to run around in other places, and who tempt others to go to other places shall be given severe criticism. If repeated education fails to change them, they shall be turned over to an agricultural producers' cooperative for supervised labor.

## ITEM 108

This item is an authoritative recommendation that a very troublesome type of urban resident be given controlled production (that is, supervised labor) in the countryside. A former public security officer has reported that an unpublished decree subsequently implemented this recommendation.

[Teng Hsiao-p'ing (General Secretary of the CCPCC), "Report Relating to the Rectification Movement" (Sept. 23, 1957), p. 18]

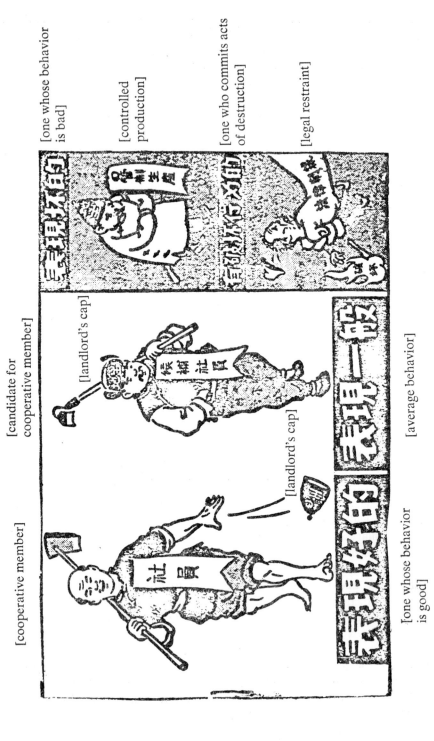

[cooperative member]

[candidate for cooperative member]

[landlord's cap]

[landlord's cap]

[landlord's cap]

[one whose behavior is bad]

[controlled production]

[one who commits acts of destruction]

[legal restraint]

[one whose behavior is good]

[average behavior]

Some hooligans who undermine social order in cities may also be sent to rural villages of that province and the government may individually authorize cooperatives with the facilities to control their production. As for problems relating to this matter, appropriate measures which have been suggested to the State Council for study shall be proposed to the National People's Congress for scrutiny and decision.

## ITEM 109

This item suggests some kinds of conduct that have resulted in a person's designation as a "bad element," subject to supervised labor.

[Ts'ui Ch'eng-hsüan,[6] "How We Defended the Safety of Hsing-fu People's Commune," *CFYC*, 6:62 (1958)]

3. During the commune movement some unlawful bourgeois elements and other bad elements resorted to corruption, theft, concealment of property, and other measures to resist and undermine the commune movement. Besides attacking those who committed serious acts of sabotage, we carried out controlled production over the ordinary elements who would not accept reform, and through supervision by the masses gradually reformed them into self-supporting laborers.

## ITEM 110

Many rightists received supervised labor (see Item 91). Together with "landlord, rich peasant, counterrevolutionary, and other bad elements," they were called the "five types of elements." This item relates the case of a public security officer who was found to be a rightist and was given this sanction.

[Interview]

Shih was a public security officer attached to a subbureau in Canton. In 1950, when the land reform team came to his native village, it accused his father, who was a minor landlord, of owing a "blood debt" to the masses because of his participation in the disposition of a case that arose in the village in 1948, prior to the Communist takeover. A petty thief had been caught, and, rather than send the thief to court for punishment, the head of the administrative village had called together the important people in the area to handle the case according to the local "village rules." The group, which included Shih's father, had approved the recommendation of the village head that the thief be buried alive. By the time of land reform, the former village chief and his principal assistants had fled from the area. Although Shih's father had played only a subsidiary role in the handling of the case, the land reform team held him responsible for the thief's death and had him executed.

This family background did little to promote Shih's career in the public security force. In 1955 he was transferred from the subbureau to serve as a secretary in a public security station. During the latter part of the movement

6. In a footnote to this article, the author is said to work in the people's court of the city of Hsin-hsiang.

to liquidate counterrevolution in early 1956, when the station cadres were engaged in "study" of state policy toward political crimes, at one of the discussions Shih stated that according to the directives of the central government his father should not have been executed since he had only been an accomplice rather than a principal offender. While nothing was said against Shih at the time, his attitude was recorded for future reference.

During the antirightist movement Shih was declared a rightist because of his landlord background and his previously expressed dissatisfaction with the handling of his father's case. He was expelled from the Youth League and the government and was sent to controlled production on a state farm that was run by the political-legal organs.

## ITEMS 111A–111C

In addition to providing further examples of the types of persons who are given supervised labor, these items present the official version of the procedures by which such determinations are purportedly made.

## ITEM 111A

[Hsü Yu-shan, "The Work of Reforming Bad Persons Is Actively Being Done Well," *Kuang-ming jih-pao* (Enlightenment daily), July 4, 1958, p. 3]

The Ling-shui federated agricultural cooperative of the administrative village of K'o-mu in Ching-chiang county [Fukien province], has organized a production team. Through productive labor and political education, the team has actively reformed landlord, rich peasant, counterrevolutionary, and bad elements and has already had very good results.

This cooperative has eighty-four landlord, rich peasant, counterrevolutionary, and bad elements. After having undergone education and reform for the past several years, 65 percent of them have become self-supporting laborers. But there still are some who even now refuse to engage in labor, who like to eat but are too lazy to work, who spread rumors, and who commit theft and sabotage. The masses are extremely dissatisfied with them, saying: "We plant grain for these bad eggs to eat, and feed them so that they can come back to undermine production." During the double-anti, double-comparison movement, the members of the cooperative all wrote large character posters asking the leadership of the cooperative to adopt measures to reform these persons. In the middle ten days of May, based on the requests of the masses, the committee of the cooperative organized the masses to discuss the matter and to propose names [of those who should be reformed], and, with the approval of the people's council for the administrative village, thirty landlord, rich peasant, counterrevolutionary, and bad elements who had not thoroughly reformed were organized into one supervised production team. They plowed the hillsides and reclaimed barren fields on the Ling-yuan mountain of the cooperative.

Within one month, this team . . . [There follows a list of its production feats and plans.]

This supervised production team has been managed according to the mass line. The masses debated and proposed names and convened a meeting of [the supervised elements'] family members to discuss and study the matter. The supervised elements wrote out applications and guarantees. In order to achieve the supervision and reform of these elements, the agricultural cooperative also sent sixteen members of the cooperative and two Party cadres to the team to serve as team leader, group leaders, defense personnel, and technical guides. This team strove for collective labor and the same compensation for the same work. It also set up ten rules and a management system.

## ITEM 111B

[Ch'en Kuo-liang, "Wu-ling Cooperative Strictly Controls the Enemy," *T'ung-ch'uan jih-pao* (T'ung-ch'uan daily), April 17, 1958]

After the completion of rectification in Wu-ling cooperative in the administrative village of Yü-hsi in Pa-chung county, it was discovered that during spring ploughing and production, some landlord, rich peasant, counterrevolutionary, and bad elements had begun to raise their tails defiantly. Some cursed the cadres and would not accept work assignments, while others made excuses to go to other places and would not participate in productive labor.

In order to ensure the smooth progress of spring ploughing and production, the cooperative held successive meetings of Party and Youth League members, leaders of security groups, and cadres who served the cooperative. They decided to strengthen the supervision and reform of class enemies and not to let them engage in sabotage activity. On the night of March 20, the cooperative convened the landlord, rich peasant, and counterrevolutionary elements in separate groups to receive instructions and ordered them to write out statements in which they guaranteed to obey the law. These were read to meetings of production teams and were discussed and passed by the masses, who supervised their enforcement. The cooperative also decided to make semimonthly examinations of how these guarantees to obey the law were being fulfilled. If there was any unlawful activity, the violators were handed over to the masses for struggle or were punished according to law. After these systems were discussed and passed by the cooperative, the members all rigorously strengthened the control of landlord, rich peasant, and counterrevolutionary elements who in the past did not observe the law or who had fled to other places.

## ITEM 111C

[Shang Yin-pin, "Fully Develop the Militant Role of the Basic Level Security Defense Organizations" (1958), pp. 71, 72]

On a foundation of attacking landlord, rich peasant, counterrevolutionary, and bad elements and extensively and intensively launching propaganda about the legal system, they [the basic level security defense organizations] organized the masses to conduct a great debate on the subject of how to implement security, so as genuinely to convert security slogans into actual conscious conduct of the vast masses. The requests put forth by the vast masses for the purpose of realizing security greatly stimulated the energy of the security defense cadres. For example, in the administrative village of Ho-tung-chai in Ch'in-huang-tao, during the debate on the supervised production of landlord, rich peasant, counter-revolutionary, and bad elements, the masses reported the situation of a certain bad element named Li. When cadres were present he carried four buckets of water, but when they left he slowed down — carrying only two half-empty buckets of water. Under these circumstances, after debate by the masses followed by adoption of the measures of the two undertakings (undertake regulation and undertake reform), the two investigations (investigate reporting for work and investigate behavior) and the end-of-the-month evaluation, they thereby created a new situation in which "everyone regulates bad people" and "everyone engages in security."

. . . In the early part of this year, when the socialist education movement and the struggle to attack landlord, rich peasant, counterrevolutionary, and bad elements had already won very great victories, those problems that had not yet been resolved were immediately brought to light after the preliminary launching of the great leap forward in industrial and agricultural production. In addition to certain landlord, rich peasant, counterrevolutionary, and bad elements who during labor evaded heavy work, picked easy jobs, and cunningly and lazily did not honestly take part in production, in Tientsin and in the special district of T'ung-hsien witches and wizards were still sporadically manufacturing magic water and medicine and had become tumors in the great leap forward in production. In order to mobilize all positive factors and to sweep away obstacles to the great leap forward in production they [the basic level security defense organizations], under the leadership of the basic level Party committees, spontaneously experimented with collective training work. After we expressed our support for and extended [the scope of] this creation, it very quickly developed throughout the entire province and became a new method of social reform work. As another example, during the period for repairing water utilization [facilities], on the one hand they educated the masses to pay attention to safety and to prevent incidents of injuries to workers, and on the other they arranged for activists to supervise counterrevolutionary and bad elements in order strictly to prevent sabotage by them . . .

From the standpoint of the circumstances of how they have executed the Act pertaining to the work of the security defense committees, in executing the task of "conduct[ing] among the masses regular propaganda-education about preventing treason, espionage, arson, and theft and suppressing counterrevolutionary activity," they have already been able to use various situations and forms, and they themselves have even made cartoons and held small-scale exhibits to conduct propaganda work among the vast masses at various times and places. When confronted by dishonest landlord, rich peasant, counterrevolutionary, and bad elements, they have made use of the masses' production rest periods and right in the fields or at the side of ditches they have convened small-scale meetings, conducted debates, and combined this with educating the masses about the legal system. With respect to the tasks of "organizing and leading the masses in assisting the government and public security organs in denouncing, supervising, and controlling counterrevolutionaries" and "conducting the work of education and thought reform among members of families of counterrevolutionaries," they have already assumed complete responsibility for the social reform work among landlord, rich peasant, counterrevolutionary, and bad elements and their family members.

## ITEM 112

This item, based on an interview with a former public security officer who participated in the case, provides an insider's view of the decision-making process concerning supervised labor. Although the consequence of the struggle meeting described was obviously unintended, such abuses have occurred with sufficient frequency, especially in rural areas, to present a problem to a government that seeks an orderly sanctioning system and yet does not want to dampen the "revolutionary enthusiasm" of the masses.

[Interview]

Chiao had been adjudged a historical counterrevolutionary in 1951 and had received three years of control. After his "cap" was removed in 1954, he reverted to the status of middle peasant and had no further difficulty with the law until 1960. At that time a movement to suppress "anti-Communist reseizures" was launched in the countryside around Canton. The special office that had been set up in Chiao's commune to handle the movement sent a work group down to his brigade, and someone reported to it that Chiao had been complaining about the very difficult economic situation in the commune. The work group reported this to the special commune office and recommended that Chiao be given detention to be followed by supervised labor. The special commune office endorsed the recommendation and sent it on for the consideration of the chief of the relevant public security subbureau of Canton. The latter approved giving Chiao ten days of detention and then supervised labor. As was usual in the area in such cases, the chief ordered that the imposition of the sanctions be preceded by a struggle meeting, at which they would be announced.

After making preparations, the leader of the work group convened a meeting of the brigade masses and introduced the facts of Chiao's case. He then ordered Chiao, who was standing on the platform with his hands tied behind him, to make a full "self-examination." Before Chiao could speak, however, the chief of the brigade's militia unit shouted at him: "You won't confess?" and with that kicked him in the groin. Chiao fell over and did not move. When he failed to respond to an order to get up, the militia chief kicked him again. After it became clear that Chiao could not move, he was carried home, where he died within a few hours.

As a consequence of this incident, the leader of the work group that was handling the movement in Chiao's brigade was removed from his position but was given no other administrative, criminal, or Party sanctions. And the militia chief who had actually kicked Chiao received only private criticism from the chief of the local public security station. The incident did, however, become the subject of a report that was circulated to all cadres concerned with the movement.

## ITEM 113

The following account, given by the "controlled element" who is its protagonist, describes what both the administrative and criminal sanctions studied in this chapter are like in practice.

[Interview]

In Canton in September 1958, a people's court sentenced Chu, a former government cadre, to two years of control. He was placed under the control of the public security station in his residential area. There every Monday evening he joined with over one hundred other "controlled elements" to report his activities of the previous week and to engage in "study" of current Communist documents and newspaper articles. The controlled elements were of a diverse sort. Some, like Chu, were "historical counterrevolutionaries" or other minor criminals who had been sentenced by a court. Others were "rightists," "bad elements," and more minor offenders, who had been given "controlled production" by the public security bureau itself. The reporting and study of both categories of offenders usually took place in small groups that were organized according to the principle of putting similar types of offenders in the same group.

In addition to these weekly meetings, the various controlled elements, who were all allowed to live at home, were subjected to other restrictions. They were not permitted to leave the city or to stay overnight within the city elsewhere than at home. If visited by anyone with a "political problem," they were required to report the visit and the conversation immediately after the visitor's departure. Before 1959, those who were under control in Chu's area also had to make periodic progress reports to the member of the security defense committee in their neighborhood. Beginning in 1959, these progress reports had to be made instead to a meeting of their residents' small group, and the controlled elements had to ask these neighbors to give them their views and criticisms. They also had to perform unremunerated labor upon demand by the chief of the public security station. On evenings of study they had to clean the lavatories and gather fuel for the furnace that heated the station. They were also frequently called upon to take part in mass sanitation campaigns and in local projects such as building a community dining hall. On state holidays they were obligated to march in public parades and meetings. Worst of all was the stigma — felt by both categories of offenders — of being branded a controlled element, which created a social abyss between the controlled and his neighbors and friends, especially in political cases.

In June 1960, many of those in Chu's area who were subjected to control or to controlled production were "mobilized" to go down to the countryside for "supervised labor." First they were told at a meeting at the public security station of the state's need for their labor in the agricultural communes. Then they were taken down to have a look at a commune which was about a three hours' bus ride from Canton. On their return a few days later, the station chief asked them at another meeting whether they were willing to go back and labor in that commune for a time. Everyone "agreed," for, as Chu believed and as the station chief broadly hinted, anyone who did not agree would be subjected to night after night of criticism until "persuaded" or arrested. Besides, they were told that this "steeling" experience would speed their reform and the end of their control. To preclude the possibility that any of them might succumb to second thoughts, the station chief announced that their household registrations would be sent to the commune in advance of their arrival. Their spouses were also "mobilized" to accompany them to the countryside, but few of them went, since they were not coerced to do so.

The controlled elements found life in the commune to be more difficult than life in the city. They were interspersed in production brigades of ordinary peasants and lived in poor shacks. Generally they labored ten hours a day in work that was identical to that of the peasants, but they received only 25 percent of the work points that the peasants received. Unlike the peasants, they had to spend many of their evenings in study, meetings, or special labor projects. If they were not sufficiently active in labor, they were not only deprived of labor points, as were the peasants, but they were also subjected to sharp criticism and violent struggle sessions. They had less leisure time than in the city, and what they had was even more closely restricted than their city leisure had been. In order to leave the brigade on the one day off they were allowed each month, they had to obtain the approval of both their brigade leader and the chairman of the security defense committee, while others only required the approval of the former. And all visitors had to be reported to an SDC member.

Even though Chu's two-year term of control expired within a few months of his going to the countryside, he spent slightly more than a year in such supervised labor, since the public security authorities told him that he could not hope to end his control until he had reformed. Although he wanted to seek review by the court, he feared that it would only lead to further punishment. He returned to Canton to live after falling ill as a result of overwork and poor food and sanitary conditions. He was still under control at the time of his escape from China in early 1962.

1. Item 113 appears to represent an instance of the implementation of Teng Hsao-p'ing's proposal in Item 108. While it is one thing to undergo supervised labor at one's customary place of employment or residence, as Item 113 demonstrates, it is quite another thing to be sent from the city to labor in a strange rural setting, even if one still is better off there than he would be in rehabilitation through labor. How does this transplanted supervised labor compare with the treatment currently accorded to parasites in the Soviet Union (see p. 273)?

2. After reading Item 113, to what extent do you believe the differences between supervised labor and control to be significant?

# Chapter VI   The Definition of Criminal Conduct

Originally, sir, I had hope in you, but now that is all over. Anciently, the early kings conducted their administration by deliberating on matters [as they arose]; they did not put their punishments and penalties [into writing], fearing that this would create a contentiousness among the people which could not be checked. Therefore they used the principle of social rightness (*yi*) to keep the people in bounds, held them together through their administrative procedures, activated for them the accepted ways of behavior (*li*), maintained good faith (*hsin*) toward them, and presented them with [examples of] benevolence (*jen*) . . .

But when the people know what the penalties are, they lose their fear of authority and acquire a contentiousness which causes them to make their appeal to the written words [of the penal laws], on the chance that this will bring them success [in court cases] . . . As soon as the people know the grounds on which to conduct disputation, they will reject the [unwritten] accepted ways of behavior (*li*) and make their appeal to the written word, arguing to the last over the tip of an awl or knife. Disorderly litigations will multiply and bribery will become current. By the end of your era, Cheng will be ruined. I have heard it said that a state which is about to perish is sure to have many governmental regulations.

> Shu-hsiang, "Letter of Protest to Tzu-ch'an (Prime Minister of the State of Cheng) Who in 536 B.C. Had Ordered 'Books of Punishment' to be Inscribed on a Set of Bronze Tripod Vessels" [1]

1. Translated in Bodde, pp. 381–382.

Today, our country's legal system is, to be sure, still incomplete but the situation certainly is not, as some people claim, that "there is absolutely no law to go by." . . . [W]e have already adopted many important laws . . . In the early days of the foundation of our country and especially during the period of transition, the political and economic situation changed very quickly, and it was difficult to adopt laws of a fundamental character and of long-term applicability. For instance, it was difficult to adopt a civil or a criminal code prior to the basic completion of the socialist reform of the system of private ownership of the means of production and the complete establishment of the system of socialist ownership. Under these circumstances it was necessary and appropriate for the state to promulgate provisional acts, decisions, instructions, etc., as work standards for common observance. Only on a foundation of their effective enforcement could we summarize experience and adopt laws of long-term applicability . . . Now the socialist reform of the system of private ownership of the means of production has been basically completed, the system of socialist ownership has been established, and the state has obtained definite experience in the various aspects of work practice. Thus, while setting in order past laws and regulations, we are able to adopt various kinds of socialist laws on a foundation of summarized past experience. For example, we already have a preliminary draft of the criminal code, and the civil code and the Security Administration Punishment Act are in the process of being drafted.

Chou En-lai, "Report on the Work of
the Government" (June 26, 1957)[2]

At various places Chapters I–V shed light upon the contemporary Chinese views of the nature of criminal conduct, the processes by which it is defined, and the principal acts that are actually regarded as criminal. This chapter seeks to provide a more explicit and detailed presentation of these views in order to facilitate an understanding of Chapters VII–XI. In reading the materials that follow one should inquire:

1. To what extent is the public given fair warning that given acts are deemed to be criminal? By what modes is warning given?

2. To what extent do legislative bodies define criminal acts?

3. What other agencies define criminal acts?

4. To what extent are police, procurators, and judges empowered to decide that given acts are criminal? More precisely, what substantive restrictions are placed on these officials?

## A. ABROGATION OF LAWS OF THE NATIONALIST GOVERNMENT

Unlike their Soviet elder brothers, whose "first decree on the courts had instructed the new people's courts to use as a guide the laws of the ousted government to the extent that they had not been revoked by the Revolution and were not contrary to the revolutionary conscience and revolutionary consciousness of the judges," [3] after their assumption of power the Chinese Communists sought to wipe the slate clean.

2. (Given at the 4th meeting of the 1st session of the NPC), *FKHP*, 6:93, 94.
3. John N. Hazard, *Settling Disputes in Soviet Society* (New York, 1960), p. 16.

## ITEM 114

Despite the ambiguous wording of the following provision of the Common Program, the fundamental charter of government of the PRC from 1949 to 1954, it has been universally accepted as having completely abrogated the laws and decrees of the Republic of China.

[COMMON PROGRAM OF THE CPPCC (passed at the 1st plenary session of the CPPCC, Sept. 29, 1949), *FLHP* 1949–1950, 1:19]

Article 17. All of the reactionary Kuomintang government's laws, decrees, and judicial systems that oppress the people shall be abolished. Laws and decrees that protect the people shall be adopted, and the people's judicial system shall be established.

## ITEM 115

[INSTRUCTIONS OF THE CCPCC RELATING TO ABOLISHING THE COMPLETE SIX LAWS OF THE KUOMINTANG AND ESTABLISHING JUDICIAL PRINCIPLES FOR THE LIBERATED AREAS (February 1949); quoted in the *Lectures*, pp. 20–21]

Under the government of the people's democratic dictatorship led by the proletariat on the basis of the worker-peasant alliance, the Complete Six Laws of the Kuomintang shall be abolished. The people's judicial work can no longer be based on the Complete Six Laws of the Kuomintang but shall be based on the new law of the people. Before the people's new law is systematically promulgated, judicial work shall be based on the policies of the Communist Party and the programs, laws, orders, acts, and resolutions issued by the people's government and by the People's Liberation Army. At present, in circumstances where the people's law is not complete, the judicial organs shall handle matters in accordance with the following principles: where there are provisions in programs, laws, orders, acts, or resolutions, they shall act in accordance with these provisions; where there are no such provisions, they shall act in accordance with the policies of the new democracy.

Recall the National Agricultural Development Outline for 1956–1967 (revised draft) (Item 105). Despite the fact that this document had been issued by the CCP alone and had not yet been promulgated by the government, its provisions were put into effect. If a rule set forth by an "unofficial" agency is habitually obeyed by officialdom and the bulk of the populace and if those who disobey it are subjected to official sanctions, is it "law"?

### B. CRIMES PROSCRIBED BY PUBLISHED LAW

#### 1. Counterrevolutionary Crimes

During its early years the PRC was necessarily preoccupied with meeting the continuing and serious problem of how to stamp out counterrevolutionary conduct. This subsection presents the principal legislation relating to the definition of counterrevolutionary crimes as well as some information about the kinds of conduct actually punished on the basis of these provisions.

## ITEM 116

[COMMON PROGRAM OF THE CPPCC (Sept. 29, 1949), p. 17]

Article 7. The People's Republic of China must suppress all counterrevolutionary activity and severely punish all Kuomintang counterrevolutionary war criminals and other leading incorrigible counterrevolutionaries who collaborate with imperialists, betray their mother country, and oppose the undertakings of the people's democracy. Reactionaries in general, feudal landlords, and bureaucratic capitalists, after having their arms taken away and their special powers eliminated, must be deprived of their political rights in accordance with law for a necessary period. But at the same time they shall be given a way to earn a livelihood and also shall be compelled while at labor to reform themselves so as to become new persons. If they continue to conduct counterrevolutionary activity, they must be given severe punitive restraints.

## ITEM 117

[*Lectures* (September 1957), pp. 21–22]

.     .     .     .

In the early period of the liberation of the entire country, the remnant counterrevolutionary force was still extremely rampant. Moreover, domestic and foreign enemies collaborated with each other in conducting various antipeople sabotage conspiracies that were intended to overthrow the recently established revolutionary regime and to disrupt social order. In order to consolidate and extend the people's victory and to safeguard the smooth conduct of various social democratic reform movements, suppression of counterrevolution thus became at the time an important task of the state. The Party and the government led the people throughout the country in conducting the full-fledged mass movement for suppression of counterrevolution and on the basis of the provisions of Article 7 of the Common Program and the experience summarized from the movement for suppression of counterrevolution, promulgated in February 1951 the Act of the People's Republic of China for Punishment of Counterrevolution. The military courts and people's courts of the various places thoroughly implemented this Act and attacked in a concentrated way secret agents, bandits, local despots, backbone elements of reactionary parties and youth leagues, heads of reactionary societies, and various other kinds of counterrevolutionaries, and thereby severely attacked counterrevolutionary activity, consolidated the people's democratic dictatorship, safeguarded the smooth conduct of the land reform movement, the "resist America and aid Korea" movement, and various other social reform movements, and safeguarded the restoration and development of the national economy.

## ITEM 118

[ACT OF THE PRC FOR PUNISHMENT OF COUNTERREVOLUTION (approved at the 11th meeting of the Central People's Government Council, Feb. 20, 1951; promulgated by the Chairman of the PRC, Feb. 21, 1951), *FLHP* 1951, 1:3–5]

Article 1. In accordance with the provisions of Article 7 of the Common Program of the Chinese People's Political Consultative Conference, this Act is specially adopted in order to punish counterrevolutionary criminals, suppress counterrevolutionary activity, and consolidate the people's democratic dictatorship.

Article 2. All counterrevolutionary criminals whose goal is to overthrow the people's democratic regime or to undermine the undertaking of the people's democracy shall be punished in accordance with this Act.

Article 3. Those who collaborate with imperialists to betray their mother country shall be punished by death or life imprisonment.

Article 4. Of those who incite, entice or buy public employees, armed military units, or people's militia to conduct insurrection, the principal elements and leaders of the military units used in the insurrection shall be punished by death or life imprisonment. Others who participate in the inciting, enticing, buying, or insurrection shall be punished by not more than ten years of imprisonment; where the circumstances of their cases are major they shall be punished with increased severity.

Article 5. In a mass, armed uprising, the ringleaders, commanders, and others whose evil crimes are major shall be punished by death. Other active participants shall be punished by not less than five years of imprisonment.

Article 6. Those who engage in any one of the following acts of espionage or of aiding the enemy shall be punished by death or life imprisonment; where the circumstances of their cases are relatively minor they shall be punished by not less than five years of imprisonment:

(1) Stealing or searching for state secrets or supplying intelligence to a domestic or foreign enemy;

(2) Instructing enemy planes or enemy ships about bombardment targets;

(3) Supplying domestic or foreign enemies with weapons, ammunition, or other military materials.

Article 7. Those who participate in organizations of counterrevolutionary secret agents or spies, and whose cases include any one of the following circumstances shall be punished by death or life imprisonment; where the circumstances are relatively minor they shall be punished by not less than five years of imprisonment:

(1) They have been sent by a domestic or foreign enemy for [conducting] covert activities;

(2) Since liberation they have organized or participated in organizations of counterrevolutionary secret agents or spies;

(3) Before liberation they organized or led organizations of counterrevolutionary secret agents or spies and committed other major evil crimes, and since liberation their behavior has not established their merit and atoned for their crimes;

(4) Before liberation they participated in organizations of counterrevolutionary secret agents or spies, and since liberation they have continued to participate in counterrevolutionary activity;

(5) After registration with and voluntary surrender to the people's government, they have continued to participate in counterrevolutionary activity;

(6) After being educated and released by the people's government, they have continued to link themselves with counterrevolutionary secret agents and spies or to conduct counterrevolutionary activity.

Article 8. Those who make use of feudal societies to conduct counterrevolutionary activity shall be punished by death or life imprisonment; where the circumstances of their cases are relatively minor they shall be punished by not less than three years of imprisonment.

Article 9. Those who, with a counterrevolutionary purpose, plot or execute any one of the following acts of sabotage or murder shall be punished by death or life imprisonment; where the circumstances of their cases are relatively minor they shall be punished by not less than five years of imprisonment:

(1) Robbing or destroying military facilities, factories, mines, forests, farms, dams, communications, banks, warehouses, safety equipment, or other important public or private property;

(2) Spreading poison, spreading germs, or using other methods that cause major disasters involving people, livestock, or agricultural crops;

(3) Under instructions from a domestic or foreign enemy, disrupting the market or undermining finance;

(4) Attacking, killing, or injuring people or public employees;

(5) Improperly using the name of military or government organs, democratic parties, or groups or people's organizations and forging official documents to engage in counterrevolutionary activity.

Article 10. Those who, with a counterrevolutionary purpose, commit any one of the following acts of provocation or incitement shall be punished by not less than three years of imprisonment; where the circumstances of their cases are major they shall be punished by death or life imprisonment:

(1) Stirring up the masses to resist or to undermine the enforcement of grain levies, tax levies, public service, military service of the people's government, or other government orders;

(2) Provoking dissension among the various nationalities, democratic classes, democratic parties and groups, people's organizations or between the people and the government;

(3) Conducting counterrevolutionary propaganda and agitation and making and spreading rumors.

Article 11. Those who, with a counterrevolutionary purpose, secretly cross the borders of the state shall be punished by not less than five years of imprisonment, life imprisonment, or death.

Article 12. The organizers and ringleaders of mass prison raids or violent prison breaks shall be punished by death or life imprisonment; other active participants shall be punished by not less than three years of imprisonment.

Article 13. Those who harbor or conceal counterrevolutionary criminals shall be punished by not more than ten years of imprisonment; where the circumstances of their cases are major they shall be punished by not less than ten years of imprisonment, life imprisonment, or death.

Article 14. In any one of the following situations, all those who commit crimes [enumerated] in this Act may, according to the circumstances, be given light punishment, reduced punishment, or may be exempted from punishment:

(1) They have taken the initiative in going to the people's government and in sincerely and voluntarily surrendering and repenting;

(2) Before or after they have been exposed or denounced, they have sincerely repented and established their merit and atoned for their crimes;

(3) They were coerced or deceived by counterrevolutionaries, and their crimes were really involuntary;

(4) Before liberation their counterrevolutionary crimes were definitely not major, since liberation they have really repented and reformed, and they have severed their links with counterrevolutionary organizations.

Article 15. The punishment of all those who commit several kinds of crimes, except those sentenced to death or life imprisonment, shall, according to the circumstances, be fixed at less than the aggregate punishment [that is possible for all the crimes] but more than the most severe punishment [for any one of those crimes].

Article 16. Those who, with a counterrevolutionary purpose, commit crimes not covered by the provisions of this Act may be given punishments prescribed for crimes [enumerated] in this Act which are comparable to the crimes committed.

Article 17. Those who commit crimes [enumerated] in this Act may be deprived of their political rights, and all or a portion of their property may be confiscated.

Article 18. The provisions of this Act also apply to those who were counterrevolutionary criminals before this Act was put into effect.

Article 19. Anyone has the right to expose or secretly to report counterrevolutionary criminals to the people's government, but no one harboring resentment may make maliciously false accusations.

Article 20. Those who commit crimes [enumerated] in this Act shall, during periods of military control, be tried in accordance with this Act by military courts that are organized by various military district headquarters, military control commissions, or command organs for combatting banditry.

Article 21. This Act shall be put into effect on the day it is approved and promulgated by the Central People's Government Council.

1. Is the Act reasonably precise in defining the kinds of conduct that come within its reach?

a. Is any act committed with a counterrevolutionary purpose a crime?

b. How could you improve upon the Act's draftsmanship?

2. Does the Act provide any guidance to legal personnel who are charged with the responsibility of handling nonpolitical crimes?

a. Is the conduct to which Article 12 refers necessarily counterrevolutionary?

b. What of ordinary crimes against the person or against property?

c. What is the dividing line between counterrevolutionary and ordinary crimes?

Recall the provisional measures of the PRC for control of counterrevolutionaries [Item 100].

## ITEM 119

This item reflects the change in political climate that had taken place in China by late 1956, following the completion of the third great movement against counter-revolutionaries — the famed "liquidation of counterrevolution." Does it merely prescribe more lenient methods of handling urban counterrevolutionaries, or does it alter the definition of what constitutes counterrevolutionary conduct?

[DECISION OF THE STANDING COMMITTEE OF THE NPC OF THE PRC RELATING TO DEALING LENIENTLY WITH AND PLACING REMNANT CITY COUNTERREVOLUTIONARIES (passed at the 51st meeting of the Standing Committee of the NPC, Nov. 16, 1956), *FKHP*, 4:243–245]

A decisive victory has already been won in our country's struggle to suppress counterrevolution, and the extremely small number of remnant counterrevolutionaries is becoming increasingly isolated and divided. In order to give remnant counterrevolutionaries an opportunity to repent of their crimes and to start life anew, further to isolate and to liquidate remnant counterrevolutionaries and to mobilize all forces that can be mobilized to participate in the socialist construction of the state, we now make the following Decision with respect to methods for dealing leniently with and placing remnant city counterrevolutionaries.

1. Counterrevolutionaries who before liberation only committed ordinary crimes and who since liberation have not conducted sabotage activity and against whom there is no great popular anger, or ordinary counterrevolutionaries who after liberation, although they committed crimes, have now stopped this activity shall not be blamed for the past if they thoroughly confess and admit their guilt.

2. Counterrevolutionaries whose cases still have not been brought to court and handled according to law and who before liberation committed serious crimes and against whom there was very great popular anger, or counterrevolutionaries who since liberation have engaged in serious sabotage activity shall be called upon to confess quickly and to admit their guilt to the people's government. Of these counterrevolutionaries, those who thoroughly confess and admit their guilt may be dealt with leniently: those whose crimes should be punished by death shall all be exempted from being punished by death; those whose crimes are such that they should be sentenced to imprisonment shall be given a light sentence or shall be exempted from punishment; those who establish their merit may diminish their guilt; and those who establish great merit may be given rewards.

3. Counterrevolutionaries who have escaped to the cities, whether they thoroughly confess and admit their guilt on the spot or after returning to their original places, shall all be dealt with according to the principle of leniency for those who confess. Those who, after confessing, are not willing to return to their original places to be dealt with shall be appropriately dealt with on the spot and must not be compelled to go back to their original places.

6. Ordinary members of reactionary organizations and persons who held

reactionary positions but who really did not commit counterrevolutionary crimes shall not be counted as counterrevolutionaries.

Persons who righteously revolted during the revolutionary war, even though historically they participated in counterrevolutionary organizations or committed counterrevolutionary crimes, shall not be counted as counterrevolutionaries if since their righteous revolt they have not engaged in counterrevolutionary activity.

Personnel of the old army and government who have participated in the People's Liberation Army and who have been demobilized, changed their professions, and been sent home shall, even more decidedly, not be treated as counterrevolutionaries.

The above three categories of persons shall have the same opportunities to labor and to get employment as the masses of people, and they may not be discriminated against.

7. As for elements who have been exempted from criminal sanctions and who already have employment and as for elements who still are controlled, the principle of the same compensation for the same work shall be put into effect, and they shall be given the salary that they ought to receive.

8. Members of families of counterrevolutionaries who have not participated in counterrevolutionary activity shall have the same opportunities for getting employment and for studying as the masses of people, and they may not be discriminated against.

9. Current counterrevolutionaries who conduct various kinds of sabotage activity shall be punished according to law. As for counterrevolutionaries who before liberation committed serious crimes and against whom there was very great popular anger and counterrevolutionaries who since liberation have engaged in serious sabotage activity, those whose cases have not previously been brought to court and handled according to law and who still refuse to confess and admit their guilt shall, after verification through examination of the evidence, be punished according to law. Counterrevolutionaries who, after being dealt with leniently, continue to conduct sabotage activity, shall be severely punished according to law.

## ITEM 120

Interviews have established that unpublished directives have frequently supplemented the published documents defining counterrevolutionary crimes. Yet, despite such efforts to provide precise guidance, considerable confusion continues to exist over what constitutes a counterrevolutionary crime, as is conceded by Chairman Mao in the following evaluation of the problem in 1957.

[Mao Tse-tung, "Problems Relating to the Correct Handling of Contradictions Among the People" (Feb. 27, 1957), pp. 12, 14]

### 2. Problems of Liquidating Counterrevolution

The problem of liquidating counterrevolutionaries is a problem of the struggle of contradictions between the enemy and us. There are, among the people, some who hold somewhat different views about the problem of liquidating counterrevolutionaries. There are two kinds of persons whose opinions differ from ours. There are persons of rightist ideology who make no distinction between the enemy and us and consider [those who are our] enemies as [those among] us. They consider as friends the people whom the vast masses consider as enemies. There are persons of "leftist" ideology who enlarge contradictions between the enemy and us to the extent that they also regard certain contradictions among the people as contradictions between the enemy and us and regard as counterrevolutionaries persons who in truth are not. These two views are erroneous. Both of them are inadequate for correctly handling the problem of liquidating counterrevolutionaries or correctly assessing our work in this.

．　　．　　．　　．　　．

At present the circumstances relating to counterrevolutionaries can be explained by using these two sentences: there still is counterrevolution; but there is not much. In the first place, there still is counterrevolution. Some people say that there is no longer any [counterrevolution] and that all is at peace, that we can pile our pillows high and go to sleep. This is not in keeping with the facts. The facts are that there still are [counterrevolutionaries] (naturally, this is not to say that each place and each unit has them), and we must continue to struggle against them. It must be understood that the unliquidated hidden counterrevolutionaries are not ones to lose heart but will certainly take every opportunity to create havoc. United States imperialism and the Chiang Kai-shek group are still constantly sending secret agents here to conduct sabotage activity. Although the counterrevolutionaries that originally existed are liquidated, new ones may still possibly emerge. If we lose our vigilance we will be greatly fooled, and we will suffer greatly for it. It does not matter where counterrevolutionaries emerge to create havoc; they should be eliminated with firmness. But from the point of view of the entire country, there are really not many counterrevolutionaries. If it is said that now there are still many counterrevolutionaries this opinion is also erroneous. If this assessment is accepted, the result also will be to breed confusion.

## ITEM 121

One of the important functions of *Political-Legal Research* is to provide legal personnel with explanations to supplement the guidance received in the form of legal documents, study manuals, and policy directives and speeches. Item 121, for example, offers many concrete illustrations of the kinds of conduct that were regarded as counterrevolutionary when, in the latter half of 1957, the pendulum again swung back toward an intensified campaign against counterrevolutionaries. It also constitutes a justification of the renewed harshness of judicial policy.

[Li Lo, "A Talk on Problems of Defending Socialist Construction in the Rural Villages," *CFYC*, 1:46–47 (1958)]

The few remaining counterrevolutionary elements and the reactionary elements and various categories of bad elements among landlords and rich peasants have [since last year's rectification] launched frenzied attacks on socialism and have viciously sabotaged it on the battleground of the rural villages.

They first engaged in political sabotage, sharply and concentratedly directed against the policies of the Party and the people's government and against socialist political power. In this period, cases of propagandizing and agitating by the dissemination of reactionary posters and leaflets greatly increased. Not only did these reactionary posters and leaflets contain strong political agitation but many were also openly distributed and pasted up in public places, viciously attacking the Communist Party and undermining the socialist road. Once, at the exit to a movie house in Hopei province's Mi-yün county, forty-one reactionary posters were found, and their contents were extremely reactionary. In this period the murder of basic level cadres and activists and other cases of blood-letting and terrorism occurred ceaselessly. In the Shih-ch'iao district of Hsiang-yang county in Hupei province, reactionary landlord Chang Ming-t'ang intensely hated agricultural cooperativization. In May of last year he used an ax to kill a production team leader and the leader of a woman's organization in the co-operative. Moreover, he insanely pursued other members of the cooperative in order to kill them, attempted to create an atmosphere of political terror, hindered the implementation of various socialist policies, and destroyed the activism of the masses in constructing socialism. In this period many cases of organizing counter-revolutionary groups, stirring up armed rioting, and other such conspiracies to subvert the regime were also discovered. They established this or that kind of organization, put forth this or that kind of program, and the flame of reaction was rather frenzied. In Chekiang province's Chin-hua county a counterrevolu-tionary group [which was organized] for armed rioting was discovered. Seventeen counterrevolutionary bandits attacked the district Party committee, wounded cadres, robbed a bank, and called upon the masses to resist the Communists and incited them to abandon their own regime. In this period in many districts cases of restoration by reactionary societies occurred. From January to July of last year in Anhwei province, thirty-two reactionary societies were discovered conducting restoration activity that involved many counties. In some places some reactionary societies were even discovered to have "cooperativized." They had borrowed production cooperative names. They did not call themselves society leader, master of the temple, and disciples but called themselves "brigade leader," "team leader," and "team members," and attempted secretly to sabotage socialist political and economic construction.

The consequences of economic sabotage have also been extremely serious. These have consisted mainly of sabotaging the means of production of the agricultural cooperatives, the fruits of their labor, and the property of the peasants in the cooperatives. At present the most conspicuous danger is in reseizure cases and arson cases. Since last year, in Hupei province's Chien-li county, fifty-eight cases were discovered of landlords and rich peasants reseizing a total of thirty-nine houses, eleven *mou* of land, thirty-six agricultural implements, three boats, and twenty-five pieces of furniture. Since the opening of the struggle against counterrevolutionary and bad elements and against unlawful landlord and rich peasant elements in Hunan province, eighteen cases of counterrevolutionary arson have occurred. Twelve of them alone destroyed sixty-three peasant houses, over 17,700 catties of food grain, over 1,600 agricultural implements, and twenty-nine head of livestock, a loss of over 40,000 yuan. Damaging agricultural implements, injuring livestock, damaging crops, sabotaging water utilization [facilities], stealing property, and other such sabotage activity are commonplace. Although they [these acts of sabotage] directly result in major production losses for rural villages, they also have clear political goals. Their demoralization and destruction of the peasants' socialist activism cannot be taken lightly. These acts of economic sabotage in reality are [acts of] political restoration and political sabotage.

At the same time they engage in the above-mentioned sabotage, they even more actively engage in ideological sabotage. As for the problem of whether to walk the socialist road or the capitalist road, in order to make the agricultural cooperatives collapse and hinder the peasants' walking the socialist road, they make use of the capitalist ideology of some rich middle peasants, regularly spread rumors, utter fallacies, provoke dissension, corrode and win over the peasants, adopt all kinds of methods to confuse the peasants' senses and to sabotage the unity between the peasants and between the cooperatives. In the suburbs of the city of Huang-shih in Hupei province some landlords and rich peasants spread a large number of rumors and fallacies, to the extent that some peasants and cadres no longer actively took part in production. Even some cadres from the cooperatives no longer wanted to serve. These acts of sabotage were especially apparent during the stage of rectification among the entire people and the great blooming and contending. Some landlords would not go to the fields and take part in production. They went to tea houses and bars and wantonly spread reactionary arguments. Some of them intentionally wore beautiful clothes and paraded back and forth in the villages. People asked them why they did not go out to work and whether they knew the meaning of rectification. They said: "You'll know in these two days"; "the rectification told us to attack the cadres." For a brief period this created doubt and unrest among some of the peasants. There were also some landlord, rich peasant, and bad elements who enticed insecure persons among the peasants and cadres from the cooperatives to engage in corruption, theft, speculation, and other such activities, and their role in the ideological corrosion of these persons was rather serious. It should be pointed out that the evil consequences of this ideological sabotage have already brought forth much danger and loss to construction and production in rural villages.

### 2. Crimes of Corruption

A second major concern of the regime has been the enormous task of eliminating public corruption. The drive against corruption that began in early 1952 was a principal part of the "three-anti" movement to create an honest, efficient bureaucracy and was intimately bound up with the "five-anti" movement to achieve complete domination over private business. Items 122–125 present the principal legal provisions defining crimes of "corruption," and suggest the circumstances that gave rise to this legislation.

ITEM 122

[COMMON PROGRAM OF THE CPPCC (Sept. 29, 1949), p. 19]

Article 18. All state organs of the People's Republic of China must rigorously maintain a revolutionary work demeanor that is pure and frugal and that serves the people. They must severely punish corruption, prohibit waste and oppose the bureaucratic demeanor that causes state organs to separate themselves from the masses of people.

ITEM 123

[*Lectures* (September 1957), p. 22]

.    .    .    .    .

The Chinese national bourgeoisie is a class which has the dual nature of progressiveness and backwardness. After liberation, they [the members of this class] played an active role in restoring and developing production and in resisting America and aiding Korea. But because they have a rotten and degenerate side that is putrid and backward, they sought only profit, benefited themselves at the expense of others, and utilized public resources for private gain, and many of them felt uneasy operating their businesses under the principle of benefiting the national economy and the people's livelihood. Economically, they attempted to expand along the capitalist road without limitations. They used every method wantonly to engage in the "five-poison" activities to endanger the interests of the state and the people, and they wildly attacked the Communist Party and the worker class. Also, some state personnel could not withstand the attacks of "sugar-coated shells," and engaged in corrupt and rotten business which violated the law and disrupted discipline. In order to drive back this kind of attack, the Party and the government in 1952 led the people of the entire country in launching the "three-anti" and "five-anti" struggles. Also, in April of the same year the Central People's Government promulgated the Act of the People's Republic of China for Punishment of Corruption, imposing punitive legal restraints on criminals who are corrupt, who steal, etc. These struggles played an active role in consolidating the leadership of the worker class and in promoting and safeguarding the smooth conduct of the undertakings of the state's socialist reform and socialist construction.

ITEM 124

[ACT OF THE PRC FOR PUNISHMENT OF CORRUPTION (approved at the 14th session of the Central People's Government Council, April 18, 1952; promulgated by the Chairman of the PRC, Apr. 21, 1952), *FLHP* 1952, pp. 25–28]

Article 1. This Act is specially adopted in accordance with the provision for severely punishing corruption in Article 18 of the Common Program of the Chinese People's Political Consultative Conference.

Article 2. All acts of embezzling, stealing, obtaining state property by fraud or by illegal speculation, extorting property of others by force, accepting bribes and other acts of unlawful profit-making that utilize public resources for private gain, [committed] by personnel of all state organs, enterprises, schools and their subordinate institutions, shall be considered crimes of corruption.

Article 3. Those who commit crimes of corruption shall be punished on an individual basis in accordance with the seriousness of the circumstances of their cases and in accordance with the following provisions:

(1) If the amount involved in an individual's corruption is 100,000,000 yuan of people's currency[4] or more, he shall be sentenced to not less than ten years of imprisonment or to life imprisonment; if the circumstances of a case are especially serious, he shall be sentenced to death.

(2) If the amount involved in an individual's corruption is 50,000,000 yuan or more and less than 100,000,000 yuan of people's currency, he shall be sentenced to five to ten years of imprisonment.

(3) If the amount involved in an individual's corruption is 10,000,000 yuan or more and less than 50,000,000 yuan of people's currency, he shall be sentenced to one to five years of imprisonment, to one to four years of labor service, or to one to two years of control.

(4) If the amount involved in an individual's corruption is less than 10,000,000 yuan of people's currency, he shall be sentenced to not more than one year of imprisonment, labor service, or control; or he may be exempted from criminal punishment and given the administrative sanction of expulsion, removal from office, demotion in office, demotion in grade, demerit, or warning.

Group corruption shall be punished on an individual basis according to the amount involved in each person's corruption and the circumstances of his case.

Property that has been obtained through corruption shall be recovered [from the guilty party]; when his crime is especially serious, a part or all of his property may also be confiscated.

Article 4. In any one of the following situations, those who commit a crime of corruption may be punished severely or with increased severity:

(1) They seriously endanger the undertakings of the state and of society and the safety of the people;

(2) They put up for sale or search out state economic intelligence;

(3) They are corrupt in a way which involves the intentional misapplication of law;

(4) They practice extortion;

(5) They organize group corruption;

(6) They commit [the crime] repeatedly and fail to change;

(7) They refuse to confess or they prevent others from confessing;

(8) They damage public property in order to eliminate traces of the crime;

(9) They shift the blame to another person in order to cover up their [own] crime of corruption;

(10) They do not thoroughly confess and after having been sentenced,

4. The yuan was subsequently (March 1, 1955) revalued on the basis of 10,000 to 1. As noted previously, according to the Chinese official exchange rate, a yuan is now valued at approximately U.S. $0.42.

they are again denounced by people who reveal other serious circumstances of their cases;

(11) Their act of committing the crime has other special, evil circumstances.

Those who, because they have been corrupt, have committed other kinds of crimes, shall be given a combined punishment.

Article 5. In any one of the following situations, those who commit a crime of corruption may be given light punishment, reduced punishment, or suspension of sentence, or they may be exempted from criminal punishment and given administrative sanctions:

(1) They take the initiative in confessing before they are discovered;

(2) After having been discovered they thoroughly confess, sincerely repent, and also take the initiative in handing over as much of the property involved in their corruption as possible;

(3) They establish their merit by denouncing others who have committed crimes [enumerated] in this Act;

(4) They are relatively young in age or their past is pure, they committed a crime of corruption on [one] occasion, and they sincerely want to repent and reform.

Article 6. All those who bribe state personnel or who introduce bribers to them, after the provisions of Article 3 of this Act are consulted, shall be punished according to the seriousness of the circumstances of their cases. When the circumstances are especially serious, a part or all of their property may also be confiscated. Those who thoroughly confess and who also denounce the person who accepted the bribe may be sentenced to a fine and exempted from other criminal sanctions.

All those who bribe to evade taxes shall pay the unpaid taxes and a fine according to law, and they shall be punished for their crime of bribery in accordance with the provisions of this Act.

All those who coerce or tempt another to accept a bribe shall be punished severely or with increased severity.

All those who, because [they are victims] of extortion, give property to state personnel and who have no unlawful gain shall not be treated as having bribed. The property that is extorted from them by threat shall be returned to the original owner.

Article 7. Those who, before promulgation of this Act, adhered to the evil habits of the old society by giving a small kickback to state personnel in a fair transaction, shall not be treated as having bribed. But, after promulgation of this Act, if a small kickback is sent or accepted in a transaction with state personnel, the one who sends it and the one who accepts it shall both be punished separately for bribery or for accepting a bribe.

Article 8. When those who are not state personnel embezzle, steal, or obtain state property by fraud or by illegal speculation, the unlawfully obtained property shall be recovered from them. Also, after the provisions of Articles 4 and 5 of this Act are consulted and the circumstances of their cases evaluated, according to the amount of their unlawful gain, they may be fined or ordered to pay compensation for other losses of the state created by their crime. When the circumstances are especially serious, after the provisions of Article 3 of this Act are consulted, they also may be given criminal sanctions or may have a part or all of their property confiscated. Those who thoroughly confess, if the circumstances of their cases are minor, shall be exempted from punishment.

Article 9. All those who, in order to scheme for their private interest, buy or obtain by force state economic intelligence shall, after Articles 3, 4, 5, and 8 of this Act are consulted, be punished according to the amount of their unlawful gain and the seriousness of the circumstances of their cases.

Article 10. If there is no way to recover property involved in [a crime of] corruption or other unlawful gain that should be recovered, adjudication organs or organs which deliberate on punishment may confer with administrative organs in charge and, considering the circumstances, may make another appropriate disposition of the case.

Article 11. Those who commit crimes [enumerated] in this Act may be deprived of a part or all of their political rights according to the circumstances of their cases.

Article 12. Those who are not state personnel but who collaborate with state personnel in [crimes of] corruption shall be punished with reference to the provisions of Articles 3, 4, 5, 10, and 11 of this Act.

Article 13. All leading personnel of all state organs, enterprises, schools, and their subordinate institutions who discover corruption on the part of their personnel and who intentionally conceal it or do not expose it shall be given criminal or administrative sanctions according to the seriousness of the circumstances of their cases.

Article 14. Any person has the right to denounce those who commit crimes [enumerated] in this Act to the competent administrative departments, people's supervision organs, people's public security organs, people's procuracies, people's courts, or other organs or department heads considered by him to be appropriate.

All those who attack or retaliate against such denouncers shall be given criminal or administrative sanctions according to the seriousness of the circumstances of their cases.

Article 15. The provisions of this Act shall apply to personnel of social organizations who commit crimes of corruption.

Article 16. The provisions of this Act shall apply to revolutionary soldiers on active duty who commit crimes of corruption.

Article 17. After promulgation of this Act, those who continue to commit a crime [enumerated] in this Act [the commission of which began prior to promulgation] or who again commit a crime [enumerated] in this Act [which they had committed prior to promulgation], shall be punished severely or shall be given punishment of increased severity.

Article 18. This Act shall be approved and promulgated by the Central People's Government Council.

1. Is this Act reasonably precise in defining the kinds of conduct that come within its reach? How could you improve upon the draftsmanship?

2. Does the Act provide any guidance for legal personnel who are charged with the responsibility of handling ordinary cases of theft, fraud, and extortion that have no connection with public property?

## ITEM 125

[P'eng Chen (Deputy Chairman of the Political-Legal Committee of the Government Administration Council of the Central People's Government), "Explanation of the Draft Act of the PRC for Punishment of Corruption," *Hsin-hua yüeh-pao* (New China monthly), 31:23–24 (May 1952)]

Mr. Chairman, members and comrades:

The Draft Act of the People's Republic of China for Punishment of Corruption, having had the benefit on many occasions of all kinds of opinions and having been revised, has been passed by the Government Administration Council of the Central People's Government at its one hundred and thirtieth meeting on government affairs. Now I am going to make the following report about the basis on which this Act has been adopted and about the Act itself, and I will present this Act to the Central People's Government Council for its examination and approval.

This Act has been adopted in accordance with the provision for severely punishing corruption in Article 18 of the Common Program of the Chinese People's Political Consultative Conference, the facts that have been exposed, and the experience that has been accumulated during the "three-anti" and "five-anti" movements.

The "three-anti" and "five-anti" movements were great mass movements that relied on the vast masses of people, under the leadership of Chairman Mao, the Central People's Government, and the worker class, to clean up the dirty poisons that had been left over from the old society. During this recent period the vast masses of people throughout the country, in order to restrain violations of law and disruption of discipline by corrupt elements, to restrain the wild attacks of lawless bourgeois elements, and to defend and thoroughly implement the line of the Common Program, have carried out an intense struggle and won a great victory. With the exception of those state personnel who are major criminals, who commit crimes of corruption, and who have completely violated law and disrupted discipline and those of the industrial and commercial world who are major thieves and who have completely violated the law, this kind of a struggle is still a struggle within the people's democratic united front; the forms that it takes are those of the mass movements and of criticism and self-criticism; and it uses the principles of the Common Program to reform the bad demeanor of society and of state personnel. It is a struggle of the vast masses who support the Common Program against unlawful acts that violate the Common Program. It is a struggle of the vast [number of] state personnel's revolutionary demeanor that is pure, simple, and in the service of the people against the evil demeanor of those state personnel who are decadent and rotten, corrupt, wasteful, and bureaucratic elements. It is a struggle of the lawful way of operation in private industry and commerce that is consistent with the Common Program and the state's laws and decrees against the unlawful way that bribes, evades taxes, steals state property or obtains it by fraud, cheats in workmanship and material, and steals state economic intelligence. To put it simply, with the exception of the struggle against major criminals who commit crimes of corruption and against major thieves, this is a struggle within the people's democratic united front between the two kinds of demeanor and the two roads. Following our country's three great movements of "resist America and aid Korea," land reform, and the suppression of counterrevolution, this is another social reform movement of a mass nature that possesses great historical significance.

During this movement people, for simplicity, call corruption, waste, and bureaucratism the "three evils"; and they call the unlawful acts of bribery, tax evasion, stealing state property or obtaining it by fraud, cheating in workmanship and materials, and stealing state economic intelligence the "five poisons." The five poisons are the principal forms in which the unlawful bourgeois elements are at present carrying out their wild attacks against the state and the people, and the three evils are principally the consequences caused by the wild attacks of the unlawful bourgeois elements.

Of course, the three evils also have other historical origins. That is to say, they are all also dirty poisons that are left over from the exploiters and reactionary rulers of the old society, but the unlawful bourgeois elements are the principal social class base which has inherited and which supports these dirty poisons.

Due to the fact that in the last three years we have been busy suppressing and eliminating the remnant forces of the U.S.-Chiang bandits, resisting America and aiding Korea, carrying out land reform, restoring the economy and culture, and developing all kinds of construction enterprises, we have not yet had time systematically to eradicate these dirty poisons. The thieves among the bourgeoisie and the corrupt elements among state personnel, on the other hand, seized the moment to make use of this lapse of ours to collaborate in unrestrainedly developing their unlawful conduct.

But this definitely is not to say that all members of the bourgeoisie have violated the law to the same extent. During this past period, if we look at the situation in the large cities, of the total number of petty bourgeoisie (this refers to ordinary independent handicraft units that do not employ workers or shop employees, and family commercial units; it does not include street hawkers) and bourgeoisie, those who observe the law represent about 10 percent; those who basically observe the law but commit minor unlawful acts represent about 60 percent; those who are semi-lawful and semi-unlawful represent about 25 percent; those who are seriously unlawful and those who are completely unlawful represent about 5 percent, and these include capitalists who are very big speculators or who are complete speculators; but the wildest and most evil speculators represent about one percent of the total number of industrial and commercial units, a figure that cannot be considered great. This last group of persons are the so-called major thieves; they are no longer our friends but are criminals. Thus, with the exception of those who confess, repent, and reform and who establish their merit, they must be given punitive legal restraints. Of the above-mentioned ratios, the units which observe the law and the units which basically observe the law represent approximately 70 percent of the total number in industrial and commercial circles. Most of them are petty bourgeois elements, but there are also many bourgeois elements. Moreover, there are a few major industrialists and businessmen.

The wild attacks of the unlawful bourgeois elements and the erosion caused by the dirty poisons left over from the old society have produced many corrupt elements among state personnel. Of these, a small number are the most serious and most evil, major corrupt elements, who no longer are our comrades but are criminals who steal the wealth of the state and the people. Thus, with the exception of those who confess, repent, and reform and who establish their merit, they must be cleaned out of our ranks and given punitive legal restraints.

Before the start of the "three-anti" and "five-anti" movements, corruption among state personnel and theft in industrial and commercial circles were very serious. But because our state has the Communist Party and the worker class to lead it, has a determined and strong leadership backbone which has already been steeled as Chairman Mao has instructed, and has the enthusiastic support of the vast masses of people, as soon as the call was sounded by Chairman Mao and the Central People' Government, the "three-anti" and "five-anti" movements were immediately launched throughout the country, and the vast [number of] laboring people, the revolutionary intellectuals and the vast [number of] active work cadres quickly united and responded to the state's call. Finally, the personnel, industrialists, and businessmen who had washed their hands also united with us and formed the great united front of the "three-anti" and "five-anti." This caused the major corrupt elements within state organs and the major thieves in society to be isolated completely and to suffer severe attacks and punitive restraints. The tendency of the unlawful bourgeois elements to go in the opposite direction from the state and the people has been effectively curbed and corrected. Also, because the bourgeoisie itself is led and supervised by the worker class; because a part of the bourgeoisie observes the law, is progressive and positive; and because a struggle has been launched against the unlawful, backward, and negative part, the entire bourgeoisie has received education on this occasion. After going through the "three-anti" and "five-anti" movements, we can clearly see that our country's people's democratic united front and people's democratic dictatorship are very consolidated, that the financial and economic situation is very much improved, and that the intellectuals' old thinking that did not favor the undertakings of the people has reformed or is in the midst of reform.

Now, in order to punish corrupt elements and thieves individually, consolidate the victories already won by the "three-anti" and "five-anti" movements, and continue to conduct a determined and unrelenting struggle against all corruption and theft, it is entirely necessary to adopt this law.

Does P'eng Chen's "Explanation" shed further light upon the circumstances in which criminality is to attach for corrupt practices? What weight should those who administer the Act attach to his "Explanation"?

## 3. The Overall Legislative Situation

### ITEM 126

Both the Act for Punishment of Counterrevolution and the Act for Punishment of Corruption were promulgated when the campaigns that spawned them were already well under way. They were products of a good deal of experimentation more than vehicles for initiating experimentation, and as such are typical of the laws and decrees adopted by the PRC. This item describes representative law-making processes.

[*Lectures* (September 1957), p. 32]

Preliminary drafts of many of our country's important laws and decrees, including criminal laws and decrees, were presented by the state's leadership nucleus, the Chinese Communist Party, after examination and study of the actual work, summarization of the people's experience in struggles, and concentration of their revolutionary will. Afterwards, the Party sought from various walks of life opinions which gradually were incorporated into the drafts. After discussion and revision by state organs, some of these, still in draft form, were transmitted to local state organs and people's organizations down to the county and administrative village levels, and the masses were broadly roused to conduct discussions. Other drafts were put into effect experimentally for a given period of time, and then became formal laws and decrees after further scrutiny and passage by legislative organs of the state.

### ITEM 127

The Act for Punishment of Counterrevolution and the Act for Punishment of Corruption are the principal criminal laws promulgated by the PRC. There are also a few provisions of relatively narrow applicability such as the Provisional Act for Punishment of Crimes That Endanger State Currency.[5] In addition, numerous laws, such as the Marriage Law (see Item 23A), simply state that their violation shall be punishable. This item summarizes the situation.

[*Lectures* (September 1957), pp. 23–25]

At the same time, on the basis of the resolution made on September 26, 1954, at the first meeting of the first session of the National People's Congress, prior to the promulgation of the Constitution, "all current laws and decrees adopted and approved by the Central People's Government since the founding of the People's Republic of China on October 1, 1949, shall continue in force unless in conflict with the Constitution."

To sum up, it can be seen that *the criminal law of our country was produced by the struggle to destroy the old law and was established and developed following the needs of state construction and through summarizing the experience of the people's struggles. All laws and decrees adopted by the people's democratic regime to struggle against crime through the use of methods of criminal punishment are the criminal law of our country.* Of these laws and decrees, some were

5. FLHP 1951, 1:149–150.

adopted not only by the highest organs of state authority, such as the National People's Congress and its permanent organ, the Standing Committee, and the former Central People's Government Council; some were also promulgated by the highest administrative organs of the state, such as the State Council or the former Government Administration Council, and by local administrative organs, such as the former regional people's governments or military government committees and the provincial level organs; and some even include instructions issued by the highest judicial organs, such as the Supreme People's Court, which are for the correct implementation of criminal [law] policies and which have the nature of laws and regulations. Next, these laws and decrees are not only seen in the separate documents dealing with special criminal laws and regulations but also in other laws, instructions, and resolutions, such as Article 12 of the previously mentioned Arrest and Detention Act and the provisions in Articles 62–64 of the Election Law. Thirdly, of these laws and decrees, not only were there some [which existed] before the promulgation of the Constitution, there were also some [which existed only] after the promulgation of the Constitution. Finally, some of these laws and decrees are relatively complete and specific, such as the Act for Punishment of Counterrevolution and the Provisional Act for Punishment of Crimes That Endanger State Currency. Some are in the nature of programs and principles such as the Order Relating to Putting into Effect the Planned Purchase and Supply of Food that was issued by the former Government Administration Council in October 1953. Paragraph 9 [of that Order] prescribes that speculators who violate the Order and state personnel who violate the law shall be "punished severely" or "given punishment of increased severity." Other relevant decrees which prescribe "punishment according to law" also are of this nature.

These circumstances, manifested by the criminal law of our country, are determined by the concrete historical conditions of our country and conform to the law of development of our country's revolutionary legal system. In the early period of the country's founding, the main tasks of the state were: "to liberate the people from reactionary rule, to liberate the productive forces of society from the bondage of the old production relations," "to destroy the reactionary order and to establish the revolutionary order." [6] Class struggle was extraordinarily sharp and complex and the balance of power between the enemy class and us changed extremely rapidly. Therefore "we could only prescribe some provisional laws in the nature of programs by following the policies of the Party and the people's government." [7] "At that time it was not fitting hastily to adopt some 'complete,' 'detailed' set of premature and not urgently needed laws and regulations which would be unworkable or would bind the hands and feet of the masses. We should put mature experience into fixed form according to the central tasks of the present and the problems of the people that urgently need to be resolved and on the basis of the possible and the necessary; and by reporting and synthesizing the typical experience of various places, systems and legal pro-

6. Liu Shao-ch'i, *Political Report of the Chinese Communist Party Central Committee to the Eighth National Party Congress.*
7. *Ibid.*

visions will be gradually formed and then gradually developed from simplicity into complexity, from general rules into detailed rules, from separate laws and regulations into a complete set of criminal law and civil law." [8] After the state entered the period of large-scale and planned economic construction, because of the change in the state's political and economic circumstances, the people's democratic legal system also had to meet this change and gradually become strong and complete. Our country's Constitution promulgated in 1954 further unified legislative jurisdiction. Article 22 of the Constitution prescribes: "The National People's Congress is the only organ that exercises the legislative authority of the state." Thus, the criminal laws adopted by the highest organ of state authority, the National People's Congress, and its permanent organ, the Standing Committee, will gradually become the main part of our country's criminal law. The criminal code of our country, which is at present being drafted on the basis of the demands of strengthening daily the legal system of the state, will in the future become the most fundamental component of our country's criminal law after it is passed by the National People's Congress.

## C. CRIMES NOT PROSCRIBED BY PUBLISHED LAWS: THE BORDERLINE OF CRIMINALITY

As mentioned in Part I, the draft criminal code referred to in Item 127 was being seriously considered in June 1957, but as a result of the antirightist movement it was neither enacted nor otherwise made public. Thus, more than seventeen years after the founding of the PRC, no criminal code or comprehensive set of criminal laws exists. Yet the Soviet Union enacted a criminal code within five years of the Bolshevik revolution and has subsequently devoted a great deal of effort to its improvement.

1. What might account for this significant difference in the legal development of the two major communist states?

a. Are there echoes here of the earliest Chinese attitudes toward the promulgation of criminal laws? Recall Shu-hsiang's letter of protest, which introduces this chapter.

b. Because of factors such as differing educational background and revolutionary experience, might the Chinese Communist leadership be more skeptical than their Soviet counterparts about whether, from the viewpoint of a totalitarian revolutionary regime, the advantages of published rules outweigh the disadvantages?

2. Interviews have established that in China unpublished regulations define murder, rape, arson, and many other common crimes and set forth the maximum and minimum penalties for each. Occasional oblique references in published sources confirm this. Can an unpublished proscription amount to "law"?

3. Assuming that it provides adequate guidance to administrators of the system, can an unpublished proscription give fair warning to the public? Note that judicial decisions are not systematically made public in the PRC but that there is a highly developed, all-encompassing system of mass communications. Is this likely to compensate for failure to publish the formal documents that embody rules created by legislative, administrative, and judicial agencies?

8. P'eng Chen, "Report Relating to Circumstances of Political Work and Current Tasks," May 1951.

4. Although people may need to be told what conduct comes within the ambit of newly defined crimes such as "counterrevolution" and "corruption," do they not already know that acts such as murder are wrong and criminal? Yet the criminality of immoral conduct is not always so clear, as this section illustrates.

### 1. Fornication and Adultery

1. Recall the relevant provisions of the Marriage Law (Item 23A). Do they proscribe adultery or fornication?

2. Recall the statement made by the author of Item 47 that, although it violates socialist morality, engaging in "illicit sexual relations . . . does not constitute a crime." What types of conduct might he have had in mind?

### ITEM 128

This article appears to have been written with a view to influencing the criminal code that was being drafted in 1957.

[Tung Ching-chih et al., "A Discussion of Bigamy and Adultery," *Fa-hsüeh* (Legal science), 4:36, 37–38 (1957)]

#### The Concepts of Bigamy and Adultery

Bigamy refers to "the act whereby a man and a woman both of whom have a marriage relationship (a spouse), or only one of whom has a marriage relationship, again register with the government to marry [and thereby obtain their marriage certificate] or whereby they have a joint economic relationship and openly reside together in the status of husband and wife for the purpose of living their lives together" . . .

Adultery refers to "the act whereby a man and a woman both of whom have a marriage relationship, or only one of whom has a marriage relationship, consent to and engage in sexual intercourse." First, a prerequisite is the marriage relationship. This is the same as in bigamy. Next, both parties consent to and engage in sexual intercourse. That is to say, both the man and the woman must engage in sexual intercourse voluntarily and not under circumstances in which a participant is subject to violence, threat, or coercion or is unconscious. Engaging in sexual intercourse once or many times constitutes adultery. Third, both parties to the adultery have not carried out the procedure for marriage, their purpose is not to live their lives together, and they do not openly reside together in the status of husband and wife. Therein lies the difference between bigamy and adultery.

#### Are Bigamy and Adultery Crimes

What are crimes? Crimes are "all acts which endanger the people's democratic system, undermine the legal order or are socially dangerous and, according to law, should be subject to criminal punishment." That bigamy is a crime is at present already undebatable. As for adultery, we believe that it should not be treated as a crime . . .

Second, why is adultery not considered a crime? What is the object of infringement in adultery? Some people believe it is the family, but we cannot agree. The family is composed of: (1) blood relative relationships such as grandparents, parents, children, brothers, and sisters; (2) the marriage relationship, that is, husband and wife; (3) foster relationships, such as parents and their adopted children and [other] dependents. The aim of an adulterer is only to engage in sexual intercourse. This causes discord between that person and his or her spouse, which infringes only the marriage relationship and cannot be said directly to infringe blood relationships or foster relationships. Some people say that if there is discord between husband and wife, then the family is being infringed. But it should be understood that the direct object of a crime refers to a concrete social relationship which is encroached upon by a concrete act. Marriage is an important part of the family, but it cannot be said that marriage and the family are the same ([though] sometimes a newly formed family is limited only to two people, husband and wife, and there are no parents, children, or others). Therefore, to say that the object of infringement in adultery is the marriage relationship is more accurate.

The damage from adultery is the discord between the adulterer and his or her spouse. Marriage is based on affection, and it is necessary for husband and wife to strive together to maintain this affection. If a person who has a spouse is willing to engage in sexual intercourse with another, then his (or her) affection is already in question . . . Even though a person lapsed once in his thinking and on [one] occasion did wrong by committing adultery, after an honest husband and wife discussion, if that person repents and reforms and the spouse is willing to forgive, the affection between the two parties can be restored to its previous state. It cannot be thought that by using an outside coercive force, affection between husband and wife can be created or sustained. Therefore, we believe that the degree of social danger from adultery is relatively small and that it is not necessary to use criminal punishment to punish it. Punishment actually is unable to resolve problems involving the quality of people's affection, thinking, and morality. Some people say that among the serious consequences of adultery are abortion, drowning babies, mistreatment, desertion, murder, suicide, etc., and that since the social danger is very great, it would not be good not to use criminal punishment to punish it. We say that, with the exception of suicide, all the rest are criminal acts and are prohibited by criminal [law] policy. But they all constitute crimes and the objects of their infringement are not the same as with adultery. These criminal acts are not the result of adultery.

Some people say that in accordance with the concrete circumstances of China our present marriage policy is in the process of reforming the old family and establishing a new family and that a third person who undermines the family should be punitively restrained. Others say that for a husband and wife who continue their marriage relationship, no matter how much their affection has deteriorated, so long as they do not get divorced, there is still a possibility that things will change for the better. They say that since the danger of adultery is that it precludes this possibility, adultery cannot be thought of as not dangerous. We cannot agree with this. First, the marriage policy's reform of the old family and its establishment of the new family is directed at the very many marriages that still exist in present society which were entered into in accordance with the old marriage system. The only methods for reforming the old family are persuasion-education and propaganda about the spirit of the Marriage Law, enabling the masses to be clear about how to treat marriage and the family, gradually changing their old ideological demeanor and taking the initiative in improving husband and wife relationships and family relationships. Punitive legal restraints are inadequate for improving husband and wife relationships or family relationships. Next, whether or not affection between husband and wife can change for the better is determined by both the husband and the wife. Both parties to adultery have free will and act voluntarily. To believe that the cause of adultery is a third person's undermining is not realistic.

Since the problem of adultery involves the quality of affection, thinking, and morality and also involves the struggle between new and old ideologies, we should prevent and eliminate adultery. We should energetically spread education about Communist morality in order to enable people to strengthen this aspect of their character. At the same time, following changes in the economic base, people's ideological consciousness also will begin to change. Thus, as the undertakings of socialist construction gradually grow and the people's political awareness is gradually heightened, the problem of adultery can gradually be resolved to the point of being resolved at the roots. Even if individual situations occur, they will only be the abnormalities of individual persons who retain remnants of the ideological consciousness of the exploiter class. We should still rely for correction of these defects on the pressure of public opinion and on education about morality. They cannot be resolved by criminal punishment.

1. Note that the authors are concerned with adultery but not with fornication. Should we infer that fornication is not a crime in the PRC?

2. Are the authors arguing that adultery is not a crime or that it should not be?

3. Recall Item 44. According to the irate husband, what was the crime committed by his wife's lover?

## ITEM 129

[Interview]

Hung was the chief of the security section of the public security bureau of a small city. In 1959 he was accused of right-wing thinking, transferred out of public security work, and sent down to serve as a government employee in the countryside. Hung's pretty wife, Chiao, worked in the state bank in their city, and she remained on her job instead of joining him in the countryside. In Hung's absence Chiao developed a fondness for Wang, a widower who was secretary of the branch of the Communist Youth League in the bank and chief of the bank's savings division.

Hung did not like rural life and after about six months he resigned from the government and returned home. By that time Chiao had become visibly pregnant as a result of her relations with Wang. Hung wanted revenge for his wife's unfaithfulness, but was too embarrassed to go to his former associates at the public security bureau to bring a complaint. But his mother, who lived with them and cared for their two children, felt no such constraint. She began going to the bureau every day until the security section agreed to investigate the case. It then notified the city's basic level court of the complaint, and the court designated an official to join in the investigation. Upon completion of the investigation a report was made at a meeting of the bureau chief and the court president. They decided that especially since Wang was a widower the case was not serious enough to warrant criminal prosecution, but that Chiao and Wang should both receive administrative sanctions. The bureau chief and court president did not specify in detail the sanctions to be meted out, but they recommended that Chiao be demoted in grade and that Wang be removed from his position as chief of the savings division and demoted in grade. The local Party organization bureau and the Youth League branch, whose task it was jointly to decide upon sanctions in this case, followed these recommendations. They demoted Chiao and Wang two grades each and expelled both of them from the League. Wang was also transferred to another city.

The case was resolved when Hung sued for divorce, which was granted on the following terms: Hung was to retain custody of their two children, Chiao was to retain custody of her as yet unborn child, and each was to support the children in his custody, with the exception that Wang was required to support the unborn child for one year after birth. Chiao subsequently married a third man.

## ITEMS 130A–130B

In Item 129 the reason that the public security bureau notified the court to take part in investigating the charge of adultery was that, as Item 129 illustrated, many such cases are not deemed of sufficient importance to merit prosecution. Their criminal aspect is considered to be a mere adjunct of what is essentially a civil, family relations dispute. It is, therefore, left to be disposed of according to the exclusive discretion of the court.

Items 130A–130B are actual judgments of people's courts. They were subsequently presented to the government of Hong Kong as evidence of the eligibility for a second marriage of one of the parties to each of the cases.

## ITEM 130A

[Civil Judgment of the People's Court for Kiangsu Province]

Civil No. ———

Appellant: Ting —, male, age 28, of [address]
Respondents: Chin —, female, age 24, of [address]
           Li —, male, age 27, of [address]
Case: Divorce

The case of divorce between appellant Ting — and respondent Chin — was heard by the people's court of Nanking, and judgment was given allowing the divorce, Judgment No. ——— of this year of that court. Ting has appealed the judgment.

First of all, Ting says that his marital relationship with Chin was always harmonious. At present affection between them has dwindled because of the enticement of the second defendant, Li —, and his undermining of their relationship. He asks that Li be given the sanction that he deserves.

According to the investigation that has been carried out and to the statement Ting previously made, after Ting and Chin were married in 1947, their relationship was certainly not harmonious. They often quarreled and fought with each other. Ting's mother controlled Chin in a feudalistic manner, and thus relations between mother-in-law and daughter-in-law were also very nasty. In 1951, less than a month after Chin gave birth to their second child, quarrels again broke out, and Chin angrily took the children with her and returned to live in the home of her parents in Nanking. In August of that year Ting went to take part in work in the Northeast, and the two parties continued to remain apart. The old affection between husband and wife was dissipated even further. Ting's statement that their husband-and-wife-relationship has always been harmonious does not accord with the facts.

In the summer of 1952 Li began to do accounting work at the Chin family's confectionery factory. Thus, Li (who already had a wife) came to sympathize with Chin's suffering over her unhappy marriage. Soon he and Chin began to have an illicit love affair. This was wrong. In the lower court, after judgment was pronounced, Li's wife, Tse —, stated: "Relations between my husband and Chin have been severed. Now our marriage relationship is very good." Also, when Li was questioned by the court, he admitted his wrong and criticized himself. For these reasons he avoided any sanctions. But the court below failed to point this out clearly in accordance with the law, and this was improper. Here we must clearly state that the illicit love affair between Li and Chin added to the deterioration of marital affection between Chin and Ting. It could not but have an influence. But we also must realize that the basic reason for the final dissipation of affection between Chin and Ting was that for a long time there had been differences and contradictions between them that could not be ironed out.

Let us also emphasize the present state of affairs. The two parties have not been living together for two years. In an effort to save the marriage the lower court gave the parties a limited time within which it hoped that the original relationship between them would be restored, but feelings between them did not improve. They continued to quarrel. Once they even had to go to court because of a fight. Thus they finally broke with each other as husband and wife. It would be unfortunate if the relationship were to go on and the two parties continue to suffer. For the sake of the future happiness of both parties this court agrees with the judgment below permitting a divorce.

Next, Ting had given Chin funds for traveling and the care of the children amounting to almost one million yuan. He wanted this sum returned. This was not a loan and should not be returned. Moreover, since a portion of this sum was for the care of the children, it is even more unreasonable to ask for its return.

Third of all, under the judgment below each party was to receive custody of one of their children. Now Ting asks for the custody of the four-year-old boy, which had been given to Chin. Chin agreed to this during the court hearing. But Chin still has the obligation to give the children as much care as proves necessary. She cannot give up her obligations to her children simply because Ting has been given their custody.

November 4, 1953
(Seal of the People's Court for Kiangsu Province, 2d Adjudication Division)
    Chief Judge: Chia K'ai Wen
    Assistant Judge: Chou Kai Jan
    Clerk: Ch'en Pi
This is the final judgment. No appeal is allowed.

## ITEM 130B

[Judgment of the Hsin-ch'eng District People's Court of Shanghai]

Civil No. ———, 1954

Marriage Dispute
Plaintiff: Li —, female, age 27, of [address]
Defendants: Ch'en —, male, age 32, of [address]
           Fang —, male
Relevant person: Wang —, female, of [address]

Li — married Ch'en — in Shanghai in 1947. They have two sons. Ch'en was a seaman and often went abroad. In 1950 he went to Hong Kong, and they have been apart for a long time. Ch'en wrote to say that he was too busy to come to Shanghai. Li — came to know Fang —, who was her schoolmate at an accounting school. She began living with him in May 1953 and later gave birth to a son. She has now applied for permission to divorce Ch'en. We hold that the two parties should no longer continue their marriage, but that Li — was wrong in living with another man before a divorce was granted. Fang — was wrong in living with a woman whose marriage had not yet been dissolved. Both therefore shall be given criticism-education.

    This is the judgment:
    1. Li — is permitted to divorce Ch'en —.
    2. Their two sons shall be returned to Ch'en for rearing and education. Ch'en — asks that Wang — be permitted to care for the children during the time that he remains in Hong Kong, and this is approved.
    3. All of Li —'s clothing that is in possession of Wang — must be returned to Li.

August 29, 1954
(Seal of the Hsin-ch'eng District People's Court of Shanghai)
Judge: Sheng Heng
Clerk: [illegible]

An appeal may be brought in this court within 10 days of receipt of this judgment. Certified true copy.

## ITEM 131

[Interview]

As a young girl Wu was sent to live in the Pao family, to be reared with one of its sons; according to a traditional Chinese practice, they were supposed to marry upon reaching adulthood. By 1956, Wu was prepared to marry, but Pao was reluctant. Having previously joined the Communist Party, he entered the People's Liberation Army and was assigned to a post outside the province. At that time, although their obligation to marry was not considered to be broken, Wu returned to her parents' household. During Pao's absence Wu began seeing a good deal of one of their close friends, a worker named Tiao. He was estranged from his wife, Ch'en, a Party member who lived on a state farm outside the county seat. An affair developed, and when Wu became pregnant the matter came to the attention of Pao's mother. She wrote him of these events.

By the time that Pao was demobilized and returned home in 1959, Wu had given birth to Tiao's child. Pao, having lost face in his community, was furious and announced that he would bring a complaint against Tiao with the public security bureau, charging him with adultery. For weeks mutual friends of Tiao and Pao in the bureau and in the office of the county Party committee tried to dissuade him from this course. They told him that the bureau would have to act if a demobilized serviceman brought such a complaint in these circumstances and that Tiao was sure to get a minimum of eighteen months in prison, which would do no good to anyone. These friends also tried to persuade Ch'en to give Tiao a divorce so that he could marry Wu and thus perhaps resolve the existing frictions. Ch'en not only refused, but she also brought a complaint about Tiao's adultery. She complained to the county court rather than to the bureau, because she believed Tiao's friends within the bureau would try to discourage her from initiating action against him. The court transferred her complaint to the bureau, by which time Pao had also brought his complaint.

Upon receipt of these complaints the bureau's security section investigated. Because he was married and especially because he had interfered with the family relations of a member of the People's Liberation Army, it decided that Tiao had to be prosecuted but that no action need be taken against Wu. Tiao was convicted and sentenced to eighteen months of imprisonment. After he served the sentence, Ch'en gave him a divorce, and he married Wu. [For details on Tiao's release, see Item 315.]

## ITEM 132

[Interview]

In investigating a fist fight among a group of men in his rural production brigade the chief of a security defense committee discovered that the fight had resulted from a dispute over the affections of a married woman named Liao, who had been having sexual relations with all of them. Since only one of the men was married and since Liao had taken the initiative in these liaisons, the

SDC chief and the chief of the commune's security office recommended that no action be taken against the men. Liao, on the other hand, deserved prosecution, it was felt. Her husband, who as a result of the investigation found out about her activities, took a similar view. He brought a complaint to the public security bureau and also sued for divorce. The divorce was granted shortly after Liao was arrested, convicted of adultery, and sentenced to six months of imprisonment.

In the bureau's detention house she was assigned to cook for the short-term prisoners who were confined there. After five months of this "reform" through labor, she was discovered to be pregnant, and investigation revealed that she had been having an affair with one of the guards. Even though the guard was a bachelor and Liao herself was single at that point, the bureau could not allow this violation of prison discipline and corruption of a cadre to go unpunished. Accordingly, Liao received an additional one-year term of imprisonment. Two months before her child was expected she was temporarily released, and four months after the child was born she had to return to the detention house to finish serving the sentence. The guard received no criminal sanction but was expelled from both the Party and the government.

## ITEM 133

[Interview]

Hsia was the manager of a company that manufactured food products for the city commerce bureau. In the course of an investigation to determine why damage was occurring to the company's products, it was incidentally discovered that Hsia, a married man, had been using his position to seduce young women. He had seduced five such women, two of whom were married, with promises of giving them good jobs with the company. Hsia was expelled from the Party and the government and was arrested and convicted of "utilizing the powers of his office to commit seduction." He was sentenced to seven years in prison.

On the basis of the cases related in Items 129–133:
1. How would you summarize the law relating to fornication and adultery?
2. Do the legal organs appear to have discretion whether or not to prosecute and convict in adultery cases? If so, what are the factors that seem to condition the exercise of their discretion?

## ITEM 134

[Edgar Snow, *The Other Side of the River, Red China Today* (London, 1962), pp. 452–453]

.    .    .    .    .

"Do you have many requests for instruction in birth control?"
"We provide it when required."
"Do you encourage it?"
Dr. Wu hesitated, "We don't oppose it. We advise it if the woman's health is affected or she already has enough children — three or four, for example."

"Are contraceptives available to unmarried people?"

The question produced a puzzled silence. [Party] Secretary Shen Yao had rejoined us. It was he who spoke up.

"Our people are always married when they have sex relations."

"Always? You never have any cases of premarital intercourse?"

This colloquy produced (as on a few other occasions) a distinctly uncomfortable if not painful atmosphere.

"This may be a problem in capitalist societies. It is not so here."

"Capitalism? I lived for several years in the Soviet Union. Premarital sex is about as common there as in any industrialized society. I know that in former times it was a rare thing among peasant women in China, when marriages were arranged early. Now, with women's rights, freedom of choice, sex equality — hasn't it changed any?"

"It has changed for the better. In feudal days young maidens frequently would be raped or seduced by landlords; sometimes the landlord claimed 'first rights.' That is gone. Now everybody can get married; the legal age is twenty-one for men and eighteen for girls; there is no need for sex before then. But I won't say it never happens. We have had only two or three cases that I remember, in the whole commune. Social opinion is strongly against it."

"What punishment is provided?"

"There is no law against it. We persuade people to get married."

"What if they simply don't want to get married?"

Shen Yao looked seriously at the others, who seemed depressed by this conversation.

"Usually they respond to education — their duties. I will say there was one such case. It was solved when the young man went to the city to work in a factory. Later, the girl moved to the city also."

"If a child were involved, what then?"

"The man would be held fully responsible as the legal father, of course. They would certainly be married."

"What if they were under legal age?"

"Special permission would be granted by the court."

"And adultery? Is that a crime?"

"It is not a crime unless the injured husband or wife wants to bring it to court. We had some cases at the time the marriage law went into effect but not in recent years. It is very rare now."

2. Hooliganism

ITEM 135

This item provides further illustration that the line between criminal and non-criminal conduct is a difficult one to draw in many contexts. A perplexed and unhappy relative wrote a letter to the editor of a Shanghai newspaper, asking for an explanation of what he thought to be the unjustified conviction of his kinsman. The editor transmitted this inquiry to one of the lawyers on the staff of Shanghai's

No. 1 office of legal advisers, who investigated the matter and submitted the following opinion.

["Is a Ten-Year Sentence Appropriate for Hooligan Demeanor?" *Hsin-wen jih-pao* (Daily news, Shanghai), May 5, 1957]

.     .     .     .     .

Two problems can be seen in the judgment of the intermediate people's court of the city of Nanking: the first is the way to view the criminal acts of hooligans and hoodlums and the morality of youth; the second is the problem of the facts. Even on the basis of the "crimes" stated in the written judgment, "the facts of the commission of the crimes" of the defendant Wang Jen-shan constitute a problem of education and cannot be treated as hooliganism. Hooligan elements generally refer to those who do not engage in proper employment, do evil, regularly insult or rape women, look for fights and make trouble, seize things forcibly, swindle, fight, etc. These acts seriously interfere with public order, and damage social morality, and undoubtedly should be punished according to law.

But Wang Jen-shan's "crimes" obviously are different in principle from these acts. For example: the situations where Wang Jen-shan "secretly took a certain [Miss] Lung's picture as she was going to school," "secretly took the Yeh sisters' picture" and where "Wang Jen-shan, learning that [Miss] Lung would return home late, used match sticks to stuff in the lock of her front door . . ." of course were all immoral. But even if they are exaggerated to the maximum, they can only be [considered] a kind of ordinary hooligan demeanor. This kind of behavior not only cannot cause personal harm, it also cannot interfere with the security of society. In addition the facts are these: [Miss] Lung was a girl friend of Wang Jen-shan, and one of the Yeh sisters was his fiancée. In view of this, how can his secretly taking pictures constitute a criminal act?

There is more: "Wang has kissed a certain [Miss] Yu by force," and "has used the excuse of studying the form of a brassiere to play with [Miss] Kao's breasts." Even if this is factual it can only be said that it is improper behavior. But the two above-mentioned victims both deny these facts.

The judgment that his "writing a letter to Miss Lung's organization, saying that she was living a wild life in Nanking," was for the purpose of venting his personal anger is even more untenable. Wang Jen-shan's writing the letter to Miss Lung's organization was completely within his "freedom of correspondence," and in fact Miss Lung's organization correctly handled the matter precisely on the basis of Wang Jen-shan's disclosure. It should be said that in writing the letter, Wang Jen-shan to some extent played the positive role of a denouncer. Is this not a good thing? The original judgment which treated this as a crime is absolutely astonishing.

From the point of view of the facts and of humanity and reason, the judgment of the intermediate people's court of the city of Nanking is incorrect. The reason for this is that it [the court] conceptually confused criminal acts of hooliganism with ordinary immoral acts, to the point of making an error in a hasty judgment.

The above is only a personal view. I invite everyone to study it to determine whether or not it is correct.

Chao Ming-chung

## D. THEORETICAL FRAMEWORK FOR DETERMINING CRIMINALITY

### 1. General Principles

It is not unusual in the PRC for the enforcement sections of regulatory legislation to contain a provision with respect to violators, similar to that of Item 81, which merely states: "If the circumstances of the case are serious and if the violation constitutes a crime, the violator shall be pursued for criminal responsibility by judicial organs in accordance with law." The problem confronting legal personnel, of course, is to determine whether the conduct in question should be regarded as constituting a crime.

In the following excerpts the authors of the *Lectures* attempt to provide a comprehensive framework of analysis to aid legal personnel in distinguishing criminal from noncriminal conduct.

### ITEM 136

[*Lectures* (September 1957), pp. 56–59, 60–65, 67, 68]

.    .    .    .    .

On the basis of our previous statements concerning the concept and class nature of the criminal law of our country, we may describe the concept of crime in the criminal law of our country as follows: *all acts which endanger the people's democratic system of our country, undermine the social order, or are socially dangerous and, according to law, should be subject to criminal punishment are crimes.*

Now let us analyze and explain this concept as follows:

First, a crime is a socially dangerous act. The social danger of an act is the most essential characteristic of a crime. A person's act is considered a crime because it is socially dangerous. An act not socially dangerous cannot be considered a crime.

In our country, whether or not an act is socially dangerous is determined by the will of the vast [number of] people of the entire country led by the worker class. To build a socialist society is the common desire of the vast [number of] people of our country. The people's democratic system of our country is a guarantee that our country can eliminate exploitation and poverty and can build a prosperous and happy socialist society through peaceful roads. But the smooth conduct of the undertaking of socialist construction is impossible without the safeguard of a good social order. Therefore, from the viewpoint of the interests of the vast [number of] people of the entire country, an act endangering the people's democratic system and undermining social order is a socially dangerous act.

By directly pointing out that from the standpoint of the concept of crime, the social danger of an act is the most essential characteristic of a crime, we have thus answered, from the standpoint of the class nature of crime, the question why certain acts are considered criminal.

Next, a crime is an act which, according to law, should be subject to criminal punishment. We say that social danger is the most essential characteristic of crime, but this certainly is not to say that all socially dangerous acts are crimes. Rather, only socially dangerous acts which, according to the viewpoint of the criminal law of our country, should be subject to criminal punishment, are crimes.

According to the viewpoint of the criminal law of our country, socially dangerous acts which should be subject to criminal punishment must be acts committed by the actor intentionally or negligently. This is because [the purpose of] criminal law punishment in our country is to reform criminals so that they will not again commit crimes; and it certainly is not to retaliate or to redress objectively created danger. Therefore, when a danger is objectively created but does not arise from the actor's intention or negligence, criminal punishment should not be applied to him.

But certainly not all socially dangerous acts that are committed by the actor intentionally or negligently should be subject to criminal punishment. Because the degrees of social danger created or possibly created by the acts differ, the methods of punitive restraint also cannot be alike. Criminal punishment is one of the most severe coercive methods of the state. Therefore, only when the social danger of an act is relatively serious should methods of criminal punishment be applied for punitive restraint. Crime and criminal punishment are intimately linked. The judgment of the state on the degree of social danger of criminal acts is manifested in criminal punishment.

At the same time, what kind of socially dangerous act should be subject to criminal punishment is prescribed by the criminal law of our country. Only when a socially dangerous act is recognized by the criminal law can it be considered a criminal act. In our country, the social danger of an act and its unlawfulness are united. Therefore, a crime is an act which on the one hand is socially dangerous and at the same time is also a violation of criminal law. Here it must be pointed out that [the term] "violation of criminal law" cannot be understood only as violation of criminal legislation. Under circumstances in which the law is still not complete, relevant resolutions, decisions, orders, instructions, and policies of the Party and the government are also bases for determining whether or not a crime has been committed.

A crime is an act which, according to law, should be subject to criminal punishment. This is another characteristic of a crime; it shows on the one hand that a socially dangerous act is a criminal act only when it becomes relatively serious and on the other hand it shows how to recognize a socially dangerous act that should be subject to criminal punishment. Therefore, in deciding whether an act of a certain person is or is not a crime, the judge can only handle the case in accordance with law. This is a manifestation of the principle of the legal system in the criminal law of our country.

The foregoing is an analysis of the characteristics of the concept of crime. A correct understanding of it has extremely great significance because many of the problems in criminal law are intimately linked to the concept of crime. It determines the establishment of some of the basic systems in our criminal law. For example, since a crime must be a socially dangerous act, if a certain act is not in fact socially dangerous, it cannot be considered a crime although in form it conforms to the requirements of specific provisions prescribed by a given criminal law or regulation. If an act of a certain person is in fact socially dangerous, but criminal law provisions for it have not directly been prescribed, the person should be convicted and sentenced by comparison [of that act] with the most similar [act proscribed by any] provision . . .

An important problem in the theory of the criminal law of our country which should be resolved is related to the boundary between crime and noncrime. Especially under circumstances in which the criminal law of our country has not yet been promulgated, the resolution of this problem has even more current significance for judicial practice.

Only from the fundamental viewpoint stated before can we reach a correct understanding of this problem: the social danger of an act is the most essential characteristic of crime and the degree of social danger is the criterion for differentiating crimes from other unlawful acts.

Since the degree of social danger is the criterion for differentiating crimes from other unlawful acts, the boundary between crime and noncrime is in substance a question of what determines the degree of social danger. We believe that it is mainly determined by the three intimately interrelated factors stated below:

First, the nature of the act itself: if the nature of the act committed by a person is itself serious, then the degree of social danger of this act is also great. A judgment as to what kind of act is a serious act can generally be made on the basis of peoples' social practice. In judicial practice, we regard as criminal acts counterrevolutionary acts which infringe the people's democratic system of our country, homicide which infringes the lives of others, robbery, rape, etc. The reason for there being no doubt about these acts is that the seriousness of these acts themselves is very obvious. It is just for this reason that the difficulty in the problem of demarcating the boundary between crime and noncrime does not occur in all general circumstances but only occurs in individual circumstances.

In judicial practice, demarcating the boundary between crime and noncrime is felt to be difficult mainly in situations in which the forms of the acts are the same but, because other factors are different, the degree of social danger is also different: for example, between crimes resulting from neglect of duty and administrative misconduct resulting from bureaucratism; between stealing property and taking advantage in a small way (such as picking some vegetables in another person's garden for one's own use); between backward words and deeds and counterrevolutionary provocation and incitement. The reason for feeling it difficult to demarcate these types of problems is mainly that too high an estimate of the significance of the form of the act is made in demarcating crime and noncrime, and the degree of social danger is ignored. The boundary between crime and noncrime is determined not only by the difference in the form of the acts but also by whether or not the results created by the acts are serious as well as by some factors involving the actor's subjective state. This situation frequently occurs: although the form of an act is the same as others, because other factors are different, some acts are crimes and some are not.

Second, the existence and amount of damage: the existence and amount of damage are also factors that determine the degree of social danger — for example, acts involving neglect of duty by state personnel; certain acts violating the rules of operation in a factory, mine, or enterprise; or minor acts of theft may be dealt with as if they were not crimes under circumstances in which there was no damage or the damage was very minor. Here, the boundary between crime and noncrime is determined by the existence and amount of damage.

In judicial practice, the question of whether or not stealing one yuan is a crime has arisen for some judges. Some people consider that since stealing is an act prohibited by law, any stealing is a crime and that the amount stolen certainly does not affect the establishment of a crime. This understanding is erroneous because it ignores the fact that a crime is not only a violation of law in form but must also be an act that in substance has a rather serious degree of social danger.

But in demarcating the boundary between crime and noncrime the significance of the existence and amount of damage cannot be understood mechanically and in isolation. Rather, it must be considered in conjunction with the scope of damage which an act can cause and the characteristics of the actor himself. For example, a certain person forged a check in an attempt to obtain 10,000 yuan by fraud. Although his attempt was discovered before it was successful, this act could have caused great damage, and therefore we cannot consider it not a criminal act on the ground that it had not yet caused damage. As another example, when a certain mine worker was taking a rest at the bottom of a mine shaft, the air coming in from a ventilator made him feel very cold and he covered up the ventilator with a cloth, disregarding the safety of other workers in the mine shaft. Then he fell into a deep sleep. When other workers discovered these circumstances, the mine was already filled with gas. It was only because they immediately took [preventive] measures that a major incident caused by the explosion of the gas did not occur. We cannot consider this mine worker's act not a criminal act on the ground that it had not yet caused damage. That we should consider to be crimes these acts which have not caused damage is a result of considering the existence and amount of damage in conjunction with the scope of damage which an act can cause. As another example, there are two persons, A and B. A is a rotten, decadent, and hardened hooligan, and B is a young person of fifteen or sixteen years, who on [one] occasion is influenced by hooligans. If both of them are arrested for attempted theft, A's act should be considered a crime, while B's act might not be considered a crime. This is a result of considering the existence and amount of damage in conjunction with the characteristics of the actor himself.

It can be seen from this that it would be incorrect to take the existence and amount of damage as the sole factor in differentiating crime from noncrime.

But not to give due consideration to this factor could result in an erroneous conclusion to deal with ordinary unlawful acts as criminal acts.

Third, factors involving the actor's subjective state: the degree of social danger is also determined by some factors involving the actor's subjective state, such as whether the actor acted intentionally or negligently or what his purpose was in committing a certain act. For example, intentional destruction of another's property is a criminal act, but negligent destruction of another person's property might not be dealt with as a crime. Here, intent or negligence becomes a factor for differentiating crime from noncrime. For another example, Article 12 of the Arrest and Detention Act of the People's Republic of China prescribes: "People's procuracies shall investigate officers responsible for unlawful arrest or detention of citizens. If this kind of unlawful act arose from malicious, retaliatory, corrupt, or other personal motives, they [these officers] shall be pursued for criminal responsibility." This provision clearly points out that the actor's purpose is a factor for differentiating crime from noncrime. In judicial practice, some backward words and deeds are sometimes erroneously dealt with as counterrevolutionary crimes mainly because a deep examination and study of the actor's purposes is ignored. For a counterrevolutionary crime to be established, the actor must have a subjectively counterrevolutionary purpose, and [one who is guilty only of] backward words and deeds certainly does not have such a purpose.

The factors involving the actor's subjective state, however, are not the only factors for differentiating crime from noncrime. They must be considered in conjunction with other factors. For example, homicide, the overturning of a passenger train or ship, or other such act which seriously sabotages communications, may constitute a crime even though it was a negligent act. This is the result of considering the actor's subjective state in conjunction with the question of whether or not the nature of the act itself is serious. For another example, although two acts which are intentionally committed in violation of the rules of safe operation are identical, because the existence and amount of damage differ, one may be considered a crime and one an ordinary unlawful act. This is the result of considering the actor's subjective state in conjunction with this factor of damage.

From the explanation of the foregoing three factors, it can be seen that the degree of social danger, as the criterion for differentiating crime from noncrime, is the result of dialectically and uniformly considering these three factors in conjunction with one another. In other words, the degree of social danger is determined by all the objective and subjective circumstances of the act. Crime is differentiated from noncrime on the basis of substance rather than form.

In circumstances in which there are already provisions of criminal law or where the criminal law has already been promulgated, what kind of socially dangerous acts should be subject to criminal punishment has already been comprehensively considered by the legislators and, from the point of view of the interests of the people of the entire country led by the worker class, written into provisions. Therefore, judicial workers only have to follow provisions of the criminal law to resolve the question of crime or noncrime; an act which meets the requirements prescribed by any provision of the criminal law of our country should be considered a criminal act. Any departure from the criminal law and arbitrary determination as to what are crimes and noncrimes are not permitted. Yet it is possible to have this situation: although an act that is committed by a given person in form conforms to the requirements prescribed by a certain provision of the criminal law of our country, on the basis of a consideration of the above-mentioned circumstances, its social danger in substance certainly does not require the application of criminal punishment. Then, on the basis of the most essential characteristic of crime, that is, the concept that the social danger of the act must be fairly serious, this act ought not to be considered a crime. For example, a certain state employee on [one] occasion corruptly takes five yuan. Although in form this conforms to the provisions of the Act of the People's Republic of China for Punishment of Corruption, if the damage he planned to create or could possibly have created is only to that extent, then it might not be considered a criminal act.

If we are able to get a clear understanding of the above explanations of the various aspects of crime and noncrime it will help us to demarcate crimes and noncrimes in cases of specific problems.

But, very obviously, merely understanding these few principles is by no means enough, because the degree of social danger of an act is certainly not static. It follows the changes in the state's political and economic situation and the standard of awareness of the masses as well as the development of social culture. For example, in the early period after the founding of our country, negligent violations of labor discipline or of rules of operation that created incidents of loss to state property by staff and workers in factories, mines, or departments of basic construction, were generally not dealt with as crimes unless the circumstances of the case were especially serious or evil. But since entering the period of planned economic construction, incidents occurring in individual departments have had greater effect on the plans of other departments. Thus the degree of social danger of the above-mentioned acts increases every day. At the same time, under the Party's education, the awareness of the vast masses of staff and workers has been steadily rising. Also the various kinds of equipment, rules, and systems have become more complete every day. Therefore, whether or not this type of act that creates serious consequences can be dealt with as a crime is worth considering. For example, Article 7 of the Act of the People's Republic of China for Punishment of Corruption prescribes: "Those who, before promulgation of this Act, adhered to the evil habits of the old society by giving a small kickback to state personnel in a fair transaction, shall not be treated as having bribed. But, after promulgation of this Act, if a small kickback is sent or accepted in a transaction with state personnel, the one who sends it and the one who accepts it shall both be punished separately for bribery or for accepting a bribe." This provision, which, on an individual basis, considers the same act a crime or not a crime according to the time of its commission, is a creative provision of legislation based on the change in the socio-political and economic situation of our country and the difference in the degree of awareness of the masses of people.

.     .     .     .     .

In resolving the problem of the boundary between crime and noncrime, the fact that our country is a country of many nationality groups also should be considered . . .

It can be seen from this that in dealing with concrete problems we must start out from reality, act appropriately for the time and place, and correctly and thoroughly implement state policies, laws, and decrees. Only by so doing can we achieve the goal of handling matters properly. This is just what Comrade Tung Pi-wu, President of the Supreme People's Court pointed out: to act appropriately for the time and place is a characteristic of our people's democratic legal system.

Here it should be pointed out that to act appropriately for the time and place certainly does not imply that an act which is uniformly prescribed as a crime by the criminal [law] legislation of our country can be considered a crime in district A and not a crime in district B (except in districts where national minority groups live together). When the criminal [law] legislation of our country defines certain acts as crimes, it does so uniformly throughout the country. But in dealing with concrete cases, that is, in determining the degree of social danger of a certain act, we must consider the complex circumstances of the act and the concrete circumstances of the time and place. Only in this way can we correctly use law and consolidate the people's democratic legal system.

The principle of clearly demarcating the boundary between crime and noncrime is of great significance, whether in the theory of criminal law or in judicial practice. From the standpoint of the theory of criminal law, this principle is a natural conclusion of the concept of crime in the criminal law of our country, and it is the implementation and application, in the struggle against crime, of the substantive characteristics derived from the concept of crime. From the standpoint of judicial practice, because of this principle, the courts, the procuracy, and the public security organs will not be disturbed by minor cases which do not require the application of criminal punishment; in this way they can concentrate their strength in the struggle against criminal acts which are actually socially dangerous.

## ITEM 137

[*Lectures* (September 1957), p. 132]

For another example, engineer Li was operating a train. Before reaching the crossroads at Hao-chia-wan, he blew the warning whistle and proceeded in accordance with the rules of railway operation. But because there were buildings near the crossroads which blocked his line of vision, he could not see whether there were, on the sides of the crossroads, any vehicles which were [about] to cross, so that when his train reached the crossroads, it collided with an automobile that was just crossing. This created a major incident in which seven people were killed or injured and which affected railway operation for two hours. The local people's court considered that engineer Li's operation at the time was normal and that in light of the specific circumstances, it was impossible for him to foresee the collision between the train and the automobile. Therefore, the court determined that the incident was completely accidental and that engineer Li was not criminally responsible.

When determining whether an incident that occurs in an industrial or mining enterprise is a natural incident or an incident of responsibility, the criterion should be whether or not the party could foresee it. If it is certain that he could not have foreseen the incident, then it is a natural incident. If the party should have foreseen it but did not, or the party foresaw it but carelessly thought that it could be avoided, then it is an incident of responsibility.

## ITEM 138

[*Lectures* (September 1957), p. 91]

In judicial practice, a certain basic level court made an erroneous judgment in the following case: peasant Chang had a quarrel with Li's wife, Chao, over a small matter. Chang got angry and hit her with his fist. At this point, their neighbors persuaded them to break it up. She then helped her husband work in the fields as usual. There certainly were no indications of abnormality. That night, because Li was on watch in the fields, he did not go home. Next morning when he got home, he found his wife unconscious in bed. Emergency aid was without effect, and she died. In the beginning the cadres of the local basic level court did not investigate deeply. They decided that the death of Li's wife was caused by Chang's act of striking her. In other words, they decided that a cause-effect relationship existed between Chang's act of striking Li's wife and her resulting death. They, therefore, considered that there was an objective basis for Chang's criminal responsibility for this result. But after an on-the-spot examination it was found that Li's wife, Chao, had had asthma and on that night it had recurred . . . and she had suffocated. The recurrence of the illness was certainly not the result of Chang's having hit her with his fist. Therefore, they could not consider that a cause-effect relationship existed between Chang's act and Chao's death, the result [of asthma]. In this case Chang could only be held responsible for the act of striking Chao, and could not be held criminally responsible for Chao's death. The erroneous judgment of the local basic level court at the beginning of the case was due to the fact that between Chang's act and Chao's death came another matter — the recurrence of Chao's illness. Therefore, the question of the cause-effect relationship was not so clear.

1. What weight should legal personnel attach to texts such as the *Lectures*?

2. Do the principles espoused in Items 136–138 substantially circumscribe the discretion of police, procurators, and judges? Is a criminal code likely to do so to a greater degree?

3. To what extent do the principles espoused in Items 136–138 make it necessary to resort to the doctrine of analogy? For what purpose?

## 2. Analogy

ITEM 139

Before reading the following excerpt, recall SAPA Article 31 (Item 66).

[*Lectures* (September 1957), pp. 69–72]

.     .     .     .     .

In the criminal law of our country, analogy is the application of a provision of current criminal legislation [proscribing the act] most similar to a socially dangerous act for which there is no direct provision in order to convict and sentence a person who has committed such an act.

Analogy is a problem that occurs under circumstances in which written criminal laws have been adopted and especially under circumstances in which a criminal code has been promulgated. According to the general principles of the criminal law of our country, an actor is held criminally responsible only when his act coincides with the provisions prescribed by the criminal law and should be subject to criminal punishment. However, there are also individual situations where an actor's act is socially dangerous in substance and should be subject to punishment, but for which there is no direct provision of criminal law. In such situations the criminal law of our country permits the application of the provision of current criminal legislation [proscribing the act] most similar to the socially dangerous act in order to convict and sentence the actor.

The fact that the criminal law of our country permits analogy is intimately related to the present political and economic situation in our country. Our country is now in the period of transition to a socialist society. Everything is in the midst of ceaseless development and transformation. The criminal acts committed by the enemy and other criminals are of all types. These are difficult to calculate at the time criminal laws are adopted. Therefore, the present criminal laws of our country cannot include all the types of criminal acts which may possibly appear or are appearing. Although such acts occur separately, in order to guarantee [the continuance of] the struggle against those acts which are in substance socially dangerous but for which there are no direct provisions of current criminal legislation, it is necessary that judges be allowed the use of analogy in the conduct of their work. For this reason, the Act of the People's Republic of China for Punishment of Counterrevolution has provided for analogy. In order to struggle against crime effectively, the provision of analogy should be affirmed in the future in the criminal code of our country. But the present political and economic situation of our country already differs from that which existed when the Act of the People's Republic of China for Punishment of Counterrevolution was adopted. Therefore, conditions for the application of analogy should be more strict than before. At the same time, we believe that after several years, following the development of the socialist construction of the state and the daily enrichment of experience in struggling against crime, under circumstances in which the criminal code is even more thorough and complete, we may consider abolishing the system of analogy.

In the application of analogy certain conditions must be strictly observed. Otherwise, the legal system would be in danger of being undermined. On the basis of the circumstances of our country's political and economic development and of its experience in judicial practice, the following conditions should be observed in applying analogy:

First, an act for which there may be conviction by analogy must be an act that is socially dangerous and one that should be subject to criminal punishment. It has been mentioned above that the most essential characteristic of a criminal act is that the degree of its social danger is rather serious. If a certain act is not socially dangerous, or the degree of its social danger has not reached the point where the application of criminal punishment is necessary, then it cannot be considered a crime. Therefore, an act for which conviction is by analogy also must have this characteristic. Otherwise, there would be no basis for imposing criminal responsibility on people, and the question of conviction by analogy would therefore never be reached.

Second, an act for which there may be conviction by analogy must be one for which there is no direct provision in current criminal legislation. Only when there is no direct provision in criminal legislation for a certain criminal act can analogy be applied. If such a criminal act already is covered by an express provision of law, there is no basis for not applying this provision and applying another provision by analogy. Otherwise, the situation would be created in which, on the pretext of analogy, the criminal responsibility that should be imposed on a criminal would be decreased or increased in severity and the legal system would be undermined.

Third, conviction and sentence must be based on comparison [of the act committed] with the most similar act proscribed by any provision of current criminal legislation. This is to say that an act for which there may be conviction by analogy must be analogized to the certain provision of existing criminal legislation [proscribing the act] to which it is most similar. Most similar refers to both *the nature of the act* and *the severity of the criminal punishment* corresponding to it. Therefore, provisions for counterrevolutionary crimes cannot be analogically applied to acts which destroy public property (*the object cannot be analogized*); provisions applicable only to state personnel cannot be analogically applied to those who are not state personnel (*the subject cannot be analogized*); provisions relating to intentional criminal acts cannot be analogically applied to negligent criminal acts (*the subjective aspect cannot be analogized*). Also, the scope of criminal responsibility should be limited strictly to the legally prescribed punishment of current criminal legislation.

Besides the above three conditions, whether the application of analogy must be approved by high people's courts or by the Supreme People's Court is a question worth studying. We believe that it is appropriate to add such a condition to the application of analogy because this can be very useful in unifying the legal system, in promoting legislation, and in preventing erroneous judgments. Although this condition is certainly not prescribed in the Act of the People's Republic of China for Punishment of Counterrevolution, yet, just as has been previously mentioned, the present political and economic situation in our country is already different from the time when the Act for Punishment of Counterrevolution was adopted. At present the demand for strengthening and preserving a uniform legal system is already becoming more conspicuous every day. Therefore, conditions for the application of analogy must be more strict than previously. Naturally, this condition differs from the three conditions spoken of before. The three aforementioned conditions are explained from the standpoint of criminal law theory, and they must be observed in applying analogy. But the condition that the application of analogy be approved by a high people's court depends on whether or not the criminal legislation of our country so prescribes. Before criminal legislation clearly prescribes this condition, the approval of a high people's court is not necessary.

Strict observance of certain conditions will help to place the application of analogy upon a foundation of precise observance of the legal system. In this way, under conditions where the principle of the legal system is not violated, the application of analogy will be of more benefit in the struggle against crime and in the implementation of the substantive concepts relating to crime in the criminal law of our country.

From this it can be seen that analogy in the criminal law of our country is fundamentally different from analogy in the criminal law of the exploiter class. In the criminal law of feudalism, "comparison of the facts of one case to the facts of an already decided case and the application of the law of the latter to the former" is in fact a kind of arbitrary judgment. In their criminal codes, although there are generally no analogy provisions, the bourgeoisie exercise this doctrine under the guise of extending the interpretation of criminal law. In order to protect its own class interests, a bourgeois court can disregard the implications and provisions of the law, and with an "extensive interpretation," can make judgments which benefit the preservation of bourgeois rule.

1. Article 1 of the Criminal Code of the Republic of China provides:

"An act is punishable only if the law in force at the time of its commission expressly so prescribes." [9]

2. In 1958 the Soviet Union abolished the doctrine of analogy. Article 7 of the Criminal Code of the RSFSR that went into effect in 1961 provides in pertinent part:

"Article 7. *The concept of crime.* A socially dangerous act (an action or an omission to act) provided for by the Special Part of the present Code which infringes the Soviet social or state system, the socialist system of economy, socialist property, the person, or the political, labor, property, or other rights of citizens, or any other socially dangerous act provided for by the Special Part of the present Code which infringes the socialist legal order, shall be deemed a crime." [10]

3. The laws of the Ch'ing dynasty provided:

a. "Section XLIV. — Determination of Cases not provided for by any existing Law.

9. In Chang Chih-pen, ed., p. 233.
10. Berman and Spindler, *Soviet Criminal Law and Procedure,* p. 147.

"From the impracticability of providing for every possible contingency, there may be cases to which no laws or statutes are precisely applicable; such cases may then be determined, by an accurate comparison with others which are already provided for, and which approach most nearly to those under investigation, in order to ascertain afterwards to what extent an aggravation or mitigation of the punishment would be equitable . . ." [11]

b. "Section CCCLXXXVI. — Improper Conduct not Specifically punishable.

"Whoever is guilty of improper conduct, and such as is contrary to the spirit of the laws, though not a breach of any specific article, shall be punished, at the least, with 40 blows; and when the impropriety is of a serious nature, with 80 blows." [12]

To what extent is the contemporary Chinese attitude toward analogy likely to be a reflection of the traditional respectability of this principle?

## ITEM 140

This is part of an overall criticism of the *Lectures* that was written after the antirightist movement had terminated the law reform efforts of 1956–1957.

[Fan Ming, "Some Opinions about *Lectures on the General Principles of Criminal Law of the PRC*," *CFYC*, 4:73 (1958)]

.    .    .    .    .

For example, in the fourth lecture, on the problem of "Analogy," the *Lectures* assert that at present the system of analogy is necessary, but they [the authors] believe that: "after several years, following the development of the socialist construction of the state and the daily enrichment of experience in struggling against crime, under circumstances in which the criminal code is even more thorough and complete, we may consider abolishing the system of analogy" (*Lectures*, p. 70). I believe this inference is worth studying because the phenomenon of crime and the class struggle are both extremely complex and also because, following the development of the class struggle, it [the phenomenon of crime] will inevitably and ceaselessly change. Even if after several years the criminal code is completed, we estimate that it will be very difficult for its provisions to be comprehensive and without omissions and completely to foresee changes that are yet to come. From the point of view of the demands of the dictatorship over the enemy and of benefiting the struggle against crime, to propose now the future abolition of analogy is not only unrealistic, it is also futile.

1. In view of the limited amount of published legislation relating to nonpolitical crimes, is it possible for legal personnel to make widespread use of the doctrine of analogy?

11. G. T. Staunton, trans., *Ta Tsing Leu Lee; being the Fundamental Laws and a selection from the Supplementary Statutes of the Penal Code of China* (London, 1810), p. 43.
12. Staunton, p. 419.

a. To what can the conduct in question be analogized?

b. Do the above discussions presuppose resort to unpublished regulations? To the aborted criminal code?

2. Is it more important that the law be clear about what conduct is criminal than about what punishment is likely to be imposed for given criminal conduct?

3. Is resort to the doctrine of analogy likely to make a substantial difference in the administration of criminal justice?

a. Are the authors of the *Lectures* right in pointing out that, in countries that do not permit analogy, equivalent results are reached through extensive interpretation? Consider the following:

"In an age chiefly characterized by rapid change in the political, economic, and social spheres, the criminal law can fulfil its functions only if some mechanism is devised to make it more readily adaptable than it has been so far . . . [T]here are only three debatable alternatives in which this can be achieved: first, by the use of general terms; second, by the admission of analogy in the interpretation of criminal statutes; and, third, by a complete revision of the main body of criminal law at regular intervals of, say, one year in order to keep up with any economic and other changes that may have occurred. Each of these alternatives is bound to come into conflict with at least one of the old-established principles of traditional law and jurisprudence." [13]

b. What doctrines does our own criminal law provide to guard against the possibility of extensive interpretation? Consider the following:

"First, it has to be stressed that punishment by analogy seems to constitute no essential characteristic of totalitarian legal systems. The Penal Code of Fascist Italy of 1939 prohibits it explicitly, whereas a democratic country like Denmark admits analogy . . .

"The unfettered admission of analogy, it cannot be disputed, is incompatible with the ideal of certainty and predictability which figures so predominantly in the arguments of the Dicey-Hewart-Hayek school of thought. What the adherents of this school are too readily inclined to assume is, however, that the prohibition of analogy is in itself capable of maintaining those safeguards of civil liberty. Actually, as no lawyer with inside knowledge of the work of criminal courts in whatever country can honestly deny, this is nothing but an illusion. Where statutes have to be interpreted, a considerable margin of uncertainty is, and will always be, inevitable. Even the line of demarcation between what is still permissible as extensive interpretation and what becomes prohibited analogy is only too often shrouded in darkness. The practical difference between the two systems is, therefore, far less important than often claimed by many theorists and outsiders . . .

"It is not our purpose to advocate the unrestricted admission of analogy — this would indeed be tolerable only in a perfectly homogeneous society where law and social morality have become identical — but merely to show the problem in its proper perspective. The fate of civil liberty depends on the men

13. Hermann Mannheim, *Criminal Justice and Social Reconstruction* (London, 1946), p. 204.

who have to administer criminal justice much more than on this or any other legal formula." [14]

4. Given Chinese tradition and the needs and perspectives of the Communist regime, is it unreasonable for China's present leaders to sacrifice predictability and fair warning to the individual for the attainment of other values? What values might these be? Consider the following provisions from the Uniform Code of Military Justice of the United States:

"Article 133. Conduct Unbecoming an Officer and a Gentleman. 'Any commissioned officer, cadet, or midshipman who is convicted of conduct unbecoming an officer and a gentleman shall be punished as a court-martial may direct.'

"Article 134. General Article. 'Though not specifically mentioned in this chapter, all disorders and neglects to the prejudice of good order and discipline in the armed forces, all conduct of a nature to bring discredit upon the armed forces, and crimes and offenses not capital, of which persons subject to this chapter may be guilty, shall be taken cognizance of by a general, special, or summary court-martial, according to the nature and degree of the offense, and shall be punished at the discretion of that court.' " [15]

### 3. Some Special Problems of Responsibility

The *Lectures* also provide legal personnel with specific guidance on other problems relating to the definition of criminal conduct that are usually dealt with by the "general part" of a criminal code. The following items include a representative sampling of the *Lectures* relating to particular problems of criminal responsibility. A few illustrative cases are also presented. Care should be taken to compare each of these items with the relevant provisions of the Security Administration Punishment Act and the case histories relating to their application (Chapter III, section E).

### ITEM 141. VOLUNTARINESS

[*Lectures* (September 1957), pp. 86–87]

. . . . . .

For an actor to be held criminally responsible for his own socially dangerous act, it is necessary to find out whether that act was a manifestation of the actor's own will, or, in other words, whether the actor committed the act in accordance with his desire. If a person's act is not committed in accordance with his own desire, then he cannot be held criminally responsible for that act. Acts which are not committed in accordance with the actor's desire are of two kinds: one is committed under circumstances in which there is physical coercion; and one is committed under an irresistible influence. Under these two kinds of circumstances, the actor commits acts which are against his own will. Even though these cause some loss, they cannot be considered criminal acts.

Acts committed under circumstances in which there is physical coercion are acts committed by a certain person under circumstances in which there is

14. Mannheim, at pp. 208, 210–211, 212–213.
15. Arts. 133–134, in *United States Code,* Title 10, sects. 933–934 (1965).

physical coercion from an external force. For example, one day A saw B, an enemy whom he wanted to kill, standing on a riverbank. At the same time, about a foot behind B stood another person, C. A intended to push B into the river but was afraid of getting close and being discovered by B. So A pushed C with great force, causing C to shove B into the river, and B drowned. Under these circumstances C shoved B into the river under physical coercion from an external force. He was only A's tool, and his act was committed against his own will. Therefore, he cannot be held criminally responsible for the result, B's death. Rather, A rightly should be held criminally responsible.

Acts committed under an irresistible influence are acts committed by a certain person under circumstances in which he himself is without the power to overcome an obstacle. For example, a supply officer of a work site was not able to send building materials to the work site on time. As a result of the delay the work project stopped, causing a major loss. But the reason for the supply officer's not being able to transport the building materials to the work site on time was that at that locality a flood had occurred and the railroad tracks were flooded. There was no way to transport the materials. This kind of obstacle was beyond his power to overcome. In other words, his act of not sending the building materials to the work site was against his own will. Therefore, he has no criminal responsibility to speak of.

Recall SAPA Article 20(2) (Item 72A) and Item 72B.

## ITEMS 142A–142C. MENTAL ILLNESS

### ITEM 142A

[*Lectures* (September 1957), pp. 110–111]

The subject of a crime must be a person who has the capacity to assume responsibility. The person who has the capacity to assume responsibility is a person who has the capacity to understand the nature of and to control his own acts. Only when a person who has the capacity to assume responsibility commits a socially dangerous act can he be held criminally responsible. A person without the capacity to assume responsibility cannot be held to criminal responsibility, even though he has committed a socially dangerous act.

When determining that a person is without the capacity to assume responsibility, the following two conditions must be fulfilled: (1) he must have been mentally ill when he committed the socially dangerous act; and (2) because of this illness he was unable to understand the nature of or to control his own act. It is necessary that these two conditions be simultaneously fulfilled for it to be possible to determine that a person is without the capacity to assume responsibility. It is possible to have this situation: although a person is mentally ill, the illness has still not reached the level where he is unable to understand the nature of and to control his own act. This person cannot be considered to be a person without the capacity to assume responsibility.

Inability to understand the nature of and to control his own act should be understood in this way: "inability to understand the nature of his own act" refers to an actor who does not understand the actual circumstances of his own act or its social significance; "inability to control his own act" refers to an actor who, when committing a socially dangerous act, has insufficient capacity to check himself. This is to say, under the circumstances at the time, his act was against his own will. Generally, a mentally ill person is one who has the above-mentioned characteristics. For example, a mentally ill mother choked her baby to death, and she still considered that it was an affectionate act of caressing. Since this act was committed under circumstances in which the actor was not able to understand the nature of her own act, of course it was against her own will.

A mentally ill person who commits a socially dangerous act while he is without the capacity to assume responsibility is not criminally responsible. However, there is a kind of person who is mentally ill intermittently; if he commits a criminal act when he is in a sane condition but after commission of the crime again goes insane and becomes a person without the capacity to assume responsibility, he still should be held criminally responsible for the criminal act he committed. However, until he recovers from mental illness, proceedings in the case should be suspended.

When it is determined that a person who has committed a socially dangerous act is without the capacity to assume responsibility, this should be verified by a court-affiliated doctor or by a medical specialist. Adjudication officers and procurators cannot make the decision arbitrarily.

Although we cannot treat as criminals people without the capacity to assume responsibility who commit socially dangerous acts, and although we cannot impose criminal punishments upon them, leaving them uncared for would interfere with the safety of society. In order to protect the safety of society, we should order members of their families or guardians to watch over them strictly and provide them with medical treatment. In districts where conditions permit, people without the capacity to assume responsibility and whose social danger is relatively great may be sent to medical institutions for compulsory medical treatment.

## ITEM 142B

[Interview]

Shih was a schoolteacher whose husband worked as secretary of the local people's council. In 1958 he was labelled a "rightist" and sent off to rehabilitation through labor. This had a profound effect upon Shih, who had previously suffered one period of mental instability. While at school she began openly cursing and reviling the Communist Party, the government, her school principal, and others. When this persisted the school reported her to the city education bureau, which summoned her for an interview. When she began to curse the chief of the education bureau, he notified the public security bureau, which asked him and Shih to come to the PSB to discuss the matter. There the chief of the PSB's security section noted that Shih's response to his criticism of her conduct was odd. She often laughed and did not seem to appreciate the significance of the case. He decided to send her to the county hospital for a mental examination.

That night the hospital doctor who had examined her called the security section to say that it appeared to be a case of mental abnormality, and he held to this view the next day after a second examination of Shih, who was confined in the hospital. On the third day the doctor saw her again and then put this view in writing. After approval by the director of the hospital, who was not a medical man but a Party administrator, this report was sent to the PSB as the hospital's report. It certified that Shih suffered from "mental abnormality" but not "mental illness" and that she would require several months of rest and care. On the basis of this report the security section of the PSB decided that, because of her abnormality, Shih should not receive any punishment but should remain in the county hospital for treatment. It notified the hospital and the education bureau of this decision.

Several months later, after Shih's condition had improved, she was released by the hospital and was sent home for further rest. She subsequently returned to teaching and at that time voluntarily wrote a letter of "self-examination" to the PSB, asserting that her conduct had been caused by mental abnormality and that she did not harbor any anti-Communist, antigovernment feelings.

## ITEM 142C

[Interview]

Wang was an overseas Chinese who had returned from Indonesia and had been settled on a state farm. In 1960 he decided that he preferred life in Indonesia and applied for an exit permit to return there. His application was rejected. Wang applied again and again but without success. One day, while discussing his case with the Party secretary of the state farm, he suddenly attacked the secretary, knocked him unconscious, and bloodied his face. After detaining and questioning Wang, the county public security bureau, which was familiar with his background because of his exit applications, summoned a doctor to examine him. The doctor and the bureau agreed that the frustrations of receiving repeated denials had affected Wang's mental equilibrium to such an extent that he did not know what he was doing in attacking the secretary. Accordingly, the bureau did not recommend that Wang be prosecuted but sent him to the provincial mental hospital. He was released as cured two months later.

1. Recall SAPA Article 27 (Item 78A) and Items 78B and 78C.
2. In the contemplation of the *Lectures,* the decision that a person charged with a socially dangerous act is mentally irresponsible is one that is made by "judges and procurators." The *Lectures* urge such officials to seek the aid of a court-affiliated doctor or a medical specialist. Nothing is said about the role of public security personnel. How would you characterize their participation in this decision-making process?

## ITEMS 143A–143B. YOUTH
## ITEM 143A

[*Lectures* (September 1957), pp. 112–115]

The subject of a crime must be a person who has reached a given age: to have reached a given age is one element of the subject of a crime. A youngster who has not reached a given age cannot become the subject of a crime because only a person who has reached a given age has the capacity to understand the nature of and to control his socially dangerous acts and thereby become a person with the capacity to assume responsibility. But a person's capacity to understand the nature of and to control his acts grows gradually, and the pace of this growth is intimately linked to the circumstances of the education he receives and the social activities in which he participates. Therefore the solution to the problem relating to the age at which a minor assumes criminal responsibility should meet these circumstances by dividing age into several stages. At the same time, the division into specific ages is not static. Under different historical conditions there are often different methods of resolving the problem.

Because our country's criminal code has not yet been promulgated, we lack a uniform criterion for the specific age at which minors assume criminal responsibility. But this problem was involved in the 1952 Reply of the Former Commission on the Legal System of the Central People's Government Relating to Whether Minors Who Have Been Used by [Nationalist] Bandit Agents To Commit Arson and to Spread Poison Should Be Punished, in the provisions of Article 21 of the Act for Reform Through Labor promulgated in 1954 and in the 1956 Joint Notification of the Supreme People's Procuracy, the Supreme People's Court, and the Ministries of Interior, Justice, and Public Security on Problems Concerning Limitations on Commitment to Custody, Procedures of Arrest, and the Disposition of Juvenile Offenders. In view of these documents, the point is relatively clear that the age at which a minor assumes criminal responsibility is divided into three stages. These three stages are: the period of complete assumption of criminal responsibility, the period of relative assumption of criminal responsibility, and the period of complete nonassumption of criminal responsibility. But there is no agreement as to how to divide the specific ages of these three stages. A synthesizing study of these documents on the basis of the order of their date of publication and in keeping with the spirit of their substance can provide this general conclusion: a person who commits a crime when he has already reached fifteen years of age is in the period of complete assumption of criminal responsibility and should assume criminal responsibility for all criminal acts; a person who has already reached thirteen years of age but who has not yet reached fifteen years of age is in the period of relative assumption of criminal responsibility and assumes criminal responsibility only for certain crimes that are easy to recognize and the social danger of which is relatively great. These crimes are: murder, infliction of serious bodily injury, habitual theft, and crimes that are dangerous to the public (for example, serious sabotage of transportation and communication facilities and arson). A person who has not yet reached thirteen years of age is in the period of complete nonassumption of criminal responsibility and does not assume criminal responsibility for doing any socially dangerous act. A minor who does not assume criminal responsibility for a crime that he has committed should be handed over to the head of his family for discipline.

The above-mentioned ages of criminal responsibility are [based on] the summary of experience of the struggle against crime throughout the country and generally can be used as applicable criteria. But it must be noted that because the territory of our country is vast and the circumstances of the development of the economy and culture in the various districts is extremely unbalanced, sometimes there is a great gap in the level of development of mental and intellectual capacity between minors in cities and those in the countryside and in mountainous areas. Therefore, in judicial practice, it would not be fitting to understand the above-mentioned legal ages as absolutes. In individual situations, we should determine a minor's capacity to understand the nature of and control his own acts on the basis of the theory of determining the legal age of criminal responsibility, proceeding from the facts and paying attention to his psychological characteristics. As for an individual minor in an individual district, if his mental or intellectual development is relatively slow and he cannot recognize the social significance of his own acts, or if he lacks the capacity to control his own acts, then we should consider a socially dangerous act committed by him to have been committed while he was without the capacity to assume responsibility and, therefore, we should not consider it a criminal act.

Compare SAPA Article 26 (Item 77A) and Item 77B with the analysis and recommendations of the *Lectures*. Are they consistent?

## ITEM 143B

[Interview]

In 1959, Leng, a fifteen-year-old boy who lived in Canton, borrowed a large sum of money from a friend who was the son of a wealthy, returned, overseas Chinese. When Leng proved unable to meet the friend's requests for repayment, an argument ensued. Leng decided to end the problem by desperate means. He lured his friend into an isolated field in the suburbs, killed him, and stole his wristwatch, bicycle, and other articles.

Investigation soon led the police to Leng, who confessed when confronted with evidence that had been assembled against him. Because of Leng's age, the public security bureau did not turn the case over to the procuracy for criminal prosecution but instead sent Leng to the local center for the rehabilitation of children. He was still confined in that institution in the spring of 1962 [when the informant left China].

The center for rehabilitation of children referred to above is a counterpart, at a juvenile level, of rehabilitation through labor camps. Just as the public security organ decides to send certain persons who have committed serious antisocial acts to rehabilitation through labor and to recommend that other such persons be given criminal punishment, so too does it exercise its discretion in the case of juvenile offenders and decide to send some to "noncriminal" rehabilitation while recommending that others be given criminal punishment.

In the case above, did the public security bureau follow the strictures of the *Lectures?*

## ITEMS 144A–144B. DRUNKENNESS
### ITEM 144A

[*Lectures* (September 1957), pp. 111–112]

.     .     .     .     .

In adjudication practice, it is possible to meet the problem of whether or not a person who commits a criminal act while in a state of drunkenness is to be considered a person without the capacity to assume responsibility. The solution to this problem is that a drunkard should be held criminally responsible for a criminal act committed by him while in a state of drunkenness and he cannot be considered a person without the capacity to assume responsibility. This is because drunkenness usually only can weaken a person's capacity for control but does not make him lose it completely. Therefore, he should be held criminally responsible for the criminal acts he commits. At the same time, drunkenness is an abnormal phenomenon, a vice remaining from the old society. Therefore, we should struggle against criminal acts committed under circumstances of drunkenness.

### ITEM 144B

[Interview]

Han was a young militiaman in a rural production brigade. One night in 1958 he got drunk and unsuccessfully tried to rape a young woman who had been refusing his advances. He was prosecuted and convicted of attempted rape, but, because he had been under the influence of alcohol, the basic level people's court at the county seat sentenced him to only one year of imprisonment instead of to the customary three-year term.

Compare SAPA Article 28 (Item 79A) and the attitude expressed in the *Lectures* (Item 144A) with the actual cases in Items 79B–79D and Item 144B. Does there appear to be any discrepancy between theory and practice?

## ITEM 145. LEGITIMATE DEFENSE

[*Lectures* (September 1957), pp. 137, 138, 139, 140, 141]

.     .     .     .     .

A legitimate defense is an act of defense used to avoid the encroachment of a person who is unlawfully [attempting to] encroach upon one's person or rights, the person or rights of another, or the public interest.

When a person commits an act of legitimate defense, it might look like a criminal act from its outward appearance. But because the purpose of this act was to prevent the realization of an unlawful encroachment, it should be considered lawful, and naturally we cannot even talk of the problem of criminal responsibility. For example, a person kills a robber in order to avoid the robber's attack; or a woman, in the course of defending herself, seriously injures a man [attempting to] rape her. Both of these are acts of legitimate defense. From their outward appearance, they might look like criminal acts in that they caused another person's death or serious injury. But because the purpose of these acts was to prevent the realization of unlawful encroachments, not only can they not be considered criminal acts but, rather, they should be considered lawful acts in the struggle against unlawful encroachments.

.    .    .    .    .

1. An act can only be a legitimate defense if it is committed against an unlawful act of encroachment . . .

2. An act can only be a legitimate defense if it is committed against an encroachment which is being carried out at the time and which actually exists . . .

An imaginary or presumed encroachment means that he [the person who commits the act of defense] does not know whether or not an unlawful encroachment really exists. He may mistakenly believe what is actually not an act of unlawful encroachment to be such an act and [as a result] defend himself. In this case, the defense cannot be considered legitimate. Under these circumstances the problem of the actor's responsibility should be resolved in accordance with the principle of mistake of fact. For example, cadre A went to the country to inspect some work. Late at night when he was walking in the outskirts [of a village] a militiaman ordered him to stop and prepared to examine him. A mistakenly thought that the militiaman was a bandit, and thus shot him to death with a pistol. Here, A misunderstood [mistakenly thought] an unlawful encroachment really existed. Therefore, the problem relating to his responsibility should be resolved in this way: if on the basis of the specific circumstances at the time, A should have foreseen that could not be an unlawful encroachment, he is criminally responsible for this act of negligent homicide.

.    .    .    .    .

3. An act can only be a legitimate defense if it is committed against a person who is committing an act of unlawful encroachment . . .

4. An act of defense should not exceed what is necessary.

## 4. Retroactivity

### ITEM 146

[*Lectures* (September 1957), pp. 44–47]

.    .    .    .    .

Except in some special circumstances, the criminal law of the People's Republic of China has [allowed] retroactivity in all cases involving criminal acts which have occurred after the People's Republic was established and which have not been adjudicated or in which judgment has not been rendered. The individual criminal laws and regulations promulaged after the People's Republic was established summarize our country's struggle against crime and embody the policies of the Party and the state. From the standpoint of the significance of their uniform applicability to the entire country, this is only a beginning. Therefore, there is no question that they should be applied to criminal acts committed before these laws were put into effect. Of the criminal laws promulgated after the founding of the People's Republic, some expressly prescribe that they are retroactive. For example, Article 18 of the Act of the People's Republic of China for Punishment of Counterrevolution prescribes: "The provisions of this Act also apply to those who were counterrevolutionary criminals before this Act was put into effect." Others do not themselves have express provisions, but their retroactivity is pointed out in the legislative explanations of those laws. For example, the Act of the People's Republic of China for Punishment of Corruption certainly does not itself clearly prescribe that it is retroactive. But the Explanation Relating to the Draft Act of the People's Republic of China for Punishment of Corruption points out: "Under this Act those who have in the past committed crimes covered by this Act may be pursued [for criminal responsibility]. The time limit for pursuing them should be figured from the date on which the People's Republic of China was established, that is, October 1, 1949. But where the circumstances of cases of corruption and theft are serious and evil or popular resentment is great, the time limit for pursuing them may go back to the date on which the large cities and provincial capitals in the various places were liberated. In places where liberation came after the People's Republic of China was established, the time limit for pursuing them should be figured from the date of their liberation." Some, such as the Provisional Act for Punishment of Crimes That Endanger State Currency, do not themselves have express provisions for retroactivity, nor do they have explanations and interpretations. In theory, this is the first law for the punishment of crimes that endanger state currency promulgated by the state and uniformly applied throughout the entire country. Therefore, although Article 11 of the Act prescribes that "this Act shall be put into effect on the date of its promulgation," it should be retroactive with respect to criminal acts endangering the state currency committed before the promulgation of that Act. This is because, before promulgation of this Act, every citizen knew that counterfeiting or alteration of state currency was an unlawful act. Also, Article 39 of the Common Program, which was the provisional constitution of our country, prescribed: "Whoever engages in financial speculation or undermines the financial undertakings of the state shall receive severe punitive restraints." Thus people's courts naturally have reason to apply the provisions of the Act to punish criminal acts endangering the state currency committed before the promulgation of that Act.

Whether in theory or practice, the criminal legislation of our country is retroactive with respect to all criminal acts committed after the People's Republic of China was established. But as said above, because the criminal legislation of our country develops and changes with the development and the change of the state's political and economic circumstances, when the law is applied, it is still possible that the following three problems that need to be resolved will arise: (1) an act which the law [in force] at the time the act was committed did not consider a crime but which the law [promulgated] after the time it was committed considers a crime; (2) an act which the law [in force] at the time the act was committed considered a crime but which the law [promulgated] after the time it was committed does not consider a crime; and (3) an act which the law [in force] at the time the act was committed considered and the law [promulgated] after the time it was committed also considers a crime but for which the severity of punishment is different. Now these three problems are explained individually as follows.

(1) An act which the law [in force] at the time the act was committed did not consider a crime but which the law [promulgated] after the time it was committed considers a crime: on the basis of the development of political and economic circumstances, the state may at certain times designate as crimes and may punish acts which were not considered crimes in the past. This demonstrates that when the law was adopted, the social danger of these acts had increased. At the same time it, of course, also shows that before the law was prescribed, the state did not consider them to be criminal acts, and it was also impossible for citizens to know that these acts would become criminal acts afterwards. Therefore, to punish these acts would be meaningless and not in conformity with the spirit of the people's democratic legal system of our country. Thus, we may draw a conclusion: a newly promulgated law should not be retroactive with respect to an act which, according to the law [in force] at the time the act was committed, was not considered a crime but which, according to the new law promulgated after the time it was committed is considered a criminal act. It should be pointed out that, because the criminal legislation of our country is still incomplete, the problem of deciding whether or not certain acts are crimes at the time they are committed should be resolved on the basis of Party and state policies and the situation at the time. Naturally, it is no problem to decide whether or not those acts for which there were no express provisions of law in the past but which the ordinary citizen knew were crimes, such as murder, theft, and rape, were, at the time of their commission, criminal acts. After their promulgation, the new laws should be applied to these criminal acts. One cannot, because there were no express provisions at the time the acts were committed, not consider them as criminal acts and thus reject the application of the new law. The principle that a new law is not retroactive with respect to a crime which, according to the law [in force] at the time the act was committed, was not considered a crime, but which, according to the new law [promulgated] after the time it was committed, is considered a criminal act, has already been expressed in the current legislation of our country. For example, Article 7 of the Act of the People's Republic of China for Punishment of Corruption prescribes: "Those who, before promulgation of this Act, adhered to the evil habits of the old society by giving a small kickback to state personnel in a fair transaction, shall not be treated as having bribed. But, after promulgation of this Act, if a small kickback is sent or accepted in

a transaction with state personnel, the one who sends it and the one who accepts it, shall both be punished separately for bribery or for accepting a bribe."

1. What do the authors of the *Lectures* mean by retroactive application of law? Do they mean retroactive application of punishment and not retroactive proscription of criminality?

2. What is the relationship of retroactivity to analogy?

a. If law enforcement officials are permitted to apply the doctrine of analogy, is it necessary that they be able to apply legislation retroactively?

b. If legislation can be applied retroactively, is it necessary to resort to analogy?

## ITEM 147

[Fan Ming, "Some Opinions about *Lectures on the General Principles of Criminal Law of the PRC*" (1958), pp. 72–73]

In the third lecture, on "Problems of the Retroactivity of the Criminal Law," the *Lectures* advocate that, with respect to a situation in which an act was considered a crime by the law [in force] at the time the act was committed and by the law [promulgated] after the time it was committed but is punished more severely by the new law," . . . in principle the new law is not retroactive," that is, "generally the lighter punishment of the old law should be applied." "When it is considered necessary to make retroactive the new law's punishment of increased severity, this can be clearly prescribed in the new law itself." (*Lectures,* p. 47.) I believe that retroactivity should be subject to the needs of the struggle against crime. I think that it is permissible on the basis of policy and in accordance with the new law, to sentence [the defendant] to the relatively heavier punishment, even though the new law has not prescribed retroactivity.

## ITEM 148

["The Principal Criminal Who Persecuted the White-Haired Girl of I-pin Is Executed," *Szu-ch'uan jih-pao* (Szechuan daily), Jan. 15, 1959]

Six criminals, including T'ao T'ien-chen, who had persecuted Lo Ch'ang-hsiu, the "white-haired girl of I-pin," were sentenced to death or to imprisonment in I-pin city on January 6.

After the case of the "white-haired girl of I-pin" became widely known, the intermediate people's court for I-pin district and the county people's court received over 1,000 letters from all over the country demanding severe punishment for the murderers and a remedy and revenge for the wrongs done to Lo Ch'ang-hsiu. Many persons who attended the trial brought along demands that the criminals be punitively restrained in accordance with law.

The "white-haired girl," Lo Ch'ang-hsiu, attended the public trial meeting. She had just given birth to a child, and Mao Shih-feng of the women's federation of I-pin county represented her at the trial. Mao Shih-feng angrily accused T'ao T'ien-chen and the other criminals of monstrous crimes. Twenty-two years ago (1937) T'ao T'ien-chen and the other local despots and landlords plundered the house of Lo Ch'ang-hsiu and beat to death her father, Lo Szu-ming. They also forced Lo Ch'ang-hsiu, who was then sixteen years old, and her older brother, Lo Ch'ang-pao, to work for T'ao T'ien-chen. They suffered mistreatment and hardship at his hands. Once after hanging Lo Ch'ang-hsiu up and beating her, T'ao T'ien-chen stripped her of her clothes and drove her out of the house. Lo Ch'ang-hsiu had nowhere to go but to Tuan-t'ou mountain. T'ao T'ien-chen and the others searched the mountain several times and finally seized Lo Ch'ang-hsiu. They hung up Lo Ch'ang-hsiu together with Lo Ch'ang-pao and cruelly tortured and beat them. Afterward, Lo Ch'ang-pao fled to Yunnan and Lo Ch'ang-hsiu to Tuan-t'ou mountain, where she lived an inhuman existence for seventeen years. Everyone who attended the trial was infuriated by the criminal acts of the criminals, and they all gnashed their teeth, shook their fists, and created an uproar demanding severe punishment for the criminals.

At the meeting, the intermediate people's court of I-pin district in accordance with law sentenced the murderer T'ao T'ien-chen to death, with immediate execution of the sentence. The other five criminals were sentenced to life imprisonment, or to lesser terms of imprisonment. The masses were jubilant and unanimous in their support of the judgment. Over thirty representatives of Lo Ch'ang-hsiu's native place, the Feng-i People's Commune of I-pin, expressed their gratitude and support to the Party and the government. They said that the Party and the government had redressed the grievance of Lo Ch'ang-hsiu and obtained revenge for her and had also uprooted the evil. From now on we must heed the words of the Party and the government more than ever, actively engage in production, and do a good job of managing the people's commune.

## ITEM 149

["Chao Feng-hsiang, Principal Criminal in the Murder of Li Kung-pu, Is Executed," *JMJP*, March 26, 1959, p. 6]

On the 24th of March in the city of Ch'ang-sha, Chao Feng-hsiang, principal criminal in the murder of Mr. Li Kung-pu, was executed.

In June and July 1946, Huo Kuei-chang, head of secret agents and commander of the military police for the Kuomintang in Yunnan province, actively carried out the so-called "secret punitive restraint" conspiracy of Chiang Kai-shek against Li Kung-pu, Wen I-to, etc. He directed Wang Tsu-ming, chief of the investigation office, to convene a meeting of the backbone secret agents Chao Feng-hsiang (head of a secret agent group), Ts'ui Chen-san (head of a group), Ts'ai Yün-ch'i (leader of the Kuomintang intelligence group of the city defense command of Kunming city), etc., and secretly assigned them to assassinate Li Kung-pu and Wen I-to. Afterward, Chao Feng-hsiang immediately sent secret agents especially to watch the movements of Li Kung-pu and Wen I-to. On the afternoon of July 11 of the same year, Chao Feng-hsiang led secret agents T'ang Shih-liang, Wu Po-yün, etc., to fire upon and attack Mr. Li Kung-pu as he returned home. Mr. Li Kung-pu passed away at the hospital the next day as a result of his severe wounds. Afterward, the secret agent organs gave these murderers a large "reward," and Chao Feng-hsiang was promoted from captain to major.

The criminal Chao Feng-hsiang was from Hunan province's Hsiang-tan county.

From 1943 to 1949 he was successively a member and then head of the intelligence group of the "investigation office" of the Kuomintang army headquarters and the investigation office of the military police command of Yunnan province. In May 1949 criminal Chao secretly returned from Hupeh's Ch'ang-sha city to Hsiang-t'an county, made up a false history, and for a long time concealed his evil crimes. In the first half of 1958, denunciations by the masses and investigation by the public security organs finally brought the matter to light. After criminal Chao was arrested by the public security bureau of Hsiang-t'an county and confronted with reliable evidence, he could not but admit his crimes. The high people's court of Hunan province sentenced Chao Feng-hsiang to death in accordance with law, the sentence was approved by the Supreme People's Court, and he was shot on the 24th in the city of Ch'ang-sha.

1. Under what laws were the defendants in Items 148 and 149 convicted?
2. Should these two cases be viewed as raising problems both of retroactivity and of nonapplicability of what we would call a statute of limitations?
Consider this criticism made of the *Lectures:*

"The twentieth lecture, on 'The Time Limit For Prosecution,' in its discussion of the time limit for prosecution for counterrevolutionary crimes, after asserting that prosecution for counterrevolutionary crimes is not subject to a time limit, states that in the future 'we may consider applying a time limit to ordinary counterrevolutionaries whose crimes are minor' (*Lectures,* p. 264). It is my understanding that 'not prosecuting them for any of their past acts' is, under the policy of liquidating counterrevolution, a lenient measure for certain situations. It certainly is not by nature related to the question of a time limit for prosecution. Otherwise, would it not mean that if the time limit had expired and these counterrevolutionary criminals had not thoroughly confessed and admitted their guilt, we would then be unable to prosecute them? Therefore, I believe that we still should assert that prosecution for counterrevolutionary crimes should never be subject to a time limit. There should be no exceptions." [16]

16. Fan Ming, pp. 74–75.

# Chapter VII   Formal Criminal Processes:
## Pretrial Proceedings

The prisoner is supposed, however, to be protected by one safeguard. No one accused of crime can be convicted except on his own confession; he not only must plead to the charge, but in practice must plead guilty; and to allow him to "stand mute" would be held as impeding the administration of justice, in the eyes of the Chinese law during the factory days and to-day, as in former centuries it was in the eyes of English law. No prisoner, however innocent, could be allowed to defeat the purpose of the judge or the interests of justice, and it invariably happens, in a Chinese court of law, that the confession of guilt, which is a necessary condition precedent to conviction, is forthcoming.

H. B. Morse,
*The International Relations of the Chinese Empire*[1]

"The principle of officiality" is also worth study. Students of Kuomintang criminal litigation call it "the doctrine of state prosecution." Mainly it asserts that, except for some minor criminal cases in which a complaint may be

1. (London, New York, Bombay, and Calcutta, 1910), p. 114.

brought by the victim or his relatives, ordinary criminal cases are all prosecuted by the state, that is, by the procuratorial organs. The task of prosecution that the procurator in the Kuomintang court performed was without doubt a counter-revolutionary activity that oppressed the people. Naturally, in order to realize his task of suppression, he limited the participation of the masses of people in this litigation activity. At the same time, the masses of people would not participate in the reactionary activity, the so-called "prosecution," because the point of its suppression was turned mainly toward members of the Communist Party, people who had taken part in the revolution, and the other masses of workers and peasants. We firmly oppose this reactionary "doctrine of state prosecution." Although in most criminal cases in our country the public security and procuratorial organs investigate and the people's procuracy initiates and supports the prosecution, this activity is conducted on the basis of the mass line, which has the active participation and support of the vast masses of people. It is not an activity that the public security and procuratorial organs conduct in isolation. We adopt the basic principle of the mass line of combining specialized organs and the vast masses under the absolute leadership of the Party. Therefore, it is one-sided and incorrect to suggest that "the principle of officiality" is the principle of our country's public security and procuratorial organs and courts in the struggle against the enemy.

> Chang Hui et al., "These Are Not
> the Basic Principles of Our Country's
> Criminal Litigation" (1958)[2]

We have seen that for many kinds of antisocial conduct the PRC imposes a variety of "noncriminal" sanctions. In many cases it does so because the conduct in question is not considered grave enough to warrant criminal punishment and the sanctions actually imposed are relatively mild. In other cases, although the conduct in question is deemed to be relatively grave and the sanctions imposed are comparable to criminal punishment in their severity, the regime has insisted on categorizing these sanctions as "noncriminal." At least to its own satisfaction, this has relieved it of having to comply with the procedures for imposing criminal punishment. From the viewpoint of the public security force, what are the inconveniences of resort to the formal criminal process? From the viewpoint of a suspected offender, what safeguards are unique to the formal criminal process? This is the subject of our inquiry for the remainder of Part II. Chapter VII deals with pretrial proceedings.

## A. INVESTIGATION AND APPREHENSION OF SUSPECTED CRIMINALS

### 1. Investigation: Cooperation between the Masses and Police

Items 150–152 illustrate the close cooperation that is said to exist between the police and the masses in the investigation of major criminal cases and suggest a few of the investigative techniques which they employ.

2. *CFYC,* 4:79 (1958).

## ITEM 150

[Shang Yin-pin, "Fully Develop the Militant Role of the Basic Level Security Defense Organizations" (1958), pp. 71–72]

.    .    .    .    .

The basic level security defense organizations were created during the mass movements of struggle against the enemy, and they were "born and raised locally." It is just because they possess this characteristic of being "born and raised locally" that, under the leadership of the Party, they can at any time and at any place reflect the feelings and requests of the masses. Last year when the rightists attacked the Party, and when the landlord, rich peasant, counterrevolutionary, and bad elements raised their heads, some of them [the members of the basic level security organizations] directly sought out the county [Party] committees and the county public security bureaus and requested the leadership to support the masses and to decide things for them. After the start of the struggle to attack landlord, rich peasant, counterrevolutionary, and bad elements, they [the members of these organizations] were the first to be inspired by this struggle and to go enthusiastically into action. Many comrades traveled long distances in very bad weather to assist the public security organs in investigating and arresting landlord, rich peasant, counterrevolutionary, and bad elements. Some of them, in order to clarify the circumstances [of a case] involving counterrevolutionaries and bad elements, even took along their own corn flour cakes and dried yams and traveled tens of *li* or even hundreds of *li* to examine the evidence. Since the great leap forward in public security work, in order to sweep away obstacles to the great leap forward in industrial and agricultural production, they further summoned their soaring energy and started a red flag competition movement to evaluate what is advanced, to strive for what is advanced, and to exceed what is advanced . . .

Here we can also see that, following the rapid development of basic level security defense work, the scope of the actual work of these organizations has already far exceeded their old scope. From the standpoint of their activity in solving cases, in the last two or three years they have progressed from their original role of assisting the public security organs in solving cases to being able directly to engage in the work of solving cases. Moreover, the proportion of cases solved by them has also been gradually increasing, especially since the great leap forward in public security work in the spring of this year; since that time they themselves have directly solved 62 percent of all the cases solved in our entire province. The proportion of cases solved by them in the special districts of Ts'ang-hsien, T'ang-shan, and Chang-chia-k'ou has already reached 70 percent; and in Ch'ien-an and Ching counties and in many other counties it has already reached 80 percent or more. The method of rousing the masses to bloom and contend and to write large character posters, adopted by the security defense committee in the administrative village in Ts'ang-hsien, solved all of the old and new criminal cases that had not been solved during the past six years. For example, in the past they only could solve some minor cases, but today they can solve some major ones; in the past the scope of their activity in solving cases was limited to only certain criminal cases, but today they can help the public security organs in investigating and solving cases of a political nature such as those involving reactionary posters or societies. In struggling against cunning enemies, these security defense cadres who had been "born and raised locally" learned how to use all kinds of "local methods" for on-the-spot investigation and for protecting the scene of a crime, such as placing a basin [upside down] to preserve traces [of the crime], using blades of grass to measure footprints, and using the smoke of kerosene lamps to take fingerprints. Thus, the whereabouts of Wang Fu-shan, a counterrevolutionary who had escaped from prison in the administrative village of Hsi-ch'eng-fang in Cho county, was discovered through a clue, the traces made by his "wolf-claw" shoes when he was committing crimes at night. When this counterrevolutionary was arrested many years after he had escaped, in addition to his being found with some homemade pistols and a knife during a search of the place [where he was apprehended], it was confirmed that during the period that he had been in hiding in a cave he had more than nine times engaged in sabotage activity including arson, rape, and theft.

## ITEM 151

["Security Defense Organizations Have Developed Their Role in All Factories and Mines in the City of Pen-hsi," *Hsin-hua t'ung-hsün-she* (New China news agency), March 8, 1955]

Many model units and persons have emerged from the struggle to prevent espionage, prevent theft, etc., in all the factories and mines in the city of Pen-hsi. Forty-seven persons who are security models, one model security unit, and nine security groups received awards from the public security organs of the city of Pen-hsi.

Many mass security defense organizations in the factories coordinated with security departments of the factories and mines and reported hidden counter-revolutionaries. Once Li K'o-yü, member of the security defense group of T'ai-p'ing-kou pyrite mine, discovered eight counterrevolutionaries led by Tung Teng-k'uei attempting to carry out sabotage. The security defense organization immediately reported the situation to the public security department. After the public security department's investigation verified this report, the counterrevolutionaries were quickly arrested, and two shotguns were seized. The mass security defense organizations have also developed a very great role in the struggle against thieves. After a cooperative in a steel plant in the city of Pen-hsi was robbed, Wang Fu, a member of the security defense group, actively investigated, discovered a clue, and turned it over to the public security organs. As a result they quickly broke the case, and the five robbers were all caught.

## ITEM 152

[Ch'en Huai-ning, "People's Policewomen Who Closely Rely on the Masses"]

. . . . .

As soon as the public security station was established, they [the young police-women] launched a surprise attack handling of the accumulated civil and criminal cases. In the process of handling these accumulated cases they undertook deep and detailed examination and study and consulted with the masses and activists. There was a case of theft that had occurred in October 1956 which had still not been solved. After the establishment of this public security station composed of people's policewomen, the deputy station chief, Lei Te-fang, assumed responsibility for solving the unsolved case of theft that had occurred in October 1956. First of all, she called a mass meeting and related the facts of the case in great detail. She also held two informal discussion meetings in the neighborhood of the family that had suffered the theft, exhorting everyone to try to recall whether or not there were any clues among the persons with whom they had contact at that time. Later she conducted a number of individual interviews, talked with the masses, gathered together and studied all the clues which the masses had bit by bit provided, and continued to investigate on the basis of these clues. After she conducted this kind of repeated examination and study, the truth was finally brought to light.

### 2. Apprehension by Means of "Detention"

Items 153 and 154 represent typical situations in which, as a result of cooperation between the police and the security defense committees, the criminal process is initiated through the detention of suspected offenders.

### ITEM 153

[Ko I, "A Group of Counterrevolutionaries Seized Because of a Letter — About Kuan Kuan-hui, an Advanced Mass Security Worker," *Kuang-chou jih-pao* (Canton daily), Feb. 26, 1955]

Kuan Kuan-hui, Chairman of the fifth security defense committee of North Yung-han street of the North district, has always enthusiastically engaged in security work. He lives in Kuan-chia temple at Hsiao-ma station.

One morning late last November, Kuan Kuan-hui discovered a letter sent to "Yen Shih-liang" in the public letter box of Kuan-chia temple. He thought: "I've lived in Kuan-chia temple for over ten years. Of the more than one hundred families and more than three hundred people who live here, there isn't one I have not met, man or woman, young or old. But there is no 'Yen Shih-liang.' Can it be that 'Yen Shih-liang' has relatives or friends here and that this letter has been left for him by his relatives or friends? But there are no words such as 'c/o' written on the envelope." Kuan Kuan-hui felt that there was something wrong about this letter, and he decided to clear up its origin. He did not take the direct approach of opening this strange letter but waited for the person to whom the letter was sent.

One day, two days — at the end of the fourth day, all the other letters in the box had been taken, and only this letter remained unclaimed. At noon on the fifth day, suddenly a twenty-six- or twenty-seven-year-old male arrived at Kuan-chia temple. He looked in all directions and, when he thought that there was no one paying attention to him, he swiftly took the letter addressed to "Yen Shih-liang," turned, and left. But his every movement had been observed by Kuan

Kuan-hui from the start. Just when the man put the letter in his pocket and began to walk away, Kuan Kuan-hui suddenly appeared before him and said: "Brother, is that letter yours?" This self-styled "Yen Shih-liang" stood transfixed. He said he was a coal-coking worker from a city suburb who was a friend of "Chou Lin." "Chou Lin" had asked him to go there to look up another friend, and thus a letter had been sent to him there.

Kuan Kuan-hui knew that there certainly was no such person named "Chou Lin" in Kuan-chia temple and grew more suspicious than ever. He then said: "We here don't know you. If you want to take this letter, come with me to the public security station and make out a statement." That young man could not but follow Kuan Kuan-hui to the public security station. Investigation by the public security organs revealed that Yen Shih-liang was a counterrevolutionary who was fleeing from arrest in Yang-chiang county. On the basis of the criminal Yen's statement and prudent investigation, the public security organs also arrested a number of accomplices.

Kuan Kuan-hui has been chairman of the security defense committee since 1955. His vigilance is very high, and he knows how to link himself intimately with the masses. During the last year he has helped the public security organs arrest nine wanted counterrevolutionaries; he collected thirty-five copies of security materials about the "seven evils" and turned them over to the public security organs, and investigation by the public security organs proved some of these persons to be criminals. He also seized a pistol and over thirty bullets. In addition, he also roused the masses to improve the situation with respect to over forty places that represented sources of fire and fire dangers and played an active role in guaranteeing safety. Recently, Kuan Kuan-hui was chosen as an advanced mass security worker for Canton for 1958.

## ITEM 154

["The Masses Cleverly Recognize a Bandit; the People and Police Cooperate in Seizing a Criminal," *JMJP*, Feb. 25, 1959, p. 6]

One afternoon Comrade Li Feng-hsiang, a people's policeman of the Tung Ch'eng-chiao public security station of Han-tan city in Hopei province, was on duty at the station. Suddenly Li T'ung-shan, chairman of the security defense committee for the area outside of the east gate, came in to report: "There are two persons who are buying rags staying in my shop. Yesterday a man brought them a twenty-five-catty watercart chain and sold it to them. Today the same man brought in another chain over thirty catties. Both were new ones. Since quite a few sets of watercart chains were stolen a few days ago, I strongly suspect him."

After hearing this, Li Feng-hsiang immediately went with the chairman of the security defense committee to investigate. When they met the man, Li Feng-hsiang pretended to be a cadre from an iron industry commune and asked him: "Do you still have some chains? I'll buy a few." The man said: "There are no more." Old Wei, who had bought the rags, then said: "The chain that you sold me yesterday wasn't heavy enough. Let's go to the shop and weigh it." As they reached the door of the shop, the criminal may have felt that something was going to happen. He drew a pistol (a single-shot, local variety) from his waist, pointed it at Old Wei and said: "Stand still. Don't move." At that, Old Wei got very alarmed. Li Feng-hsiang, seeing that the situation was tense, rushed to grab the gun. He did not succeed, and the man fled.

When Li Feng-hsiang saw the man flee, he chased him, shouting as he ran. At that time, T'ieh Fu-lin, a member of the people's militia, heard the shouting and rushed in with a gun. Su Yü-chen, a cart-puller, used an iron shovel to bar the criminal's escape. When the criminal saw that he could not escape, he then waved his gun threateningly. This startled Comrade Feng-hsiang; but he quickly remembered that a people's policeman must protect the people from harm and that it is glorious to die in the struggle against the enemy. He ran forward a few steps, and, without waiting for the criminal to fire, he kicked him in the foot, twisted him around, and grabbed his gun. After a struggle, he finally managed to wrest the gun away. At that moment Su Yü-chen and the masses who followed them pressed forward in droves and took the criminal away.

Through interrogation they learned that this criminal was named Lu Chin-te, that he was a habitual robber left over from the old society and that he had done a lot of evil things. He had just started to go into action again when he was caught.

Lien Wen [a citizen]

### 3. Distinction between "Detention" and "Arrest"

ITEM 155

[CONSTITUTION OF THE PRC (passed at the 1st meeting of the 1st session of the NPC, Sept. 20, 1954; promulgated by the Presidium, Sept. 20, 1954), *FKHP*, 1:28]

Article 89. Freedom of the person of citizens of the People's Republic of China may not be infringed. No citizen may be arrested except by decision of a people's court or with the approval of a people's procuracy.

ITEM 156

In Items 153 and 154 did the manner in which the suspects were apprehended violate the Constitution? Does the following statute suggest the answer to the above question?

[ARREST AND DETENTION ACT OF THE PRC (passed at the 3d meeting of the Standing Committee of the NPC, Dec. 20, 1954; promulgated by the Chairman of the PRC, Dec. 20, 1954), *FKHP*, 1:239–242]

Article 1. According to the provisions of Article 89 of the Constitution of the People's Republic of China, freedom of the person of citizens of the People's Republic of China may not be infringed. No citizen may be arrested except by decision of a people's court or with the approval of a people's procuracy.

Article 2. Counterrevolutionaries and other offenders who may be sentenced to death or to imprisonment shall be arrested immediately after a decision of a people's court or approval of a people's procuracy.

If the offender to be arrested is seriously ill, pregnant, or a woman nursing her own baby, the measures of obtaining a guarantor pending trial or of residential surveillance may be used instead.

Article 3. A people's court, a people's procuracy, or a public security organ shall arrest offenders whose arrest has been decided upon by a people's court or approved by a people's procuracy.

When a public security organ requests [authority] to arrest an offender, the request shall be submitted to a people's procuracy for approval.

Article 4. When arresting an offender the arresting organ must possess a warrant from a people's court, a people's procuracy, or a public security organ, and the warrant of arrest must be read to the arrested person. After arrest, the arresting organ shall inform the members of the arrested person's family of the reason for the arrest and the place in which he is confined in custody, except in situations where this will be an obstacle to the investigation or where there is no way to give notification.

Article 5. In any one of the following situations, a public security organ may adopt emergency measures to detain immediately [without obtaining a warrant] an offender whom it is necessary to investigate:

(1) He is preparing to commit a crime, is in the process of committing a crime, or is discovered immediately after committing a crime;

(2) He is identified as a criminal by the victim or by an eyewitness;

(3) He has evidence that he has committed a crime discovered on his person or at his residence;

(4) He is planning to escape or is [in the act of] escaping;

(5) He may destroy or fabricate evidence or may collude with others regarding statements to be made [with respect to a case];

(6) His status is unclear or he has no definite residence.

Article 6. Any citizen may immediately seize the following offenders and take them to a public security organ, a people's procuracy, or a people's court to be dealt with:

(1) One who is in the process of committing a crime or is discovered immediately after committing a crime;

(2) One who is wanted for arrest;

(3) One who has escaped from prison;

(4) One who is fleeing from arrest.

Article 7. When a public security organ detains an offender, within twenty-four hours after detention it shall notify the people's procuracy of the corresponding level about the facts of and the reasons for detention; within forty-eight hours after receipt of notification, the people's procuracy shall either approve or not approve an arrest; if the people's procuracy does not approve an arrest, the public security organ shall release the detained person immediately upon receipt of notification.

If a public security organ or a people's procuracy has not handled the matter in accordance with the provisions of the previous paragraph, the detained offender or members of his family may ask the public security organ or the people's procuracy to do so.

Article 8. Officers who arrest or detain may adopt appropriate methods of coercion for an offender who resists arrest or detention, and when necessary they may use weapons.

Article 11. Organs that arrest or detain shall conduct an interrogation of an arrested or detained offender within twenty-four hours after arrest or detention; when they discover that they should not have arrested or detained a person, they must immediately release him. One whose crime is relatively minor may obtain a guarantor pending trial.

Article 13. A public security organ shall not apply the provisions of this Act to a detention that is an administrative punishment for a citizen who violates security administration rules.

## ITEM 157

The following exegesis of the above statute fails to mention SAPA detention because the SAPA was not enacted until eight months after this essay was published.

[Harbin Office of Legal Advisers No. 3, "Arrest and Detention," *Hei-lung-chiang jih-pao* (Heilungkiang daily), Feb. 23, 1957]

Arrest and detention are coercive measures used by investigation and adjudication organs for a defendant or criminal suspect in criminal litigation. The essence of the coercive measure of arrest is that it deprives the person against whom the complaint is brought of his personal freedom in order to prevent his escaping or his having an accident during the period of investigation, and it confines him in custody. Detention is the preliminary arrest of a suspect; it is an emergency measure used before his status has been made clear, before a decision (or order) to arrest him has been made, and before it is announced that he has become a defendant.

The difference between the two is that detention is used for a suspect and arrest is used for one who has been accused and who has already become a defendant. The goal of detention is to make clear in a very short period the status of a suspect and, before it is decided to arrest him, to guarantee that he can be investigated and tried. The time cannot exceed seventy-two hours (it is decided in the seventy-two hours whether to release or arrest him). But with the coercive sanction of arrest, the confinement in custody of the defendant continues from the time the defendant is investigated and tried right through to the execution of sentence. It can be applied throughout the entire litigation process. Detention is generally used by public security organs without the prior approval of the procuracy. But generally, arrest can only be used by investigators and procurators after obtaining the approval of the chief procurator. The court may also use it.

But any citizen may, on the basis of the Arrest and Detention Act of the People's Republic of China, immediately seize one who is in the process of committing a crime or is discovered immediately after a crime, one who is wanted for arrest, one who has escaped from prison, or one who is fleeing from arrest, and take him to a public security organ, a people's procuracy, or a people's court to be dealt with.

1. In Items 153 and 154, did the manner in which the suspects were apprehended violate the Arrest and Detention Act?
2. Under the Act, in what circumstances would it be unjustifiable to apprehend a suspect by means of "detention"?
3. From a practical point of view, when is it likely to be necessary to apprehend a suspect by means of an "arrest"?

### 4. Apprehension by Means of "Arrest"

## ITEM 158

[Interview]

On his return from a meeting at the county seat in the spring of 1959 the chief of the security defense committee of a commune production brigade received a secret "tip" that the secretary of the brigades' Party branch and the brigade leader were the ringleaders of a group of important brigade cadres who had surreptitiously slaughtered oxen belonging to the brigade and sold the meat for their private profit. He immediately telephoned this report to the chief of the security section of the county public security bureau. Because this was obviously an important and delicate case, the section chief went with the bureau chief to report it to, and to seek instructions from, the secretary of the county Party committee.

The Party secretary determined that it was necessary to send a work group down to the brigade to investigate the matter. Among the group that was selected were four cadres from the bureau — a deputy bureau chief, who was appointed group leader, the chief of the security section, who was made a deputy leader, one of the secretaries of the security section, and an investigator. There were also a procurator, a judge, a representative of the Party organization bureau, a representative of the Party supervision commission, who was made a deputy leader, a representative of the Party agriculture department, two cadres from the office of the county Party committee, and a cadre from the women's federation. In order to avoid arousing the suspicions of the suspects and creating a situation in which the masses might become too frightened to cooperate with the investigation, this political-legal work group was designated as a "spring plowing work group of the county Party committee," a temporary Party organization the task of which was to lead and to supervise spring plowing.

After arriving at the brigade, the members of the investigating group dispersed among the various production teams, laboring with the peasants by day and taking part in meetings at night. In the course of conducting propaganda on the needs of production at these meetings, they gradually exhorted the team members to find out why there were insufficient oxen to take care of the plowing. At first the peasants, fearing the consequences of implicating their leaders, were reluctant to give any information about the matter, but in a few days the investigators began to earn their confidence, and conversations with individual peasants enabled them slowly to piece the facts together. After almost three weeks of investigation, the group was prepared to accuse the principal culprits — the branch secretary, the brigade leader, the leader of the brigade militia, the women's chairman, and two other cadres, all of whom were Party members. The accusations were made at a meeting of the brigade Party branch. The accused admitted having ordered the slaughter of the oxen but denied having done it for profit. They claimed that the oxen had been old, sick, and unfit for work and that the whole matter had been too insignificant for them to report to the commune.

After the meeting the investigators then undertook a series of intensive private, individual talks with the accused in an attempt to "mobilize" them to confess. Care was exercised not to frighten them about the consequences of their conduct, because the investigators did not want them to commit suicide, as often happened in such situations. Leniency was promised to those who made full confessions. After a few days of "mobilization," the women's chairman finally told the entire story. Having checked her confession, the group convened another meeting of the branch, at which the women's chairman gave all the details of the offense. When the other accused heard this, they too confessed.

Following this branch meeting there was a meeting of the members of the investigating group who were most knowledgeable about the disposition of such cases: the political-legal cadres and the representative of the Party supervision commission. The representative of the Party organization bureau, who normally would be present at such a meeting, did not attend, since he was deemed to be an inexperienced newcomer. The group discussed the case and prepared recommendations with respect to the sanctions to be given to each of the culprits, who included four non-Party members: a brigade accountant who had had custody of the proceeds of the sales and three peasants who had done the actual slaughtering of the oxen. The leader and deputy leaders of the group then returned to the county seat to submit the materials in the case to the public security bureau and to report orally to a meeting of the county Party secretary, the head of the county Party secretariat, and the bureau chief, the chief procurator, and the court president.

This five-man body approved the recommendations made by the investigation work group, which were as follows: the money that had been collected from the sale of the slaughtered oxen had to be surrendered to the brigade. The secretary of the Party branch, who was the instigator of the scheme, was to be expelled from the Party and arrested. It was understood that arrest meant criminal punishment, although no decision was yet made on the length of the sentence. The brigade leader was to be expelled from the Party and removed from his brigade position. Because it was clear that he had not taken the initiative in the plot but had followed the lead of the branch secretary, he was not to be arrested but was to be given ten days of detention for violation of the SAPA. The leader of the brigade militia was to be expelled from the Party and removed from his brigade position, but he was to receive no punishment. Although her responsibility was deemed to be as great as the militia leader's and although her confession had not been spontaneous, the only sanction to be received by the women's chairman was a demerit on her Party record, because she had been the first to confess. The two other Party members had played minor roles and thus were to receive mere warnings from the Party. The accountant was to be removed from his position because he had improperly used it to safeguard the illegal proceeds. The peasants who had killed the oxen were only to receive criticism from their production teams in view of the fact that they had acted under orders. While they were not considered innocent, their responsibility was deemed to be greatly diminished.

Because the case was thought to have great educational significance, it was decided that, in addition to publicizing it in a bulletin to be circulated among all cadres in the county, disposition of the case should be announced at a forthcoming enlarged meeting of the important Party cadres of the county, commune, and brigade levels. Before the meeting took place the Party supervision commission was notified of the decisions with respect to those culprits who were Party members, and it prepared expulsion documents in the appropriate cases. Also, the commune Party secretary was informed about those who were to be removed from their brigade positions. The public security bureau's security section made out an application for an arrest warrant for the branch secretary and, after the application was approved by the bureau chief and by the procuracy, it made out the actual warrant. It also prepared a detention warrant for the brigade leader.

At the meeting the Party members who were involved in the incident were ordered to stand on the platform. They had all remained at large until that time and were ignorant of their fate. The secretary of the Party supervision commission briefly introduced the facts of the case and announced what Party sanction was meted out to each of the members involved and the reasons underlying it. Then the deputy chief of the public security bureau, who had led the investigating team, briefly stated why the branch secretary had to be arrested, and he read aloud the arrest warrant, which charged the branch secretary with undermining production. At that point a people's policeman put handcuffs on the accused and led him away to the detention house. The chief of the bureau's security section then rose to state why the brigade leader had to receive detention. After he read off the detention warrant, a people's policeman led the brigade leader away, but without the use of handcuffs.

## B. CONFINEMENT

### ITEM 159

[ACT OF THE PRC FOR REFORM THROUGH LABOR (passed at the 222d meeting of the Government Administration Council, Aug. 26, 1954; promulgated by the Government Administration Council, Sept. 7, 1954), *FLHP* 1954, pp. 33–40]

*Chapter 1. General Principles*

Article 3. Detention houses shall be established in order to hold offenders whose cases have not been adjudged . . .

Article 5. Organs of reform through labor shall put into effect strict control over all counterrevolutionary and other criminal offenders during the period that they are being held, and the organs must not be apathetic or relax their vigilance. Mistreatment and corporal punishment shall be strictly prohibited.

Article 6. Organs of reform through labor shall be led by people's public security organs, shall be supervised by people's procuratorial offices of the various levels, and, in matters relating to judicial business, shall be guided by people's courts of the various levels.

Article 7. The work of organs of reform through labor in holding and educating offenders whose cases are being investigated and adjudicated shall accord with the work of investigation and adjudication.

## Chapter 2. Organs of Reform Through Labor

### Section 1. Detention Houses

Article 8. Detention houses shall be mainly [used] for confining in custody offenders whose cases have not been adjudged . . .

Article 9. Detention houses shall be responsible for being informed about the circumstances of offenders whose cases have not been adjudged. Where the circumstances of the case are major, offenders whose cases have not been adjudged shall be kept in solitary confinement and those who are involved in the same case or in related cases shall be isolated [from one another] in order to meet the needs of investigation and adjudication organs in quickly closing the case.

Offenders whose cases have not been adjudged shall be organized to engage in appropriate labor under conditions that do not hinder investigation or adjudication.

Offenders whose cases have already been adjudged and who are being held in a detention house on behalf of another [institution] shall be kept in custody separately from those whose cases have not been adjudged . . .

Article 11. Detention houses shall be established with the central government, the province, the city, the special district and the county as units, and shall be under the jurisdiction of people's public security organs of the various levels.

Detention houses of [different] units that are located in the same place may be merged with consideration to local circumstances.

When necessary, detention houses may be established by public security subbureaus of city-administered districts in cities directly under the central authority and in provincial capitals.

Article 12. Detention houses shall each have a director, one or two deputy directors, and a number of staff members and guards.

## Chapter 5. System for Regulating Offenders

### Section 1. Commitment

Article 36. The commitment of offenders to custody shall require a written judgment, a written order for execution [of sentence], or a warrant for commitment to custody. Without the above-mentioned documents, commitment to custody shall not be permitted. If the material recorded in the above-mentioned documents is discovered to be not in conformity with the actual circumstances or is incomplete, it shall be explained or supplemented by the organ that originally sent the offender into custody.

Article 37. A health examination shall be given to offenders who are committed to custody. Except for major counterrevolutionary offenders and other offenders whose criminal acts are major, commitment to custody shall not be permitted in any one of the following situations:

(1) Mental illness or acute or malignant contagious disease;

(2) Serious illness that may endanger the life of the offender while he is being held in custody;

(3) Pregnancy or childbirth six months or less before the time of commitment.

Offenders who under the preceding items may not be committed to custody shall, after the organ that originally ordered their commitment to custody has considered the situation, be sent to a hospital, turned over to a guardian, or put in another appropriate place.

Article 38. For offenders who are committed to custody there shall be established, on the basis of the actual circumstances, multiple occupancy cells, single occupancy cells, women's cells, cells for the sick, and other such cells for holding offenders on an individual basis. There shall be female guards in places where female offenders are held.

Article 39. Female offenders shall not be permitted to bring their infants into prison with them. As for infants whom the offenders really cannot give to another for care, civil affairs departments of local state administrative organs shall entrust them to residents, orphanages, or nurseries. Necessary expenditures shall be paid out of social relief funds.

Article 40. A thorough examination shall be made of offenders who are committed to custody. Contraband articles shall be sent to the people's court for confiscation. Articles which are not of daily use shall be kept on the offenders' behalf; a receipt shall be given to them and the articles shall be returned at the time of their release. But when they have a proper use for them, the offenders may be permitted to use the articles. If materials are discovered that contribute to investigation and adjudication, they shall be sent to the organs in charge of investigation and adjudication.

Female offenders shall be examined by female guards.

Article 41. The name, sex, age, race, place of origin, address, [social] origin, occupation, cultural level, special abilities, type of crime, term of imprisonment, health circumstances, family circumstances, the people's court that determined judgment, etc., of an offender who is committed to custody shall be recorded item by item in his status identification booklet. When necessary a photograph may be glued in.

Article 46. When there is a possibility of escape, violence, or other dangerous acts on the part of offenders, upon special instructions from investigation organs or with the approval of the responsible officials of organs of reform through labor, instruments of restraint may be used. But when the above-mentioned situation is eliminated, they shall be immediately removed.

### Section 4. Receiving Visits and Correspondence

Article 56. Before receiving visits from family members, offenders whose cases have not been adjudged shall secure the approval of the organ that originally sent them into custody or of the adjudication organ.

Article 58. Mail sent and received by offenders whose cases have not been adjudged shall be examined by the organ that originally sent them into custody or by the adjudication organ, or an organ of reform through labor may be authorized to make the examination. If situations of collusion regarding the [presentation of] circumstances of a case or of hindering education and reform are discovered, it [the mail involved] shall be held back.

Article 59. In special circumstances an offender's receipt of visits and receipt of articles sent by family members and the sending and receipt of mail, etc., may all be further limited or stopped

### Section 5. Obtaining a Guarantor

Article 60. When an offender is in any one of the following situations, he may be permitted to obtain a guarantor and serve his sentence outside of prison, but this must first be reviewed and approved by the people's public security organ in charge, and the people's public security organ at the place in which the offender is located must be notified to place him under supervision. The period that the offender is outside of prison [during his term of imprisonment] is counted as within his term of imprisonment.

(1) Except for an offender whose crime is heinous, one who is seriously ill and for whom it is necessary to obtain a guarantor and seek medical treatment outside of prison;

(2) One who is fifty-five years of age or more or is physically disabled, whose term of imprisonment is five years or less and who has lost the capacity to endanger society.

The provisions of Paragraph 1 above also apply to offenders whose cases have not been adjudged, but the matter must first be submitted for the approval of the organ that sent them into custody, and the people's public security organ at their place of residence must be notified to place them under supervision.

## C. INTERROGATION BY POLICE

### ITEM 160

This item describes a process of interrogation that lasted for ten months beginning in the summer of 1953. It thus took place in the period just prior to the enactment of the Constitution, the Law for the Organization of People's Procuracies, the Law for the Organization of People's Courts, and the Act for Reform Through Labor in September 1954, and the Arrest and Detention Act in December 1954. The provisions of that body of legislation should be viewed against the background of the practices described below.

[Deposition of Father André Bonnichon (former Dean of the Faculty of Law of the Catholic University Aurore at Shanghai) before the Committee on Criminal Law of the International Congress of Jurists (Athens, Greece), in André Bonnichon, *Law in Communist China* (The Hague, 1956), pp. 24, 26–32]

[O]n June 15th, 1953, at half past ten in the evening, the police invaded the little house where I was living. After having closed in on me in my room, they showed me the warrant of arrest.

For there was a warrant of arrest issued in my name. It was drafted in Chinese and was very brief. It was composed as follows: "Bonnichon", then my name in Chinese, "imperialist element, arrested for anti-revolutionary activity". I was immediately placed in prison where I had to remain for ten months . . .

For 19 days, I waited for my first interrogation. I was then introduced into one of the rooms of the prison known as the "tribunal". It was a small room in which I found myself before a military judge [interrogator] in uniform, his name visible on a small piece of white cloth on the left side of the chest, as typical of Chinese armies, communist or otherwise. He was accompanied by a clerk and an interpreter.

He asked me first if I wished the service of an interpreter. I replied that I did. It is true that I speak Chinese, but the differences between dialects are too great, so much so that one is never certain to speak the same dialect as the judge or, more particularly, to understand him. And then, I must confess that I preferred to assure myself the slowness of pace afforded by the intermediary of an interpreter. Subsequently, with only one exception, I was always questioned in the presence of an interpreter.

The judge spoke to me at great length and, in my opinion, his discourse is of capital importance if one wishes to understand penal procedure such as it is practised in China. Moreover, as with all prisoners, foreigners and Chinese alike, it was repeated to me over and over again. I expected to be accused of specific acts: I would have denied or confessed, or would have explained myself according to the circumstances. But such was not the case.

The judge said to me: *"If you have been arrested, it is not without reason, for the government acts always in the right.* It has observed your anti-revolutionary activity for a long time. It has gathered the witnesses and the accusations necessary. *It is, therefore, certain that you are guilty.* Two paths lie open to you: either you confess your crimes, whereupon the government will be able to act with extreme clemency toward you, because, although judges previously had to pass sentence in accordance with the former procedure based on the code, we are now able to act with clemency. *Or, on the other hand, you refuse to confess, thus resisting the government, in which case the severest of punishments awaits you."*

I naturally declared my innocence and asked of what crime I was accused. I received the characteristic reply: "you are not to ask questions. You are to accuse yourself." And this statement subsequently became the basis and the tenor of all the procedure to which I was subjected . . .

One day, the judge, indicating a thick package of papers, said to me: "I have a pile of accusations **against you as high** as that." I asked who my accusers were. He then replied: "*You do not have to know them.* You must simply confess."

Naturally, I adopted the only position possible, that of speaking the truth. At all times, I replied in the same form, that I had not broken the laws of the people's government, and that I had not opposed the government, which was true.

I was questioned for approximately a month, once every two days, sometimes more often. I must have gone through 25 interrogations in all, each of about three hours' duration. Only once did the judge order me to remain standing; on all other occasions I was permitted to sit. Unlike a good many others, I was not subjected to wilfully exhausting interrogations . . .

On one occasion, the judge accused me of having said in class at the University that China was not a semi-colony. I said, as a matter of fact, that, during the period which saw China as a member of the League of Nations, she could not be considered as a semi-colony but, on the contrary, as a sovereign state. I specified that it was a technical question of no political significance. The judge then retorted: "But this term has been employed by our President Mao-Tse-tung". I expressed regret at having contradicted the President who must have used the term in an oratorical and quasi-political sense during a public address. And I added that I would not change my opinion on the subject. Finally, they passed on to other matters.

On another occasion, the judge accused me of having listened to American radio broadcasts. I could have replied as an Occidental would have, that this had never been prohibited, for there was no regulation forbidding the population to listen to the Voice of America. I took great care not to make this reply and said that I had not listened to the Voice of America because I had no radio. The judge, feeling he had committed an "error", recovered himself by saying: "The government knows very well that you have no radio, because it knows all. But it is quite possible that you may have listened to American broadcasts in the home of a French or Chinese friend."

After a certain time, I felt that, in the face of my denials and my refusal to confess "my crimes", the interrogations of the judge were beginning to exhaust themselves. I had been subjected to a few bursts of anger on his part, but there were also moments in which he revealed a certain amiability. At such moments, he would say to me: "Be reasonable, the government is concerned only with your well-being. Confess. You are the only one who has not done so because all the other priests have already made confessions. *Don't force the government to punish you.*" This last statement is unquestionably a true pearl of humour!

The reproaches made against me were always vague. I was reproached for being an imperialist, a foreign agent, but never for a single specific act. The principle of the procedure is, as a matter of fact, that the accused must remain ignorant of the accusation aimed at him. The same applied as to the identity of his accuser. Thus, after having changed prisons, and judges as well, I said to my second judge, during an interrogation, that I was aware of the fact that certain of my former students had made accusations against me. He was very much taken aback and asked: "How do you know that some of the accusations come from your former students?" I replied frankly that the first judge had told me so. There was then a significant exchange of glances between the judge and the clerk which clearly showed that the first judge had committed a "technical" error. For he never should have told me that the accusations, the contents of which he had never revealed to me, came from my former students . . . *You do not know who accuses you, you do not know of what you are accused, you must simply accuse yourself* . . .

I come now to the question of prison life. In my first prison, I shared a cell with four other prisoners. There was no maltreatment, but life was hard: we were obliged to remain in a squatting position on the ground along the wall during the entire day, that is, 16 hours out of 24. During 8 hours only were we able to stretch ourselves out on the ground to sleep. The rest of the time, we were not allowed to doze, nor to speak, and the squatting position without budging was sheer agony, especially in mid-summer because there was very little air or light in the cell. During my stay in prison, there were only three twenty-minute periods of interruption during which we could move about in the cell which was very small.

Later, I was moved to another prison where I was placed in a cell of fifteen. Here, as in the previous one, there were no beds, chairs or tables. We were still obliged to sleep on the ground and pass the entire day in silence in a squatting position along the wall.

Every evening, the prisoners were obliged to discuss, in small groups for a period of two and one-half hours, the policy of the government, and especially, matters which concerned us directly, that is, the obligation to denounce ourselves. We were supposed to urge one another mutually to be frank with the government. And I must say that all my prison mates, who were prisoners such as myself, accused of the only existing political crime — anti-revolution — spoke as true and sincere communist servants. Indeed, they had been told that the only way of getting out of prison was by reforming their ways of thinking . . . I, myself, went through approximately three hundred of these sessions during which prisoners praised the regime, expressed satisfaction at having been placed in prison because it afforded them — or so they said — an opportunity to reform their ways of thinking. They declared themselves ready to do anything the government might ask of them, including forced labour.

I was the only one to reply sincerely to the questions posed. During the first few days, my replies created such astonishment that one of my co-prisoners asked me if I were communist or no. When I answered in the negative, there was a moment of sheer stupor, because *to say in a Chinese communist prison that you are not communist is to defy the government.* And similarly, you defy the government in declaring that you are not guilty.

·     ·     ·     ·     ·

My prison mates were submitted to the same procedure as I, that is, they were invited to confess. Most of them did confess and, asking for paper and pen, squatted along the wall and wrote down their confession. However, I have seen them remain in prison afterwards for six, eight, and ten months, having to reaffirm their confessions under the pretext that they were not sincere.

We were also supposed to accuse other persons, such accusations being considered as proof of sincerity. For this purpose, there were, in prisons, printed forms of denunciation which could be obtained by asking the guard at the wicket-gate. On the right-hand side of the form, you place the name of the person whom you wish to accuse, his address and the nature of the accusation. On the reverse side, there is space for developing in greater detail the accusation. Here, of course, we are still concerned with political accusations and with the offence of anti-revolutionary tendencies. I have seen my prison mates fill dozens and dozens of these forms.

The same forms are also used during periods of "thought reform" to which, one day or another, entire schools, hospitals, factories, entire branches of industries are submitted. They were the official forms for denunciation.

In our case, it is difficult to say whether we came under a jurisdiction concerning instruction or a jurisdiction in which judgment was to be passed. Nothing is known about this political procedure which exists absolutely without any text. The judge who questioned me, a young man of 23 years dressed in military uniform, might have resembled what we call an examining magistrate. Among my prison mates, there reigned the conviction that, to be sentenced, you were placed in another prison where there sat a tribunal which condemned you to death or to forced labor.

Father Bonnichon's vivid description is of more than historical interest. Except for the facts that military officials subsequently came to play a less prominent role in the administration of criminal justice and that in many areas small group discussions among persons awaiting trial ceased to take place, it accurately portrays the techniques of a process of interrogation that continued to be employed throughout the period covered by this study.

## ITEMS 161A–161B

These items record more recent accounts by those who, prior to their departure from mainland China, were subjected to criminal investigation.

## ITEM 161A

[Interview]

In the autumn of 1956, Chang was a student in Peking University's department of journalism. He had a strong desire to go abroad to study and to see the outside world. Not being a Party or Youth League member, he felt that he had no chance to visit other "socialist" countries. He thought that it might be possible to obtain permission to study in certain of the "capitalist countries" such as Sweden or India if an opportunity presented itself. Since he knew of no organization that could aid him in this ambition, like a number of his classmates, he wrote letters to the embassies of Sweden and India inquiring about prospects. He received what he deemed to be encouraging responses from them. But before negotiations could go very far, the department of journalism called a meeting of all its students at which the chairman of the department denounced such "activity." He named no names and urged all students who had "abused their freedom" by expressing an interest in study in capitalist countries to "hand over their hearts" after the meeting. Those who did, he said, would have no difficulties.

Although he knew that some students had followed the chairman's advice, Chang did nothing. A few weeks later a staff member of the university's Party committee summoned him and asked him why he had had no "activity" to report. Chang made excuses and protested the innocence of his interest in studying abroad. He was severely scolded and was told that the best way to go abroad was to become very "active" and "heighten his awareness" and thereby become eligible to go to the Soviet Union.

One of Chang's friends at Peking University was a young official of the embassy of a nonaligned country who took courses in Chinese on a part-time basis. Despite the criticism that he previously received because of his foreign contacts, Chang, along with six or seven other students, continued to go to parties at the official's quarters in the embassy compound. About six weeks after being criticized by the Party committee, Chang was called to the office of his department and told to report to the public security subbureau for a talk.

In a small room at the subbureau he was questioned by a plainclothes detective with no one else present. The interrogator sat behind a desk, and Chang sat on the other side of the desk. "Do you know why you are here?" the interrogator began.

Chang professed ignorance of any misconduct.

The interrogator became angry and accused Chang of dishonesty. "Why were you called before the university Party committee?" he demanded.

Chang explained the innocence of his interest in going abroad to study.

The interrogator then asked, "What did you do last Saturday evening?"

"I went dancing," Chang replied.

"There's no harm in that, certainly," the interrogator remarked, "but where did you go dancing?"

"At the Embassy," Chang admitted.

"Then why do you say you do not know why you are here? We know everything you've done. We've been following you for over a month."

"Then why do you ask me to tell you?"

"Because we want to see whether you are being honest. If people are honest, big things can become little things, but if they are not, little things can become big ones."

With the "help" of his interrogator Chang went over every detail concerning his visits to the embassy compound. The interrogator then persisted in asking him what other contacts he had with foreigners and which plot he was involved in. Chang insisted that he had given the entire story. "You'd better stay here awhile and think it over," the interrogator concluded. With that he asked Chang to sign a statement that summarized his answers and then ordered a guard to take him off to the subbureau detention house, which was located in another building.

There he was placed in a small cell with over thirty others. He was warned not to utter a word while in the cell, and, since the other inmates were under similar orders, silence prevailed. Apart from leaving the cell in a group to use the toilet several times a day and to go to their individual interrogations, the inmates remained in the cell at all times. Their only activity was to study documents connected with their "reform" that were posted on one wall of the cell. These admonished them to confess freely and fully and thereby to obtain lenient treatment and move ahead with their becoming "new persons." There were no meetings or discussions, nor were the inmates asked to write anything while in the cell. Chang witnessed no brutality in the cell except that anyone who failed to keep his head bowed while outside the cell would usually be hit in the head with the butt of a gun.

Chang remained in the cell for almost two months. During this period he was taken out for interrogation approximately fifteen times. His interrogator was always the man who had first questioned him, although occasionally another man would also be present and ask supplementary questions. The questioning covered not only Chang's activities but also those of his friends. Chang repeatedly denied any undisclosed activities, and he claimed to know little of his friends' conduct. This "resistance" often provoked the interrogator, who sometimes cursed him, struck the desk with his hand or took his pistol out of its holster and put it on the table. Sometimes the interrogator would stand over him and threaten him with harsh imprisonment unless he confessed everything. He told Chang that his companions had already made a clean breast of things. Chang occasionally cried uncontrollably. The interrogator never struck him, nor did he ever order him to be handcuffed or put in leg irons, although Chang estimated that perhaps 25 percent of those in detention at the time were being subjected to one or both of these restraints. One day, while waiting in the hall for the interrogator to finish questioning another suspect, he heard them shouting at each other concerning the suspect's defiant refusal to confess counterrevolutionary conduct. The interrogator ordered a guard to put handcuffs and leg irons on the suspect. That night the inmates heard shots from what they took to be a firing squad, and there was whispered speculation that the presumed victim might have been the defiant suspect. Through these interrogations Chang persisted in repeating essentially the same story that he had told at the outset.

Finally, after another of what had by then become standard interrogation sessions, Chang was instructed to remain in the room to write out two documents. The first was to discuss his life history, his misconduct, and the effect that his detention experiences had had upon him. The second was to be a "guarantee" that he would not repeat his misconduct. After reading these documents the interrogator told Chang that for the moment he could go home and renew his university study. He warned Chang, however, that no conclusion had yet been reached in his case and that he would subsequently be summoned to return to the public security subbureau. Chang said that he would not try to run away, agreeing with the interrogator that such an attempt would be fruitless and lead to more serious consequences. Chang was given a document that stated that he had been in detention for the period in question and had been lawfully released.

Upon his return to the university he did not resume his foreign contacts and was never recalled to the public security subbureau. A few of his companions were released in similar circumstances within one to four months of their detention, while several others went to rehabilitation through labor and had not yet been released prior to his departure from Peking in the fall of 1962.

## ITEM 161B

[Interview]

Chu was a young economist who prior to liberation had served briefly with the Nationalist [KMT] government, and had been active in the KMT Youth Corps. In 1950, after three months of political "training," he was employed by the state bank in Canton. During the movement to suppress counterrevolution in 1951, he was sent along with many other cadres for six months of "thought reform" at Nanfang University. He later returned to his post with the bank. But in April 1953, he was sent off with a group of others who had "political problems" for what was to be six months of further "study," this time at a "new life school." Actually he was held for two years in that institution while his "problem was being resolved." Upon his release, although he was no longer a cadre, Chu considered himself lucky not to have been sentenced to control or to imprisonment as many of his "classmates" had been. He and a few friends started a small private factory, but within a few months it was converted into a "state-private jointly operated enterprise." Chu then left this enterprise and applied for a license to start another similar one. After his application was denied, he managed to start such an enterprise by resorting to the unused license of a friend, who became nominal head of the firm. In October 1957 the Canton city government closed this firm down on the grounds that it had been illegally organized and that Chu had failed to accept socialization of industry. He was required to pay a large fine.

In February 1958, Chu was arrested at his home. The arrest warrant charged that he was a "historical counterrevolutionary." He was interrogated on only three occasions during his first three months in the public security bureau's detention house. Otherwise he remained in a very crowded cell where he had to take part in rather desultory "study" and criticism meetings. At the end of the third month his interrogator told him that the investigation had concluded and that the bureau had decided to prosecute him for violation of the state's economic laws by refusing to accept socialist reform. Chu was permitted to look at a copy of the bill of prosecution and was asked whether he agreed with its charge. He confessed to this charge, as he had during previous interrogations, and signed the bill of prosecution. When the interrogator asked him what sentence he wished, Chu said that he hoped for a light sentence that would permit him to return quickly to serve the state-private jointly operated enterprise that he had previously abandoned. The interrogator replied that he would ask the head of the enterprise whether this might be feasible. The next day another interrogator questioned him about what sentence he would like, and Chu gave the same answer.

Chu remained in detention for five more months after this. During that time he decided that it would be wise "voluntarily" to turn over to the state some rights that he held to an invention. Finally one day he was notified by the bureau that the people's court had sentenced him to two years of control and that he would be released immediately. He was instructed to go to the bureau the next day for his certificate of release and, when notified that it was ready, to pick up the judgment in his case at the court. The judgment stated that Chu had fifteen days in which to appeal, but he had no interest in doing so. [For details of Chu's control, recall Item 113.]

1. Do the material suggest that a suspect or accused has a right to keep silent?
2. Does he have a right to see or otherwise to maintain contact with family, friends, or counsel?
3. Is the distinction between detention and arrest relevant for these purposes?

### D. IMPLEMENTATION OF PROTECTIONS AGAINST PROLONGED PRETRIAL CONFINEMENT

1. What guarantees against prolonged pretrial confinement does the Arrest and Detention Act (Item 156) provide for:
    a. "Detained" persons such as Chang (Item 161A)?
    b. "Arrested" persons such as Chu (Item 161B)? Does the PRC appear to have any rule similar to the following provision of the RSFSR Code of Criminal Procedure?

"Article 97. *Periods of confinement under guard.* Confinement under guard in connection with the investigation of a case may not continue for more than two months. Only by reason of the special complexity of the case may this period be prolonged up to three months from the day of confinement under guard by a procurator of an autonomous republic, territory, region, autonomous region, or national area, or by a military procurator of a military region or fleet, or up to six months by the RSFSR Procurator or the Chief Military Procurator. Further prolongation of a period of confinement under guard may be carried out only in exceptional instances by the USSR Procurator General for a period of not more than an additional three months." [3]

2. What opportunities does the Arrest and Detention Act provide the police to evade the Act's restrictions upon their power to subject persons to prolonged pretrial confinement?
3. Does the following provision of the Act for Reform Through Labor ease the plight of detained or arrested persons?

"Article 42. When investigation or adjudication has not yet been concluded and the commitment to custody of an offender whose case has not been adjudged

3. Berman and Spindler, *Soviet Criminal Law and Procedure,* p. 288.

already exceeds the legally prescribed limit, the detention house shall promptly notify the organ that sent the offender into custody to deal with the case quickly." [4]

To what might "the legally prescribed limit" refer?

Article 11 of the Act for Reform Through Labor states that "Detention houses . . . shall be under the jurisdiction of the people's public security organs of the various levels." [5] The "organ that sent the offender into custody" is usually the public security organ. How much weight is notification by the detention house likely to carry with the public security organ?

### 1. Complaint by Confined Person

The person confined can, of course, complain to the detention house authorities and to his interrogators. He can also attempt to communicate with higher levels of the police and with the procuracy, the court, and other agencies. The Constitution of the PRC has the following provision.

### ITEM 162

[CONSTITUTION OF THE PRC (Sept. 20, 1954), p. 29]

Article 97. Citizens of the People's Republic of China shall have the right to present written or oral complaints to state organs of the various levels with respect to any violation of law or dereliction of duty by personnel of state organs.

Are such complaints likely to improve the confined person's lot?

### ITEM 163

The following criticism was voiced during the "blooming and contending" in the spring of 1957.

[Roderick MacFarquhar, ed., *The Hundred Flowers Campaign and the Chinese Intellectuals* (London, 1960), p. 229]

.    .    .    .    .

*Handling of Complaints*

PEKING: *Chiu San Society*                                          June 5

Chu Tsung-jang [Ministry of Health] thinks that to pass back people's letters of complaint to the organisations complained about is not the correct way to deal with such matters, because the persons who wrote the letters are bound to be retaliated against by the organisations concerned which are bedevilled by bureaucracy and sectarianism.

Recall Item 95.

4. *FLHP* (1954), p. 38.
5. *FLHP* (1954), p. 34.

## 2. General Supervision by Procuracy

If the suspect is not able to take the initiative in protecting himself against prolonged police confinement, can he look to the intervention of outside agencies? In the Soviet Union, because of its power to exercise general supervision over the legality of administrative actions, the procuracy has become known as the "watchman" or "guardian of legality." Consider, for example, the commentary in Berman, *Justice in the U.S.S.R.*:

"The procurator also is supposed to supervise the legality and correctness of actions of the state security organs as well as of the Republican Ministries of Protection of Social Order (the former Ministries of Internal Affairs), the police, the organs of criminal investigation, and the corrective labor institutions . . .

"The function of the Procuracy in supervising the legality of administrative (as contrasted with judicial) acts is, potentially at least, its most important aspect, for here the work of the Procuracy bears upon the adherence of the Soviet bureaucracy to standards of justice laid down in the Soviet Constitution and Soviet laws . . .

"It should also be stressed that in practice the Procuracy was totally ineffective in supervising the multitude of illegal acts of the top Soviet leadership under Stalin. These acts were committed to the jurisdiction of the Ministry of Internal Affairs (or Ministry of State Security), which had its own Procuracy. The post-Stalin regime has emphasized the control of the Procuracy of the U.S.S.R. over the state security agencies, and has reduced the powers of these agencies. Also, through a 1955 statute on Procuracy Supervision in the U.S.S.R., the first comprehensive statute defining the rights and duties of the Procuracy as an agency of supervision of administrative and judicial legality in Soviet history, the duty of Procuracy supervision over places of detention of criminals has been re-emphasized, and procurators have been made "liable" for the observance of legality in those places. It is very doubtful, however, that the Procuracy could exert more than a moral influence against a return to a policy of terror at the highest level." [6]

Items 164 and 165 introduce the Chinese procuracy and the notion of general supervision that is embodied in published legal documents. Item 166 indicates what has happened to general supervision in practice in the PRC.

### ITEM 164

[CONSTITUTION OF THE PRC (Sept. 20, 1954), pp. 26–27]

Article 81. The Supreme People's Procuracy of the People's Republic of China shall exercise procuratorial authority over the various departments belonging to the State Council, local state organs of the various levels, personnel of state organs, and citizens to see whether they observe the law. Local people's procuracies of the various levels and special people's procuracies shall exercise procuratorial authority to the extent prescribed by law.

6. Pp. 238–239, 245, 246.

Local people's procuracies of the various levels and special people's procuracies shall conduct their work under the leadership of higher level people's procuracies and they shall all conduct their work under the unifying leadership of the Supreme People's Procuracy.

Article 82. The term of office of the Chief Procurator of the Supreme People's Procuracy shall be four years.

The organization of people's procuracies shall be prescribed by law.

Article 83. Local people's procuracies of the various levels shall exercise their powers independently, and they shall not be subject to interference by local state organs.

Article 84. The Supreme People's Procuracy shall be responsible to and also shall report its work to the National People's Congress; during periods when the National People's Congress is not in session, it shall be responsible to and also shall report its work to the Standing Committee of the National People's Congress.

## ITEM 165

[LAW OF THE PRC FOR THE ORGANIZATION OF PEOPLE'S PROCURACIES [7] (passed at the 1st meeting of the 1st session of the NPC, Sept. 21, 1954; promulgated by the Chairman of the PRC, Sept. 28, 1954), *FKHP*, 1:133–138]

*Chapter 1. General Principles*

Article 1. The People's Republic of China shall establish the Supreme People's Procuracy, local people's procuracies of the various levels, and special people's procuracies.

Local people's procuracies of the various levels shall be divided into people's procuracies of provinces, autonomous regions, cities directly under the central authority, autonomous *chou,* counties, cities, and autonomous counties. People's procuracies of provinces, autonomous regions, and cities directly under the central authority may establish subprocuracies in accordance with their needs. People's procuracies of cities directly under the central authority and of districted cities may establish people's procuracies for city-administered districts in accordance with their needs.

The organization of special people's procuracies shall be [covered] by provisions separately issued by the Standing Committee of the National People's Congress.

Article 2. People's procuracies of the various levels shall each have a chief procurator, a number of deputy chief procurators, and a number of procurators.

Chief procurators of people's procuracies of the various levels shall lead the work of people's procuracies.

People's procuracies of the various levels shall each establish procuratorial

7. For purposes here, the parts translated have been reordered in the following manner: Chapter 1, Articles 1–2; Chapter 3, Articles 20–21; Chapter 1, Articles 6–7, 3–4; Chapter 2, Articles 8–9.

committees. Under the leadership of chief procurators, procuratorial committees shall deal with important questions relating to procuratorial work.

## Chapter 3. Appointment and Removal of Officers of People's Procuracies

Article 20. The Chief Procurator of the Supreme People's Procuracy shall be elected by the National People's Congress for a term of office of four years.

Deputy Chief Procurators of the Supreme People's Procuracy shall be appointed and removed by the Standing Committee of the National People's Congress.

Procurators of the Supreme People's Procuracy and members of its procuratorial committee shall be proposed by the Chief Procurator of the Supreme People's Procuracy for appointment and removal by the Standing Committee of the National People's Congress.

Article 21. The appointment and removal of chief procurators, deputy chief procurators, procurators, and members of procuratorial committees of people's procuracies of provinces, autonomous regions, and cities directly under the central authority shall be recommended by the Supreme People's Procuracy to the Standing Committee of the National People's Congress for approval. The appointment and removal of chief procurators, deputy chief procurators, procurators, and members of procuratorial committees of subprocuracies of provinces, autonomous regions, and cities directly under the central authority and of people's procuracies of counties, cities, autonomous *chou,* autonomous counties, and city-administered districts shall be recommended by people's procuracies of provinces, autonomous regions, and cities directly under the central authority to the Supreme People's Procuracy for approval.

## Chapter 1. General Principles

Article 6. Local people's procuracies of the various levels shall exercise their powers independently, and they shall not be subject to interference by local state organs.

Local people's procuracies of the various levels and special people's procuracies shall conduct their work under the leadership of higher level people's procuracies, and they shall all conduct their work under the unifying leadership of the Supreme People's Procuracy.

Article 7. The Supreme People's Procuracy shall be responsible to and also shall report its work to the National People's Congress; during periods when the National People's Congress is not in session, it shall be responsible to and also shall report its work to the Standing Committee of the National People's Congress.

Article 3. The Supreme People's Procuracy shall exercise procuratorial authority over the various departments belonging to the State Council, local state organs of the various levels, personnel of state organs, and citizens to see whether they observe the law.

Article 4. Local people's procuracies of the various levels shall exercise the following powers in accordance with procedure prescribed in Chapter 2 of this Law:

(1) To put into effect supervision with respect to whether or not resolutions, orders, and measures of local state organs are legal and whether or not personnel of state organs and citizens observe the law;

(2) To conduct investigations of and to initiate and support prosecution of criminal cases;

(3) To put into effect supervision with respect to whether or not the investigatory activities of investigation organs are legal . . .

*Chapter 2. Procedure for the Exercise of Powers by People's Procuracies*

Article 8. When the Supreme People's Procuracy discovers unlawful resolutions, orders, and measures of departments of the State Council or of local state organs of the various levels it shall have the power to protest.

When local people's procuracies of the various levels discover unlawful resolutions, orders, and measures of state organs of corresponding levels, they shall have the power to request correction. If the request is not accepted, they shall report to people's procuracies of the next higher level [in order for the latter] to protest to [state] organs of the next higher level [than those initially involved]. When local people's procuracies of the various levels discover unlawful resolutions, orders, and measures of departments of the State Council or of local state organs of higher levels, they shall report to people's procuracies of higher levels [in order for the latter] to deal with the matter.

People's procuracies shall not have the power directly to annul or change unlawful resolutions, orders, and measures or to suspend their execution.

The state organs concerned must be responsible for dealing with and answering requests and protests of people's procuracies.

Article 9. When people's procuracies discover that unlawful acts have been committed by personnel of state organs, they shall notify those organs to correct the situation. If the unlawful acts constitute crimes, people's procuracies shall pursue the offenders for criminal responsibility.

## ITEM 166

[T'an Cheng-wen, "Absorb Experience and Teaching, Impel a Great Leap Forward in Procuratorial Work," *CFYC*, 3:34–37 (1958)]

*On the Problem of Dogmatism*

Under the leadership of the Party Central Committee and the Party committees of the various [other] levels, our procuratorial work has had very great accomplishments and has accumulated considerable experience during the various great revolutionary movements. This is basic and central, and it is also the thing that is in the dominant position and the main current. But because of a lack of experience in our work and because our level of Marxism-Leninism is not high, some comrades have been particularly confused in their emphasis and, with mistaken concepts of a one-sided and extreme nature, have paid relatively more attention to the Soviet Union's experience and have paid relatively little attention to combining our country's concrete circumstances and characteristics with a summary of their own actual work experience. Thus many comrades have consciously or unconsciously committed errors of dogmatism to differing degrees. Some comrades have been intimidated by dogmatists and have lost their direction on some problems; there are even some comrades who, for a certain period and on some problems, have been captured by the dogmatists. Naturally, the number of persons who engage in serious dogmatism is extremely small, to the point of being only a few individuals. But this phenomenon really is rather widespread, and the form of its manifestation is also serious. In ideological method a special characteristic of dogmatism is subjectivism and in work demeanor it is separation from reality and from the masses. The concrete manifestations in our procuratorial work can be mainly generalized [as follows]:

1. In studying the advanced experience of the Soviet Union. Naturally, we definitely study the Soviet Union's advanced experience, and this is unshakeable. But the problem is how to study it. And there is also a problem of what kind of method and attitude to adopt in studying it . . .

2. In adopting rules and systems for procuratorial work they [the dogmatists] are unable to conduct thorough examination and study, summarize experience, and start out from the needs of the struggle against the enemy on the basis of Party guidelines and policies, but rather they "build their wagon behind closed doors" [are impractical]; revere their [Soviet] textbooks as "classics," swallow [the contents] without chewing and apply them in their original form; and make a set of trivial procedures. For example, with respect to some experimental measures and investigating procedures that we have adopted, we cannot say that some of them are completely useless, but most of them are copied from books. There are only a very few provisions that have really been adopted by combining our actual work and by summarizing the actual experiences of the past. Especially in investigation procedure they [the dogmatists] repeatedly and indiscriminately applied things from two small books, "An Investigation Handbook" and "The Leadership and Supervision of Investigation." In this way "higher levels mechanically transmit, and lower levels mechanically apply." This situation existed in both investigation supervision and adjudication supervision. The result is that our hands and feet are bound to such an extent that the activism of the masses in the struggle against the enemy is injured. It is even of less use to speak of the set of procedures for general supervision. The dogmatists will not look at or do not have confidence in the experiences of the struggle of the masses but only look at and have confidence in textbooks. There are even individual comrades who, except for listening to the words of books, will not listen to anyone, to the extent that they question the instructions of the Party and the instructions of responsible comrades in the Central Committee. We think that this kind of "only believe books" demeanor has become so serious that even the words of the Party are not heeded. The dogmatists only believe in book learning;

they apply some legal provisions and "strut around and use these to intimidate people." The result is to increase their separation from politics, their separation from reality, their separation from the masses, their separation from the present actual struggle, etc., and this really has been seriously injurious to others . . .

The bourgeois rightists hidden within the procuratorial organs planted the banner of studying the experience of the Soviet Union and falsely made use of "vertical leadership" and "general supervision" to oppose Party leadership over procuratorial work. They say that "the procuratorial organs are judicial organs, are only responsible to the law, should not be responsible to the Party, and that the procuracy cannot be the yes-man of the Party committee"; their insolence is such that they want to supervise and put themselves above the Party committee. The rightists also plant the sign of constructing a well-ordered legal system. They distort the correct working relations of division of labor and responsibilities and mutual restraints that the procuratorial organs have with related departments, unlawfully transform the procuratorial organs' functions of investigation supervision and adjudication supervision, specially investigate "unlawful acts" of the public security and judicial organs in the struggle against the enemy, and bind the hands and feet of the public security and procuratorial organs. Particularly, it is the debate over the work of general supervision that has become the focal point of the two-road struggle in the work of the procuracy. According to the Law for the Organization of [People's] Procuracies, the procuracy has the power of general supervision; but actually this is a weapon that is held in preparation only for use upon discovery that state organs and personnel have resisted the leadership or that serious unlawful acts have occurred. But at present our country is unprecedentedly unified. The various levels of state organs and personnel actively support and observe the Constitution and the laws. Therefore, we do not want general supervision to be the regular work of the procuracy and be universally developed. When, under certain circumstances we want to exercise the function of general supervision, the work must be conducted on the basis of the Party's instructions. But the rightists nevertheless exaggerate the unlawfulness of the state cadres. They advocate putting "supreme supervision" and "supervision of supervision" into effect over state organs and cadres, and they try to change this weapon into an instrument by means of which the bourgeois rightists can attack state organs and cadres. In summary, in order to open up the road to the restoration of capitalism, and through [attacking] the procuratorial organs, to attempt to make a crack in the political-legal front, they unlawfully attempt to transform the dictatorial function of the procuratorial organs and direct the point of the struggle against the state organs and the people.

1. Do the Constitution and the Law for the Organization of People's Procuracies contemplate a Soviet-style system of general supervision?

2. How do the Chinese and Soviet systems of general supervision seem to compare in practice?

3. What factors might account for the differences?

### 3. Inspection by Legislators

Can the confined person rely on other institutions or practices to stimulate the police either to release him or to deliver him for trial? Items 167–169 suggest another possibility.

## ITEM 167

[CONSTITUTION OF THE PRC (Sept. 20, 1954), pp. 12, 15–16]

Article 27. The National People's Congress shall exercise the following powers:
(3) To supervise enforcement of the Constitution . . .

Article 35. The National People's Congress, or its Standing Committee during periods when the National People's Congress is not in session, may, when it considers it necessary, organize committees to investigate specific questions.

All state organs, people's organizations, and citizens concerned shall be obliged to supply necessary material to these committees when they conduct investigations.

Article 36. Deputies of the National People's Congress shall have the right to present questions to the State Council, or to the various ministries and committees of the State Council, and the questioned organ must assume responsibility for answering.

## ITEM 168

[LAW OF THE PRC FOR THE ORGANIZATION OF LOCAL PEOPLE'S CONGRESSES AND LOCAL PEOPLE'S COUNCILS OF THE VARIOUS LEVELS (passed at the 1st meeting of the 1st session of the NPC, Sept. 21, 1954; promulgated by the Chairman of the PRC, Sept. 28, 1954), *FKHP*, 1:143]

Article 17. When local people's congresses hold meetings, questions presented by the deputies to people's councils of corresponding levels or to work departments of people's councils of corresponding levels shall be forwarded by the presidium to the questioned organ. The questioned organ must assume responsibility for answering during the meeting.

## ITEM 169

[DECISION OF THE STANDING COMMITTEE OF THE NPC OF THE PRC RELATING TO INSPECTION OF WORK BY DEPUTIES OF THE NPC AND DEPUTIES OF PEOPLE'S CONGRESSES OF PROVINCES, AUTONOMOUS REGIONS AND CITIES DIRECTLY UNDER THE CENTRAL AUTHORITY (passed at the 20th meeting of the Standing Committee of the NPC, Aug. 6, 1955), *FKHP*, 2:66–67]

1. In order to understand work conditions in all places, to make more intimate the links with the masses and attentively to listen to the opinions and requests of the masses, deputies of the National People's Congress and deputies of people's congresses of provinces, autonomous regions, and cities directly under the central authority shall generally inspect work twice each year. The suitable times of inspection shall generally be after spring plowing and after autumn

harvest. It is permissible for deputies who are advanced in years or physically weak or who really cannot leave their work posts not to go out on inspection or to inspect in places near which they live.

2. . . . . Deputies may conduct inspection of work in groups or separately.

3. When inspecting work, deputies . . . may go to the relevant personnel of local people's councils, people's courts, and people's procuracies to understand conditions; they may attend meetings of local people's congresses and of local people's councils; and they may receive visits from local people's deputies and interview the masses of people.

4. When they arrive at the district to be inspected, deputies . . . may contact the local people's council and obtain its assistance. People's councils in the various places and other relevant departments shall facilitate the deputies' inspection of work.

5. When inspecting work, deputies shall not deal with problems directly; problems that are discovered shall be turned over to local people's councils, people's courts, or people's procuracies for them to deal with. When necessary, deputies of the National People's Congress may report by letter problems that they discover to the Standing Committee for it to deal with, and deputies of people's congresses of provinces, autonomous regions, and cities directly under the central authority may report by letter problems that they discover to the people's council of their province, autonomous region, or city directly under the central authority for it to deal with.

As stated in Part I, although deputies of the people's congresses at various levels do make occasional inspections of detention facilities and, among other things, do inquire into the length of time that confined persons have been awaiting disposition of their cases, the police receive ample advance notice of such visits and have little difficulty in shielding from view those cases that involve unduly prolonged confinement.

### 4. Review by Ad Hoc Committee

## ITEM 170

Item 170 describes one instance of a practice that has occasionally provided relief against prolonged pretrial confinement.

[Interview]

In response to widespread discontent over excesses in the criminal process that took place during the 1955–1956 movement to liquidate counterrevolution, and earlier movements, committees composed of representatives of the police, procuracy, and courts were secretly established in at least some areas in late 1956 to review the disposition of certain categories of cases of political crimes. One of these categories concerned confined persons whose cases had not yet been concluded despite the passage of considerable time.

After reviewing cases in this category, one such committee, which in a certain county of a southern province was called the evaluation committee, recommended that some of the confined persons be released and the charges dropped for lack of evidence and that the prosecutions of others proceed to conclusion.

These recommendations were followed by the county's political-legal organs [see Chapter XI for a detailed description of the procedures of this evaluation committee]. This evaluation committee left only one case unresolved. It involved a man named Li who had been arrested sometime prior to 1955 on a charge of being a historical counterrevolutionary. Li admitted that in another province prior to liberation he had served as the chief of a military affairs section in the provincial government, but claimed that he had only done what he was told and had acted under the coercion of superior orders. Repeated investigation had failed to uncover reliable evidence concerning Li's activities, because the relevant witnesses could no longer be located. Because of the lack of solid evidence other than Li's limited confession, the public security force was reluctant to terminate its investigation and to bring the case to trial. Yet it was also reluctant to release him, since it did not want to be responsible for failing to punish a fairly important historical counterrevolutionary. The evaluation committee succumbed to the same dilemma. Li was known still to be awaiting trial in early 1961.

## E. SEARCH AND SEIZURE

### ITEM 171

[CONSTITUTION OF THE PRC (Sept. 20, 1954), p. 28]

Article 90. The homes of citizens of the People's Republic of China shall be inviolable, and privacy of correspondence shall be protected by law.

### ITEM 172

[ARREST AND DETENTION ACT OF THE PRC (Dec. 20, 1954), p. 241]

Article 9. In order to find evidence of a crime, when arresting or detaining an offender, the arresting or detaining organ may search his person, his possessions, his residence, or other relevant places; if it believes that another person concerned may be harboring an offender or concealing evidence of the crime, it may also search his person, his possessions, his residence, or other relevant places. At the time of the search, except in emergency situations, they [those who search] shall have a search warrant from the arresting or detaining organ.

A neighbor or another witness and the person searched or a member of his family shall be present at the time of the search. After the search a written record shall be made of the evidence of a crime that was searched for and taken into custody, and a neighbor or another witness, the person searched or a member of his family, and the officers executing the search shall sign their names to it. If the person searched or the members of his family have escaped or refuse to sign their names, this shall be noted on the record.

Article 10. When the arresting or detaining organ considers it necessary to take into custody mail or telegrams of an offender who has been arrested or detained, it may notify the postal and telecommunications organs to do so.

1. Does either Article 9 or Article 10 of the Arrest and Detention Act violate Article 90 of the Constitution?

2. Does the Act authorize an arresting officer to search an arrested person without a search warrant?

3. In Items 153 and 154, if the police had wanted to search the detained suspect's residence, would a search warrant have been required?

4. Recall Item 73C, especially the third paragraph. Although the requirement is frequently ignored, the approval of a people's court or a people's procuracy is necessary for a valid arrest. Does a similar requirement apply to the issuance of a search warrant?

## ITEM 173

The following essay suggests that questions such as the above are not merely academic. This essay was published in response to a letter to the editor written by a bus passenger who inquired whether, in the circumstances related, it was lawful for the police to search him and his fellow passengers without a search warrant.

["Is It Right for the Public Security Organ To Do This?" *Hsin-hua jih-pao* (New China daily, Nanking), Oct. 28, 1956]

Editor's note: With respect to the question raised in Comrade Yü Ch'en's letter, we have referred it to Comrade Chung Yu for a reply. We believe that in addition to the value of studying the question raised in Comrade Yü Ch'en's letter, there are two other points which are worth our serious attention. First, he is full of political enthusiasm and is able actively to supervise public security organs. We hope that all our readers can be as active as he in supervising state organs and in helping them ceaselessly to overcome their shortcomings and to do their work even better. Second, by treating the newspaper as his own bosom friend, he is able courageously to raise a question which in his own thoughts is not clear and to study it with comrades in the editorial department. We heartily welcome our readers to study questions with us as intimately as Comrade Yü Ch'en has done, and we are willing to do our utmost to help our readers in resolving the various ideological problems of life in society.

*My View    Chung Yu*

The editorial department has referred Comrade Yü Ch'en's letter to me and has told me to reply publicly to the question. After receiving the letter I immediately visited the people's procuracy and the public security bureau of the city of Nanking and the preparation committee of the lawyer's association of Kiangsu province, and I studied the question with the comrades concerned. I also investigated the events. Now I will discuss my own view.

### A Question of Principle Worth Studying

The central question raised by Comrade Yü Ch'en is: In an emergency situation, by directly conducting a search of the person without having [first] obtained the approval of the people's procuracy, is the public security organ infringing rights of the person? As I understand it, when the matter occurred, of the more than fifty passengers on the bus, some supported the search by the public security organ, and some indicated dissatisfaction with it. Was it correct, ultimately, for the public security organ to have done this? What attitude should a citizen who meets a special situation like this adopt? This is a question of principle which is really worth our study.

Before replying to this question, I believe that it is necessary to discuss the events in detail.

## The Events in Detail

The person who lost the money, Wang Chung-lin, boarded the bus at the Hsin-chieh-k'ou stop. As the bus passed the stop at Ch'ang-chiang street he bought a ticket, and after buying the ticket he put the remaining forty-three yuan in his pants' pocket. As the bus approached the stop at Chu-chiang street, he discovered that the money which he had just put in his pocket had been stolen. Since the conductor did not see a people's traffic policeman, the bus drove to the stop at Ku-lou before finding a people's traffic policeman, to whom a report was made. When the public security officers arrived, the conductor and the driver of the bus and the person who lost the money reported three basic circumstances as follows: (1) the money was definitely stolen between the stop at Ch'ang-chiang street and the stop at Chu-chiang street, (2) the three passengers who got off the bus at the stop at Chu-chiang street had been a great distance from the person who lost the money and could not be suspected, (3) a stolen bill had the address and the name of a friend written on it by Wang Chung-lin himself. The public security officers, after analyzing and examining these circumstances, adopted emergency measures in accordance with law and, dividing the passengers into groups, searched them. Many passengers who had their identification cards were allowed to go after a brief look at the cards. When the search of the fourth group began, a passenger who was wearing a blue Sun Yat-sen suit suddenly began to yell anxiously: "This is not right. You should not search us; it infringes rights of the person and violates the Constitution." Following this some other passengers also began to yell. After the public security officers gave them all an explanation and continued their search, the person who was wearing the blue Sun Yat-sen suit withdrew to the rear and tried to evade the search. A search revealed that he had the money. That person was named Li Cheng-fang (alias Ts'ui Ching-hsüan) and was a habitual thief. He had been stealing on transportation lines for more than ten years. The public security organ detained him at the scene in accordance with law and returned the illegally obtained money to the person who lost it. The people at the scene praised the public security organ highly for being able to solve the case so promptly and were angry about the habitual thief's rousing the masses to resist the search.

### The Search Was Advantageous to the People and Disadvantageous to the Habitual Thief

It can be seen from the events that when this theft case suddenly occurred on the bus, if the public security officers who immediately reached the scene had not promptly adopted emergency measures and conducted the necessary search, not only could the illegally obtained money not have been promptly returned, but, after escaping, the habitual thief inevitably would have continued to endanger the security of society. Thus, to oppose the search by the public security organ under these special circumstances was to fall into the trap set by the habitual thief, Li Cheng-fang. Obviously, it is necessary and correct for a cadre of a state organ or for an ordinary citizen to support a search and prompt solving of a case by the public security organ in this special situation. Some persons have written letters saying that the public security organ should not search many passengers to protect the interests of one person who lost money. This is not a correct view. How can the number of people whose interests were endangered by the habitual thief, Li Cheng-fang, in the past ten years be limited to just a few more than fifty! If he had not been promptly arrested, he would have endangered the interests of how many more people! Thus, the public security organ did this not only to protect the individual interests of the person who lost the money, but also to protect the interests of the entire society.

### In an Emergency Situation the Public Security Organ May Adopt Emergency Measures

From the point of view of the matter itself, the method adopted by the public security organ started from the interests of the entire society. From the point of view of the law, there was not the slightest infringement of the people's democratic rights. The Arrest and Detention Act of the People's Republic of China prescribes that, in special emergency situations, a public security organ may adopt emergency measures. Article 5 of this Act prescribes that a public security organ may detain immediately [without obtaining a warrant] a person in any one of six situations, for example, when "[h]e has evidence that he has committed a crime discovered on his person or at his residence" or "[h]is status is unclear or he has no definite residence." On the basis of the provisions of Article 9 of this Act, a public security organ may in accordance with law decide to conduct a search. Such a search certainly does not require the approval of a procuratorial organ (it is not the same as arrest). The same article also prescribes that the public security organ, "[a]t the time of the search, except in emergency situations . . . shall have a search warrant from the arresting or detaining organ." That is to say, in emergency situations, public security officers cannot delay the conduct of their work on the ground that there is no way of obtaining in a given time a search warrant from the arresting or detaining organ. It is very likely that if emergency measures were not adopted in emergency situations, criminals would get away or a change in the scene [of the crime] would increase the difficulty of solving cases. Thus, in these extremely few and special situations, although the actions of some persons may be temporarily restricted, it [search without warrant] should not be considered an infringement of the freedom of the person or of the people's democratic rights. A search of the person conducted directly by the public security organ in an emergency situation, without having [first] obtained the approval of the people's procuracy, is a lawful and expedient measure. It should be actively supported.

Here it is necessary to explain emphatically that although it is necessary and correct for public security personnel to adopt such emergency measures in such emergency situations, it was unlawful for them to let the person who lost the money search some of the passengers (according to our understanding, there was a slight discrepancy between the facts and Comrade Yü Ch'en's mention of the public security officers' "want[-ing] the youth who had lost the money to search each passenger"). The public security organ has the authority to adopt emergency measures, but the person who lost the money certainly does not have the authority. According to what the public security personnel who handled this matter said, they let the person who lost the money search some of the passengers because they feared the possibility that if they did not find anything, they would disappoint the person who lost the money. This demonstrates that it is necessary for the average cadres and the masses, as well as public security officers, to establish a clear view of the law. Furthermore, inasmuch as the public security officers did not give good enough explanations while performing their task, I suggest that in the future the public security organ pay attention to improving.

## ITEM 174

[Interview]

A county public security bureau received several confidential reports in 1956 that Ch'en, a resident of an outlying administrative village, had a pistol hidden in his house. Since unauthorized private possession of guns was prohibited and since Ch'en had been a policeman under the Nationalist government, the bureau treated these reports seriously. Agents of the bureau questioned Ch'en on several occasions, but he always denied having any weapons. Yet the reports persisted. The bureau chief finally decided to approve a search warrant for a search of Ch'en's home and persuaded the chief procurator to approve the issuance of a blank arrest warrant, it being understood that Ch'en's name would be filled in and Ch'en arrested if a gun was discovered as a result of the search.

Two policemen then took the warrants and set off for Ch'en's administrative village. Upon arrival they checked in with the chairman of the local security defense committee and went with him and a neighbor to Ch'en's house. There they knocked on the door, announced their presence, and, when Ch'en appeared at the door, read off the search warrant. Because they were searching for a gun and wanted to avoid suspicion, the policemen then gave their own pistols to the SDC chairman to hold. They ordered Ch'en to remain outside the house with the SDC chairman and proceeded to search the entire house thoroughly in the company of the neighbor. But no gun was found.

After consulting with the SDC chairman, the policemen decided that the gun was probably being kept at the home of Ch'en's close friend, Pao. They had no search warrant for Pao's house and feared that by the time they went back to the bureau, got one and returned to the village Pao would have had ample time to dispose of the weapon. They, therefore, telephoned to the bureau, informed the security section of the predicament and suggested that they immediately search Pao's house while the bureau prepared and sent out a search warrant. When this course was approved, they went to Pao's house, announced that an emergency search had to take place, and, with the same precautions as had been taken at Ch'en's house, searched the premises. Within a few minutes a pistol was found. Pao was immediately detained on the grounds of unauthorized possession of firearms and concealing evidence of a crime at his residence.

Before leaving the premises the policemen made out two copies of a statement which asserted that at the time and place in question they had conducted a search and had seized a pistol. They read this statement to Pao and to the neighbor who had been in attendance and asked each whether this was accurate and, if so, to sign their names to it, which they did. One copy of the statement was left with Pao's family, and Pao was taken back to the bureau by two local militiamen. The policemen then returned to Ch'en's house, filled in the arrest warrant, and arrested him. Shortly thereafter, the search warrant for Pao's house arrived and was presented to the SDC chairman, who in turn gave it to Pao's family.

Because Ch'en had steadfastly refused to admit possessing the pistol and because of his history, he was sentenced to three years of imprisonment for unauthorized possession of arms. Pao, on the other hand, who had no history and had been merely helping a friend, was only given ten days of detention under the SAPA.

1. Was the search of Pao's house legal?
2. Was his detention legal?
3. Was Ch'en's arrest legal?
4. Who decides such questions and what might be the consequences of a finding of illegality?

## F. EVALUATION OF EVIDENCE BY POLICE

Items 175–180 indicate the types of evidence that may be used and the methods of analysis and the standards which the police, and also the procuracy and the courts, are admonished to apply in determining whether the evidence is sufficient to warrant conviction of crime. Item 180 attempts to articulate how conviction standards differ from the standards that the police are supposed to apply when deciding whether (a) to detain or (b) to arrest a suspect.

## ITEM 175

[Chang Tzu-p'ei,[8] "Several Problems Relating to the Use of Evidence To Determine the Facts of a Case in Criminal Litigation," *CFYC*, 4:13–15 (1962)]

### 4. Emphasize Evidence, Do Not Be Gullible with Respect to the Statement of the Defendant

Chairman Mao has said: "We should firmly forbid corporal punishment of any offender, and we should emphasize evidence and not be gullible with respect to the statement of the defendant." [9] This is an important guiding principle for our use of evidence and our determination of the facts of a case. Particularly, it reveals the correct attitude and policy for treating the defendant's statement.

The statement of the defendant (offender), the testimony of witnesses, the conclusions of experts, real evidence, documentary evidence, etc., all are evidentiary material for the determination of the facts of a case. But the characteristics of the defendant's statement and the question of whether or not it can be treated correctly often constitute the key problems in determining whether the adjudication of a case will be correct or erroneous.

In order to make correct use of the statement of the defendant in the determination of the facts of a case, we must first analyze the characteristics of his statement. Generally, the defendant's is the oral or written statement that the defendant makes to a public security organ, a procuracy, or a court. Its contents should include [statements made at the time of] voluntary surrender, confessions, admissions of guilt, and denunciations of others, as well as requests, clarifications, rebuttal evidence, and doubts which pertain to his denial of guilt. The statement has two fundamental characteristics:

First, the probability that the defendant will intentionally make a false statement is relatively great. The defendant is the person whose interest in the outcome of the case is greatest. After his conviction punishment will be imposed on him. Because of his personal interest in the outcome, he will attempt to avoid the punishment that he should receive and often will deny or minimize his guilt and make false statements. There are also some who make false statements admitting their guilt, and there are even some who make maliciously false accusations against good people in order to conceal the crimes of joint offenders, conceal their followers, and conceal the criminal activity that they themselves continue to conduct; it is also possible that there are some who, due to external influences, falsely state the facts of the crime, etc. With other evidentiary material it is not the same. It is possible for all evidentiary material

---

8. The author reportedly is of peasant origin and served with the Communist guerrilla forces during the Anti-Japanese War. After "liberation" he served as chief of a public security bureau and was subsequently assigned to supervise ideological education of cadres at Peking's Political-Legal College, where he pursued his own studies in criminal law and evidence under the guidance of Soviet experts. He has since become a faculty member of the institution.

9. "On Policy," in *Selected Works of Mao Tse-tung*, II (Peking, 1952), 764.

to have this or that kind of error, but other evidentiary material does not [come from sources that] have a direct interest in the outcome of the case and, even if in some cases some witnesses have an interest in the outcome of the case, they do not have so close a connection to the case as the defendant. At the same time, the awareness of the masses of people in our country is increasing daily. The great majority of people certainly would not give false evidence because of an interest [in the case]. Besides, giving false evidence is an unlawful act. Therefore, there is a greater possibility of intentional falsification in the statement of the defendant than there is in other evidentiary material.

Second, the defendant knows better than anyone else whether he committed the crime of which he is accused and how he committed it. Therefore, his statement is also intimately linked to clearing up the facts of the case. Often, the lack of certain evidentiary material does not actually affect the normal conduct of investigation and adjudication. But it frequently is not possible to think of clarifying the facts of the case without listening to the defendant's statement. Investigators, procurators, and adjudication officers cannot but study the statement of every criminal defendant; in order to pinpoint the circumstances, to adopt measures, and to clarify the facts of the case, they need to know what the defendant has said about the case, what concrete reflections he has of the crime of which he has been accused. In a situation where the defendant has not been found, it generally is not possible to proceed with prosecution and adjudication, and sometimes such a situation can cause a temporary suspension of the investigation.

According to the characteristics of the defendant's statement, our guiding thought and principle should be: firmly prohibit corporal punishment of the defendant, oppose belief in coerced statements, emphasize evidence, and not be gullible with respect to the defendant's statement. Statements [of defendants] and [other] evidentiary materials must all be checked. Therefore, we should have a correct attitude in treating such statements.

First, the probative role of statements of defendants must be analyzed and cannot be overestimated. Whether the statements admit or deny guilt, for all kinds of reasons the probability of falsity is relatively great. Therefore, we cannot adopt an attitude of blind gullibility. If we are gullible with respect to statements in which defendants deny guilt, it is easy to indulge criminals; if we are gullible with respect to statements in which defendants admit guilt, it is easy to create erroneously decided cases and cases the judgments of which are unjust, and it is easy to be lax about [the real] criminals. Actually, situations of gullibility with respect to statements that deny guilt are relatively few, while situations of gullibility about statements that admit guilt are relatively numerous.

·    ·    ·    ·    ·

But we cannot because of this go to the other extreme and adopt an absolutely negative attitude toward the defendant's statement. Whether the statement admits or denies guilt, it plays a significant role in clarifying the facts of a case during the process of investigation, prosecution, and adjudication. First of all, the role of statements made at the time of voluntary surrender and statements of confession and of admission of guilt mainly consists of: (1) helping to study and determine the scope of investigation and to collect evidence relating to the crime; (2) possibly revealing new facts of the crime and new criminals who have not yet been discovered and enlarging clues for investigation; (3) helping to verify other evidentiary materials in order to be even more certain about the facts of the case and to arrive at a conclusion for handling it; and (4) helping to judge and to determine the degree to which the defendant has repented and reformed. Naturally, we must heighten our vigilance, not limit ourselves to the statement [of the defendant], and not relax the work of making a comprehensive examination and study. Furthermore, even statements that deny guilt have a role, which lies mainly in: (1) establishing a contrary view to stimulate investigators, procurators, and adjudication officers, to examine and study the material more comprehensively, and to avoid subjective biases; (2) helping to discover defects in investigation, prosecution, and adjudication and to prevent erroneously decided cases or errors in the determination of a part of the evidence or facts of the case; (3) after the falsity of the statement has been verified, further strengthening the certainty that there is evidence of guilt and determining the facts in the case; and (4) helping to understand the attitude of the defendant toward repentance and reform. Therefore, the work of questioning a defendant is very important.

To summarize what has been said above, we may come to the following conclusions:

First, we should strictly prohibit corporal punishment of a defendant and must oppose belief in coerced statements;

Second, we cannot always be absolutely negative about arguments and rebuttal evidence that deny the defendant's guilt; we should listen to them, study them, and make necessary checks;

Third, we should not convict the defendant of a crime if we do not obtain other accurate and thorough evidentiary material but only rely on a statement admitting guilt;

Fourth, after obtaining accurate and thorough evidence, we may convict and punish the defendant even if he refuses to admit his guilt. But we must be careful. When the defendant firmly denies his guilt or recants, we must check it repeatedly to see whether it corresponds to the facts;

Fifth, when contradictions occur between the statement of the defendant and other evidentiary material and these create doubts about the reliability of the evidentiary material, or when the evidence is insufficient, we must not be in a hurry to force a positive or negative conclusion.

Actually, this is not only true of the statement of the defendant. All other evidentiary material must be checked before it can serve as the basis for handling the case.

According to the author of Item 175:

1. Can the defendant be convicted on the basis of his confession alone without any corroborating evidence?

2. How much corroboration is necessary?

## ITEM 176

The account below of a conversation with his cellmates by an American who was convicted of counterrevolutionary espionage in China suggests that admonitions such as those quoted in Item 175 have some relation to actual practice.

[Allyn and Adele Rickett, *Prisoners of Liberation* (New York, 1957), pp. 149–151]

· · · · ·

Finally, driven to a point of angry desperation, I exploded, "Well, I don't see why I couldn't have had a lawyer."

Immediately shouts came flying from all sides. What did I want a lawyer for? What had I to defend? Was I or was I not a spy?

"The only reason you want a lawyer," broke in Liao, "is so you can avoid having to pay for your crimes. That's the way it is in a capitalist society. If a man has money he can hire a lawyer to get him out of almost anything, while the poor man goes to jail. And what's more, if this were the old China you wouldn't even have had to hire a lawyer. All you'd have had to do was call your Consulate friends and they'd have had you out in no time."

I was silent. How could I answer such an attack? What they said might be true, but to my mind it was irrelevant. According to our traditions, whether a man was guilty or not he had a right to a lawyer.

As if to answer this unexpressed thought, Liao went on, "If you had committed an ordinary crime and this were a civil court, you would have a right to a lawyer and organized defense. But you're forgetting that we're not only living through a revolution here at home. There is also a war going on in Korea. You have been guilty of counterrevolutionary espionage. That puts your case under martial law and before a military tribunal a person has little in the way of normal legal rights.

Academically speaking, I could see his point. A revolution by its very nature is the antithesis of formal legality. It is a social explosion which takes place when one part of society rises up and forcibly asserts its will over its former ruler. To disagree with such a situation is like disagreeing with the universe. However, when it was a matter of my own life being involved, academic logic seemed cold and barren, and I could find little satisfaction in it.

"Incidentally," spoke up Ma suddenly, "since you seem to have so much resentment about not having a lawyer, what about it? Was your confession true or not?"

"I vehemently denied that there was any question about the veracity of my confession. Heaven knows the government had been painstaking enough in searching for the truth during those endless hours of intensive questioning. Every point had been gone over and over, yet the investigating judge [interrogator] had never tried to put words in my mouth. In fact, once when I had tried to accept the blame for an affair in which I had been involved but for which I had not actually been responsible, he had reprimanded me for not taking my confession seriously enough and had crossed that part out of my statement.

My quick response to Ma's question seemed to satisfy him, for the moment at least, but he had no way of knowing what was seething in my mind. Actually what I objected to but did not dare put into words was the very idea of having to make a confession. To me this was a violation of basic civil rights, without which there could be no safeguard for justice. Supposing I had not been guilty but had been arrested on the basis of false evidence? If I had refused to confess, what would have happened? I would have run the risk of being shot. Under the pressure of knowing this a person might very well decide to play safe and confess to something he had not done, in the hopes of pleasing the authorities.

This same point has often been raised by people we have met since our return home. Actually, as I came to realize later on, the court did not determine a person's guilt on the basis of his confession alone. It had to be substantiated by extensive outside evidence. Furthermore, his case was reviewed once a year until final sentence was passed, and even then every prisoner had the right to appeal.

Especially from the latter part of 1952, the government seemed to become increasingly aware of the danger of false confessions. Not only was every confession checked and rechecked for corroboration of the facts, but, in order to avoid undue pressure, prisoners were no longer allowed to "help" each other with their confessions or even discuss the details of their cases in the cell. The use of handcuffs and leg irons as punishment for those people who refused to confess to what the government felt it had substantial proof of was also greatly reduced. Prisoners were frequently encouraged to think over their cases and make any rectifications which would bring their statements more in line with the facts, and it was stressed that any deviation from the facts, whether by way of exaggeration or concealment, was equally dishonest.

It became clear to me that the confession itself served not so much to verify a prisoner's guilt as to give him a chance to make his first step toward reform. That is one of the reasons why the authorities were so careful to see that it adhered strictly to the facts, for only if the prisoner made a really accurate confession could he begin to appreciate what he had done. If he admitted to something he had not done, then, to excuse his reluctance to reform, he would certainly use the rationalization that he was being treated unjustly.

My four years' experience in prison led me to the conclusion that, in spite of the tense internal situation which led to counterrevolutionary and espionage cases being handled by military courts — with the resulting restrictions on normal legal rights — the Chinese government sincerely attempted to see that justice was done. Injustices certainly occurred, as has been admitted by the government itself, but as the internal situation has improved many of the more severe restrictions have been done away with, and at the recent meeting of the National Congress in the summer of 1956 the Chief Justice of the Chinese Supreme Court asserted that the treatment of counterrevolutionary cases was being further liberalized.

## ITEM 177

[Ho Shuang-lu, "Several Problems Relating to Evidence in Criminal Litigation," *CFYC*, 2:32–33 (1963)]

. . . . .

1. The testimony of witnesses is one kind of evidence that is often used in litigation. Almost every case has some. There is true testimony of witnesses, and there is false testimony. When using testimony we must be clear about this; otherwise, the correctness of the determination of the facts of the case will be affected. An important way of judging the truthfulness of the testimony of a witness is to explore the source of that testimony. The extent to which testimony is [considered] true should not be the same for something that the witness directly saw, for something he heard from another person, and for common gossip. The witness's age, cultural level, ideological awareness, memory, powers of discernment, and other concrete factors also affect the truthfulness of the testimony. For example, because their understanding of the problem is not clear or their memory is mistaken or they rely on impressions, some witnesses unintentionally give testimony that does not conform to the facts. Whether a witness has an interest in the disposition of the case or in one of the parties frequently affects the truth of the testimony. For example, in a case involving the spreading of poison, the defendant admitted spreading the poison. The poison had been stolen from a witness, but the witness persistently refused to admit that the poison had been stolen from him because he feared being held responsible [for possession of poison]. From this it can be seen that we can only believe testimony [of a witness] if we can definitely verify it and check it against testimony [of other witnesses], against other evidence, and against the defendant's statement.

In actual work, testimony of a companion in the commission of a crime and testimony of the victim are used relatively often. These two kinds of testimony come from personal experience and things personally seen. Generally speaking, such testimony is relatively concrete and can directly prove the facts of the case, but whether it proves or disproves the defendant's crime, we cannot be blindly gullible when using it. We should note that some testimony of companions in the commission of a crime is based on [self-]interest; they give false testimony in order to reduce their own criminal responsibility, to shift responsibility for the crime to another defendant, or, together with another defendant, to conceal the crime. In addition, because some victims hate the defendant, they make inaccurate statements in order to increase his criminal responsibility. Although this type of evidence looks very powerful and can directly and concretely explain problems, we usually must depend upon other evidence for determination.

2. The statement of the defendant is one kind of evidence . . .

3. Real evidence is also a kind of evidence that we frequently encounter and use in adjudication. Real evidence includes any weapon, used to commit a deadly

act, bloody clothes, poison, articles left behind after a crime, illegally obtained money, etc. Real evidence has great significance in exposing crime and in proving whether or not a crime was committed. In dealing with real evidence we first must take a look at its source — whether it was obtained at the scene of the crime, found during a search, or handed over. Different sources differ in reliability. Whether the real evidence that is obtained is linked to the facts of a case and can in truth play a probative role is the key to examining the genuineness of real evidence. Ignoring this point and simply being satisfied with obtaining real evidence will result in treating those articles which are unrelated to the facts of the case as evidence and in ignoring the collection of genuine and reliable evidence, to the point of affecting the correct use of evidence in making a determination about the case. This is something that we have been taught by experience in adjudication practice.

4. Documentary evidence is a kind of real evidence and is regularly met in the form of letters, posters, account books, contracts, etc. It plays a very great role in proving guilt. As for cases of some hidden counterrevolutionaries' writing reactionary posters or sending reactionary letters, the defendant's letters, his diary, and other such documentary evidence can further clear up the motive and purpose of the crime. As for crimes of speculation and corruption in which the thieves forge negotiable instruments, alter itemized accounts, carve official seals without authorization, forge certificates, etc., these documents all can serve as the basis for proving guilt.

When using documentary evidence we must pay attention to combining it with the actor's motive, purpose, and other relevant evidence in a comprehensive analysis and determination. At the same time we also must rely on expert scientific opinion. For example, some reactionary letters are written to oppose our people's democratic regime, while some are written to give vent to personal anger and to harm others. These two kinds of letters are very different in nature. Other examples are expert accounting opinion on account books and negotiable instruments in a corruption case, and expert opinion on the handwriting in reactionary posters and reactionary letters in a counterrevolutionary case. With expert scientific opinion we can prove guilt even more accurately and reliably.

5. Expert opinion material. In practice we regularly encounter expert opinion on handwriting, blood types, fingerprints, footprints, traces left behind (scrape marks, tire marks, etc.), accounting, and technology, etc. Expert opinion is an important weapon in the investigation process, and especially now, with science increasingly developing, expert opinion has an important role in exposing crime and in determining [the identity of] the criminal. Under ordinary circumstances expert scientific opinion is reliable. Therefore, it is wrong only to believe one's own investigation and not to believe expert scientific and technological opinion. But the source of the expert opinion material, the level of the technician, and the technical equipment will usually affect the quality of the expert opinion. Therefore, we cannot blindly believe expert opinion material and let expert opinion serve as the only basis for the adjudication of cases so that a correct determination of the case completely turns on the correctness of the expert opinion. This would improperly substitute expert opinion for the active role

of the judge and would ignore the role of the mass line. It would seriously endanger the correct handling of the case and would obviously be erroneous. We need to have a correct and truth-seeking scientific attitude in treating expert opinion. Even though it be expert scientific opinion, we should examine it in detail to see whether it is consistent with other evidence and whether there are contradictions, and we must believe it only after detailed examination reveals no errors.

6. The record of an on-the-spot examination is a kind of evidence in written form that accurately and comprehensively reflects the objective circumstances at the time a crime was committed. It has very great significance for analyzing the facts of the case, for exposing the crime, and for determining [the identity of] the criminal. The circumstances that it reflects are generally the circumstances at the scene of the crime. When the testimony of witnesses, the statement of the defendant, and other real evidence are used for verification of the on-the-spot examination of the scene of the crime, the facts that have been determined are generally [found to be] genuine and reliable. In some cases the problems are difficult to see from the statement and the testimony, but going through an on-the-spot examination of the scene [of the crime] reveals the contradictions, and going through detailed examination and study of it resolves the contradictions and avoids having an erroneously decided case. But in some on-the-spot examinations of the scenes of crime, because of limitations in professional level, technical level, and other such conditions or because of one-sided knowledge, some of the material from these on-the-spot examinations which should be there is not there or the material is [from the outset] incomplete or inaccurate, etc. Consequently, this makes investigation and adjudication work difficult when it should not be, even to the point of creating situations in which cases are difficult to solve. The scene of the crime exists objectively, but after time passes and conditions change, it is very possible that it will lose its objective, genuine nature, and then it can only serve as a reference for analyzing and studying the case and cannot be used as evidence. Therefore, in conducting an on-the-spot examination of the scene of the crime, we must be objective and prompt.

ITEM 178

[Chang Tzu-p'ei, "Several Problems Relating to the Use of Evidence To Determine the Facts of a Case in Criminal Litigation" (1962), pp. 15–17]

.        .        .        .

5. *All Evidentiary Material Should Be Checked* . . . [*The reasons for this are:*]

First, the intentional giving of false evidentiary material.

.        .        .        .        .

Second, the errors produced by subjective mistakes and mistakes in work. This kind of situation is relatively complex. Put simply it is that:
Because of subjective mistakes, even well-intentioned witnesses may give

erroneous testimony. For example, because of the limitations imposed by a witness's age, occupation, or level of knowledge or because his sight or hearing is not strong or because he was excited at the time and his power of attention was insufficient, etc., his observations of the event can lead to misapprehension. It is possible that because the witness's memory is not strong, he remembers incorrectly; or because the elapsed time is too long, his recollection is erroneous. It is also possible that the witness is upset at the time he is interrogated and omits important circumstances of the case or that he has certain fears and does not reveal all of the facts, etc.

In most situations the conclusions of experts are correct. But it is also possible for errors to occur because the material on which the expert opinion is based is insufficient or unreliable, the level of specialized knowledge which the expert has on the questions he must answer is insufficient, the technical equipment used by the expert has defects, or the methods he used are improper, the expert's carelessness, at the time he makes his evaluation, leads to negligence, etc.

It is also difficult for investigators, procurators, and judges to avoid making this or that kind of error collecting, keeping, studying, and evaluating the various kinds of evidentiary material.

Third, the influence of external and natural conditions can also create errors in evidentiary material. For example, natural conditions at the time the witness observed an event can affect the correctness of his testimony. Whether the witness is far away or near, whether it is day or night, cloudy or clear, rainy or foggy, and the size, appearance, color, and smell of the object in question all will affect the witness's observation. Material traces at the scene of the crime also can undergo natural changes due to wind, rain, sunlight, etc., and real evidence that is collected can change in nature and form if it is not kept properly.

From this it can be seen that it is very important for the various kinds of evidentiary material to be conscientiously checked. How should the material be checked? This requires differential treatment according to the different circumstances of the different evidentiary material. That is to say, we should make concrete analyses and checks by combining the concept of Marxist-Leninist dialectical materialism with the characteristics of the various kinds of evidentiary material. The methods that are frequently adopted are:

First, make an analysis that synthesizes and compares all the evidentiary material and the objective circumstances relating to a case, and then expose and eliminate contradictions. Absolutely avoid fearing contradictions and concealing them. Examine whether there are contradictions between the evidentiary material and the facts of the case; whether there are contradictions among the statement of the defendant, the testimony of witnesses, the real evidence, the documentary evidence and the conclusions of experts; and whether there are contradictions between testimony of witnesses, between statements of joint offenders, and between [different items of] real evidence, etc. Upon discovery of contradictions, there should be further examination and checking of evidence. It cannot be carelessly done and easily dropped. This is the most fundamental method of examining evidentiary material.

### 6. The Use of Direct Evidence and Indirect Evidence

Evidence is divided into direct evidence and indirect evidence. The actual significance of this is something that is worth study. But I also think that there is a definite significance in studying the use of this classification to resolve the probative relations between the evidence and the facts of the case — how facts that serve as evidence prove the facts of a case.

Direct evidence is evidence that directly verifies the facts of a case, while indirect evidence cannot independently and directly verify the facts of a case. This classification is based on the probative relationship of the evidence to the facts of a case. The facts of a case refer to all problems in the case that need to be clarified. The problems that need to be clarified in all concrete cases are not completely the same. What usually needs to be clarified is: whether a crime occurred and what kind of crime; [the identity of] the criminal and his origin, history, previous behavior, and attitude after committing the crime; the time, place, method, means, purpose, motive, surroundings, and dangerous consequences of the crime; whether it was committed intentionally or negligently; whether it involves a contradiction between the enemy and us or a contradiction among the people; and whether all evidentiary material relating to the facts of the case is reliable; etc. Since there are many aspects of the facts of a case that should be clarified, to which facts in the case do direct and indirect refer? This [the answer to this question] requires dividing the facts that should be clarified into two categories, principal facts and ordinary facts. [The term] "principal facts" refers to the problem of "whether or not the defendant is guilty." It also refers to the problem of "whether a crime was committed and [if so] by whom it was committed." Besides these, the [other] facts that should be clarified are ordinary facts.

As for the principal facts of a case, evidence that directly affirms or negates that a certain person is guilty is called direct evidence; evidence that indirectly asserts or negates that a certain person is guilty is called indirect evidence. Direct evidence is thus independent evidence that, if factual, can prove that a certain person is guilty; indirect evidence is thus independent evidence that, although factual, cannot prove that a certain person is guilty.

For example, if a witness sees the defendant viciously beat a certain child to death or if the defendant admits that he beat a certain child to death, this is direct evidence. If in a homicide case a witness proves that there are bloodstains on the defendant, the defendant admits that these are bloodstains, chemical analysis verifies that this was human blood of the same type as the victim's and an item of proof that is found near the scene of the crime is the defendant's handkerchief, etc., all of this is indirect evidence.

. . . . .

To use direct evidence to prove that a certain person committed a crime is relatively simple, but to use indirect evidence to prove that a certain person committed a crime is more complex. Therefore, in the usual determination of the facts of a case, not only is there indirect evidence, but there also is direct evidence. If we only rely on indirect evidence to decide a case, then we must understand the following two points:

First, it is necessary for indirect evidentiary material to have an intrinsic relationship to the facts of the crime; if it is not possible for it to have an intrinsic relationship to the facts, it cannot serve as evidence to prove guilt. If in a homicide case a bloodstained vest is seized under the defendant's bed, but the result of chemical analysis proves that the blood on the vest is not human blood but the blood of a domestic animal, there is no intrinsic relationship between the blood of a domestic animal and the facts of this crime. Thus, this cannot serve as indirect evidence. For another example, what are frequently called "abnormal emotions," "panic," and "bad facial expressions and red eyes," cannot serve as indirect evidence. Actually, when persons who have not committed crimes are suspected or are confronted by investigators and judges, it is also possible for all kinds of "abnormal" phenomena to occur and for some real criminals in the same situation to behave in a normal way as if there were nothing wrong. Therefore, when necessary in the process of investigation, "abnormality" may serve as a point of reference for further collection of evidence and checking on the criminal, but it cannot serve as a basis for deciding the case.

Second, even though we only rely on indirect evidence, we can decide that a certain person is guilty; but we must have several items of indirect evidence that constitute a mutually harmonious chain and exclude the various possibilities that other persons committed the crime or that no crime was committed. This requires that: (1) the indirect evidence is accurate and there is a possible intrinsic relationship between it and the facts of the case; (2) there are several items of indirect evidence; (3) there are no contradictions among the items of indirect evidence; (4) they [the items of indirect evidence] exclude the possibility that another person committed the crime; and (5) they exclude the possibility that there was no crime. Actually, if the indirect evidence is reliable, when the defendant is confronted with it, he is often likely to admit the crime, and after he does so there is direct evidence. Therefore, there are very few circumstances in which only indirect evidence is used to decide a case.

It would seem that using direct evidence to prove the principal facts is not so complex as using indirect evidence, but actually neither is it so simple. Direct evidence that can directly prove that a certain person is guilty must be accurate and reliable. The reliability of direct evidence in a case depends on combined proof from other items of indirect and direct evidence. Actually, in a concrete case, we cannot rely only on an individual item of direct evidence to decide the case. A case can only be finally decided by combining the use of varying amounts of evidence with the use of several items of indirect evidence. For example, a detailed account in which the defendant admits killing a person is direct evidence. But we still must check whether his statement is consistent with the circumstances at the scene of the crime, whether there is other evidence to prove that he was at the scene, where the instruments [of the crime] and [any] illegally obtained goods were put, whether there are contradictions with other evidentiary material, etc. Only when the statement [of the defendant] is checked and found to be in complete agreement with the facts of the crime can it be proved to be factual and serve as a basis for deciding the case.

In addition to clarifying the principal facts, the ordinary facts must also be clarified.

## ITEM 179

[Ho Shuang-lu, "Several Problems Relating to Evidence in Criminal Litigation" (1963), p. 37]

.    .    .    .    .

But after determining the truth and reliability of those facts that serve as indirect evidence and that also have an objective connection with the case, we still cannot immediately reach an affirmative or negative conclusion about the facts of the crime. This is because these items of evidence are only clues to individual facts or are fragments among them. We still must combine these facts and with respect to the evidentiary material in the entire case discard what is worthless and false and keep what is valuable and genuine, and in a penetrating, deductive, and detailed manner analyze and study the material. Only then can we reach a conclusion about the facts of the crime. Here I will give an example for concrete analysis and explanation:

On December 3, 1952, a certain Liu discovered that some clothing that had been stored in a trunk for a friend was missing. He immediately went to question a certain Chao who was temporarily living in the room where the clothing had been stored. At that time Chao admitted that he had sold the clothing. Later he denied it, and because of this Liu made a complaint to the court.

This is a theft case. Who could possibly have committed the theft? By means of investigation, evidence was obtained in the following three areas. The first was: (1) the defendant had previously been sentenced twice for theft; (2) after his release, he relied on his maternal uncle for a livelihood and had no other financial sources; also, 200,000 yuan (old currency) was found during a search of his person; (3) the trunk with the missing clothing had been placed in the room in which he lived. All of these could serve as a basis for determining that the defendant had possibly committed the act of theft. But this was only a "possibility." We still were far from being able to reach the conclusion that this Chao had committed the theft. The second area in which evidence was obtained was: (1) a witness named Li proved that the defendant had admitted to the complainant that he had sold the clothing; (2) in November 1952 the defendant had borrowed the complainant's household registration booklet, saying that he was going to use it in order to be admitted to a school entrance examination, but investigation disclosed that he definitely had not taken any examination; (3) in November 1952 he also stole and used his older sister's household registration booklet and secretly returned it when he had finished using it; (4) recently the defendant had frequently gone out to eat and drink and had spent money very freely. These items of indirect evidence showed that the defendant was an important suspect in this theft. On the basis of the above circumstances, we could make the following inference: it is possible that the defendant obtained the household registration booklets of others by deceit and theft in order to sell the illegally obtained goods and that his money came from their sale. But, ultimately, could it be said what the true use of the household registration booklets was? And where was the true location of the illegally obtained goods? None of these had yet been clarified, and the possibility that others had committed the theft had also not yet been excluded. Therefore, this determination of the case was still a "possibility" that required other evidence before the facts of the crime could be further clarified. The third area in which evidence was obtained was: (1) in November 1952 the defendant had sold clothing through a certain commission firm, and the sold clothing was the same as some of the missing clothing; (2) at the same time there was also a man who had used the name of the defendant's older sister to sell clothing at another firm, and it too was the same as the clothing that the complainant was missing; (3) the handwriting on the tax-exemption slip from the sale of clothing, made through use of the household registration booklet of the defendant's older sister, was the same as the defendant's handwriting; (4) a sales clerk in the second firm verified that the person who used the name of the defendant's older sister to sell clothing was the defendant. After evidence obtained in this area was combined with evidence in the other two areas for analysis and study, the facts of the case became clear and comprehensible. The indirect evidence was like a chain, each link joined to another to prove that the defendant Chao had stolen the clothing in Liu's trunk, had used deceit and theft as means to obtain the household registration booklets, had gone to the commission firm to sell the clothing, and had thus obtained money to spend.

In this case we still can see that contradictions among items of evidence always can emerge. When we meet this situation, we must seize the contradictions and resolve them. If we do not resolve the contradictions, we cannot reach a conclusion about the facts of the crime. For example, in the above-mentioned case it was discovered that the name on the slip for the commission firm's sale of the illegally obtained goods was that of the defendant's sister. This contradicted the evidence that the defendant had sold the illegally obtained goods. Why were the illegally obtained goods sold under the name of this Chao's sister? Was there a possibility that two people had collaborated in committing the theft? If there had been no other evidence, this contradiction would not have been easy to resolve. After we saw the expert opinion on the handwriting; [considered] the defendant's theft, his use of his older sister's household registration booklet, and the testimony of the sales clerk of the second firm; and made an evaluation [of all the evidence], we were able to reach the conclusion that the defendant had stolen and used the household registration booklet to sell the illegally obtained goods. In this way we were enabled to resolve the contradiction among the items of evidence.

## ITEM 180

[Chang Tzu-p'ei, "Several Problems Relating to the Use of Evidence To Determine the Facts of a Case in Criminal Litigation" (1962), pp. 17–18]

.    .    .    .    .

We should explain that when investigators, procurators, and judges determine the facts of a case, the different processes of investigation and adjudication require that there be differences in the degree of thoroughness and reliability of the evidentiary material. Adjudication is the time for the final decision of a case, and we must have sufficient and reliable evidence as a basis before we can make a judgment. Therefore, when hearing a case the court must conscientiously examine the evidentiary material. When the evidence is insufficient or subject to doubt, the court itself should examine the case or return it to the departments concerned for supplementary investigation. But because comprehensive and reliable evidence cannot be found the moment the process of investigation begins, such a requirement cannot be made of the evidentiary material at the time that a decision to arrest or to detain is made during the process of investigation. But there should be a minimum requirement. The minimum evidentiary material requirement for purposes of arrest demands that: although the suspect does not admit his guilt, direct testimony and real evidence actually can prove the principal facts of the crime; or the admissions and confession of the suspect have been analyzed, studied, and repeatedly evaluated and the facts have been checked, and they are consistent with the on-the-spot investigation of the scene of the crime, the expert technical opinion, and the circumstances of the case [as set forth] in the victim's petition; or although no direct evidence has been obtained, indirect evidence in various respects proves who the criminal is; or other similar circumstances. The minimum evidentiary material requirement for purposes of detention is also different from the [minimum] requirement for the purpose of arrest. Article 5 of the Arrest and Detention Act of the People's Republic of China has specific provisions for this.

According to the author of Item 180, how does the arrest standard for appraising evidence differ from the conviction standard?

## G. REVIEW BY PROCURACY OF POLICE RECOMMENDATION TO ARREST AND TO PROSECUTE

We have seen that, in practice, the limited constitutional and legislative provisions for protecting a suspected criminal from unduly prolonged confinement by the police have proved to be ineffective. Since the enactment of the Constitution, however, the power of the police to dispose of a suspected criminal's fate has been subjected to certain restrictions both in theory and practice. It is true, of course, that the police continue to enjoy unfettered power to impose SAPA sanctions, rehabilitation through labor and supervised labor, as well as the variety of informal sanctions that culminate in struggle meetings. Moreover, they can require hospitalization for an indefinite period of criminal suspects whom they find to be mentally ill, and they can require suspected juvenile offenders to be confined indefinitely in centers for rehabilitation of children. But the police can no longer sentence an accused to death or to any other criminal punishment, as they often did during the 1949–1954 period, but must submit the charges and the evidence for scrutiny and approval by the procuracy in most cases and for adjudication by the people's court in all cases.

Review by the procuracy of the police recommendation to prosecute may take several forms. According to the model contemplated by the pertinent 1954 legislation, the police ask the procuracy to approve a warrant for the suspect's arrest either prior to his apprehension or within twenty-four hours thereafter; assuming that approval of the arrest is granted, after an unstated period of further investigation, if prosecution appears appropriate, the police submit their recommendation for the procuracy's determination of whether or not prosecution is in order. In practice, however, the situation is more complex. In some cases, of course, the arrest procedures contemplated by the legislative model are followed. In many other cases the police issue their own arrest warrant and only notify the procuracy of the case when the investigation is completed and the case is thought ready to submit to the procuracy for approval of prosecution. Often in cases of importance the police do apply to the procuracy for an arrest warrant but do not do so until completion of the investigation. In these circumstances approval of the application, which is frequently considered by a representative of the court together with a representative of the procuracy, signifies approval of initiation of prosecution. Thus the two stages of procuratorial review originally contemplated are often telescoped into one.

## ITEM 181

The following excerpt and the provisions of the Arrest and Detention Act quoted in Item 156 form the legislative framework for review by the procuracy.

[LAW OF THE PRC FOR THE ORGANIZATION OF PEOPLE'S PROCURACIES (Sept. 28, 1954), p. 135]

Article 10. When a people's procuracy discovers and confirms the fact that a crime has been committed, it shall initiate a criminal case and, in accordance with procedure prescribed by law, conduct an investigation or turn it over to public security organs to conduct an investigation; when after completion of the investigation it considers that it must pursue the defendant for criminal responsibility, it shall initiate prosecution before a people's court.

Article 11. If a public security organ, after completion of an investigation in a criminal case initiated by it, considers it necessary to initiate prosecution, it shall, in accordance with the provisions of law, send the case to a people's procuracy for examination and decision whether or not to initiate prosecution.

Article 12. Except where there is a decision of a people's court the arrest of any citizen must be approved by a people's procuracy.

Article 13. When a public security organ considers erroneous a decision by a people's procuracy not to approve its request for an arrest or a decision by a people's procuracy not to initiate prosecution in a case that the public security organ sent to the procuracy, it has the right to present its opinion or bring a complaint [against the procuracy] to a people's procuracy of the next higher level.

## ITEM 182

[Rickett and Rickett, *Prisoners of Liberation* (1957), p. 272]

.    .    .    .    .

*Rick:* By late spring of 1955 it had become clear that my long-awaited release was near at hand. In April I was informed that Dell [Mrs. Rickett] had left and that my own case would soon be settled. Then one evening in late August, 1955, I was called out of the cell and directed toward a big room near the interrogation offices. As I entered, the guard remained on the outside and I found a man and woman waiting for me there.

The man stood up, bowed politely, and asked if I were Li Ko. When I replied in the affirmative, he motioned to a comfortable chair and said pleasantly, "We are from the Procurator-General's office. The Public Security Bureau has turned your case over to us and we would like you to tell us about your crime. You should speak freely and you may disregard any statements you have made before."

I told him that my last statement written in the summer of 1954 was correct to the best of my knowledge. I then proceeded to give him a rough outline of my relations with the Consulate and the British Negotiation Mission.

When I had finished he leaned back for a moment and asked, "Have you any complaints or requests which you would like to make?"

I faltered, "What do you mean? Requests or complaints about what?"

"About the way you were treated and the handling of your case."

I told him that I considered my treatment fair and my punishment just, but that I hoped that some day I would be able to return to the United States.

"Well," he said, standing up by way of dismissal, "we think your wish will probably come true."

## ITEM 183

["Kwangtung Province Deals with Eight U.S.-Chiang Secret Agents, Four Are Not Prosecuted, Four Are Sentenced to Prison," *Ta Kung Pao* (Great public daily, Hong Kong), Feb. 12, 1964]

Recently the people's procuratorial organs of Chung-shan and Tung-kuan counties separately announced that four U.S.-Chiang secret agents who had been sent to the mainland and who had voluntarily surrendered were dealt with leniently and exempted from prosecution.

These four secret agents who were dealt with leniently were sent by U.S.-Chiang Kai-shek espionage organizations from Hong Kong and Macao within the last year. They were assigned by these espionage organizations to sabotage factories, railways, bridges, sluices, and other important installations, to distribute reactionary pamphlets, to develop espionage organizations, and to steal military information. However, after they smuggled themselves into the mainland, they saw the great accomplishments made in the building of socialism in the mother country, the ubiquitous scene of prosperity, and the happy and fortunate life the people were leading. They realized that they had been deceived by the propaganda of the espionage organizations and saw their future clearly. Meanwhile awed by the strength of the people's democratic dictatorship and the high degree of vigilance of the masses of people, they voluntarily surrendered to the people's government and thoroughly handed over their plans for sabotage. Taking into consideration that these spies were brave in correcting their errors and could rein in on the brink of the precipice by voluntarily surrendering after smuggling themselves into the mainland, the people's procuratorial organs of Chung-shan and Tung-kuan counties decided to deal with them leniently and exempted all of them from prosecution. The competent department of the people's government also made proper arrangements for them to get employment.

## ITEM 184

The following is a sample form which, according to a Soviet authority on Chinese law, is used by the procuracy to record its decision not to initiate prosecution. The last two paragraphs are explanatory statements by Chugunov.

[Vladimir E. Chugunov, *Ugolovnoye Sudoproizvodstvo Kitayskoy Narodnoy Respubliki* (Criminal court procedures in the People's Republic of China, Moscow, 1959); translated in *JPRS,* no. 4595 (Washington, D.C., May 8, 1961), pp. 235–236]

. . . . .

*Resolution on Discharge from the Obligation to be Turned Over to the Court*

This procurator's office has conducted an investigation and is terminating the investigation in the case of _____
(name of accused)
On the basis of the materials gathered in this, the following facts are established:
1) Established facts and evidence in the case are
2) listed here
3)
4)
On the basis of the above facts and in accordance with Article — we have resolved to free the accused _____ without further prosecution of the
(name)
case.

If the law provides no instructions on the possibility of dropping prosecution of a case, the resolution contains the bases used for arriving at such a decision.

At the end of the resolution it is duly indicated if the institution, organization, enterprise, or citizen who submitted the petition to institute criminal proceedings is not in agreement with the above resolution, they may petition for a second check of the materials by a higher procurator's office.

## ITEM 185

Interviews suggest that private citizens rarely invoke the procedure described below to challenge a procuracy's decision not to prosecute.

["What Is One To Do If One Disagrees with the People's Procuracy?" *Kung-jen jih-pao* (Workers' daily, Peking), Feb. 21, 1957]

Comrade Editor:
Last year, on the afternoon of May 11, my fourth brother was working in a certain mine in Luan-hsien while the head of the mine production work group was

drilling a hole for explosives. Before exploding the charge he did not notify the workers on the scene to leave the danger area. As a result my fourth brother was struck by a flying stone and killed. This matter was investigated and handled by the Luan-hsien people's procuracy, and recently they notified me of the result. The person who was derelict in his duty was given only an administrative sanction, and that was the end of the matter. Prosecution was not initiated before a court. I do not accept this kind of decision but I am now living in Peking. Where should I go to bring a complaint? What procedures are there?

Peking   Chang Tzu-wen

Comrade Chang Tzu-wen:

As for the matter of your fourth brother's being struck by a flying stone and killed, the worker who was derelict in his duty is responsible. But because your discussion of the circumstances was relatively brief, there is no way of giving a specific answer to the question of how responsible. I can only reply to the question about litigation procedure.

If you do not accept the decision not to initiate prosecution, you may write a letter to the Luan-hsien people's procuracy giving your reasons and request it to transmit the letter to a higher level people's procuracy for study and handling. On the basis of current criminal litigation procedure, all cases of incidents involving responsibility for serious injury or death generally should be investigated by the people's procuracy, which should decide whether or not to initiate prosecution. But when the victim or other citizen directly brings his accusation to a people's court or when, in a case in which a people's procuracy has decided not to initiate prosecution or to exempt from prosecution the person who was responsible, and the victim again brings his accusation directly to a people's court, the people's court should receive the accusation and then send it to the people's procuracy for handling and inform the accuser [of its having done so]. Therefore you also may bring your accusation directly to a court. Both the place where this matter occurred and the worker against whom the accusation is to be made are in Luan-hsien, so the matter should be handled by the Luan-hsien people's procuracy. If you do not have time to go to Luan-hsien you may draft a bill of prosecution and mail it with a copy to the Luan-hsien people's court and request them to handle the matter. If you yourself cannot write a pleading, you may authorize a lawyer to draft it for you.

Editor

## ITEM 186

In most cases no serious dispute arises between the police and the procuracy over questions of arrest and prosecution. Differing views are usually harmonized through informal consultation and negotiation. Indeed, as Item 158 illustrates, in important cases cadres from the court as well as the procuracy often cooperate with the police from the start of the investigation through participation in joint "work groups." What factors might account for smooth cooperation among these legal organs?

Occasionally, however, conflicts do arise. They occurred more frequently during the 1956–1957 era than in recent years, for reasons suggested by Item 186.

[T'an Cheng-wen, "Absorb Experience and Teaching, Impel a Great Leap Forward in Procuratorial Work" (1958), pp. 37, 38, 41, 42]

.     .     .     .     .

The rightists not only spread reactionary arguments, they also use the powers that they have usurped to indulge counterrevolutionaries. For example, when in 1957 rightist Li Jui, former deputy chief procurator of Anhwei province, went to Tang-tu county to inspect some work, he ordered the county procuracy not to approve the arrest of five criminals who should have been arrested, and he ordered the county court to release nine criminals who had already been sentenced or who should have been sentenced for their crimes.

Under the leadership of the Party Central Committee and the Party committees of the various [other] levels, during the last half year or more of the antirightist struggle, many rightists in the procuracy have been discovered through investigation. These included Liu Hui-chih, deputy chief procurator of the transportation procuracy of the Supreme People's Procuracy; Wang Li-chung and P'eng Jui-lin, chief of the first department and chief procurator of the Chekiang provincial procuracy, respectively; Yang Hsiao-ch'un and Li Jui, chief procurator and deputy chief procurator of the Anhwei provincial procuracy, respectively; and Lin Fang, deputy chief procurator of the Kwangsi provincial procuracy, all of whom were rightists who usurped important offices. Major victories have thus been won in the two-road struggle in procuratorial work. But the antirightist struggle still has not concluded. Units that have already concluded the struggle should pay attention to the question of whether or not there have been any in the procuracy who have been overlooked. The struggle must be carried out to the end. There must be a thorough and complete victory. The rightists must be completely dug up and the organization of the procuratorial organs purified . . .

Many of those who "favor the defendant in litigation activity relieve criminals of criminal responsibility in the following ways:

1. They one-sidedly emphasize the application of [the concept of] "attempt." They do not distinguish cases according to their nature but emphasize the uniform application of "attempt." For example, after liberation, a counterrevolutionary who owed blood debts habitually sabotaged agricultural cooperativization, gathered together more than ten backward members of the masses, tried to make the basic level organizations of the regime collapse, and tried to murder our cadres. Those who "favor the defendant" believe that this was an "attempt to commit a crime" by this counterrevolutionary. Can it be said that this is not absolutely absurd? Attempt, as we apply it, has a definite scope and it may not be recklessly used. Attempt definitely cannot be applied to counterrevolutionary criminals. This is a fundamental principle, because the purposes of counterrevolution are to sabotage our dictatorship of the proletariat, and our socialist system and to try to overthrow our state. Would it not be a mess if counterrevolutionary sabotage were allowed to succeed? There should be the same kind of understanding with respect to murder and other such crimes.

2. They excessively emphasize and even distort the motives and purposes for which the crime was committed in order to open the door of convenience to the criminal. They say that intentionally slashing and injuring oxen belonging to an agricultural cooperative by "landlord, rich peasant, counterrevolutionary, and bad elements" "is not for the purpose of sabotaging the agricultural cooperative's production." They say that the sabotage activity of counterrevolutionaries "is not for counterrevolutionary purposes." They "push off" the crimes of historical counterrevolutionaries as "crimes committed in the line of duty." They say that the counterrevolutionaries' writing reactionary posters and spreading rumors is [only] "backward thinking." They "push off" the crimes of capitalists who steal state property by [saying that] "those capitalists originate from the bourgeoisie and are accustomed to it [the life of the bourgeoisie], and that now conditions have changed, they have no money to spend." They believe that theft is [only] "unjust enrichment," and so forth. There are even some who believe that, when a middle peasant does not sell his excess grain and a cadre who goes to mobilize and educate him is slashed by the peasant's son, this is not murder but "legitimate defense." In this way, by considering the criminal's motives and purposes and by pushing these back and forth, they push all criminals into [the category of] "not guilty." It should be clearly pointed out that in analyzing the motives and purposes for which crimes are committed, we must proceed from what is beneficial to the dictatorship of the proletariat, from what is beneficial to an accurate and prompt attack on criminals, and from what implements the various policies and guidelines of the Party and the state. The only correct way is to proceed from what is beneficial to the smooth conduct of [activities for] protecting the social order and the various undertakings of socialist construction and from what is beneficial to the development and consolidation of all revolutionary undertakings. It is erroneous to depart from these and to talk of the motives and purposes for which crimes are committed. This cannot be permitted.

3. They emphasize the "consequences" of the crime and always use "there were no consequences" or "the consequences were not serious" to relieve criminals of criminal responsibility. For example, with respect to a capitalist who beat up a labor union cadre and who was about to kill him with a knife, they believed that this was "an ordinary dispute, the consequence was not serious and it did not constitute a crime." With respect to a criminal who used a gun to try to kill someone, they believed that because the gun did not fire, "there were no consequences." With respect to some criminals undergoing reform through labor who, committing arson, set fire to the prison, they believed that because someone reported it and the criminals were unsuccessful, "there were no consequences." This is a "key method" by means of which those who "favor the defendant" use "consequences" to relieve criminals of criminal responsibility. The consequence of a crime is something that should be considered, but the decision must be based on the nature of the case. Moreover, consideration of the consequences can only serve as a reference for deciding upon punishment. It definitely cannot go beyond this and serve as the standard for determining whether or not a crime has been committed.

. . . . .

5. They also emphasize trivial legal procedures and the rights and position of the criminal and open the door of convenience to the criminal. In litigation activity they one-sidedly or improperly emphasize the completeness of "procedure" (certain procedures are necessary) and erroneously emphasize the rights and position of the defendant. For example, they cunningly proclaim that they do not want to worsen the position of the defendant, and they also say that the defendant has the right to lie and is free to remain silent. All of these violate our criminal [law] policy. The procedure that we adopt is for the purpose of accurately, promptly, and lawfully attacking the enemy and not for the purpose of binding our own hands and feet. We should pay attention to the lawful rights of criminals, but this definitely cannot serve as a pretext for indulging criminals.

Besides this, they also one-sidedly emphasize that the defendant is "young," is "old," is "a woman," is "an offender of [only one] occasion," has "good [class] status," and has a "clear history," and they call an admission a "confession," etc. For example, new counterrevolutionaries who everywhere write and post reactionary posters and conspire to conduct sabotage activity are believed to be people "without any problems of origin or history" or people "without counterrevolutionary status," and the problems are viewed as "problems of contradictions among the people." "Youth," "age," etc., may be considered with respect to ordinary criminals, but they likewise can only serve as a reference for deciding upon the severity of the sentence. Criminals should not be indulged because these points are considered.

. . . But in their concrete work do the public security and procuratorial organs and the courts have problems and contradictions? Naturally they have. When there are contradictions, do not be afraid. If there are contradictions, think of a way to resolve them correctly. Do not, because of the fear that contradictions will [adversely] affect relations, compromise and not dare to hold firmly to principles. This is a vulgar way of thinking. It is natural for there to be contradictions and problems in the work of the three organs. It must be ideologically clear that these contradictions involve relations of right and wrong within the three organs and problems of correctness and error. Therefore, I believe that they should be resolved mainly through the methods of discussion and study. Usually there will not be situations in which criminals are concealed. Under our system such situations do not easily occur. If, occasionally, an individual situation of this kind really does occur, that is another problem.

. . . One aspect of the exercise of procuratorial power by procuratorial organs, the principal and basic aspect, is the development of the role of dictatorship and investigation of the sabotage activity of all enemies — counterrevolutionary and bad elements and other criminal elements. Another aspect, and one which supplements the principal aspect mentioned above, is supervision with respect to whether or not the enemy has been indulged — for example, whether those who should have been arrested were not arrested, whether cases which should have been adjudicated were not adjudicated and whether those who should have been heavily sentenced were lightly sentenced. Naturally, they should also investigate whether those who according to policies and laws should not have been seized have been seized and whether cases which should not have been adjudicated were adjudicated. When in the course of investigation it is possible to arrest or not to arrest, to adjudicate or not to adjudicate, or to kill or not to kill, and they themselves are not very clear about the policy limits or there is a dispute or disagreement with [other] relevant departments it should be discussed and studied as much as possible with the relevant departments and the Party committee should be asked for instructions concerning resolution.

.        .        .        .        .

The special privilege thinking of some cadres of our procuratorial system who are "self-designated supervisors" has already been basically resolved by the rectification and the antiright-wing [movements]. But at present there has emerged among individual comrades a kind of crude and careless fear of assuming responsibility. For example, upon receiving cases of application for the approval of arrest, they do not conscientiously and responsibly examine them but, after giving them a perfunctory examination, immediately send them to the Party committee for examination and approval. This demonstrates a lack of revolutionary responsibility. Because of this we must be conceptually clear that, under the absolute leadership and supervision of the Party, procuratorial organs must accept the supervision of the masses, state organs, relevant departments, and higher level professional departments in all aspects. Only in this way can we complete the serious task that the Party and the state have given us.

1. Is it any wonder that some comrades in the procuracy fear assuming responsibility for decision-making?
2. According to the author of Item 186, in what circumstances should a procurator consult the Party committee? How should a model procurator fulfill his responsibility?

### ITEM 187

Criticisms such as those voiced in Item 186 prepared the procuracy for the demands that were to be made upon it shortly thereafter in the "great leap forward." Item 187 demonstrates the impact of the leap upon the procuracy.

[Chang Wu-yün, "Smash Permanent Rules, Go 1,000 *Li* in One Day," *CFYC*, 5:58 (1958)]

.        .        .        .        .

The leap forward is something that has emerged in unprecedented fashion; the work during this period in both quality and quantity has exceeded that done in any period of the past. In order to strive for higher goals and fulfill their tasks ahead of schedule or overfulfill them, the energy of the procuratorial cadres of the entire province [Kweichow] has been very great. They have taken the initiative in working overtime, fought bitterly, and attacked suddenly. For example, the accumulated cases for the entire province have been cleaned up and concluded within a few short days. In the past accumulated cases pressed down so heavily that we could not raise our heads; now we strongly take the initiative. The procuracy of the autonomous *chou*, Ch'ien-nan, originally needed thirty-three days to finish handling, in accordance with the permanent rules method of disposition, accumulated cases of [arrest] applications which had to be examined for approval and accumulated cases involving the initiation of prosecution. Now, with one leap forward, they have finished in three days. Prior to the Kweiyang city's political-legal meeting, the city procuracy, in order to present a gift to that meeting, raised its average efficiency in handling cases involving the initiation of prosecution eleven-fold within five days. On the basis of the records for the first ten days in April, of the ninety-one units in the entire province, fourteen can finish handling a case of an application for approval of arrest within thirty minutes and forty-eight can finish handling it within one hour; forty-four units can examine a case involving the initiation of prosecution within approximately one hour and six units can examine it within three hours; twenty-two units can appear in court and prosecute a case within thirty minutes and thirty-five units can do it within approximately one hour. Efficiency in handling cases has increased several times and even several tens of times. Perhaps some people are doubtful: when a case is handled within thirty minutes or within an hour or so what is the quality like? According to the results of a re-examination of fifty-one units, the quality of the case [handling] is good. A re-examination of the Tu-shan county procuracy proved that 100 percent of the cases were correctly handled. Of the offenders who were arrested and who were prosecuted, some were counterrevolutionaries with plenty of blood debts who had evaded suppression many times in the past or who had sneaked in from other places; some were secret agents in hiding who attempted to seize opportunities to conduct sabotage activity; some were counterrevolutionaries and criminals who had engaged in serious current sabotage activity.

## ITEMS 188A–188D

The antirightist movement and the "great leap forward" did not completely convert the procuracy into a mere echo of its more powerful sister agency. These items are recent examples of the relatively isolated instances in which contradictions between the two organs continued to occur. They illustrate the various procedures employed for resolving such contradictions.

## ITEM 188A

[Interview]

Liao was a petty thief of no fixed address who wandered all over his county pilfering minor items. He had twice previously received detention for violations of the SAPA. In early 1958 he was caught in the act of another petty theft and detained at the county public security bureau's detention house while the security section considered the best way of handling him. It was the section chief's view that SAPA detention would prove ineffective, as it had in the past. Rehabilitation through labor, although it was already on the books, was not yet a feasible alternative, since preparations for its implementation had not yet been completed in this area. Neither supervised labor nor control seemed practicable since Liao had no residence. Therefore, the section chief decided that Liao ought to be arrested, convicted, and sentenced to imprisonment for his reform. Accordingly, the bureau applied to the basic level procuracy of the county for authorization to arrest him.

The procurator to whom the application was assigned, however, thought the case too minor to deserve criminal prosecution and orally recommended to the chief procurator that the application not be approved. Without consulting the file, the chief procurator agreed, and the application was returned to the bureau. The section chief complained to the bureau chief about this lack of cooperation on the part of the procuracy and prevailed upon him to pay a call on the chief procurator. When queried about the case, the latter said that the facts failed to justify arrest, although he admitted that he had not studied the matter in any detail. Receiving no satisfaction from the procuracy, upon returning to his office the bureau chief found his section chief adamant. He, therefore, reported the matter to the deputy secretary of the county Party committee whose duties included political-legal affairs. As a result, this secretary called an enlarged meeting of the important cadres from the "three families" to discuss the problem.

The meeting was held at the public security bureau. It was attended by the bureau cadres who served at the level of chief and deputy chief of the various sections and above; by the chief procurator, his deputy, the regular procurators, and the secretary of the procuracy, and although the court was not immediately concerned, by the president and vice-president of the court. At the meeting the representatives of the bureau's security section pressed their case for arrest, while the procurator who had initially handled the application gave his reasons for recommending that it not be approved. The bureau chief and the chief procurator did not enter into the detailed discussion of the merits, preferring to leave responsibility with the cadres at the operating level. When the matter had been thoroughly explored, the deputy secretary of the Party committee, who could have made a decision, simply asked the chief procurator to restudy the case in the light of the discussion and the Party's current policy.

After further study the chief procurator still could not bring himself to approve the arrest but was no longer certain of the wisdom of not approving it. He therefore decided to ask the intermediate people's procuracy to consider the case. The bureau had also reported the case to its superior, the public security division. The chief procurator of the intermediate level procuracy then met with the division chief. Although, at the meeting, each tended to support the views of his own cadres, afterward the chief procurator instructed the county procuracy to approve the arrest. He cited as his reason the Party's newly enunciated policy of "attack crime and protect the people's commune."

## ITEM 188B

[Interview]

Tou was a twenty-year-old youth who had recently become friendly with Wu, an attractive eighteen-year-old girl. One night in 1960 Wu burst into the local public security station in a disheveled and distraught condition and claimed that Tou had raped her. After interviewing her, the secretary on duty sent her to the hospital for a physical examination and an examination of her clothing. Several policemen were sent after Tou, who admitted having had sexual intercourse with Wu, but said that no force had been involved. Tou was also sent to the hospital for tests, while investigators checked the scene of the incident. The hospital tests indicated that intercourse had occurred and that Wu had previously been a virgin. Her torn clothing suggested that there had actually been a struggle.

On this basis the security section of the county public security bureau detained Tou for intensive questioning, during which he continued to refuse to confess to rape. After a day of questioning, the security section still did not want to release him, but it did not yet feel certain enough of the rape charge to apply for an arrest warrant. It therefore gave Tou fifteen days of detention for having violated Article 10(1) of the SAPA by "acting indecently" with a woman. This provided additional time for inquiring into the backgrounds of Tou and Wu, their previous relations, and other factors. After a few days the security section concluded that this was a genuine instance of rape and applied for an arrest warrant.

The procurator to whom the case was assigned studied the file and then personally went to interview Wu and Tou. His investigation led him to doubt that there could have been sexual relations without Wu's consent. Accordingly, the procuracy asked the security section to study the case further. Dissatisfied with this response, the chief and a secretary of the security section went to the chief of the public security bureau and asked for his assistance. He invited the procurator who had handled the case and the chief procurator of the office to join them in a discussion of the problem. When this conference failed to result in agreement, it was decided to ask the "higher-ups" at the special district level to consider the case.

After the public security division and the intermediate level people's procuracy were notified of the case, they sent a work group composed of one representative of the former and two of the latter to undertake a comprehensive investigation. During this investigation Tou's fifteen-day term of detention expired, but the security section gave him fifteen days more on the theory that his stubborn refusal to admit his guilt constituted bad behavior in the detention house, which was an aggravating circumstance within the meaning of Article 21 of the SAPA. Before the expiration of the second fifteen-day term, the work group reported that this appeared to be a true rape case, and the intermediate people's procuracy approved arrest and prosecution. Tou was subsequently sentenced to serve three-and-one-half years of imprisonment.

## ITEM 188C

[Interview]

In 1960 four cadres who had been "sent down" [10] to perform staff work in a people's commune were reported to have embezzled some commune welfare funds. Investigation by a team of public security cadres verified the report, and the security section of the county public security bureau decided that the offense was serious enough to warrant criminal prosecution. Accordingly, it applied to the procuracy for approval of an arrest warrant. The procuracy, however, returned the application with a request that the matter be given further

10. The "sending down" movement was begun in 1956–1957 as an attempt to spread Party cadres more evenly among the working masses and prevent excessive centralization and inertia of the Party bureaucracy. For an interesting analysis of the movement and its distinctive jargon see T. A. Hsia, *A Terminological Study of the Hsia-Fang Movement* (Studies in Chinese Communist Terminology, no. 10; Berkeley, 1963).

study. It asked the security section to bear in mind that this was a case of corruption and not of theft and that, unless a very large sum was taken, detention under the SAPA was the proper sanction.

The security section reviewed the file again and persisted in its belief that criminal sanctions were necessary. It was obvious that it would take a few days to resolve the matter of arrest. Although the suspected cadres had all confessed, they had not yet been taken into custody. The security section believed it unwise to allow them to remain at large pending a decision on arrest, since they might flee or commit suicide because of the disgrace and the certainty of receiving some sanction and since it was also feared that the appearance of favoring the offending cadres might have an adverse impact on the opinion of an outraged citizenry. For these reasons the security section decided to give these cadres fifteen days of detention for violation of Article 11(1) of SAPA, which would allow ample time for resolution of the arrest problem. Because these were state cadres, before they were detained the security section informed the Party organization bureau of its proposed action. Since two of the cadres were also Party members, it also notified the Party control commission. After receiving prompt responses from these Party institutions that the offenders had been expelled from the government and the Party, as a result of their involvement in this case, the security section detained them.

After their detention the security section asked the chief of the public security bureau to call an enlarged meeting of the principal cadres of the bureau, the procuracy, and the court to discuss the arrest problem. At the meeting the chief of the security section spoke with fervor of the popular anger against swivel-chair cadres who through accounting tricks could by a stroke of the pen deprive the masses of their hard-earned welfare accumulation. In reply the chief procurator did not say that he would not approve the arrest but argued that corruption had to be distinguished from theft. At the close of the meeting the bureau chief said that the best solution would be to ask the intermediate people's procuracy to consider the problem.

After the intermediate procuracy received the materials, it sent a procurator to the county level to investigate. He talked with the bureau chief, the chief procurator, and the other officials involved and then called a meeting of the Party general branch committee of the three legal organs. After a two-hour discussion the meeting recessed to allow members of the committee to study the matter informally. During the recess the chief of the bureau and the procurator from the intermediate procuracy thought of a compromise solution — the two offenders who were not Party members would be arrested but the two Party members would merely receive detention since, having been expelled from the Party, they had already suffered the most severe sanction that could be meted out for their offense. All four offenders would also be required to make restitution of the embezzled funds to the extent that their economic circumstances permitted. When the meeting reconvened the general branch committee approved the proposal. The two non-Party offenders were promptly arrested and tried; they received prison sentences of sixteen and eighteen months, respectively.

## ITEM 188D

Item 188D gives an overall view of the interaction of the public security organ, the procuracy, and the court in "breaking" a major criminal case.

[Interview]

T'ang, the deputy Party secretary of a rural commune in Fukien province, disappeared in 1959. Five days later he was found bound, gagged, and wrapped in a burlap bag floating in a lake near the production brigade which he had been inspecting at the time of his disappearance. T'ang had previously served as a cadre of that production brigade. There were no clues to his death, and for the first four months the case remained a complete mystery. This was peculiarly embarrassing to the county public security bureau, because, in the "great leap forward" atmosphere, public security organs, like all other units, were required to make a leap forward in their work. The bureau chief subjected the cadres of the security section to a constant barrage of criticism for failing to break the case, and Huang, the deputy section chief who was also chief of the section's criminal investigation group, came in for especially heavy criticism because the case was his direct responsibility.

For some time Huang had suspected three young men who worked in the brigade and who were known to have had a grudge against T'ang. But since there was no evidence linking the three to the crime and they had had no previous difficulties with the law, Huang had not detained them for questioning. One night, however, the three were caught stealing a small amount of grain from the brigade for their personal use. Although normally in such cases persons with a clear record would only receive criticism, Huang seized upon the opportunity and gave the suspects seven days of detention for petty theft under the SAPA. Each of them was then intensively interrogated for almost the entire week by two-man teams. Although they were given a sufficient amount of food, because of the time pressure they were allowed only minimum amounts of sleep. The three suspects admitted their theft, but steadfastly denied any connection with the murder.

At the same time as they were being questioned, other public security men questioned members of the brigade about the three suspects' possible involvement in the crime. Several people, including Liao, a Party member and the secretary of the local branch of the Communist Youth League, said that these three had a motive for the murder, but no one revealed any evidence. With the time for the suspects' detention about to expire, Huang, a Party veteran of the Anti-Japanese War who made up in zeal what he lacked in education, yielded to the "leap forward" psychology and prepared an application for the arrest of the three on a charge of murder. The bureau chief approved the application and happily announced to his superiors at the special district and provincial levels that the case had finally been solved.

The county procuracy, however, had difficulty with the arrest application. When the procurator in charge questioned the suspects, they remained adamant in their denials, and his outside investigation uncovered no firm evidence of guilt. He checked with the chief procurator, who did not want to reject the bureau's application and thereby perhaps reveal "right-wing" thinking but who also did not want to approve the application and thereby risk exposing himself to criticism for professional incompetence. The chief procurator consulted the bureau chief in order to obtain assurances, and the bureau chief, himself unwilling to take the responsibility, called in Huang, who asserted that he was "certain" that the three suspects had committed the crime. After this the chief procurator felt that he had to approve the arrest, because the murder of a cadre was not the kind of case that he could afford to take lightly. After giving its approval, the procuracy made out the bill of prosecution and sent the file to the court.

In the company of a representative of the bureau's trial preparation section, the judge who was assigned to the case questioned the defendants on a number of occasions. His study of the case led him to conclude that the court could not convict on the existing evidence. He talked with the court president, who decided to take the case up with the chief procurator, the bureau chief, and the deputy secretary of the local Party committee. This group, which constituted the political-legal Party group for the county, decided to send a joint investigating team down to the production brigade under the leadership of the deputy bureau chief. When after three weeks of further investigation no further evidence was discovered, the political-legal Party group decided that the case had to be disposed of, since the higher authorities were inquiring about why so much time had elapsed since the case had been "solved." Because of uncertainty over the defendants' guilt, rather than give them the death sentence, the political-legal Party group agreed to give one of them life imprisonment and the two others fifteen years of imprisonment. The judgment was written out, and arrangements were already made to announce it when the first break in the case occurred.

A militiaman overheard Liao, the CYL secretary, tell his wife that the police really had no way of solving this case. He reported this remark to the investigating team. Since Liao had been one of those who had confirmed the bureau's suspicions of the defendants, the team became suspicious of him and began inquiring into his background. It heard that Liao had once been engaged to marry T'ang's wife. The victim's wife confirmed this, stating that T'ang, a more important cadre, had wooed her away from Liao. But when the team leader dropped in on Liao and casually asked whether he had ever been close to Mrs. T'ang, he claimed that he hardly knew her. During this visit the team leader noted a burlap bag similar to the one in which T'ang had been wrapped. At this point, although the county Party committee believed that there was not yet enough evidence to justify the arrest or detention of a Party member, it felt that enough had been produced to justify "asking" Liao to come up to the committee office for questioning. While Liao was kept there for four days, the investigating team decided that, since the murder could not have been committed alone, his brother Lin-tse might have helped him and that, being younger and more impulsive than Liao, Lin-tse might respond to intensive interrogation more readily than Liao. The difficulty it confronted was that there was no basis, other than sheer suspicion, for detaining Lin-tse. Moreover, having already made one serious mistake in detaining suspects in the case, the investigators did not want to lose face again, as they would if they detained Lin-tse on suspicion and he later turned out to be innocent.

They met this problem by resorting to a ruse. They arranged for the chairman of the Women's Federation of the brigade "accidentally" to meet Lin-tse in the street and to start an argument by accusing him in front of a group of being a hooligan and a loafer. As anticipated, his temper got the better of him, and he replied in kind, cursing and insulting the woman. The chairman of the security defense committee then used this as a pretext for requesting Lin-tse's detention under the SAPA. When after two days in detention Lin-tse still had not made any admissions, and Liao was also stubbornly holding out, their interrogators told each that the other had confessed and had implicated him. Liao did not fall for the trick but Lin-tse did and made a full confession. But when he was subsequently asked to repeat the confession in front of his brother he completely recanted and claimed that he had been forced to sign a false confession.

Dissatisfied with this state of affairs, the investigating team decided to go after Liao's wife. It detained her and told her that both Liao and Lin-tse had confessed and had implicated her and that she had better make a full confession or suffer the consequences. Mrs. Liao quickly broke down and told all. She was subsequently brought into a room where, unknown to her, Liao and Lin-tse could hear her but not see her, and she repeated her confession. When they were subsequently confronted with her, they admitted their guilt. Mrs. Liao, who had played only a passive role in the crime, was then released. With the approval of cadres from the public security division and the intermediate level court, who had been sent down by the special district to make certain that the case was not bungled a second time, it was decided to apply for a warrant for the arrest of the Liao brothers on a charge of murder. The procuracy, which was already familiar with the facts because of its participation in the joint investigating team, promptly approved the arrest after Liao was expelled from the Party and sent the file on to the court. [For the judicial processing of the Liao brothers, see Item 252. For the sanctions administered to the cadres who handled this case, see Item 286, and for the circumstances in which the three original defendants were released, see Item 281.]

## ITEM 189

["A Procuracy's Bill of Prosecution . . ." *Hsin-wen jih-pao* (Daily news, Shanghai), June 4, 1957]

Defendant Chiang Yeh-wei, male, twenty-seven years old, a native of Kiangsu, was formerly the assistant manager of the state-private, jointly operated Szuming-t'ang medicated liquor store. He lives in this city at 74 West Hsi-tsang street.

On March 20, 1957, citizen Ch'en Chi (manager of the Szu-ming-t'ang medicated liquor store in this city) came to this procuracy to present a petition: Chiang Yeh-wei, the assistant manager of said store, at 10:00 A.M. on March

11 stabbed him with a knife and wounded him in the arm while he was in his store; he requested that we handle it [the case]. This procuracy participated in the investigation of this case conducted by the Huang-p'u subbureau of the city of Shanghai's public security bureau. When the investigation was concluded it [the file in the case] was sent to this procuracy. After examination [it has been determined that] the facts are as follows:

Defendant Chiang Yeh-wei originally was a worker in the Szu-ming-t'ang medicated liquor store in this city. Since the "five-anti" movement, his relationship with Ch'en Chi, the manager of said store, has not been good. After March 1957, when said store became a state-private, jointly operated store, defendant Chiang Yeh-wei served as assistant manager, but his work relationship with manager Ch'en Chi was not harmonious. On March 9, after being summoned by the district store for a talk about problems of his daily time schedule, Ch'en Chi received criticism. He, suspecting that the defendant had reported him, indicated his dissatisfaction. When Ch'en Chi returned to the store he was very irritated and said that it was reprehensible for a worker to make a report because of animosity. Because of this the defendant was worried and feared that something might happen, so he reported it to the district store. The defendant also suspected that Ch'en Chi had a pistol so, on March 10, he bought a wooden-handled fruit knife (including the handle it was twenty-two centimeters long) and hid it in his right pants' pocket, just in case. At 10:00 A.M on March 11, defendant Chiang Yeh-wei went to work at the store and saw that Ch'en Chi was sitting inside the store and that his manner was unusual. Chiang Yeh-wei was afraid that something would happen, so he went out through the rear door and reported these circumstances to the district store and the public security station. Ch'en Chi saw the defendant returning to the store and questioned him: "Why do you go out through the rear door and not through the front — the door is not closed . . ." At that time, the defendant saw Ch'en Chi put his right hand into his shirt, and he [the defendant] mistakenly thought that Ch'en was reaching for a weapon. He immediately became nervous and quickly moved forward, using his left hand to seize Ch'en's right hand. Seeing this situation, Ch'en Chi swung his left hand toward the defendant's face, knocking the defendant's glasses to the floor. At that time, the defendant became even more nervous, and he took the fruit knife out of his pocket, intending to stab Ch'en's right hand. Ch'en Chi used his left hand to prevent this, and the outside of his left arm was wounded. The length of the wound was twelve centimeters and the depth about one to two millimeters (there is a doctor's diagnosis and a court-affiliated doctor's expert opinion). Hsü Chiang-ch'ing, another worker who was on the scene at the time and who saw this situation, hastily intervened, and he wrested the knife from the defendant's hand. There were no serious consequences.

During the course of the investigation, the people who were on the scene and who were interrogated were Hsü Chiang-ch'ing and the witness Yang Yüan. They verified the above facts. When the defendant was interrogated, he admitted the fact of wounding the person with the knife.

On the basis of the above facts, this procuracy believes that for his act of wounding a person with a knife the defendant Chiang Yeh-wei should bear criminal responsibility for infliction of bodily injury. In order to protect state discipline and the rights of a citizen's person, we request that it [the case] be handled according to law.

Hereby submitted to the Huang-p'u district people's court in the city of Shanghai

Chief Procurator    Wang Hsin-min
May 24, 1957

# Chapter VIII Formal Criminal Processes: Trial Proceedings

The masses were so pleased with this trial procedure that they sang:
> When new leaps-forward are on their way,
> Trials in villages become the news of the day.
> The august courts were once places to abhor,
> But cases are now brought to our door.
> Even judges carry manure, when they hear cases,
> Resting in fields at tables cut from boulder faces,
> And on earthen stools, as the old and young,
> Of both sexes testify in words sharp and strong.
> When the villains startled at truth from witness chair,
> The virtuous folks found it just[,] jocund and fair.

For it spoke well of harvests sure and abound,
So fairly vouched in good words safe and sound.

> Chao Yuan (President
> of the High Court of
> Fukien Province), "Re-
> port on a Year's Work
> of the People's Court of
> Fukien Province" (Feb.
> 13, 1959)[1]

[B]ecause of cooperation among our three families — the procuracy, the public security organs, and the courts — we have launched a security movement, [the implementation of] which has served as a goal of the political-legal departments' joint struggle. Since a joint leap forward is our major objective and a leap forward in the business of each department is our secondary objective, the direction is clear, and we are marching in unison. What is even more important is that when the three departments, under the unified leadership of the Party committee, divide their labor and cooperate, they are more united internally. As a result, the three departments become one fist and attack the enemy even more forcefully.

> Chang Wu-yün, "Smash Permanent
> Rules, Go 1,000 *Li* in One Day"
> (1958)[2]

At the same time the [bourgeois] courts and judges take orders from the police bureau, stand together with the representative of officialdom, the procurator, and only try one party to the case, the defendant. In this situation there is basically no such thing as an "independent court" that is only "subject to law" and there is no such thing as the equality of both parties in litigation.

> Chang Hui et al., "These Are Not the Basic
> Principles of Our Country's Criminal
> Litigation" (1958)[3]

This chapter is concerned with court procedures for reviewing the recommendation of police and procuracy that the defendant be convicted of a crime. After introducing the constitutional and legislative framework for the organization of the courts, the chapter presents the basic rules prescribed during 1954–1957 for the conduct of public trials as well as eyewitness accounts of how a number of these experimental trials were carried out. It then provides examples of the secret trials that continued to prevail even in the constitutional era, before going on to trace the consequences of the antirightist movement and the great leap forward for the budding public trial system and to illustrate the types of judicial procedures that in recent years have been denominated "trials" in the PRC. The final part of the chapter deals with the question of judicial independence.

1. *Fu-chien jih-pao* (Fukien daily); translated in *JPRS*, no. 1077-D (Dec. 17, 1959), p. 8.
2. P. 60.
3. P. 77.

## A. ORGANIZATION OF THE COURTS

### ITEM 190

[CONSTITUTION OF THE PRC (Sept. 20, 1954), pp. 25, 26]

Article 73. The Supreme People's Court, local people's courts of the various levels, and special people's courts shall exercise the power of adjudication in the People's Republic of China.

Article 74. The term of office of the President of the Supreme People's Court and presidents of local people's courts of the various levels shall be four years.

The organization of people's courts shall be prescribed by law.

Article 79. The Supreme People's Court shall be the highest adjudication organ.

The Supreme People's Court shall supervise the adjudication work of local people's courts of the various levels and special people's courts; higher people's courts shall supervise the adjudication work of lower people's courts.

Article 80. The Supreme People's Court shall be responsible to and also shall report its work to the National People's Congress; during periods when the National People's Congress is not in session, it shall be responsible to and also shall report its work to the Standing Committee of the National People's Congress. Local people's courts of the various levels shall be responsible to and also shall report their work to local people's congresses of corresponding levels.

### ITEM 191

[LAW OF THE PRC FOR THE ORGANIZATION OF PEOPLE'S COURTS (passed at the 1st meeting of the 1st session of the NPC, Sept. 21, 1954; promulgated by the Chairman of the PRC, Sept. 28, 1954), *FKHP*, 1:123–130]

*Chapter 1. General Principles*

Article 1. The power of adjudication of the People's Republic of China shall be exercised by the following people's courts:

(1)  Local people's courts of the various levels;

(2)  Special people's courts;

(3)  The Supreme People's Court.

Local people's courts of the various levels shall be divided into basic level people's courts, intermediate people's courts, and high people's courts.

Article 2. Recommendations for establishing high people's courts and special people's courts shall be submitted by the Ministry of Justice[4] for the approval of the State Council. Recommendations for establishing intermediate people's courts and basic level people's courts shall be submitted by judicial administrative organs of provinces, autonomous regions and cities directly under the central authority for the approval of people's councils of provinces or cities directly under the central authority, or of organs of self-government of autonomous regions.

4. The Ministry of Justice was abolished in 1959. See Chapter II, note 43.

Article 3. The task of people's courts shall be to adjudicate criminal and civil cases and by adjudication activity, punish all criminals and resolve civil disputes, in order to defend the people's democratic system, protect public order, protect public property, protect the rights and lawful interests of citizens, and safeguard the smooth conduct of the undertakings of socialist construction and socialist reform of the state.

People's courts shall use all their activities to educate citizens to be loyal to their mother country and consciously to observe the law.

Article 14. The Supreme People's Court shall be responsible to and also shall report its work to the National People's Congress; during periods when the National People's Congress is not in session, it shall be responsible to and also shall report its work to the Standing Committee of the National People's Congress. Local people's courts of the various levels shall be responsible to and also shall report their work to the people's congresses of corresponding levels.

The adjudication work of lower people's courts shall be supervised by higher people's courts.

The judicial administrative work of people's courts of the various levels shall be administered by judicial administrative organs.

## Chapter 2. Organization and Powers of People's Courts

### Section 1. Basic Level People's Courts

Article 15. Basic level people's courts shall include:
  (1) People's courts of counties and cities;
  (2) People's courts of autonomous counties;
  (3) People's courts of city-administered districts.

Article 16. Basic level people's courts shall each be composed of a president, one or two vice-presidents, and a number of judges.

Basic level people's courts may each establish a criminal adjudication division and a civil adjudication division, each division having a chief judge and, when necessary, associate chief judges.

Article 17. A basic level people's court may, on the basis of the conditions of the district, its population, and its cases, establish a number of people's tribunals. A people's tribunal shall be a component part of the basic level people's court, and its judgments and orders shall be the judgments and orders of the basic level people's court.

Article 18. Basic level people's courts shall adjudicate criminal and civil cases of first instance; but cases for which laws and decrees have [made] separate provisions shall be excepted.

When a basic level people's court considers that a criminal or civil case that it has accepted is a major case and should be adjudicated by a higher people's court, it may request that the case be transferred to the higher people's court for adjudication.

Article 19. Basic level people's courts, besides adjudicating cases, shall handle the following matters:

(1) Deal with civil disputes and minor criminal cases for which adjudication in court is not necessary;

(2) Guide the work of people's mediation committees;

(3) Administer judicial administrative work within the scope of powers authorized by higher judicial administrative organs.

### Section 2. Intermediate People's Courts

Article 20. Intermediate people's courts shall include:

(1) Intermediate people's courts established according to districts in provinces and autonomous regions;

(2) Intermediate people's courts established in cities directly under the central authority;

(3) Intermediate people's courts of relatively large cities;

(4) Intermediate people's courts of autonomous *chou*.

Article 21. Intermediate people's courts shall each be composed of a president, one or two vice-presidents, a number of chief judges, a number of associate chief judges, and judges.

Intermediate people's courts shall each establish a criminal adjudication division and a civil adjudication division and, when necessary, may establish other adjudication divisions.

Article 22. Intermediate people's courts shall adjudicate the following cases:

(1) Cases of first instance that are prescribed by laws and decrees as being within their jurisdiction;

(2) Cases of first instance transferred from basic level people's courts . . .

When an intermediate people's court considers that a criminal or civil case that it has accepted is a major case and should be adjudicated by a higher people's court, it may request that the case be transferred to the higher people's court for adjudication.

### Section 3. High People's Courts

Article 23. High people's courts shall include:

(1) High people's courts of provinces;

(2) High people's courts of autonomous regions;

(3) High people's courts of cities directly under the central authority.

Article 24. High people's courts shall each be composed of a president and a number of vice-presidents, chief judges, associate chief judges, and judges.

High people's courts shall each establish a criminal adjudication division and a civil adjudication division and, when necessary, may establish other adjudication divisions.

Article 25. High people's courts shall adjudicate the following cases:

(1) Cases of first instance that are prescribed by laws and decrees as being within their jurisdiction;

(2) Cases of first instance transferred from lower people's courts . . .

*Section 5. The Supreme People's Court*

Article 28. The Supreme People's Court shall be the highest adjudication organ.

The Supreme People's Court shall supervise the adjudication work of local people's courts of the various levels and the adjudication work of special people's courts.

Article 29. The Supreme People's Court shall be composed of a president and a number of vice-presidents, chief judges, associate chief judges, and judges.

The Supreme People's Court shall establish a criminal adjudication division, a civil adjudication division, and other necessary adjudication divisions.

Article 30. The Supreme People's Court shall adjudicate the following cases:

(1) Cases of first instance that are prescribed by laws and decrees as being within their jurisdiction and cases of first instance that it considers it should try.

## ITEM 192

[DECISION OF THE STATE COUNCIL OF THE PRC ON ABOLISHING RAILROAD AND WATER TRANSPORTATION COURTS (passed at the 56th plenary meeting of the State Council, Aug. 9, 1957; issued, Sept. 7, 1957), *FKHP*, 6:297–298]

The State Council approves the report of the Ministry of Justice on abolishing railroad and water transportation courts and agrees to abolish the already-established nineteen railroad and water transportation courts and the thirty-one branch tribunals. It also decides:

1. After transportation courts are abolished, ordinary criminal cases with transportation aspects shall be dealt with on an individual basis by basic level courts at the place in which the case occurred; criminal cases that directly endanger transportation shall be dealt with by intermediate level people's courts at the place in which administrative bureaus or subbureaus of the transportation system are located.

## ITEM 193

[Wang Kuang-li (President of the High Court of Honan), "How Judicial Work in Honan Province Serves the Central Work" (1958), p. 46]

.   .   .   .   .

Our province has a population of forty-eight million. It occupies third place in the entire country behind Szechuan and Shantung [provinces]. Through the last nine years of effort the organizational structure of judicial work has been ceaselessly strengthened. At present in the entire province there are 139 courts, 232 people's tribunals, four judicial sections and divisions and a total of 1850 cadres engaging in the work of adjudication and of judicial administration. After the rectification and the antirightist struggle, we cleaned up the rightists and further purified the organization within the judicial work system.

## B. PUBLIC TRIAL: CONSTITUTIONAL MODEL

### ITEM 194

[LAW OF THE PRC FOR THE ORGANIZATION OF PEOPLE'S PROCURACIES (Sept. 28, 1954), p. 136]

Article 14. With regard to cases the prosecution of which is initiated by a people's procuracy, the chief procurator or a procurator assigned by him, shall appear in court as the state prosecutor to support the prosecution and to supervise the adjudication activity to see whether or not it is lawful. The chief procurator may also send someone to participate in, and to put into effect supervision over, the adjudication of cases that are not prosecuted by the people's procuracy.

When a people's court decides that the people's procuracy must send someone to appear in court, the chief procurator or a procurator assigned by him shall appear.

### 1. Preparatory Session

### ITEM 195

The following excerpt is from an article that was one of the first to bring to public attention the Soviet-style procedure with which the courts began to experiment after adoption of the Constitution on September 20, 1954.

["Answering Questions from Readers: On Trial Procedure in Criminal Cases," *Kuang-ming jih-pao* (Enlightenment daily), March 11, 1955, p. 3]

*Question:* What does the court's trial procedure in criminal cases amount to? *Answer:* When we refer to regularized trial procedure in criminal cases we mean the prescribed procedure through which a case must pass — from the preparatory examination to the final pronouncement of judgment. This rather regularized trial procedure is put into effect in order to expose criminal activity precisely, to attack criminals, and to guarantee that punishments are decided upon in accordance with law, giving criminals punishments that fit their crimes. On the other hand, it is also designed to guarantee that citizens are not subjected to court trial and are not erroneously made to assume criminal responsibility in situations where the evidentiary basis of their having committed a crime is lacking.

Now, on the basis of the accepted trial procedure developed by the people's courts and a consideration of the regularized trial procedure of the Soviet Union, people's courts have already begun to put into effect on an experimental basis rather regularized trial procedure for the trial of criminal cases in the first instance. This procedure may generally be divided into the preparatory examination (or preparatory) stage and the formal trial stage.

The preparatory examination stage is the first stage at which the court handles the case. It is conducted by one judge and two people's assessors who together constitute a preparatory examination session. The chief procurator or a procurator participates in the preparatory examination session and reports on the investigation conducted by the procuratorial organs and on the facts and evidence of the defendant's crime.

During the preparatory examination stage the judge and the people's assessors make a detailed examination of whether the procuratorial organs, in the course of their investigation, have made a comprehensive investigation, whether the facts are complete and the investigation clear, whether the evidence is accurate, and whether there was any unlawful conduct during the course of the investigation. On the basis of the results of this examination, they decide whether the act of the defendant constitutes a crime and whether or not they should prosecute (if the proof is insufficient, the procuratorial organs may make a supplementary investigation and prosecution may again be initiated). With respect to cases which are to be prosecuted, they [the judge and the people's assessors] fix the date of formal trial and the list of persons to be summoned to court, and they decide whether to have a public hearing.

1. If at the preparatory session the court performed all the activities mentioned above, what remained to be done at formal trial?

2. Was defense counsel supposed to participate in the preparatory session?

### 2. Role of People's Assessors

The Chinese have proudly proclaimed that their use of people's assessors constitutes a clear manifestation of the participation of the masses in the administration of justice. Items 196–199 introduce the official version of the assessors' role. Later materials will provide additional official information and will suggest the significance of the assessors in practice.

### ITEM 196

[CONSTITUTION OF THE PRC (Sept. 20, 1954), p. 25]

Article 75. People's courts shall, in accordance with law, put into effect the system of people's assessors when adjudicating cases.

### ITEM 197

[LAW OF THE PRC FOR THE ORGANIZATION OF PEOPLE'S COURTS (Sept. 28, 1954), pp. 124–125, 132]

Article 8. Except for simple civil cases, minor criminal cases and cases for which the law has [made] separate provisions, people's courts shall put into effect the system of people's assessors for adjudicating cases of first instance.

Article 9. People's courts shall put into effect the collegial system when adjudicating cases.

When people's courts adjudicate cases of first instance other than simple civil cases, minor criminal cases, and cases for which the law has [made] separate provisions, the adjudication shall be conducted by a collegial panel composed of a judge and people's assessors . . .

The president of the court or the chief judge shall assign one judge to serve as presiding judge of the collegial panel. When the president of the court or the chief judge participates in adjudicating a case, he himself shall serve as presiding judge.

## Section 2. People's Assessors

Article 35. Citizens who have the right to vote and to stand for election and have reached the age of twenty-three may be elected people's assessors; persons who have been deprived of their political rights may not be elected.

The number, term of office, and methods of selection of people's assessors for people's courts of the various levels shall be [covered] by provisions separately issued by the Ministry of Justice.

Article 36. People's assessors, during the period they perform their duties in people's courts, shall be constituent officers of the adjudication division in which they participate, and shall have equal authority with judges.

Article 37. People's assessors must perform their court duties at the time assigned by people's courts.

During the period they discharge their duties, people's assessors shall continue to be paid salaries as usual by their regular work units. People's assessors who have no salary or income shall be given appropriate subsidies by people's courts.

## ITEM 198

[INSTRUCTIONS OF THE MINISTRY OF JUSTICE OF THE PRC RELATING TO THE NUMBER, TERM OF OFFICE AND METHODS OF SELECTION OF PEOPLE'S ASSESSORS (July 21, 1956), *FKHP*, 4:239–241]

Since the promulgation of the Constitution of the People's Republic of China and the Law of the People's Republic of China for the Organization of People's Courts, people's courts in the various places have called attention to the establishment of the system of people's assessors and have thereby further advanced the development of this work. At present, according to incomplete national statistics, over two hundred thousand people's assessors have already been elected throughout the country, not including those who have been invited to serve temporarily. This has served nicely in attracting the masses of people to participate in state administration and in the supervision of the courts' adjudication work, in making more intimate the links between the people's courts and the masses, and in increasing adjudication strength. In the process of selecting people's assessors, the various places have already accumulated some elementary experience about the number, term of office, and methods of selection. According to the provision of Article 35, paragraph 2, of the Law for the Organization of People's Courts, this Ministry should adopt measures regarding these items. However, the widespread establishment of the system is still a recent matter, work experience is still not mature, and there are still difficulties in deciding upon the perfect number, term of office, and methods of selection. For this reason, we have first specially made the following Instructions:

1. Because our country is vast, the population density varies greatly from place to place and the volume of cases received by courts in the various places is not the same, at present it is very difficult to prescribe a nationally uniform, concrete figure [for the number] of people's assessors. People's courts of the various levels may calculate and propose the number of people's assessors according to (1) the number of cases in which assessing is required as prescribed by law, (2) the principle that a judge shall be accompanied by two people's assessors, and (3) [the principle that] the period of time that each people's assessor spends in court participating in the hearing of cases shall generally be ten days a year.

The number of people's assessors proposed by each basic level people's court for the people's courts of its county or city shall be sent to the provincial or city judicial organs for review and then to the people's councils of the same level for approval.

The number of people's assessors for intermediate people's courts shall be formulated by the organ of judicial administration of the same level in conjunction with the intermediate people's court, and shall be reported to the people's council of the same level for approval. If a people's council of the same level and its organ of judicial administration have not been established, after formulating the number by itself the intermediate people's court shall submit it to the organ of judicial administration of the next higher level for approval.

The number of people's assessors for high people's courts shall be formulated by the organ of judicial administration of the same level in conjunction with the high people's court and shall be reported to the people's council of the same level for approval and to the organ of judicial administration of the next higher level for the record.

2. In principle the period of time that a people's assessor spends in court performing his duties shall not exceed ten days a year. But if the hearing of a case in which he is participating has not concluded and if the [continuing] participation of the original people's assessor is necessary, the period may, in the exercise of discretion, be extended.

3. The term of office of all elected people's assessors shall uniformly be provisionally fixed at two years.

4. According to the provision of Article 35 of the Law of the People's Republic of China for the Organization of People's Courts, people's assessors shall be selected in accordance with the principle of election. For the election simple and practicable measures may be adopted. But faithful attention shall be paid to the representative and broad nature of people's assessors. The methods of selection are as follows:

(1) After the total number of people's assessors to be selected for basic level people's courts of the various places is determined, the basic level people's courts shall allocate, according to the number of residents, the number of people's assessors that should be elected by administrative villages (rural villages) and districts (cities). Then the assessors shall be elected by the people's

congresses of the administrative villages (towns) or of the city-administered districts or by the residents directly.

(2) People's assessors for city intermediate people's courts and for intermediate people's courts established in cities directly under the central authority may be elected, according to the allocated number, by the people's congresses of the various districts under the jurisdiction of these cities. They may also be elected within the staff and workers of [state] organs, people's organizations, and enterprises of the same level.

All or some of the people's assessors for intermediate people's courts established according to districts in the various provinces and autonomous regions may be elected by the city or country in which the court is located or by a nearby county at the same time that the city or county elects its people's assessors. Some or all may also be elected from among the staff and workers of organs, people's organizations, and enterprises of the same level.

(3) People's assessors for high people's courts and people's courts of autonomous *chou* may be elected from among the staff and workers of people's organizations and enterprises of the same level.

People's courts of the various levels may arrange and proceed with [the implementation of] the above methods of selection of people's assessors on the basis of the above provisions and in accordance with concrete local circumstances.

5. The selection of people's assessors for people's courts of the various levels in national autonomous regions and minority nationality districts may, on the basis of actual local circumstances, be [covered] by separately issuing provisions or by making supplementary provisions. [In either case] the provisions shall be formulated by local organs of judicial administration of the provincial level, submitted to the people's council of the same level for approval, and also sent to the Ministry of Justice for the record.

6. People's courts shall faithfully develop the role of people's assessors in adjudication and may not turn over to them work unrelated to adjudication. Also, they shall pay more attention to and show more concern for the study and the way of life of people's assessors.

The number, term of office, and methods of selection of assessors for the Supreme People's Court and for the special courts shall be [covered] by separately issued provisions.

It is hoped that in executing the above Instructions the various places, whenever they summarize experience and discover problems, will report them to this Ministry, so that experiences and problems can be concentrated and a foundation laid for adopting relatively mature methods.

## ITEM 199

["Fifth Group of People's Assessors Elected in Kwangtung," *Nan-fang jih-pao* (Southern daily, Canton), Nov. 19, 1963]

The fifth group of people's assessors of Kwangtung [province] has been elected in conjunction with this year's basic level elections. According to statistics returned by 104 counties and cities, more than 11,900 people's assessors have been elected.

The overwhelming majority of people's assessors elected this year are activists in various political campaigns and various tasks. Most of them are Communist Party members or CYL members. Having rendered outstanding services during their last term of office, more than 2,700 of these assessors have been elected again for another term of office.

The newly elected people's assessors realized that this was the greatest trust and honor that the Party and the people had conferred upon them and all said that they would seriously do the work of an assessor well. Tseng Szu, a people's assessor in the city of Canton, said: "Before the liberation, we women suffered every oppression and humiliation and were basically deprived of our freedom and rights. Today, I have been elected a people's assessor. This honor is conferred upon me by the Party and the people. Though I am of a low cultural level and am not very familiar with the work of an assessor, I have the will to serve the people. In the future, I will link myself intimately to the masses and report to the authority concerned the views of the masses on the judgments handed down." Yeh Hsien-fa, a people's assessor of Hsin-hsing county, said: "Before liberation, I saw how a case was judged in a counterfeit [KMT] court. At that time, one who had money and influence would always win, and nothing could be considered to be right or wrong. At present, however, before the people's court proceeds with a case, it must conduct investigations among the masses and study the facts carefully. Moreover, when a hearing is in progress, the masses are allowed to attend, and the defendant may defend himself. A special characteristic is that the people's assessors are elected to participate in court. This is really a mass-line method. Now that I have been gloriously elected a people's assessor, I must take care and try my best to do the work of an assessor, so that I do not betray the trust that the Party and the people have placed in me!"

How unusual is it for a country to resort to lay assessors in criminal cases? The courts of the Soviet Union and some western European countries employ assessors. Do Anglo-American jurisdictions have anything comparable? Consider the following news item:

"Vermont has a unique tradition by which laymen make certain they control those 'goldurn judges.'

"It is the assistant judge system, and its members are known as side-judges. This is because they flank the superior court judges in cases tried in county courts. The system is a throwback to the days when anything slightly reminiscent of Merrie Olde England was immediately suspect.

"When Vermont joined the original 13 colonies, it carried with it a deep distrust of the British judicial system. Although the system was adopted, it was saddled with some strict reservations that have never been discarded.

"To be a side-judge in Vermont, you don't have to qualify as a lawyer, you don't have to be a man and you don't have to know who Louis Nizer is.

"The closest thing to a requirement is that you should be somewhat advanced in years.

"For it is mainly retired folk who get elected. There are two in each of Vermont's 14 counties.

"Flanking the superior judge, the side-judges pose a problem. Vermont law states non-jury cases must be settled by the three judges and the laymen can overrule — and sometimes do — the decision of the trained jurist.

"The side-judges act as a buffer to the 'book-larned judges' — and often speak up when the superior judge exercises what they feel just isn't good, common, country horsesense.

"The superior judge knows what side his bread is buttered on. In this case, both sides. He has to be wary of the side-judges — knowing they can upset his decision. He usually manages to be friendly enough with one of them so he has a majority." [5]

Do Vermont side-judges sit in criminal cases?

### 3. Right to Make a Defense

## ITEMS 200A–200D

These items present the legal provisions upon which the institution of "people's lawyers" was erected during the 1953–1957 period.

## ITEM 200A

[CONSTITUTION OF THE PRC (Sept. 20, 1954), p. 26]

Article 76. The defendant shall have the right to have a defense.

## ITEM 200B

[LAW OF THE PRC FOR THE ORGANIZATION OF PEOPLE'S COURTS (Sept. 28, 1954), p. 124]

Article 7. The defendant shall have the right to have a defense.

The defendant, besides exercising the right to defense himself, may entrust a lawyer with his defense, may be defended by a citizen who has been introduced by a people's organization or who has secured the permission of a people's court, or may be defended by a close relative or guardian. A people's court may also, when it considers it necessary, assign a defender to defend him.

## ITEM 200C

[DECISION OF THE STANDING COMMITTEE OF THE NPC OF THE PRC RELATING TO WHETHER PERSONS WHO HAVE BEEN DEPRIVED OF POLITICAL RIGHTS MAY SERVE AS DEFENDERS (passed at the 39th meeting of the Standing Committee of the NPC, May 8, 1956), *FKHP*, 3:179]

Having discussed at its thirty-ninth meeting on May 8, 1956, the problem presented by the Supreme People's Court relating to whether persons who

5. Ronald E. Cohen, "Colonial Era Throwback: Side-Judges Part of Vermont Courts," *Boston Globe,* Oct. 16, 1964, p. 13. Quoted by permission of the United Press International.

have been deprived of political rights may serve as defenders, the Standing Committee of the National People's Congress decides: persons who have been deprived of political rights may not serve as defenders during the period in which they are deprived of political rights. But if a person who has been deprived of political rights is a close relative or guardian of the defendant, he may serve as defender.

## ITEM 200D

[PROVISIONAL MEASURES OF THE PRC FOR RECEIPT OF FEES BY LAWYERS (approved at the 29th plenary meeting of the State Council, May 25, 1956; promulgated by the Ministry of Justice, July 20, 1956), *FKHP*, 4:235–238]

Article 1. Lawyers are furnished in order to give legal help to the people. On the basis of the present standard of living of the people and the degree of complexity of a case and putting into effect the principle of to each according to his labor, lawyers may receive fees from parties as compensation for labor in accordance with these Measures.

Article 2. The amount of the fee to be received shall be agreed upon by the Director of the Office of Legal Advisers and the party.

Article 3. After agreement has been reached on the amount of the fee, the party shall pay it to the accountant of the Office of Legal Advisers, and the Office shall issue a formal receipt to the party.

Article 4. A portion of a lawyer's total income shall be given to the Lawyers' Association for its expenses, but that portion may not exceed 25 percent of his income.

Article 5. A lawyer who gives legal help to a [state] organ, enterprise, or organization may receive a fee in accordance with the contract concluded between the Office of [Legal] Advisers and the organ, enterprise, or organization.

Article 6. In any one of the following situations a lawyer shall give legal help without fee:

(1) Cases relating to a request for payment of compensation for injuries suffered because of a production incident;

(2) Cases relating to a request for alimony or payments for child-care expenses;

(3) Cases relating to a request for survivor benefits;

(4) Except where oral opinions are provided about specific cases that are being litigated, instances relating to a party who requests legal help and is given an oral answer;

(5) Cases in which it is proved that the party is in actual economic difficulties and is unable to pay.

Article 7. When a party requests oral help of a legal nature in a specific case, a lawyer shall receive a fee in accordance with the following standards:

(1) When the subject matter of a specific case does not involve property relations or, although it does involve property relations the facts of the case are simple, the fee in each case may not exceed one yuan;

(2) When the subject matter of a specific case involves property relations

or, although it does not involve property relations the facts of the case are complex, the fee in each case may not exceed two yuan.

Article 8. When a party requests that documents be written in his behalf, a lawyer shall receive a fee in accordance with the following standards:

(1) When an application is written in his behalf, the fee in each case may not exceed one yuan; when a contract, agreement, document for the partitioning of property, declaration, will, or other document that involves a legal act is written in his behalf, the fee in each case shall be two to five yuan;

(2) When a pleading is written in his behalf, the fee in each case may not exceed two yuan; when an appeal is written in his behalf the fee in each case may not exceed three yuan.

Article 9. When a criminal case is handled in court, a fee shall be received in accordance with the following standards:

(1) The fee for handling a case at the first instance level may not exceed twenty yuan;

(2) When the lawyer does not handle the case at the first instance level but does handle the case at the second instance level, the fee may not exceed fifteen yuan;

(3) When the lawyer has handled the case at the first instance and second instance levels, the fee that is received for the second instance handling may not exceed ten yuan;

(4) A lawyer who defends several defendants in the same case: when there are two defendants, the fee received from each shall be 65 percent of the fixed amount; when there are three or more defendants, the fee received from each shall be 50 percent of the fixed amount.

Article 10. When a civil case is handled in court, a fee shall be received in accordance with the following standards:

(1) When handling a case in which there is no amount in litigation, or, although there is an amount in litigation, it is 1,000 yuan or less, the fee may not exceed 10 yuan;

(2) When handling a case in which the amount in litigation is 3,000 yuan or less, the fee may not exceed 30 yuan;

(3) When handling a case in which the amount in litigation is 5,000 yuan or less, the fee may not exceed 50 yuan;

(4) When handling a case in which the amount in litigation is 10,000 yuan or less, the fee may not exceed 100 yuan;

(5) When handling a case in which the amount in litigation is 10,000 yuan or more, the fee may not exceed 150 yuan.

Article 11. When handling a complex criminal or civil case, the amount fixed in accordance with the provisions of Articles 9 and 10 of these Measures may, in the exercise of discretion, be increased, but the increased amount may not exceed twice the originally prescribed amount.

Article 12. When a lawyer goes to another place to handle a case, in addition to the fee prescribed by Articles 9, 10, and 11 of these Measures, he shall receive payment for daily living and transportation expenses from the party.

Article 13. The fixed amount to be received as a fee as prescribed by

Articles 7 and 8 of these Measures refers to the fee to be received by a lawyer not for participating in litigation procedure but only for orally providing legal opinions and for writing pleadings on behalf of a party; the fixed amount to be received as a fee as prescribed by Articles 9 and 10 includes the entire fee to be received for orally providing legal opinions, writing pleadings, and appearing in court.

Article 14. In accordance with these Measures, the departments and bureaus of justice in all provinces, autonomous regions, and cities directly under the central authority may formulate supplementary provisions that are based on actual circumstances and submit them to the Ministry of Justice for approval.

## ITEM 201

The above documents do not indicate the full extent to which lawyers were subject to regulation by the regime even during the Constitutional era. No one was permitted to practice law outside an OLA. The OLA in each city was under the local lawyers' association, which regulated admission to practice. This "social organization" was in turn directed by the local office of the Ministry of Justice. At least in some cities, lawyers were not allowed to be compensated in accordance with the provisions of Item 200D but were paid on the basis of a salary scale that was assimilated to that of government employees. As Item 91 demonstrated, each OLA was actually controlled by the Party, which did not hesitate to invoke available administrative and criminal sanctions against deviant OLA personnel.

Yet even though these "people's lawyers" cannot be said to have constituted an independent bar and even though their activities as defense counsel were severely circumscribed, their introduction into Chinese Communist society required a considerable educational effort by the regime. Lawyers and legal scholars did their best to explain the desirability of the adversary system of criminal adjudication and the need for professional defense counsel to implement it. They were met with doubts, disagreement, and even contempt. What need did a Communist government have for lawyers? Why should a lawyer be permitted to defend someone whom both the police and the prosecutor had already investigated and believed guilty of crime? Hasn't a lawyer who takes such a case lost his "political standpoint"? Don't defense counsel drag out trials unnecessarily? Such questions were asked not only by the ignorant masses but also by Party members, police, procurators, and even members of the judiciary.

The answers given, with the aid of Soviet textbooks, recited arguments that are familiar in the West. The adversary system helps the court reach a correct decision. If a court merely listens to the procurator and his witnesses, it too easily slips into a one-sided and often mistaken view of both the facts and the law. Only by allowing the defendant actively to present his side of the case can the court thoroughly and comprehensively analyze it. The defendant, however, cannot conduct his own defense, because he is often confined pending trial and is generally too uneducated and afraid to speak up in his own behalf. Although Chinese legislation permits a close relative or a representative of a mass organization to defend the defendant, full implementation of the adversary system requires his defender to be a lawyer. Lawyers alone have the legal knowledge and professional experience necessary to handle a criminal case. Also, because they understand better than laymen the significance of the right to make a defense, only they have the courage to risk charges that they have lost their "political standpoint" by making a vigorous courtroom presentation and by appealing an erroneous decision of the trial court. Moreover, the knowledge that lawyers will be participating in criminal litigation itself stimulates police and procurators to prepare their cases better and causes judges to act with circumspection. The discussion in the following excerpt, taken from one of the principal pamphlets published on the subject, is typical of the argumentation employed.

[Huang Yüan, *Wo-kuo jen-min lü-shih chih-tu* (Our country's system of people's lawyers; Canton), December 1956, pp. 8–9]

Lawyers, participating in litigation, will play a supervisory role in judicial work and will stimulate judicial organs to pay attention to raising the quality of their work. The lawyer, in the role of a defender, participates in the public trial session and, by bringing forth material that favors the defendant, helps the court to clarify the facts of a case. This cannot but stimulate the organs that initiate prosecution to consider carefully, before they initiate prosecution, such questions as whether their reasons are sufficient, their evidence adequate . . . etc., and to strive to raise the quality of their work so that the contents of the bill of prosecution are completely based on fact and law and cannot be overthrown or refuted. Next, the lawyer attends the public trial session and participates in litigation, and because he has legal knowledge about litigation, he is able to use [his knowledge of] the law to evaluate the activity of the court; and he dares to present his views about shortcomings in the work of the court. If a court's judgment in a case injures the lawful rights and interests of a defendant, the lawyer may, after obtaining the consent of the defendant, initiate an appeal. This also cannot but stimulate the officers who comprise the court strictly to observe the law in every aspect of litigation activity. Also, when a lawyer receives visits from the masses, he discovers shortcomings and errors in the court's adjudication work, which he promptly reports to the court. This stimulates the court to eliminate the shortcomings and errors quickly and to improve its work.

## ITEM 202

The available evidence suggests that, contrary to the impression which the government sought to create after the antirightist movement, the newly established system of "people's lawyers" was favorably received by the ordinary people who came in contact with it. In interviews two lawyers who practiced in China during the period immediately preceding the antirightist campaign asserted that the Communist experiment with the bar had proved a popular success. They reported that on many occasions criminal defendants who had initially mistrusted their counsel expressed satisfaction with his efforts at the conclusion of the public trial. Moreover, the masses who attended such trials were often enthusiastic about having someone able and willing to present the plight of a hapless defendant and the views of the common people, especially in cases when they felt the procurator was acting in a one-sided and high-handed fashion. Because their help to the public elicited warm appreciation, those who served as lawyers were developing a sense of mission and professional self-esteem. As one ex-lawyer stated with pride, "Every day people formed lines to see us." This item is one of many laudatory accounts that appeared in the press prior to the antirightist movement.

["This Year There Are Over 3,000 Lawyers Serving the Masses," *Kuang-ming jih-pao* (Enlightenment daily), Jan. 14, 1957]

A responsible official in the Ministry of Justice told a reporter from the New China News Agency that in 1957 there will be about 3500 lawyers in various places throughout the country serving the masses in the area of law. The organ through which the lawyers' business is handled, the office of legal advisers, will increase the number of its offices to about 1000. In 1956 there were over 2100 full-time lawyers in the entire country, and the office of legal advisers had over 670 offices.

The responsible official in the Ministry of Justice said that, on the basis of the provisions of the Constitution and the Law for the Organization of People's Courts relating to the right of the defendant to have a defense and on the basis of the urgent need of the masses of people for the work of lawyers, the work of lawyers in the new China began to be established relatively broadly this past year. Now, with the exception of Tibet, of the various cities throughout the country that are directly under the central authority, of the cities (counties) in which the various provincial (regional) people's councils are located or in which intermediate people's courts are located, and of the cities that have a population of 300,000 or more, the great majority have already established offices of legal advisers. The city of Shanghai, which has already established six offices of legal advisers, now has 122 full-time lawyers; Shantung province has 45 offices of legal advisers and 153 lawyers. Thirteen provinces (regions) and cities — Kiangsu, Fukien, Shensi, Peking, Shanghai, etc. — already have established preparation committees for lawyers' associations.

The offices of legal advisers in the various places have received the widespread welcome of the local people. From April to the end of November of last year, over 31,000 people went to the five offices of legal advisers in the city of Shanghai for information. The lawyers wrote over 9,000 legal documents on behalf of the masses, served as agents for parties in civil matters over 1,000 times, and served as defenders for defendants in criminal cases over 1,400 times.

## ITEM 203

This item illustrates the limited pretrial role of defense counsel. Before reading it recall Item 176.

[Rickett and Rickett, *Prisoners of Liberation* (1957), pp. 272–274]

.     .     .     .     .

September 11 [1955], was a Sunday. Han and I had a big project afoot. My Chinese-English dictionary had become so battered it was falling apart. Han, who had once lived next door to a bookbindery, had suggested that we try to rebind it ourselves. Saturday evening we had spent dismantling the volume and twisting cotton threads to sew the pages together again. We had just started arranging the guide strings Sunday morning when Supervisor Shen appeared at the door.

"Li Ko, put on some presentable clothes and come along," he said.

He stood waiting while I scrambled into a pair of clean slacks and shirt and then led me over to his office, where a blue-uniformed cadre presented me with a typewritten sheet bearing the stamp of the Superior Municipal Court of Peking.

"These are the charges against you," he said. "Read them over and see if they are correct."

I read them carefully. I had been charged with supplying information to the American Consulate and the British Negotiation Party, as well as carrying on activities intended to sabotage the revolution.

After assuring him that they were correct and signing the statement, I was led out to the courtyard where a jeep was waiting. We rode through the streets of Peking to the Municipal Court Building, where I was ordered into a small waiting room. In a few minutes the little interpreter who had accompanied us ushered in a man whom she introduced in English as Professor Wang of the Peking University Law School.

"He is to act as your lawyer," she said.

"I don't need a lawyer," I replied in Chinese. "I'm guilty of the charges against me."

"That's not the point," broke in the professor. "Let me explain. In the first place, since this is not a military court, the law entitles you to legal advice. If you are not satisfied with me, you can choose anyone you want to represent you. Expenses will be taken care of by the government. Secondly, you may plead guilty or not guilty. But even if you plead guilty you still want to have your sentence reduced as much as possible. There are a number of points which can be argued in your favor."

"What?" I asked.

"The fact that you made a full confession and that your attitude since arrest has shown that you regret your past actions. And then, too, perhaps there were extenuating circumstances which forced you to commit your crime. All of these factors should be considered by the court."

We discussed my case for about half an hour and he then left with the interpreter, whose services had not been needed.

About twenty minutes later an attendant appeared to summon me to the courtroom.

At the time that he was permitted to see a lawyer, the defendant in Item 203 had been in prison awaiting trial for over four years. Within minutes of this interview with the lawyer who had been assigned to him, he was brought to trial (see Item 210B).

If counsel had had an opportunity to interview the defendant at some substantial interval prior to trial, to what extent might this have enhanced his capacity to render effective assistance at trial?

### 4. Right to Public Trial and Other Protections

## ITEM 204

[CONSTITUTION OF THE PRC (Sept. 20, 1954), pp. 25–26]

Article 76. Except in special circumstances prescribed by law, people's courts shall conduct all hearings of cases in public.

Article 7 of the Law for the Organization of People's Courts contains an identical statement.

## ITEM 205

This item provides the official criteria for determining whether or not a trial should be public. They are similar to the Soviet standards. At the time of its promulgation this decision represented more a goal that was gradually to be reached than an inflexible guide to action, not only because of the politically sensitive nature of certain cases but also because judicial authorities lacked the manpower, education, and experience to hold public trials in all criminal cases.

[DECISION OF THE STANDING COMMITTEE OF THE NPC OF THE PRC RELATING TO CASES THE HEARING OF WHICH IS TO BE CONDUCTED NONPUBLICLY (passed at the 39th meeting of the Standing Committee of the NPC, May 8, 1956), FKHP, 3:178]

Having discussed at its thirty-ninth meeting on May 8, 1956 the problem presented by the Supreme People's Court on which cases may be heard nonpublicly, the Standing Committee of the National People's Congress decides: cases relating to state secrets or to the intimate lives of the parties or cases in which juveniles who have not reached the age of eighteen have committed a crime may be heard nonpublicly by people's courts.

## ITEM 206

The following article is one of many that sought to explain the significance of the right to a public trial. Ironically, by the time that it appeared in this provincial newspaper, the antirightist movement that was to bring an end to most public trials was already under way in the major population centers.

[Ling Hung-chin, "Why Public Trial Should Be Put into Effect," *Pao-t'ou jih-pao* (Paotow daily), Oct. 13, 1957]

.    .    .    .    .

Public trials may be divided into two kinds: one that is public with respect to the parties to litigation and one that is public with respect to society. Public with respect to the parties to litigation means that the complainant, defendant, defender, agent, guardian, etc., are allowed to go to court to petition and to present arguments and are allowed to know the reasons for the bringing of the complaint. Public with respect to society means not only that the above-mentioned persons are allowed to participate when a case is being heard, but also that the masses of people are allowed to attend and listen [to the proceedings], and newspapers are allowed to publish news and material relating to the case when it is in the process of being heard. When we talk of public trial we ordinarily refer to a trial which is public with respect to society. But although cases are not public with respect to society, if the law prescribes that there shall be no public trial, they are public with respect to the parties.

Why should the people's court put the public trial [system] into effect? What is the significance of it? The people's court puts the public trial [system] into effect because the people's court, in trial [work], represents the greatest interests of the greatest majority of people and also represents truth and justice. If a trial is just, then there is nothing that cannot be told. The public trial system can only truly be put into effect in a country led by the worker class. The significance of public trial is that it puts the trial work of people's courts directly under the supervision of the masses. In this way it can stimulate adjudication officers (judges and assessors) to raise their sense of responsibility and to prevent the mistake of subjectively forming opinions without foundation and obtaining statements by coercion or by enticement; it can stimulate experts conscientiously and responsibly to give accurate expert opinion; and it can stimulate witnesses and defendants so that they do not dare to conceal the true circumstances but rather help adjudication officers to examine the evidence even better, to clarify the facts of a case and to guarantee the accuracy of the trial. The significance of public trial is also that, through trial activity, it gives propaganda-education about the legal system to the people and it strengthens the sense of law observance in the masses of people. At the same time, it serves as a warning to those few persons who are preparing to commit crimes so that they do not dare to walk the road of crime.

Items 207 and 208 represent other rights that were widely publicized during the constitutional era.

## ITEM 207

[CONSTITUTION OF THE PRC (Sept. 20, 1954), p. 26]

Article 77. Citizens of the various nationality groups shall all have the right to use their own spoken and written languages in conducting litigation. People's courts shall interpret for a party who is unacquainted with the spoken and written language commonly used in the locality.

In districts in which a minority nationality group lives together or in which many nationality groups live together, people's courts shall conduct hearings using the spoken language commonly used in the locality, and written judgments, public notices, and other documents shall be issued in the written language commonly used in the locality.

## ITEM 208

[LAW OF THE PRC FOR THE ORGANIZATION OF PEOPLE'S COURTS (Sept. 28, 1954), p. 126]

Article 13. If a party to a case considers that an adjudication officer has a personal interest in the case or for any other reason cannot adjudicate fairly, he shall have the right to request the adjudication officer to withdraw. The president of the court shall decide whether or not an adjudication officer should withdraw.

### 5. Conduct of Public Trial

Item 209 completes the description of procedure in public trials that was begun by Item 195.

ITEM 209

["Answering Questions from Readers: On Trial Procedure in Criminal Cases" (March 11, 1955), p. 3]

.    .    .    .    .

After a case has passed through the preparatory hearing stage it enters the formal trial stage. This stage is the crucial link in the entire trial process. At this stage the court conducts a formal, public trial of the case, makes a final examination of the facts and the evidence in the case and passes judgment on the person tried.

At the formal trial stage there are one presiding judge and two people's assessors, who together conduct the public trial session. From the opening of the hearing to the pronouncement of judgment the public trial session goes through four stages: the preparatory stage, the examination stage, the argument stage, and the pronouncement of judgment stage.

At the preparatory stage, in addition to engaging in certain preparatory activities for guaranteeing that the examination at the public trial is correctly and smoothly conducted, the presiding judge of the public trial session must also tell the defendant of his rights, such as the right to request that an adjudication officer withdraw from the case, the right to have a defense, the right to present new evidence, and the right to make a final statement, in order to protect the exercise of these rights by the defendant. If there are to be witnesses or experts participating in the hearing, the presiding judge must inform them of their responsibilities.

At the examination stage of the public trial the main items are the presiding judge's reading aloud the bill of prosecution, questioning the defendant about whether he admits the crimes charged in the bill of prosecution (and about the defendant's views concerning them), examining the evidence and the defendant's previous statements, hearing the statements of witnesses and experts, and examining whether there are discrepancies between the defendant's statement and the statements of the witnesses and experts, in order, in the end, clearly to ascertain the true circumstances.

Following this is the argument stage. At this stage the main items are the statements about the defendant made to the court by the state prosecutor (the chief procurator) and the defender on the basis of the circumstances revealed by the examination at the public trial, and the proposals that they make, on the basis of the circumstances of the defendant's crime, for deciding upon punishment. The state prosecutor and the defender may argue these issues. After the arguments have been completed, the defendant may make a final statement.

Pronouncement of judgment is the final stage. It has to resolve the questions of whether or not the defendant is guilty and what law should apply. Actually, this stage includes two stages — deliberation and pronouncement of judgment.

After the presiding judge announces the conclusion of the argument stage he and the people's assessors retire to deliberate the case. During this deliberation, the presiding judge and the people's assessors have equal authority. If their views are not unanimous, the minority yields to the majority (but the minority view must be recorded and appended to the file). After deliberation the court is reconvened and the presiding judge publicly reads aloud the written judgment and tells the defendant of his right to appeal.

At this point the trial procedure for criminal cases in the first instance concludes.

## ITEMS 210A–210E

### ITEM 210A

["Hearing of the Szu-ming-t'ang Medicated Liquor Store Case," *Hsin-wen jih-pao* (Daily news, Shanghai), June 4, 1957]

The case of Chiang Yeh-wei, former assistant manager of the Szu-ming-t'ang medicated liquor store who wounded manager Ch'en Chi with a knife, was heard yesterday at 1:45 P.M. at a session of the Huang-p'u district people's court in the city of Shanghai.

*Chiang Yeh-wei's Statement*

After Judge T'ao Yung-k'ang declared the court in session, Procurator Ch'eng Ch'en-han of the Huang-p'u district people's procuracy read aloud the bill of prosecution . . . After the bill of prosecution was read, the judge asked defendant Chiang Yeh-wei: "You have heard the bill of prosecution. Do you have any views?" Chiang Yeh-wei said: "Yes. I took out the knife, but I did not stab him (referring to Ch'en Chi). I was only preparing [to defend myself], nothing else."

The judge then wanted Chiang Yeh-wei to relate the facts of his wounding Ch'en Chi on March 11. So Chiang Yeh-wei related the events. The judge asked: "Did your glasses fall off?"

Chiang Yeh-wei replied: "Yes, they fell off."

Question: "Do you know when Ch'en Chi's arm was wounded?"

Answer: "I do not know. At the time I did not notice it."

Question: "You did not stab him?"

Answer: "I did not."

Question: "At the time what did you suspect he was reaching for?"

Answer: "I suspected he was reaching for a gun."

Question: "What understanding [of your actions] do you have now?"

Answer: "I was wrong in taking out the knife and for this I can be dealt with in accordance with law. But the objective reason should be analyzed — was it to kill a person or to protect myself — and it should be studied in accordance with law."

People's assessor Ch'en Shao-chung then asked Chiang Yeh-wei: "You said that Ch'en Chi threatened you, saying that you were young and he was already over sixty years old and that if he fought you to the death, he would still be the winner [because he had lived a longer life than you]. When were these words spoken?"

Chiang answered: "In 1954, again in 1955, and again recently."

The judge asked the procurator whether he had any questions. The procurator asked Chiang: "When you went to the store did you have the knife?"

Answer: "Yes."

The procurator then asked: "When you went to attend the meeting were you also carrying it?"

Answer: "Yes, I used newspaper to wrap it up."

The judge asked Chiang Yeh-wei's defense lawyer, Li Kuo-chi, whether he had any questions.

The lawyer replied that he had, and he asked Chiang: "When you grabbed Ch'en Chi's hand, did he try to stop you?"

Answer: "He did not."

The lawyer then asked: "Did you stab and wound him with the knife?"

Answer: "I did not stab him."

### Ch'en Chi's Statement

After the judge had finished questioning Chiang Yeh-wei, he asked the victim, Ch'en Chi: "Chiang Yeh-wei has already related the facts. Do you have any different views?"

Ch'en said: "I am his teacher. He is my apprentice. This affair occurred three months ago, and there is so much to it. Now that we are in court I do not want to debate it with him again."

The judge said: "The court wants to clear up the facts. Today you are the victim and also a witness. Therefore you should make a statement that is in accordance with the facts."

So Ch'en Chi related the events: "When Chiang Yeh-wei returned to the store, I asked him: 'Where are you coming from?' Before a second sentence was spoken, he took out a knife. I blocked and ducked and then went outside and yelled for help."

The judge asked: "Did you reach into your clothes with your hand?"

Ch'en answered: "I do not clearly remember that."

Question: "Do you know when your arm was wounded?"

Answer: "I know." Then he said: "When I was at the public security sub-bureau and at the procuracy I requested that he should not be punished. But I requested that a judge determine who was right and who was wrong and that an explanation be published in the newspaper."

At that time, people's assessor Li Kuo-k'ang asked Ch'en Chi: "When Chiang Yeh-wei came in [the store] you only asked him one question?"

Ch'en Chi answered: "Only one. He took out a knife and stabbed at me, and I ducked down and ran outside."

Li then asked: "Is there a basis for your belief that Chiang Yeh-wei intended to stab you?"

Answer: "He said to me after the five-anti [movement] that he did not approve of my being his teacher. That was one inflammation [which rankled him]; second, there was the matter of salary; third, there was the question of the gun.

There were these inflammations. But to sum up, we have a teacher-apprentice relationship. I do not want him to be punished."

Chiang Yeh-wei's defense lawyer asked to talk with Ch'en Chi: "Is what you call inflammation, hatred?"

Ch'en Chi said: "There is no hatred between him and me."

*The Statement of the Witness Hsü Chiang-ch'ing*

The witness Hsü Chiang-ch'ing was summoned to come before the court. The judge wanted him to relate what he saw on March 11. Hsü said: "On the morning of March 11, I was the only person in the store. Ch'en Chi came at about ten, and at the time he did not have too nice an expression on his face. I was reading the paper. He sat down angrily. Not long after, Chiang Yeh-wei came in. Later, Chiang went to the rear. Ch'en Chi also went to the rear. When he came back, he took off his leather jacket and tied an apron around his waist. Not long after, Chiang Yeh-wei came back. Ch'en asked him: 'Where did you go?' Chiang said: 'I had business.' Chiang asked why he had not told him. In this way they began to struggle. When I raised my head to take a look, Chiang had a knife in his hand. I went up to them and grabbed Chiang's hand and pushed it down. I said that if there was something to be said he could say it but that he could not use a knife, and then some people came."

The judge asked: "Do you know when Ch'en Chi was wounded?"

Answer: "I do not know."

The defense lawyer asked Hsü: "Did Chiang Yeh-wei stab forward with the knife?"

Answer: "When I saw the knife, I pushed it away."

*The Statement of the Witness Yang Yüan*

The witness Yang Yüan (Ch'en Chi's daughter-in-law) was then summoned to come before the court. The judge asked Yang Yüan whether among the events of the day of March 11, she saw Hsü Chiang-ch'ing grab Chiang Yeh-wei.

Yang answered: "I saw it." And she also said: "I saw Ch'en Chi and Chiang struggling, and at that time I saw Hsü Chiang-ch'ing grab Chiang Yeh-wei's waist."

The defense lawyer asked the witness Yang Yüan: "Were you upstairs?"

Answer: "Yes."

He also asked: "When Ch'en Chi blocked with his hand, did he knock Chiang Yeh-wei's glasses off?"

Answer: "Yes."

Yang Yüan also related some things concerning the gun.

After the witnesses had been summoned and questioned, the judge, in response to the defense lawyer's request, read aloud the diagnosis of Ch'en Chi's knife wound, which was written by Dr. Ch'en Kuo-shou, a surgeon at the Jen-chi hospital, and he read aloud the expert opinion of the court-affiliated doctor. The procurator then asked the defendant, Chiang Yeh-wei, some questions relating to that.

### The Arguments

At this point, the judge announced: "The examination of this case has been completed. The arguments will begin." The procurator spoke first. He believed that from the investigation, from the questioning of the witnesses and the victim, and from the defendant's statement, it should first of all be determined as "a fact that the defendant had a knife in his hand on March 11 and that Ch'en Chi's arm was wounded by stabbing." He also said that "since the expert conclusion of the court-affiliated doctor was that the wound was a knife wound, the defendant, because he wounded the victim with a knife, should be held responsible for infliction of bodily injury. In our country, one's person is protected by law, and encroachment upon it is not permitted. To stab and wound with a knife is unlawful. Therefore, according to law the defendant should be given appropriate sanctions." The defense lawyer, Li Kuo-chi, then defended defendant Chiang Yeh-wei . . .

The hearing went on until six P.M. The judge and the people's assessors then deliberated the case. After deliberation, the judge announced: "We believe that some of the facts need further study and analysis. Later, a time will be set to pronounce judgment."

### ITEM 210B

[Rickett and Rickett, *Prisoners of Liberation* (1957), pp. 274–275]

I walked down a broad corridor to a side door of a long, narrow room. To my left across the back of the room was a gallery of about twenty-odd people some of whom I seemed to recognize. They were probably witnesses called to testify against me if I should plead not guilty. Toward the front of the room on either side were long tables. I was motioned to take a chair at the foot of the table nearest me, where I noticed my lawyer sitting. The young woman on the other side of him turned out to be the court stenographer.

At the table opposite us sat the man from the Procurator-General's office who had interviewed me a few weeks before in prison. Next to him sat a clerk from his office and the interpreter.

I had hardly sat down when the court was called to order and three men filed in to take their places at the bench on the dais which filled the front of the room. The man in the middle, a heavy-set person of forty or so with a fierce-looking mustache, announced in a clear Peking accent that the court was about to consider my case and told me to stand up. He first asked me if I wished an interpreter, and when I declined, he introduced himself as the judge and the men on his right and left as people's asseyors [assessors]. From their appearance they might very well have been college professors. After he had ascertained that I was represented by counsel, the trial got under way.

The man from the Procurator-General's office read off the charges. I was asked whether I pleaded guilty or not guilty.

"I wish to plead guilty," I stated.

The judge then told me that I was free to make any statement in my defense.

I declined, but my lawyer stood up and made a plea for clemency. He cited the points which he had mentioned to me before. I was again asked if there were anything I wished to say and after I had declined for the second time the court record was read back to us and I was asked to sign it. The judges filed out and I was led back to the waiting room. The whole trial could not have taken more than half an hour.

I sat watching the clock as it ticked off the minutes. When twenty-five of them had gone by, the attendant appeared again to lead me back to the court-room. This time I was ordered to stand in the center of the room.

The judge and two jurors [assessors] returned to take their places again on the dais. After clearing his throat the judge began to read off the decision, a lengthy document. I was guilty on two counts but in view of my record since arrest, the plea for clemency was granted in part and my sentence was six years, dating from the time of arrest.

"Six years!" I thought, a little stunned. Perhaps I had not heard right. I had been so sure that I was already on my way home. But when I was asked to sign the decision and given a copy, I could see it clearly in black and white — six years.

Court was adjourned and I was led out. By the time I had reached the waiting room the initial shock had worn off.

"Six years is not so bad. I could have been given much more," I thought. "With only two more to go, I'll be home in no time."

While waiting for someone to take me back to prison, I began making plans as to how I would spend those next two years. The list of books I would ask Dell to send me was already taking shape in my mind. Much to my surprise, however, the court attendant reappeared to direct me to a small room opposite the courtroom. It seemed filled with people.

As I stood at attention, a man informed me that I was now before the Peking Lao-gai Wei-yüan Hwey (Labor Reform Committee, which acts as a sort of parole board). My case had been referred to the committee and in view of my record it was decided that my six years' sentence should be commuted to immediate release.

Mumbling some sort of thanks, I left the committee room in a state of joyous confusion and as I almost flew back to the waiting room my lawyer had a hard time catching up with me to explain that I had three years or three days (I was too excited to hear him clearly) to appeal my sentence. In any case I assured him that no appeal would be necessary.

## ITEM 210C

[Jules Chome, "Two Trials in the People's Republic of China," *Law in the Service of Peace,* new series, 4:105–108 (June 1956)]

·     ·     ·     ·     ·

The Court sat on a raised dais. On both sides of the dais, but on the same level as the accused, were tables reserved for the prosecutor and counsel for the defense, Maître Ma Lu Chen, fresh from the Peking Institute of Legal and Political Sciences, who had been designated for the defense by the Court.

After the prisoner had been invited to challenge, if he wished, any of the three judges, the presiding judge explained to him his legal rights, and pointed out in particular that he could demand the right to bring witnesses if he thought it would be useful. In that event the case would be adjourned.

The presiding judge then read the bill of indictment [bill of prosecution].

The accused was a peasant forty-six years old. In 1942, when he was a gendarme in the service of the Japanese, he had assassinated a man in order to assist his superior officer to take that man's wife. Later, as a gendarme in the service of the occupying power, he had arrested a certain Tien, a member of the People's Army, of whom nothing more was heard after his arrest.

The accused, invited to defend himself, repeated the admissions he had made to the Parquet in the course of the preliminary inquiry. He admitted having joined the gendarmerie in 1942 in the service of the occupying Japanese. He pleaded in defense his necessitous condition.

The man for whom he had agreed to commit this crime was his superior officer. This man had already asked him once to kill the husband of the woman he desired, and he had at first refused. Then, on the insistence of his chief, he had agreed to do it. He went with his superior officer to a tea house. There he met his victim, who was a rickshaw man. The accused took the rickshaw, and directed the man to take him to the country. Once there, and beside a river, he had shot the man dead with his revolver. The body had been buried. Although the matter came to the ears of the Japanese authorities, they did nothing about it.

Some months after the crime, his superior officer had married the widow of the victim.

The crime would have remained unpunished, if a certain Hiang, a colleague of the accused, who had been approached by the superior officer first, had not decided to give information against him at the end of the year 1955.

The accused pleaded in defense that he had benefited in no way from this crime, that he had done it to please his superior officer, and that he had been afraid to refuse.

In so far as the second case was concerned, the accused declared that he had been sent, with another policeman, to a village to effect the arrest of a bandit who was preying on the peasants. He had genuinely thought he was dealing with a criminal, and had no idea that a member of the People's Army was involved. Moreover, he declared, it was not he himself who had arrested this man, but his colleague. He had simply guarded an exit of the house.

The presiding judge then asked the prosecutor if he wished to cross-examine the accused. The answer was no, and the presiding judge then asked the counsel for the defense if he had any questions to put.

Counsel for the defense asked three questions.

Q. — Had the accused known the rickshaw man before he killed him?
A. — No.

Q. — Who was his direct superior?

A. — The instigator of the crime.

Q. — Why had he in particular been called upon to arrest Tien?

A. — It was simply chance that it was he who had been sent to arrest a criminal.

The prosecuting counsel then made the closing speech for the prosecution. In the name of the State and the Chinese people, he declared, he wished to draw the attention of the Court to the social gravity of these crimes, which had indisputably occurred and had not been denied. The accused, not content with putting himself at the disposal of the enemy, had abused the authority with which he had been improperly invested, to commit, not simply a murder, but an assassination which had been premeditated and carried out according to a meticulously prepared plan.

"He is completely responsible for this crime," the prosecutor declared.

As for the second charge, the prosecutor pointed out that he had arrested a member of the People's Army, who had disappeared after the arrest. There was every presumption that he had been turned over to the enemy, but proof was lacking. However that might be, this arrest had done harm to the activities of the People's Army, and constituted a counter-revolutionary act.

"The accused," said the prosecutor, "had not been honest. He had first denied everything, and had only finally admitted the facts when confronted with the informer and his former chief, the instigator and beneficiary of the crime."

The defense was then called on.

The defending counsel analyzed the evidence, and attempted to enlist the understanding of the Court for the position in which the accused had found himself when he committed these crimes.

"Who decided on the crime? Not he. He was simply a private in the gen·· darmerie. The instigator was an officer. He was all-powerful at that period. The accused feared to refuse him. He did not know his victim; he received no reward for his crime. He was only a more or less passive instrument of the assassination and the principal author of the crime was the officer, who in a way might be described as commanding him to do it."

In the second case, the defense stressed that the accused did no more than guard a door. "Nothing gave him any reason to believe he was dealing not with a criminal, but with a soldier of the People's Army."

"The accused, moreover," said the defense, "had been a gendarme for only six months, and the two acts with which he was charged had both taken place in that short period. They were in addition committed on the orders of his superiors.

"The accused subsequently lived for six years in a district occupied by the Kuomintang, before the Liberation, and during the whole of this time, and since the Liberation, he had not committed a single blameworthy act. That, he hoped, would earn him the leniency of the Court, in virtue of Article 14.4 of the law on treasonable and counter-revolutionary activities" [Act for Punishment of Counterrevolution].

This article of the law allowed for considerable extenuating circumstances in the case of those who committed, before the Liberation, crimes covered by this law, but who freely and of their own accord had broken off every connection with counter-revolutionary organizations.

The prosecutor demanded the right of reply.

He protested with vehemence that Article 14.4 was not applicable to this type of offense. He invoked a decision of a higher court in a Southern province which determined that these provisions only applied to cases of treason or counter-revolutionary activity as such; and could not be invoked to cover crimes of common law perpetrated during the commission of treasonable or counter-revolutionary acts.

Referring to this case, he described it as an act of "counter-revolutionary despotism," an abuse of the authority conferred on him by the enemy, and such an act should be punished with exemplary severity.

Counsel for the defense made the closing speech.

He asked the Court not to accept the court decision cited by the prosecutor. "This decision," he said, "added to the clear and formal text of the law a distinction which is not contained in it. The conditions for the application of Article 14.4 are indisputably fulfilled, since the accused left the gendarmerie and the service of the Japanese of his own free will and had lived many years in territory governed by the Kuomintang without committing the slightest counter-revolutionary act."

The presiding judge then asked the accused if he had anything to add in his defense. He likewise asked the public if anyone had anything to say on the subject. The wife of the accused was heard. She spoke of her children, but knew nothing about the facts under discussion. A neighbor had nothing to say, and demanded loudly that he be allowed to leave.

The Court then retired to consider the verdict.

The hearing was resumed an hour later, when the presiding judge read the verdict standing before the accused and the public, who all remained standing while it was read.

This verdict, naming the accused and giving an account of the crimes with which he had been charged, surveyed and analyzed the facts of the case. The Court accepted the argument put forward by the defense, and rejected the restrictive interpretation of Art. 14.4. After stressing the gravity of the crimes in a long statement, it admitted considerable extenuating circumstances for the accused. He was sentenced to three years' imprisonment.

The presiding judge, in closing the session, informed the accused that he, as well as the prosecution, had five days in which to appeal.

We were also present at other trials, in particular the pleadings in a case of industrial sabotage before the Nanking High Court, an appeal from a death sentence before the Criminal Division of the Shanghai Appeal Court (the accused, a commander in the Kuomintang Army, who had landed secretly in China from Formosa in 1955 and carried on spying and counter-revolutionary activities, had his sentence reduced to eight years' imprisonment).

Wherever we went we had the impression of a justice dispensed with calm, dignity and deep humanity.

Unquestionably it was a matter of regret that the barristers acting in criminal cases had each time been briefed only a few days before the public hearing. I had the impression that this was a temporary difficulty owing to the present shortage of lawyers. The Chinese bar, I understood, is in the process of re-organization. I was told that a series of regulations dealing with the legal profession has just been enacted.

However that may be, the lawyers I saw and heard plead were fully briefed, despite the little time they had at their disposal to prepare the case. They disputed on obviously equal terms with the Public Prosecutor, and defended their clients not only with considerable energy, but also, in all the cases where I was present, with remarkable success.

## ITEM 210D

[Ishijima Yasushi, "A Pickpocket Case in Peking, Actualities of a Criminal Trial in China," in *Chūgoku no hō to shakai* (Chinese law and society; Tokyo, 1960), pp. 64–71][6]

Our delegation visited the people's court in Peking on the afternoon of August 22 [1959] . . .

I . . . had an opportunity personally to see the actualities of a Chinese criminal trial. Through a description of this trial I should like to explain a bit about Chinese criminal trials and the Chinese policy toward criminals.

First, I will introduce you to the courtroom.

The building of the Peking people's court is probably the same building that served as a courthouse in preliberation days. The gray walls, dark corridors, and courtrooms on both sides of the corridor all reminded me of the atmosphere of Japanese courthouses.

The courtroom that we entered seemed as large as the Japanese courtrooms that are used for single judge trials.

On the front wall there was a portrait of Chairman Mao Tse-tung. Under it we saw the judge's bench, which was elevated a step. (In the courtroom for civil cases, on the other side of the corridor, I saw that the judge's bench was on the same level as the floor. I suppose there is some reason for this difference.) Attached to the front of the judges' bench there were two big "red stars." The defense lawyer sat on the left of the bench and the procurator on the right (the reverse is true in Japan). Each had a small table and chair set at an angle toward the spectators' section.

The spectators' section is in the same place as in Japanese courtrooms. It had four rows of seats and could hold about thirty people. There was no bar separating this section from the rest of the courtroom.

On the left side of the room there were windows, and on the wall on the right there was a framed poster containing "Rules for the Courtroom." These rules were:

1. Quiet should be maintained in the courtroom.

6. I am grateful to Professor Toshio Sawada and the late Judge Kohji Tanabe for this translation.

2. Minors are not permitted to attend.

3. When the court is in session, no one may make a statement at will without permission of the judge.

4. The parties to the case should rise when the judgment is rendered.

. . . Among these provisions the third rule, namely, "When the court is in session, no one may make a statement at will without permission of the judge," particularly drew my attention. This illustrates a unique Chinese system whereby a spectator may make a statement in court with permission of the judge. Since there were no Chinese spectators at this trial I could not observe how this is done. I later heard (from my fellow delegates) that in a civil trial in the Shanghai court, the spectators had been very active in expressing their opinions.

Then the judges — more precisely, one professional judge and two assessors — entered the courtroom, along with the procurator and defense counsel . . . The judge, Chang Shih-jung, aged thirty-two or thirty-three, was a judge of the Peking intermediate court. The two assessors were both men who looked like workers of about forty-five and thirty, respectively. The procurator was a woman of about thirty named P'an Te-huai. The defense lawyer was a young man of about thirty-four or thirty-five.

On the judges' bench the professional judge sat in the center, with the assessors on either side of him. To the right of the judges sat a clerk, who was also a woman in her thirties.

The defendant entered the room without handcuffs, accompanied by a young man in the uniform of the people's police. The defendant was a tall, unshaven man with a crew cut. He was thirty-eight. (I shall keep him anonymous.)

The hearing began. At the beginning, the judge identified himself, the two assessors and the clerk, and told the defendant that he had the right to challenge them . . .

According to what we heard before the courtroom trial began, the personal history of the defendant was as follows: he began working when he was fifteen or sixteen as a coolie and also as a shepherd. When he was seventeen or eighteen he began to work as a butcher without a license. When he was twenty-seven or twenty-eight, just before liberation, he worked for a year for the T'e-wu, which was the intelligence service of the Kuomintang. During that period he took people's property through extortion and informed against those who offered food to the liberation army and caused their arrest. He was tried twice by the Nationalist regime for working as a butcher without a license and for gambling. His present occupation was said to be that of butcher for a food supply enterprise.

In the opening procedure there was one more thing which interested me. It was that in the course of the examination of the defendant for identification purposes he stated in response to a question about his family that he had two wives. This examination took place after the arraignment procedure, which had followed the reading of the bill of prosecution by the procurator. . . . The defendant was charged with eighteen separate pickpocket offenses during a four- or five-month period.

He had allegedly stolen bags and purses eighteen times in buses or trolleys from November of last year (1958) until March 8th of this year when he was caught in the act.

. . . Then the bill of prosecution was read, and the defendant was arraigned. He admitted all the facts alleged. The judge began the examination by questioning him about his family background, his monthly income, etc. His entire career was reviewed. After that, the judge said: "Admit before the court all the facts of the thefts alleged."

The defendant then stated his eighteen offenses so fluently that we were all surprised how well he had remembered them. ". . . I stole a purse with sixty-eight yuan from the rear pocket of a man in a bus on such and such a route on such and such a day, [I stole] a black bag with fifteen yuan, a bankbook with five yuan, and a gold ring, from a woman of about twenty-four or twenty-five in such and such a bus on such and such a day . . ."

. . . In his story I heard that he had stolen a purse, then entered a movie theater and threw the purse under the seat after taking the money out . . . Pickpockets are the same everywhere, I thought. Whenever he found a bankbook in a stolen bag he returned it to the victim with a letter, he said. This attitude, I felt, was typically Chinese. One of these letters was admitted as evidence and also cited in the argument of the defense counsel. All these things interested me immensely.

When the defendant's confession was over, the judge asked: "Have you confessed everything?" Then an interesting examination was begun by both the judge and the assessors in turn. This examination focused on whether the defendant had made sufficient self-criticism. Some of the questions and answers were as follows:

Judge: "For what purpose did you steal?"

Defendant: "To pay back a debt."

Judge: "Why were you in debt?"

Defendant: "I liked to have more luxurious things than others, so I embezzled money with which I had been entrusted."

Judge: "Do you smoke or drink?"

Defendant: "No, I do not."

Judge: "But you had some wine in you when you were caught, didn't you?"

Defendant: "I used to drink."

Judge: "When did you begin drinking?"

Defendant: "When I began stealing."

Judge: "Is your life very hard?"

Defendant: "No, not very hard."

Assessor: "You stole eighteen times in four or five months, causing trouble and disrupting production. You partially confessed, but you are still not very honest. You have the pickpocket's technique of choosing rush hours. I cannot fully believe your story. I suspect you have been trained to be a pickpocket. Tell us more clearly why you stole!"

Defendant: "To live a luxurious life."

Assessor: "Didn't you get on street cars to steal money?"

Defendant: "No."

Assessor: "Did you know your victims would suffer [by the loss of money]?"

Defendant: "When I stole a [transportation] ticket I became remorseful and thought of returning it."

Judge: "If you had been remorseful you would have stopped stealing. Is it not because you were not remorseful that you continued stealing?"

. . . . .

Then the judge showed the defendant for identification some pieces of evidence such as a purse and the letter written by defendant when he mailed back the bankbook. He also read aloud some documentary evidence including a statement of a victim, a report of damage to the police, a complaint against the defendant and the report of the arresting officer, and asked the defendant to verify them.

After this, the judge resumed the examination.

Judge: "Why doesn't your confession agree with the reports of the victims with respect to the total amount of money stolen?"

Defendant: "I think it must."

Judge: "The victims well know the sums stolen. Did you make a mistake, or are you holding back information?"

Defendant: (no response)

Judge: "Where did the money you stole come from?"

Defendant: "From the sweat of labor."

Then the judge asked the procurator whether he had any other evidence and also asked the defense counsel whether he had something to ask the defendant.

Lawyer answered: "There are some vague points," and asked some questions.

Lawyer: "What did you tell the government after you were arrested?"

Defendant: "The government said it would treat me generously if I confessed."

Lawyer: "Did you confess only a part of your offenses the first time?"

Defendant: "Yes."

Lawyer: "Afterwards did you make further confessions voluntarily?"

Defendant: "Yes."

Lawyer: "How many times did you confess?"

Defendant: "Three times."

Lawyer: "What did you do with the rest of the money?"

Defendant: "I surrendered it to the government."

Lawyer's examination ended. The judge then asked defendant again: "Don't you have anything else to confess?" He said no.

They permitted the defendant to sit down, and the argument of the procurator took place. He stated that all the accusations had been proved by the evidence and that not only had the defendant committed many offenses, but also that the way he committed them was vicious and there was nothing extenuating in his account of his motives. The procurator's argument was similar in form to that of a Japanese prosecutor. The contents of the argument, however, fully reflected the criminal policy and fundamental ideas of justice in new China.

The procurator referred to the career of the defendant before liberation and pointed out that "The defendant lived his life in the old society, trampling on the interests of others. Under the protection of the Kuomintang he repeatedly committed crimes against the people. Yet after liberation the government did not punish him but gave him a job. Nevertheless, without any reflection he committed thefts. These offenses after liberation were caused by his evil thoughts which were deeply rooted before liberation." As to the essence of this crime [the procurator continued]: "Now the Chinese people are all absorbed in working for progress. In this country labor is regarded as the highest honor, and rewards for labor are guaranteed by law. The conduct of the defendant damaged the social order of this country, which respects labor. People now consider thieves as the worst people. Among the victims were foreign representatives and members of minority nationality groups. Therefore these offenses had bad political effects in our capital." The procurator went on to discuss the motive of these offenses. "He lived a middle-class life, not a hard life. He admitted this himself. These offenses originated in a mind that wanted a hedonistic life. Although he received education for several years after liberation, his evil thoughts and bad habits were not changed at all." Finally he concluded that he would "propose a fairly long term of imprisonment for the defendant" because such a person "should be given an opportunity for complete reform."

The procurator's argument was indeed scathing.

The defense lawyer argued for the defendant: "Defendant sent back the bankbook he had stolen. Therefore this theft was harmless although legally it was certainly a theft. Moreover, he confessed voluntarily, and his confession fundamentally fits the facts. The attitude of the defendant is serious" . . . "Now he has made up his mind to reform himself. The sentence should be generous for a man who is genuinely repentant."

Honestly, I could not help smiling because his argument was so similar to that of Japanese counsel provided by the state.

The defendant was then given an opportunity to make his final statement. He said: "I have nothing to say. I disrupted the people's interest. Freedom made me a bad man. I did not think. Please punish me!" This big man began to weep as he was making his plea.

The trial ended, and the defendant was ordered out. There was a twenty- or thirty-minute intermission for consultation. Court was then resumed, and the sentence was immediately pronounced.

It was impressive that the judge stood up when pronouncing sentence.

The opinion of the court referred to the career of the defendant before liberation, as had the procurator, and pointed out: "Defendant did not go straight but did much wrong, for example, gambling and working for the intelligence service of the Kuomintang. He was given a good job by the government. He received criticism-education. While he should have observed the law, he did not try to recognize his faults or to improve himself." The judge stated that the facts alleged by the prosecutor had been proved fully by the evidence and continued. "This bill of prosecution is correct. We also took the opinion of defense counsel into consideration. Defendant substantially confessed and has basically begun to reflect upon his situation. He is somewhat repentant. However, his conduct comes from the bad customs of the old society, where he used to obtain great rewards without any labor. This conduct, interfering with the normal [pattern of] earning through labor, damaged the daily lives of our people and our social order, which is based on labor; it damaged labor itself, which is the supreme value in our country." The judge concluded: "Therefore, the defendant must reform himself through labor." He sentenced the defendant to six years of imprisonment.

The judge also stated that this six-year term would run from the date of arrest and that an appeal may be filed within ten days of the service of the written judgment. It took about two hours from the opening of the trial to sentencing.

## ITEM 210E

[René Dekkers, *Lettres de Chine* (Letters from China; Brussels, 1956), pp. 116–117, 78–80]

.    .    .    .    .

Scarcely had I arrived in Peking [in May 1956] . . . when I was informed that a criminal trial was about to take place.

It involved thefts and embezzlements committed by an employee of a construction firm. I hoped finally to attend a preliminary hearing; unfortunately for me, again the defendant confessed.

The matter should have lasted an hour; it took three and a half. The *pièce de résistance* was the questioning of the defendant (a man of forty-three, who looked fifty-five and was dirty and badly shaven and wore a mustache) by the presiding judge (a woman of about thirty with an intelligent face, closely set eyes, and a large mouth). She managed the matter with a calm authority. The questioning focused less on the truthfulness of facts than on the methods the defendant had used, especially the falsification of documents. The speeches of the prosecutor and of the defense lawyer each took only ten minutes. The sentence: four years (since he was a recidivist).

Other noteworthy aspects: the seats and the benches of the defense lawyer and of the prosecutor were turned toward the public . . . In fact, the prosecutor spoke more to the public than to the members of the tribunal. He particularly deplored the inadequacy of the Chinese accounting system: it seemed to permit too many frauds.

During the questioning one of the spectators (there were about twenty of us) belched magnificently. No one cracked a smile.

Always the same correctness in the proceedings.

.    .    .    .    .

This morning three of us went to hear a criminal case.

It took place in a small white room with dark brown furniture. The members of the court were at the end of the room, on a platform. Against the wall on the left sat the defense lawyer. Against the wall on the right sat the procurator (which is better than in our country, where the procurator sits right next to the court, even though he takes part in the proceedings). Between them was the defendant. Behind him were a dozen or so benches for the public (about thirty people).

When we entered the defense lawyer and the procurator (he had an enormous jaw but there was nothing malicious about him) were already in their respective seats. In came the clerk, a woman in her thirties. Then the members of the court entered: a presiding judge (with an intelligent and gentle countenance) and two workers (this was a court of first instance).

The defendant was brought in. She was a nurse who had stolen watches and medicines from the hospital where she worked. Next came the complaining witnesses. After establishing their identity, the presiding judge reminded them of their duty; then they temporarily withdrew from the room.

The defendant confessed. She claimed to have stolen in order to support her family (five children and her sister), and in order to provide for one of the children, who had bronchitis. Her husband worked far from Shanghai and returned only on holidays.

The presiding judge reproached her for badly managing her affairs.

"You and your husband earn 120 yuan a month; isn't this plenty to live on?"

"Yes, your honor. But what would you have me do? My children like the good things of life, and I do too. I abhor streetcars and like pedicabs." [A streetcar only costs six cents while a pedicab costs thirty.] "But you can be sure that I have learned my lesson. If only I can continue to work, I'll pay back the money regularly."

The prosecutor then spoke. "These are grave crimes, gentlemen. The stolen watches belonged to workers who came to the hospital for treatment. If the word gets around that there is stealing in hospitals, the workers will hesitate to go there. It will create an atmosphere of mistrust that could be harmful to production. As to the thefts of the drugs, these concerned the resources of the community, which is even more serious. If this mother really had household difficulties, shouldn't she have taken them to the welfare agencies? They are there to aid her. Finally, I am keeping her five children in mind, and I will be satisfied with a moderate punishment."

It was then defense lawyer's turn to rise. "The facts are clear, and it is not on them that we should concentrate but on the defendant herself. She is forty. Until liberation she led the life of the exploited, where stealing was common and was regarded as a means of defense. Since then she has not had the time to re-educate herself. She has many debts and stole in order to pay them off. Is it really feared that these larcenies will harm production? Isn't this pushing the imagination a little far? Let us remember the great principle that dominates the criminal law: punishment must tend to rehabilitate the criminal. Now this goal is already attained, since the defendant regrets her conduct and wants to make up for it."

The court withdrew for a quarter of an hour to deliberate. Then the presiding judge pronounced the judgment. He reviewed all the facts. He scolded the defendant for having misused the nurse's position which the government had obtained for her: she deserved punishment. Taking account of the fact that she had confessed and that she wanted to make amends, she would be sentenced to only six months of imprisonment and to a suspended sentence of ten months. Naturally, she would have to make reimbursement for those of the stolen articles that had not been recovered.

"You have eleven days to appeal."

It took at least ten minutes to hand down the judgment. Was the proceeding over? No; one of the witnesses asked for and received permission to speak again. He was the director of the hospital, and he seemed dissatisfied. He claimed that the defendant had not confessed everything. The presiding judge told him: "Sir, talk to the assistant prosecutor, since he too can appeal the judgment."

1. Do Items 210A–210E suggest generalizations about the respective roles in Chinese public trials of the presiding judge, the people's assessors, the procurator, the defendant, and the defense lawyer?

2. What purposes were served by these public trials?

3. What inferences can be drawn from the fact that in each of these trials the defendant fully confessed and only sought mitigation of punishment? Does this support the accusation that the PRC is a "police state"? Consider the following:

a. "The closing argument of the defense [in Japan] is generally aimed mainly at the reduction of the sentence suggested by the procurator.

"From experience, defense counsel well knows that it is strategically more effective to appeal to the emotions rather than to the reasoning processes of the judge. Of course, if guilt is seriously in doubt, defense counsel will try to persuade the judge to render a favorable judgment, or at least a moderate sentence, by attacking logically and factually the weak points of the prosecution's case. In most cases, however, it is wiser for the defense to admit the guilt of the accused and to place the accused on the mercy of the court. The defense counsel often resorts to the favorite technique of presenting a witness who appeals to the softheartedness of the judge; it is particularly important to show the judge that the defendant is remorseful and is making efforts to rehabilitate himself. Thus an able and eloquent defense counsel sometimes succeeds in obtaining a very lenient sentence for a man whose personality and background, if examined scientifically, would prove in fact too questionable to warrant early release from prison." [7]

b. "[In the United States] the typical method of conviction is by the accused's plea of guilty, with no trial required. In the federal courts, the guilty plea receives the heaviest use, 86 percent in the fiscal years 1960 through 1963, while in the state courts, the use of the plea trails by 5 to 10 percent." [8]

4. What was there about trials such as those described in Items 210A–210E that might have led the Party generally to abandon its experiment with public trials?

7. Haruo Abe, "The Accused and Society: Therapeutic and Preventive Aspects of Criminal Justice in Japan," in A. T. von Mehren, *Law in Japan* (Cambridge, Mass., 1963), p. 330.

8. Jerome H. Skolnick, *Justice without Trial* (New York, London, and Sydney, 1966), p. 13.

## C. SECRET TRIAL: ENDURING REALITY

### 1. Secret Trial During the Preconstitutional and Constitutional Eras

#### ITEM 211

Even during the constitutional era, of course, in most cases the defendant did not receive a public trial in the constitutional sense. In Item 211 a judge of a rural people's tribunal that served as a branch of a county basic level court describes two of the cases that he handled in ordinary fashion, one from the preconstitutional period and one from the constitutional period. It is significant that this judge's description of his experiences was published in 1959 as a contemporary model for judicial personnel.

[Liu Tse-chün, "Realizations from My Adjudication Work," *CFYC*, 1:50–51 (1959)]

At two o'clock on an autumn night in 1955 two members of the masses came to our [people's] tribunal to talk to me. In the town of Lan-ch'eng there was a case of a person having been crushed to death by a wagon. They asked me whether it would be necessary to conduct an on-the-spot examination. By questioning them I found out that the deceased was named Hsiu Kuei-lan and the driver of the wagon was her husband, Ch'ang Chung-hsiao. I remembered that they had tried to get a divorce. At daybreak I left to go to Ch'ang's house, together with two health officers. At that time not only did Ch'ang Chung-hsiao and some cadres suggest that we not examine the corpse, but the father of the deceased firmly refused to agree to the examination. He said the entire responsibility was on him. If people had any suspicions and wanted to accuse someone, let them accuse him. I thought to myself: "Human life is sacrosanct." We must be responsible to the revolution and to our work. In order to get to the truth of this irregular case of death, I used all my persuasiveness on the father of the deceased, and we examined the corpse. We also conducted an on-the-spot examination of the scene of the incident. As a result of my examination I discovered five suspicious points: (1) the deceased had five wounds, all of them on her head; she had no other wounds elsewhere on the body, so it did not seem as if she had been crushed to death by a wagon; (2) the northern and western boundaries of the scene of the incident were hills and on the eastern and southern sides tall crops were growing, so that no one from any of these sides could see what was going on in the interior, which was really a convenient place for the activity of a criminal; (3) the harness of the donkey that had pulled the wagon was not broken but seemed to have been loosened; if, as Ch'ang said, the donkey had run wild, the harness would have been broken; (4) there was blood at the place where the deceased had fallen from the wagon, and this was very far from the place the wagon had overturned; moreover, there was no blood at the place where the wagon had overturned; (5) Chang's statement that he was 100 meters away at the time the wagon overturned was incredible. Thus I was suspicious of Ch'ang Chung-hsiao but I did not show it at that time. I only ordered him not to bury the corpse for a certain period. Then I returned to the tribunal to make a telephone report to the court. The county public security and procuratorial departments immediately sent two comrades to join me, and we asked a doctor to conduct a second on-the-spot examination. This proved that the wounds of the deceased did not result from her having been crushed but resulted from her having been beaten. After Ch'ang was brought back to the county [seat] it was only through interrogation that we learned that the deceased had not been crushed to death by the wagon but that Ch'ang Chung-hsiao, because he had had illicit sexual relations and had unsuccessfully tried to divorce his wife, had deliberately killed her and then disguised it as a wagon accident. At the time the death sentence of the criminal, Ch'ang, was executed, the father, maternal uncle, and younger sister of the deceased personally come to the tribunal and, weeping so hard they could hardly be heard, said: "If it had not been for the government, we could never have had revenge for our hatred." The father of the deceased also said: "If the head of the tribunal had not taken charge, I would have wronged my daughter by not inquiring into the circumstances of her death." This gave me the profound realization that punishing criminals is protecting the interests of the masses and inspired me with even greater confidence in my struggle against the phenomenon of crime. In 1953, not long after I came to the court, I handled the case of Hsü Wan-jung, who [was charged with having] forced Liu Chin-ling to commit suicide. Hsü was Liu's nephew. Liu lived in Hsü's house. The village cadre reported that Hsü and Liu had fought before Liu committed suicide and that Liu had been forced into it. The cadres brought Hsü to the court. Through my interrogation I did not find anything that indicated Liu had been forced to kill himself, but rather the more I inquired the more I discovered that Hsü was not closely connected with Liu's death. After I reported this situation to the leadership, I twice sent people down to investigate. The cadres and witnesses all reported that Liu had been forced by Hsü to kill himself. But the only evidence that they could point to was that: (1) before the deceased's suicide, he and Hsü had a fight; and (2) when the case became known Hsü suddenly returned to his native county of An-tzu. I repeatedly thought to myself that these two points of "evidence" certainly did not prove that Liu had been forced by Hsü to kill himself. At that time Hsü's mother came to visit him in prison. From the side, I purposely observed her, and the scene of the mother and son embracing and crying bitterly was extremely moving. I felt that if an error were made in this case and a good person were wronged, it would do a great deal of harm to that family. Although at the time I had just come to the court and had never yet gone down to an administrative village to investigate a case, these circumstances stimulated me to request the leadership to send me down to the administrative village to make a third investigation. After being sent down to the administrative village I convened an informal discussion meeting of the cadres. At first the cadres persisted in their previous story. I then gave them a lecture on policy, and I pointed out that every cadre should feel himself responsible for this problem. I continued by questioning two cadres who had persisted in their opinion. Their story then became shaky. I went down and interviewed some of the masses and also conducted an on-the-spot examination of the site of the incident. I discovered that Liu Chin-ling's entire family had been buried alive by bandits and that Liu had become mentally ill after that happened. The reason that he committed suicide by hanging was that his illness had recurred. On the two previous occasions when our people went down to the administrative village to investigate, they always talked to the village cadres and the witnesses the cadres produced. Because Hsü Wan-jung usually did not obey the village cadres, they disliked him, and this is why there was an untruthful report about him. Although Hsü and Liu had fought, the fight had occurred eleven months, not two days, before Liu committed suicide. This fight was unrelated to the suicide. As for Hsü's returning home, this took place nine days before the suicide. After my investigation had cleared things up, I again convened a discussion meeting of the cadres and the masses. Everyone recognized that Hsü had not forced anyone to commit suicide, so we let him go. Hsü movingly said: "If it had not been for this people's court, I would have died as a result of being wronged."

How can we make sure that "bad people do not get away and good people are not wronged"? My realization is that in hearing cases we must understand principles and not be careless about making judgments. We must understand the four do nots of judging, namely: do not make a judgment if the facts are not clear; do not make a judgment if the evidence is not sufficient; do not make a judgment if the nature of the case is still vague; and do not make a judgment if the policy is unclear. If we act in this way we can prevent judgments which unjustifiably acquit criminals and judgments which erroneously convict innocent persons. In order conscientiously to implement this method in my actual work, I never want to relax with respect to any file involved in my daily work. To avoid errors I always scrutinize every word and every sentence. I always examine the documents drafted by clerks. In order to facilitate examination work, our tribunal has established [a system of] recording its business meetings, a diary of our working day and twelve charts so that the work can be conducted in an orderly way.

## ITEM 212

Contrary to the implication in Item 206, even during the constitutional era defense lawyers did not frequently participate in cases that were not publicly tried. However, during that era in some instances the defendant was offered the services of a lawyer but declined because the surrounding circumstances led him to believe that resort to counsel might prejudice his prospects and could not improve them. This item illustrates this situation.

[Interview]

Li was a cadre of the department of commerce of the Kwangtung provincial government. He was dissatisfied with conditions in China, and in conversations with a few trusted friends he did a good deal of complaining and even made some anti-Communist statements. One of these friends, a man named Ai, was subsequently transferred to a government post in Wuchang, and in July 1955, after the outbreak of the movement to liquidate counterrevolution, Li received a letter from Ai warning him that Ai was already being subjected to struggle meetings and that Li should expect the same. Li decided to leave Canton to try to sneak across the border into Hong Kong. He was caught at the border, however, and taken to the nearest public security station. He spent several hours there while the authorities decided what to do with him. He was not questioned, because the station chief said that the case of an escaping cadre had to be investigated by "higher-ups."

Li was then taken to the detention house of the public security bureau of Canton. He remained there for ten days, and on three occasions during that period he was taken from his cell to a small hearing room where he was interrogated by a plainclothes public security officer in the presence of a secretary. The first interrogation concerned his motives for attempting to leave China. The second and third sessions inquired into his possible connections with Nationalist or American agents. Li admitted that he had tried to leave because of dissatisfaction with economic conditions. But although his interrogator claimed that the bureau knew all about him and his associations, Li said nothing of his hostility to the regime, nor did he mention his relations with other dissatisfied cadres.

Following the third interrogation Li was sent to the public security bureau of the city of Wuchang, since it was deemed desirable to have him in the same area as his friend Ai, who was not under arrest but who had been placed under informal house arrest [residential surveillance] by his government unit. In this way it was hoped that their stories could be easily compared and that they could thus be played off against each other. In the Wuchang detention house Li was questioned on numerous occasions about suspected counterrevolutionary activity. Although he was subjected to no physical coercion, he was told repeatedly that if he made a full confession and established his merit by revealing all others who had joined in his plot, he would be assured of lenient treatment. Li believed that these promises were designed to trap him into providing evidence that the bureau did not have. In the statements of confession that he was required to write, he admitted only the obvious and made no mention of anti-Communist utterances that could be deemed evidence of counterrevolutionary activity. While the interrogation proceeded, public security investigators were tracing Li's connections with people in Shanghai and even Peking as well as those in Wuchang and Canton.

Four months after his arrival in the Wuchang detention house, Li was presented with a copy of a bill of prosecution that charged him with two crimes: attempting to cross the national border illegally and promoting a counterrevolutionary organization. Although the bill of prosecution was signed in the name of the procuracy, Li had never spoken with a procurator. Li was asked whether he wanted to be represented in court by a member of the Office of Legal Advisers, but he declined. "Nobody wanted a lawyer; we all knew that they were mere window dressing and couldn't really defend us, because they would be accused of having 'lost their standpoint' if they did." Moreover, Li believed that any attempt to defend himself in court would only result in his receiving a harsher sentence than otherwise. The sole defense in which he had confidence was to provide as little information as possible during the pretrial interrogations without giving the appearance of "resistance."

What puzzled Li was that these interrogations continued on an occasional basis for another sixteen months after he received a copy of the bill of prosecution. Finally, in March 1957, he was summoned to the usual hearing room in the detention house for what he thought would be another routine session. But this time there was no public security interrogator but a judge from the Wuchang people's court, a court secretary, and a court policeman. The judge announced that the court had studied his problem and had reached a conclusion. He then read aloud a written judgment that declared Li guilty of attempting illegally to cross the border but that dismissed the charge of counterrevolutionary activity. The judge sentenced Li to eighteen months of imprisonment but said that since he had already been detained for a longer period, he would be released immediately. Li was told that if he disagreed with the judgment, he could appeal within three days.

1. Of what did Li's "trial" consist?
2. If Li had accepted the offer of counsel it is very likely that his case would have been publicly tried. What difference might this have made?

## ITEM 213

The following account by Mrs. Adele Rickett (see Item 176) refers to the pre-constitutional era and provides further evidence that even in the "trials" of that period a conscientious effort was often made to determine the accuracy of the accusation.

[Rickett and Rickett, *Prisoners of Liberation* (1957), pp. 214–215]

[I]n the eight months I spent in cell No. 9 I learned much from her [Jeng Ai-ling].

She never talked much about her crimes, except for the fact that she had been involved in smuggling and the misuse of government funds. One day, however, she described part of her investigation, and said that in one instance there was a question about the placing of responsibility for some point in her crime. She maintained that the matter had not been her responsibility, but there were several witnesses who said it was. For eleven months the People's Government investigated this one point, and she was summoned to court sixteen or seventeen times to be confronted by witnesses. Each time she was asked to state her version of the story. A witness would then be brought in and asked to state his version. When he had finished, Jeng Ai-ling spoke again in her own defense, and in each case the witness backed down and admitted that he might have been wrong. Jeng Ai-ling remained steadfast during the questioning and in the end the People's Government told her they were satisfied that she was telling the truth. In telling us of her experience, she paced up and down the cell, her eyes sometimes crinkling at the sides with laughter, sometimes shining bright with excitement as she related the flustered shame of each witness as he admitted his mistake.

She then continued, "It does happen sometimes that mistakes occur and it takes a lot of stamina to see the thing through until truth is established."

## ITEM 214

This article vividly illustrates the value, even without a public trial, of judicial verification of the bill of prosecution.

[Yang P'eng and Lin Ch'ih-chung, "Investigate Deeply, Handle Cases Conscientiously," *Fu-chien jih-pao* (Fukien daily), Aug. 14, 1956]

At the end of last year, Judge Kao Hsing-kuang of the Fu-an county people's court received the counterrevolutionary case of Su Shun-ch'ing from San-k'eng village in the administrative village of Chi-k'eng.

Kao Hsing-kuang, as usual, first carefully looked over the entire file of the case from beginning to end: the letters of denunciation from the masses, the public security bureau's preparatory investigation record, the procuracy's bill of prosecution, and real evidence such as a writing brush. In the preparatory investigation record, he saw the paragraph from Su Shun-ch'ing's statement: "At five P.M. on the eighteenth of December when I was on my way to Su Ming-sheng's home in the village to see him about his illness I used a brush for writing prescriptions to write the reactionary slogans on a panel of the door of the agricultural cooperative." He [Kao Hsing-kuang] thought: in broad daylight he wrote reactionary slogans on the door of the agricultural cooperative. Could it be that he was not afraid of being seen by passing pedestrians? Furthermore those letters of denunciation contradicted each other in places: some said the reactionary slogans were written with a brush, and others said they were written with charcoal. Therefore, before bringing up defendant Su Shun-ch'ing for hearing, he took advantage of the fact that there was an enlarged cadres' meeting being held in the county, and he sought out the secretary of the Party branch in the administrative village of Chi-k'eng, the head of the administrative village and the head of the work group in order to understand the facts of the case. They all said that the reactionary slogans were written with a brush. The head of the administrative village also added that the assistant head and the principal of the people's school both personally had seen Su Shun-ch'ing writing the reactionary slogans. It looked as if there were nothing wrong. But after returning to the court, he became suspicious of something else: if some people had personally seen Su Shun-ch'ing writing the reactionary slogans why had they not seized him at the scene? Entertaining these suspicions, he had Su Shun-ch'ing brought from the detention house for a talk. During the talk, Su Shun-ch'ing again repeated from beginning to end the admission he made during the public security bureau's preparatory investigation. When Kao Hsing-kuang began to question him some more, Su Shun-ch'ing said this: "Upright judge, I can only say that I really did this thing. Make a judgment quickly and let me go to reform through labor!"

At that time Kao Hsing-kuang thought: this case has passed through [the stage of] preparatory investigation by the public security bureau, and the procuracy has investigated it and has initiated prosecution. Witnesses and real evidence are complete, and the defendant also has already admitted [the facts charged] without reservation, so that it can be said that there is no problem. But when he [Kao] was about to take up his pen to write the judgment, he again felt that his suspicions had still not been resolved. In particular [the evidence] that Su Shun-ch'ing had personally been seen writing the reactionary slogans by the assistant head of the administrative village and the principal of the people's school had not been checked. I cannot make a judgment in this way. But I do not have sufficient reasons for not making a judgment and sending the case back to the procuracy. He thought and thought. When he thought about the responsibility of the state's judges and when in particular he thought about the spirit of the Party Central Committee's instructions "to heighten vigilance, to liquidate all special agents, to prevent mistakes and not to wrong a good person," he determined to go down to the administrative village personally to investigate the case deeply. His idea was supported and approved by the president of the court.

On February 28 of this year Kao Hsing-kuang arrived at the administrative village of Chi-k'eng. After he had arrived, he first held an informal discussion meeting with the important cadres of the administrative village. At the meeting, as the cadres described the solving of the case, he discovered that the [defendant's] statement had been obtained by enticement and coercion. Furthermore, an important problem was verified at the meeting, namely, that the assistant head of the administrative village and the principal of the people's school had not seen Su Shun-ch'ing write the reactionary slogans. After the meeting, Kao Hsing-kuang went to the scene of the crime in San-K'eng village for an on-the-spot investigation. He discovered that the position of the panel of the door on which the reactionary slogans were written was very high and that it would not have been easy for Su Shun-ch'ing, who was very short, to have written characters on such a high place. Although the characters of the reactionary slogans had already faded, it could vaguely be seen that charcoal had been used to write them. When he was investigating, a people's assessor named Su Sheng-ti reported that last summer when he was cooling off in a place opposite that building, he saw those characters, but because he could not read he did not know they were reactionary slogans. The fact completely contradicted the defendant's statement. After understanding these circumstances, he penetrated the masses in order to continue to investigate. Four of Su Shun-ch'ing's neighbors, including peasant Su Shou-ch'üan, all said that on the afternoon of December 18 they saw Su Shun-ch'ing and his niece's husband, Chao T'ung-ti, go into the fields together to sow wheat and that the two did not return home until the sun had gone down. When Kao Hsing-kuang went to Su Ming-sheng's home to ask some questions, both the father and the son said that Su Shun-ch'ing went to his [Su Ming-sheng's] home to see him about his illness twice on December 16. At that time Su Shun-ch'ing used an already prepared herb medicine, and he certainly was not carrying a brush for writing prescriptions. After examining all this evidence, the facts were clarified. The next day he [Kao] took this circumstantial evidence and the door panel on which the reactionary slogans were written and he returned to the court. After the leadership had studied the results of his investigation, Kao Hsing-kuang brought up Su Shun-ch'ing for several hearings and carefully explained to him the government's policies. This time Su Shun-ch'ing finally told the truth and clarified the facts of the case.

This is what had happened: in December of last year, when the principal of the people's school in Fu-an county's San-k'eng village discovered the reactionary slogans, he reported it to the government of the administrative village. The government of the administrative village suspected it was the work of Su Shun-ch'ing, who had served as a *pao* head [see Item 9] in the counterfeit [KMT] government, so they called him in for a talk and encouraged him to confess. Certain individual cadres also erroneously tried to obtain a statement from him by enticement, telling him that there would be no problem if he just cleared up the matter. At the same time they summoned the masses to the government [office] to await his confession and told him that if he did not confess, they [the masses] would not let him return home. So it became a situation of obtaining a statement by coercion. Su Shun-ch'ing had served as a *pao* head in the counterfeit government before liberation, and he was afraid of being struggled by the masses. After listening to the cadres of the administrative village, he admitted it [writing the slogans]. When he was [subsequently] seized by the public security bureau, he was afraid that if he "recanted" he would be dealt with with increased severity, so he persisted in refusing to speak the truth.

After the facts of the entire case were clarified, the county people's court quickly gave the order to release Su Shun-ch'ing.

### 2. The Antirightist Movement Ends the Constitutional Experiment

For all practical purposes the antirightist movement of mid-1957 terminated the constitutional experiment with public trials. Since that time, apart from minor criminal cases that are closely related to civil disputes, such as bigamy and adultery, a public trial has been held only when a case is considered to have unusual educational significance or when an effort is made to comply with the request of a visiting foreign delegation, as in Item 210D. See section C, subsection 4, this chapter. This sudden abandonment of the constitutional model required the PRC to expend considerable resources in re-educating its judicial personnel to accept the abrupt shift in policy and the revised standards of judicial behavior.

### ITEMS 215A–215B

These articles are examples of many that appeared in 1958 and 1959 redefining the role of defense lawyers so that, to the extent that they continued to be employed, their activities became more circumscribed than ever.

### ITEM 215A

[Su I, "Should a Defender Attack Crime or Protect Crime?" *CFYC*, 2:76–77 (1958)]

In its fourth issue for 1957, Political-Legal Research published Comrade Wu Lei's article, "A Study of the Position of the Defender in Our Country's Criminal Litigation." It mainly discusses the problem of how defenders (principally lawyers) should handle the situation when they discover new facts about the defendant's crime which he has not confessed to an investigating organ or court. The author's opinions are like this: "Because of his position and function in litigation, the defender absolutely may not do anything that is unfavorable to the defendant. When in the course of performing his duties the defender discovers new facts about the crime of a defendant which the defendant has not confessed to an investigating organ or court, he should rouse and persuade the defendant to confess in an effort to obtain lenient treatment. When this is without effect, the defender may not reveal the facts. All other forms of revealing facts about the defendant's crime that supposedly do not affect the defense system should be strictly prohibited. Only in this way can the defense system be correctly and smoothly implemented."

In order to prove his own point of view the author gives these reasons: (1) from beginning to end the defender is the person who is always most trusted by the defendant; he may not during litigation do something that is unfavorable to the defendant; (2) to reveal and to prove that the defendant has committed a criminal act are the responsibilities of the public security and procuratorial organs; if the defender reveals and proves that the defendant has committed a crime, this will undermine the defense system; (3) if the defender reveals the crime, the defendant will become suspicious of the defender; will believe that the defender, the court, and the investigating organs are members of one family; and thus will not treat the defender as the person whom he trusts most; (4) to reveal the crime is, with respect to the people, a kind of deceit. From the above points it can be seen that Comrade Wu Lei long and comprehensively considered this problem of how the defendant is to be given increased benefits and how his confidence in the defender is to be increased. Comrade Wu Lei's understanding of the goals of the defense system is not the same as ours, and I believe that his basic point of view is erroneous.

Now I want to talk about the following points:

1. What are the goals of the defense system? I believe that the goals of the defense are: proceeding from objective truth and based upon the policies and laws of the state, to present, with respect to factual or legal matters, evidence or reasons that are sufficient to prove or to explain that the defendant is not guilty or that the crime is minor; to refute accusations that are incorrect or are not completely correct; to protect the lawful rights and interests of the defendant; to assist the courts in exercising the power of adjudication more correctly; to protect the socialist legal system; to enable the weapons of the people's democratic dictatorship to attack the enemy more forcefully than ever; and "not to let a bad person run rampant and not to wrong a good one" . . .

2. What does undermining the defense system mean? Comrade Wu Lei believes that for the defender to reveal the crime of the defendant is to undermine the defense system. First, he believes that to reveal and to prove that the defendant has committed a criminal act is the responsibility of the public security and procuratorial organs. Actually, to reveal and to prove the defendant's crime is the responsibility of the public security and procuratorial organs, but

Comrade Wu Lei has forgotten that our state organs are intimately linked to and rely on the masses. This is a principle that is prescribed in the Constitution. Intimate links with and reliance on the masses are in the excellent tradition of our country's judicial and public security organs. Moreover, our country's Constitution prescribes that every citizen has the responsibility to denounce all criminal acts that infringe the public interests of the state and the undertakings of socialist construction. Why can a people's lawyer who serves as a legal worker be an exception? Comrade Wu Lei says: "When the procuratorial organs conduct their struggle against criminal acts, they very much hope that the vast masses can provide them with clues, but they certainly do not hope nor ask that the defender obtain facts about the crime [for them] from the defendant." Our procuratorial organs actually do not ask the defender to obtain facts about the crime because this is not a goal of our defense system. But why, when the defender clearly knows of a concealed crime that the defendant has not confessed and for which he has not been punished as he should have been, should the defender "keep the secret forever" for him? Let me ask: is there a legal or moral basis for this? I see no basis for it. Next, Comrade Wu Lei says that "from beginning to end the defender is the person who is always most trusted by the defendant . . . if he discovers new facts about the crime of the defendant which the defendant has not confessed, and he then reveals them, the defendant will become suspicious of the defender; will believe that the defender, the court, and the investigating organs are members of one family; and thus will no longer treat the defender as the person whom he trusts most." I believe that the defender cannot be "from beginning to end . . . the person who is always most trusted by the defendant." The defendant should trust our country's defense system. He should have confidence that the defender will protect his lawful rights and interests. Moreover, many defendants in fact do have such confidence. This is because of the strength and consolidation of our people's political power and the lofty prestige of the Party and the government. But is the defender then the person most trusted by the defendant? This is not possible, because criminals, those who sabotage socialist construction and reform, are still hostile to socialism and the people's democratic legal system. Although they submit to the policy of confession, have a way out indicated to them, receive all kinds of education from the public security and procuratorial organs, and repent, it is not very likely that they abandon their standpoint at one stroke. Because of this it is not possible for them completely to trust an upright people's lawyer who protects the socialist legal system. As to the problem of whether or not the defender, the court, and the investigating organs are members of one family, if these "members of one family" refer to organizational structure, our answer is negative; if it refers to politics, then they are "members of one family," because their common goal is to protect and to consolidate the socialist legal system. We are not afraid of anyone's having doubts about this problem of "members of one family." If the defendant has doubts, this should not affect the defender in any way. What should determine the defender's conduct is the interests of the people and the state and not whether the defendant has doubts. Finally, I believe that the problem of whether or not the defense system is undermined should be considered from the point of view of the interests of the people. Whatever is favorable to the people protects the defense system and will also earn the praise and support of the people.

From the above it can be seen that our views and those of Comrade Wu Lei are fundamentally different. Why do we have these differences? I believe that in the final analysis it is a problem of standpoint. Comrade Wu Lei takes the standpoint of the defendant. Everything starts out from what is beneficial to the defendant. Although Comrade Wu Lei says that the defender "has an independent position in criminal litigation and is an independent subject in litigation" and that the defender "takes the standpoint of the state and the people," when it comes to concrete problems he [the defender] has gone over to the defendant's side. Moreover, Wu Lei even says that to reveal a crime that the defendant has not confessed is, "with respect to the people, deceit." Our view is exactly the opposite. Not to reveal it is deceit with respect to the people and the state!

## ITEM 215B

[Wu Lei, "An Examination of the Article 'A Study of the Position of the Defender in Our Country's Criminal Litigation,'" CFYC, 2:78 (1958)]

. . . . .

My article, "A Study of the Position of the Defender in Our Country's Criminal Litigation," was published in the fourth issue of Political-Legal Research for 1957. Because of dogmatism in my personal methods of thinking and the existence of the concept of idealism, [my discussion of] the problem of whether a defender may reveal new facts about the crime that he has discovered while performing his duties was dissevered from practice, did not start out from reality, and dealt rigidly with provisions of law. Therefore, errors occurred with respect to many questions. At present, the nature of these errors is not only a matter of debate in academic theory, it is also a matter of political standpoint of a fundamental nature. These erroneous concepts must be conscientiously examined and thoroughly censured.

## ITEMS 216A–216B

Not only did the role of the defense lawyer undergo redefinition during the post-1957 period, but so did the "right to defense" generally, as these items indicate.

## ITEM 216A

[Chang Hui et al., "These Are Not the Basic Principles of Our Country's Criminal Litigation," CFYC, 4:77–78 (1958)]

. . . . .

In our country's criminal litigation the position and the rights of the prosecutor and the defendant are not equal. Because the people's procuracy serves as the state prosecutor, complete equality cannot be asked for. The procuratorial organ is the instrument of the dictatorship of the proletariat. Its task is, through the handling of cases, to attack the enemy, to protect the people, and to prevent crime. The defendants whom it prosecutes are basically all enemies of the people. If we demand that the position and the rights of the enemies of the people be equal to the state prosecutor, this will of necessity weaken the role of the struggle against the enemy.

When a people's court adjudicates cases, it definitely cannot maintain a neutral position between the prosecutor and the defendant. A people's court is a weapon of the dictatorship of the proletariat and, although there is a division of labor and responsibility between it and the public security and procuratorial organs, the three organs perform the common task of suppressing enemies, punishing criminals, and protecting the people. A court cannot serve as a "just" arbitrator between the prosecutor and the defendant, and even less can it maintain neutrality. It should actively take the initiative in investigating criminals and in punishing them. Therefore, the concept of the so-called "clear separation between the adjudication function and the prosecution function" is erroneous. From the point of view of judicial practice it is difficult strictly to separate a court's [function in] adjudication and prosecution because in court adjudication it is mainly the adjudication officers who take the initiative in examining the evidence of the defendant's crime and who, when the evidence is insufficient, take the initiative in investigating and obtaining new evidence, in questioning the defendant and witnesses, etc. When they discover new criminals or new facts about the crime they promptly investigate them. Moreover, when the state prosecutor does not appear in court to support the prosecution, the court then also performs the activity of the prosecutor. The court certainly does not render a judgment favorable to the defendant because the prosecutor did not appear. Of course, we cannot confuse adjudication and prosecution. Adjudication is conducted by the court, initiation of prosecution and support of the prosecution are mainly conducted by the procuracy. From this it can be seen that the concept of a clear separation between the adjudication function and the prosecution function is a concept that is favorable to the defendant. We believe that the adjudication and prosecution functions should be both separated and not separated.

## ITEM 216B

[Shen Ch'i-szu, "Censure 'the Principle of Debate' in the Criminal Litigation of the Bourgeoisie," *CFYC*, 1:33–34 (1960)]

[B]ut counterrevolutionary and bad elements, because of their reactionary nature and vain hope of escaping punishment, will resort to all kinds of conspiracies and plots to oppose prosecution by the procuratorial organs and adjudication by the courts. Therefore, it is not difficult to understand that the trial of counterrevolutionary and bad elements is a sharp face-to-face struggle to put dictatorship into effect against the enemy. In this struggle if, as some people advocate, we "let the defendant have equal rights with the procuratorial organ" and let him "freely" make reactionary speeches and distort the facts, policies and laws, this can only mean giving shields and weapons to these enemies, enabling them to block people's courts and people's procuracies from putting their dictatorial power into effect over them and to conduct a counterattack . . .

So, after all, what is the reality and the significance of our country's provision that "the defendant shall have the right to have a defense"?

We know that our entire investigation, procuratorial, and adjudication systems are powerful weapons for the political-legal organs to use to attack the enemy, punish crime, and protect the people. The provision in the Constitution and in the Law for the Organization of People's Courts that "the defendant shall have the right to have a defense" is a similar kind of system. We believe that this system provides that in court adjudication it is permissible for criminal defendants (criminals) to defend themselves, with the precondition that they not violate policies and laws and not distort the facts. The significance of this provision lies in the fact that through questioning and through the criminal's defense the criminal's crime can be further examined and his guilt proved; and through his defense his attitude toward admitting his guilt of the crime can be observed, and this is helpful to us in determining his punishment. In summary, the only purpose for prescribing that "the defendant shall have the right to have a defense" is to attack the enemy even more fiercely, accurately, and firmly.

## ITEM 217

[Chang Hui et al., "These Are Not the Basic Principles of Our Country's Criminal Litigation" (1958), pp. 78–79]

.        .        .        .        .

The procedure of uninterrupted adjudication of the bourgeois countries and of the Kuomintang is incompatible with the principles and procedure of our adjudication. In our investigation and adjudication we adopt the principle of promptness in order effectively to suppress the enemy, to punish crime, to safeguard the realization of the central task of a given period, and to prevent crime. But this promptness must be [only] the greatest possible promptness and speed of handling cases consistent with the objective of correctness. Except for those few cases in which the facts are simple and which can be resolved after one hearing, the correct adjudication of the majority of cases requires a certain period of interruption between receipt of a case and pronouncement of judgment, because criminal cases usually require investigation and a number of court sessions before the facts are clarified. Also, after the court makes a judgment, it must be examined and approved. These processes inevitably interrupt adjudication. During the period of interruption, the handling of many other cases should be fitted in. We absolutely cannot cease work and await the conclusion of one case before handling another case. Actually, the Kuomintang certainly did not handle cases in accordance with what the law prescribed. Delay in litigating cases was a characteristic of their adjudication.

Frequently their cases dragged on for three to five years with no conclusion to adjudication.

. . . . .

Is adjudication by the collegial panel of courts of first instance an application of the "principle of directness"? This requires concrete analysis. Cases that are adjudicated by the collegial panel of courts of first instance are all handled on the basis of deeply penetrating the masses and examining, studying, and clearing up the facts before forwarding them to a court for adjudication. When a court tries the defendant, whether or not it will notify the witnesses and experts to come to court depends on the concrete circumstances. For example, when the opinions of the witnesses and experts are already in written form and no doubts or contradictions have been discovered in the course of examining them, or when they live very far from the court, the place of adjudication, it is permissible not to summon them; when there are a number of witnesses in a case it is permissible not to summon for interrogation secondary witnesses whose connection with the case is not too great. Persons who have denounced the crime normally cannot be summoned to court to testify. When the investigation and adjudication officers already understand a witness and have clarified the circumstances, there is no need to notify him to appear in court.

### 3. Impact of the Great Leap Forward

### ITEMS 218A–218D. PROPAGANDA IMAGE

The advent of the great leap forward in the spring of 1958, before the antirightist movement had run its course, signaled a new development in the system of judicial trials. Items 218A–218D are representative selections from the large number of articles in which the courts, as well as the procuracy and police, were said to be vigorously applying the newly re-emphasized mass line. Some of the innovations discussed were superficial and temporary while others proved to be significant and enduring.

### ITEM 218A

Two of the basic principles of the newly re-emphasized mass line in judicial work stressed the importance of relying on the masses for "on-the-spot" adjudication and the importance of enhanced judicial cooperation with the police and procuracy. This item reveals what these principles were usually said to entail.

[Chang Wu-yün, "Smash Permanent Rules, Go 1,000 *Li* in One Day" (1958), pp. 58–59]

. . . . .

What methods are used to handle cases well and fast? What is especially worth mentioning here is the method of coordinating the mass line with the specialized organs, namely, cooperation among the "three families" (the public security and procuratorial organs and the courts), handling of cases by the "three officers" (the officer in charge of preparatory examination, the procurator and the judge), combined debate, thoroughly rousing the masses, denouncing and exposing crime, on-the-spot arrest, initiation of prosecution, and adjudication. This is a new creative experience in the handling of cases that has occurred since the leap forward, and at the same time, it is also a traditional method of handling cases that has a national style. For example, in Chien-ho county, under the leadership of the county Party committee, the procuracy, the public security organ, and the court sent a work group composed of three officers to penetrate deeply into Nan-ming and Wench'üan, two large and complex administrative villages along the border. After arriving there they immediately made a report to the local Party committee about material they had obtained relating to the circumstances of the enemy, and they informed themselves about new material relating to current activity. After approving arrests, they concentrated all the offenders in an administrative village, conducted a preparatory examination, and checked the material. After the legal documents of the preparatory examination of the case had been completed, the offenders were taken to a place for an on-the-spot hearing. When hearing the case of a certain Hsü who was both a counterrevolutionary and an opium offender, before the court was convened they [the three officers] determined the facts of the crime and discussed their views about deciding upon the sentence with cadres from the cooperative, with Party and Youth League members and with activists, and sought their opinions. Later they used the rest period of over a thousand members of the masses who were repairing a road to convene the court for a hearing. Doing it in this way not only reduced the time wasted in traveling and greatly increased the speed of handling the case, it also punished the criminal promptly and forcefully, made propaganda for the legal system and educated the masses. For example, during the adjudication of the case of a certain Shao, who sabotaged [state] unified purchasing and marketing, after the procurator read aloud the bill of prosecution, the masses said that the defendant had committed still other evil crimes and immediately exposed two crimes. One of them was participation in a killing and, after an examination of the reliability [of the facts], he was sentenced to nine years [of imprisonment]. After the criminal Shao's sentence was pronounced, the masses denounced two criminals on the spot who, after examination of the evidence, were promptly arrested. Under the intimidating influence of the masses, one of the opium offenders handed over 220 ounces of opium on the spot, and the other handed over 198 ounces of silver that was used as capital for their opium trade. When accumulated cases were cleaned up in Jen-huai county, a work group composed of a procurator, an officer in charge of preparatory examination, and a judge took along the files, took the offenders into custody, and went up to the mountains or down to the administrative villages to examine the evidence and handle cases on the spot. They propounded the militant slogan of: "eat quickly, run down the road, smoke little, sleep little, do not rest, work at night, make the work site the office and rocks and clumps of mud the benches, unite into one heart, and clean up the accumulated cases." Because the three officers cooperated in their efforts in the three kinds of work procedure — preparatory examination, initiation of prosecution, and adjudication — they simplified the procedures for returning cases for supplementary investigation and for preparatory examination sessions, etc.; when convening court for prosecution they also adopted the practice of collectively informing the defendant of his litigation rights. Within twelve days at the work site this one work group, by investigating, conducting preparatory examinations, initiating prosecution, convening court, and adjudicating, all at the work site, cleared up seventy-three accumulated cases. Doing things this way not only increased efficiency in handling cases but also made it possible to obtain thorough evidence and to close the cases promptly. For example, there was the case of a certain Chang who sabotaged an agricultural cooperative. During two interrogations by the procuracy he completely denied having committed the crime. Behind the procurator's back he said: "If they want to clear up my case, Pao Kung[9] must be re-born . . ." We had an even more intelligent method than Pao Kung had. We took Chang down to the administrative village. After an examination of the evidence and, under face-to-face exposure with the masses, the offender could not but bow his head and admit his guilt. Thus prosecution was promptly initiated, and the offender was handed over for adjudication. Because the comrades can deeply penetrate local areas and eat and live together with the masses, sharing their joys and sorrows, the handling of cases not only does not [adversely] affect production but, on the contrary, it stimulates production and receives the enthusiastic welcome of the masses. After they get to the local area, the secretary of the Party branch arranges a time and notifies the witnesses. The masses take the initiative in reporting the situation, and the secretary of the Party branch says, "In the past we were opposed to your handling of cases behind closed doors. It is very good that you are now doing things this way." Under the unifying arrangements of the Party committee the people's procuracy of Chin-sha county took seven days' time and handed over to the masses for debate the cases in which it had approved applications for arrest. On the basis of penetrating debate of the facts of the crime, thorough debate of reactionary thinking, and foul-smelling debate with the criminals, they convened mass meetings at work sites and in the fields and carried out searches and arrests in a concentrated manner. This not only educated the masses, but it strengthened their activism in the struggle against the enemy, attacked crime, and caused the disintegration of the enemy. As the above-mentioned situation has convincingly demonstrated, only by smashing permanent rules and by having the courage to innovate can our work leap forward; also, only by wiping out superstition and liberating thinking can we create some flexible methods for handling cases.

## ITEM 218B

In this item the model judge of a rural people's tribunal reveals to his fellow cadres some of the secrets of his success in implementing the mass line.

[Liu Tse-chün, "Realizations from My Adjudication Work" (1959), pp. 49–50]

.    .    .    .    .

(1) Combine on-the-spot adjudication with the central work . . . For example, during the plowing of fields in an all-out operation to sow wheat, in

9. Pao Kung was a famous judge in Chinese history.

the western cooperative plowing brigade of Ch'ien-liu-wu-ying village, there was a landlord element named Ting Chien-ch'ang, who took advantage of the early mornings, while it was still dark, to engage in undercover sabotage of the plowing and sowing work. He also influenced two other cooperative members to conduct this undercover deception. When the tribunal heard of this, after asking the Party committee for instructions, it immediately rushed to the work site and combined plowing with learning about the circumstances of the case. At noon it took advantage of the cooperative members' lunch period to conduct a public hearing on the spot, so that the cooperative members could combine their plowing with discussion [of the case]. The second time the cooperative members took their rest I adopted the method of a meeting at the scene to handle the case in front of the masses. I arrested and sentenced the bad element Ting Chien-ch'ang. I gave the two other cooperative members criticism. At the same time I combined the work of sowing wheat with lectures on law. I commended the good people; I also vigorously criticized those who were not good without mentioning their names. Thus I stimulated the plowing efforts of the cooperative members, and they were unusually satisfied with this.

(3) Combine on-the-spot adjudication with discussion in order to lay a foundation for launching debate. In this way we can give cooperative members time to think so that they are prepared to speak at the time of our debate. A part of the cooperative members' rest period is used to conduct a hearing, which is combined with a clear discussion of the circumstances of the case. For example: What do you think about the facts of this case? Are there still things about which he [the defendant] is not telling us? We discuss their views on handling the case. The cadres deeply and with selected emphasis penetrate each group of laborers to inspire them; before the next rest period they report the discussions of each group and its views on handling the case, and they wait for the second rest period to conduct a debate. In this way they can promptly inform themselves about the requests of the masses in the cooperative and about their views on handling the case.

(4) Combine on-the-spot adjudication with debate. To combine adjudication with debate we must adjudicate on the spot. If we adjudicate at a formal public trial session, since that is not in the village where the masses live together, they cannot understand the circumstances of the case, and there can be no debate. If we combine on-the-spot adjudication with debate, not only can we distinguish right from wrong, we can also make unlawful elements bow their heads and admit their guilt in front of the masses. For example, in the district of Tung-chen-chuang in on-the-spot adjudication of a case in which Wang Yü-jung beat someone up, the defendant not only would not admit beating him up, he also would not even admit speaking abusively to him. After the debate among the cooperative members, one cooperative member, Liu Feng-chün, pointed out right there: "By not admitting you beat him up you are really not being honest. That day when you hit him I pulled you away, and you gave him another two kicks. I got very worried." After hearing the proof presented during this debate the defendant bowed his head and admitted his wrong.

(6) Combine on-the-spot adjudication with investigation. When we go down

to the administrative village to adjudicate on the spot we should take along those cases in that district that require investigation so that we can combine on-the-spot adjudication with conducting investigations. This saves more time than specially going to the village for investigation. Generally, while investigating cases, we can at the same time solve some of them.

(7) Combine on-the-spot adjudication with [the work of] the departments concerned. Doing this will result in "more people, prompter action, and greater care, and it will come close to satisfying both sides." For example, when we investigated the transportation situation in a certain village, we combined with ten people from the market administration committee, the commodity exchange, and other departments concerned. In two days we clarified a situation of transport speculation involving fifty men in four villages, so that the case was promptly handled.

## ITEM 218C

In this report the president of the high people's court of Shantung province recognizes that it is not always suitable to send judges to try cases among the masses. In these circumstances he advocates bringing the masses to the judges.

[Wang Yün-sheng, "How Adjudication Work Implements the Mass Line," *CFYC*, 6:38, 39 (1959)]

Adjudication work implements the mass line. This is an important sign of how our country's socialist judicial work differs from the judicial work of all capitalist countries.

. . . In the great leap forward in judicial work, apart from the relatively ordinary cases in which on-the-spot investigation and on-the-spot adjudication (mediation) are put into effect, the courts in the various places broadly adopted the method of adjudication which combines adjudication in court with debate by the masses, further developing the fine tradition of the mass line.

Combining adjudication in court with debate by the masses is a new development in implementing the mass line in judicial work; it is a concrete application to adjudication work of the Party's mass line work method of great blooming, great contending, and great debates. The results of using debate by the masses to handle cases prove that: (1) It further facilitates reliance on the masses in clarifying the facts of a case and in correctly handling the case. As for criminal cases, it directly rouses the masses to expose crimes; it results in the acquisition of thorough evidentiary materials; it deprives criminals, when confronted by the masses, of any way of cunningly denying their guilt; it effectively isolates and attacks the arrogant manner of criminals; it educates the masses clearly to demarcate the boundary between the enemy and us; and it heightens revolutionary vigilance. The action of the masses even further narrows the sphere of activity of the enemy and of all kinds of criminals and thereby attains the goal of preventing and reducing crime . . . (2) By using living facts it carries out propaganda-education of the masses and heightens the masses' awareness, establishing the direction for Communist morality. Its results are even better than those achieved by simply lecturing to the masses about law or by drawing the masses into participation as spectators in court, and it enables the policies and laws of the Party and the state to penetrate even deeper into the hearts of the people. (3) Because the opinions and views of the masses are listened to from all angles, the people's court can consider the cases that it handles even more comprehensively, and this effectively guarantees the quality of the case, raises work efficiency, and avoids and prevents the possibility that certain short-comings and errors will occur. (4) It can do an even better job of placing adjudication work under the supervision of the vast masses and of obtaining their assistance and support. Many judges realize through practice that the concentrated wisdom of the masses is the greatest wisdom and that the law can be correctly executed and develop its strength only if it is understood by the masses.

. . . Since the great leap forward, combining adjudication with productive labor in the various places has been one of the best methods. By laboring to-gether with the masses, judges understand the circumstances and conduct adjudication in their leisure time. Among the methods of adjudication activity are the informal discussion meeting; debate meeting, both small-scale and large-scale; mediation and giving judgment. This not only does not hinder production by the masses but also makes handling cases both fast and good.

## ITEM 218D

This article deals with the theme of enhanced judicial cooperation with the police and procuracy but says nothing of the role of the masses in the judicial process.

["Canton's Political-Legal Departments Experiment with Cooperation in Case Han-dling," *Nan-fang jih-pao* (Southern daily), March 30, 1958]

The public security bureau, the people's procuracy, and the intermediate people's court of the city of Canton have recently experimented with uniting in handling cases. By resolving their mutual problems of coordination and co-operation and improving their work methods, they have raised their average efficiency in handling cases four and a half times higher than last year. The ex-periment proves that all political-legal work can leap forward.

In the past, these three organs handled cases with complicated procedures. Their thinking was not unified, they could not coordinate closely, and in handling cases each organ managed one section. Some systems of rules were already out of date and did not meet the actual circumstances; some were misapplications of doctrine which mechanically used viewpoints of the old law. Handling a complete case (from arrest to judgment) required sixty-four procedures, steps, and proc-esses and ordinarily required 131 working hours.

In order to organize a great leap forward in political-legal work and to develop even further the power of the weapons of dictatorship, on the 19th of this month the city's public security bureau, procuracy, and court studied how the three units could coordinate, cooperate, and unite in the struggle against the enemy, and they also studied the questions of how procedures and steps in the handling of cases could be reduced, how methods of handling cases and legal documents could be improved, and how efficiency in handling cases could be raised. They selected seven different cases with which to conduct an experiment, courageously eliminated thirty-seven unnecessary procedures and steps and made it twenty-eight [sic]. At the same time, they improved and eliminated some unnecessary legal documents and they improved methods of handling cases, that is, reading case files and interrogating. With respect to methods of handling cases, they created the method whereby four officers (investigator, procurator, officer in charge of preparatory examination, and judge) get together and directly handle the case; three officers (or four) assemble, and the three chiefs (chief of the public security bureau, chief procurator, and president of the court) decide to divide the work; in doing that part of the work they have undertaken to do, they keep in direct touch with each other, overcoming the past shortcoming of individual management of each section and not asking about anything else and not cooperating. Now they impel each other, coordinate with each other, and act unitedly.

The results of the experiment with the seven cases show that one case, from arrest to judgment, requires only twenty-nine hours and forty-nine minutes to pass through the three units — the public security organ, the procuracy, and the court. The efficiency in handling cases is four times higher than last year. From the point of view of public security the efficiency in handling counterrevolutionary cases is fourteen times higher than last year. The procuracy's efficiency in handling cases is 21.7 times higher than last year. And it is about 40 times higher than that of a few days ago when the procuracy experimented with handling cases alone. Adjudication of the seven experimental cases by the court proved that the quality and speed [of the work done] was good.

## ITEMS 219A–219B. OPERATIONAL CONSEQUENCES OF THE LEAP

Interviews suggest that published accounts such as Items 218A–218C exaggerate the role of the masses in the adjudication of cases even during the period of the great leap forward. As in the past, information provided by the masses continued to be considered and weight continued to be attached to the attitude of the masses toward the defendant, but in cases of any importance neither the masses nor lower level cadres who came in contact with them appear to have exercised the powers attributed to them. Decisions were actually made by responsible court and Party officials, often in consultation with leaders of the police and procuracy. This cooperation continued after the leap subsided. Thus, the aspect of the leap discussed in Item 218D introduced some significant innovations.

### ITEM 219A

This item illustrates a type of cooperation among the law enforcement agencies that frequently occurs in cases of special importance or difficulty.

[Interview]

While on duty one night in 1959 in the countryside, K'o, two other people's militiamen, and the deputy leader of their production brigade's militia unit found a dead pig and decided to have a feast. Much wine was consumed, and K'o especially became thoroughly intoxicated. After the feast the deputy leader and K'o picked up their rifles and went out to resume their joint patrol. Shortly thereafter K'o saw someone in the shadows and shot him dead. The victim was the brother of the girl K'o had planned to marry. The county public security bureau promptly detained K'o and the deputy, questioned them thoroughly, and investigated the case. It decided that the deputy should receive thirty days of detention under the SAPA for having negligently permitted K'o to go out on armed patrol while K'o was highly intoxicated. Because the deputy himself had been intoxicated, his responsibility was deemed to be diminished, and he was for that reason exempted from criminal sanctions.

The bureau found K'o's case much more difficult to dispose of. Although it recognized that the degree of his intoxication precluded the killing being deemed murder, it was reluctant to hold that drinking had so diminished his responsibility as to make mere administrative punishment appropriate. Not to mete out a prison sentence for the taking of a human life in these circumstances, it was feared, would leave the public with a very bad impression. On the other hand, the mother and sister of the deceased had repeatedly come to the bureau to ask for leniency for K'o on the ground that he had had no intention of shooting anyone. Prior to reaching a decision about whether to arrest K'o, who was in detention, the bureau chief, recognizing the delicacy of the case, discussed it with the chief procurator and the president of the county people's court. This group decided that K'o had to be sentenced to one year of imprisonment because of the importance of deterring others and of avoiding popular dissatisfaction. The bureau then obtained the procuracy's formal approval of an arrest warrant, the procuracy made out a bill of prosecution, and the case was quickly transferred to the court for completion of the details of adjudication and sentencing. K'o was found guilty of "unintentional killing as a result of intoxication."

## ITEM 219B

Although "trial" has generally continued to take place behind the scenes rather than in public, the aura of the mass line has been maintained by frequently pronouncing sentence before the masses, as in this item.

[Ts'ui Ch'eng-hsüan,[10] "How We Defended the Safety of Hsing-fu People's Commune" (1958), p. 62]

Following the establishment of the communes, in Hsin-hsiang city there was a high tide in which everyone produced iron and steel. Some delinquent elements in society took advantage of the opening provided by everyone's being mobilized to produce iron and steel to steal public and private property. This directly affected the masses' production morale and the completion of iron and steel tasks. In order to defend the commune's iron and steel production we publicly handled a batch of theft, fraud, and other cases of current sabotage. In order to broaden the impact we also selected two groups of thieves, took them into the streets, to the train station, and to the iron and steel work sites, and pronounced their sentences en route, combining the pronouncement of sentences with broadly developing [the use of] propaganda. Over 6000 members of the masses were educated. This warned the delinquent elements, educated the masses to heighten

10. See Chap. V, note 6.

their vigilance, and powerfully defended the smooth operation of the commune and iron and steel production. The masses were very much satisfied with this method.

### 4. Public Trial Exceptions

Certain criminal trials continue to be conducted in public. Recall the constitutional-type trial witnessed by the delegation of Japanese lawyers that visited the PRC in 1959 (Item 210D). Item 220 is an example of a situation in which a public trial is held because the case is thought to have unusual educational significance. Item 221 illustrates that public trials continue to be held in cases formally denominated "criminal" but considered to be essentially civil in nature. Note that in neither account is any mention made of the role of lawyers, either for the prosecution or defense.

### ITEM 220

[Sun Chia-hsing (Judge of the People's Court of Li-shu County, Kirin Province), "Realizations from Participating in Production and Defending Production," *JMJP*, May 13, 1959]

.    .    .    .    .

Last year on October 30, just when a "satellite" was launched in a factory, the thief Lo Yü-chiang used that opportunity to steal the oil line of a diesel engine. When I watched them start the oven for production, I discovered that the oil line had been stolen. I quickly telephoned the relevant department and sent men to intercept the thief. The thief was caught at the railroad crossing at Kuo-chia-tien street on the same day. With the approval of the Party committee, various groups selected representatives and organized them into a meeting of over one hundred persons at the scene of the theft, and I had a public hearing of the case and sentenced the defendant to three years of imprisonment. In order broadly to educate the masses and to prevent the recurrence of this type of case, we had the representatives of the groups transmit the pronouncements of the judgment to their groups, printed and distributed to the groups over 300 large character copies of the written judgment, and organized the workers to conduct discussions of the judgment.

### ITEM 221

[Interview]

Several years prior to liberation Tu and Wang had married in customary fashion in Fukien province. After the Communist takeover they fled to Singapore. In 1954 Tu returned to his home on the mainland without Wang. In 1957 he and Li fell in love and decided to marry. Li's mother opposed the plan and went to the county basic level court to complain that the marriage should not be allowed on the ground that Tu already had a wife in Singapore. The court summoned Tu and Li and inquired into Tu's marital status. Tu claimed that he and Wang had dissolved their relationship prior to his return from Singapore. On this basis the judge stated that he could see no objection to the marriage, which took place shortly thereafter.

But in 1959 Wang came back from Singapore, claimed that she was still married to Tu, and was outraged at the news of his new marriage. She went to the public security bureau and charged Tu with the crime of bigamy. The bureau, however, advised her to take the case directly to court. Wang went to the court and made an oral complaint. The judge who had previously handled the matter investigated it further and then summoned the parties. Tu, who had run away when Wang arrived from Singapore, was prevailed upon by friends to return and attend the hearing.

The judge explained to Wang that at the time that the case first came before the court, because Wang was out of the country, the court had no way of verifying Tu's assertion that his marriage to her had terminated. The judge said that if she insisted on proving that the marriage had not terminated he would be obligated to find Tu guilty of bigamy and sentence him to imprisonment. He would also grant her a divorce if she desired one, he said. But he cautioned her that sending Tu to prison would benefit no one and that she might find it difficult to return to Singapore, as she wished to do, once her marital status had changed. The judge advised her to think these matters over carefully before taking definite action.

Several weeks later when the case was heard again, through more of the same reasoning, the judge succeeded in persuading Wang to withdraw her complaint and to return to Singapore without altering the situation.

## D. THE QUESTION OF JUDICIAL INDEPENDENCE

Article 78 of the Constitution of the PRC states that "People's courts shall conduct adjudication independently and shall be subject only to the law." [11] Article 4 of the Law for the Organization of the People's Courts is identical. The final segment of this chapter is devoted to exploring the meaning given to this provision at the time of its promulgation and during the postconstitutional era.

### 1. Inferior Position of the Individual Judge

Although the Constitution provides that the courts shall conduct adjudication independently, it says nothing about individual judges. Article 112 of the Constitution of the USSR, on the other hand, states that "Judges are independent and subject only to the law." [12] Is this a significant difference?

In China may a judge who handles a criminal case decide that case without consulting his superiors within the court? Can a judge afford to act contrary to the wishes of other government agencies and the Party?

## ITEMS 222A–222E. SUBJECTION TO SUPERIORS WITHIN THE COURT

Items 222A–222B confirm that the judge in charge of a criminal case of any significance must clear his proposed decision with the chief judge of his division,

11. P. 26.
12. Constitution (Fundamental Law) of the Union of Soviet Socialist Republics (Moscow, 1960), p. 97.

the president of the entire court, and on certain occasions with the court's adjudication committee.

## ITEM 222A

[Chang Hui et al., "These Are Not the Basic Principles of Our Country's Criminal Litigation" (1958), pp. 77, 78]

.    .    .    .    .

"The principle of oral presentation" cannot serve as a principle of litigation for public security organs, procuratorial organs, or people's courts in the struggle against the enemy. No matter what kind of social intercourse there is between nations and between people, one cannot use only written materials and not resort to oral communication to exchange thoughts and conduct relations. Criminal litigation activity is no exception. But in the investigation and adjudication conducted by our public security and procuratorial organs and by our courts, written and oral communications are combined. For example, there are the various records of investigation and adjudication, and then those of prosecution, written orders, and written judgments. In particular, when the adjudication committee of a people's court discusses and decides cases, or when a high court and the Supreme Court review or make the judgment in death penalty cases, or when a court of second instance adjudicates certain cases, all this is conducted on the basis of the case files, and the parties are not summoned for oral argument. To establish the principle that there must be an oral presentation would not be consistent with the actual situation and would affect the prompt attack against the enemy and the punishment of crime. Even though it is not established as a principle, in the struggle against the enemy the public security and procuratorial organs and the courts cannot but use speech to understand the circumstances. [However,] the principle of oral presentation is deceitful juggling by the bourgeois states. It is our view that if we use this trivial form, it will not benefit that struggle against the enemy but, on the contrary, will bind our hands and feet.

.    .    .    .    .

A people's court cannot bind itself by using the hypocritical bourgeois rule that the officers of a court [judges and people's assessors] cannot be replaced while they are adjudicating a case. In judicial practice these officers are not often replaced during adjudication. But when a replacement is made, adjudication is not and need not be started over again from the beginning, because the new adjudication officer can understand the circumstances of the case through the file, the record of adjudication, or through the explanation of other adjudication officers. Erroneously decided cases will therefore not be created. For the adjudication to start anew only because of the replacement of an individual judge or assessor and without regard to whether or not it can be correctly handled would be a formalistic and wasteful method of doing things. It would not only affect the prompt attack against the enemy and the punishment of crime, but it would also inevitably cause resentment among the people who participate in the case. It would be frivolous and laughable.

.    .    .    .    .

What is the "principle of directness"? The "principle of directness" demands that the judges personally examine the origin of the evidence; directly interrogate the witnesses, the experts, and the defendant himself; read aloud the written evidence in court; and not be limited to the evidence which both parties present.

.    .    .    .    .

"The principle of directness" conflicts with the spirit of the Law for the Organization of People's Courts which prescribes: "People's courts shall conduct adjudication independently and shall be subject only to the law." "People's courts shall conduct adjudication independently and shall be subject only to the law" is not the same as "judges are independent and subject only to the law." The system of people's courts independently conducting adjudication differs in two respects from the independence of judges. First, people's courts establish adjudication committees. Adjudication committees discuss and decide important and difficult cases and cases of legally effective judgments in which the president of the court has discovered an error in the application of the law or in the determination of the facts. Second, the president of the court and the chief judge lead the collegial panel. With the exception of relatively minor criminal cases, the judgment in all cases which the collegial panel adjudicates can only be pronounced after examination and approval by the president of the court and the chief judge. The discussion and decision by the adjudication committee and the examination and approval by the president of the court and the chief judge are all made on the basis of the case file and the oral report by the judge and not on the basis of direct examination of the evidence itself or interrogation of the witnesses or the defendant. Therefore, we certainly do not demand application of "the principle of directness."

## ITEM 222B

[Chang Tzu-p'ei, "Censure the Bourgeois Principle of 'the Judge's Free Evaluation of the Evidence," *CFYC*, 2:43, 44, 47–48 (1958)]

"The judge's free evaluation of the evidence" liberated the "judge's consciousness" from the system of formalistic evidence and enabled him to rely on his own "good sense," "freely" judge the evidence, and analyze the facts. This is because the class interests of the bourgeoisie and the interests of the circulation of capital required a more mature judge than the feudal era had in order better to meet the demands of the bourgeoisie's development and required a more "rational" method of judging the evidence. But the system of formalistic evidence could not guarantee that the interests of the bourgeoisie would obtain the protection and development they ought to have. "The judge's free evaluation of the evidence" met the tide of bourgeois liberalism and the integrated ideological system that it established and was one of the slogans of the struggle to establish and consolidate the political rule of the bourgeoisie and to realize bourgeois "democratic principles."

. . . "The judge's free evaluation of the evidence" still actively serves the rule of the bourgeoisie for the following reasons: the main reason is that "the judge's free evaluation of the evidence" is most beneficial to the bourgeoisie's unfettered oppression of the laboring people and progressive forces, because the judge can, according to his "good sense," "freely" judge the evidence and determine the facts of the case. That is to say, he can distort the facts, change black into white, and make a judgment that harms the laboring people, the Communist Party, and progressive persons. Even though there is actually no basis for political persecution, the judge is under no necessity to explain the reasons for his determination of the facts . . . The principal characteristic of "the judge's free evaluation of the evidence" refers to the judge's judging the evidence and determining the facts. The deceitful bourgeois slogan of "the judge's free evaluation of the evidence" which Chia Ch'ien and other rightists suggest should serve as a principle of our adjudication work has as its goal resistance to Party leadership and distortion of the essence of the meaning of "people's courts shall conduct adjudication independently and shall be subject only to the law."

. . . . . . .

The bourgeois "judge's free evaluation of the evidence" is not only antagonistic to Party leadership over people's courts, it also violates the spirit of Article 78 of our country's Constitution, which prescribes that "people's courts shall conduct adjudication independently and shall be subject only to the law." The system of organization by which people's courts conduct adjudication independently and are subject only to the law is a system which is determined by a combination of the organizational principles of democratic centralism, collective leadership, and individual responsibility. According to the provisions of this system, a people's court has a president, chief judges, and judges. When adjudicating cases, it puts into effect the collegial system, and it establishes an adjudication committee. The president of the court and the chief judge lead collegial panels. Criminal cases of first instance are all adjudicated by a collegial panel, which makes its decision (judgment) on the basis of the principle of the minority obeying the majority. Except in some minor criminal cases, generally these judgments all must be examined and approved by the chief judge and the president of the court before judgment can be pronounced. Important and difficult cases and legally effective judgments and orders of the court in which the president of the court has discovered some definite error in the determination of facts or the application of law are discussed and decided by the adjudication committee. Decisions of the adjudication committee must all be executed by the president of the court, the chief judge, and the collegial panel. But under the bourgeois principle of "the judge's free evaluation of the evidence," the judgments which are made by the adjudication division are final decisions which cannot be changed except after appeal to an appellate division. Therefore, the bourgeois "judge's free evaluation of the evidence" which the rightists suggest should serve as a principle of our adjudication would violate our country's Constitution and the Law for the Organization of People's Courts. Their goal is to eliminate or to weaken the function of the president of the court, the chief judge, and the adjudication committee in leading collegial panels.

Do the authors of the above articles, both of which were published in 1958, accurately portray the role originally intended for the adjudication committee? Items 222C and 222D present the theory and practice of the adjudication committee during the constitutional era.

## ITEM 222C

[LAW OF THE PRC FOR THE ORGANIZATION OF PEOPLE'S COURTS (Sept. 28, 1954), p. 125]

Article 10. People's courts of the various levels shall set up adjudication committees. The tasks of adjudication committees shall be to summarize adjudication experience and to discuss major or difficult cases and other problems relating to adjudication work.

Members of adjudication committees of local people's courts of the various levels shall be recommended by the presidents of local people's courts for appointment and removal by people's councils of corresponding levels. Members of the Adjudication Committee of the Supreme People's Court shall be recommended by the President of the Supreme People's Court for appointment and removal by the Standing Committee of the National People's Congress.

Meetings of adjudication committees of people's courts of the various levels shall be presided over by the presidents of people's courts; the chief procurators of people's procuracies of corresponding levels shall have the right to attend such meetings.

## ITEM 222D

[Interview]

Hung was a railroad worker who in 1956 was discontented with his lot. His wages were low, and he was often criticized for being backward in his work. One day a "friend" who was visiting Hung's room in Harbin saw a piece of paper on which Hung had written "Mao Tse-t'ung is dead." The friend secretly picked up the paper and took it to the local public security station. After a brief investigation Hung was arrested and prosecuted for current counterrevolutionary activity.

The president of the railroad transportation court assigned a judge to handle the case. After studying the file, the judge talked the matter over with the president of the court. The two of them were puzzled about how to dispose of the case. On the one hand, Hung had in effect cursed the Chairman of the People's Republic and the Party, and this could not be tolerated. On the other hand, Hung was a worker, he had no history of counterrevolutionary activity, he had not circulated the statement in any way, and he had no counterrevolutionary motive or purpose. He was simply a backward type who had lost his temper in the privacy of his home. Because of the difficulty of the case the president of the court convened a meeting of the court's adjudication committee, which was composed of all the judges of the court.

After the problem was put to them, the committee members agreed that Hung could not be considered a counterrevolutionary. But they were also of the view that he could not go unpunished. Several members suggested that he was guilty of defamation, a crime that was generally punishable by a sentence of from six months to two years of imprisonment, which seemed an appropriate punishment in the circumstances. A court secretary, who was a recent graduate of the Peking Political-Legal College and who, because of his advanced legal training, was normally invited to attend meetings of the adjudication committee, said nothing when the suggestion was first made. But during the luncheon intermission he consulted some materials on Soviet law that were in the possession of the court. He noted that both the criminal code of the RSFSR and a leading text on Soviet criminal law stated that circulating was an essential element of the crime of defamation. When the committee reconvened he spoke up and pointed out that a serious legal obstacle to Hung's conviction was the absence of any evidence of publication of the offensive words. The committee members were unreceptive to the idea of having to acquit the defendant on "a technicality." But after patient explanation by the secretary and long discussion, the president of the court agreed that there could be no conviction without evidence of publication and that if the court failed to uncover such evidence, the case would have to be dismissed. With some grumbling the committee members acquiesced.

The judge in charge of the case then interrogated Hung in a room at the public security detention house and later went to talk to Hung's neighbors and co-workers but found no indication that he had expressed any counterrevolutionary views. Accordingly, Hung was released and was given a copy of a judgment that dismissed the charge of counterrevolutionary activity and stated that what he had written had amounted to a "backward opinion" for which he had been appropriately criticized.

During the antirightist movement in 1957, when a review was conducted of of the political cases that the court had handled, both the president of the court and the secretary who had provided the legal advice were severely criticized for the "right-wing tendencies" they had shown in the disposition of the case.

### ITEM 222E

Since the great leap forward little information has appeared concerning adjudication committees. Interviews have suggested that these committees may have become largely vestigial as a result of the procedural simplifications made during the leap; often the kinds of cases that were formerly considered by the adjudication committee have subsequently been allocated to joint decision-making by the "three chiefs," that is, the heads of the relevant court, procuracy, and police units, with advice from professional Party personnel when necessary. Recall Item 219A, for example. This innovation, however, has not altered the requirement that an ordinary judge who has been assigned to handle a case must submit his proposed decision for approval by higher officials within the court. In the following excerpt, published in 1959, the model judge points out the advantages of this requirement.

[Liu Tse-chün, "Realizations from My Adjudication Work" (1959), p. 51]

.     .     .     .     .

In August 1953 when I heard that I was going to be transferred by the organization to work in the courts, I was a bit frightened. I believed that the responsibility of doing judicial work was great. At the same time I also believed that judicial work was "mysterious" and could not be done by ordinary men. The secretary of the county Party committee said to me: "You will have difficulties in the beginning but do not be afraid of them. Remember one word — 'study.' Study hard and ask many questions." I thought to myself: I am a member of the Communist Party. I cannot bow to difficulties. Thus I made up my mind to follow the Party committee's instructions, to ask many questions, and to study hard. After I arrived at the court, I observed others when they presided in court. When I presided in court I asked the leaders and my comrades to watch, and after adjudication I asked my comrades for their suggestions. I did not know how to write a judgment so I watched how other comrades did it and copied various types of judgments. When I wrote a judgment myself, I let other comrades correct it, and then I gave it to the president of the court for his examination.

1. Does the fact that the individual judge cannot render a decision without the approval of higher court officials make the process arbitrary? Is such a procedure more likely to make the process ad hoc? Is it possible that the shortage of politically and legally competent cadres accounts for resort to this procedure?

2. To what extent can an analogy be drawn between the position of the Chinese judge and that of the trial examiner in the administrative process in the United States?

## ITEMS 223A–223D. SUBJECTION TO OTHER GOVERNMENT ORGANS

Like other government personnel the Chinese judge is subject to a variety of disciplinary sanctions that may be imposed by his administrative superiors. But his removal from office, like his appointment to office, is governed by special constitutional and legislative provisions, which are reproduced in these items.

### ITEM 223A

[CONSTITUTION OF THE PRC (Sept. 20, 1954), pp. 12, 13, 14, 22, 25]

Article 27. The National People's Congress shall exercise the following powers:
(7) To elect the President of the Supreme People's Court;
(8) To elect the Chief Procurator of the Supreme People's Procuracy . . .
Article 28. The National People's Congress shall have the power to remove from office the following personnel:
(4) The President of the Supreme People's Court;
(5) The Chief Procurator of the Supreme People's Procuracy.
Article 31. The Standing Committee of the National People's Congress shall exercise the following powers:
(9) To appoint and remove vice-presidents, judges, and members of the Adjudication Committee of the Supreme People's Court;
(10) To appoint and remove deputy chief procurators, procurators, and members of the Procuratorial Committee of the Supreme People's Procuracy . . .
Article 59. People's congresses of county level and above shall elect and shall have power to remove from office presidents of people's courts of corresponding levels.

Article 74. The term of office of the President of the Supreme People's Court and presidents of local people's courts of the various levels shall be four years . . .

## ITEM 223B

[LAW OF THE PRC FOR THE ORGANIZATION OF LOCAL PEOPLE'S CONGRESSES AND LOCAL PEOPLE'S COUNCILS OF THE VARIOUS LEVELS (Sept. 28, 1954), p. 140]

Article 6. Local people's congresses of the county level and above shall exercise the following powers in their respective administrative areas:

(6) To elect presidents of people's courts of corresponding levels; people's congresses of provinces and cities directly under the central authority [shall exercise the power] to elect presidents of intermediate people's courts.

## ITEM 223C

[LAW OF THE PRC FOR THE ORGANIZATION OF PEOPLE'S COURTS (Sept. 28, 1954), pp. 131–132]

*Chapter 3. Adjudication Officers and Other Personnel of People's Courts*

*Section 1. Presidents, Chief Judges, and Judges*

Article 31. Citizens who have the right to vote and to stand for election and have reached the age of twenty-three may be elected presidents of people's courts, or appointed vice-presidents, chief judges, associate chief judges, judges, and assistant judges; but persons who have been deprived of political rights shall be excepted.

Article 32. Presidents of local people's courts of the various levels shall be elected by local people's congresses of the various levels; vice-presidents, chief judges, associate chief judges, and judges are appointed and removed by local people's councils of the various levels.

Presidents of intermediate people's courts established according to districts in provinces and in cities directly under the central authority shall be elected by people's congresses of provinces or of cities directly under the central authority; vice-presidents, chief judges, associate chief judges, and judges shall be appointed and removed by people's councils of provinces or of cities directly under the central authority.

Presidents, vice-presidents, chief judges, associate chief judges, and judges of local people's courts of the various levels in areas in which nationality groups are autonomous shall be elected, appointed, and removed by the organs of self-government of the various levels.

The President of the Supreme People's Court shall be elected by the National People's Congress; vice-presidents, chief judges, associate chief judges, and judges shall be appointed and removed by the Standing Committee of the National People's Congress.

Article 33. The term of office of presidents of people's courts of the various levels shall be four years.

People's congresses of the various levels shall have the power to remove from office presidents of people's courts whom they elect.

Article 34. People's courts of the various levels may, according to their needs, have assistant judges.

Assistant judges of local people's courts of the various levels shall be appointed and removed by judicial administrative organs of the next higher level. Assistant judges of the Supreme People's Court shall be appointed and removed by the Ministry of Justice.

Assistant judges shall help judges conduct their work. Assistant judges may, upon passage by the adjudication committee of a recommendation of the president of their court, temporarily perform the duties of a judge.

## ITEM 223D

[DECISION OF THE STANDING COMMITTEE OF THE NPC OF THE PRC RELATING TO THE PROBLEM OF APPOINTMENT AND REMOVAL OF ASSISTANT JUDGES OF THE SUPREME PEOPLE'S COURT AND LOCAL PEOPLE'S COURTS OF THE VARIOUS LEVELS (passed at the 12th meeting of the Standing Committee of the 2d session of the NPC, Jan. 21, 1960; promulgated by the Chairman of the PRC, Jan. 21, 1960), *FKHP*, 11:120]

In accordance with the proposal of Hsieh Chüeh-ts'ai, President of the Supreme People's Court, relating to the problem of appointment and removal of assistant judges of the Supreme People's Court and local people's courts of the various levels, the twelfth meeting of the Standing Committee of the second session of the National People's Congress decides: assistant judges of the Supreme People's Court shall be appointed and removed by the Supreme People's Court; assistant judges of local people's courts of the various levels shall be appointed and removed by people's courts of their respective levels.

1. According to the above documents what is the term of office of an ordinary judge?
2. Who may remove him from office?
3. On what grounds?

## ITEMS 224A–224C. SUBJECTION TO THE PARTY

Although formally the power to appoint and remove judges is lodged with legislative and executive organs of government, that power is actually exercised upon the orders of the Party. Moreover, since the antirightist movement, virtually all judges are Party members and therefore subject to Party disciplinary sanctions as well as to those applicable to government personnel. These items illustrate the significance of Party membership for judicial service and the consequences of failure to heed, or sometimes to anticipate, the Party line.

## ITEM 224A

["What Shortcomings Are There in the Work of the Supreme People's Court?" *JMJP*, May 21, 1957, p. 2]

Wu Yü-heng, adviser of the Supreme People's Court and deputy chairman of the Peking city committee of the democratic league, talked about the internal contradictions within the Supreme People's Court. He believed that the major contradiction in the Supreme People's Court is the contradiction between the leadership and the led, that is, the contradiction between the Party and the masses. He said that in implementing the cadres' policy the Supreme People's Court has displayed sectarianism. In recent years, non-Communist cadres have been uplifted and reformed. But thus far not a single non-Communist cadre has served as a judge or an assistant judge. He also said that former judicial personnel had not been fully utilized.

## ITEM 224B

["The Supreme Court Wins a Great Victory in the Struggle against the Rightists," *JMJP*, Dec. 12, 1957, p. 4]

Recently the entire staff of the Supreme People's Court held fifteen antirightist struggle meetings in succession, launching a determined struggle on two roads of the people's judicial front and thoroughly exposing and censuring the anti-Party, antisocialist words and deeds of four rightists. They are Chia Ch'ien (chief judge of the criminal division and member of the Communist Party), Lu Ming-chien (director of the research office and member of the Communist Party), Chu Yao-t'ang (associate chief judge of the criminal division and member of the Communist Party), and Lin Heng-yüan (associate chief judge of the criminal division and member of the democratic league). This struggle greatly benefited the people's courts in further developing their appropriate role of consolidating the people's democratic dictatorship and defending the socialist revolution and the task of construction. This struggle revealed in a more concentrated fashion the reactionary visages of these four rightists who opposed the Communist Party's leadership over adjudication work and who tried to change the nature of people's courts unlawfully.

## ITEM 224C

[Wu Te-feng (Vice-President of the Supreme People's Court), "Struggle in Order To Defend the Socialist Legal System" (a speech broadcast Jan. 19, 1958, on the Central People's Broadcasting Station), *CFYC*, 1:10 (1958)]

*1. The Struggle Between Two Roads — the Socialist Legal System and the Bourgeois Legal System*

Since its start in the middle ten days of June of last year, the various levels of political-legal departments throughout the country have successively entered into the antirightist struggle in the legal world. Up to the present in the political-legal organs at the central level and in some of the units at the provincial and city level the antirightist struggle has basically concluded and has changed into readjustment and reform. The struggle continues penetratingly to be developed in some of the provincial and city units and in most of the special districts and counties. This struggle uninterruptedly exposes rightists who have usurped important posts in the central, provincial, and city political-legal organs, organizations, and schools. They are: Ch'ien Tuan-sheng, Yang Chao-lung, Chang Ying-nan, Yang Yü-ch'ing, Yü Chung-lo, Wang T'ieh-yai, Wu Chuan-i, Ch'en T'i-ch'iang, T'an T'i-wu, Lin Heng-yuan, Lo Pang-yen, Liu Wen-t'ao, Chiang Chen-chung, Li Hsiang-jo, T'ang Hsien-chih, Chang Hsüeh-yen, Ho Kung-kan, etc. There were also some rightists hidden within the Communist Party. Among them are: Wang Han, Chia Ch'ien, Lu Ming-chien, Chu Yao-t'ang, Liu Hui-chih, Wang Li-chung, Pai Pu-chou, Pao T'ing-kan, Wu Chia-chen, Ch'en Jen-kang, Peng Jui-lin, Lin Fang, etc. Except for these, we cannot list one by one all the rightists who have been exposed in the political-legal departments of the various levels. This situation, on the one hand, shows the acuteness and complexity of the struggle. On the other hand, it reflects the breadth and depth of the antirightist struggle in the legal world. Coming after the judicial reform movement [of 1952], this is another great victory.

### 2. Inferior Position of the Court

We have seen that judges are far from independent in their status and in the conduct of their duties. But the Constitution, after all, guarantees that the courts, rather than individual judges, "shall conduct adjudication independently."

1. Does this provision mean that the courts act independently of legislative organs? Executive organs? The procuracy? Mass organizations? The Party? The parties to the case?

2. What is the scope of the courts' independence?
   a. Can they independently decide specific cases?
   b. Can they independently formulate judicial policies?

3. If the courts cannot independently decide specific cases, by what means is their independence curbed? According to what criteria?

4. Does whatever interference that takes place render judicial adjudication arbitrary? Ad hoc?

## ITEMS 225A–225E. SUBJECTION TO OTHER GOVERNMENT ORGANS

At both the central government level in Peking and at local levels, the Constitution of the PRC separates the courts, and also the procuracy, from the legislative organs and from the executive organs that exercise power in behalf of those legislative organs. (By contrast, the Ministry of Public Security is regarded as an agency of the executive branch at both the central and lower levels of government.) However, this independent identity of court and procuracy does not imply their freedom from control by other government organs. The provisions concerning appointment and removal of judges presented in Items 223A–223D and other constitutional and legislative provisions reproduced in Items 225A–225B indicate that courts are to some largely undefined extent subject to control by legislative organs and, through them, by executive organs.

## ITEM 225A

[CONSTITUTION OF THE PRC (Sept. 20, 1954), pp. 14, 26]

Article 31. The Standing Committee of the National People's Congress shall exercise the following powers:

(5) To supervise the work of the State Council, the Supreme People's Court and the Supreme People's Procuracy . . .

Article 80. The Supreme People's Court shall be responsible to and also shall report its work to the National People's Congress; during periods when the National People's Congress is not in session, it shall be responsible to and also shall report its work to the Standing Committee of the National People's Congress. Local people's courts of the various levels shall be responsible to and also shall report their work to local people's congresses of corresponding levels.

## ITEM 225B

[LAW OF THE PRC FOR THE ORGANIZATION OF LOCAL PEOPLE'S CONGRESSES AND LOCAL PEOPLE'S COUNCILS OF THE VARIOUS LEVELS (Sept. 28, 1954), p. 140]

Article 6. Local people's congresses of the county level and above shall exercise the following powers in their respective administrative areas:

(8) To hear and examine reports of the work of people's councils and people's courts of corresponding levels.

## ITEM 225C

[DECISION OF THE STANDING COMMITTEE OF THE NPC OF THE PRC RELATING TO THE PROBLEM OF WHETHER PRESIDENTS OF LOCAL PEOPLE'S COURTS OF THE VARIOUS LEVELS AND CHIEF PROCURATORS OF LOCAL PEOPLE'S PROCURACIES OF THE VARIOUS LEVELS MAY CONCURRENTLY SERVE AS CONSTITUENT OFFICERS OF PEOPLE'S COUNCILS OF THE VARIOUS LEVELS (passed at the 26th meeting of the Standing Committee of the NPC, Nov. 10, 1955), FKHP, 2:71]

Having discussed at its twenty-sixth meeting on November 10, 1955, the problem presented by the people's council of Fukien province and the people's council of Hupei province relating to whether presidents of local people's courts of the various levels and chief procurators of local people's procuracies of the various levels may concurrently serve as members of people's councils of the various levels, the Standing Committee of the National People's Congress decides: presidents of local people's courts of the various levels and chief procurators of local people's procuracies of the various levels can in no case concurrently perform duties in people's councils of the various levels.

Upon what principle would this decision appear to have been based?

Items 225D and 225E represent subsequent attempts to interpret the relation of the courts to the other organs of government.

## ITEM 225D

[Ch'i Wen, "We must Thoroughly Liquidate the Bourgeois Ideological Influence of 'Independent Adjudication,'" CFYC, 2:56 (1960)]

The people's exercise of the various kinds of state power is completely realized under the unifying leadership of the Party. On the other hand, as for relations between people's courts and administrative organs — people's councils of the same levels — we should make clear that on the basis of the provisions of the Constitution and the report of Chairman Liu Shao-ch'i on the draft Constitution, the various levels of local people's councils are not only the executive organs of the various levels of local people's congresses, they also perform the duties of standing organs of people's congresses. Thus, since the various levels of people's courts are responsible to people's congresses of their corresponding levels and report their work to them, naturally they also must be responsible to the standing organs of the latter — people's councils of the same levels. At the same time, since the various levels of local people's councils are responsibe for concretely organizing all aspects of the work of the nation's economy, politics, culture, education, health, etc., at all times the central work of the Party is concretely and thoroughly carried out by it. Therefore, in order to enable the adjudication work of people's courts, under the unifying leadership of the Party, effectively to serve politics and the central work, people's courts must also accept the leadership of people's councils of the same level and regularly report their work to it. From this it can be seen that our country's system of people's congresses and relations between people's courts and people's councils of the same level are fundamentally different from "the separation of the three powers" and "the independent adjudication" proclaimed by the bourgeoisie.

## ITEM 225E

[Wu Te-feng, "Struggle in Order to Defend the Socialist Legal System" (Jan. 19, 1958), p. 14]

.    .    .    .    .

Our country's Constitution has the provision that "people's courts shall conduct adjudication independently and shall be subject only to the law." [The term] "conduct adjudication independently" means that a court conducts its adjudication work independently and impartially. It means that a court "uses facts as the basis and law as the standard" during adjudication work and is not affected by the parties' views. It means that during adjudication work the court may not be subjected to the unlawful interference of other state administrative organs, people's organizations, or individuals. Nevertheless, people's courts in our country are created by the organs of state power and should be responsible to these organs. Therefore, they cannot act "independently" of the organs of state power. The Communist Party is the leading nucleus of our state organs. People's courts are state organs. Naturally, courts cannot act "independently" of the Party either.

It would be interesting to attempt to determine whether local courts are actually more independent of local people's councils than are local public security units, which are ostensibly under the direction of people's councils but which operate with a great degree of freedom.

## ITEMS 226A–226G. SUBJECTION TO THE PARTY

Item 225B suggested what has been apparent throughout these materials—that Party control of the courts is far more important than legislative and executive control. Since the antirightist movement, Chinese publications on law have openly and repeatedly advocated and justified Party control. Items 226A–226D are representative selections of the kinds of advocacy employed and the efforts to reconcile the postconstitutional mass line with the wording of Article 78 of the Constitution. In view of Wu Te-feng's position as president of the Political Science and Law Association and a vice-president of the Supreme People's Court, Item 226D has particular significance.

## ITEM 226A

[Chang Tzu-p'ei, "Censure the Bourgeois Principle of 'the Judge's Free Evaluation of the Evidence' " (1958), p. 47]

.        .        .        .        .

The Communist Party is the nucleus of the dictatorship of the proletariat. Without the leadership of the Communist Party there would be no proletarian dictatorship, and naturally there even more certainly would be no socialism. The Party's leadership over people's courts is comprehensive and concrete and is not an abstract slogan. The Party's leadership is manifested not only in the Party's adoption of guidelines, policies, and laws but also in its supervision of the concrete implementation of these policies, guidelines, and laws by people's courts. Party leadership is manifested in political-ideological leadership and should be carried out in concrete adjudication work, including "inquiry into specific cases." Party leadership not only refers to leadership by the Party Central Committee but also to leadership by various local level Party committees over people's courts of the same levels. Not recognizing that the Party leads all aspects of people's courts is tantamount to denying Party leadership. If the "meaning" of "the judge's free evaluation of the evidence" suggested by Chia Ch'ien and other rightists is followed, Party leadership will be completely denied. This is because the hypocritical explanation of the bourgeois "meaning" of "the judge's free evaluation of the evidence" is: the judge is not subject to legal restraints in judging the evidence and determining the facts of the case; other organs or individuals cannot inquire into this; and the judge need not report the reasons for and methods of determining the facts of the case. The judge only follows his "good sense" in "probing" materials of the case and, on the basis of the impression created by his own "reasoning," reaches a conclusion (in reality it is not like this). Therefore, according to the bourgeois "meaning" of "the judge's free evaluation of the evidence," the policies and guidelines of the Party and the laws of the state play no role; the Party cannot inquire into cases decided by judges; nor do judges explain the reasons for their judgments or the methods for making them; that is to say, they do not ask instructions of or report to the Party committee. This method completely rejects Party leadership and is the anti-Communist substance of "the judge's free evaluation of the evidence" which the rightists suggest for our country of the dictatorship of the proletariat.

## ITEM 226B

[Chang Hui et al., "These Are Not the Basic Principles of Our Country's Litigation" (1958), p. 78]

.   .   .   .   .

"The principle of directness" is antithetical to concrete leadership by Party committees over the adjudication work of people's courts of the same levels. Concrete leadership by Party committees over the adjudication work of people's courts of the same levels is without a doubt extremely necessary in order to guarantee the correct, lawful, and prompt handling of cases. One of the important aspects of concrete leadership by Party committees of the adjudication work of people's courts is the examination of cases for approval. When a Party committee examines a case for approval, it not only conducts an examination of the policy, the law, and the punishment decided upon, but it also examines the facts of the case. The method by which a Party committee examines the facts of a case is not personally to conduct an on-the-spot examination of the scene, interrogate witnesses and the defendant, etc., but it is done through examination of the written file or through an oral report by comrades of the court's Party organization. Party committees cannot and need not substitute themselves for people's courts in directly examining the evidence. Thus, "the principle of directness" implies the rejection of Party leadership because the examination of cases for approval by Party committees is contrary to the so-called "principle of directness."

## ITEM 226C

[Ch'i Wen, "We Must Thoroughly Liquidate the Bourgeois Ideological Influence of 'Independent Adjudication' " (1960), p. 55]

If separated from the leadership of the Party, adjudication work will not be well done and it will also change in nature. Whether there are 1,000 legal provisions or 10,000, the leadership of the Party is the first provision. All work is like this and adjudication work is no exception.

The Party's leadership over adjudication work is comprehensive and includes leadership over the line, guidelines, and policy, and leadership over political ideology, organization, and concrete adjudication work. The Party's leadership is unified. Not only should people's courts be absolutely obedient to the leadership of the Party Central Committee and the other higher level Party committees, but they should also be absolutely obedient to the leadership of Party committees of the same levels.

Some people outwardly seem to recognize Party leadership but actually believe the Party's concrete leadership over the business of adjudication to be "interference" with adjudication work that [adversely] affects "the independence" and "active initiative" of the judges. This kind of argument is absolutely absurd. It is absolutely clear that only the Party's concrete leadership over the adjudication of cases can guarantee that the Party line, guidelines, and policies will be correctly, concretely, and thoroughly implemented, and only this can guarantee that the courts handling of specific cases will be correct, lawful, and prompt, attacking the enemy even more accurately and fiercely and serving the Party's central work even better. Therefore, if we insist on asserting that the Party's concrete leadership over the business of adjudication is "interference" and that it affects "the independence" of judges, then opposing and overcoming this kind of "independence" is just what we need. This "interference" is a synonym for strengthening Party leadership while this "independence" is actually a synonym for "doing away with Party leadership" and "becoming independent of the Party."

ITEM 226D

[Wu Te-feng, "Struggle in Order To Defend the Socialist Legal System" (1958), pp. 13, 14, 15, 16]

### 3. The Leadership of the Party is the Fundamental Guarantee for Strengthening the Socialist Legal System

. . . Naturally, when we emphasize the role of Party leadership, we certainly do not imply that the Party should arrange everything. There certainly is no contradiction between discussion and decision by the Party concerning the important problems in the work of the legal system and various professional departments concretely conducting their work. On the contrary, the Party has always opposed unnecessary intervention in and substitution for the concrete work of the professional departments, and at no time will a Party committee organ itself arrest a person or adjudicate a case. Thus, when the rightists say "there is no separation between Party and government" and "the government is replaced by the Party," they intentionally distort the facts. Experience proves that they should say "no separation between Party and government in the first instance, and a separation between them only in the second." That is, the Party puts forth policies and guidelines in accordance with the overall situation, and then, in accordance with these policies and guidelines, the state organs prescribe measures of enforcement. This is the correct attitude that we should have in treating problems of Party-government relations.

Second, another problem put forth by the rightists is that "the Party committee does not understand law" and "does not understand professional work" and therefore that the Party cannot lead the work of the legal system, and that persons "within the field" should lead it. This kind of talk itself exposes the insolent ignorance of those rightists who are self-proclaimed "legal experts." We have already said above that law is not some "mysterious" thing. It is no more than the manifestation of the will of the ruling class and is the product of irreconcilable class struggle. The class nature of law was exposed only after the creation of Marxism-Leninism, which provides a scientific explanation. In our country the people's law is under the leadership of the Communist Party and it is created according to the Marxist-Leninist theory of state and law and a summary of the experience of the masses in the class struggle. Therefore, who best understands the Marxist-Leninist theory and who has the most experience in leading the masses in the struggle? Very obviously it is the Communist Party and not the rightists . . .

On the problem of "independent adjudication" there is still one point, the relationship between policy and law, that needs explanation. Because the rightists have the distorted view that independent adjudication "is subject only to the law," they say that to be "subject only to the law" means that they need not be concerned with policy. Some rightists in people's courts have even publicly shouted that "courts administer law, they do not administer policy." This so-called "do not administer policy" amounts to opposing policy. In essence it amounts to wanting to oppose and to throw off the leadership of the Party because the adoption of guidelines and policies for work is an important aspect of the tasks of the Party's leadership of the state. Can good judicial work be done if it is not based on the policy of the Party and the state? Our answer is negative, because policy is the soul of law and law is the embodiment of policy. One aspect of the mutual relationship between the two is the preliminary generalization of the people's will into policy which, after undergoing testing through practice, is adopted as law. Another aspect is that after its promulgation a law must fit the changes in the objective situation and, on the basis of the policy determined by the Party and the state, correctly develop its role. Policy and law thus mutually reinforce each other. From this it can be seen that for people's courts to apply the law on the basis of policy not only is absolutely necessary for work but also conforms to the leading principles prescribed by law. Therefore, the guideline according to which policy guides the law is absolutely unshakeable.

Another manifestation of the rightists' distortion of "independent adjudication" is that they verbally recognize that a Party committee may politically lead a court, but in reality they do not want the Party committee to "inquire into specific cases." They say that the Party can only be concerned with leadership in the adoption of laws and cannot supervise the enforcement of the laws. Otherwise this "hinders the cadres' activism." Everyone knows that the Party's leadership is comprehensive and cannot be weakened or limited. If one only vocally recognizes the Party's political leadership but rejects its supervision and examination of work, in reality this amounts to denying the Party's leadership, especially with respect to the adoption and execution of the law. Our country's ancestors said: "The law is not self-executing." In the same way, no matter how superior the people's law is, if we do not rely on the Party's leadership and on persons who are loyal to the undertakings of the people to understand it, if we do not at all times examine and correct shortcomings and errors in its execution, then no matter how good the provisions of the law, there will be the possibility of its being distorted and misused. The many cases of distorting law, secretly applying the old law, and indulging criminals, which were exposed in various places during the judicial reform and antirightist struggles, thoroughly demonstrate this point. Correct activism should be supported; erroneous activism should be prohibited. Let me ask: what is wrong with hindering a bit the "activism" in indulging counterrevolutionaries and the "activism" in opposing the Party? Here I also want to explain the so-called problem of "Party committees inquiring into specific cases." Party committees do not need to, nor are they able to, inquire into all cases, whatever their magnitude, that are heard by courts. The problem is that in their work Party members or Party organizations in courts in some cases need to ask Party committees for instructions in order to be able to sentence correctly and to conform to the needs of the present struggle. This is completely necessary from the point of view of Communist Party members and organizations. Since Party committees better understand the present overall political situation and are more capable of striking an overall balance of interests and of considering problems, doing this may greatly reduce the subjective and one-sided nature of adjudication work, be helpful in correctly applying the law, and be beneficial to the present struggle against the enemy. From this it can be seen that for courts to rely on Party leadership is completely consistent with being "subject only to the law." At the same time, since the hearing of the case is conducted independently by courts and judgment is also made independently by them, the courts' reliance does not hinder their "conduct[ing] adjudication independently." Therefore, for the Party comprehensively to lead courts fits the circumstances and is reasonable, lawful, and completely necessary.

. . . [T]he Party is a complete entity. Party leadership is carried out on a unified basis through Party committees of the various levels. Therefore, in accordance with the Party's organizational principles, all of the Party organizations in the various departments within a certain district should, without any exception whatever, accept the leadership of the Party committee in that district and should periodically report to it about work and ask it for instructions. Party groups in all state organs must be even more obedient to Party committees on all questions. This is all specifically prescribed in Chapters 2 and 9 of the Constitution of the [Chinese] Communist Party. Violating these provisions amounts to violating the Party Constitution and undermining Party unity. This should result in severe disciplinary sanctions for Communist Party members and Party organizations. These provisions of the Party Constitution are completely consistent with principles prescribed by law. The Constitution of our country prescribes the right of the Party to lead the state, which naturally includes the central and the various local level Party committees. Therefore, personnel of all state organs, in order to fulfill the obligation of "loyalty to the people's democratic system and obedience to the Constitution and the law" (Article 18 of the Constitution), should first obey the provisions of Article 1 of the Constitution and accept the Party's leadership.

## ITEM 226E

The following selection from the essay by the model judge illustrates for the benefit of other judicial personnel the actual application of Party control and the benefits that flow from it.

[Liu Tse-chün, "Realizations from My Adjudication Work" (1959), pp. 48, 49]

In August 1953 I was transferred to Yung-ch'ing county to do adjudication work in the people's court; when the people's tribunals were established in

February 1955 I was again transferred, this time to work in the Pieh-ku-chuang people's tribunal.

In recent years I have adjudicated a total of 1592 criminal and civil cases. Of these, 967 cases were settled through mediation while 625 proceeded to judgment. Of the latter, appeal was initiated in 26 cases. After hearing these appeals, the intermediate people's court basically affirmed the original judgments. In addition, according to the provincial department of justice, the results of a selective examination of my cases by the intermediate people's court and an examination of the files of all my cases by the county Party committee have not yet revealed one erroneously decided case. I have compiled a report on my work methods and some of my realizations of the last few years for presentation to my comrades. There are certainly many errors and shortcomings in it, and I hope that my comrades will correct them.

First, I realize that judicial work must be absolutely obedient to the leadership of the Party. The Party is the nuclear force that leads us in all of our undertakings. Any work that departs from the Party's leadership will lose direction. Since the political and ideological nature of judicial work is very pronounced, it should, in particular, be absolutely obedient to the leadership of the Party. In the last few years, apart from simple and minor civil and criminal cases, when cases I have handled required arresting and sentencing, had a relatively strong policy nature, or involved village or cooperative cadres, I asked instructions from the Party committee both before and during the process of handling the cases, and afterward I reported to the Party committee. Similarly, in my other work I persisted in this system of asking instructions of and reporting to the Party committee. Whenever the Party committee gave me instructions, I conscientiously studied and thoroughly implemented them. When the county Party committee and other responsible comrades from the county level came to our Pieh-ku-chuang people's tribunal to do their work, if they had a little free time I would seek them out in order to report to them and to ask them to give me instructions for my work. In my work, apart from those times when I directly asked instructions of [the member of] the county Party committee residing in our administrative village and received the leadership of the county Party committee through the county people's court, I always absolutely obeyed the leadership of the Party committee of the administrative village in which the tribunal was located and regularly reported to it the circumstances of the people's tribunal, our summary of special problems, and the morale of the court business meetings. When I went to another administrative village to handle cases and do my work I always reported to its Party committee on the circumstances of the work in the people's tribunal and of the cases to be handled, and I asked the committee for instructions and listened to its views. When I went to the villages and cooperatives to do my work, I paid attention to and respected the views of the Party branch committee. For example, in April of last year I handled a case in the village of Feng-chia-ch'ang involving Jen Chih-p'ing, who stirred up the masses to riot over food. When I arrived at that village, I first sought out the Party committee of the administrative village in order to inform myself about the circumstances and to ask for its instructions and views on handling the case (if the [alleged] circumstances were true I would prepare to make an arrest and to handle the case according to law). Then I investigated further; finally, I asked for instructions from the Party committee of the administrative village and the county people's court on the basis of the new circumstances and of their views for handling them. I also solicited the views of the village Party branch. They all agreed with my view, so that this case was correctly handled.

In recent years I have come to appreciate deeply the importance of absolute obedience to the Party leadership. In my work, every time that I encounter difficulties or problems which are unclear from an ideological standpoint, after asking the Party committee for instructions and after receiving its instructions and support, I feel strengthened and have more confidence with which to complete the task which the Party has assigned us. When I report to the Party committee and ask it to instruct me in my work, I first clarify the circumstances and present the committee with my own ideas and views on the problems so that it may instruct us on the basis of the actual circumstances of our work. I also deeply feel the Party's concern and loving care for the cadres. Once I became ill in the midst of adjudicating a case; I was so dizzy that I almost collapsed. Just at that time the secretary of the county Party committee arrived at the tribunal and told me to take a good rest. On my behalf he personally explained things to the party involved and straightened out his thinking so that the problem was satisfactorily resolved. This not only demonstrates the Party committee's unmatched concern for the cadres, it also demonstrates its strong mass point of view, which gave me a great education and inspiration and increased my strength and confidence in my work.

.     .     .     .     .

Through work practice I also realized that law is the concentrated expression of the will of the masses. When we execute the law we must act on the basis of this spirit; if we rely on the masses and accept their correct views, we will correctly implement policy and execute the law. In many of the cases that I have handled, before reaching a judgment, I solicited the views of the cadres of the village and the cooperative, of the departments concerned, and of the masses. I humbly adopted those views that were correct and resorted to persuasion and explanation with respect to those that were not. In mediating cases where the facts were relatively complex, I also invited participation by members of the mediation committee, assessors, reputable members of the masses, and cadres of the village and the cooperative. In March of this year I handled a case of bodily injury involving Kao Yung-liang. Kao was the child of a rich peasant. He had been struggled against and was dissatisfied with us. This time he had beaten and injured the deputy chief of a production team and had been sent to the tribunal. At first I still thought this was an ordinary case of bodily injury, and I was prepared, after learning the facts of the case, to sentence Kao to only a few months of imprisonment. The facts of the case which the defendant admitted during questioning were inconsistent with those of the complainant's accusation. In order to clarify the facts of the case I went down to the administrative village to investigate and discovered some witnesses who had been afraid [to testify about the case]. I therefore repeatedly conducted investigations, adopting the method of going to the work sites to take advantage of the peasants' rest period by combining casual chats with individual interviews. Only in this way did I find out that many of the cadres and masses hated both Kao and his mother. They not only indicated that it was a fact that Kao had beaten and injured the person, they also pointed out that the deputy chief of the production team was the public security representative. Kao had not only disobeyed his command but had also beaten him up. This was an act of class hatred. Everyone demanded his punishment. The Party committee of the administrative village also instructed me to handle the case in this way. I followed the instructions of the Party committee of the administrative village and the views of the masses, and, with the approval of the county court, I sentenced him to a year and one-half of imprisonment.

1. Recall the quotation from *Izvestia* reprinted on p. 57 above. Consider the following:

"Leading jurists in the Soviet Union are pressing a campaign to establish unchallenged integrity of law and independence of the courts.

"Growing criticism is being directed at Soviet newspapers and prosecutors for a widespread practice of whipping up public opinion against defendants before their cases have been heard in court.

"Prosecutors and police officials, who find newspaper attacks and denunciations of defendants by 'indignant citizens' helpful in obtaining convictions, are strongly resisting the demands that the courts be shielded from outside influences. They assert that a prohibition of public pressure on judges would isolate the courts from the people and thereby violate 'Socialist democracy.'

"To support their demands for strict adherence to the law, Soviet jurists cite numerous instances in which defendants have been unjustly convicted by courts yielding to the clamor of local passions and pressures.

*Innocent Man Doomed*

"In one such case an innocent man was sentenced to be shot for murder and was saved only when his appeal was heard by a higher court in another city.

"The latest jurist to speak out in the debate on the integrity of law, which has been under way in the pages of the Government newspaper Izvestia for several months, was Dr. Ilya D. Perlov, a Moscow authority on criminology.

"The sovereignty of the courts is guaranteed by Article 112 of the Soviet Constitution, Professor Perlov wrote Wednesday, and this must not be considered a hollow declaration.

"Soviet courts, he added, have an inviolable obligation: 'to carry out correctly and unswervingly the requirements of law, not to retreat from law under any circumstances, not to succumb to influences and "pressures", regardless of how strong and from whatever source.'

"Despite the Constitutional guarantee, the professor protested, Soviet courts frequently are brought under pressure to convict a defendant or to levy harsh sentences unjustly and sometimes illegally.

### Prosecutors Accused

"All too often, he said, the campaigns are stirred up by prosecution officials pretending to represent an 'outraged public opinion.'

"Judges must be wary of so-called public opinion, Professor Perlov warned. He added: 'Calmness, sobriety and sound reasoning are needed not only by judges but also by the public when demanding a harshening or lessening of punishment for a defendant. Passion, public or otherwise, only interferes with an objective, businesslike weighing of a case.'

"The professor condemned Soviet newspapers for publishing articles attacking defendants and insisting 'in the voice of the people' that the courts pass down severe penalties.

"This position is criticized by Ilya S. Galkin, chief criminal investigator in the Russian Republic. Deriding jurists' protests that newspaper attacks on defendants tend to influence courts, Mr. Galkin wrote in Izvestia:

" 'In those rare instances when citizens are in legal proceedings against law-breakers, then the calmness, sobriety and sound reasoning of the judges will cool off these passions.'

"Scorning the demand that courts be permitted to deliberate free of outside influences, the criminal investigator asserted:

"[']Such a demand contradicts the basic principles of Socialist democracy and also contradicts the task of educating citizens to feel a personal responsibility in maintaining public order.' " [13]

2. Does the model judge advise his colleagues to seek the approval of the Party committee in all criminal cases? If the Party is asked to consider all such cases, might this not prove to be a heavy burden?

### ITEM 226F

The author of this selection offers another set of criteria for determining when the Party committee should be consulted.

[Li Mu-an, "Censure Independent Adjudication That Proceeds from Concepts of the Old Law," *CFYC*, 1:26 (1958)]

.     .     .     .     .

There is also the rightist argument that for the courts to send individual important cases, especially counterrevolutionary cases, to the Party committee for examination and approval and for instructions, is Party "interference in independent adjudication" and leaves "no separation between Party and law." This argument proceeds from the old law's concept of independent adjudication. We

---

13. Raymond H. Anderson, "Courts' Freedom Urged in Soviet," *New York Times,* July 3, 1966, p. 14. © 1966 by the New York Times Company. Reprinted by permission.

believe that the concrete leadership of the Party over guidelines and policies of judicial adjudication work can only truly be realized through its examination for approval and its instructions with respect to specific cases. To reject the Party committee's inquiry into specific cases is, in reality, tantamount to denying the concrete leadership of the Party over adjudication work. Naturally, there is no necessity for the Party committee to examine every case for approval or to issue instructions in every case without regard to the magnitude and nature of the case. Generally, this is only necessary in important cases such as cases during a movement, political cases, and cases of an important policy nature and of far-reaching implications. Moreover, examining these important cases for approval and issuing instructions with respect to them guides the adjudication of ordinary cases. Examining specific important cases for approval and issuing instructions is one of the main methods by which the Party committee manifests its leadership and supervision over the courts. This is beneficial and not harmful in assisting the courts in handling cases. It is especially necessary in the struggle against the enemy and also is consistent with the spirit of the Constitution. Is there anything objectionable about "no separation between Party and law"?

## ITEM 226G

In Item 226E the model judge was careful to point out that when he asked the Party committee for instructions he always presented it with his own "ideas and views on the problems so that it may instruct us on the basis of the actual circumstances of our work." As a result of the extreme emphasis upon obtaining Party approval of court decisions and the fear of making mistakes that might offend Party leaders, apparently many courts simply handed cases over to the Party without submitting an appropriate analysis of the file and a recommendation for disposition. This item also inveighs against this practice.

[Ts'ui Ch'eng-hsüan, "How We Defended the Safety of Hsing-fu People's Commune" (1958), p. 63]

Absolute obedience to Party leadership is the fundamental guarantee of doing our work well. In every link of our work in defending the commune, because we promptly report each situation to the commune Party branch and conscientiously listen to the instructions of the branch, we are able to understand the overall situation in the commune's development and closely coordinate it with the entire work of construction; and we are able to take the initiative in forcefully attacking the sabotage activity of the enemy and in defending the smooth development of the commune movement. In addition, in the comprehensive leap forward, the tasks of the Party branch in leading production (especially iron and steel production) are complex and heavy. When we ask the branch for instructions in our work we must present it with concrete proposals. We cannot simply extend our hands to the Party and ask for a method, thus adding to the burdens of the branch.

In appraising the Manchu legal system, one authority has written:

"The real weakness of the Chinese system sprang from the fact that the application of the law was entrusted to the administrative officers of the Empire.

The court of law was, like the militia, part of the machinery for maintaining order and good behaviour throughout the district. It provided no check on the executive power." [14]

To what extent might the same be said of the judicial system of the PRC?

14. Van der Sprenkel, p. 70.

# Chapter IX  Formal Criminal Processes: Sentencing

A. Principles Governing Imposition of Sentence

B. Specific Types of Punishment
1. Reprimand
2. Fine
3. Confiscation of Property
4. Deprivation of Political Rights
5. Suspension of Sentence
6. Control
7. Detention
8. Imprisonment for a Fixed Term
9. Life Imprisonment
10. Death Penalty

C. Special Problems of Sentencing

When punishments are heavy, people dare not transgress, and therefore there will be no punishments.

Anonymous Legalists,
3d century B.C.[1]

In the light of these developments, people's courts, acting under the leadership of the party and government, put into effect the program to purge all the counter-revolutionaries and the policy of "blending leniency with punishment." They also carried out a lenient program which stresses control and transformation instead of apprehension and killing. In cooperating with the public security and procuratorial organs, they mobilized the masses to beat back these sabotage operations, and took further steps to screen and punish the remnant counter-revolutionaries, tightened our struggle against the enemies along the sea coast, and provided safeguards for the success of the socialist construction undertakings and the people's communalization drive in our province. The broad masses of people were so pleased that they sang in praise:

> May the rays of socialism shine in bright, radiant light,
> And the purge of counter-revolution tighten up the fight.
> Happy life comes as we weed out the landed guys,
> Rich farmers, the undesirables and counter-revolutionary spies.

The criminal and civil cases of the first instance adjudged by our provincial people's courts at all levels in 1958 covered a great variety of offenders. Some

1. In J. J. L. Duyvendak, trans., *The Book of Lord Shang* (Chicago, 1963), p. 288.

were bloody criminals who had incurred public wrath and covered up their offenses without confessing ever since the liberation. Some were the American-Chiang secret service spies who had engaged in grave sabotage operations, such as gathering information on our military and political conditions, murder and other destructive operations. Some were landlords, wealthy peasants, counter-revolutionaries and undesirable elements engaged in active sabotage operations. Some were incorrigible criminals left over by the old society, who were guilty of robbery, theft or deceit. Others were those who had resisted transformation and maintained their reactionary stand during reform through labor, and continued their sabotage activities. We have meted out death sentences to a small number of vicious counter-revolutionary and criminal elements because nothing else was good enough to calm down public wrath. Others have been imprisoned, placed under control or released after weighing carefully the development of our struggles, the nature of their crimes and the extent to which they had confessed and repented.

> Chao Yuan (President of the High Court of Fukien Province), "Report on a Year's Work of the People's Court of Fukien Province" (Feb. 13, 1959)[2]

Although sentencing is actually part of the adjudication process, the subject is sufficiently important and the materials are sufficiently ample to warrant independent treatment. In reading this chapter, consider to what extent the theory and practice of sentencing appear to implement the goals of the criminal law set forth in Chapter I. Also, how would you characterize the degree of discretion that the courts exercise in imposing sentence? Is there anything peculiarly Communist about the way in which these problems are handled?

## A. PRINCIPLES GOVERNING IMPOSITION OF SENTENCE

Item 227 spells out for the benefit of judicial cadres factors that should be considered in passing sentence in a concrete case. What is the relation of these factors, and others mentioned in subsequent materials, to the goals stated in Item 5?

### ITEM 227

[*Lectures* (September 1957), p. 216]

.     .     .     .     .

How can the principle of handling matters on the basis of the facts and in accordance with the law be implemented in the work of deciding upon criminal punishment? The several items [discussed] below can explain this:

(1) The principle of assuming the criminal responsibility prescribed by law must be followed, and punishment must be applied within the scope of

2. *Fu-chien jih-pao* (Fukien daily); translated in *JPRS*, no. 1077-D (Dec. 17, 1959), pp. 2–3.

punishments prescribed by law . . . With respect to crimes for which the law does not prescribe punishment, punishment should be determined on the basis of the spirit of our policies and with reference to our experience in actual adjudication.

(2) Punishment must be decided upon on the basis of the complete circumstances of the crime after evaluating the seriousness of the circumstances of the case and examining the amount of social danger.

It should be understood that when we decide upon punishment for [two] crimes of the same nature, because the circumstances of the cases are different and because there are differences in the amount of social danger, one punishment may be light and the other heavy. Problems in this area [of deciding upon punishment] are: the damage caused by the crime (sometimes we must consider direct damage and indirect damage, material damage, and political damage, etc.), the means and methods of committing the crime (whether or not they are evil, contemptible, vicious, cruel, etc.), the motive of the crime (whether or not it is contemptible or evil, etc.), the time, place, and circumstances of the crime, etc. Only by examining all these circumstances completely and concretely can we possibly make a correct evaluation of the social danger of each crime and thereby impose a suitable punishment. Naturally, the scope of this evaluation can only be in accordance with provisions of law and the spirit of policy.

(3) To assist in determining punishment it is necessary to refer to the personal circumstances of a criminal and to examine the degree of his social danger.

The personal circumstances of a criminal include his [class] status, [social] origin, history, cultural level, age, ideological quality and demeanor, living conditions, whether or not he previously committed crimes, behavior prior to committing the crime, and attitude after committing the crime. By linking these circumstances for study and examination, it is possible to expose the moral visage of the criminal, further decide the degree of his social danger, and thereby help in correctly deciding upon punishment. For instance, there should be a difference in deciding upon punishment for a criminal who, before committing the crime, customarily labored [diligently] and observed the law but who slipped up on [one] occasion and in deciding upon punishment for a criminal who, before committing the crime, was a habitual loafer who did not engage in labor and who repeatedly broke the law . . . Here it should be pointed out that although the status, origin, and history of a criminal are one part of his personal circumstances, only when they are linked to the crime that has been committed will they have a definite reference value in deciding upon punishment and a definite influence on the decision. Otherwise it [the decision] cannot be changed because of the person. For example, when a bicyclist negligently hits and injures a person, the actor should be dealt with in the same way, whether he is a landlord, a capitalist, or a laboring person. The severity of punishment is determined by the degree of social danger of the crime and not by the status, origin, or history of the criminal. To consider the question only or mainly on the basis of the criminal's status and to make that the main basis for deciding upon punishment is the status theory viewpoint and is an error.

Article 85 of the Constitution of the PRC states that "Citizens of the People's Republic of China shall all be equal before the law." [3]

Article 5 of the Law for the Organization of People's Courts elaborates upon this by providing:

"In the adjudication of cases by people's courts, the law shall be applied uniformly to all citizens irrespective of their nationality, race, sex, occupation, social origin, religious belief, level of education, property status, or duration of residence." [4]

## ITEM 228

[Interview]

Chu was a capitalist who had undergone socialist reform and had subsequently been assigned to work in the warehouse of a state export company in Canton. One day in 1959 he smoked a cigarette while in the bathroom, tossed the match into a corner and left. This started a fire that destroyed the warehouse. The city public security bureau immediately detained all the employees who had been on duty at the time and interrogated them over a three-day period until Chu admitted having been careless with the match. At that point the other employees were released, and Chu was subjected to intensive interrogation.

He steadfastly insisted that his conduct had only been negligent. The investigators, on the other hand, were equally insistent in accusing him of being a "dissatisfied capitalist" who had intended to damage the warehouse. Despite the fact that Chu refused to confess to this accusation and that investigation failed to uncover other evidence, the bureau finally turned the case over to the procuracy on a charge of current counterrevolutionary activity, and he was prosecuted, convicted, and sentenced to life imprisonment. The sentence was publicly pronounced at a meeting of Chu's fellow warehouse employees, who showed no enthusiasm for it, since they had regarded Chu as a friendly and reliable person and did not believe that his conduct had amounted to more than criminal negligence.

## ITEM 229

As Item 228 suggested, in practice the class status of the defendant is a critical factor in the determination of the degree of guilt and the severity of punishment. The following item appears to be another example of a "mirror image" characterization.

[*Lectures* (September 1957), p. 35]

The criminal law of the countries of the exploiters, like that of the feudal countries, openly manifests inequality. Decisions are arbitrary and involvement [of the innocent] is extensive. Although the criminal law of capitalist countries differs from that of feudal countries in that it [the former] does not expressly prescribe that a certain class will have privileges but declares that all people are equal before the law, it only uses the form of equality to cover up its extremely unequal substance.

3. P. 27.
4. P. 124.

Consider the following commentary on traditional Chinese law:

"In accordance with the spirit of the *li,* the codes provide penalties which differ sharply according to the relative class status of the offender and his victim. As one of countless examples, let us see how the Ch'ing code treats the offense of striking or beating another person. The lowest degree of this offense, as defined in the code, is a blow or blows delivered solely by the hand or foot and resulting in no wound (defined as inflammation or discoloration of the skin or other more serious injury). Such an act, when occurring between equals (a commoner striking a commoner or a slave a slave), is punishable by twenty blows of the small bamboo. This constitutes the standard or normal penalty. For a slave who beats a commoner, however, this normal penalty is increased by one degree to thirty blows, whereas for a commoner who beats a slave, it is decreased by one degree to only ten blows. Decapitation is the penalty for a slave who strikes his master (irrespective of whether or not injury results), whereas no penalty attaches to a master who injures a slave, unless this leads to death. The penalty for beating the presiding official of one's own locality is three years of penal servitude, whereas for beating an official belonging to another district the penalty ranges from two years downward depending on the official's rank." [5]

## ITEM 230

[Interview]

After successfully mediating a violent dispute that had occurred between construction workers and peasants in the outskirts of Canton in late 1955 [see Item 24B], public security cadres undertook an investigation to discover whether hostile elements had surreptitiously fomented it. They questioned each of the forty-odd men who had been involved in the fight. All of them were ordinary members of the masses with the exception of a man named Huang, who had a "history." Huang had been a middle peasant who had served as head of the local *pao* under the Nationalist government's *pao-chia* system. After the Communist forces took over the area in 1949, he was found guilty of counterrevolutionary activity and sentenced to five years of reform through labor. Upon his release in 1954 he was given "controlled production," but after one year of good behavior his counterrevolutionary "cap" was removed and the "controlled production" terminated. It was only shortly thereafter that he became involved in the outburst of violence.

In the course of their investigation the public security cadres learned that Huang had said to another peasant who had been struck by a worker: "Let's go after them." Although other peasants and workers had uttered similar remarks and although there was no evidence that Huang had done anything else to incite violence, the public security cadres singled him out for prosecution. The problems of the other peasants and the workers were deemed to be problems from "among the people" but, because of his "history," Huang's problem was not. He was arrested for "provoking dissension," convicted, and, in front of a mass meeting of local residents, sentenced to five years of reform through

5. Bodde, p. 389.

labor. The public security station cadres subsequently heard muffled grumblings of resentment on the part of some of Huang's neighbors who considered the treatment to be too harsh, but nothing was done to alter the sentence.

### ITEM 231

Recall SAPA Article 26 (Item 77A) and the case interpreting it (Item 77B). Are they consistent with the principles advocated in this item?

[*Lectures* (September 1957), pp. 114–115]

.    .    .    .    .

Even under circumstances where a minor assumes criminal responsibility, we still should pay attention to the fact that the development of a minor's mental and intellectual powers has not completely reached maturity and that therefore he is more susceptible to external temptation, education, and reform than an adult. Thus we should not apply criminal punishment to him in completely the same way as to an adult. In the aforementioned Reply of the Former Commission on the Legal System of the Central People's Government, it was pointed out that when a criminal is a minor who has not reached the age of eighteen, he may be punished lightly in comparison with a criminal who is over the age of eighteen, or the [prescribed] punishment may be reduced. The Act of the People's Republic of China for Reform Through Labor prescribes that in the course of executing the punishment of offenders who are minors over the age of thirteen and below the age of eighteen, houses of discipline for juvenile offenders shall be established. Houses of discipline for juvenile offenders shall emphasize educating these offenders in politics, the new morality, and basic cultural and production skills, and shall make them engage in light labor under circumstances where concern is shown for their physical development. From these documents it can be seen that in struggling with crimes committed by minors the criminal law of our country clearly embodies a spirit of concern for minors, is based on their characteristics, and has correctly implemented our country's criminal [law] policy: the spirit of "combining punishment with education."

### ITEM 232

[*Lectures* (September 1957), pp. 224–227]

.    .    .    .    .

According to the special circumstances of a case, if a people's court considers that sentencing a criminal to the minimum punishment prescribed by law is still too severe, it may sentence him to a punishment that is less than the punishment prescribed by law. If it considers that sentencing him to less than the lightest punishment prescribed by law is also unnecessary, it may remit criminal sanctions. But reductions and remissions of punishment must be handled on the basis of state policy and the law, and the reasons should be explained in the written judgment.

What are "special circumstances" of a case? From the standpoint of our country's judicial practice, certain above-mentioned circumstances for light punishment also can become circumstances for reduction or remission of punishment. For example, if a counterrevolutionary whose evil act is not serious voluntarily surrenders, sincerely confesses, or has behavior which establishes his merit, his punishment may be reduced or remitted. Even if he is a counterrevolutionary whose evil act is relatively serious, if he sincerely confesses and has behavior which establishes his merit, his guilt may be offset by his merit, and his punishment may be reduced or remitted. For another example, if the crime is not serious and if, after commission of the crime, the criminal voluntarily eliminates or reduces the danger, punishment may be reduced or remitted. An example of such a case would be if, after stealing public property, he returned it to its original place because he repented or feared criminal sanctions. In addition, for acts of legitimate defense which exceed the limits of necessity, punishment may also be reduced or remitted according to the circumstances.

Reducing punishment is different from punishing lightly. Punishing lightly is within the scope of punishments prescribed by law. Reduced punishment is a sentence less than the minimum punishment prescribed by law or a sentence of another kind of even lighter criminal punishment. For example, the punishment prescribed by a provision of a certain law is one to ten years of imprisonment. If we sentence lightly, we may sentence [a criminal] to three or four years of imprisonment, but not to less than one year. Reduced punishment, on the other hand, would be a sentence of more than six months but less than one year of imprisonment and may even be a sentence of detention, control, or some other lighter criminal punishment as a substitute for imprisonment for a fixed term.

When punishment is reduced according to the special circumstances of a case, the appropriate degree to which it may be reduced can, naturally, only be resolved by an examination and an evaluation of the complete circumstances of the case. But without appropriate control and restrictions it might create the danger of undermining the legal system and damaging the dignity of the law. In practice, some people have suggested that the minimum punishment prescribed by law be taken as the standard: if the minimum punishment is life imprisonment, it may be reduced to imprisonment for not less than ten years; if the minimum punishment is imprisonment for less than ten years, it may be reduced to two or three years, or six months, according to the length of the minimum punishment, or reduced to detention, control, or reprimand; if the minimum punishment is detention or control, it may be reduced to reprimand or remission of punishment. We believe that this suggestion may serve as a general reference, but we still must continue to summarize our experience.

·    ·    ·    ·    ·

We believe that in principle it is unsuitable to use [the doctrine of] sentencing to more than the maximum punishment prescribed by law, that is, the so-called punishment of increased severity. This is because when the law prescribes a principle for punishing a certain crime, it already indicates the most severe degree of punishment on the basis of a consideration of all the circumstances of that crime. The maximum point in the range of [prescribed] punishments resolves the problem. Therefore, if it is necessary to give a severe punishment to a criminal, dealing with him severely is permissible and also resolves the problem. If sentencing beyond the punishments prescribed by law is allowed, the legal system will be undermined. It is wrong to consider that since, in addition to light punishment, there is reduced punishment, there also should be punishment of increased severity in addition to severe punishment. This improperly symmetrizes [the idea of] encouraging the self-reform of criminals to [the idea of] strictly punishing criminals. In our country's Act for Punishment of Corruption there is a provision relating to punishment of increased severity. There are special circumstances for this. We know that this Act is an individually issued regulation to punish crimes of corruption. The severity of punishment was prescribed according to the amount of money [involved in the corruption] fundamentally to meet the circumstances of the "three-anti" and "five-anti" movements and specifically to resolve questions [arising out] of these movements. Moreover, very specifically, the range of punishments to be decided upon, as prescribed by the various clauses of Article 3, is relatively small. Therefore, the provision establishing punishment of increased severity is necessary and has significance. It would be inappropriate to disregard these circumstances and to treat the provision of the Act for Punishment of Corruption that relates to punishment of increased severity as a universal principle of criminal law.

With respect to principles of mitigation and aggravation, recall the statutes that appear as Items 118, 119, and 124 and the cases in Items 210D–210E and 219A. Also recall SAPA Articles 20 and 21 (Items 72A and 73A) and the materials that illustrate their application (Items 72B and 73B–73C).


## B. SPECIFIC TYPES OF PUNISHMENT

For an introductory comment, see Item 6.


### 1. Reprimand

Recall Item 54 and the comment that follows it.

### ITEM 233

We have previously read the bill of prosecution and the account of the judicial hearing of this case. (See Item 189 and Item 210A.) The current item reports the outcome of the process.

["Hearing of the Szu-ming-t'ang Case Concluded," *Chieh-fang jih-pao* (Liberation daily, Shanghai), Aug. 31, 1957]

The hearing of the Szu-ming-t'ang case has been concluded. Yesterday the Huang-p'u district people's court, in accordance with law, gave defendant Chiang Yeh-wei the sanction of reprimand.

After the occurrence of the incident, the true facts of the case were clarified by the Huang-p'u district people's court at a public hearing. The court held that: defendant Chiang Yeh-wei's act of wounding a person with a knife was an infringement of the rights of a citizen's person and constituted the crime of infliction of bodily injury which, according to law, should be punished. But before the incident occurred the defendant made a report to the district store and public security station in order to avoid the occurrence of an incident. It was when he returned to the store that a controversy arose between him and Ch'en Chi, his glasses were knocked off and in a moment of excitement he pulled out a knife and wounded Ch'en Chi. Furthermore, he did not deliberately inflict injury, and the result was not serious. For these reasons he can be dealt with leniently and can be given the sanction of reprimand.

## 2. Fine

### ITEM 234

[*Lectures* (September 1957), pp. 205–207]

. . . . .

When used as a method of criminal punishment, a fine differs from an ordinary administrative fine. The former is applied to a criminal by a court. The latter is applied to an ordinary violator of law by the organ concerned (such as a tax organ). Although both of them belong to the category of legal coercive sanctions, they differ in legal nature. We cannot confuse them. A fine also differs from compensation for damage. Although some compensation for damage, such as a criminal's paying for medical expenses or living expenses for a given period of time to a victim who has been injured, also is occasioned by a criminal act, this is a question of supplementary civil compensation in a criminal case and is not a punishment.

A fine, when applied independently, is a relatively light method of punishment. It is only applicable to criminals whose crimes are relatively minor in nature and circumstances. It can only serve as a supplementary punishment and cannot be applied independently in [cases of] major crimes.

According to our current criminal [law] legislation (such as the Act for Punishment of Corruption and the Provisional Act for Punishment of Crimes that Endanger State Currency) and according to judicial practice, a fine is mainly applied to crimes motivated by pecuniary gain, such as speculating, smuggling, evading taxes, unlawfully buying or selling gold and silver, bribing or accepting bribes, gambling, purchasing stolen property, manufacturing, selling or transporting opium, or extorting property through use of the marriage relationship. The aim of criminals in committing these crimes is to get unlawful benefits. As a result, supplementary application of this kind of punishment, directed at this contemptible exploiter class ideology, can, by depriving them of their money, more realistically play a punitive and educative function with respect to these criminals and can stimulate them to repent and to reform themselves.

To impose fines for crimes which are not motivated by pecuniary gain and are not of great social danger, such as imposing a given fine on a criminal whose crime is ordinary interference with the administrative order of society, amounts to punishing by [imposing a sentence of] uncompensated labor for a given period of time. For instance, A's monthly salary is one hundred yuan. If he commits a certain crime and is punished by a fine of fifty yuan, this amounts to punishing him by [imposing a sentence of] half a month of uncompensated labor.

In the past, because of their lack of understanding of the significance and the role of the fine as a punishment, some judges applied it abusively. For example, they imposed fines for crimes of negligent homicide, infliction of bodily injury, and adultery. This is wrong. Facts have proved that this way of doing things cannot achieve the goals of punishing and educating offenders. On the contrary, it encourages those bad elements who have money to continue to do evil, and it also arouses the dissatisfaction of the masses. When the sentence is a fine, we must start out from the point of view of punishing criminals and preventing crime, and the decision whether or not the sentence should be a fine must be based on the nature of the crime and the circumstances of the case. When the sentence may be a fine, in deciding the amount we must also consider the criminal's property status. We cannot fine with the point of view of increasing the income of the national treasury. A fine may only be imposed on a criminal as supplementary punishment in a situation where sentencing to punishment that deprives him of freedom is not sufficient to punish and educate him and, therefore, where it is necessary to sentence him to a fine as a supplementary punishment directed at his motive of pecuniary gain. Only in this situation is a fine appropriate.

When the sentence is a fine, the time limit for payment and the issue of whether payment is to be made once or in several installments should, on the basis of concrete circumstances, be prescribed in the written judgment. One who has not paid by the expiration of that time should be coerced to pay. If in the course of executing judgment, circumstances indicating the criminal's inability to pay are discovered, such as his really being unable to pay because of the occurrence of a disaster which he could not control, at such time a people's court may, considering the situation, reduce or remit the fine. In the past, some people's courts quite often resolved this problem by the method of substituting [a sentence of] labor service (actually it was detention). We believe that this deserves consideration because when the sentence is a fine, people's courts should thoroughly consider the financial capacity of the sentenced person and should not create the possibility that the problem of inability to pay will occur afterwards. If he has encountered unexpected circumstances, since these were not desired by the criminal himself, the court, following the spirit of revolutionary humanitarianism, should reduce or remit the fine and show concern for his livelihood and production. Substituting a severe punishment for a light punishment or substituting a punishment that deprives the criminal of freedom for a fine is not in conformity with the principle of punishment in our country. Likewise, in our country's criminal law substituting a light punishment for a severe punishment, [such as] substituting the imposition of a fine for detention, as is the way in bourgeois countries, is not permissible. In bourgeois countries this way of punishing lets wealthy criminals redeem themselves from punishment by using money. It is a method for freeing capitalists from criminal responsibility and is incompatible with the nature of punishment in our country.

### 3. Confiscation of Property

ITEM  235

[*Lectures* (September 1957), pp. 208–209]

.      .      .      .      .

Confiscation of property is the coercive, uncompensated nationalization of a part or all of the property personally owned by a criminal. In our country's current criminal [law] legislation, such as the Act for Punishment of Counterrevolution, the Act for Punishment of Corruption, the Provisional Act for Punishment of Crimes that Endanger State Currency, and the Regulations Relating to Confiscation of Property of Counterrevolutionary Criminals, there are provisions relating to confiscation of property.

According to criminal [law] legislation and judicial practice, confiscation of property is mainly applied to those counterrevolutionary criminals whose crimes are serious — criminals guilty of major crimes of corruption, thieves, major opium offenders, major smugglers, and criminals whose speculation is serious. Applying confiscation of property to these criminals punishes and educates them on the one hand and thoroughly eliminates the possibility of their continuing their criminal activity on the other. Because most of the property of these criminals has been acquired by criminal means and because the criminals use this property as capital for engaging in even more crime, confiscation of their property is completely reasonable and necessary. Confiscation of property is a relatively severe punishment and is only applied as supplementary punishment for certain serious crimes. In the future, in order to facilitate control [over this punishment], legislation may prescribe those crimes to which this punishment can be applied.

Only in the Regulations Relating to Confiscation of Property of Counterrevolutionary Criminals is there a provision for the independent application of the punishment of confiscation of property. But we believe that this provision was established only for situations where counterrevolutionary criminals are [in the act of] escaping. In the future, it will be necessary for the criminal law to limit the scope of the application of confiscation of property to the point where it is only supplementary punishment.

When [the punishment of] confiscation of property is applied, a part or all of the property may be confiscated according to the concrete circumstances. But the confiscated property can only be the property personally owned by the criminal. Property which is not personally owned by the criminal should not be confiscated. In the Regulations of the Government Administration Council of the Central People's Government Relating to Confiscation of Property of Counterrevolutionary Criminals, it is pointed out: "The property of his [the counterrevolutionary's] family members who are not living with him and the property personally owned by his family members who are living with him shall not be confiscated." In the confiscation of property, if only part is to be confiscated, the judgment of the people's court should specify which part it is to be. If all of it is to be confiscated, funds for living expenses should, in the exercise of discretion, be left for his family members. There is also a provision for this in the above-mentioned Regulations: "When all of a counterrevolutionary criminal's property is confiscated, the means of production and the means of earning a livelihood shall, in the exercise of discretion, be left for his family members who are living with him and who did not actively participate in his counterrevolutionary activity so that they can maintain their livelihood." This provision embodies the humanitarian spirit of our country's criminal law and at the same time stabilizes the life of those family members who have relied on the criminal for a livelihood and who have no other source of livelihood. This provision is also in the interest of stabilizing the social order.

The above-mentioned Regulations also point out: "If among the confiscated property of a counterrevolutionary criminal there is property of the people that was embezzled, taken by force, or robbed by the counterrevolutionary criminal, and if the original property [in its original form] still exists, it shall be returned to the original owner upon his request and after the truth [of his claim] has been verified" (fourth paragraph). "If a counterrevolutionary criminal's legitimate debts should be paid out of the confiscated property, they may be paid within the proper limits of the confiscated property upon the request of the creditor and after the truth [of his claim] has been verified" (fifth paragraph). It can be seen from this that the property of victims should be returned to them from the confiscated property and that legitimate debts may properly be paid. But matters must be handled on the basis of the above-mentioned legally prescribed conditions and procedures in order to prevent situations of abuse in making payment and of wrongful receipt [of payment] from occurring.

The above-mentioned principles for applying [the punishment of] confiscation of property which were established by the former Government Administration Council in the Regulations Relating to Confiscation of Property of Counterrevolutionary Criminals are also applicable to other criminals whose sentence prescribes the confiscation of their property.

Recall Item 60.

## ITEM 236

[Mou Min, "Enemy Property Concealed by Ma Po-sheng Confiscated in Accordance with Law," *Ta-chung jih-pao* (Masses' daily), Aug. 10, 1957]

On the eighth of this month the high people's court of Shantung province publicly tried the case of Ma Po-sheng, who had concealed enemy property.

Defendant Ma Po-sheng was general manager of the Jen-feng Yarn Mill in Chi-nan before liberation. After Japan occupied Chi-nan and imposed a military administration on the Jen-feng Yarn Mill, Ma Po-sheng and others lost [control over] the administration of the mill and received very little profit from it. At that time Ma Po-sheng secretly conspired with the great traitor Yin T'ung (superintendent of the general office of construction of the counterfeit [puppet] North

China Government Administration Commission) to collaborate with the Japanese robbers, and they maneuvered to make the Jen-feng Yarn Mill a Chinese-Japanese jointly operated mill. In 1941 they signed a contract of joint operation. In the investment agreement it was provided that the Chinese investment would be the land, plant, tools, etc., of the former Jen-feng Mill, the value of which was set at two million yuan of the counterfeit government's currency, and that the Japanese investment would be two million yuan in cash, to be paid by the Chung-yüan Company, a Japanese imperialist enterprise in China.

After Japan surrendered, Ma Po-sheng bribed officials of the KMT and secretly combined the two million yuan of the counterfeit government's currency invested by the Japanese robbers with the Jen-feng mill's property. In addition, in 1937 the Jen-feng Yarn Mill had borrowed 500,000 yuan of the counterfeit government's currency from the state bank, and it still owed this amount. The debt had never been cleared up. After liberation, Ma Po-sheng continued to conceal the facts and did not report them. When the people's government cleared up the affairs of the Jen-feng mill in accordance with law, Ma not only refused to confess the true facts, but he also incited some stockholders jointly to request that the government return the property rights of the Jen-feng mill to them. For these reasons, in January of 1952 Ma was incarcerated by the government in accordance with law. While in custody, he was educated by the government, and he confessed all the facts. As a result, having obtained a guarantor, he was released pending disposition of his case.

At the public trial session, defendant Ma Po-sheng admitted all the above-mentioned facts. After the arguments, the court held that Ma Po-sheng's concealing of enemy property constituted a crime which should be punished. But Ma Po-sheng, having been educated by the government, was able to bow his head and admit his guilt. Therefore, in keeping with the spirit of the "five-anti" period policy of dealing leniently with this type of case, the court announced that the defendant was to be exempted from criminal sanctions but that the concealed enemy property and public property was to be confiscated in accordance with law.

#### 4. Deprivation of Political Rights

ITEM 237

[*Lectures* (September 1957), pp. 210–213]

.     .     .     .     .

Deprivation of political rights is deprivation of the rights to participate in the administration of the state and in its political life, rights which the criminal enjoyed as a citizen of the People's Republic of China. This criminal punishment is applied mainly to counterrevolutionary criminals who are hostile to the people's democratic system and criminals whose crimes are serious. Very obviously, the people's democratic rights can only be exercised by the people, not by the enemies of the people. To deprive these persons [counterrevolutionaries and criminals whose crimes are serious] of their political rights can prevent them from using these rights to endanger the people's democratic system and the undertakings of socialist construction and socialist reform. This is completely necessary and correct. Because deprivation of political rights is by nature a relatively serious punishment, we must adopt a very serious and careful attitude in considering whether or not it is necessary to deprive other criminals [whose crimes are not serious] of their political rights. We believe that it is necessary only when the nature of a crime and the circumstances of the case are relatively serious and when all the circumstances of the case indicate that it would be inappropriate for the criminal to exercise these rights for a given period of time. It is not fitting to apply this punishment to ordinary, relatively minor crimes.

Based on the needs at the time of adopting the Provisional Measures for Control of Counterrevolutionaries the political rights of which one can be deprived were prescribed as: (1) the right to vote and to be elected; (2) the right to hold administrative office in a state organ; (3) the right to participate in the people's armed forces and in people's organizations; (4) the right to freedom of speech, publication, assembly, association, correspondence, [choice of] residence, movement of household, demonstration, and procession; and (5) the right to enjoy the people's honors. Today, in view of present circumstances, some of these provisions are no longer suitable. For example, the right to freedom of correspondence, [choice of] residence, and movement of household of the fourth item cannot be called political rights. At the same time, from the point of view of actual circumstances in the past few years, there have been difficulties in implementing provisions related to the fourth item. Therefore, we consider that the contents of that item need not be listed [as political rights of which one can be deprived]. As for the third item, Article 103 of the Constitution of our country prescribes that military service is an honorable obligation of citizens of our country. If this also is treated as a political right, then it is not in conformity with the spirit of the Constitution's provisions. Thus, the third item also is worth considering. There is no question that a criminal who is deprived of political rights does not have the right to vote or to be elected; to hold administrative office in a state organ; and to enjoy the people's honors, that is, to enjoy state medals, decorations, military titles, or honorary titles. In addition, we believe that a criminal who is deprived of political rights cannot serve as judge, assessor, procurator, lawyer, or leader of any people's organization. These questions can be resolved in the future by legislation. At present, we should handle matters according to the spirit of state policies and the instructions of each period.

When one is sentenced to deprivation of political rights it may be to deprivation of all political rights or to a part of them. On the basis of the provisions of the Provisional Measures for Control of Counterrevolutionaries, a counterrevolutionary criminal should be deprived of all political rights. Other criminals who should be deprived of political rights may, on the basis of concrete circumstances, be deprived of a part or all of them. If they are deprived of a part, those rights of which they are deprived should be specified in the written judgment.

Current criminal [law] legislation still has no express provisions relating to the period of deprivation of political rights. On the basis of experience in judicial practice, it ordinarily is between one and five years. We believe that this minimum and maximum period can serve as a reference. If criminals are in a state of not having political rights for too long a period and cannot lead the normal political life of ordinary citizens, it will affect their activism in striving for self-reform as urged and encouraged by us. Naturally, it would not be suitable if the period of deprivation were too short. For example, in a few months the function of punishment of deprivation of political rights cannot be developed and the objective of punishing and educationally reforming offenders cannot be attained.

The period of deprivation of political rights is calculated from the day on which execution of the principal punishment is completed or the day on which the criminal is conditionally released. Only when the principal punishment is control can [the punishment of] deprivation be executed simultaneously with the principal punishment. In practice, some [judges] fix the period of deprivation of political rights at ten, fifteen, and even twenty years, partially because this point is not clear and they [the judges] include the period served in prison in the calculation. Relevant to this problem, the Central Ministry of Justice in its Interpretations Relating to Problems of Conditional Release, Suspension of Sentence, and Deprivation of Rights of Citizens (a reply to the people's court of Chahar province) on May 20, 1950, pointed out: "Imprisonment and deprivation of rights of citizens (that is, deprivation of political rights) are two different matters. One who is sentenced to imprisonment is not automatically deprived of his rights as a citizen . . . During his term of imprisonment he is not automatically without these rights, but in fact he cannot exercise them. Whether or not he is deprived of these rights should be decided in the judgment. Because he is sentenced to imprisonment he is not automatically without them." It can be seen from this that sentencing to imprisonment and depriving of political rights cannot be confused to mean the same thing. One who is sentenced to imprisonment and also deprived of his political rights has no political rights during the term of imprisonment. One who is sentenced to imprisonment but not deprived of his political rights is in principle considered as one who still has political rights during the term of imprisonment, but in fact he cannot exercise them.

Whether or not it is necessary simultaneously to announce that a criminal who is sentenced to death or to life imprisonment is deprived of his political rights for life is also a controversial question. In judicial practice, there is no consistency. Some [judges] simultaneously announce deprivation of political rights; some do not. We believe that for criminals who are sentenced to death, the deprivation of any state medals, decorations, military titles, or honorary titles that they may have should be announced at the time the judgment is given. As for other political rights, they cannot in fact be enjoyed by criminals who are sentenced to death, and to make a *pro forma* announcement of the deprivation of these rights would be meaningless. As for an offender who is sentenced to life imprisonment, a decision should be made at the time of judgment as to whether or not to deprive him of political rights, because afterwards the question of his conditional release or reduction of his sentence may arise. If the deprivation of his political rights is simultaneously announced, naturally he has no such rights while serving his term in prison. If he is conditionally released or released [unconditionally] after a reduction of his sentence, the court should decide the period for which he is to be deprived of his political rights. If the deprivation of his political rights was not announced in the original judgment, he should be deprived of such rights after being conditionally released or released [unconditionally] after reduction of his sentence.

Finally, it should be explained that the deprivation of political rights that we have here discussed is a method of criminal punishment. It differs from the deprivation of political rights that is a revolutionary administrative measure of the state in its enforcement of dictatorship. Article 19 of the Constitution of the People's Republic of China prescribes: "The state shall deprive feudal landlords and bureaucratic capitalists of political rights for a definite period of time according to law." This is a revolutionary administrative measure which the state has put into effect against all the hostile elements of the overthrown classes. As long as there are feudal landlords and bureaucratic capitalists, whether they have committed crimes or not, they will all be deprived of political rights by the state for a definite period of time according to law. This is entirely necessary for the protection of our people's democratic state. This revolutionary measure is directly proclaimed by our Constitution. But deprivation of political rights as a method of criminal punishment is a punishment that is put into effect against individual criminals. It is prescribed by criminal law and realized through adjudication.

### 5. Suspension of Sentence

### ITEM 238

[*Lectures* (September 1957), pp. 239–241, 242, 243–244, 247, 248, 249–250]

.     .     .     .     .

If the criminal's social danger is relatively small, a people's court may decide, on the basis of certain conditions and situations, not to execute a sentence of detention or imprisonment for a fixed term if within a prescribed test period the sentenced criminal does not commit a new crime. This conditional nonexecution of the punishment imposed by the original sentence is called suspension of sentence. Its basic characteristics are a punishment [set forth] in a sentence and a decision not to execute that punishment, but the possibility of executing it is maintained for a given period of time. It uses the method of nonexecution of punishment to achieve the purpose of punishment.

Since suspension of sentence is a conditional nonexecution of punishment, then ultimately, under what conditions can sentence be pronounced suspended? This is an important question which must first be studied.

On September 28, 1953, the Supreme People's Court pointed out in a reply to its former East China branch court relating to several questions about which instructions were sought and opinions given: "Suspension of sentence is generally applicable to a defendant whose social danger is not great and whose sentence is relatively light and may temporarily not be executed because of other concrete circumstances . . ." With respect to conditions for applying suspension of sentence these instructions propose a relatively clear principle and scope.

. . . Some people believe that suspension of sentence is only applicable to criminals whose sentence is no more than five years of imprisonment. Others believe it applicable only to those whose sentence is no more than three years. Still others believe it applicable only to those whose sentence is no more than two years. It is, of course, possible that the defect of misuse of suspension of sentence would arise if it were only applicable to those whose term of imprisonment was very long. But suspension of sentence would be too limited if it were only applicable to those whose term of imprisonment was very short and this would be equally disadvantageous to our struggle against crime. Especially with the degree of awareness of the people of our country increasing every day, conditions for applying suspension of sentence are even more complete. Under these circumstances, it would not be in conformity with the interests of the state and of the people if the scope of suspension of sentence were too limited. On the basis of the experience of our country's adjudication practice, suspension of sentence has been applied only in a very few individual cases in which the term of imprisonment was three years or more. Unquestionably, in most cases it has been applied to those whose term was no more than three years. This is worth our attention. Generally speaking, if a criminal has been sentenced to three years or more of imprisonment, his crime can no longer be considered a minor crime, and consequently, his social danger cannot be considered relatively small. Therefore, we advocate that suspension of sentence only be applied to criminals who have been sentenced to no more than three years of imprisonment or detention.

Next, it should be noted that the fact that the scope of suspension of sentence is prescribed as being applicable to criminals sentenced to no more than three years of imprisonment naturally does not mean that sentence may be pronounced suspended for all those criminals. The length of the term of imprisonment is only a condition for evaluation. The criminal's attitude after commission of the crime, his behavior before its commission, and various other aspects also should be considered comprehensively from the point of view of the nature of the crime and the circumstances of the case in order to evaluate the degree of his social danger and [to determine] whether or not to apply suspension of sentence.

(1) The nature of the crime: suspension of sentence is mainly applied [in cases] where the general nature of the crime is relatively minor. From the point of view of practice, sentence has been pronounced suspended mostly in cases of mistreatment, negligent infliction of bodily injury, theft, violation of labor discipline and labor protection, adultery, etc. Generally, sentence will not be suspended in [cases of] relatively serious crimes. Sentence should not be suspended for counterrevolutionary criminals, especially current counterrevolutionary criminals, because the nature of their crimes is especially serious. There-

fore, before a decision is made whether or not to suspend sentence, the nature of each specific case must be carefully considered and studied.

.    .    .    .    .

In addition to this, in our country's adjudication practice, the following circumstances also serve as reasons for the application of suspension of sentence: hardship for the family [of the criminal] in earning a livelihood [without him]; having young children whom it is necessary to take care of; being a pregnant woman; business or production necessity; being relatively young of age; having serious illness, etc. But these circumstances can only be regarded as secondary conditions for suspension of sentence. They must be considered together with the conditions for suspension of sentence explained above before the applicability of suspension of sentence can be finally determined. These [secondary] circumstances certainly cannot clarify the question of the criminal's social danger. Therefore, if a sentenced criminal does not demonstrate even the slightest repentance and reform after committing a crime and may possibly continue to endanger society, and suspension of sentence is inappropriate, sentence should not be suspended despite hardship for his family in earning a livelihood, etc.

.    .    .    .    .

What is an appropriate length for the term of the suspended sentence? In practice, most [judges] have advocated that the length of that term maintain a definite proportionate relationship to the term of the original sentence. But there are different views as to how to determine this proportionate relationship. For example, some have advocated that "the term of the suspended sentence should be longer than the term of punishment." Others have advocated that "it should be shorter than the term of punishment." Still others have advocated that "both terms should be equal," or "if the term of punishment is relatively long, the term of the suspended sentence may be the same; if the term of punishment is relatively short, the term of the suspended sentence may be longer than that." We believe that it would be reasonable if the term of the suspended sentence met the degree of social danger of the crime. When the degree of social danger of the crime is relatively great, the term of punishment is relatively long, and the term of the suspended sentence also ought to be relatively long. On the other hand, when the degree of social danger of a crime is relatively small, the term of punishment is relatively short, and the term of the suspended sentence also should be shorter. But considering the nature and function of suspension of sentence, it would be even more appropriate to prescribe that the term of the suspended sentence be a little longer than the original term in the sentence in order to ensure full development of the influential role of education which suspension of sentence should play. If the term of the suspended sentence and the term of punishment were the same, particularly if the term of punishment were very short (such as no more than six months), the purpose of testing criminals surely could not be achieved because the test period would be too short. Therefore, there must also be a limitation on the minimum term of the suspended sentence.

On the basis of our understanding of the above and on the basis of the suggestion that suspension of sentence only be applicable in circumstances where criminals are sentenced to detention or to no more than three years of imprisonment, we advocate that it would be proper if the term of their suspended sentence generally were no less than the term of the original sentence and no more than five years. The maximum term of the suspended sentence would be five years. If it were more than five years, it would impose an unnecessary mental burden on the sentenced person and would affect the activism of the offender in self-reform. We say "generally," which means that this can only serve as a principle. Since actual circumstances are so very complex, it may not be in the interest of the work if the term of the suspended sentence is fixed too rigidly. Therefore, after considering all the circumstances of a case and the personal circumstances of the criminal, if a people's court believes that the term of the suspended sentence should be shorter than the term of punishment imposed by the [original] sentence, it may set a lower term. But it would not be suitable if the minimum term of the suspended sentence were shorter than six months. Otherwise, as said above, the suspension of sentence would have no effect. On the basis of our understanding of the above, we can see that the term of the suspended sentence of those whose sentence is no more than six months and for whom sentence is pronounced suspended cannot be less than six months.

.    .    .    .    .

The system of suspension of sentence has been extensively and effectively used in our country's adjudication practice. In some people's courts, judgments in which sentence is suspended account for approximately 10 percent of total criminal judgments. In some basic level people's courts the percentage is even larger . . .

Suspension of sentence cannot be confused with a stay of execution of punishment. A stay of execution of punishment refers to a situation after the determination of judgment in which the court decides to stay execution of the sentenced person's punishment because of certain special circumstances which prevent execution, such as serious illness and pregnancy. Execution begins when such circumstances disappear. Although the situation in which suspension of sentence is revoked and the punishment imposed by the original sentence is executed has certain similarities to the stay of execution of punishment, from the above explanation it can be seen that in nature and in significance they [suspension of sentence and stay of execution] are obviously different . . .

To take suspension of sentence for remission of punishment is equally erroneous. In the case of remission of punishment, a people's court adjudges the defendant guilty according to provisions of law and the special circumstances of his case, and at the same time announces the remission of his punishment. Therefore, the problem of execution does not exist. In the case of suspension of sentence the judgment not only declares that the defendant is guilty, it also simultaneously imposes punishment. But the court prescribes a test period. The possibility of executing the punishment is certainly not lost. Once the sentenced person violates legally prescribed conditions during the test period, this possibility will be realized.

.    .    .    .    .

Finally, we should explain the problem of supervision of persons whose sentence has been suspended during the term of the suspended sentence and the problem of the simultaneous imposition of suspension of sentence and supplementary punishment.

The problems of whether or not it is necessary during the term of the suspended sentence to supervise persons whose sentence has been suspended and how to supervise them is worth study. In practice, some [judges] have imposed no restrictions [on persons whose sentence has been suspended]; others have imposed control; and still others have prescribed a reporting system for supervising and examining them. The methods vary. There are still no express provisions in law dealing with this problem. We believe that it is necessary to supervise and examine persons whose sentence has been suspended during the term of the suspended sentence. Appropriate supervision and examination can strengthen the educative influence of the suspension of sentence upon a person whose sentence has been suspended, stimulate a criminal to attain reform, and achieve the anticipated effects of suspension of sentence. But control is a method of criminal punishment in our country. To use the method of control to supervise a person whose sentence has been suspended is to confuse suspension of sentence with control. In view of the purpose and significance of suspension of sentence, it is inappropriate to apply too severe a method of examination to a person whose sentence has been suspended or to prescribe too many limitations. In order to supervise a person whose sentence has been suspended, the court may, we believe, notify the public security department or the department for which he [the person to be supervised] originally worked of the judgment of suspended sentence. This department may examine his behavior in production or work and educate him in political ideology and in observance of law. In addition, limitations on his freedom to move his household should be imposed. When a person whose sentence has been suspended wants to move his household, he should get the approval of the people's court that originally adjudicated the case. This point is clearly prescribed in the State Council's Instructions Relating to the Establishment of a Regular Household Registration System which was promulgated in June 1955.

With respect to the problem of the position and salary of criminals whose sentence has been pronounced suspended, the Ministry of Justice in a reply to the City of Peking Bureau of Justice and the High People's Court of Kansu province on December 30, 1956, pointed out: "A defendant whose sentence has been pronounced suspended, if not deprived of political rights, may keep his position . . . He shall be paid a salary on the basis of the principle to each according to his labor and in accordance with his duties."

## ITEM 239

[Interview]

Hsia was a factory worker who lived in Canton while his wife remained in the countryside. In 1958 he set up housekeeping with Kao, an attractive woman who, while her husband was in prison, had been engaging in sexual relations with a number of men in return for their financial support. Shortly after they moved to a production brigade in a rural commune, Kao was ordered to join the brigade's rehabilitation through labor unit [see Item 93]. At the same time, because of his relations with Kao, Hsia was prosecuted and convicted of adultery in violation of the Marriage Law and was sentenced to eighteen months of imprisonment. Since he was a worker, had no record of prior crimes, and had done no great harm by his conduct, the basic level court decided to suspend the execution of the sentence for eighteen months on condition that Hsia and Kao separate, which they agreed to do.

## 6. Control

Recall Items 100–104 and 113.

## ITEM 240

["A Group of Unlawful Elements Are Sentenced to Control by the Ku-yüan County Circuit Tribunal," *Ku-yüan jih-pao* (Ku-yüan daily, Kansu province), Jan. 10, 1958]

Editor's note: The circuit tribunal which was sent by the Ku-yüan county people's court to Chang-i district tried some bad elements on the spot and then announced the disposition of their cases. This not only linked the masses with reality and educated them about the legal system, it also promptly attacked bad elements and effectively developed the role of the people's democratic dictatorship. Therefore, this is a good method.

In the last ten days of November 1957, in order to protect production, to safeguard the security of society, and to consolidate the people's democratic dictatorship, the circuit tribunal which was sent to Chang-i district by the Ku-yüan county people's court sentenced to control seven unlawful elements who had damaged production. They were handed over to the agricultural cooperative for supervision and reform.

Among the unlawful elements were four unlawful landlord and rich peasant elements. For example, the unlawful landlord element, Yang Fu-tsan, continued to spread rumors and to conduct sabotage activity after agricultural cooperativization. After entering the cooperative, he did not obey the leadership of the cooperative. On two occasions he secretly used a donkey that belonged to the cooperative to carry lily leaves for his own benefit and told the cooperative to record work points for him. He also illegally bought ten strips of second-class fur and went out to engage in speculation. He was sentenced to two years of control. After entering the cooperative, unlawful rich peasant element Ma Kung tried to beat up Huang Pao-Li, the director of the cooperative's supervision committee. He refused to pay his public grain contribution for 1955–1956 . . . He did not obey the leadership of the cooperative and twice went out to engage in secret speculation, making more than seventy yuan profit. Moreover, he deliberately increased the burden of the [cooperative's] donkey. He was sentenced to three years of control. Five other criminals were sentenced to control in accordance with law and were handed over to the cooperative for supervised labor.

## ITEM 241

[Interview]

Wu was a badly crippled man of twenty-eight who sold books and periodicals at a street corner stand in Canton. In 1959 he developed a friendship with a ten-year-old girl who frequently came to look for stories, and after a time they became intimate. When the girl's mother discovered the relationship, she reported it to the public security station. After a prompt investigation, Wu was prosecuted and convicted of seduction. Although the crime is normally punishable by a long prison sentence, since Wu was too disabled to take part in regular reform through labor, the basic level court sentenced him to three years of control.

### 7. Detention

Recall Item 59.

### 8. Imprisonment for a Fixed Term

## ITEM 242

[*Lectures* (September 1957), pp. 198–199]

.    .    .    .    .

Imprisonment for a fixed term is a method of criminal punishment whereby criminals are held for a definite period of time for reform through labor. In keeping with the purpose of punishment in our country, this method of punishment is mainly applied to [cases involving] various relatively serious crimes. Those who have committed major crimes may be sentenced to long-term imprisonment, and those whose crimes are not very serious may be sentenced to short-term imprisonment.

With respect to the minimum term of imprisonment, there are no express provisions in law relating to it, and in practice there is no uniformity. Some [minimum terms] are one or two months. Others are five or six months. Considering that imprisonment for a fixed term is a relatively severe punishment, and at the same time, considering imprisonment for a fixed term in connection with detention, we believe that it would be more appropriate to fix the minimum term of imprisonment at six months.

With respect to the maximum term of imprisonment, in practice it is generally fifteen years. In a few cases, it is twenty years, and in isolated cases, it reaches twenty-five years. In order to make the maximum term of imprisonment uniform, the Supreme People's Court and the Central Ministry of Justice, in a reply to the former East China branch court dated June 11, 1953, pointed out: "Until the central government makes express provisions, the maximum term of imprisonment generally may not exceed fifteen years, but in a special situation it may be raised to twenty years." We believe that this is appropriate. But "a special situation" should be understood to mean a situation in which there is combined punishment for several crimes.

The problem of calculating the term of imprisonment is not handled completely consistently in our practice. Some [judges] calculate it from the day on which the defendant is [first] confined in custody. Others calculate it from the day on which judgment is rendered. Calculating it from the day on which the defendant is [first] confined in custody is inappropriate because confinement in custody prior to the rendering of judgment is a coercive sanction used during criminal litigation. At that time it has not yet been determined that the person confined in custody is a criminal. If calculated from the day on which the defendant is [first] confined in custody, criminal punishment and coercive sanctions used during criminal litigation become confused. From the point of view of both theory and practice, it is only proper to make the day on which judgment is rendered the date from which the term of imprisonment is calculated.

The period of confinement in custody prior to the rendering of judgment should be deducted from the term of imprisonment. The standard for deduction is pointed out in the Opinion of the Supreme People's Court Given to the Former East China Branch Court Relating to the Problem of Judgment When the Defendant Dies during Litigation and the Problem of Deduction of the Number of Days of Confinement in Custody Prior to Judgment, of June 25, 1951: "On the problem of deducting from the defendant's term of imprisonment the period of confinement in custody prior to the rendering of judgment, we believe that in the future it should be explicitly noted in every judgment that one day shall be deducted for each day of confinement in custody, so that it is clear and the prison authorities are not neglectful in calculating the term of imprisonment."

## ITEM 243

["People's Tribunal Protects the Rights of the Person. Wang Shao-ch'ing To Serve Imprisonment for Hitting Others," *Chung-ching jih-pao* (Chungking daily), Apr. 23, 1957]

On the afternoon of April 17, at a meeting attended by 500 or more of the Chungking Steel Company's staff and workers and their family members, the Ta-tu-k'ou people's tribunal of the Chiu-lung-p'o district people's court publicly tried Wang Shao-ch'ing for violation of the rights of people.

The defendant Wang Shao-ch'ing, a worker in the third workshop of the Chungking Steel Company, always behaved crudely and frequently hit others over trivial matters. On March 19 of this year at about seven o'clock in the evening Wang Shao-ch'ing's wife fell ill and was taken by the head of the division of workers' family affairs, Wu Pen-yü, and others for treatment at the company's hospital for staff and workers. After Wang returned home, he immediately rushed to the hospital. At that time, Wu and the others were carrying the patient and were waiting to get some medicine. After helping them to get the medicine, Wang intentionally asked the nurse on duty, P'an Yu-ku: "Where is my wife? Where is my wife?" P'an explained to him that, since there were so many patients, she did not know where his wife was. Wang viciously asked "What are you doing here?" and made a threatening gesture. A staff member of the hospital, Liu Ch'ing-sung, came over to explain things to him, but Wang would not listen, grabbed Liu's collar and pushed him away. At that moment Dr. Tai T'ien-chun (a woman), who was making her rounds, came out to try to settle the matter, but Wang reached out for Tai's chest and tore her uniform. Wang then hit her with his fist, but, because many persons had come over to persuade him to stop, he only managed to hit Tai's left wrist. He also hit nurse Ts'ao Shui-chen with his fist. When the director of the company's health office, Yang Kuang-min, heard what was happening, he rushed to the spot to try to settle it. Wang Shao-ch'ing became more arrogant and said: "I was just looking for you, Director!" Then he hit Yang twice in the chest. Just as he was about to hit Yang again, he was dragged away by the masses who had gathered around. But Yang's neck had already been scratched in several places, and his clothing had been torn. What was particularly bad was that when some patients who had been waiting for diagnosis had come over to try to settle the matter, they too were pushed and hit. After the incident, the personnel of the hospital for staff and workers, the patients awaiting diagnosis, and the masses of workers were all furious and unanimously demanded that Wang be punished in accordance with the law.

On the basis of the above stated facts, the people's tribunal, in order to safeguard state law and discipline and to protect the rights of people from infringement, sentenced Wang Shao-ch'ing to six months of imprisonment in accordance with law.

The masses who attended the trial unanimously expressed their satisfaction.

## ITEM 244

[Snow, *The Other Side of the River* (1962), pp. 570–572]

.    .    .    .    .

The courtroom was in a former missionary compound in the Hongkew district of Shanghai, an area which China once offered as a territorial concession to the United States . . . The room held about forty people, dressed in working clothes, who were already seated and quiet as church when the young judge, Mo Pen-wan, entered. He was accompanied by two "people's representatives" [people's assessors] in their thirties, with whom the law requires a judge to confer before pronouncing sentence. I learned from my companion that Judge Mo was a machinist and labor union leader who had been given special training in a school operated by the judicial department to teach the relatively simple legal codes of the People's Courts.

Yang Kuan-fu was the name of the prisoner, aged thirty-nine. A lean, sallow-faced man with a receding chin, he was escorted into the room and stood at attention before the elevated bench. Yang and his defense lawyer listened as the prosecutor read his summation of the charges:

"You were arrested on September 14, 1960. As a former special policeman under the Kuomintang regime you intrigued with gangsters to blackmail, intimidate and rob citizens, having in instances beaten them. After liberation you stayed on in Shanghai, failed to report your past misdeeds, donned civilian clothes, and took a job with the light and power company. Your duties were to collect bills owed for repairs and maintenance. During the past two years you embezzled 1,527 yuan by falsifying receipts. These facts were first reported by your fellow workers. After your arrest an investigation confirmed the facts, to which you have confessed. Accordingly you are brought to trial under Article Three of the Legal Code.[6] Do you admit your guilt and acknowledge your confession?"

After the prisoner had replied in the affirmative Judge Mo questioned him directly:

Q. "What did you do before Liberation?"

A. "I was a policeman in Chiang Kai-shek's Loyalty Gendarmerie, engaged in political and intelligence work. Aside from that I arrested and tortured people to extract money from them, part of which I kept for myself. I helped carry out some looting also. With others, I took part in a few highway robberies . . ."

This curious confession, indicating a reversal of roles between policeman and criminal, may be explained by conditions at the end of Kuomintang rule (to which I have referred earlier), when the gendarmerie seized, tortured and extracted gold and precious articles from prominent citizens before Shanghai was evacuated.

Q. "When did you take your present job?"

A. "In 1957. I began embezzling on a small scale but soon took as much as thirty yuan at a time. My method was to write one figure on the top receipt but a different and lower one on the carbon copy."

Several witnesses appeared against the accused. Judge Mo instructed them briefly: "Tell the truth. Do not exaggerate. Do not try to protect the accused." The first witness was a worker who asserted that Yang had come to his factory thirty-five times to collect for repairs. A total of 487.82 yuan had been paid to him. The next witness, an accountant in Yang's office, testified that the accused had remitted only 109.34 out of the total mentioned. Becoming suspicious, he had gone to the factory, compared receipts, and discovered the discrepancy. Two more factory representatives provided similar evidence. Most of the audience consisted of men and women workers from the defrauded factories and organizations. They were attending the trial to see that justice was done and to report back to their groups.

6. This is apparently a reference to Article 3 of the Act for Punishment of Corruption, Item 124.

When the defendant had admitted all the accusations the Judge asked him whether he realized that he had been robbing the working people and his own family, and whether he realized the seriousness of his crime. He said that he did, and added: "While the whole country is going forward I have been leaping backward. The government had given me a new way of life despite my corrupt past life. I was not satisfied with ample wages. I was greedy and wanted more."

The prosecutor then demanded maximum punishment in accordance with the law. The accused had not voluntarily confessed his crimes. Even after his fellow workers had discovered the first instance of embezzlement, the previous May, he had refused to help them by admitting his other crimes. Only after they had gathered all the evidence and had him arrested had he confessed to the police.

Judge Mo next heard from the defense attorney, who spoke in the following sense:

"The accused has confessed and expressed his regret. Article Three is two-sided. It provides for punishment but also for reform through education. With us it is a principle to be lenient to those who repent and to be severe with those who do not. After his arrest the accused did quickly confess and confess thoroughly. After a trip in the countryside he himself has seen how everyone is working to build the country up while he was tearing it down. This is true even in his own family. Now he feels ashamed. We should consider the corrupt life he formerly lived and make allowances. I consider his attitude relatively good. I would recommend leniency."

Judge Mo turned to the prisoner, who was visibly shaking. "Have you anything to say?" Yang replied in a quavering voice with one sentence only: "I shall do my best to carry out whatever punishment is given to me and to reform myself into a morally fit citizen."

Court was recessed while the judges conferred. It took no longer than a cigarette smoke. In the courtyard I spoke to a young electrician who knew some English. He had worked in the same office with Yang. I asked him what Yang had done with the money he stole.

"He spent it on expensive restaurants where capitalists go. Of course, when someone saw him in those places we began to get suspicious. He got hold of some bad women, too, and he wanted money to sleep with them. Prostitutes? No. But there are still some women around who will make love for money."

Yang could have got ten years for embezzlement. I asked the worker what his group thought would be fair in this case. "If he had confessed to us when we first got the evidence on him he might have been given only a year. Now — he may get five years." When court reconvened, Judge Mo again reviewed the facts. Then he compared life in the corrupt Shanghai of the past with the present and said that allowances must be made.

"The crime was serious, but the prisoner has now fully confessed and seems ready to rehabilitate himself. We consider that after some re-education he can still do something useful in society. Our sentence," he ended, "is three years."

The prisoner was notified that he had a right to file an appeal within ten days. The court then adjourned. Everyone seemed satisfied.

## ITEM 245

["Severely Punish Wandering Thieves, Safeguard Security and Order in Society," *Ta-nan-shan jih-pao* (Ta-nan-shan daily, Kwangtung province), Dec. 11, 1959]

On the sixth and seventh of this month, in the villages of Li-hu, Chan-lung, and Hsin-liao, the Pu-ning county people's court publicly tried the cases of three wandering thieves, Ch'en Wen, Yuan I-hsiung and Ch'en Ping-ch'eng.

Habitual thief Ch'en Wen, also named Ch'en Tse-yüan, assumed names Ch'en I and Ch'en Hui, was a thirty-year-old male of Ch'ing K'an village in Hai-feng, Pu-she-mei commune. Beginning in 1944 this offender served as a soldier of the counterfeit [KMT] government until he returned home in 1948. He never engaged in proper employment. After liberation, he frequently committed acts of theft. In 1955 he was sentenced to five years of imprisonment. In 1957 he received a conditional release and returned home, but he still had not thoroughly reformed. He wandered among Chieh-yang, Lu-feng, Liu-sha, and Li-hu of this county, continuing to steal. One after another he stole bicycles, mosquito netting, clothes, cash, fountain pens, scissors, shoes, bicycle tire tubes, etc. At the same time he also dared to steal an official seal used by Lung-tang reservoir in Lu-feng to buy things and with it he made false documents to buy the "three birds" [chicken, duck, goose] and small pigs, hoarding them and interfering with market control. Even more serious was what happened on October 6 when he was stealing at Ho-po. He was seized by the local public security station and detained. On October 9 he broke out of jail and secretly returned to Liu-sha. He broke into hotels and shops on several occasions to commit theft and also broke into the bank of Liu-sha and stole a batch of one-fen notes worth eighteen yuan. He was discovered and seized by bank officials. The character of this criminal is extremely evil. He is always stealing and seriously undermining public order. Thus, he was sentenced to fifteen years of imprisonment in accordance with law.

Thief Yuan I-hsiung, also named Yuan O-ying, assumed names Ch'en Jo-ming, Lin Chung, Lin Hsiao-ch'uan, and Yang Hsiao-p'ing, thirty years of age, comes from Tung-shan village of Li Hu commune in this county. Since June 1957 he has stolen cotton cloth, woolen sweaters, clothing, fountain pens, flashlights, and other things from the villages of An-jen, Chiao-nei, Li-hu, and Chang-mei of this county. In 1958 the masses subjected him to a speak reason struggle, but he still did not repent and reform. He wandered from Ch'ieh-yang to Mien-hu to Hung-ch'eng stealing and undermining the security of society. Thus, he was sentenced to seven years of imprisonment in accordance with law.

Thief Ch'en Ping-ch'eng, also named Ch'en Ta-tu, a twenty-seven-year-old male, comes from Shen-shan village in Nan-ching commune in this county. When he was eighteen years old and at Swatow, he was sent to ten months of rehabilitation through labor [this is perhaps an erroneous reference to reform through labor] for theft. Afterward he continued to steal and was sentenced to three years of imprisonment. In 1953 he was conditionally released and returned home, but he continued to steal bananas, ginger, and other crops. On the night of November 2 of this year, when he was in Hsin-liao village of Chang-sung commune, he sneaked into a goose shed, used a bamboo weapon to beat to death ten geese that belonged to the commune, stole eight of them, and caused an estimated damage of 600 yuan. This damaged livestock production, and the consequences of the situation were very serious. Thus, he was sentenced to twelve years of imprisonment in accordance with law.

### 9. Life Imprisonment

### ITEM 246

[*Lectures* (September 1957), pp 200–201]

.    .    .    .    .

Life imprisonment is a criminal punishment which deprives a criminal of freedom for life. It is a method of punishment second in severity only to the death penalty. On the basis of the provisions of Articles 13 and 14 of the Act for Reform Through Labor [the punishment of] life imprisonment is executed in prison. Criminals must be strictly controlled and closely guarded. If necessary, they may be kept in solitary confinement. Under the principle of strict control, they are separated according to their different circumstances, and they engage in compulsory labor and [receive] education.

Life imprisonment is applicable to those counterrevolutionary criminals and other major criminals whose crimes are serious enough to require that they be permanently separated from society but not serious enough to require that they be sentenced to death.

In the view of our country's criminal [law] legislation and judicial practice, life imprisonment is one of our effective means of struggling against counter-revolutionary criminals and other major criminals. It plays a very great role in such matters as attacking the enemy's sabotage activity, rousing the masses to initiate a struggle against the enemy, and warning other criminals not to violate the law. Although at present the period of intense class struggle is past in our country, the class struggle situation both at home and abroad is still very complex. Therefore, we believe that for a certain period in the future it will be necessary to retain this punishment. Meanwhile, since there is a big difference between the death penalty and imprisonment for a fixed term, the retention of this intermediate punishment of life imprisonment not only ensures more flexibility and convenience in adjudication practice, but also has a positive function in implementing the policy of "less killing."

In our country's criminal law, life imprisonment is not simply punishment. An offender who is being held for life and who is in the process of reform through labor still has an opportunity for repentance and self-reform and for making himself into a new person. On the basis of the provisions of Article 68 of the

Act for Reform Through Labor, if a criminal has been sentenced to life imprisonment, has labored actively and striven to reform, and if he has behavior which really establishes his merit or indicates his repentance and reform, he may, after serving a considerable period of time [in prison], have his sentence reduced or be conditionally released. As a matter of fact, many offenders who have been sentenced to life imprisonment have had their sentences reduced in the past few years. Some people believe that this just proves that imprisonment for a fixed term has replaced life imprisonment and that life imprisonment exists only in name. This statement is incorrect. It confuses two problems which are different in nature — sentencing to punishment and reduction of sentence. When we sentence to punishment, we cannot and should not predetermine whether or not a sentenced criminal can have his sentence reduced. The circumstances of a criminal at the time of adjudication and the sincere repentance and reform of a reformed criminal are two different things. It is illogical to say that the factual basis for the punishment of life imprisonment can be retained only if the sentence of life imprisonment is executed to the very end.

Life imprisonment does not extinguish the offender's hope, nor does it block his prospects for reform. Compared with the death penalty, it might be said that life imprisonment is a relatively light punishment. Some people have said that life imprisonment is even more inhumane than the death penalty. This is not in conformity with reality.

Life imprisonment is not applicable to minors. The intellectual powers of minors are still not completely mature. Compared with the evil of adults who commit the same kinds of crime, the evil of minors is less, and they can also be reformed more easily. Therefore, even though they have committed serious crimes, the sentence of life imprisonment is not applicable to them. This conclusion is based on the essence of our country's criminal law, on state policy, and on the circumstances of judicial practice.

### 10. Death Penalty

ITEM 247

[*Lectures* (September 1957), pp. 201–205]

.    .    .    .    .

The death penalty is a criminal punishment by which a criminal is deprived of his life. It is the most severe method of punishment in our country. This punishment is applicable only to those extremely few counterrevolutionaries who seriously endanger the people's democratic dictatorship, whose crimes are heinous, and whose death alone can pacify the people's anger, and to other criminals whose danger to the interests of the state and the people has reached the most serious degree. In the early period of our country's liberation and in the period of restoration of the state economy, counterrevolutionaries violently resisted and the dregs of the old society also conducted various sabotage activities. At that time, the class struggle was very intense and sharp. In order to protect and consolidate the people's democratic political power and to safeguard the people's security and interests, the state had to suppress this resistance and these sabotage activities. The death penalty was applied to those counter-revolutionaries whose crimes were heinous, who were persistently hostile to the people, and who adamantly refused to repent and reform. Only by so doing could we attack the enemies' vicious power and consolidate the fruits of the revolution. At the same time, the death penalty was applied to those who committed crimes of corruption, major opium offenders, habitual robbers, murderers whose crimes were especially serious, and criminals who sexually violated young girls — those major criminals who seriously endangered state economic construction or the people's interests. If the death penalty were not applied, state law and discipline could not be dignified, social justice could not be extended, and the anger of the masses could not be pacified. The facts of history have proved that because of the timely suppression of enemies and the timely elimination of harmful elements on behalf of the people, the political power of the people's democratic dictatorship was consolidated and the activism of the masses of people in the revolution and in production had a great upsurge. From this it can be seen that the death penalty as a punishment in our country is a necessary means to suppress the resistance of domestic and foreign enemies and to protect the interests of the state and the people. To use the death penalty is not only necessary but also just. One cannot confuse our country's death penalty with that of the exploiter countries and discuss them as if they were the same.

A correct estimate of the death penalty's active role in the struggle against crime by no means implies the need to retain the death penalty forever. On the contrary, our country is in the process of creating conditions for the gradual abolition of this penalty. The existence or the abolition of the death penalty is not something which can be determined by our subjective desires alone; it is determined mainly by the needs of the class struggle.

In keeping with the spirit of Party and state policies, we should strictly understand the principle of "less killing" in handling matters in our country's judicial practice. In dealing with the death penalty, we have habitually adopted a serious and careful attitude. Moreover, in the past we have prescribed special procedures for execution of the death penalty that are different from methods of executing other punishments. For example, the provisions of Article 7 of the General Rules for the Organization of People's Tribunals promulgated in July 1950 are concerned with the authority to approve the death penalty for local despots, bandits, secret agents, counterrevolutionaries, and criminals who resist land reform laws and decrees. The Instructions Relating to Suppression of Counterrevolutionary Activity promulgated in the same year and the provisions relating to the establishment of the people's tribunals for the "three-anti" and "five-anti" movements in 1952 also prescribed the authority to approve the death penalty for counter-revolutionary criminals, criminals who commit crimes of corruption, and thieves. Paragraph 5 of Article 11 of the Law for the Organization of People's Courts of 1954 prescribes: "If a party does not accept the judgment or order of last instance of an intermediate people's court or a high people's court in death penalty cases, he may apply to the people's court at the next higher level for review. A judgment of a basic level people's court and a judgment or order of an intermediate people's court in death penalty cases shall, if the party does not appeal or apply for review, be submitted to the high people's court for approval before execution." These provisions in the organizational system have guaranteed correct application of the death penalty and have prevented deviations. They thoroughly show our serious and careful attitude toward the application of the death penalty.

In addition to this, in our practice of struggle against counterrevolution, we have also created the method of "sentencing to death, suspending execution of sentence for two years, compelling labor, and observing the consequences." If immediate execution of sentence is not necessary, this gives those counterrevolutionary criminals whose offenses are great and who, according to the law, should be sentenced to death, an opportunity to repent and reform. After a two-year test period, the question of whether or not to execute sentence will be decided on the basis of his [the criminal's] behavior during reform through labor. If, during the period of suspension of execution, concrete facts demonstrated in reform through labor are sufficient to indicate his sincere repentance and reform, his death sentence may be reduced in accordance with certain procedures to life imprisonment or to long-term imprisonment. If he refuses to reform, then the death penalty will be executed. Practice in the past few years has proved that most counterrevolutionary criminals who were sentenced to death but whose sentence was suspended for two years demonstrated their repentance and reform during the period of suspension of execution. Thus, they were resentenced to life imprisonment or to long-term imprisonment. This method has not only guaranteed the healthy development of the movement to suppress counterrevolution but has also embodied to a high degree the spirit of revolutionary humanitarianism in our country's criminal law and the state's policy of "uniting suppression with leniency."

It is wrong to regard the two-year suspension of execution of the death penalty as an independent punishment. It [the suspension] is merely a measure adopted by the state in executing the death penalty, for during the period of suspension of execution it has not been determined that the death penalty will not be executed. After the expiration of the period of suspension of execution, the death penalty may be executed or the criminal sentenced to death may be resentenced to life imprisonment or long-term imprisonment, this decision depending on his behavior during the period of suspension of execution. Because "suspended death" has played an active role in our judicial practice, local people's courts in the various places have in the past few years also applied this system to other criminals who have been sentenced to death and not merely to counterrevolutionary criminals.

Since our country entered the period of planned economic construction, the scope of application of the death penalty has been reduced from what it was previously. Especially as a result of the application [of the method] of suspending the execution of the death penalty for two years, the scope of actual application of the death penalty has been greatly reduced. Following the decisive victory in the undertaking of our country's socialist reform, the situation in our domestic politics has undergone a fundamental change. This has created the possibility for further reducing the scope of the death penalty. In his political report to the Eighth National Party Congress, Comrade Liu Shao-ch'i pointed out: "The Party Central Committee believes that we should not sentence to death any other criminals except the extremely small number of criminals who must be sentenced to death because their heinous crimes have aroused the people's anger . . . Any case belonging to [the category of] required death penalty cases should be decided by judgment of or approved by the Supreme People's Court. In this way, we will gradually be able to achieve the goal of abolishing the death penalty. This is in the interests of our socialist construction." To implement these instructions, in legislating our future criminal code, we should limit as much as possible provisions applying the death penalty to an extremely small number of crimes. In present judicial practice, we should strictly observe the spirit of "less killing" in dealing with counterrevolutionary criminals or other major criminals, though we cannot yet completely abolish the death penalty. Our country is still in a period of transition. Imperialism still exists, and counterrevolutionaries still exist. Domestic and foreign enemies are trying every possible means to sabotage our country's socialist construction. The struggle is still complex and serious. Therefore we should not fail to consider this point and limit ourselves [by abolishing the death penalty]. Application of the death penalty to that extremely small number of criminals whose heinous crimes have aroused the people's anger is also in the interests of our country's socialist construction. We are retaining the death penalty while in the process of gradually abolishing it, and we are reducing the scope of the application of the death penalty to a minimum. But at present we still are using this punishment. It should be clear that this use or retention of the death penalty is just for the purpose of its final abolition. To [try to] understand these two problems by placing them in opposition is inappropriate. In order to achieve the goal of gradually abolishing the death penalty, besides strictly limiting the scope of its application, we should, as proposed by the Party Central Committee, concentrate the authority to decide by judgment and to approve of death penalty cases completely in the Supreme People's Court. To have the highest adjudication organ of the entire country controlling this is a very wise and thorough method.

In keeping with the spirit of our country's criminal [law] policy, the death penalty is not applicable to pregnant women or to minors. As for the former, the department of justice of the former East China Military Government Council in its Reply to the People's Court of Fukien Province Relating to Methods for Sentencing Pregnant Women to Death and for Pronouncement of Execution of Sentence, which was approved by the Ministry of Justice, pointed out: "For the protection of the life and normal development of the child in the womb a criminal who is pregnant generally shall not be sentenced to death. If death alone can pacify the people's anger, it [the death penalty] shall be pronounced one year after the birth of the child, and shall be executed [only] in accordance with certain procedures." The reason for not applying the death penalty to the latter [minors] is the same as the aforementioned reason for not applying life imprisonment to them.

## ITEM 248

[Lo Jui-ch'ing (Minister of Public Security), "The Struggle of the Revolution against Counterrevolution in the Past Ten Years," *JMJP*, Sept. 28, 1959, p. 3]

Among the criminal punishments of our country there is one which prescribes "sentencing to death, suspending execution of sentence for two years, compelling labor, and observing the consequences." Imperialists have denounced this as the greatest cruelty. We say that this is the greatest humaneness. The criminals themselves understand this. Sentencing them to death and suspending execution of their sentence gives to these persons, allowed to live on under the sword of the people's government, a last opportunity to reform. In fact most of the criminals who are dealt with this way are spared. Where was there ever in ancient or modern times, in China or abroad, so great an innovation? Where could one find in the capitalist world so humane a law?

## ITEM 249

[Snow, *The Other Side of the River* (1962), p. 369]

When asked whether I would like to question any other prisoner I chose a political offender under suspended death sentence.

He was a Shantung man, rugged in build, heavy-featured, middle-aged and solemn. I asked him what he had done. He answered that as a Kuomintang policeman in Tsinan he had led an anti-Red squad and arrested many suspects. Urged by Wang to elaborate, he added, face downcast, that he had personally killed four revolutionaries, one of whom was a pregnant woman. His crime was graver because he had not come forward after the revolution when everyone was given an opportunity to confess, repent, and ask for punishment. Instead, he had gone north, taken a job in a Peking textile mill, and pretended to be an ordinary worker. One day in 1958 he was recognized by another Shantung man who denounced him and had him arrested. Did he feel he had been fairly treated?

"I ought to be dead," he said. "I deserved death but instead I have been given back life. I am being educated and I can now handle machines and do useful work. I am doing my best to remold myself to show my gratitude." He seemed thoroughly humbled and remorseful, and deep tension was written on his face. One needed little imagination to share some of the awareness that must have filled his days that one bad mistake might be his last. To know with reasonable certainty that salvation depended entirely on his own repentance and reform must in some ways have placed far heavier burdens on him than would be on a condemned man in an American prison. Realizing that nothing he can do by way of inner awakening can alter matters, the latter need not undergo the agony of attempted self-reform but can hold society or his lawyers at least partly responsible for his fate.

When the prisoner and his unarmed escort left, Wang said that he was a good worker. He had been in jail for two years; his sentence would probably be altered to life imprisonment.

Is the suspended death sentence an innovation worthy of emulation in other countries?

For an interesting account of the Soviet experience with the death penalty, see Leon Lipson, "Crime and Punishment; Execution: Hallmark of 'Socialist Legality,' " *Problems of Communism*, 11.5:21–26 (September–October 1962).

## ITEM 250

["Criminal Judgment of the Nanchang City People's Court," *Chiang-hsi jih-pao* (Kiangsi daily), June 29, 1955]

(54) Criminal Judgment File No. 1145

Authority Sending the Case: Nanchang City Public Security Bureau

Criminal: Chang Chien-hsin. Male. Age: 39 years old

Native Place: Nanchang City, Kiangsi.

> Personal background: hooligan, professional swindler
> Cultural level: three years [of education]
> No fixed address

Criminal Chang Chien-hsin, also known by the name of Chang Yung-seng and the aliases of Sung Hua, Liu Pin, T'an Yu-chun, Hsü Chen-ch'iu, and others, has been, before liberation, a traveling merchant, a navigator of a ship, and a sergeant of a Kuomintang police bureau. After liberation, he operated a grocery store which he often used to swindle property from boatmen by pretending to charter ships for transporting goods or to buy goods for boatmen. In June 1950, one such act [of swindling] was discovered, and he was arrested by the city public security bureau. He was released after receiving education. In August of the same year, he was sentenced to one year of labor service by this court for swindling property from boatmen T'ang Te-tzu, Ting Hsi-k'o, and others. After performing this labor service, he was released but again engaged in swindling. On October 16, 1952, he was caught by a victim, Tai Chin-hsi, and later was sentenced to three months of labor service by this court. He continued to engage in swindling after release. In May 1953, he was sentenced to two years of imprisonment for swindling boatman Wan Chang-shun. During the period of his reform through labor, however, he escaped and fled to Wuhan . . . and other cities. He still made his living by swindling and was caught thirteen times. In December of the same year, he was caught and sent to the public security organ of the place of the offense for swindling 200 yuan from the family of boatman Hsiao Chun-ch'uan. After being taken into custody and educated, he was released. From then on, this criminal used an alias and pretended to be an agent of the Wuhan City Trading Company, the Anking Kerosene Company and . . . some other cooperatives. He chartered boats for the above-mentioned units, pretending to transport goods, and fraudulently caused boatmen to purchase "low price" rice, flour, oil, salt, and other foods from him. In total, he swindled . . . several hundred yuan from boatmen. On May 7, 1954, while he was swindling boatman Lo Chang-yin, he was caught on the spot by the public security organ and was sent to this court to be dealt with.

The consequences caused by this criminal's swindling have been serious. For instance, the money that he swindled from Wan Chang-shun was a loan from the people's bank to the mutual aid group of the fourth village of Feng Lin administrative village, third district, Keng-cheng county, for the purpose of shipping camphor boards to Nanchang for sale. After being swindled, Mr. Wan was suspected by other members of the group, and they held him responsible for compensation. As it was difficult for him to raise the money, a member of his family tried to commit suicide by hanging himself. This criminal swindled forty-one yuan from Mei Shao-t'ing, who had earned the money through diligent labor, and thus caused Mei's wife to jump into the river several times in an attempt to commit suicide. Fortunately, she was rescued by others and did not drown. The victims all expressed their deep hatred of this criminal.

It is evident that since liberation Chang Chien-hsin has habitually engaged in swindling. He has been caught five times by the people's government, confined, and educated. However, he has not demonstrated a bit of repentance or reform, and during the periods of his confinement he has insulted the people's government and resisted reform. The above-mentioned criminal acts of this offender have seriously undermined security on the river, interfered with boatmen's production, and endangered the interests of the people. In order to safeguard state law and discipline, to maintain the security of society, and to protect the safety of peoples' lives and property, this court sentences criminal Chang Chien-hsin to death in accordance with law and deprives him of political rights for life.

This is the judgment.

President: Ou-yang Ming
Vice-President: Yü Hung-yang

June 28, 1955

(The case was appealed to the high people's court of Kiangsi province by criminal Chang Chien-hsin. The high people's court in its final judgment, criminal file no. 10, affirmed the original death sentence of this court and ordered that it be immediately executed.)

## ITEM 251

[REPLY OF THE STANDING COMMITTEE OF THE NPC OF THE PRC TO THE SUPREME PEOPLE'S COURT RELATING TO PROBLEMS OF HOW TO EXECUTE THE RESOLUTION THAT DEATH PENALTY CASES SHALL BE DECIDED BY JUDGMENT OF OR APPROVED BY THE SUPREME PEOPLE'S COURT (Sept. 26, 1957), FKHP, 6:297]

Supreme People's Court:

We have received the report of July 26, 1957, relating to how to execute The Resolution of the Fourth Meeting of the First Session of the National People's Congress Relating to Death Penalty Cases' Being Adjudged or Approved by the Supreme People's Court. The Standing Committee believes: Death penalty cases which, according to the Law for the Organization of [People's] Courts, high people's courts are responsible for approving or for deciding by a judgment of last instance shall still be decided by judgment of or reviewed by high people's courts. In a case in which a high people's court believes that the defendant should be punished by death, the judgment shall be executed after it has been submitted to the Supreme People's Court for approval. A case in which a high people's court believes that the defendant should not be punished by death shall, in accordance with the provisions of law, be remanded by it to a lower people's court for readjudication or shall be adjudicated at the higher level. This is the reply.

Chairman Liu Shao-ch'i
Secretary-General P'eng Chen

## ITEM 252

[Interview]

In 1959 Liao and his brother Lin-tse were arrested and prosecuted on a charge of murdering the deputy Party secretary of a rural commune [see Item 188D]. Since one of the county basic level court judges had participated in the joint investigating team that had prepared the case for adjudication and was already familiar with the file, the county court quickly completed its consideration of the case. In view of the fact that the case was important and involved a capital offense, the chief judge and the president of the court could not decide upon the sentence by themselves but presented the problem to the political-legal Party group consisting of the president of the court, the chief of the public security bureau, chief procurator, and the deputy party secretary for legal affairs. It decided to sentence Liao to death and Lin-tse to fifteen years of imprisonment. These sentences were discussed with and approved by the first secretary of the county Party committee.

Liao's sentence had to be presented to the intermediate court and the high court for approval. Because one of its judges had supervised the arrest of the Liaos, the intermediate court was familiar with the case and promptly gave its approval. The high court, however, was less conversant with the facts, and, since the case had already been mishandled once, one of its judges went down to investigate in the company of an official of the provincial public security department. They carefully questioned Liao and Lin-tse and made a general check of the circumstances.

After the provincial level cadres had completed this review but before they returned to the provincial capital, the county court held what purported to be a public trial of the defendants in its courtroom. The judge in charge of the case served as chief judge, with two people's assessors participating. A procurator appeared, but the defendants had no defender. In addition to the provincial level cadres, the audience was composed of Liao's wife, representatives of his production brigade, and people from the county seat. The trial consisted only of questioning the defendants, who admitted all the details of the crime. The court then adjourned, stating that the judgment would be announced at a later date.

After the provincial level cadres reported their findings, the high court approved Liao's death sentence, and it notified the Supreme Court as well as the lower courts of its approval. Upon receipt of the high court's approval, the county political-legal Party group scheduled a "mass trial." This was held in a large field in the suburbs of the county seat. Several thousand persons and approximately forty representatives of Liao's brigade attended. On the platform the president of the court, two judges, and the two assessors who had previously participated in the case were seated together. The procurator and court clerks sat nearby. The defendants stood under guard on one side of the platform. The president of the court introduced the facts of the case and then gave the representatives of Liao's brigade an opportunity to "present their views." A number of them bitterly attacked the defendants, especially Liao. Neither of the defendants spoke. The president of the court then announced the sentences, stating that the death sentence for Liao had already been approved by the Supreme Court. The meeting adjourned, and Liao was taken to a nearby field and executed by a firing squad in front of a large number of curious spectators.

Did the procedure in the Liao case comply with the letter and spirit of the Reply of the Standing Committee of the NPC (Item 251)? What about the procedure in the cases in Items 148 and 149?

## ITEM 253

[Fan Ming, "Some Opinions about *Lectures on the General Principles of Criminal Law of the PRC*" (1958), p. 74]

In addition, in this lecture on "Types of Punishments," it is asserted that at present we need to retain the death penalty, but it is also said that "[w]e are retaining the death penalty while in the process of gradually abolishing it" (*Lectures,* p. 205). I believe that a comprehensive and concrete explanation should be made of this proposal. Moreover, to avoid creating ideological confusion, it should be clearly pointed out that we should still insist on sentencing to death those criminals who must be sentenced to death.

.     .     .     .     .

The sixteenth lecture [section 2], on "Principles for Combined Punishment for Several Crimes," mentions that "if a defendant is sentenced to several terms of life imprisonment . . . only one can be executed" (*Lectures,* p. 230). Since he has committed several crimes punishable by life imprisonment, he is obviously extremely evil. Why can he not be sentenced to death? I believe that, in circumstances where the struggle against crime requires, it should be possible to decide to execute the death penalty against a criminal who has been sentenced to several terms of life imprisonment.

.     .     .     .     .

## ITEM 254

[Snow, *The Other Side of the River* (1962), pp. 352–354]

.     .     .     .     .

The People's Republic publishes no comprehensive crime statistics. I asked Judge Wu Teh-fang, chairman of the association of politics and law, why it wasn't done. His reply was, "The figures are so low that they would not be believed abroad." There was Chou En-lai's statement several years ago that 830,000 "enemies of the people" had been "destroyed" during the war over land confiscation, mass trials of landlords, and the subsequent roundup of counter-revolutionaries which ended, as a "campaign," in 1954. (Incidentally, the term *hsiao-mieh*, usually translated as "destroyed," literally means "reduced," "dispersed" or "obliterated," but not necessarily physically liquidated.) This figure, according to the Chinese, was merely used as a basis for "fantastic distortions and exaggeration by our enemies."

No nation ever resorts to violent revolution unless the old order has exhausted all its means of orderly solutions. Class war is the most tragic of all wars. It can be justified only if, as with all emunctory processes, nature itself finds no alternative for survival. There was a bloody civil war and class war combined in China which took millions of lives on both sides* and the wounds are far from healed. Hundreds of thousands of ex-Kuomintang soldiers who allegedly turned bandit after the war were reported as "destroyed"; yet many of them were later sent to Korea. Since the early and party-led mass trials and executions of landlords, scores of thousands have been punished in varying degrees by "people's courts" during half a dozen campaigns against "counterrevolutionaries," "rightists" and private businessmen.

Eight hundred thirty thousand is far from a bagatelle in human life, but the figure, *if true,* is not large in proportion to the population — about 14 per million† — compared to the costs of other catastrophes, such as the American Civil War, the French Revolution, and the Russian Revolution, not to mention Hitler's Germany. Counterrevolutionaries are still being arrested. I was told by Judge Wu that they are executed only if their action has caused the death of a citizen. Notices of executions appear in the provincial newspapers — apparently *pour encourager les autres* — and Western correspondents keep a tally on them. In 1960 these executions varied from eight to twelve a month, mostly cases of allegedly well-paid assassins and saboteurs caught in Fukien or Kwangtung, across the strait from Taiwan.

There are two other types of capital crimes: 1) murder or assault with intent to kill motivated by class hatred, or violence of an especially cruel nature; and 2) rape, of a victim under the age of fourteen. In such cases the death penalty is now said to be suspended for two years, during which the prisoner may repent and reform. At the end of that period his case is reviewed and he may receive a reduced sentence.

* [Mr. Snow's note:] In reply to an inquiry I made concerning the total casualties on *both* sides during the two civil wars in China, Rewi Alley, who was in China throughout the whole conflict, wrote to me from Peking on May 19, 1956: "I have myself estimated that the deaths through political executions, Kuomintang 'cleaning up' in Kiangsi, Fukien, etc. [1930–34, during five anti-Communist expeditions], in man-made famines [blockades] in Hunan, Honan, etc., in 'incidents' [armed clashes or 'border warfare' before the outbreak of renewed major civil war in 1948] and following the KMT-CP breaking of armistice negotiations, then in the general [civil war] struggle subsequently, all add up to something like fifty million from the break [counterrevolution] in 1927 up until 1949."

† [Mr. Snow's note:] On a population base of 600,000,000.

## C. SPECIAL PROBLEMS OF SENTENCING

### ITEM 255

[*Lectures* (September 1957), pp. 227, 228–229, 230–231]

.      .      .      .      .

### 1. The Concept of Combined Punishment for Several Crimes

In adjudication practice, in addition to meeting cases in which a person has committed one crime, we often meet cases in which a person has committed several crimes. Besides following the general principles for deciding upon punishment, we must also apply the principles of combined punishment for several crimes to cases in which a person has committed several crimes.

.      .      .      .      .

When punishing a person who has committed several crimes, we should first convict him separately [for each of his crimes], decide upon the punishment for each, and then determine the punishment that should be applied by considering them [the individual punishments] collectively. In 1952, the Supreme People's Court in its instructions, How To Decide Upon the Punishment of a Person Who Has Committed Several Crimes, pointed out: "When trying a defendant who has committed several crimes, in principle the court shall first pronounce the punishment to which he is sentenced for each separate crime and then pronounce the punishment to be executed, except when the sentence is death or life imprisonment." Doing things this way is good because it clearly shows how the judge convicted the defendant and how he fixed punishment. If the case is appealed, the appellate court can see whether or not the conviction and the punishment decided upon are proper. If it is discovered that [guilt for] some of the crimes cannot be established, then this can readily be corrected. If the period of limitation for prosecution of some of the crimes has expired, then they can readily be dealt with separately. Therefore, this method of deciding upon punishment is relatively scientific.

But in our country's judicial practice, some judges in the past adopted the method of "gross estimate," that is, they did not separately convict and decide upon the punishment for each of the several crimes, but rather they determined the punishment by considering the crimes collectively. This is related to the [following] circumstances: the incompleteness of our country's criminal [law] legislation; the definite difficulty in separately convicting and deciding upon punishment; and the fact that at the time most of the criminals were dregs remaining from the old society and many of them had committed several crimes. But this also shows that certain judges did not have sufficient knowledge of the meaning of the scientific method of deciding upon punishment. Following the strengthening of the people's democratic legal system, our country's criminal [law] legislation is becoming more and more complete every day. This demands that when convicting criminals who have committed several crimes and when deciding upon their punishment a people's court should strictly observe the provisions of law so that the convictions and punishments decided upon will be even more precise. This will be advantageous in increasing the accuracy and the effectiveness of the struggle against crime. Therefore, the method of "gross estimate" should be changed.

## 2. Principles for Combined Punishment for Several Crimes

Before judgment is pronounced in a case where a person has committed several crimes the court should separately convict and decide upon punishment for each of the several crimes and then pronounce the punishment that should be executed. [The question is] then: "On the basis of what principles should the [separate] punishments be combined into the punishment to be executed?"

.    .    .    .    .

As for the principle for combining imprisonment for a fixed term with lesser punishments, our country's current criminal [law] legislation and the leading organs concerned already have express provisions and instructions. Article 15 of the Act of the People's Republic of China for Punishment of Counterrevolution prescribes: "The punishment for all those who commit several kinds of crimes, except crimes for which the sentence is death or life imprisonment, shall, considering the circumstances, be fixed at less than the aggregate punishment [that is possible for all the crimes] but more than the most severe punishment [for any one of those crimes]." In the relevant instruction of the Supreme People's Court quoted earlier, it is pointed out: "Therefore, if all of the several crimes are punishable by imprisonment for a fixed term, the punishment to be executed shall be fixed at less than the aggregate punishment for these several crimes but more than the most severe punishment for the one [most serious] crime." It can be seen from the above provisions and instructions that in our country the principle adopted for combining punishments for several crimes is a principle for limiting the increase in severity of punishment, that is, after the punishments for the several crimes are separately pronounced, the most severe punishment is taken as the minimum combined punishment and the aggregate punishment is taken as the maximum, and the punishment which should be executed is properly determined within this scope. Adopting this principle will enable judges to follow the specific circumstances of a case and to apply punishment flexibly within a given scope. It is not only in the interests of the struggle against crime, but it also embodies the principle of the legal system. The principle of totalling all the punishments and the principle that serious crimes absorb minor crimes (that is, sentencing according to the most serious of the several crimes) cannot be general principles of combined punishment for several crimes in our country's criminal law. If the principle of totalling all the punishments is taken as a general principle, on the one hand judges will have no flexibility in fixing punishment, and on the other hand it may result in sentencing criminals to unnecessarily severe punishment. This is not in conformity with the purpose of punishment in our country. If we take the principle that serious crimes absorb minor crimes as a general principle, criminals who commit several crimes will wrongly be punished too lightly. This is not in the interests of the struggle against crime. But in special circumstances the principle of absorption is not completely unusable. For instance, the principle that serious crimes absorb minor crimes may be adopted with respect to one whose two or more related acts constitute different crimes.

How might the authors of Item 255 explain the sentence meted out in Item 250?

Generally, how does Chinese practice square with Chinese theories of sentencing? Can you rank the goals of punishment in the order of the priorities actually accorded to them?

# Chapter X  Formal Criminal Processes: Appeal, Postconviction Review, and Problems of Mistakes and Abuses

A. Appeal

B. Postconviction Review

C. Vindication of the Accused

D. Sanctions against Officials

Some [lawyers] encourage offenders to appeal. They say that "appeal only has good points and has no bad points, that in appeal cases the higher level courts can only reduce the sentence," etc. As a result, they have caused criminals in some places unreasonably to make trouble and ceaselessly to pester us and have caused our work to remain on the defensive.

> T'an Cheng-wen, "Absorb Experience and Teaching, Impel a Great Leap Forward in Procuratorial Work" [1]

Comrade:

If a party considers as erroneous the judgment or order rendered by an intermediate people's court in an appealed case, can he appeal to a high people's court? Please reply.

> Huang Yüan-hsiang

Comrade Huang Yüan-hsiang:

The judgment or order rendered by a people's court at the next higher level in an appealed or protested case is the final judgment or order, that is, a legally effective judgment or order. Therefore, the case mentioned in your question . . . cannot be appealed to a high people's court . . .

However, the foregoing explanation does not mean that no further opinion can be submitted with respect to a legally effective judgment or order. On the contrary, if a party considers erroneous a judgment or order rendered by a people's court, he may submit his opinions to a people's procuracy or to the president of the people's court. If the people's procuracy or the president of the people's court finds that there really is an error in that judgment or order, it will be handled in accordance with adjudication supervision procedure. If there is no error, the matter will be explained to the party. Adjudication in our

1. P. 42.

country is perfectly responsible to the people. If an error is found in a legally effective judgment or order, even if the party himself does not bring it up, the president of the court, a people's court of a higher level, a people's procuracy of a higher level, the Supreme People's Court, and the Supreme People's Procuracy all have the power to correct the error in accordance with adjudication [supervision] procedure.

> "What Is 'the System of the Court of Second Instance as the Court of Last Instance'?" [2]

We have already adopted or are now adopting steps to correct all errors that have been discovered in the work of liquidating counterrevolution. As for those not yet discovered, we are prepared to correct them as soon as they are discovered. Whatever the extent to which the errors originally made were publicized, their correction should be publicized to the same extent. I propose that the work of liquidating counterrevolution be completely examined once this year or next to summarize experience, spread a spirit of uprightness, and attack wrongful tendencies . . . When examining the work, we should not pour cold water on the vast [number of] cadres and activists, but rather we should help them. It is not right to pour cold water on the vast [number of] cadres and activists, but errors which are discovered definitely should be corrected. Public security departments, procuratorial departments, judicial departments, prisons, or organs that administer reform through labor all should adopt this attitude.

> Mao Tse-tung, "Problems Relating to the Correct Handling of Contradictions Among the People" [3]

## A. APPEAL

The materials in this section shed light on the following questions:
1. What are the functions of a criminal appeal in the PRC?
2. Who may appeal?
3. On what grounds?
4. What procedures must be observed in submitting an appeal?
5. What procedures do appellate courts employ?
6. How does an appeal differ from adjudication in the first instance?
7. To what extent can an appeal affect the original judgment and sentence?
8. To what extent do persons who have been convicted of crime avail themselves of their right to appeal?
9. What factors might account for whatever reluctance such persons show?

### ITEM 256

[LAW OF THE PRC FOR THE ORGANIZATION OF PEOPLE'S COURTS (Sept. 28, 1954), pp. 124–125, 128, 129, 130]

Article 9. In cases of appeal and protest in people's courts, adjudication shall be conducted by a collegial panel composed of judges.

2. *Kung-jen jih-pao* (Workers' daily, Peking), Jan. 26, 1957.
3. Pp. 13–14.

The president of the court or a chief judge shall assign one judge to serve as presiding judge of the collegial panel. When the president of the court or a chief judge participates in adjudicating a case, he himself shall serve as presiding judge.

Article 11. In the adjudication of cases, people's courts shall put into effect the system of the court of second instance as the court of last instance.

In cases of first instance, parties may appeal judgments and orders of local people's courts of the various levels to a people's court of the next higher level in accordance with procedure prescribed by law. People's procuracies may protest the judgments and orders to a people's court of the next higher level in accordance with procedure prescribed by law.

In cases of first instance, judgments and orders of local people's courts of the various levels shall become legally effective if, in the period for appeal, the party does not appeal and the people's procuracy does not protest.

Judgments and orders of intermediate people's courts, high people's courts, or the Supreme People's Court in cases of second instance, and judgments and orders of the Supreme People's Court in cases of first instance, shall be judgments and orders of last instance, that is, legally effective judgments or orders.

Article 22. Intermediate people's courts shall adjudicate the following cases:

(3) Cases of appeal of and protest against judgments and orders of basic level people's courts . . .

Article 25. High people's courts shall adjudicate the following cases:

(3) Cases of appeal of and protest against judgments and orders of lower people's courts . . .

Article 30. The Supreme People's Court shall adjudicate the following cases:

(2) Cases of appeal of and protest against judgments and orders of high people's courts and special people's courts . . .

## ITEM 257

[LAW OF THE PRC FOR THE ORGANIZATION OF PEOPLE'S PROCURACIES (Sept. 28, 1954), pp. 134, 136]

Article 4. Local people's procuracies of the various levels shall exercise the following powers in accordance with procedure prescribed in Chapter 2 of this Law:

(4) To put into effect supervision to see whether or not adjudication activities of people's courts are legal . . .

Article 15. When, in a case of first instance, a local people's procuracy considers erroneous a judgment or order of a people's court of the corresponding level, it has the right to protest the judgment or order in accordance with appeal procedure.

## ITEM 258

[Interview]

Hsüeh was the deputy leader of a commune production team that in 1959 had been assigned by the commune to construct a reservoir in some nearby mountains. Men and women members of the team lived in sex-segregated temporary quarters. On warm nights in the summer many slept in the open. One night screams were heard on a hillside, and shortly thereafter Hu, an attractive married woman whose husband had not been assigned to reservoir construction, reported that Hsüeh had attempted to rape her while she slept outside. Hsüeh, whose wife had remained back in the village, was taken to the county public security bureau and detained for questioning. He steadfastly denied any intention to rape Hu but said that he had merely taken a few liberties with her in a flirtatious fashion. The bureau decided otherwise, and an arrest warrant was obtained.

Hsüeh was brought back to his team's mountain location for an "on-the-spot" trial because the case was deemed to have educational significance. The political-legal organs wanted to make it clear to women — and men — that women who helped to build socialism in the countryside would be protected. Despite the fact that Hsüeh still refused to confess, at the conclusion of the trial, which was actually a struggle meeting, he was convicted of attempted rape and sentenced to three years of imprisonment. His sentence would have been even heavier had he not had a clear record and a brother in the People's Liberation Army.

But Hsüeh and his family thought the sentence unfair. Since he had been told he could appeal, he asked the guards in the detention house how this could be done. They suggested that his family ask a literate friend to write the appeal, which they did. The appeal argued that the facts did not support a criminal conviction for rape, but only a SAPA punishment for "acting indecently" with Hu. Copies of the statement of appeal were handed to the detention house authorities, who kept one and forwarded the other to the intermediate court.

After receiving the appeal, the intermediate court sent a judge to investigate the case. He interviewed Hu, Hsüeh, members of the team who were in the area on the night in question, the police investigators, and the president of the county court. After he reported his findings, the intermediate court decided that the judgment below was correct. Because Hsüeh had refused to confess it also decided that its affirmance of the judgment below should be handed down in a public court session. Accordingly, the judge who had investigated the case and two other, lesser functionaries of the intermediate court went down to the county seat and pronounced judgment in the county court. Representatives of mass organizations located in the county seat and representatives of Hsüeh's production team were summoned to attend, as were Hsüeh's family and someone from Hu's family. In reading the judgment aloud the judge recited the facts of the case, Hsüeh's ground for appeal, and the results of the appellate court's investigation — that from all the surrounding circumstances it appeared that the factual determination of the county court should be upheld. Hsüeh was then asked whether he wanted to present any "opinions," but he declined to do so and was led out of the court.

## ITEM 259

[Interview]

The administrative village of Ch'eng-ch'i in the mountains of Fukien province had two advanced agricultural producers' cooperatives whose principal crop was pineapples. In early 1958 higher echelons of government announced plans to build a dam in the middle of Ch'eng-ch'i's fields in order to capture the rain water that fell in the mountains that towered over the area. As part of the project canals were also to be built to enable the water to irrigate the entire surrounding countryside. Although the announcement of this much needed project was greeted with favor elsewhere in the area, it met with a hostile reaction in Ch'eng-ch'i, because the dam and canals would preclude the people there from farming their most profitable land and because the government had offered the two cooperatives what they deemed to be grossly inadequate compensation. Delegations from Ch'eng-ch'i went to remonstrate with the authorities at both the county and special district levels. Wherever they went, they were told that it was unfortunate but the dam and canals could not be placed elsewhere due to the topography of the land. The cadres of Ch'eng-ch'i were admonished to educate their people to accept the principle of the greatest good for the greatest number.

While some of the cadres accepted this explanation, the principal ones, Party veterans who had served as guerrilla fighters during the Anti-Japanese War when Ch'eng-ch'i had been part of a Communist base, decided to oppose the project in every way possible. Their view was that they had loyally served the Party since the darkest days of the revolution and that Party bureaucrats could not simply cast their interests aside. The secretary of Ch'eng-ch'i's Party branch, a man named Lin, let it be known that those who took part in building the dam ran the risk of physical attack. One day, after thousands of workers had arrived to start construction, a group of local residents set fire to the houses that had been built for these workers, destroying a large amount of supplies and personal possessions. Shortly thereafter, the chief of the workers was ambushed and badly beaten up.

The county Party committee then sent a number of work groups down to Ch'eng-ch'i to try to improve the situation. One of these groups was composed of representatives of the three legal branches. Its assignment was to educate the populace in the importance of obedience to the law and to find out who was responsible for sabotaging construction. After living with the masses for a while, this group began to obtain information from some of the younger activists, who were less prone to "localism" than their seniors. Eventually even one of the "old cadres" who had participated in the incidents was persuaded to describe them. The investigation made clear that Lin, the local Party secretary, had inspired and organized the sabotage. This was reported to the county committee, which decided that the time was not ripe to handle Lin because this would only aggravate the situation. But the inaction of his superiors emboldened Lin, who felt confident of the justice of his cause and his credentials as a Party veteran. One night he organized a group of over thirty men to damage much of the construction work that had already been done. Local people also began beating up workers on the job. Its patience exhausted, the county committee sent the political-legal work group back to Ch'eng-ch'i to investigate further. Upon receipt of the second investigation report, the county committee ordered Lin's arrest. When he was taken back to the county seat for questioning he freely admitted the facts. He was also subjected to intensive education about why the Party could not tolerate his obstructionist tactics.

Although Ch'eng-ch'i sent representatives to each of the legal branches to plead for Lin's release, he was taken back to the administrative village for a public sentencing, because the county cadres believed it desirable for purposes of educating the villagers and satisfying the anger of the substantial number of workers who had been harmed by Lin's tactics. Lin was sentenced to three years of imprisonment for sabotaging production.

Most of the Ch'eng-ch'i leaders stubbornly refused to yield and decided to fight the battle on two peaceful fronts: to try to persuade higher authorities to cancel the project and to seek a reversal of the judgment in Lin's case. They dispatched a two-man delegation to take up both problems with the special district. One delegate talked with the Party secretary and the other with the president of the intermediate court. They were met by polite lectures on why even veteran cadres had to obey the law and Party policy. Many of the villagers then contributed to a fund to send these delegates to the provincial capital, where they talked with the deputy chief of the public security department and the president of the high court. Although they met with the same lectures, they were told that if they insisted on seeking a reversal of the judgment in Lin's case they should file an appeal with the intermediate court. The literate villagers then cooperated in writing a lengthy appeal, copies of which were sent to the intermediate and the high court. Many people also wrote letters to the legal branches at the special district and provincial levels, requesting Lin's release.

The high court and the intermediate court sent a joint investigating group down to Ch'eng-ch'i. Since the case was already familiar to officials at their levels, they promptly completed the investigation. Shortly thereafter at a mass meeting held in Ch'eng-ch'i the intermediate court announced affirmance of the judgment below and used the occasion to conduct further propaganda about the reasonableness of the government's policy and the need to obey it.

A group of senior cadres decided to push the case to the last resort and pooled their resources to send the two oldest guerrillas among them to Peking to take the case up with the central authorities. There they went to the office of Chang Ting-ch'eng, chief procurator of the Supreme People's Procuracy, who had been governor of Fukien province in the early years after liberation. He gave them a warm reception and said that they need not have come personally to complain but could have written him a letter. He turned them over to some subordinates for detailed talks, after which the delegation returned home with a promise that the central level would investigate.

Within a few weeks a three-man team from Peking composed of a procurator, a construction cadre, and a representative from the Party's rural work department arrived in Ch'eng-ch'i along with cadres from the province and special district. They finally concluded the affair by awarding satisfactory compensation to the two cooperatives and by making some land of neighboring cooperatives available for their use. No change was made in Lin's sentence.

## ITEM 260

How would you characterize the appellate review conducted in the cases described in Items 258 and 259? During the "blooming and contending" period of 1957, Yu Chung-lu, an adviser to the Supreme People's Court, "objected to the fact that the majority of the appeal courts had adopted the system of dealing with cases in writing. He said: 'The appeal courts should hold "factual trials" based on the principle of direct hearings as in public debates.'"[4] Does this item suggest that Yu's criticism was heeded?

[Chang Hui et al., "These Are Not the Basic Principles of Our Country's Criminal Litigation" (1958), p. 78]

.    .    .    .    .

"The principle of directness" also is not appropriate for adjudication of cases of second instance and the review of death penalty cases. In adjudication by courts of second instance and in the review of death penalty cases, witnesses, experts, and the defendant are ordinarily not summoned, but rather an examination of the materials in the file is first conducted. If the court determines that the evidence and facts are correct, it makes a judgment. If, after examination, it discovers some problem in the determination of the facts, on the basis of the circumstances it either decides to remand the case to the court which originally adjudicated it for a readjudication or itself directly examines the evidence and questions the witnesses and the defendant. Although a small number of cases require direct examination of the evidence, this is not in response to the requirements of the principle of directness.

## ITEMS 261A–261B

In practice, can a convicted person benefit from appellate review in the PRC? These items are examples of successful appeals.

## ITEM 261A

[Rickett and Rickett, *Prisoners of Liberation* (1957), p. 215]

.    .    .    .    .

Jeng Ai-ling told (in mid-1953) about a woman who had left the prison just a few months before. She had been arrested in connection with the Three Anti's movement on a question of bribery. Her crime was a minor one and after making a full confession, she had expected to be released. It was a shock when her sentence was passed. She had been given two years.

When Jeng Ai-ling had looked at the statement of charges which the woman had brought back to the cell she was disturbed to find mistakes in it. The woman was prepared to let the matter go and work out her sentence, but Jeng Ai-ling urged her to appeal while there was still time. Just before the three-day limit was up, the woman finally gave in to Jeng Ai-ling's pressure and the appeal was sent in. The government then went back over the evidence and eventually

4. MacFarquhar, p. 116.

found that one of the witnesses, an ambitious woman cadre who had hoped to gain position by ruining the defendant, an older, more experienced worker, had falsified evidence.

Jeng Ai-ling concluded, "The result was that my cell mate was cleared of that portion of the charges which was incorrect and granted immediate release. I don't know what happened to that other woman but I wager she had to make a pretty strict accounting of herself."

## ITEM 261B

[Interview]

Yüan was an official of the food bureau of a small city. In 1958 the basic level people's court that served the entire city convicted him of a crime of corruption involving over 2000 yuan. At a large meeting of government personnel, he was sentenced to two years of imprisonment. At that time it was announced that he had three days in which to file an appeal, and the copy of the judgment that he was given said the same thing. When Yüan returned to the detention house after being sentenced, he told the guards that he wished to appeal. They gave him a pencil and paper and told him how to go about writing the appeal. On their instructions he made three copies, one for the high court, one for the intermediate court to which the appeal was directed, and one for the detention house files. These were given to the guards for appropriate distribution after passing through the office of the chief of the public security bureau. The grounds on which Yüan appealed were that his unlawful act had really amounted to the lesser offense of misappropriation rather than corruption and that in any event the fact that he was the sole support of his family of a wife, five children, and an ailing mother should be given added consideration. Yüan's family also wrote letters and made personal visits to the police, procuracy, courts, and offices of local government to ask for mitigation.

Upon receipt of Yüan's appeal, the intermediate court sent its vice-president to investigate the case. He first discussed it with the president of the city court. He then interviewed Yüan to make certain that he understood Yüan's version of the facts and the arguments on which the appeal was based. Later he went to the food bureau to check these facts and arguments with the responsible officials of Yüan's former unit. The vice-president of the intermediate court then met with the members of the local political-legal Party group — the president of the city court, the city's chief procurator, the chief of the public security bureau, and the deputy secretary of the city Party committee for legal affairs — to get their current views of the case. The discussion centered on three aspects: (1) Yüan had not taken the money in one lump sum but a little at a time over a long period. Moreover, the evidence showed that only roughly 1000 yuan had actually been taken by Yüan, while the remainder of the missing money came from unexplained deficits of minor sums. This suggested that Yüan's problem in part might have been incompetence in balancing the books or that he might genuinely have intended to return the money when circumstances permitted and thus misappropriated part of the total sum, rather than to commit a crime of corruption involving that amount. (2) Yüan's family obligations were heavy, and support of his dependents would present a legitimate problem to them and to the state. (3) Although a former Nationalist civil servant, Yüan had behaved well for the past nine years and had never evidenced disloyalty to the present regime.

After this meeting the vice-president of the intermediate court returned to his court to report his findings to the president and the ordinary judges. Their consideration of the case led them to conclude that Yüan's sentence should be reduced from two years to one, principally because of his family circumstances. Before announcing its decision the intermediate court notified the city court in writing of its intention to revise the sentence and asked whether the city court had any "opinions" to present. The city court replied that it had nothing to add. The intermediate court then made out a judgment, sending copies to the city court, the high court, and the appellant. It also sent a representative to explain to Yüan that the city court had not erred but that the intermediate court was simply showing him leniency out of consideration for his family.

## ITEM 262

Despite the fact that in certain circumstances appellate review has improved the situation of convicted persons, the limited judicial statistics that have been made public all suggest that convicted persons appeal in only a small percentage of cases. One writer has hypothesized that "[t]he small number of appeal cases despite the simplicity of the appeal procedure might be an indication that the trials in which [people's] assessors have participated may be meeting with general satisfaction." [5] What other hypotheses come to mind? This item, which represents the current Chinese attitude toward appellate review, discusses one factor that may make convicted persons reluctant to appeal.

[Wang Chao-sheng, "Refute the Principle of 'Not Making the Position of the Defendant Unfavorable in a Criminal Appeal,'" *Hsi-pei ta-hsüeh hsüeh-pao* (*jen-wen k'o-hsüeh*) (Northwestern University Journal [humanistic sciences]), 1:66–70 (July 1958)]

. . . . .

According to my understanding, the problem of the principles of appellate procedure (or the characteristics of appellate procedure) in criminal litigation has certainly been controversial. In particular, there have been different views about the principle of "not making the position of the defendant unfavorable." The essence of these differences concerns the problem of affirming or denying whether, when hearing appeals, people's courts of our country have the power to increase the punishment of the defendant in the case of an appeal that has been submitted by the defendant or his guardian, defender or close relative. All those who advocate the principle of "not making the position of the defendant unfavorable" in our country's criminal appeals deny that when people's courts hear appeals they have the power to increase the punishment of the defendant.

5. Luke T. C. Lee, "Chinese Communist Law: Its Background and Development," *Michigan Law Review*, 60:453, note 50 (February 1962).

On the basis of the facts uncovered in the antirightist struggle, in addition to those die-hard rightists who use this theory of favoring the defendant to absolve criminals of their responsibility, there are some comrades, who, due to the influence of lingering rightist thinking and old legal concepts, also advocate using the principle of "not making the position of the defendant unfavorable" in our country's criminal appeals. In order to wipe out the influence of these old legal concepts and to smash the absurd theory of favoring the defendant, this essay will refute the latter's right-wing premises.

Article 11 of the Law of the People's Republic of China for the Organization of People's Courts prescribes that in adjudicating cases people's courts shall put into effect the system of the court of second instance as the court of last instance.

An appeal may be brought by a party from a judgment or order made by a local people's court as a court of first instance to a people's court of the next higher level in accordance with the procedure prescribed by law. A people's procuracy may protest such a judgment or order before a people's court of the next higher level in accordance with the procedure prescribed by law.

In judicial practice, not only do the defendant, the public prosecutor (the people's procuracy) and a person who prosecutes as a private individual have the right to appeal or to protest; the guardian, the defender and close relatives of the defendant also are allowed to appeal, in accordance with the procedure prescribed by law, the judgment or order in a case of first instance. However, an appeal submitted by a defender or close relative of the defendant must have the consent of the defendant. If the defendant does not consent, the appeal will be handled as a petition from the masses.

Obviously, the purposes of providing procedures for appeal and conferring the right of appeal upon the persons concerned are: to correct errors which may have been committed in the not yet effective judgment or order made by a people's court of the first instance; to realize [the system of] adjudication supervision; correctly, lawfully and promptly to suppress the enemy; and to punish crime and protect the people. The purpose of establishing any adjudication system, including an appellate system, is to safeguard the correct exercise of the state's power to adjudicate.

It is erroneous to maintain the view that the only purpose of providing an appellate system and conferring the right of appeal upon the defendant is "to protect the interests of the defendant." The purpose of appeal in people's courts is to perform the task of criminal adjudication correctly, not only by correcting erroneously decided cases that result in "injustice" (such as convicting an innocent person or convicting one who has committed a minor crime of a major crime) but also by correcting erroneously decided cases that result in "evasion of justice" (such as, acquitting a guilty person or convicting one who has committed a major crime of a minor crime). The consequence of correcting an erroneously decided case that has resulted in an "injustice" may be "favorable" to the defendant, but this is certainly not our purpose in providing an appellate system and in conferring the right of appeal upon the defendant.

If we do not clearly understand this point, we must be compelled to advocate the distorted theory of "favoring the defendant." The theory of the principle of "not making the position of the defendant unfavorable" in a criminal appeal is a manifestation of such an erroneous view. There are some defenders who do not understand this point clearly. In the procedure at the first instance level they not only follow the erroneous formula of "defending a guilty person by arguing that his crime is minor," but they also maintain an erroneous view of appeal. For example, they believe that "the appeal is the final opportunity to protect the interests of the defendant before the judgment becomes effective." Thus, they are not able sincerely to educate the defendant through persuasion to accept his punishment, observe the law, and through reform through labor become a new person. Instead, without considering whether or not the judgment is correct, they intentionally or unintentionally hint or connive at appeal by the defendant. Such a way of handling the matter is a reflection of the "theory of favoring the defendant."

At present there are still some persons who do not clearly understand the nature of the right of appeal enjoyed by the defendant. They broadly describe the right of appeal (also the right of defense) enjoyed by the defendant as a "democratic right" and also consider it to be a "democratic system" determined by the "essence of the people's democracy" in our country. This view is extremely incomplete and erroneous. We all know that the law of criminal litigation in our country is a powerful weapon of the people's democratic dictatorship and that most of the defendants in criminal cases come within the scope of contradictions between the enemy and us. They are enemies of the people. The so-called enemies of the people "[a]t this stage of building socialism . . . are all those social forces and groups which resist the socialist revolution, and are hostile to and undermine socialist construction." For instance, counterrevolutionary, unlawful landlord, rich peasant and bad elements involved in criminal cases are all objects of our dictatorship.

Enemies of the people cannot enjoy the rights of citizens. By "the rights of citizens," politically we mean the rights to freedom and democracy. Therefore, the right to appeal of those criminals who come within the scope of contradictions between the enemy and us absolutely cannot be considered a "democratic right." I believe that, in essence, this right can only be deemed a litigation right that is enjoyed by criminals when they are being pursued for criminal responsibility and have to participate in criminal litigation. Despite this, we have never neglected the right of criminals to appeal; on the contrary, we have guaranteed it. Doing so is helpful to the correct, lawful and prompt realization of the task of adjudication.

For the same reason, it is also improper broadly to label the system of appeal a "democratic system." This is because "to put the democratic system into effect among the people" has nothing to do with the enemy. In discussing the essence of our country, it is improper to discuss merely the "people's democracy" aspect while leaving out the other aspect, "dictatorship." "Democracy" does have a class nature; it cannot be arbitrarily applied. It has been correctly pointed out by Chairman Mao in his paper, "Problems Relating to the Correct Handling of Contradictions Among the People": "In reality there are only concrete freedom and concrete democracy in the world. There is no abstract freedom or abstract democracy. In societies where the class struggle is being waged, there is the freedom of the exploiting classes to exploit the laboring people, but there is no freedom for the laboring people not to be exploited. There is democracy for the bourgeoisie, but there is no democracy for the proletariat and the laboring people." In a socialist country, we cannot talk of "democracy" with respect to the class enemies of the people. A view that does not differentiate the enemy from us and speaks of "democracy" for the enemy, fully reflects the rightist feelings of some persons. We should immediately rectify the deviation of "only talking democracy and not discussing dictatorship" or "talking more of democracy and less of dictatorship." We should correctly consider the system of appeal as a "system of the people's democratic dictatorship" and present the essence of our country as "a people's democratic dictatorship, led by the worker class and based on the worker-peasant alliance." We should not one-sidedly understand or emphasize a particular aspect. Only then will we not commit the errors of leftist deviation and, especially, rightist deviation. We should try to understand the people's democratic dictatorship in accordance with Chairman Mao's view, expressed in his paper, "On the People's Democratic Dictatorship," that "democracy among the people and dictatorship over the reactionaries . . . combine to form the people's democratic dictatorship."

According to Chapter 2 of the Law of the People's Republic of China for the Organization of People's Courts, except for basic level people's courts [all other courts, namely,] intermediate people's courts, high people's courts, and the Supreme People's Court have the power to adjudicate appealed and protested cases that have been submitted with respect to judgments or orders made by a lower people's court of first instance. At the same time, Article 79 of the Constitution of the People's Republic of China and Article 14 of the Law of the People's Republic of China for the Organization of People's Courts further prescribe that the adjudication work of lower people's courts is subject to supervision by higher people's courts.

According to provisions of law, an appellate court not only has the power to hear an appealed case, but it also has the power to render judgment on it. Moreover, higher courts have the power to supervise lower courts. Therefore, the jurisdiction of an appellate court is very broad. It has the power to make different decisions with respect to appealed cases. For instance, it may affirm the original judgment and reject the appeal or protest; it may change a part or all of the original judgment, either reducing or increasing the punishment (it makes no difference whether the case is appealed or protested); it may annul the original judgment and remand the case to the people's court of original instance for readjudication or further investigation; and it may even drop the case (although this rarely happens, it is nevertheless within the power of the appellate court).

In the legal provisions of our country we cannot find any provisions to the effect that an appellate court "has no authority to increase the punishment of the defendant." Nor do we find a shadow of the so-called principle of "not making the position of the defendant unfavorable."

People's courts of first and second instances are instruments of the dictatorship of the proletariat, and their task is to suppress the enemy, to punish crime and to protect the people. It is precisely because of this that it is the legally prescribed duty of people's appellate courts to put adjudication supervision into effect in order to perform the task of unifying adjudication and of correcting erroneously decided cases of lower people's courts that either result in "injustice" or "evasion of justice."

### 2.

The so-called principle of "not making the position of the defendant unfavorable" means that when a people's appellate court deals with an appeal submitted by the defendant or his guardian, defender or close relative and believes that the punishment imposed in the lower court's judgment is obviously too light, and it is necessary to increase the punishment, it should make an order annulling the judgment and remanding the case to the people's court of original instance for readjudication. Only the people's court of original instance, in the course of the new hearing, has the right to increase the punishment of the defendant. (With respect to cases which a people's procuracy has protested, if it determines that the punishment is obviously too light and it is actually necessary to increase it, the people's court of second instance may do so directly.)

What are the "reasons" for maintaining the above viewpoints? Although the various theories are different, their general spirit is the same. In short, the reasons can be summarized as follows: first, to protect the right of the defendant to appeal because the purpose of submitting an appeal by the defendant, his guardian, defender or close relative is to improve the situation of the defendant. If after an appeal the defendant would, on the contrary, be in an unfavorable position (that is, given increased punishment), this would frighten all defendants and cause them to abandon appeals. This would restrict the right of the defendant to appeal. Second, since the judgment of the appellate court is the judgment of final instance, if the punishment is increased, the defendant cannot appeal to a higher court if he believes the judgment is erroneous. But if punishment is increased after readjudication of a case which has been remanded to the people's court of first instance and if the defendant believes the judgment is erroneous, he can again appeal. Finally, if a case is remanded to the people's court of original instance for readjudication and punishment is increased, the lower court may give even more consideration to the concrete situation at the time and the place concerned and further investigate and understand the true situation.

Because of such "reasons" they [the rightists] believe that the principle of "not making the position of the defendant unfavorable" has "vital significance" in criminal litigation and that "it is absolutely necessary firmly to prescribe in future legislation on criminal litigation the principle of not making the position of the defendant unfavorable."

I believe this view is erroneous and untenable.

According to what they say, it seems that the decisions of people's appellate courts should be determined by the purposes for which the defendant appeals.

That is to say, a court should act in accordance with the hopes and views of the defendant, for to do otherwise would place restrictions upon the right of the defendant to appeal. This is nonsense. The decision of a people's court, which is the organ that executes the law for the people, should concretely manifest only what is the will of the ruling class. A court should complete the tasks that are assigned to it by the ruling class by relentlessly attacking the enemy, punishing crimes and effectively protecting the interests of the people and of socialist construction. It should certainly never render a judgment that is favorable to the defendant and unfavorable to the people.

Whether the position of the defendant can be "improved" cannot be determined according to the subjective wish of an individual, but it can be determined according to the criminal act of the defendant, the objective facts of the crime and the policies and laws that reflect the will of the ruling class. The fundamental principle that guides our adjudication activity can only be "evidence and facts are the basis, and policy and law are the standard." Even if a court imposes increased punishment upon a defendant, if it is what the crime deserves, how can it be said that it is "unfavorable"? What is there in it that is "unfavorable" to the people?

In our country, since there is no contradiction between the right to appeal and the realization of the goals of the people's democratic dictatorship, we always pay serious attention to the right of the defendant to appeal. In the course of litigation, in order to enable the defendant fully to exercise his right of appeal, we do not demand that a particular form of litigation [procedure] be employed for an appeal. An appeal may be submitted orally or in writing. It may be submitted to a higher people's court directly or to a people's court of first instance. The category of orders and judgments from which an appeal may be taken and the category of persons who may submit an appeal are both very broad. The procedure for appeal is also very simple. . . . From the point of view of both provisions prescribed by law and judicial practice, the right of the defendant to appeal is not restricted by any conditions.

There is no connection between the so-called "frightening" of the defendant and our appeal system. This can only be "sowing what you reap." Moreover, what is strange about being "frightened" if one is placed on trial as a defendant in a criminal case?

Therefore, I believe that protection of the right of the defendant to appeal is not determined by whether an appellate court has the power to increase punishment, but by the essence of the country, the purposes for which its appellate system is established and the unconditional protection in practice of the defendant's right to appeal.

Our country's system of the court of second instance as the court of last instance is an effective system that was adopted in accordance with a synthesis of the historical experience of the people's revolutionary judicial work with the specific characteristics of our country. It can enable the people's courts speedily and correctly to accomplish their tasks.

·       ·       ·       ·       ·

On what basis should the defendant decide whether or not to accept a judgment? I believe that the ultimate criterion is "truth," that is, the "correctness" of a court's judgment or order (that is, in accordance with the principle of "facts are the basis and law is the standard"), and not the subjective desire of the defendant to accept or reject the judgment. If we follow the "theory of repeated appeals," our system of the court of second instance as the court of last instance will be undermined and lose its significance. Moreover, I believe that this view stems purely from the influence of bourgeois-type democratic ideas. It gives us additional trouble, binds our hands and feet and is not beneficial to the realization of the dictatorship of the proletariat.

I also believe that such a theory is incompatible with the guidelines for building socialism: "more," "faster," "better" and "cheaper."

In practice, if it is discovered after an appeal has been submitted that the true facts of a case really have not yet been clarified, an appellate court engages in penetrating examination and study. It is not necessary to remand the case to the court of first instance for readjudication. The people's appellate court can itself clarify the facts of the case. A higher people's court can, in accordance with the procedure of a court of first instance, conduct adjudication at the higher level or on-the-spot adjudication. (Of course, if it is necessary to remand the case for supplementary investigation, that is a different matter. Here I am referring to those cases which the court can clear up without supplementary investigation.)

But after the facts of a case have been cleared up, an appellate people's court can still resentence the defendant to increased punishment. I believe that whether the facts of a case can be clarified and whether appellate people's courts have the power to increase the punishment of the defendant are two different matters. If appellate people's courts have the power to increase the punishment of the defendant, then it is relatively easy to resolve such questions as whether the facts of the case are clear, whether it is necessary to conduct further examination and study and who should conduct such examination and study, etc.

It is correct that an appellate people's court should comprehend the concrete facts of the time and the place concerned when it adjudicates a case; we certainly cannot say that only the people's court of original instance can do that. An appellate people's court can do the same thing. In view of this, why must the case be remanded to the people's court of original instance for readjudication? Does this not amount to looking for trouble?

In practice, higher level people's courts usually have an understanding of the concrete facts of the time and place known to lower level people's courts, regardless of the methods used. Such a view can be fully proved by looking at the unbending leadership and supervision exercised by higher people's courts over lower people's courts.

Therefore, the question is not whether higher people's courts are able to consider the concrete circumstances at the time and the place concerned or to clarify the facts of a case, but mainly whether appellate people's courts have the power to increase the severity of the defendant's punishment.

According to my view, this concept of "favoring the defendant" is politically reactionary, prejudicial to practical work and erroneous in theory.

According to the author of this item, all authorities agree that, upon an appeal by a convicted person, the appellate court has power to remand the case to the court of first instance for retrial and resentencing that may result in a more severe sentence than originally meted out. This undoubtedly is a factor that deters convicted persons from resorting to appeal. Is the deterrent likely to be increased substantially if the appellate court itself can impose a more severe sentence?

## ITEM 263

The fact that a number of reasons discourage convicted persons from exercising their right to appeal increases the importance of the procuracy's power to protest erroneous judgments. Following the Soviet pattern, Chinese procurators are supposed to protest not only cases in which courts have erred in favor of the defendant but also cases in which judicial error has prejudiced the defendant. This item illustrates the latter situation.

["The City Intermediate People's Court Yesterday Publicly Tried the Case of Fu Ken-lin and Decided To Annul the Judgment of the Pei-t'a District People's Court," *Hsin Su-chou pao* (New Soochow news), July 8, 1956]

.    .    .    .    .

Yesterday, the city intermediate people's court publicly heard the case of the erroneous judgment of the Pei-t'a district court which sentenced Fu Ken-lin to imprisonment. Over two hundred persons attended the session. Yesterday afternoon around three o'clock, after the intermediate people's court began the public trial, the president of the court explained the relevant matters to the complainant and the defendant, then he read the original judgment of the Pei-t'a district people's court and the protest lodged by the city people's procuracy, questioned the complainant and the defendant in detail about various facts, and, in the course of analysis and confirmation of various facts, also conducted criticism-education of Fu Ken-lin.

As a result of the trial, the court considered erroneous the judgment of the Pei-t'a district people's court which had sentenced Fu Ken-lin to two years of imprisonment, with a two-year suspended sentence, for having undermined production. It decided to annul the original judgment of the Pei-t'a district people's court, only give Fu Ken-lin criticism-education in court and not give him any other criminal sanction.

Criminal Judgment of the Intermediate People's Court of Soochow City, Kiangsu Province

Criminal Judgment No. 9001 for 1956

The official lodging protest: Li Ch'i-shan, chief procurator of the people's procuracy of Soochow city, Kiangsu province

Complainant below: Chao Chung-k'ang, representative of Hsin-su Silk Screen Factory, male, 25 years old, secretary of the Hsin-su Silk Screen Factory

Address: 3 Ma-ch'ang lane, Soochow

Defendant below: Fu Ken-lin, male, 27 years old, native of Soochow, worker in Hsin-su Silk Screen Factory

Address: 2 Lung-hsin-ch'iao, Soochow

The above defendant was sentenced on January 24, 1956, to two years of imprisonment, with the sentence suspended for two years, by Criminal Judgment No. 3007 of the people's court of Pei-t'a district, Soochow city. The people's procuracy of Soochow city, Kiangsu province, considered the judgment erroneous and lodged its protest in City Procuracy Protest No. 001 ('56). Retrial by this court has clarified the facts as follows:

The defendant, Fu Ken-lin, is a worker at Hsin-su Silk Screen Factory. On October 11, 1955, when he was operating a machine as a substitute for the worker usually on duty, Tao Yün-lun, he [caused] . . . the production of goods of inferior quality. On October 19 of the same year, while he was on daytime duty . . . he continued to use the big press iron in order to produce more work and . . . thus [caused undesirable] consequences to production, in both quality and quantity. Again, on October 20, he . . . caused the machine to stop operating for half an hour.

The above-stated consequences were caused by defendant Fu Ken-lin's selfishness and self-interest, irresponsibility in work, and lack of any idea of protecting state property. Although such acts were wrong, the consequences certainly were not serious. Nor did he intentionally undermine production. The basic method for reducing and preventing the occurrence of similar incidents is to conduct Communist education of workers and staff in order to raise their understanding so that they are voluntarily faithful to their duty, devotedly protect state property, and observe labor discipline. The original judgment in which Fu Ken-lin was sentenced to two years of imprisonment, with the sentence suspended for two years, is erroneous.

This court gives judgment as follows:

(1) Criminal Judgment No. 3007 ('56) of the people's court of Pei-t'a district, Soochow city . . . is annulled.

(2) Defendant Fu Ken-lin will be given criticism-education in court, but he will not be given any criminal sanction.

If this judgment is deemed erroneous, an appeal may be made to the high people's court of Kiangsu province within ten days of the second day after receipt of the copy of the judgment.

|  |  |
|---|---|
| Chief Judge: | Cheng Min |
| Judge: | Hsü Ch'iu-hsia |
| Acting Judge: | Yüng Chih-min |
| Clerk: | Chiao Yün-shen |

July 7, 1956

1. Note that the appellate court provides that its own judgment may be appealed. The reasons for this apparent violation of Article 11 of the Law of the PRC for the Organization of People's Courts (Item 256) are not clear. Can you think of any?

2. Recall the special procedures for review of cases in which the death sentence has been imposed (Chapter IX, section B, subsection 10).

## B. POSTCONVICTION REVIEW

The materials in this section focus on the following questions:

1. After the opportunity for appeal has expired or appeal has been exhausted and the judgment of conviction has become "legally effective," what further possibilities exist for obtaining review of the correctness of the judgment and sentence?

2. Who may initiate postconviction review?

3. On what grounds?

4. What procedures must be observed in seeking postconviction review?

5. What procedures do the reviewing agencies employ?

6. How does postconviction review differ from adjudication in the first instance and appeal?

7. To what extent can postconviction review affect the original judgment and sentence? In what circumstances?

8. To what extent do the various methods of postconviction review actually appear to be invoked?

### ITEM 264

[LAW OF THE PRC FOR THE ORGANIZATION OF PEOPLE'S COURTS (Sept. 28, 1954), pp. 126, 128, 129, 130]

Article 12. If the president of a people's court of any level discovers that, in an already legally effective judgment or order of his court, there is an actual error in the determination of facts or the application of law, he must forward the judgment or order to the adjudication committee for handling.

If the Supreme People's Court discovers that there is an actual error in an already legally effective judgment or order of a lower people's court at any level, or if a higher people's court discovers that there is an actual error in an already legally effective judgment or order of a lower people's court, it shall have the power to adjudicate the case at the higher level or to direct a lower court to readjudicate it.

If the Supreme People's Procuracy discovers that there is an actual error in an already legally effective judgment or order of a people's court at any level, or if a higher people's procuracy discovers that there is an actual error in an already legally effective judgment or order of a lower people's court, it shall have the power to protest the judgment or order in accordance with the procedure of adjudication supervision.

Article 14. . . . The adjudication work of lower people's courts shall be supervised by higher people's courts . . .

Article 22. Intermediate people's courts shall adjudicate the following cases:

(4) Cases protested by people's procuracies in accordance with the procedure of adjudication supervision . . .

Article 25. High people's courts shall adjudicate the following cases:

(4) Cases protested by people's procuracies in accordance with the procedure of adjudication supervision.

Article 30. The Supreme People's Court shall adjudicate the following cases:

(3) Cases protested by the Supreme People's Procuracy in accordance with the procedure of adjudication supervision.

Article 16 of the Law for the Organization of People's Procuracies is identical to the last paragraph of Article 12 above.

## ITEM 265

The following discussion suggests some of the complex problems that have been encountered in implementing the legislative provisions presented in Item 264.

[Wang Hsin et al., "Several Problems Relating to the Procedure of Adjudication Supervision," *CFYC*, 2:71, 72–75 (1958)]

We believe that adjudication supervision procedure is a special litigation procedure apart from ordinary adjudication procedure (procedure of first and second instances). It is a remedial procedure, begun and carried out by special state organs or public personnel empowered to supervise adjudication. Its goals are to examine the legally effective judgments and orders of people's courts to determine whether or not there are errors in [the determination of] the facts or in the application of law and, when it is discovered that there are actual errors, to annul or to revise them so that cases are correctly adjudicated.

·    ·    ·    ·    ·

### 2. Problems of Carrying Out the Procedure of Adjudication Supervision

Article 12, Section 1, of the Law for the Organization of People's Courts prescribes: "If the president of a people's court of any level discovers that, in an already legally effective judgment or order of his court, there is an actual error in the determination of facts or the application of law, he must forward the judgment or order to the adjudication committee for handling." From the above provision it can be seen that the president of a people's court of any level has the power to initiate the procedure of adjudication supervision with respect to the legally effective judgments and orders of his court, and that he also has the power to decide whether or not to forward the case to the adjudication committee for handling. After he examines the materials of the case, if he holds that there is an actual error in the original judgment, then he must forward the case to the adjudication committee for handling; he has no power to annul or to revise the judgment. If he holds that there is no error in the judgment, he has the power to terminate the adjudication supervision procedure and not forward the case to the adjudication committee for handling.

In practice, since it would be difficult for him to do all of this work personally, it is permissible for the president of a people's court of any level to authorize other judges to conduct the work of examining the legally effective judgments and orders of their court. This authorization may be made by the president on a temporary basis, or for the convenience of the work it may be fixed for a long period. But, in order to guard against preconceived prejudices, the authorized person cannot have been a member of the collegial panel which originally participated in the adjudication of the case. After concluding the examination, the authorized person should present a relatively detailed examination report and his views on handling the case, but, because of the importance of an effective judgment, only the president can decide whether or not the case needs to be submitted to the adjudication committee for handling. In accordance with law the authorized person certainly has no authority to make this kind of decision.

People's courts are established on the basis of the principle of democratic centralism, and they put collective leadership into effect. When the president of a people's court of any level holds that there is an actual error in a legally effective judgment or order of his court, the fact that he must forward the case to the adjudication committee for handling and cannot make the [final] decision himself is the embodiment of the above-mentioned principle of collective leadership, and this procedurally guarantees to the maximum extent a serious attitude in the treatment of effective judgments and orders.

In order to develop the role of the adjudication committee to an even greater degree and to make its discussion of a case even more penetrating, we believe that preparatory work should be done before the meeting, so that the entire membership understands the principal facts of the case they are going to discuss. If they are going to discuss an especially important or difficult case, when conditions permit, several members of the adjudication committee should be assigned to examine the file of the entire case. The chief procurator (or a procurator) of the people's procuracy of the same level may attend the meeting, as may the judge who originally handled the case (they have the right to speak but do not have the right to vote). This way the adjudication committee can understand the case even more profoundly and can hear opinions on all aspects, and this is helpful in correctly determining whether or not there is an actual error in the original effective judgment or order. The collegial panel [of original instance] must absolutely obey the resolution of the adjudication committee.

A supervision hearing by higher people's courts of the legally effective judgments and orders of lower people's courts involves the serious work of [deciding] whether or not to alter effective judgments and orders, and, like the hearing of a case of first or second instance, it should be conducted by a collegial panel, the panel to be composed of three judges. This [procedure] is something that has been distilled from the experience of the past few years' practice, and it also conforms to the provisions of the Law for the Organization of People's Courts. In order to implement the principles of the collegial system, after the judge who is handling the case has looked at the file of the entire case, whether or not he holds the original legally effective judgment or order to be correct, the collegial panel should deliberate and make a judgment or order after the supervision hearing.

During the supervision hearing, the parties to the case naturally have no litigation right to go to the meeting or to the court to give their opinions or make their defense. But we advocate that if the people's court believes it necessary it can in the course of the supervision hearing question the parties, witnesses, and experts and also can conduct investigations and on-the-spot examinations, etc. Doing this will be helpful in correctly determining whether or not there is an actual error in the original effective judgment or order. This is what has been done in our country's practice, and we should determine that it continue to be done.

After the supervision hearing, the following kinds of decision may generally be made:

1. Termination of the litigation or striking the case from the record;

2. Rejection of the petition for review or the protest;

3. The adjudication committee of a court may annul the original effective judgment or order and decide to form another collegial panel to hear the case anew; or, when the original effective judgment or order is a judgment or order of the second instance, it may annul the judgment or order of the first or second instance and remand the case to the lower people's court for readjudication. When necessary, some criminal cases may also be sent back to the people's procuracy for a new investigation or a supplementary investigation.

A higher level people's court may annul the original judgment and decide to adjudicate the case at the higher level or to order the lower people's court to hear the case anew (readjudication);

4. Revision of the original judgment or a change of all or a part of it.

In the Law for the Organization of People's Courts there is no provision for directly changing a judgment according to adjudication supervision procedure. This is another form of supervision that has been newly created in our judicial practice on the basis of the concrete circumstances of our country. It plays a powerful role in promptly and effectively attacking crime and correcting deviations. Practice proves that this form is necessary and practicable. But since what is being changed is a legally effective judgment or order, it must be seriously and carefully done and should have definite limits. On the basis of practical experience this form is relatively suitable in cases where the circumstances are clear, the facts have been correctly determined, and there has been an error only in the application of policies, laws, or decrees. It is not suitable in cases in which the principal facts are unclear and which must be heard anew to be clarified. Therefore, we believe that in the future the direct changing of a judgment in the course of adjudication supervision should be limited to cases in which the circumstances are clear and where the original judgment correctly determined the facts.

Another problem in adjudication supervision procedure is whether or not to annul the original effective judgment or order when it is decided to readjudicate a case or to adjudicate it at a higher level. Some people argue that the original judgment should not be annulled. Their reasons generally are: although the collegial panel of a higher level court or the adjudication committee of the original court determines after the supervision hearing that there is an error in the original judgment, at that time it still is not necessarily an actual error. The original judgment can only be annulled when, after readjudication or adjudication at a higher level, it is determined that there was an error in the original judgment. This maintains the stability of effective judgments to the maximum degree and manifests the seriousness of revising effective judgments. If we first annul the original judgment, after readjudication or adjudication at a higher level, it may still be determined to be correct, and at that time the original judgment will have to be affirmed and its legal effectiveness will have to be restored. Thus the early annulment of the original judgment will lose its significance and will create an undesirable effect.

We do not agree with the above suggestion for the following reasons:

First, Article 12 of the Law for the Organization of the People's Courts clearly prescribes that readjudication or adjudication at a higher level can only be decided upon if the president of a people's court "discovers that, in an already legally effective judgment or order . . . there is an actual error in the determination of facts or the application of law . . . ." This provision is worth our deep study. If it is held only that "there is a possible error" in the original judgment rather than that "there is an actual error," then readjudication or adjudication at a higher level cannot be decided upon; and it is then only possible to make a further study of the case in order to be able, if it is determined that the original judgment has an error, to make a decision about readjudication or adjudication at a higher level. This provision effectively guarantees the stability of effective judgments and orders and guarantees that correctly decided cases will not lightly be subjected to new hearings. When it is determined that there is an actual error in the original judgment, then it should be annulled. The suggestion not to annul the original effective judgment or order when deciding upon readjudication or adjudication at a higher level only emphasizes that we should not lightly annul effective judgments or orders. But it ignores the strict control over conducting new hearings of cases which have been adjudged. This may lead to lightly granting new hearings, which is not carefulness. Owing to the exclusiveness of an effective judgment, a case should not have a new hearing if the original effective judgment has not been annulled. Otherwise it will create a situation in which there is an effective judgment in a case at the same time that the case is having a new hearing.

Second, there really exists in practice the kind of situation in which the original effective judgment or order is annulled at the time that readjudication or adjudication at a higher level is decided upon, and then after readjudication or adjudication at a higher level it is held that the conclusions of the original judgment are correct and should still be upheld. But to uphold the conclusions of the original judgment is not the same as determining that the original judgment is completely correct. This is because the bases of the two successive judgments (or orders) are not the same; the annulled judgment or order has defects in the determination of the facts or in its reasoning, while the new judgment or order is formed from the correction of those defects.

*3. The Problem of Whether Readjudication and Adjudication
   at a Higher Level Are in the Last Analysis Parts
   of Adjudication Supervision Procedure or Are the
   Restoration of First and Second Instance Procedure.*

.     .     .     .     .

We believe that it is improper to emphasize the special nature of readjudication and adjudication at a higher level and to include them as parts of adjudication supervision procedure. This is because, first of all, ordinary litigation
procedure and adjudication supervision procedure differ with respect to court
activity and the litigation rights of the parties. Ordinary litigation procedure is
the ordinary procedure for handling cases, but adjudication supervision procedure is a remedial procedure. From practice we can see that generally the
latter can determine whether or not there is an error in the original effective
judgment or order, and when it discovers that there is an actual error it can
annul the original judgment and create the opportunity for the case to have a
new hearing. But it is not able to go beyond this scope and make a new judgment or order. For example, with respect to the litigation rights of the parties,
in courts of first and second instance the parties have various legally prescribed
litigation rights, and the courts have the responsibility of safeguarding the parties'
legitimate exercise of these rights because their legitimate exercise is bound up
with the courts' activity, facilitates correct handling of the case, and is consistent with the interests of the state. To a very great degree, whether or not the
parties exercise these litigation rights is decided by the parties themselves. In
the procedure for adjudication supervision, although the parties may be permitted to participate in the court hearing when the court deems it necessary,
the parties certainly do not have any automatic litigation right to participate
in the supervision hearing. Moreover, under ordinary circumstances, no parties
participate in the supervision hearing. This is because the two procedures differ
concretely in nature. This is also related to the right of the parties to appeal
and to the right of a people's procuracy to protest. If both readjudication and
adjudication at a higher level were part of adjudication supervision procedure,
their judgments and orders would all be the judgments and orders of the supervision hearing and would be legally effective upon being made, and none of
them would be permitted to be appealed or to be protested according to appeal
procedure. When cases are to be readjudicated or adjudicated at a higher level,
the judgments or orders of the first and second instances are annulled or the
effective judgment or order of the first instance is annulled, and the original
court of first instance readjudicates the case or the court which conducted the
supervision hearing adjudicates it at the higher level. At that time readjudication
or adjudication at the higher level actually corresponds to a new hearing in the
first instance, and it would not be sufficient if, with respect to this kind of
judgment or order [that is, the one made in the new hearing], the parties were

not given the right to appeal, the people's procuracy were not given the right to protest in accordance with appeal procedure, and the opportunity to conduct a re-examination of the judgment through appeal procedure were not provided.

.    .    .    .    .

In practice, with respect to cases in which a lower people's court has already rendered judgment, if after a hearing in accordance with adjudication supervision procedure a higher people's court holds that there is an actual error, it generally makes an order to annul the original effective judgment or order and directs the lower people's court to readjudicate the case. The higher people's court decides to adjudicate a case at the higher level only if it has national or regional significance or if it would be difficult for the lower people's court to readjudicate it. It can be seen that the question of whether to readjudicate a case or to adjudicate it at a higher level is decided by the degree of importance and complexity of the case itself. Actually, adjudication at a higher level only means raising the level of jurisdiction so that a new hearing is conducted by the higher people's court as a substitute for the new hearing (readjudication) of the case that should [otherwise] have been conducted by the lower people's court. We should say that with respect to a new hearing of a case after annulment of the original effective judgment or order, apart from the different level of jurisdiction of the courts, no difference in nature exists between adjudication at a higher level by a higher people's court and readjudication by a lower people's court. Adjudication at a higher level may be viewed as another form of readjudication. To force the classification of adjudication at a higher level and readjudication as two procedures that are different in nature would create trivialities and confusion in theory. In actual work methods, since the cases to be adjudicated at a higher level by higher courts are important or complex or are cases which lower courts would have difficulty adjudicating, in order to prevent erroneous judgments it is even more necessary in such cases to conduct the systematic activity of the court in accordance with ordinary litigation procedure so that the parties can actively participate in litigation activity. Only if there is a unification of readjudication and adjudication at a higher level in both theory and practice, with both of them serving as a new hearing of a case in accordance with ordinary litigation procedure, can the common nature of the contents of these two forms of new hearing be manifested.

. . . [D]irectly changing a judgment after a supervision hearing is based on the needs of practice and has a limited scope. It is appropriate that it still belongs to the category of adjudication supervision procedure. It is rather similar to adjudication at a higher level but also is different from the latter. The differences are that it does not involve annulment of the original effective judgment or order, and it does not involve a decision to have a new hearing (with notice to both parties) and the process of a new hearing. Moreover, as previously mentioned, they [directly changing a judgment after a supervision hearing and adjudication at a higher level] are individually applied to two different situations.

## ITEM 266

["In Response to the Demands of the People, the Canton Intermediate People's
Court in Accordance with Law Resentences Hooligan Chief Ch'en Fu-pi to Four
Years of Imprisonment," *Nan-fang jih-pao* (Southern daily), March 13, 1955]

After we published the news item "In Response to the Demands of the Vast
[Number of] People, the Canton People's Court (now the Canton Intermediate
People's Court) Punishes a Group of Hooligan Chiefs Who Corrupted Youths
and Juveniles" on December 23, 1954, a great many readers individually wrote
to us and to the people's court to express the opinion that it is extremely necessary for the Canton people's court to apply the laws of the state to punish
hooligan chiefs. They expressed deep abhorrence of the criminal acts of criminals
Ch'en Hui-shan, Ch'en Fu-pi, and others. However, they believed that giving
a sentence of two years of imprisonment to criminal Ch'en Fu-pi, who had
acted obscenely and indecently with women and had debauched and corrupted
youths, was not severe enough, and they angrily demanded that he be resentenced.

So that criminal Ch'en Fu-pi would get the punishment he deserved, we
sent these letters to the Canton intermediate people's court for handling. On
March 1, that court sent us a letter in reply, stating that it accepted the opinion
of the vast masses. The president of the court, in accordance with the provisions
of Article 12 of the Law of the People's Republic of China for the Organization
of People's Courts, examined the original judgment, found that there had been
an error in the application of law, and forwarded the judgment to the court's
adjudication committee for handling, decision, and resentencing. Now, that
court has resentenced criminal Ch'en Fu-pi to four years of imprisonment.
Criminal Ch'en Fu-pi must return to the buyers the money he received for the
obscene records he sold them and he is also required to pay fifteen yuan per
month to the complainant Ch'en Ch'i-fang.

## ITEM 267

["The Ku-lou Court of Foochow Accepts the Opinion of the Masses, Corrects the
Situation of Too Lenient Sentences and Resentences Two Criminals Who Had
Sexual Relations with Young Girls," *Fu-chien jih-pao* (Fukien daily), Nov. 29,
1957]

The Ku-lou district people's court of Foochow has accepted the demands
of the masses and, in accordance with law, has resentenced Wang Hsing-ho and
Liu Mei-hui, two criminals who had sexual relations with young girls and
whose original sentences were too lenient. On November 15 it publicly pronounced the sentences before a mass meeting of over 3000 persons.

Liu Mei-hui has been a man of lecherous and evil character. Between 1952
and July of this year, when he was arrested, he had committed by enticement,
coercion and other methods, indecent acts, or had sexual relations, with twelve
young girls in a place near his residence and thus seriously impaired the mental
and physical health of these girls. Wang Hsing-ho has already reached the age

of seventy-one. Before and after liberation, he was a [Christian] minister. Although he spoke without reservation of "behaving virtuously" and he preached to others, he secretly committed many indecent acts and often had sexual relations with his granddaughter who was only twelve years old and was under his direct education and upbringing, and this seriously impaired the health of the child. In September of this year, the Ku-lou district people's court sentenced these two criminals to seven years and five years of imprisonment respectively. After the sentences were imposed, the court received thirty-nine letters from the masses and more than 300 oral expressions of opinion which unanimously stated that these sentences were too lenient and which demanded resentencing. The president of the court accepted the opinion of the masses, undertook an examination of the original cases, and forwarded them to the adjudication committee for study. In accordance with law, the court annulled the original sentences, resentenced criminal Liu to fifteen years of imprisonment and criminal Wang to ten years of imprisonment, and thus obtained the unanimous support of the vast masses.

Are Items 266 and 267 examples of the "direct changing of a judgment in the course of adjudication supervision"? Or did the courts act after holding a new trial? Given the nature of Chinese trials, how much difference is there between the two procedures discussed in Item 265?

## ITEM 268

[Interview]

Chiang was the estranged wife of a dentist who had been having an affair with another woman. One day in 1958, in order to put a crimp in her husband's extramarital activities, she secretly entered his office and took a substantial sum of cash and gold that he had hidden there. Upon discovering the theft her husband suspected that she was the culprit and reported her to the public security bureau. When questioned by the police Chiang confessed and was promptly tried by the county court, convicted of theft, and sentenced to fourteen months of imprisonment. She filed no appeal, but her parents and older brother wrote a number of letters to the bureau, the procuracy, the court, and the county Party committee protesting the severity of the sentence in what they said was not a genuine theft case but merely a marital dispute in which Chiang did what she could to defend her home against an unscrupulous adulteress.

The county Party committee instructed the court to review the matter. The president of the court discussed it with the other members of the political-legal Party group, and they decided to form a joint investigating team to inquire into the circumstances in detail. This group subsequently reported that actually the case only involved a family quarrel. On the basis of this report the political-legal Party group ordered that Chiang, who had already served one month of reform through labor, be released. She was told that her release was a manifestation of the leniency of the government and a recognition of her good behavior in prison. She was given a certificate of release, but there was no annulment or revision of the original judgment. Although the cadres who had originally handled the case were required to conduct self-examinations before their own units and although within these units Chiang's release was called a reversal of a decision, there were no public indications that the case had been wrongly decided.

## ITEM 269

[Chugunov, Criminal Court Procedures in the People's Republic of China (1959), pp. 199–200]

.     .     .     .     .

Soon after the liberation of the entire country the people's court of Tinghsiang county of Szechwan province, at the request of Chung Kui-lan, examined the case of a counter-revolutionary organization and convicted its members. As was brought out subsequently, one of the members of this counter-revolutionary organization evaded responsibility and was not turned over to the court. Chung Kui-lan, in exposing the entire organization, learned of this counter-revolutionary and reported him to local organs of authority. But the judge who was trying the case did not study all the circumstances of the case and instead of convicting the counter-revolutionary, sentenced Chung Kui-lan to six months' imprisonment for slander and false denunciation. The convicted woman appealed the sentence to the Szechwan province people's court. But the counter-revolutionary, against whom Chung had made the charges, wrote a denunciation against her to the people's court, stating that she was discrediting state cadres, giving false denunciations, violating election laws, etc. The Szechwan province people's court, in examining this case, believed the slanderous statements and sentenced Chung Kui-lan to two years' imprisonment. Chung Kui-lan was sent to prison. One night in prison Chung Kui-lan cut her face slightly while sleeping. The prison administration, imagining that Chung had tried to escape, turned over her case to the court, which sentenced her to an additional year in prison. This case aroused the righteous indignation of private citizens, who appealed to the Party committee of Tinghsiang county. The Party committee requested the Szechwan province people's court to examine the case within the framework of judicial [adjudication] supervision. The Szechwan province people's court, examining the case of Chung Kui-lan, rescinded all three sentences, dismissed the case and freed Chung Kui-lan from prison. The state aided the freed woman with money and other means. Having established the lack of grounds for the conviction of Chung the Szechwan province court transferred the materials to the people's procurator's office for institution of proceedings against the counter-revolutionary who had slandered the honest woman.

## ITEM 270

[ACT OF THE PRC FOR REFORM THROUGH LABOR (Sept. 7, 1954), p. 38]

Article 43. As for an offender whose case has already been adjudged and who is being held by an organ of reform through labor [while serving his sentence], if that organ discovers reliable material sufficient to alter [the assessment of] the facts of the case, it shall immediately send the material to the original adjudication organ or to the people's court of the place in which the organ of reform through labor is located to serve as the basis for adjudicating the case anew.

## ITEM 271

[Interview]

In 1952 Huang was convicted of the assassination of two Communist Party guerrillas in the hills of Fukien province in 1948. The county court sentenced him to fifteen years in prison on the ground that he had been a ringleader of the assassins. While Huang was serving this sentence, in early 1956 two others were also convicted by the court of a neighboring county of having participated in the same murders. In the course of the investigation of their case it became clear that Huang had merely been an accomplice. This new evidence was sent to the court that had sentenced Huang. After verifying the evidence, it reduced his sentence to six years in prison.

## ITEM 272

[Interview]

Two counterrevolutionary posters appeared within the same week in 1959 in a production brigade of a rural commune. One said "Down with the Communist Party" and the other "Eliminate Mao Tse-tung." Investigation failed to reveal the author. Since this kind of case had to be broken, the county public security bureau assigned six men to conduct an all-out investigation. They came up with two suspects — an ex-landlord named Hsü and a youth named Liang who was of poor peasant origin but who had been heard grumbling about bad food and other conditions. Both were detained for questioning. Under intensive questioning Hsü finally admitted that he had written the first of the posters but denied authorship of the second. He was convicted of current counterrevolutionary activity and sentenced to seven years of imprisonment.

Liang persisted in denying his guilt. The bureau sent some of his school notebooks and some specimens of Hsü's writing, as well as the second poster, to one of the provincial public security department's handwriting experts for analysis. The expert reported that the characters for "eliminate" in the poster were written the same as those in Liang's notebooks, although Hsü's characters were also similar. On the basis of this report and the evidence of Liang's dissatisfaction with conditions, he was arrested and convicted. Because of his youth, his poor peasant status, and his previously pure history, he was sentenced to only three years in prison.

Liang went to reform through labor at a camp run by the special district. After he had been there a few months, Hsü, who had gone to a camp run by the province, responded to indoctrination about the advantages of full confession and admitted that he had also written the second counterrevolutionary poster. The labor camp informed the county public security bureau. It sent a team out to talk to Hsü, to Liang's relatives and friends, and to Liang himself, who had been reportedly despondent since his arrival at the labor camp. It also sent the handwriting specimens back for a second expert analysis, which reached the same conclusion as the first. The bureau made a report on the investigation to the political-legal Party group, which decided that there was a "discrepancy" in Liang's conviction. Because the approval of the special district political-legal organs had been obtained for Liang's arrest, the county level organs reported their decision to their superiors at the special district. They also reported it to the provincial public security department, because this decision reflected adversely on the conclusion reached by the department's handwriting expert.

After the special district approved his release, Liang was brought back to the county public security bureau and, in the presence of the principal cadre concerned with law enforcement in his commune, the secretary of the Party branch of his brigade, and the chief of the brigade's security defense committee, an important public security official told him that through unremitting effort the bureau had discovered that ex-landlord Hsü had written the poster in question and that Liang could therefore go free. The cadres from Liang's commune were instructed to hold a meeting of his brigade to announce that Liang was not guilty of any crime and was to be treated like an ordinary citizen rather than like a released criminal. At this meeting there was no acknowledgment that an error had been made, but emphasis was placed on the determination of the people's government to ferret out every offender such as ex-landlord Hsü and to avoid wronging innocent persons such as poor peasant Liang. Nor was any mention made of the "subsidy for living expenses" of 100 yuan which the bureau gave Liang for what had totalled five months in jail and which in its records the bureau classified as compensation for reversal of a conviction. [For the fate of the public security cadres who handled Liang's case, see Item 287].

## ITEM 273

[Interview]

On returning from a national judicial conference held in Peking in 1956, the leaders of the police, procuracy, and courts of a southern province convened a meeting of the leading political-legal cadres of the special districts and counties of the province to inform them of the need for and the methods of organizing and operating evaluation committees in all areas. The purpose of these committees, the cadres were told, was to review cases involving political crimes. Since resources were limited and the number of political cases overwhelming, within this category they were to concentrate their efforts on cases of (1) historical counterrevolutionaries; (2) leaders of reactionary societies; and (3) imprisoned defendants whose trials had not yet been concluded despite the passage of considerable time [with respect to this third category see Item 170]. The cadres were provided with unpublished, detailed standards for use in disposing of these cases.

Chang was a secretary of the security section in the county public security bureau. When the leading political-legal cadres of his county returned from the meeting at the provincial capital, he was assigned to the ten-member county evaluation committee which they organized as a secret, ad hoc joint committee.

It was composed of four representatives of the bureau — a deputy chief, the chief of the trial preparation section, a secretary of the political defense section, and Chang; two representatives of the procuracy — a secretary and a regular procurator; and four representatives of the court — the president, vice-president, and two ordinary judges.

The first stage of the committee's work was to determine which of the adjudicated cases from its area required reinvestigation. The process of selection was as follows: all the committee members except the president and vice-president of the court, who were busy with other duties, first scanned the entire list of cases that had been adjudicated by their county involving historical counter-revolutionaries and leaders of reactionary societies. On the basis of past knowledge of these cases each member noted those that might possibly merit reevaluation. These selections were pooled into a single list, and the committee then ordered the files in each of these cases to be produced. The files were then divided among the eight active members, and each had to study the files allocated to him and make notes on those cases in which it seemed that the evidence in the file was not in accord with the conviction and punishment. Each member then orally reported to the committee on each of the dubious cases he had found. If from the oral summary it appeared to the committee that the reporter's assessment was correct, after the meeting each member briefly reviewed that file to verify the accuracy of the reporter's presentation. The committee then voted on whether the case should be marked for investigation. Although the president and vice-president of the court did not take part in reading the files, they did participate in the discussions concerning selections.

The second stage of the committee's work was to investigate the selected cases. For this purpose the committee divided into two five-man groups. One was to handle all investigations that had to take place outside the province, and the other to handle all investigations within the province and to manage the committee office. Chang belonged to the first group. It extracted from the selected cases all the accusations and evidence that had come from other provinces, divided these materials according to geographic areas, and assigned them to members of the group who were to do the investigating in the different areas. Each member then went to the area assigned to him and interviewed the relevant persons such as the victim or his family, witnesses, others who made accusations, and the prisoner himself if he was confined in a labor camp outside the province. Each person signed a statement which summarized the interview, and these statements were sent back to the committee office. The second group did the same thing within the province. The only area of the country that was not visited by a committee cadre from Chang's county was the extreme north, since, being southerners, none of the members wanted to brave the extremely cold weather there. In those areas they relied instead on the cooperation of local political-legal personnel, whom they asked to undertake investigation on their behalf.

The investigation process consumed four months. When it was completed, the committee reconvened, and each of the eight regular members studied the new material in every file in order to ascertain what light it shed on the correctness of the original decision. The committee discussed each case and decided how it should be handled. A committee member then wrote a report on each case called a "statement of evaluation," which summarized the original disposition, the evidence revealed by the reinvestigation, and the discrepancies which were found between the original and the new evidence. On this basis the report presented a recommended disposition of the case.

This statement of evaluation was sent to the court that had sentenced the prisoner, in most cases the county basic level court, which automatically adopted the recommendation contained in the statement, since the president and vice-president of the court had already approved it as members of the committee. The statement was then sent for approval to the court at the level of the unit that administered the prisoner's reform through labor, which was usually the province but was sometimes the special district. That court obtained a report on the prisoner's behavior during imprisonment from the organ of reform through labor. On the basis of this report and the statement, the president of the court and the other members of the political-legal group of that level decided whether to approve the statement's recommendation or to revise it. The sentencing court and the organ of reform through labor were then notified of the decision. The latter informed the prisoner of any change in his sentence. When this process resulted in reduction of the sentence, the prisoner was always told that this was a manifestation of the leniency of the people's government rather than a confession of error.

In Chang's county the work of the evaluation committee, which was not concluded until the spring of 1957, had the following consequences for the prisoners whose convictions were reinvestigated: In one instance the reinvestigation uncovered evidence of a previously unknown serious crime which the prisoner had committed during the Anti-Japanese War — revealing the whereabouts of Communist guerrillas to Nationalist forces — and this evidence subsequently became the basis of a separate criminal prosecution that resulted in an additional five-year sentence for the prisoner. In some instances, although evidence of a new crime was uncovered, a new prosecution was not instituted, but the material was placed in the prisoner's file for possible future use. In other cases the original judgment and sentence were found to be supported by the verified evidence, and thus they were left unchanged. In most cases the prisoner was granted a reduction in sentence; and in some instances this reduction resulted in his immediate release.

## ITEM 274

[Mao Tse-tung, "Problems Relating to the Correct Handling of Contradictions Among the People" (Feb. 27, 1957), pp. 13–14]

### 2. Problems of Liquidating Counterrevolution

. . . . .

After liberation, we liquidated a number of counterrevolutionaries. Those with serious crimes were punished by death. This was completely necessary; it was the demand of the vast masses; it was [done] in order to liberate the vast masses from a long period of oppression by counterrevolutionaries and all kinds of local despots, that is to say, in order to liberate productive forces. If we had not done so, the masses would not have been able to lift their heads. Since 1956 circumstances have changed fundamentally. As for the country as a whole, the main force of counterrevolutionaries has already been liquidated. Our fundamental task has changed from liberating productive forces to protecting and developing them in [the context of] new relations of production. Some people do not understand that our present policy fits present circumstances and our past policy fitted past circumstances; they want to make use of present policy to reverse decisions of past cases and to negate the great accomplishments in the work of liquidating counterrevolution. This is completely erroneous and this the masses of people will not permit.

With respect to our work of liquidating counterrevolution, accomplishments have been paramount, but there have also been errors. There were both excesses and oversights. Our guideline is: "Where there is counterrevolution, it must be liquidated; where there is error, it must be corrected." Our line in the work of liquidating counterrevolution is the line of letting the masses liquidate counterrevolution. Naturally, even with the adoption of the mass line, defects still can occur in the work, but they can be fewer and errors can be easier to correct. The masses have gained experience in the struggle. From things done correctly they gained experience in doing things correctly. From errors committed they also gained experience in how errors are committed.

We have already adopted or are now adopting steps to correct all errors that have been discovered in the work of liquidating counterrevolution. As for those not yet discovered, we are prepared to correct them as soon as they are discovered. Whatever the extent to which the errors originally made were publicized, their correction should be publicized to the same extent. I propose that the work of liquidating counterrevolution be completely examined once this year or next to summarize experience, spread a spirit of uprightness, and attack wrongful tendencies. Centrally, this [task] should be presided over by the Standing Committee of the National People's Congress and the Standing Committee of the People's Political Consultative Conference; and locally, by provincial and city people's councils and by committees of the People's Political Consultative Conference. When examining the work, we should not pour cold water on the vast [number of] cadres and activists, but rather we should help them. It is not right to pour cold water on the vast [number of] cadres and activists, but errors which are discovered should definitely be corrected. Public security departments, procuratorial departments, judicial departments, prisons or organs that administer reform through labor all should adopt this attitude. We hope that all members of the Standing Committee of the National People's Congress and the People's Political Consultative Conference and the people's deputies who possibly can, will participate in this kind of examination. This can be of help in perfecting our legal system and in correctly handling counterrevolutionaries and other criminals.

ITEM 275

[MacFarquhar, *The Hundred Flowers* (1960), p. 48]

.    .    .    .    .

*A Commission to rectify injustices proposed*

May 22 [1957]

Lo Lung-chi [Vice Chairman, China Democratic League; Minister of the Timber Industry] in his statement today proposed that the National People's Congress's standing committee and the People's Political Consultative Conference's standing committee should jointly establish a special organisation, of a united front nature, to inspect the deviations during the past "three-anti," "five-anti" campaigns and the movement for the suppression of counter-revolutionaries. It would at the same time provide a guarantee that people who dared to "bloom" and "contend" would not be subject to attack and retaliation. Lo considered that such an organisation should be set up immediately . . . In the first place, every road leads to Peking. Some people think that all will be well if any wrong can be brought to the notice of the capital, since Chairman Mao and the highest organs of state power are in Peking . . . In the second place, the leadership machinery for the "righting of past wrongs" must be clearly distinguishable from the leadership organs in charge of the past movements, the "three-anti," "the five-anti" campaign and the suppression of counter-revolutionaries. The present committee will be responsible for the inspection and handling of cases wrongly adjudged during the past three movements. At the same time it will hear charges made by the people, so that those who were wronged and who are objects of retaliation will have a place to take their troubles to.

ITEM 276

["Anhwei [Province] Corrects Erroneously Decided Cases in Accordance with the Spirit of Chairman Mao's Speech," *Wen-hui pao* (Literary news, Shanghai), May 13, 1957, p. 1]

In accordance with the spirit of Chairman Mao's speech, "Problems Relating to the Correct Handling of Contradictions Among the People," the high people's court of Anhwei province has undertaken an examination of cases of contradictions among the people which have already been disposed of. Since April 16, it has undertaken a case by case study and examination of thirty-two judgments recently reported to it by the people's courts of ten counties, including Wu-wei, Ching-hsien, and Wu-ho.

After examining these cases, the high people's court of the province held that prompt adjudication by the courts of a batch of cases of current crimes played a positive role in stabilizing social order and protecting production. However, it also clearly observed that the handling of some cases was improper or erroneous. With respect to each of those cases that were erroneously or improperly handled, the high people's court of the province submitted concrete opinions and requested the respective courts of original instance to check them and to deal with them again.

The high people's court of the province examined the judgment of Wu-ho county people's court of March 30 relating to defendants Yüan Hung-pao, Yüan Chu-cheng, and Yüan Chu-p'in. The three defendants were each sentenced to one year of imprisonment and three months of control by the people for undermining cooperativization of agriculture by taking away their cattle and attempting to withdraw from the cooperative. After studying the case, the high people's court of the province held that Yüan Hung-pao and the other two defendants were poor peasants whose attempt to withdraw from the cooperative and take away their cattle was caused by the members' discontent with the defective administration of the cooperative which had, for example, resulted in long delays in settling accounts and in failure to resolve the shortage of cattle fodder. The high people's court, therefore, held that the county people's court should persist in the policy of persuasion-education and that sentencing them to imprisonment was a mistake. In March, the Ching-hsien people's court sentenced Wang Shao-jung to two years of imprisonment and Hu Shih-hsing to one year and six months of imprisonment on charges of convening the masses to create a disturbance and undermining cooperativization of agriculture. In the course of its examination, the high people's court of the province found that it was true that Wang Shao-jung and Hu Shih-hsing had led members to demand that the cooperative settle its accounts and thus caused a disturbance among the masses; but the members' demand for settling the cooperative's accounts was a proper demand and the disturbance created by the masses was a purely spontaneous, individual incident. Thus, the defendants should not be sentenced to imprisonment. As to the Ts'ung-yang county people's court's handling of the case of Chang Fu-lai's hitting a cadre, the high people's court of the province, after examining the case, held that the court had handled a case of backward conduct as a case of criminal conduct and thus had given the defendant more severe punishment than he deserved. Captain of the production team, Chu Liang-yuan, without submitting the matter to discussion by the majority of members, had distributed two yuan from the team's income from selling beef to himself and to two needy families (it was difficult to decide whether this was fair and reasonable). Since Chang Fu-lai did not get a share of such income, he was dissatisfied with the matter and hit and cursed Chu Liang-yuan, and they then had a fist fight. This resulted from backward, selfish motives. Although his act of hitting someone was wrong, the circumstances were not serious, and he should be given criticism-education instead of being sentenced as a criminal to two years of imprisonment.

The high people's court of the province also recently decided to develop the study of the instructions given by Chairman Mao in his "Problems Relating to the Correct Handling of Contradictions Among the People" at the various levels of people's courts in this province, to link them to actual adjudication work, to organize them to engage in an examination and recapitulation of all cases that have already been disposed of, and to correct those cases that have been erroneously handled.

## ITEM 277

[Chugunov, Criminal Court Procedures in the People's Republic of China (1959), pp. 198–199]

A higher people's court may discover errors in verdicts which have become valid by lower courts, by means of conducting planned and unexpected inspections and checks. Higher people's courts, besides exercising control over the work of lower courts within the framework of judicial [adjudication] supervision, make rather broad application of the method of spot checks of cases for making general conclusions of experience in judicial work, in order that the lower people's courts might be directed by the general conclusions in their own operations. If cases are revealed by spot check where incorrect decisions were arrived at, review of these sentences is carried out on the basis of law. Errors in people's court sentences which have become valid can be revealed also by judicial-administrative organs in checking the operations of lower courts.

Proposals by these organs can serve as a basis for reviewing verdicts which have become valid. In November 1955 the higher [high] people's court of Hopeh province and the justice administration of this province spot-checked criminal cases which had been tried in the lower people's court of Chengting, Chu and other counties, and after this study they made general conclusions of the experience of the work of the courts. The people's courts of all levels of this province, proceeding from these general conclusions, checked cases of counter-revolutionary and other crimes, for which sentences had already become valid. Fourteen thousand criminal cases were checked. On the basis of law 500 cases were reviewed in which erroneous verdicts had been reached. As a result of this great work, errors in sentences which had become valid were not only revealed and corrected in time, but the ideological-theoretical level of judicial workers was increased, as well as their knowledge of legal science, and this doubtlessly played an active part in the further increase in the quality of trying cases. With the aim of correcting possible errors in sentences which had already become valid, people's courts of all levels are systematically conducting checks of verdicts of the court. This voluminous work by the people's courts brings positive results and makes it possible to eliminate possible mistakes in judicial work rapidly and accurately. The carrying out by people's courts of various levels of reviews of verdicts which have become valid guarantees the observance of the lawful rights and interests of those persons convicted and assures the correctness of judicial repression.

## C. VINDICATION OF THE ACCUSED

The materials in the preceding section and in earlier chapters not only demonstrate the PRC's procedures for detecting mistakes in the application of the criminal process. They also suggest the efforts that are sometimes made in cases of severe hardship to mitigate the consequences of the erroneous accusation and confinement of the vindicated person. Recall, for example, Chairman Mao's statement in Item 274 that "Whatever the extent to which the errors originally made were publicized, their correction should be publicized to the same extent." Item 272 illustrated the application of this admonition to restore the status of the accused. Other measures of amelioration have also been taken, as indicated by the statement in Item 269 that "[t]he state aided the freed woman with money and other means." The following items shed further light upon such measures.

## ITEM 278

[CONSTITUTION OF THE PRC (Sept. 20, 1954), p. 29]

Article 97. Persons shall have the right to obtain compensation for losses received through infringement by personnel of state organs of their rights as citizens.

## ITEM 279

[Fukushima Masao, "Chinese Legal Affairs (Second Discussion)," in *Chūgoku no hō to shakai* (Chinese law and society; Tokyo, 1960), p. 47]

17. The existence of procedural law concerning state compensation and the actual circumstances of its application.

Article 97 of the Constitution provides that any citizen has the right to file a complaint about any official's unlawful act, and the state must pay compensation for the damage it has caused. But no statute sets forth the procedure for implementing this right. However, before promulgation of the Constitution a resolution of the Central People's Government dealt with this problem.

For example, in the case of false arrest or punishment of the innocent, upon the complaint of the party himself or the protest of the procurator's office, if such facts are clearly established, the damage caused by such an unlawful act must be compensated for by the state as follows: When the victim is a worker, he shall be paid the amount of the wages he would have earned during the period of this detention and, if he has lost his job, it shall be immediately restored. Suitable medical treatment is provided for personal injuries. If the injured person is an independent businessman, his compensation is the sum he would have earned during the period.

A question was asked concerning the actual occurrence of such cases. Until 1952 there were some cases of this nature, but after that such cases became rare and since the promulgation of the Constitution (1954) there have been almost none. Why? Because until 1952 judicial workers of the old regime remained in office and tried cases in the old way. Therefore, they often mistried cases. But in 1952 a judicial reform was completed, and all these old elements were swept away from the courts. Thereafter, erroneous judgments became scarce. Nevertheless, it can be expected that there will be a few cases of this nature. Therefore, this kind of expense, though small in amount, is set aside as part of the national budget, However, there were no such cases in 1958 and 1959.

ITEM 280

[Interview]

Lao was a former Party guerrilla fighter who in 1953 was accused of having actually served with a Nationalist guerrilla force prior to liberation. He was arrested and held in detention while the truth of his protestation of innocence was verified. After a number of his former Party comrades-in-arms confirmed his story, he was released. But the investigation had taken six months. In a private conversation the chief of the public security bureau apologized for the mistake and informed Lao that the bureau had awarded him six months' salary so that he would not suffer any economic loss from having been away from his job for that period.

ITEM 281

[Interview]

By the time that the Liao brothers were arrested for the murder of deputy Party secretary Tang [see Item 188D], the three original defendants, who had initially been detained on the pretext of their petty theft, had been in jail several months. Following the arrest of the Liaos, Huang, the principal public security official who handled the case, had a talk with each of the original defendants. He lectured them on the evils of theft, explained why the bureau had thought it reasonable to arrest them for the murder, and emphasized that the political-legal organs had been determined not to convict the innocent and that was why they were being released. Each of them, he said, would receive a subsidy for living expenses of ten yuan per month for each month spent in jail.

1. Would it appear from these materials that the state has an obligation to make compensation whenever it makes a mistake? Or only when a mistake results from unlawful conduct?

2. How does compensation appear to be calculated? What should it include?

3. What can one infer from the fact that compensation is seldom sought?

## D. SANCTIONS AGAINST OFFICIALS

We have already seen examples of cases in which sanctions have been imposed upon law enforcement officials for intentional or negligent violation of proper standards of conduct. Recall Item 112 and Item 268. Moreover, published rules governing the application of sanctions to state employees and to Party members have been reproduced in Item 46 and Item 43 respectively, and the guiding doctrinal precepts appear in Item 274. The materials in this section present other relevant legislative provisions and some additional interviews that describe how sanctions have been applied in concrete cases.

ITEM 282

[ARREST AND DETENTION ACT OF THE PRC (Dec. 20, 1954), p. 242]

Article 12. People's procuracies shall investigate officers responsible for unlawful arrest or detention of citizens. If this kind of unlawful act arose from malicious, retaliatory, corrupt, or other personal motives, these officers shall be pursued for criminal responsibility.

## ITEM 283

[PEOPLE'S POLICE ACT OF THE PRC (June 25, 1957), pp. 115–116]

Article 8. The state grades and ranks people's policemen in accordance with their present duties, political character, professional activity, and contributions to revolutionary undertakings.

Article 9. When people's policemen perform their duties with outstanding success, they shall be given, on an individual basis, commendation, material rewards, merit marks, early promotion, state decorations, medals, honorary titles, and other such rewards.

Article 10. People's policemen must observe prescribed discipline. Officers who violate discipline and are derelict in their duties may, on the basis of the individual circumstances of their cases, be given warning, demerit, confinement to quarters, demotion in grade, demotion in duty, removal from position, or other such disciplinary sanctions.

If violation of the law or dereliction of duty by people's policemen constitutes a crime, the case shall be sent to the people's court for adjudication. If this kind of crime constitutes a military crime, a military court shall adjudicate the case.

Recall Item 182.

## ITEM 284

[Interview]

In early 1956, during the "surging tide of socialism" in agriculture, an officer of a county public security bureau and a representative of the county procuracy went down to an administrative village to arrest a counterrevolutionary suspect. While the policeman led the suspect away, the procurator, a bachelor, having been attracted to the suspect's daughter, stayed behind and seduced her. The girl never made a complaint to the authorities, but the incident eventually became known and was reported to the public security organs. When questioned, the procurator admitted the wrongful conduct. He was expelled from the Party and removed from his position in the procuracy but kept his status as a state employee and was assigned to a post in a state book store. In view of the severe administrative sanctions meted out, he received no criminal punishment.

## ITEM 285

[Interview]

In 1956 several people's policemen bearing a warrant of arrest went to the home of a capitalist and arrested him on a charge of "inciting sabotage." They also thoroughly searched the premises, but did not purport to seize anything. A week later the arrested person was released on the ground that further investigation revealed that his misbehavior had been too minor to warrant punishment. Upon his return home, his wife informed him that, after the search, a number of their possessions could not be found. He thereupon wrote the public security bureau a polite letter stating that several things had been "lost" at his house subsequent to his arrest and asking the bureau to investigate. The bureau did promptly investigate and found that one of the arresting officers had stolen the missing articles. He was expelled both from the Communist Youth League and from the government, but was not subjected to criminal sanctions.

### ITEM 286

[Interview]

For his role in the case involving the murder of deputy Party secretary Tang [see Item 188D], Huang, the public security officer who directed the investigation, was put on probation by the Party for one year, was demoted one grade, and was required to make a self-examination before the personnel of the public security bureau's security section. The other cadres who had mishandled the case merely received criticism.

### ITEM 287

[Interview]

On the basis of an opinion by a handwriting expert of the public security department and some scanty corroboration, in 1959 Liang was arrested and convicted of writing a counterrevolutionary poster. Several months later the real offender confessed and Liang was released [see Item 272]. As a consequence, each of the public security officials who had handled Liang's case was required to conduct a "self-examination" within his unit. Their statements were assembled into a report on the case that was printed by the public security department and circulated to its cadres throughout the province as an object lesson. But no other sanctions were taken against any of the officials involved, because they had done their best and had made an honest mistake. As one of them put it, "If they had punished us for this, who would ever go investigate?"

What principles emerge from the materials in this section?

# Chapter XI  Formal Criminal Processes:
# Reform through Labor and Release

The tremendous achievements made in the work of reforming criminals through labor are manifest not only in the reform of large groups of criminals, but also in the transformation of nature, in the development of production, and in the mobilization of the criminals to serve China's socialist construction with their two hands.

Productive labor has enabled the criminals not only to change their reactionary nature but also to master . . . labor techniques, so that after they have served their terms, they can rely on their own labor in finding proper employment in society and becoming citizens living by their own labor. Therefore, it has provided another favorable condition for the thorough elimination of counterrevolution and all other criminal elements.

All this has obtained the enthusiastic praise and positive support from the broad masses of the people. The people generally said: "The old prisons [in the days of the Kuomintang] tortured people to death, but the new prisons turn bad people into good people." They thought that the labor reform work was "very good indeed" and was "right." Dependents of many criminals and those who have been released at the conclusion of their sentences are without exception truly grateful to the people's government for its revolutionary and humanitarian policy.

> Chou K'e-yung (Deputy Commissioner of Public Security Department of Kiangsi Province), "The Great Achievement Made in Work of Reforming Criminals Through Labor" [1]

1. *Chiang-hsi jih-pao* (Kiangsi daily), Dec. 17, 1959; translated in *JPRS*, 3349:101 (June 3, 1960).

For all criminals incarceration is the beginning of a long period of "education or re-education in the morals and purposes of socialist society." It is not enough that the sentence be served. The prisoner's jailer-teachers have failed unless he emerges a completely reformed man able "to distinguish between right and wrong" and ready to restart life with "the desire for unity." Is not this doctrine right out of old Calvinism — the supralapsarian conviction that Destiny (History) ordained the fall of man in order to create the opportunity for his redemption?

But the concept of law as an instrument of reform, education and ethical indoctrination is not wholly alien to traditional patterns of Chinese thought. Confucians generally believed that those who understood the difference between good and evil had the duty to teach others by positive example, as well as the duty to manage society, especially during periods of crisis. Mao's sense of ethical values churns the content of old teachings, but he also holds that man can be perfected by education. In this he is closer to Mencius, who believed that most men are inherently good, than he is to Han Fei-tzu, who believed that nine out of ten are bad, but even Han Fei-tzu agreed that man can be taught to be good — which is the underlying principle of thought reform.

In a casual conversation during my recent visit, Mao remarked (but without any reference to Confucian concepts), "Most men are good; only the minority is bad. Even bad men are not bad all the time and can be made better, just as good men can be made bad by negative example. The difficult thing is to discover what is good and how to teach it to others."

Edgar Snow, *The Other Side of the River*[2]

Both inside and outside of the People's Republic reform through labor is the most publicized aspect of the criminal process in China. Chinese publications have claimed that a blend of thought reform techniques and compulsory labor has achieved remarkable success in the correction and rehabilitation of criminal offenders. Some foreign observers have enthusiastically endorsed these claims. Others have indicted the system of penal administration for having cruelly subjected millions of prisoners to the worst of the abuses that are associated with the term "forced labor."[3]

In reading the materials in this chapter the following questions should be kept in mind:

1. To what extent does Chinese penal administration actually appear to promote each of the goals of punishment (recall Item 5)? For example, to what extent do those who administer punishment strive for individualization of treatment and emphasize correction and rehabilitation?

2. What incentives are used to stimulate prisoners to reform?

3. What significance is attached to the fixed terms of imprisonment in which most prison sentences are couched? Can they be altered:

a. To grant early release?

b. To keep prisoners in confinement beyond the term prescribed in the sentence?

2. P. 356.
3. See, e.g., Commission Internationale Contre Le Régime Concentrationnaire. *White Book on Forced Labour and Concentration Camps in the People's Republic of China*, 2 vols. (Paris, 1957–1958) and Karl A. Wittfogel, "Forced Labor in Communist China," *Problems of Communism*, 5.4:34–42 (July–August 1956).

4. What agencies make such decisions?

5. According to what criteria?

6. What procedures do they employ?

7. What is the relation of the courts to other agencies that participate in this decision-making process?

8. To what extent does the prisoner in question have an opportunity to be heard in the process?

9. What conditions circumscribe the activity of a released prisoner?

10. In what circumstances can release be revoked and according to what procedures?

## A. PLACES OF REFORM

### ITEM 288

[ACT OF THE PRC FOR REFORM THROUGH LABOR (Sept. 7, 1954), pp. 33–36, 38–40]

*Chapter 1. General Principles*

Article 1. In accordance with the provisions of Article 7 of the Common Program of the Chinese People's Political Consultative Conference, this Act is adopted specially in order to punish all counterrevolutionary and other criminal offenders and to compel them to reform themselves through labor and become new persons.

Article 2. Organs of reform through labor of the People's Republic of China are instruments of the people's democratic dictatorship and are organs for enforcement of punishment and reform of all counterrevolutionary and other criminal offenders.

Article 3. With respect to reform through labor of offenders, those whose cases have already been adjudged shall, in accordance with the nature of the crime and the seriousness of the crime and punishment, be held in prisons and reform through labor discipline groups individually established to handle the different types of offenders . . .

Article 4. Organs of reform through labor shall implement the guidelines of combining punishment and control with thought reform and of combining labor and production with political education when putting into effect reform through labor of all counterrevolutionary and other criminals.

Article 5. When holding all counterrevolutionary and other criminal offenders, organs of reform through labor shall effect strict control and must not be apathetic or relax their vigilance. Mistreatment and corporal punishment shall be strictly prohibited.

Article 6. Organs of reform through labor shall be led by people's public security organs, shall be supervised by people's procuratorial offices of the various levels, and, in matters relating to judicial business, shall be guided by people's courts of the various levels.

.    .    .    .    .

## Chapter 2. Organs of Reform Through Labor

### Section 1. Detention Houses

Article 8. Detention houses shall be [used] primarily for confining in custody offenders whose cases have not been adjudged . . .

Criminals who have been sentenced to two years or less of imprisonment and whom it is inconvenient to send to reform through labor discipline groups for execution of sentence, may be held by detention houses.

Article 10. If offenders whose cases have not been adjudged and who are confined to custody in detention houses are then sentenced to control or to labor service [outside of prison] but are exempted from imprisonment, they shall, on the basis of a judgment determined by a people's court, be sent back to their original place of residence or to the department where they originally worked, and the sentence shall be executed by the local people's government of that place or by the department where they originally worked.

. . . . .

### Section 2. Prisons

Article 13. Prisons shall be [used] primarily for holding counterrevolutionary offenders and other important criminal offenders whose cases have already been adjudged, who have been given suspended death sentences or life imprisonment, and for whom the execution of sentence by labor outside of prison would be inappropriate.

Article 14. Prison [authorities] shall strictly control offenders and also guard them closely. When necessary, offenders may be placed in solitary confinement. Under the principle of strict control and distinguishing the different circumstances of offenders, prison [authorities] shall put into effect compulsory labor and education.

Article 15. Provinces and cities shall establish prisons on the basis of actual needs, and they shall be under the jurisdiction of provincial and city people's public security organs.

Article 16. Prisons shall each have one warden and one or two deputy wardens and shall establish discipline, production, general affairs, and other such work departments under them.

### Section 3. Reform Through Labor Discipline Groups

Article 17. Reform through labor discipline groups shall hold counterrevolutionary offenders and other criminal offenders whose cases have already been adjudged and for whom labor outside of prison is appropriate.

Article 18. Reform through labor discipline groups shall organize offenders for planned participation in agriculture, industry, construction work, and other such production and shall combine labor and production and conduct political education.

Article 19. Provinces and cities shall establish reform through labor discipline groups on the basis of actual needs, and they shall be under the jurisdiction of provincial and city people's public security organs.

Article 20. Reform through labor discipline groups may establish platoons, companies, battalions, regiments, and corps, depending on the number of offenders and the needs of production. These groups shall each have a leader and a number of assistant leaders and, in accordance with the actual needs of discipline and production work, may establish work departments.

．　　．　　．　　．　　．

## Chapter 3. Reform Through Labor and Reform Through Education

Article 25. In order to make compulsory labor gradually approach voluntary labor and thereby attain the goal of reforming offenders into new persons, reform through labor must be combined with political and ideological education.

Article 26. In order to expose the essence of crime, to eliminate criminal thoughts, and to establish new concepts of morality, collective classes, individual conversations, assigned study of documents, organized discussions, and other such methods shall be regularly and systematically used to educate offenders about admitting their guilt and observing the law, about current political events, about labor and production, and about culture.

Offenders may be organized to engage in appropriate athletic and cultural recreation and in examination and discussion of their lives, their labor, and their study.

Article 27. Attention shall be paid to the cultivation of the production skills and labor habits of offenders. During reform through labor attention shall be paid to the full utilization of technical skills of offenders who have them.

Article 28. Production contests may be conducted among offenders in order to raise production efficiency and to promote in offenders a positive attitude toward reform through labor.

Article 29. In order to examine the circumstances of the reform of offenders a card file system shall be established for them. Moreover, there shall be special persons to administer this system and to record at any time the circumstances of the offenders' observance of discipline and their behavior with respect to labor and study. Evaluations shall be made periodically.

．　　．　　．　　．　　．

## Chapter 5. The System for Regulating Offenders

### Section 2. Guarding

Article 44. The people's public security armed units have exclusive responsibility for the armed guarding of offenders. Organs of reform through labor shall exercise professional leadership over the armed units performing that task.

Article 45. Areas around prison cells, areas around places where offenders work and relax, and routes by which they come and go shall be closely guarded.

Except for armed guard units and discipline personnel, no person who enters prison cells and places where offenders work and relax shall be permitted to carry weapons.

Article 46. When there is a possibility of escape, violence, or other dangerous acts on the part of offenders, upon special instructions from investigation organs or with the approval of the responsible officer of organs of reform through labor, instruments of restraint may be used. But when the above-mentioned situation is eliminated, they shall be immediately removed.

Article 47. When all other methods have been used and have proved incapable of checking the situation, organs of reform through labor and armed guard units may use weapons when they encounter any one of the following situations:

(1) A mass riot by offenders;

(2) An escaping offender disregards an order to stop or resists arrest;

(3) An offender possesses a deadly weapon or dangerous object, is in the process of committing a deadly act or destroying something, and disregards an order to stop or offers resistance;

(4) Someone takes an offender away by force or [otherwise] helps an offender to escape and disregards an order to stop;

(5) An offender forcibly seizes a guard's weapon. Every use of weapons shall be reported in detail for the examination of the people's public security organ in charge and the people's procuratorial organ.

If organs of reform through labor and armed guard units erroneously use weapons and such erroneous use constitutes a criminal act, they shall be held criminally responsible.

Article 48. When organs of reform through labor and armed guard units encounter natural disasters and accidents, they shall strive to rescue offenders and strengthen their guard.

Article 49. Organs of reform through labor shall conduct an inspection of offenders and prison cells daily. Every week or fortnight they shall conduct a major inspection.

### Section 3. Daily Life

Article 50. Standards for the clothing and food of offenders shall be imposed according to uniform provisions, and unauthorized reduction and appropriation shall be strictly prohibited.

In administering the food of offenders, they [the authorities] shall within the standards of supply, strive for variety and improvement. Moreover, they shall show concern for the habits of offenders from minority nationality groups.

Article 51. Supply stations may be established in reform through labor camps on the basis of actual needs in order to supply offenders with supplementary food and articles of daily use.

Article 52. The time for actual labor for offenders generally shall be fixed at nine to ten hours each day. With seasonal production it may not exceed twelve hours. The time for sleep generally shall be fixed at eight hours. The time for study may be fixed in accordance with concrete circumstances, but it shall not be permissible to average less than one hour a day. Sleep and study periods for juvenile offenders shall be appropriately extended. Offenders who do not participate in labor should have one to two hours a day of outdoor activities.

A day of rest for offenders shall generally be fixed at once every fortnight, for juvenile offenders once every week.

Article 53. In accordance with the size of their unit, organs of reform through labor shall establish medical dispensaries, hospitals, and other such institutions for medical treatment, and they shall have necessary medical equipment. But detention houses in counties (cities) that have few offenders may use the county hospital as a medical institution.

Attention must constantly be paid to seeing that offenders bathe, have haircuts, wash their clothes, use disinfectants, guard against contagious diseases, and take other such measures for cleanliness and sanitation.

Article 54. When an offender dies, a medical evaluation shall be made, and it shall be examined by the local people's court. Moreover, members of the offender's family and the organ that took him into custody shall be notified.

.    .    .    .    .

## Section 4. Receiving Visits and Correspondence

Article 56. Offenders shall not be permitted to receive visits from family members more than twice a month, and each visit may not exceed thirty minutes. In special circumstances, with the approval of a responsible officer of the organ of reform through labor, it [the time] may be appropriately extended. When receiving visits, use of secret languages or foreign languages shall be prohibited. When offenders from foreign countries receive visits from family members, there shall be an interpreter present.

.    .    .    .    .

Article 57. Articles of daily use or people's currency given to offenders by family members shall be carefully examined by organs of reform through labor, and the sending in of all unnecessary articles shall be prohibited. Organs of reform through labor shall register people's currency sent by members of offenders' families, keep it on their behalf, and issue a receipt to the offenders. When offenders have a proper use for the money, it may be given to them.

Article 58. Mail sent and received by offenders shall be examined by organs of reform through labor . . . If situations of collusion with regard to [the presentation of] the circumstances of a case or of hindering education and reform are discovered, the mail [involved] shall be held back.

Article 59. In special circumstances an offender's visits and receipt of articles sent by family members and the sending and receipt of mail, etc., may all be further limited or stopped.

Article 60. In any one of the following situations, an offender may be permitted to obtain a guarantor and serve his sentence outside of prison, but this must first be reviewed and approved by the people's public security organ in charge, and the people's public security organ at the place in which the offender is located must be notified to place him under supervision. The period of time that the offender serves outside of prison is counted as within his term of imprisonment.

(1) The offender is seriously ill and it is necessary for him to obtain a guarantor and seek medical treatment outside of prison; but an offender whose crime is heinous shall not be permitted to obtain a guarantor and serve his sentence outside of prison.

(2) The offender is fifty-five years of age or more or is physically disabled, his term of imprisonment is five years or less, and he has already lost the capacity to endanger society.

## ITEM 289

[Snow, *The Other Side of the River* (1962), p. 355]

．　　．　　．　　．　　．

Three kinds of detention are provided for: imprisonment in a municipal jail; work on a state reform farm; and restricted freedom or work under surveillance. Prisoners up for less than three years or more than ten are put in standard jails; those serving between three and ten years are assigned to state reform farms or mobile labor teams based on them; those sentenced for less than a year usually get "work under surveillance." This third category is for first offenders and minor crimes. The transgressor returns to his usual abode and work, but he is accountable for his daily behavior and movements to his street security committee or a group of ten fellow workers.

For details concerning the third category of criminal custody referred to above (work under surveillance), translated as "control," see Chapter V.

## ITEMS 290A–290B

## ITEM 290A

[ACT OF THE PRC FOR REFORM THROUGH LABOR (Sept. 7, 1954), pp. 33, 35]

Article 3. Houses of discipline for juvenile offenders shall be established to conduct the reform through education of juvenile offenders.

．　　．　　．　　．　　．

*Section 4. Houses of Discipline for Juvenile Offenders*

Article 21. Houses of discipline for juvenile offenders shall discipline juvenile offenders who are over the age of thirteen but who have not reached the age of eighteen.

Article 22. In educating juvenile offenders houses of discipline shall emphasize political education, education in the new morality, and education in basic culture and production skills. Moreover, they shall make juvenile offenders engage in light labor under circumstances that show concern for their physical development.

Article 23. Houses of discipline for juvenile offenders shall be established on the basis of the need for them, with provinces and cities as units, and shall be under the jurisdiction of provincial and city people's public security organs.

Article 24. Houses of discipline for juvenile offenders shall each have a director and one or two deputy directors, and they may arrange for a number of discipline officers in accordance with the needs of the work.

## ITEM 290B

["Notification of the State Council of the PRC Transmitting the Report of the Ministry of Public Security Relating to the Work of Preparing the Establishment of Houses of Discipline for Juvenile Offenders" (March 3, 1958), *FKHP*, 7:216–217 (January–June, 1958)]

The State Council agrees with the report of the Ministry of Public Security relating to the work of preparing the establishment of houses of discipline for juvenile offenders. Now this report is transmitted to you [provincial and city people's councils], and we hope that you will see that the relevant departments implement it thoroughly.

*Report of the Ministry of Public Security Relating to the Work of Preparing the Establishment of Houses of Discipline for Juvenile Offenders (February 21, 1958)*

According to reports from the various places, there are now altogether over 4500 juvenile offenders who have already been sentenced to criminal punishment. These child criminals, except for some who are held in custody in houses of discipline for juvenile offenders, at present are dispersed in prisons and reform through labor groups and are mixed together in custody with adult offenders. This way it is not only easy to be contaminated by all kinds of evil thoughts of adult offenders, but also the proper physical and moral development of the juvenile offenders may be affected. At the same time, it is felt that because of the dispersal of these juvenile offenders in the various provinces, cities, and autonomous regions, and the separate establishment of centers of discipline, the number of people [juvenile offenders involved] is small, there is a lack of teachers, and equipment is inadequate. This not only wastes manpower and material resources, but it also makes very good, effective reform difficult. In order to change this situation, even more effectively to strengthen the reform-education of juvenile offenders and correctly to implement the guideline of making reform through education the principal measure and light labor a supplementary measure, in January 1957 we and the Ministry of Education agreed to establish nine new or rebuilt houses of discipline for juvenile offenders in Changchun, Tientsin, Shanghai, Nanking, Wuhan, Sian, Chungking, Kunming, and Canton, and on an individual basis to concentrate in them for discipline juvenile offenders from nearby districts. It is estimated that they will be able to accommodate over 5000 persons. Now these houses of discipline for juvenile offenders are almost ready for use, and it is planned to begin concentrating and receiving juvenile offenders during the first quarter of this year. With respect to expenses and expenditures relating to juvenile offenders after concentration, our opinion is that this year they should in principle be carried by public security organs in the various places. After next year expenditures should come from production income. Any deficits should be offset from reform through labor expense funds of public security departments or bureaus of the place in which they [the houses of discipline] are located. If this proposal is considered appropriate, please approve and transmit it to provincial and city people's councils for them to see that the relevant departments handle the matter.

## ITEMS 291A–291B

## ITEM 291A

[Snow, *The Other Side of the River* (1962), pp. 366–368]

.    .    .    .    .

I could have found the Peking jail without a guide if anyone had told me that it was the old "model prison" I had last visited in 1935, when some students I knew were incarcerated there. It was built sixty years ago, a great improvement over the filthy windowless dungeons then in general use; that particular prison reform did not spread very far. The prison stands beyond the eastern suburbs and from a distance seemed unchanged: the same gray brick walls. But the outer gate was now open and I saw no sentries until we reached the inner wall, where one soldier stood in a pillbox. An unarmed guard opened the iron gate and Yao Wei and I passed through a flower garden into a reception room which fronted on part of the inner prison walls. The deputy warden, Mr. Wang, was a serious-minded party man in his mid-thirties who had had "special training" for his job. He offered me the usual tea and preliminary briefing.

There were "about 1,800 prisoners" of whom about 40 percent were "counter-revolutionaries" (aged mostly between thirty-five and forty-five); more than a hundred prisoners were women. Sixty of the inmates were under suspended sentences of death. The prison population had been as much as 3,000; in 1960, "more than a hundred" prisoners were released as contrasted to "seventy to eighty" new arrivals.

The prison operated three factories: a hosiery mill, a mill for plastic articles, and a machine and electrical shop. I was told that the prison routine was eight hours of shop work, two or three hours of study and lectures, eight hours of sleep, four or five hours for dining, physical exercise, reading, recreation and "discussion" (thought remolding). Prisoners got one holiday every two weeks, when they could receive visitors or do as they wished. They had their own band, an opera troupe, an outdoor theater, and movies once a week. Men and women ate in the same dining room and could attend plays and sports contests held inside the prison compound.

With that said we toured the prison cells and then the shops. The buildings were one-storied and made of brick, with two rows of cells on either side of a central aisle. I noticed that all bars had been removed from the windows and that every cell door was open. The rooms, with two to four long k'angs in each, were white and clean, and all had neat piles of bedding. One man, off on a free day, was lying in bed reading; his door was also open. He was in for two years for embezzlement of state funds.

The shops were all mechanized. Machinery was antique but better than in most urban commune shops I had seen. Women handled the knitting machines and a few worked in the plastics rooms with the men. They wore blue or black cotton clothes issued by the prison, with no special markings to differentiate them from other working people. They paid strict attention to their machines and did not look at us except when I paused here and there to ask a question; then they replied politely and not sullenly. I saw no marks of physical violence and people seemed in average good health. Some of the young women were rather pretty. I asked one of them why she was there. "Fraud," was the answer I got. I was puzzled, but the deputy warden later enlightened me.

What was different here was the "open door" policy, the absence of an armed-camp atmosphere. Shops were run by prisoner foremen supervised by prison staff members; I saw no armed guards among them. Prisoners also managed their own barber shop, mess rooms, a canteen, shower baths and a library. In various courtyards and grounds I saw half a dozen soldiers, but none was posted in guard towers or on the walls which enclosed gardens where prisoners cultivated vegetables. Perhaps the other guards were removed for my benefit? Perhaps. But Sing Sing would consider that rather risky as a public relations stunt.

"It looks easy enough to get out of here," I said to Wang. "Do many try it?"

"We've had several runaways in the past year. Usually they are brought back by their families."

.     .     .     .     .

Around the basketball court and a stage which prisoners had built were bulletin boards posted with *ta tzu-pao* [large character posters] such as you see before any Chinese factory; essays, rhymes, praise and mutual criticism, lists of model workers and their awards. Prisoners got no wages but received an allowance of three yuan a month pocket money, which they could double by outstanding work. The money bought a few cigarettes or other items in the canteen. The kitchen was preparing a noon meal of soup, spinach and steamed bread which looked like a Salvation Army handout.

## ITEM 291B

[Mu Fu-sheng, *The Wilting of the Hundred Flowers* (1963), p. 178]

Perhaps China is the only country in the world that has really open prisons. One mad prisoner in south China, an ex-Kuomintang officer, threatened to escape. The warden came to explain to him he was free to do so and the guards were instructed to let him pass. The erratic man really walked out, but found he could not get into a hotel without credentials, he could not buy a long-distance bus-ticket without a letter of introduction from the organization he belonged to, he could not stay with his relatives because he had no rice ration cards, he could not sell or pawn his belongings to the shops without explaining why he wanted to sell them, he could not work without a trade-union card, he could not eat in the restaurants because they were very expensive, and he could not rob or steal because members of the cadre were everywhere and they could order anyone to assist in his arrest. After a few days he went back to the prison weak and hungry and asked to be admitted.

## B. THE PROCESS OF REFORM

### ITEM 292

[Meng Chao-liang, "The Basic Situation in Reform Through Labor Work in the Last Nine Years," *CFYC*, 5:66–67, 68, 69 (1958)]

Reform through labor, a component of public security work, has been established gradually by following the instructions of the Party Central Committee and Chairman Mao and by intimate coordination with the movement for suppressing counterrevolution and the struggle attacking crime. Through the second movement for suppressing counterrevolution throughout the country during 1955, reform through labor work was further developed.

In the last nine years, the work of reforming criminals through labor has, under the correct leadership of Party committees and public security organs of the various levels, firmly and thoroughly executed the guidelines and policies prescribed by the Central Committee. Politically and economically, it has had remarkable accomplishments.

The policy of putting reform through labor into effect for criminals sentenced to imprisonment is an important aspect of the policy of liquidating counterrevolution. It is also an important means of the state for putting dictatorship into effect over the enemy and for thoroughly exterminating counterrevolution.

Our aims in reforming criminals are to eliminate their reactionary standpoint and viewpoint, to enable them to establish new ideological and moral qualities and to learn productive skills that meet the needs of society, and to do our utmost in reforming them into excellent laborers who walk the socialist road and who participate in socialist construction.

In order to realize the above-mentioned aims, we take productive labor beneficial to society as the fundamental means for reforming criminals. Because the great majority of criminals lived an exploiting and parasitic life in the past, productive labor has eliminated their reactionary standpoint and viewpoint and has played a decisive role in establishing new moral qualities.

On the basis of productive labor, we have effectively educated criminals in political ideology. In carrying out education, and in order to elevate the effect of ideological reform, we have intimately grasped fundamental principles that are related to actualities, that is, related to the facts of the offender's evil and the cause of the crime, the labor practice and the ideology of the offender during the process of reform, the rapid development of socialist construction in our country, and the change in the international and internal political situation.

In ordinary ideological education, we have emphatically educated criminals about admitting their guilt and obeying the law, about current affairs and policy, and about their future prospects. The experience of the last few years has told us that to make criminals admit their guilt and obey the law is the first sign that ideologically they are disarmed and ready to surrender. It is also the minimum condition under which they would accept reform ideologically. Therefore all organs of reform through labor have first educated offenders beginning reform through labor about admitting their guilt and obeying the law. Moreover, in coordination with the social reform movements of every period, they rouse offenders to confess and to make denunciations. This has compelled the offenders to make further confessions, admit their evil crimes, and honestly accept reform. At the same time, during the movements these offenders have also disclosed and handed over a great number of clues about enemy secret agents, hidden guns, ammunition, and other materials, and they have forcefully coordinated with the struggle for liquidating counterrevolution and attacking crime. On earth, the eastern wind has overwhelmed the western. The rapid development of socialist reform and of the undertakings of socialist construction in our country has played an extremely important role in reforming the reactionary ideological standpoint of criminals. Organs of reform through labor have for several years been using favorable domestic and foreign situations energetically and penetratingly to educate offenders about current affairs and policy. This has had a really conspicuous effect. At the same time that we have been educating criminals, we have invited people from within society to report actual circumstances to them, and we have roused members of the criminals' families, relatives and friends of the criminals, those [ex-criminals] who, having served their sentence, have been released and have become model laborers in state-operated enterprises, and activists to do the same. We have organized these criminals according to plan and have sent them into society to observe so that they see with their own eyes the rapid development of and change in our country — 1000 *li* in one day — and cannot but be really convinced. As a result of their observations many criminals, after comparing the new China with the old one, have been so moved as to cry bitterly and to express their determination to correct their past wrongs and to become new persons. They have thus profoundly realized that the leadership of the Communist Party over the entire people has already really enabled the country to walk the road of prosperity, affluence, and strength, while they themselves can have that opportunity only by relinquishing their reactionary standpoint and thoroughly reforming. At the same time, they have recognized the unity of their own reformed future and the future of socialist development. In other words, under the principle of suppressing criminals, many different forms must be adopted for the necessary and thorough reasoning-education which will enable the offenders to recognize the truth and to eliminate their reactionary viewpoint.

Combining labor and production and political education and conducting organized and planned education in production skills and cultural education play active and important roles insofar as the aim of reforming criminals into excellent laborers is concerned.

In reforming criminals suitable methods must be adopted. In the last few years we have adopted the methods of: criticizing, comparing, and evaluating periodically; launching criticism and self-criticism; launching labor competition; rousing criminals to make reasonable suggestions; in reform through labor production fully utilizing criminals who have scientific technical knowledge, rewarding criminals for inventing and creating production techniques; concretely prescribing various reward systems, thoroughly stimulating the activists among the criminals and thereby utilizing criminals who have demonstrated their activism to censure those who are backward and to set in motion those in the middle. Moreover, we have organized them to struggle with those who have resisted and undermined reform. Facts have proved that in order to reform criminals effectively we must, with compulsory reform as a possible last resort, encourage their self-awareness in accepting reform. We must, under the condition of unremunerated labor, give them the necessary guarantees for material life. While attacking the firm reactionary elements among the criminals and their activities, we should pay attention to winning over the great majority by education. These experiences tell us that without coercion and without punitive restraints upon their unlawful acts criminals cannot be reformed. At the same time, only by enabling offenders to advance from the stage of compulsory reform to the stage of voluntary reform, that is, to negate themselves, can their reactionary thinking be really eliminated and can counterrevolution be thoroughly eradicated.

Reforming the reactionary standpoint and viewpoint of the criminals is a long-term, repetitive, and difficult process of struggle, and it is also a sharp class struggle in political ideology. Facts have proved that since domestic and foreign reactionaries still exist and since class struggle still exists, the illusions of criminals in custody have still not been completely destroyed. Their political ideology has been changing with the class struggle situation and the state of the development of our work. As the class struggle situation has fluctuated, the criminals' state of being reactionary and destructive has surfaced and submerged. When their state of being reactionary and destructive surfaces, a few of them should be firmly suppressed, attacked, and punished, but the great majority should be won over by education. When their state of being reactionary and destructive is relatively submerged and when the time is favorable for hastening the reform of criminals, we should, under the principle of not relaxing our revolutionary vigilance, adopt measures for further encouraging activism and self-awareness in criminals undergoing reform through labor . . .

Reform through labor agriculture is largely established along rivers, in lake regions, in saline or alkaline regions, and in dry regions with extremely inconvenient transportation. It has encountered great difficulties in technology and material supplies. The cadres who are engaged in reform through labor work lead the offenders to scarcely populated, barren land. They eat simple food and sleep in the open. By means of hoes and ploughs they surround the lakes with fields, dig ditches for removing the alkali, open rivers and canals and ultimately conquer the rivers, lakes, salt, alkali, and dryness, reform nature, open up a large amount of barren land, and produce much food, cotton, and livestock. Reforming nature not only makes the vast [number of] cadres happy about their victory, it also makes a great majority of the criminals recognize the truth that labor creates the world. This shows that the process is as follows: in the course of reforming criminals, nature is reformed; and in the process of reforming nature, the criminals are reformed (the production of reform through labor industry and of construction work has the same significance).

In the last few years various work teams have participated in the construction of many well-known railroads and water utilization projects. House construction work teams were mainly [formed] for the purpose of serving basic construction of reform through labor production. They themselves built what they used and saved a great deal of capital. This shows that organizing offenders to engage in productive labor not only plays a decisive role with respect to their reform, it also has great economic significance.

.    .    .    .    .

The various places have responded to the present extremely favorable situation and the newly changed political ideology of the criminals by immediately following up the work of last winter and this spring, the work of attacking criminals who resisted reform. They have energetically conducted formal education and have launched an ideological reform movement the central content of which discourages destructiveness and passiveness and encourages progressiveness and activism. Moreover, they have also started productive labor competition among the offenders which discourages waste and conservatism and encourages progressiveness, speed, and thrift. They have called upon the offenders "to admit their guilt, to give over their hearts for good production and to proceed with the two-fold reform — reform through labor and ideological reform"; and they have stimulated the activism of the great majority of criminals in reform through labor. "The double-anti movement" that was launched among offenders by the various reform through labor movements of the city of Tientsin not only disclosed more than 50,000 cases of waste and of passive conduct, it stopped up the wasteful holes and also twisted the passive feelings of offenders who were attacked and struggled against last winter. This greatly heightened activism and stimulated a leap forward in production. In the first ten days of "the double-anti movement," the hardware workshop of Tientsin prison successively set fifty-nine production records. It increased the volume of production five times and modified the original production plan four times. The volume of production leaped forward from the 750,000 dozen of the original annual plan to two million dozen. Especially important is the fact that some obstinately backward offenders who in the past had passively dragged along, consistently unable to fulfill their production tasks and even feigning illness to evade labor, had begun to change in "the double-anti movement." Some groups of criminals voluntarily proposed mutual guarantees of carrying out the "five noes," namely, no nonfulfillment of the fixed amount, no passive dragging along, no resistance to reform, no flunking studies, and no work injuries or incidents. This had very great significance in eliminating the bad ideology of the offenders and in stimulating their reform. Some districts have had great results in conducting the movement for criminals to admit their guilt and give over their hearts. The Yü-lin Machinery Plant of Kwangsi, after having roused the offenders "consciously to give over their hearts" in six days came up with these problems: 284 persons thought of insurrection, 34 thought of escape, 261 were suspicious of the government and its policies, 299 had not admitted their guilt, and 22 were dissatisfied with the government and hostile toward the cadres and the masses. There were still other offenders who disclosed evil crimes which they had not confessed in the past. On the Ch'eng-ling-chi farm of Hunan province, 70 percent of the offenders wrote resolutions to the government guaranteeing "to change themselves down to their very bones," to reform themselves and to become new persons.

## ITEM 293

[Interview]

In late 1958 Tai, a university student who had been declared a "rightist" and given "supervised labor," was sentenced to two years of reform through labor for having committed theft and having failed to work hard during the period of supervision. He was assigned to a labor camp at a coal mine. By day he was required to work underground in the mine. At night he had to participate in a study group that, in addition to engaging in the usual indoctrination processes, often held struggle meetings against members of the group who were regarded as lazy or dishonest. Persons receiving "rehabilitation through labor" also served at the mine, but their work was not so arduous as that given to those who received reform through labor. Moreover, the former were paid wages while the latter were not, they were allowed to mail as many letters as they liked instead of a single postcard each month, and they were not guarded so closely as the latter.

After almost two years at the coal mine, Tai was transferred to labor in an iron mine. Shortly thereafter, he was assigned to a full-time "study class" for several weeks of intensive ideological training. This was climaxed by an interview with a Party official whose job it was to verify each prisoner's "progress." Following the interview the Party official gave Tai a note to deliver to the administration of the iron mine. It said that Tai was fit to be released and to return home. In turn the mine authorities gave Tai a document to present to his university Party committee. It stated that he was being released and was to remain under the supervision of the university Party committee. Upon returning to the university, Tai was assigned to labor on the university vegetable farm, but he was otherwise not placed under any supervision.

## ITEM 294

[A. Doak Barnett, *Communist China: The Early Years, 1949–55* (New York, Washington, D.C., and London, 1964), pp. 89–99, 102–103]

.    .    .    .    .

## GROUP INDOCTRINATION

March 1954

The revolution in China is a process of struggle. It is a struggle not only to "reform" society but also to capture and "remold" the minds of one-fifth of the human race. The Chinese Communists' aim is mass ideological conversion and creation of the "new socialist man" — a man who rejects the past and accepts an entirely new code of Communist "truth" and morality.

Indoctrination, which strikes at the innermost recesses of the mind, is therefore given equal priority with industrialization, collectivization, and similar programs that attack the political, economic, and social structure. The Chinese Communists believe that if minds can be controlled, and basic ways of thinking changed, their revolutionary struggle can be won.

Considerable attention has been devoted by the Western press to the intensive "thought reform" carried out by the Chinese Communists on a few imprisoned foreign missionaries, businessmen, and prisoners of war. Some of these men, whose minds and wills were broken by the strains of powerful mental pressures, have described how they were forced or persuaded to make false confessions.

Much less attention has been given, however, to the methods of indoctrination the Communists are using to assault the minds of their own people — not only the imprisoned minority who are considered "enemies" by the regime, but the mass of ordinary people of all sorts: workers, students, government employees, intellectuals, business employees, housewives, and farmers.

The Chinese Communists use many methods of thought control. Formal education is, of course, important. The entire educational system in China has been reorganized and its content changed. A new generation is being nurtured on strictly controlled fare rationed by the Communist leaders. Propaganda media of all sorts are important, too. The Communists attempt to control everything that is capable of conveying ideas and symbols. This control is designed to place strict limitations upon the ideas to which people are exposed, and since thought does not take place in a vacuum, the elimination of heterodox ideas from the intellectual marketplace is an important means of thought control.

One of the most distinctive and successful means the Communists are using in their ideological struggle, however, is group indoctrination. It is group indoctrination that they employ to give political training to the new elite of the country — the students, *kanpu*, government workers, and Party members. Group indoctrination is the basis for campaigns to change the outlook and attitudes of entire classes — campaigns such as the "ideological reform" of the intellectuals carried on during 1951–52. And it is also used in prisons to "reform" or at least to cow the actual or potential "enemies" of the regime — "reactionaries" and "counter-revolutionaries." In effect, virtually everyone in China is exposed to group indoctrination in some form or other. Primary attention is devoted to youth and "intellectuals" in the broadest sense, and the urban population is more thoroughly organized for indoctrination than people in the countryside, but no group is exempted.

The term used throughout Communist China for group indoctrination is *hsueh hsi* or "study" (literally, *hsueh hsi* means "to learn and practice"). The origin of this phrase is traceable to Confucius, who says, in Chapter I of the Analects (using the words *hsueh* and *hsi*): "Is it not pleasant to learn with constant perseverance and application?" But the phrase was little used in modern times until the Communists adopted it for their indoctrination methods, and it now has harsher, sterner connotations. Actually, the Communists use *hsueh hsi* to refer to all political study, including individual "self-study," but in common usage it has become almost synonymous with collective group study, which is given primary stress by the regime.

*Hsueh hsi* has become an essential part of the fabric of society and the way of life in Communist China. Every day, millions of Chinese gather together in small groups of a half-dozen to a dozen people — in factories, shops, schools, and offices — to *hsueh hsi* the ideology and policies of the Communist regime. These organizational cells are a direct link between the Communist rulers of China and the brain cells of masses of ordinary people.

During the past three years, I have talked with many Chinese refugees in Hong Kong who have taken part in *hsueh hsi* groups in Communist China. What they describe is not "study" in any sense in which the word is understood in non-Communist countries; it is a unique process of manipulating minds and organizing social pressure to force acceptance of the new philosophy and ideology sponsored by the Communists. The individual in a *hsueh hsi* group must think, but he does not think independently; his mind is shaped by the pressures within the group. Clearly, the Chinese Communists have hit upon a method of indoctrination that reveals great intuitive insight into subtle psychological principles and principles of "group dynamics," applied to political purposes.

"You can't think clearly, even if you think you can, when you are taking part in intensive *hsueh hsi*," one former newspaper editor, now in his forties, said to me. "You instinctively realize that your real thoughts will some day pop out of your mouth and that therefore to be safe you either have to change your real thoughts or not think at all."

"Most students began to change after undergoing *hsueh hsi*," said a young girl who had just been graduated from a university in Communist China. "Only a small percentage stuck to any old beliefs. That doesn't mean, however, that this 'change' was really 'conversion' in many cases. For most students, there wasn't much to convert; they had no firm or well-developed ideology; they were an ideological blank. The 'change,' therefore, was an acceptance of new ideas which filled a vacuum."

"It is difficult to know how much the Communists are able really to change people's thinking," another *hsueh hsi* participant said to me, "but there is no doubt that at least they break down almost everyone's resistance to the new ideas."

A young man who had actually joined the CCP after his indoctrination told me: "*Hsueh hsi* is very effective. I was impressed by the theory and the ideas I learned. It was only later, when I began to see differences between theory and practice, that I became disillusioned."

From these and other persons who have belonged to *hsueh hsi* groups in Communist China, one can learn how *hsueh hsi* groups operate — in what way they are organized, how they function, what they study. There are many variations in details; at one extreme, these groups are used in special training courses where *hsueh hsi* is carried on six or eight hours a day for many months; at the other extreme, in some offices or organizations, the groups may meet for a weekly one-hour session only. But there are certain basic principles that seem to apply to all *hsueh hsi* groups.

One of these, an essential, is the principle that the "study" is collective, a group effort. Not only is it possible for the regime to reach and control much larger numbers of people through groups than it could individually, but the fundamental nature of the Chinese Communists' indoctrination methods requires group action. The Communists do not trust the individual, or believe that the individual can be allowed to function as an independent unit, even in his thinking.

*Hsueh hsi* groups are small: sometimes as few as six members, rarely more than twelve. The groups have continuity. There is definite membership, and the same people meet together over an extended period of time. Their meetings are regular and periodic, whether several times daily or only once every few days. One of the most common practices of *hsueh hsi* groups, particularly in large organizations, is to meet for an hour a day, either before or after regular working hours.

Although participation in *hsueh hsi* groups is sometimes described as "voluntary," the pressures to take part make it compulsory in fact. If a person shows reluctance, he is criticized as being "backward and unprogressive," and he is not left in peace until he shows a more cooperative attitude. Often, however, there is no attempt to maintain the fiction of voluntariness; all members of a large organization are simply assigned to small *hsueh hsi* groups.

*Hsueh hsi* groups do not function as isolated or independent organizations. They are always established on the initiative of higher authorities. (In any particular area, ultimate responsibility for them usually rests in the hands of educational organs in the government and propaganda organs in the Party.) Each group is tied into a network of similar groups and is responsible to a hierarchy of leaders or committees which exercises direct supervision and control over it. In many organizations or local areas, for example, about ten small groups (*hsueh hsi hsiao tsu*) are grouped into a larger unit (*fen tui* or *ta k'o*), and above these larger units are committees linking them to the ultimate local authority for their schedule of meetings, subjects to be discussed, material to be read, lectures to be attended, and so on. And the small groups submit regular reports to the organizational hierarchy above them. When the members of any one small group gather for their regular meetings and discussion, therefore, they know in most cases that thousands of other people like them are meeting simultaneously in similar groups, discussing the same topics. They are merely one small unit in a tremendous, organized "captive audience."

Each *hsueh hsi* group has a leader, and sometimes there is also an assistant leader. In most cases, the group leader is "elected," but people who have participated in the groups report that "the Communists have ways of getting the people they want into positions of group leaders." If the group contains a Party or Youth League member, an "activist," or a known "progressive" (and where possible, they are organized so that at least one such person is included in each group), this person usually emerges as the leader. If a clearly undesirable leader is elected, the authorities veto him; in extreme cases, they may break up and reorganize a group that shows its "backwardness" by choosing a suspect leader.

The group leader is a direct link with authority, through the organizational hierarchy above the *hsueh hsi* groups. He carries out instructions from above. He supervises discussion sessions. He takes notes on the meetings and makes regular reports (sometimes written, sometimes verbal) to those above him. He is supposed to learn everything about each member in his group and watch with care the development of his ideas and attitudes. He represents the eyes and ears of the regime and is a personification of the conscience of the group.

The role of the group leader in the whole scheme of small-group *hsueh hsi* is extremely important. Responsible to authorities, he symbolizes the power of the regime, and although he is expected to lead and guide in a restrained manner, his mere presence in the group ensures control. On all questions discussed, he is the ultimate arbiter and oracle of the "correct," orthodox "truth" — or if he himself does not have the answer to a question, he is the pipeline to higher authorities who do.

Another basic principle of this group indoctrination is the fact that discussion is the essence of the process. "Studying" is not conceived of as a matter of passively listening to lectures or privately reading books and other written materials. Thoughts and ideas must be expressed verbally, and there must be interchange and interaction among all members of a group. Lectures and reading play a role in the process, but primarily to provide a springboard for group discussion. And even in lectures and reading, the emphasis is upon collective rather than individual activity. Lectures are attended en masse, and very often textual source materials are read aloud in the study groups. (One technique is for the group leader to read a text, paragraph by paragraph, with prolonged group discussion after each paragraph.)

Every member is expected to participate actively in discussion within the groups. This is extremely important. There are no passive observers; there is no neutrality or indifference. If a group member appears to stay aloof, it is the responsibility not only of the leader but also of all other members of the group to arouse and involve this laggard, to criticize his backwardness, to solicit his views. This necessity for active participation means that every member of the group is involved in the indoctrination process in a positive way, must be mentally alert throughout the meetings, and must bare his mental "self" to group scrutiny.

The pattern of discussion in the groups has peculiarities of its own. "Free discussion" and strict control are combined in a unique formula. Abstract theory is linked to personal attitudes and experience. Criticism and self-criticism are used to bring all members of the group into a complicated interrelationship in which they exert a mutual influence upon each other. The confessions involved in self-criticism give the discussion a strong emotional flavor, making it something quite different from a primarily intellectual discussion.

One fundamental premise of all the discussion is that for every problem or question there is a "correct" solution or answer. The "truth" is contained in "scientific Marxism," as defined by the Party, and the problem is to understand and accept the Communists' basic theories of historical and social change, to relate these to current social, economic, political, and international issues, and to adapt one's own behavior to this theoretical framework. It is also assumed that no one — even old Party members — has progressed as far as is theoretically possible in understanding this "truth" and in fully relating one's personal life to it.

This means that for average members of a *hsueh hsi* group, the whole aim of discussion is focused upon the necessity of repudiating past beliefs, discovering what it is that the Communist regime now requires them to believe, rejecting all competing ideas, and expressing — at least verbally — full acceptance of the "correct" dogma.

Discussion always centers on one, or a few, specific ideas or ideological problems. More often than not, they are quite abstract theoretical or philosophical questions. The following are typical examples, taken from a study outline for one *hsueh hsi* group of university students:

"Selfishness is natural; the working class is also selfish." "If the individual is slightly selfish, that is all right as long as he does not interfere with other people." Why are these thoughts the selfish and self-profiting ideology of the petty bourgeoisie? Are they influenced by feudalistic or capitalistic ideology?

The revolutionary outlook on life is one involving examination of one's life from a revolutionary standpoint. Revolution is the meaning of life. One lives for the revolution. Why? How do you understand this now? In the past?

From a class viewpoint, what is your opinion of internationalism and patriotism? Patriotism is certainly related to internationalism. Why? By what steps did you come to an understanding of this question?

Why do the ideas of "being a sympathizer with the working people" and having a "new viewpoint of showing gratitude" reveal that you really do not yet understand that the laborer is the master of history and the masses are the real heroes? Why are these ideas merely petty-bourgeois humanitarianism and salvationism? Examine yourself to see if you have such thoughts.

Of course, not all of the discussion concerns broad questions of attitude and outlook such as these. *Hsueh hsi* groups also discuss current events, government policies, and concrete problems related to the work of group members. But the broad ideological questions are looked upon as of fundamental importance.

As already stated, lectures and reading of prescribed texts (books, pamphlets, newspaper editorials, or specially mimeographed material) play a part in *hsueh hsi* and usually precede discussion. In some situations, normal procedure is for several *hsueh hsi* groups to meet together and listen to a speech, which may last two to four hours, or for all the group members to read the basic writings on a particular question, either individually or collectively.

The lectures and reading provide the raw material for discussion and pose the problems or questions to be discussed. The presentation is often highly "dialectical" — full of "on the one hand" and "on the other hand," outlining wrong answers and the right one, listing rightist and leftist deviations and defining the "correct" view.

Upon analysis, one interesting fact about this preparation for discussion becomes clear. At the very start, everyone in a *hsueh hsi* group knows what the right answer to the question under discussion is; it is contained, either explicitly or implicitly, in the speeches that group members have heard or in the material they have read. Yet the members of a *hsueh hsi* group then proceed to spend hours, and sometimes weeks, in discussion that will end where it began. In short, the discussion is not a genuine search for unknown answers to difficult questions and problems; it is a process of clarifying and obtaining acceptance of answers that are defined at the beginning.

What happens, then, during the course of lengthy discussion of a topic? Essentially, there is a detailed examination of every conceivable aspect of a question; an attempt to bring into the open and refute all possible objections, counterarguments, and doubts concerning the "correct" line; an effort to get each group member to renounce any reservations about accepting the orthodox view; and finally insistence that each member of the group openly express full acceptance of the officially sanctioned "truth" and try to relate this to his personal life.

Even if every member of a group is inclined to accept the prescribed ideas at the start of discussion on a particular subject, the process of discussion cannot be dispensed with. Group members must rack their brains to raise problems and doubts, even if they have to invent them, so that they can be properly disposed of.

If a group member genuinely disagrees with the "correct" line, and persists in resisting conversion, it is the responsibility of all members of the group to criticize him, argue against him, and prove him to be wrong. If they do not speak up, this fact may be interpreted by the group leader as indicating that they share the mistaken ideas of the maverick.

The result, therefore, is mobilization of intense social pressure within the group to achieve total conformity. In a sense, every member of a *hsueh hsi* group is a minority of one being worked on by all the rest. Some of the groups are composed of people who may all be skeptical of the Communist line, yet in these groups a remarkable phenomenon occurs: Eight or ten skeptics all exert pressure on each other to become believers — under the watchful eyes of the group leader.

Persons who have participated in *hsueh hsi* describe a subtle but deep undercurrent of tension, suspicion, and fear that exists, at least in many of the groups. Each group member realizes that the discussion is a test of his ability or willingness to accept the official ideology of the regime. He realizes also that the Communist authorities demand acceptance of their ideology and that in the long run he either must give in or risk subjection to further, more intensive indoctrination. If a person is really stubborn, he may be sent to a jail for "re-education" — or worse — and everyone knows this.

The pressures upon a group member's mind during discussion are by no means all negative, however. Constant repetition of ideas hammers them into one's mind and leads to an increasing willingness to accept and believe. Hearing the other group members argue in support of the "correct" line; a person begins to think, "Maybe, after all, they're right and I'm wrong." The pressure to verbalize arguments supporting the official line, even if one is skeptical, begins to create a readiness to accept the ideas. And all possible arguments to support the Communist-approved answers to problems are mobilized during the course of the group discussion.

The final aim of discussion on any question is open acceptance, by each and every member of the group, of the official ideas and viewpoint, and this is usually achieved. Even those who have participated in *hsueh hsi* groups, however, find it difficult to assess the real effects of all this upon members of such a group. In some cases, genuine conversion and full acceptance of the ideas are achieved. At the other extreme, verbal acceptance in some cases is obviously a fraud, and people begin living a double life mentally — espousing one set of ideas openly, but clinging to another set privately. Many people probably fall into categories between these extremes. But one thing is clearly and indisputably achieved: open expression of intellectual submission to the official line of the regime. Whether a person is actually converted or secretly persists in maintaining intellectual independence, almost all admit by their verbal acceptance of the "correct" views that they are subservient to the regime.

Discussion of any one major subject by a *hsueh hsi* group usually ends with a summary of all that has been said. In special intensive indoctrination courses, the course comes to a climax when each participant writes what is called an "ideological résumé" (*szu hsiang tsung chieh*). Criticism and self-criticism are essential components of the process of group indoctrination, and they reach their apex in these ideological résumés.

An ideological résumé is usually a long document, of several thousand words, in which an individual recounts his whole past life (childhood, class status, education, work, activities of all sorts) and previous thoughts and attitudes, confesses all those aspects that did not live up to what the Communists define as ideal, and describes how he has now renounced the past and has been converted.

Sometimes, several weeks are devoted to preparation of these documents. Each individual in a group first works alone on preparation of a résumé. The drafts are then circulated among members of the group, who write criticisms and suggestions. They are then revised, and subsequently each member reads his résumé to the group, which critically examines and discusses it in detail. The individual is probed to see to what extent he has completely revealed all of his past, confessed all of his errors, and actually presented convincing proof of having really changed and become a new man ideologically. Almost always, a résumé is rejected by the group after the first reading, and the individual is told to improve it and make it more complete. Sometimes, a person must revise and expand his résumé two or three times before it is finally accepted by the group and then by the hierarchy of authority above the group.

Everyone I have talked with who has written an ideological résumé states that it is a devastating experience, that the necessity of dissecting and denouncing one's past breaks down one's integrity as an individual. The problem of justifying oneself, and supporting the claim that genuine ideological change has taken place, puts a great mental strain upon a person. It is not uncommon for an individual to lose several pounds during the period he is preparing and defending his ideological résumé.

The final approved résumé is kept on file by the authorities, and according to some people it becomes the basis of a permanent dossier on one's thinking following a person from place to place and job to job. The sincerity of a person's claims about past and present thoughts can be periodically checked by referring to his ideological résumé and looking for inconsistencies between past and present statements.

The most effective indoctrination is obviously achieved in the full-time, intensive *hsueh hsi* schools, whose students are usually persons slated to work for the regime and whose aim is complete "thought reform." In such schools, the small group is the basis of the students' entire life; not only *hsueh hsi* as such but all other activities are carried out collectively. The schedule of activities of the schools, furthermore, is designed to occupy all of the students' time and energy, and for periods ranging from a few weeks to several months the students spend almost the whole of every day in discussion sessions designed fully to "remold" their minds.

The most intensive process of all is that applied to prisoners in Chinese Communist "re-education" [labor reform] jails. The treatment of these prisoners — including Westerners — is rather different in its psychological basis, however, from the *hsueh hsi* undergone by ordinary people. Fear, intimidation, and threats play a much greater and more obvious role here than in ordinary *hsueh hsi*, although they are certainly present in every *hsueh hsi* group . . .

The experiences of men such as these [prisoners] indicate that the Communists have developed psychological techniques that can "break" men's minds as well as "remold" them. The emphasis in most *hsueh hsi* is upon remolding minds, however, and this is what the Chinese Communists are trying to do on such a wide scale.

·    ·    ·    ·    ·

The insight into subtle psychological techniques and group pressures revealed by present methods of *hsueh hsi* also is surprising. It makes one wonder if Communist leaders in their caves at Yenan were reading Freud and Jung as well as Marx and Lenin, although there is certainly no evidence that this was the case.

Undoubtedly, the entire program developed in China slowly on the basis of both Soviet and Chinese experience, but there is no doubt that *hsueh hsi* and the great emphasis placed upon remolding the thinking of the entire population in China are now in many respects unique aspects of the Chinese Communist regime.

How effective is this group indoctrination, and how much success are the Communists actually having in their efforts to accomplish a mass ideological conversion?

One can answer, at the start, that group indoctrination has been very successful in achieving surface conformity in the thinking of the Chinese people. They are being taught the new ideology, and they are expressing verbal acceptance of it. But it is extremely difficult to know what actually goes on in the minds of those indoctrinated. How many genuinely believe the new ideology? How many people's minds are confused by a combination of partial belief and doubt? How many people "believe" only because of the unremitting psychological and social pressures upon them? What would happen if the pressures were lifted? How many have built walls around their minds and have tried to stop thinking? How many cling stubbornly to old beliefs despite the necessity of approving the new ones verbally?

It is almost impossible to answer these questions with any confidence, although undoubtedly there are people who fit each of these categories.

Recall Item 249. For another comparison between reform through labor and rehabilitation through labor, recall Item 90C.

## ITEM 295

[Rickett and Rickett, *Prisoners of Liberation* (1957), pp. 195–202, x–xiii]

.     .     .     .     .

We looked up with more than ordinary interest when a new arrival was ushered into the cell . . .

After introducing himself as Li Cheng-ming, he explained briefly in answer to Liao's questions that he had been arrested for providing information to Nationalist agents. He appeared to be a completely inoffensive little fellow, but from the first I felt there was something sly about his movements and the furtive way he avoided meeting one's gaze. During class he had little to say but would sit nervously working his long, feminine fingers, sometimes flexing the joints, sometimes rubbing the tips with his thumbs, sometimes bending them backward as if they were made of rubber. I took this as just an idiosyncrasy, although it did seem strange to me that he always picked things up between his middle and index fingers rather than with his thumb and index finger as people normally do. It did not take Liao, with his secret police training, long to spot it, however.

A couple of days after his arrival, while we were playing cards, Li picked up one of them in his peculiar manner. Leaning forward quickly Liao snatched it out of his hand. "What are you doing?" he roared. "So you're a dip. I knew there was something fishy about you from the start."

Li squirmed and looked around desperately as though trying to find escape, but as Liao pressed the point he admitted to being a professional pickpocket. From then on, every time any one of us noticed Li working his fingers or picking up things in an unnatural way we would immediately pounce on him, but all our shouting, arguing, and lecturing seemed to do little good. The crisis came one day when Li was caught with a silk handkerchief he had stolen from Han. We stopped our regular study immediately to concentrate on "helping" Li. It was a futile attempt, for his only reaction was a frightened silence.

The following day Liao took the matter up with Supervisor Shen. When he had heard the story through the supervisor nodded and said, "We know all about Li. He was trained that way as a child. These habits of his have become so ingrained they cannot be changed overnight. We'll put him in handcuffs to make him realize it's a serious matter, but when you help him, make him tell why he did it."

Shortly after Liao returned to the cell the supervisor came and took Li away to put handcuffs on him. While he was gone Liao told us what the supervisor had said. "Simply reprimanding him won't do any good," he explained. "We've got to dig deep into the reasons why he does these things."

When Li returned, hands pinned behind his back, Liao immediately began by asking, "Why did you steal that handkerchief?"

Li hung his head and replied in a weak voice, "I don't know."

"What do you mean you don't know? You took it, didn't you? You must have had a reason for it. Why did you take it?"

"Because I wanted it," was the hesitant reply.

"Wanted it!" everyone roared in unison. "Was it yours?"

"No."

"Why did you want it?"

Li was silent.

"Answer," shouted someone. "Why did you take that handkerchief?"

"Because I didn't have one."

"Is that any excuse for taking something that belongs to someone else?"

"No."

"Then why did you take it?"

On we went, trying to make Li think out himself why he was addicted to stealing, but we were able only to scratch the surface. We could go only so far and then Li would say he did not know. We still could not get him to think out why he had become a habitual criminal, how he looked upon stealing itself, or what his justifications for it were. Largely this was our fault, because at that time we knew too little about Li to be able to penetrate deep into his motivations.

After two days we gave up, on the promise from Li that he would never steal again. Then, after a long lecture by each cell member on the contemptibility of stealing, and warnings that if he kept on he was certain to be treated severely because in the new society there was no place for criminals, the matter was dropped and the handcuffs removed. A few days later Li was transferred to another cell.

It was a couple of years before I saw Li again, but in the meantime I heard that he had been caught stealing once more. This time he was put into handcuffs and ankle chains and, with help from prisoners who had come to know him better, he had been forced to make a thoroughgoing self-criticism. The question of why and the search for the chain of cause and effect had gone deep. Layer after layer of his motivations had gradually come to light, until the heart of the matter had been reached.

Li, as a child, had been abandoned by his parents and picked up by a gang of thieves. At first he was used as a beggar, and then, because of his slight build, to wriggle through small windows and openings in walls to rob houses. Later he had been taught the art of a pickpocket. Whatever he got was turned over to the gang. He was virtually their slave, and when he displeased them was beaten and starved.

He had lived in a realm of fear: fear of his masters, fear of the police, fear of everything around him. Even when he had grown up and become a full-fledged member of the gang his situation changed little. He had been caught several times and once imprisoned for many months by Nationalist police. They had let him loose only after he had paid the usual bribe and consented to work for them as a stool pigeon.

After liberation he had been arrested once as a pickpocket, but had been allowed to go after promising to reform. However, with no conception of how to work for a living, he had quickly drifted back to the only things he knew — stealing, informing, and running away. As his pathetic story had unfolded he had broken into tears and had begun to realize the hopelessness and sordidness of his former life. He realized that he had never looked upon stealing itself as something wrong. For him it was just a way of making a living. He had never really hurt anybody. Other people all had more than he had. If he could get away with it, why shouldn't he? Being a pickpocket was as much an art as that of a juggler, magician, or storyteller.

His cell mates then reasoned with him that there was nothing that did not come about through someone's labor, and that stealing the fruits of another man's work was criminal. How would he like it if he had been forced to work all day and then was given no reward for it at all? They managed to break down Li's fear a little and helped him come to understand his relationship to society and the wrongness of what he had been doing. Other people had been able to live honestly, free of fear and contempt. Why hadn't he? Partly, they said, it was because of his own desire to get something for nothing, but for the most part it was the old society which was to blame.

Thus, while never being allowed to forget that he himself had been wrong, Li developed a passionate hatred for the old society which had produced not only himself but countless others like him. The dream of a world in which there would be no fear or want became almost an obsession with him.

The authorities then did what seemed a strange thing. This spineless pickpocket, the dregs of humanity, was made leader of a cell. For the first time in his life he was given some responsibility and a position of respect. In coming to a realization of his own background he found that he could help others and in so doing help himself. His fears gradually disappeared almost completely.

I hardly recognized Li the next time I saw him, almost two years later, when we were exercising in the same compound. He seemed inches taller and when he looked at you it was straight in the eye. There was not a shadow of his former cringing self. I heard he had joined the prison literacy classes and applied himself so well that he could now read and write. Just before I was released I read in the prison newspaper that he had been given an award for a proposal he had made for increasing production in the prison sock factory. I had no doubt that he was well on his way toward building a new life and would soon be released.

Although Li's problem was a special one in that he was a habitual criminal, the process of his reform was in many ways typical of what happened to most of the men in the prison. The American reader who is acquainted with modern psychiatric techniques has undoubtedly noted strong similarities between the methods used in helping Li and the rest of us to reform through criticism and self-criticism and those used in group therapy here in the United States. Yet it was clear from my experience with both the authorities and the prisoners themselves that none of these people had any systematic training in psychology.

Indeed, as far as I know, the Chinese have never tried to work out the techniques of thought reform in the sense of a textbook science. Rather, the entire process seems to have developed in a rule-of-thumb manner based on a common-sense insight into human character, something for which the Chinese have always been noted, a concept of self-criticism borrowed from general Marxian practice and techniques which grew out of the need to reform the troops and intellectuals in the early days of the revolution.

The nearest approach to an organized theoretical basis for thought reform is to be found in Mao Tse-tung's two philosophical treatises, "On Contradictions" and "On Practice," and his various essays dealing with the practical application of Marxist principles to human relations. In these works as well as those of Liu Shao-chi, who next to Mao Tse-tung is considered China's leading Marxist theoretician, the stress is placed on the necessity for using criticism and self-criticism as a means to foster personal honesty and social responsibility. These are supplemented by numerous articles in newspapers and magazines describing particular problems, such as selfishness, graft, male supremacy, conservatism, and the manner in which certain individuals overcome them.

Though this group activity of thought reform was going on all over China, it perhaps found its most systematic application in prison, where the process was concentrated to an intense degree. Where, on the outside, participation in thought reform was largely voluntary, with the only force that of social pressure, in prison it was a matter of compulsion. Therefore the actual process could be observed more clearly there. In our discussion and talks with the authorities certain basic concepts were emphasized again and again.

The point of departure in almost every one of our discussions on thought reform was the premise that the individual is a product of his environment, both from the point of view of the historical period into which he is born and the class to which he belongs. From birth he begins to develop mental habits which reflect his material surroundings. The old, highly competitive class society presented the individual with a constant struggle for his own survival and thus instilled in him a highly self-centered set of mental habits and outlooks. At the same time this society set up certain ideals of conduct which it considered necessary for the preservation of workable human relations.

The Judeo-Christian doctrines of the Ten Commandments and the Golden Rule found their counterpart in China in the Six Confucian Standards of Behavior and the saying, "Do not do unto others what you would not have them do unto you."

It is only natural that the individual, then, would be faced constantly with contradictions between what society presented to him as morally true and what experience in daily life clearly demonstrated was pragmatically true. Such contradictions existed for everyone, but they were particularly sharp among members of the old ruling classes who had to resolve the problem of preaching industriousness, thrift, and morality to others while living in idle luxury themselves.

In order to resolve these contradictions the individual would build up a set of rationalizations which he used to justify his every action. The housewife who did not tell the butcher when he had undercharged her, the clerk who made personal use of office supplies, the politician who embezzled millions of the taxpayers' money, and the general who ordered the annihilation of a defenseless population — all had their excuses.

It was no different for any of us in prison. Even though we had been forced to confess our crimes, we too all had our excuses. Thus the first step in our reform was to break down our justifications and rationalizations and make us face up to our true selves. To do this the attack was launched on two fronts. Our study discussions provided us with a yardstick to measure the rightness or wrongness of our actions. This yardstick was basic socialist morality. That is to say, what is best for the greatest number of people in a specific historical context determines right from wrong.

Under socialism — the goal of the Chinese revolution — with the elimination of man's exploitation of man, the individual is no longer compelled to engage in a life-and-death struggle against the rest of society. It then becomes possible in practice for men to live by the ideal of the Golden Rule and seek their own personal happiness within the common good. Self-criticism forced us to take this yardstick and compare our own actions and attitudes with it by criticizing them.

Merely being able to criticize, however, did not mean that one had reformed. Mental habits are not so easily changed. It requires a long and constant struggle and a sincere desire to change on the part of the individual himself. Many people in prison, after overcoming their initial distaste for revealing their shortcomings before others, became what we called chronic confessors. They would confess endlessly but never change. Most often this was because they were not interested in reforming but only in making a good impression on the authorities. Some would also resort to confession merely to gain emotional release from the stress and strain of prison life.

Most prisoners at some time or other went through a stage in which, though somewhat conscious of it, they had no genuine understanding of their guilt. Therefore they tended to indulge in highly emotional exaggerations of their crimes without trying to bring about any real change in their character. Their situation often resembled that of the alcoholic who may be sincerely alarmed about his condition and most vehement in his promises to swear off drinking, but still, because he lacks any real understanding of his problem, is never quite able to do so.

In line with this almost every prisoner met with the problem of having his original rationalization broken down only to find he had built up a new set to justify the old habit. This again was like the alcoholic who, having come to realize the fallacy in his former rationalization "I know how to handle my liquor," substitutes as a new rationalization, "*One* little drink won't hurt."

Therefore it was only when a prisoner ceased confessing for confession's sake or setting up false rationalizations and began to understand his true self and the harm his actions had caused others that he could develop a real desire to reform. At this point he could begin to struggle against his old, selfish, anti-social habits and outlooks and replace them with a new sense of social responsibility. In describing this process the analogy was sometimes made to teaching a person to throw a ball correctly after he had acquired the habit of throwing it incorrectly. Even though such a person may realize his mistake, his instinctive reaction is to continue to throw in the old way until an entirely new set of muscles and reflexes have been developed.

For the drifter elements who made up the vast majority of counterrevolutionaries in the detention quarters reform was particularly difficult because they had spent most of their lives trying to get something for nothing. Never having taken part in productive work, they not only had to be impressed with the necessity and desirability of becoming constructive members of society but had to be taught how to do so. This was the reason for the labor reform which most of the prisoners took part in after leaving Tsao-lan-tzu Hu-tung [the prison]. The pickpocket Li was typical in the sense that his reform went through all these stages.

·    ·    ·    ·    ·

[Publishers' introduction]

·    ·    ·    ·    ·

However, admitting the pressure of jail and the moral pressure of felt guilt, readers are still left with the question as to how the Chinese could have brought about such a basic change in the political and social outlook of the Ricketts. Perhaps the "brainwashing" we have heard so much about is a reality. Is it really possible, one might ask, to deprive a person of his normal mental processes and stuff his mind full of alien ideas and principles which he will accept as his own and put into practice from then on? Our advising psychiatrist commented on this question as follows:

"The most convincing answer to this question is to read the Ricketts' own carefully documented account of their long experience in prison. It is perfectly true that the Chinese government set out to re-educate them, but this re-education was not accomplished with pills, drugs or any hocus-pocus whatsoever.

"The Ricketts and the other prisoners in the jail were re-educated in the only way that such re-education can be accomplished, namely, as a result of a long, slow, and tedious examination of themselves and their past social milieu, together with an attempt to live and practice a new type of life. In other words, they were re-educated the hard way, by a perfectly understandable process.

"The educational processes followed by the Chinese include a fascinating mixture of enlightened penal methods, work and occupational therapy, group therapy, and conventional methods of study. In reading this account one is struck by the similarity of some of these Chinese methods to the procedures developed in the early years of the Soviet Union by Makarenko in his pioneering work with juvenile delinquents. Makarenko's work is known and his principles of correction are followed in enlightened penal institutions the world over and thus were probably known to the Chinese. However, in reading this work one is impressed by the probability that the Chinese supervisory personnel were devoted and enthusiastic amateurs who learned a great deal as they went along. Their methods of re-education followed principles of general political indoctrination to be found in their own revolutionary literature.

"These principles were applied in the framework of a humanitarian, socialist morality which guided their approach to the individual prisoners. It is my opinion that this morality was the decisive force in their ability to tame, persuade and re-educate hundreds of thousands of anti-social elements. Without this morality the jails would not have been emptied in a few years."

One sees the specific applications of this morality in many different ways: the respect for the dignity of the individual prisoners; the concept of punishment *as education* and not as revenge or mere physical deterrent; the criticism of the *acts* of an individual without *condemnation* of his inner, most personal self; the constant emphasis on the ability of humans to change; the emphasis on the common, basic rights of mankind; the emphasis on the moral questions involved in every act; the emphasis on giving the prisoners something positive to work for; the emphasis on giving them first the hope and then the understanding that they, too, could be integrated into a decent world and at last be friends with their fellow man.

This morality was inherent in the dignity and self-restraint of the prison personnel; in their approachability; in their solicitude for the welfare of the individual; in their obvious attempt to handle each person as a separate and distinct problem; in their own participation in self-criticism; in the fact that prisoners could make complaints against the personnel and these complaints would be listened to and acted upon; in the fact that the prison personnel had no more heat nor better food than their charges, etc. The fact that the prison keepers lived by the same ethical principles which they were attempting to teach the prisoners was undoubtedly the largest single factor in the re-education of so many delinquent individuals.

The processes of change which took place in the Ricketts' personalities are similar to the events which take place in an individual undergoing successful psychotherapy. A change took place in their evaluation of their background; in their understanding of themselves; in their ethical concepts of life; in their attitudes and motivations, and consequently in their relationships to people. In commenting on this our psychiatric consultant wrote:

"This did not happen quickly. The process was long and painfully slow, with many backslidings. The Ricketts were under great social and personal pressure to change. Many of the stages they underwent are comparable to a person in treatment. They developed anxiety; they became introspective; they began to see things intellectually before they could feel them or apply them; they developed a true shame as contrasted to the false guilt of the neurotic. They went through stages of commencing to see their problems before they could see any solutions, and this depressed and upset them. Then, as they commenced to envisage a new way of life they also began to grasp some of the *new* problems and contradictions that would result from that way, and this created new doubts, anxieties and hesitations.

"However, it would be wrong to pursue this analogy, tempting as it may superficially appear, too far. The Ricketts were not neurotic and the Chinese government was not practicing psychiatry or psychotherapy. It was engaged in re-educating and reconstructing delinquent individuals on a wholesale basis and while individual psychotherapy is also a process of re-education and life re-construction, it is conducted by different techniques, on different types of individuals and for different purposes."

For a more comprehensive and less sanguine psychiatric evaluation of the thought reform efforts made during the PRC's early years, see generally Robert Jay Lifton, *Thought Reform and the Psychology of Totalism, A Study of "Brainwashing" in China.*

## ITEM 296

[Snow, *The Other Side of the River* (1962), pp. 369–370]

.     .     .     .     .

The theory holds, and the law supports it, that the starting point for all prisoners is sincere repentance, recognition of the crime, and welcome of the sentence as "good." Until this happened they were kept under stricter confine-ment. The next step was the "genuine desire" to reform. Many prisoners were "really ignorant and understood nothing about the revolution or what the govern-ment was trying to do for the people." Tours were organized to take them to visit communes, factories and schools, to show them the good things being done and to awaken "a sense of shame." Illiterates were taught to read and write and all attended political lectures. Much of the education and indoctrination was done by "advanced" prisoners put into cells with new arrivals and backward ones. Truly "reformed" prisoners received special privileges; the more successful their political work the better their chances of release. By means of cadres organized within the prison blocks, order and disciplined study were maintained. Political prisoners did the same shop work as others but were subjected to much more intensified thought remolding in cells led by reformed "politicos."

Mr. Wang said that in the great majority of cases prisoners who made political progress were also the best shop workers. Their chances of getting good jobs on release were improved by both their technical education and their ideological remolding. Stubborn cases might take as long as a year or two before beginning to see the light. In only a few instances did prisoners refuse to "recognize the roots of their errors"; if these silent resisters worked well and were not political prisoners they would also be released when their sentences expired, although there was no chance for a shortened term. Punishment consisted of overtime work or loss of holidays, but Wang maintained that violence was never used and that solitary confinement "in no case exceeded a week."

## C. NEGATIVE INCENTIVES TO REFORM

### ITEM 297

[ACT OF THE PRC FOR REFORM THROUGH LABOR (Sept. 7, 1954), pp. 41–42]

*Chapter 7. Rewards and Punishments*

Article 67. In order to enable offenders to establish their merit and atone for their crimes, a reward and punishment system with clearly defined rewards and punishments shall be put into effect.

Article 69. In any one of the following situations offenders may, on the basis of the different circumstances of each case, be given warning, demerit, confinement to quarters or other such punishment:

(1) They hinder the reform of other offenders;

(2) They do not take care of or they damage instruments of production;

(3) They are lazy or deliberately work slowly;

(4) They engage in other acts that violate the rules of administration.

Article 71. On the basis of the seriousness of the circumstances of each case, organs of reform through labor shall [decide whether to] recommend that the local people's court sentence, in accordance with law, offenders who commit any one of the following crimes while they are being held by those organs:

(1) Rioting or committing deadly acts or inciting others to commit deadly acts;

(2) Escaping or organizing escapes;

(3) Destroying construction work or important public property;

(4) Openly resisting labor despite repeated education;

(5) Engaging in other acts that seriously violate the law.

Article 72. When major counterrevolutionary offenders, habitual robbers, habitual thieves, and other offenders who, during the period of their reform through labor, do not labor actively but repeatedly violate prison rules, and the facts prove that they still have not reformed and that there is a real possibility that they will continue to endanger the security of society after release, before their term of imprisonment expires organs of reform through labor may submit to the people's security organ in charge the suggestion that their reform through labor be continued; after the suggestion is reviewed by the public security organ and after the offenders are sentenced by the local people's court in accordance with law, their reform through labor shall be continued.

Article 73. If, after they receive punishment, offenders really demonstrate that they have reformed and that they repent, their punishment may be reduced or terminated, according to the degree of their reform and repentance.

## ITEM 298

[Interview]

Hu was a well-educated technician of bourgeois background who worked in a factory in Canton. In 1956 he was convicted of putting up counterrevolutionary posters and was sentenced to five years of imprisonment. After an appeal was rejected, he began to speak "strange [anti-Communist] words" at labor camp. Upon the recommendation of the reform through labor authorities, the sentencing court increased the punishment in Hu's case to eight years of imprisonment. Hu subsequently escaped but was caught in Canton and sent back to the camp. As punishment for the escape the court increased his sentence by another seven years to make a total sentence of fifteen years. When informed of this, Hu began to shout reactionary slogans such as "down with Mao" and was placed in solitary confinement. One day when the guard brought his food, Hu beat him severely with a big stick and tried unsuccessfully to escape again. For this he was sentenced to death and was executed before the entire group of prisoners at the labor camp. The case also received widespread newspaper publicity.

Recall Item 269.

## D. POSITIVE INCENTIVES TO REFORM

### 1. Reduction of Sentence and Conditional Release

## ITEM 299

[ACT OF THE PRC FOR REFORM THROUGH LABOR (Sept. 7, 1954), pp. 41–42]

Article 68. Offenders in any one of the following situations may, on the basis of different behavior, be given a commendation, material reward, merit mark, reduction of sentence, conditional release, or other such reward:

(1) They habitually observe discipline, diligently study, and really demonstrate that they have repented and reformed;

(2) They dissuade other offenders from unlawful conduct, or information given by them denouncing counterrevolutionary organizations and activity inside or outside prisons is confirmed through investigation;

(3) They actively labor and fulfill or overfulfill production tasks;

(4) They have special accomplishments in conserving raw materials and taking care of public property;

(5) They diligently study technical skills and specially demonstrate inventiveness, creativity, or [ability in] teaching their own technical skills to others;

(6) They eliminate disasters or major incidents and avoid loss [to the people];

(7) They engage in other acts that are beneficial to the people and the state.

Article 70. The rewards and punishments prescribed in Articles 68 and 69 shall be announced and given after review and approval by a responsible officer of the organ of reform through labor. But, for reduction of sentence or conditional release, a recommendation of the organ of reform through labor must be submitted to the people's public security organ in charge for review and then sent to the local provincial or city people's court for approval, announcement and execution.

## ITEM 300

[*Lectures* (September 1957), pp. 185–186]

Many offenders are continuing to confess and admit offenses which they had concealed when they were questioned and are taking the initiative in denouncing counterrevolutionary and other criminals still in society who endanger the people. According to incomplete statistics from Shensi and eight other provinces, in the winter of 1953 offenders getting reform through labor training in those places revealed, through confessions and denunciations, clues to 2,503 hidden rifles and pistols, 34,276 rounds of ammunition, and 33,182 items relating to other cases. Most of these clues were verified, and played a large role in advancing and coordinating various social reform movements.

## ITEMS 301A–301B

## ITEM 301A

[Interview]

Liang was married to a Nationalist secret agent who in 1958 persuaded her to carry a bomb in her belongings on one of her trips from their home in Macao to Chung-shan county in Kwangtung province. She was instructed to plant the bomb under a bridge but became frightened en route and left it at a recreation center. It went off and injured two members of the local security defense committee. Liang was caught when the public security forces detained all those who had recently arrived from Macao, and, being inexperienced, she promptly confessed.

The High People's Court of Kwangtung province convicted her of current counterrevolutionary activity and, after approval by the Supreme People's Court, sentenced her to death. When informed of the sentence, Liang wept and revealed for the first time that she was pregnant. After a medical examination the court ordered that execution of the sentence be suspended until an appropriate time after the birth of her child.

While awaiting the child's arrival Liang unsuccessfully appealed the conviction to the Supreme People's Court. Subsequently she established her "merit" by informing on another secret agent, and after the birth of her child her death sentence was commuted to life imprisonment.

ITEM 301B

[Interview]

Mrs. Hu was convicted of beating up her mother-in-law during a violent quarrel. Because the victim had suffered serious injuries, Hu was sentenced to fourteen months of imprisonment. Hu was six months pregnant at the time of sentencing, however, so the court suspended execution of the sentence for nine months. When she gave birth to a boy, her mother-in-law's attitude toward her softened, and harmony was restored in the household. Afterward, her husband and her mother-in-law wrote letters to the public security bureau and the court detailing these favorable developments and asking that the judgment in Hu's case be annulled. The bureau and the court sent cadres down to Hu's village to investigate the truthfulness of these assertions. After receiving confirmation from these cadres, the court annulled the judgment.

ITEM 302

[Audrey R. Topping, "Through Darkest Red China," *New York Times Magazine,* Aug. 28, 1966, p. 92]

.    .    .    .    .

"[In the spring of 1966 the warden of Nanking political prison] . . . related the personal histories of some of the prisoners, among them a 62-year-old "counterrevolutionary" named Kuo Ban-pei. "He committed many crimes when he was secretary general, in Hupei, of the Nationalist Government," said the warden. "He was also chief of the Secret Service and secretary to the Minister of National Defense. Kuo was arrested in 1951 and sentenced to death.

"In jail he confessed. He showed that he wanted to change his ideology and his execution was put off and changed to a prolonged period in jail. He showed signs of improving and in 1955 we reduced his sentence to 17 years. . . . This year we were able to reduce it another two years and his prison term is now soon over." The warden seemed proud of the story.

ITEM 303

[*Lectures* (September 1957), pp. 251, 253–255]

.    .    .    .    .

Reduction of sentence reduces or shortens the punishment to which criminals in the process of reform through labor have originally been sentenced, and it is applied after they have demonstrated repentance and reform and established their merit. For example, a relatively severe method of punishment is reduced to a relatively light punishment, or a relatively long term of imprisonment to a relatively short term of imprisonment.

Reduction of sentence is not the same as changing a judgment. It does not upset the original judgment's determination of facts or the punishment [pre-scribed] in the sentence and make a new judgment. Rather, it reduces or shortens the punishment after original judgment has been rendered and is based on the new circumstances of the offender's demonstrating repentance and reform and establishing merit while serving his sentence. From this it can be seen that a reduction of sentence takes the original judgment as its basis. Changing judgment, on the other hand, is [sometimes required] because there is an error in the original judgment. Therefore the original judgment is annulled and the case is adjudged anew. They [reduction of sentence and changing a judgment] are different in principle and should not be confused.

Reduction of sentence also differs from conditional release. If a criminal is released because of a reduction of his sentence and then commits a new crime, the reduced part [of his previous sentence] cannot be executed again. Under these circumstances, however, the people's court may consider severely punishing him for the new crime in accordance with the provisions dealing with recidivists. But if a criminal who has been conditionally released commits a new crime during the period of conditional release, then his conditional release must be revoked and the remaining term of imprisonment and the punishment for his new crime combined and executed. The legal consequences of the two [reduction of sentence and conditional release] are different.

Reduction of sentence and conditional release may both be applied to a criminal. In other words, conditional release may be applied to a criminal after his sentence has been reduced.

.  .  .  .  .  .

When reduction of sentence is applied to a criminal, the questions of how much the sentence can be reduced each time, how many times it can be reduced, to what extent the original punishment can be reduced by repeated reductions, etc., are not specifically prescribed by the central government. The practices in the various places are inconsistent . . .

According to our understanding of the above and in order not to create confusing situations in the execution of punishment when reduction of sentence is applied, we believe that when an offender's sentence of imprisonment for a fixed term or his sentence of detention is reduced once or several times, the minimum term of imprisonment actually executed should not be less than one half of the original term of imprisonment. When an offender's sentence of life imprisonment is reduced, the minimum term of imprisonment actually executed should not be less than ten years of imprisonment (if it is the first reduction, the minimum should not be less than fifteen years of imprisonment) . . .

According to the provision of Article 70 of the Act for Reform Through Labor, reduction of a criminal's sentence should be recommended by the organ of reform through labor, submitted to the people's public security organ in charge for review, and then sent to the local provincial (city) high people's court for approval, announcement, and execution. In the past, some organs of reform through labor and public security organs have made their own decisions to apply reduction of sentence. This violates the procedure prescribed by law.

As for the question of calculating the term of imprisonment after reduction of sentence, on June 29, 1954, the Supreme People's Court and the Ministry of Justice in Instructions Relating to the Question of Whether the Judgment May

Be Changed in a Case in Which the Offender Has Been Sentenced to Life Imprisonment or to a Relatively Long Term of Imprisonment and [If So], after It Has Been Changed, from What Day the Term of Imprisonment Should Be Calculated, pointed out that after reduction of sentence the term of imprisonment should be calculated from the day when, after the original judgment has been rendered, sentence is pronounced. That is, [the portion of] the punishment already executed before the reduction of sentence should be included in the term of the reduced sentence. For instance, Chang was originally sentenced to life imprisonment, and his sentence was pronounced on February 1, 1950. On March 1, 1954, because he demonstrated repentance and reform and established his merit during reform through labor, his sentence was reduced to fifteen years of imprisonment. The term of his reduced sentence still should be calculated from February 1, 1950. That is, the executed four years and one month should be included in the reduced fifteen-year term of imprisonment.

## ITEM 304

["At the Request of the Reform Through Labor Department of the Public Security Bureau, the Tientsin City High Court Granted Conditional Release or Reduction of Sentence to Criminals Who Demonstrated Their Repentance and Reform," *Hsin wan pao* (New evening news, Tientsin), Aug. 5, 1956]

Recently, the responsible officer of the reform through labor department of the Tientsin city public security bureau requested the Tientsin city high people's court to grant conditional release or reduction of sentence to some of the criminals who really demonstrated repentance and reform during the period of reform through labor. After examining each case on an individual basis, the city high people's court granted early release, conditional release, or reduction of sentence to those criminals according to law. At the same time, the department of reform through labor of the city public security bureau awarded merits, material rewards, and honors to some other criminals who behaved relatively well in the course of reform through labor.

Those criminals who were granted conditional release or reduction of sentence had all committed different kinds of criminal acts endangering the people. During the period of reform through labor, they were relatively conscientious in observing discipline and diligent in study, and they actually expressed repentance with respect to the crimes they had committed. Some criminals established their merit by denouncing counterrevolutionary organizations and activity or achieving outstanding records in fulfilling production tasks, conserving raw materials, and protecting public property. For instance, in 1953 a hoodlum and traitor named Kao Po-hai was sentenced to twelve years of imprisonment. During the period of the Japanese puppets he consistently oppressed the masses, contributed money which he had exacted from the people to the Japanese in order to flatter them, and procured prostitutes for the use of the Japanese. In the past several years, because of reform through labor and the inspiration of the government's policy, he gradually came to recognize his past evils, actively participated in labor, and honestly accepted reform. Since his arrest by the government, he has denounced a great many persons, and some of this information has already been verified. Therefore, in accordance with the request of the department of reform through labor of the city public security bureau, the city high people's court ordered reduction of his sentence by four years. During the period that he held reactionary offices such as director of the second branch of the Japanese Tientsin police office, director of the first branch and director of the western suburb branch of the Peking police office, traitor Pao Hsin-yüan voluntarily served the enemy, unscrupulously oppressed the people and made use of his official position to sell opium and practice extortion. In 1951, he was sentenced to fifteen years of imprisonment. In the past several years, including the period of his reform through labor, he repeatedly fulfilled the prescribed production quotas before the deadline and actively engaged in studying skills and increasing the efficiency of his work. He courageously revealed some thefts committed by offenders while in prison and thus prevented the loss of some public property. He was treated leniently; his sentence was also reduced by four years. Ku Chin-te, who was granted conditional release, had been a feudal leader of local despots at the Ta-ku salt fields during the period of Kuomintang reactionary rule, and later had joined the "Central Statistical Bureau" [a Kuomintang intelligence organization]. He had consistently exploited workers and had seized over 120 persons for service in the Kuomintang army. After liberation, he had refused to register and had corruptly taken the dues of workers' union members valued at more than 1400 catties of corn. In 1951, he was sentenced to ten years of imprisonment. During the period of his reform through labor, he observed the discipline of reform through labor and denounced more than twenty persons. While undergoing reform through labor at the Tientsin Steel Factory, he submitted several proposals for nationalizing [production] . . . and thus increasing the capacity of the steel furnaces and saving a large amount of coal for the state. Ku Chin-te still has four years and eight months of his sentence to serve. According to the order of the city high people's court, if during the period of his conditional release, he can obey the supervision of the people and not commit a new crime, his remaining sentence will be considered served. However, if he commits a new crime, the city high people's court will not only sentence him to imprisonment according to law for the new crime but will also add the period of his conditional release to that sentence. Wu Hung-lin, who was released early, was formerly an agent of the "Central Statistical Bureau" and was sentenced to ten years of imprisonment. During the period of Kuomintang reactionary rule, he organized a counterfeit workers' union in the Tientsin Bicycle Factory, fomented disputes among workers, and sabotaged the workers' movement. After liberation, he destroyed his reactionary documents and continued to spread rumors. During the period of his reform through labor, he gradually recognized the seriousness of his own evil acts and expressed deep disgust at his criminal conduct of betraying the interests of the worker class. He therefore made a radical change in his character and actively participated in labor. He was willing to study a skill, to protect and to maintain machines, and to use waste materials to make tools. When he heard the news that he would be released four years and eight months early, he was extremely grateful for the lenient handling of the government and became speechless. He indicated that his response to the Communist Party and the people's government would be to do his best to become a genuinely useful citizen in society.

ITEM 305

[*Lectures* (September 1957), pp. 255, 256–259]

.    .    .    .    .

Conditional release[4] is the early release under given conditions of criminals sentenced to imprisonment who demonstrate repentance and reform during their term of imprisonment, prove that they have reformed, and convince the people's court that they will not again endanger society.

Conditional release is not the same as "obtaining a guarantor and serving sentence outside of prison." According to the provisions of Article 60 of the Act for Reform Through Labor, an organ of reform through labor, with the approval of a public security organ, may permit an offender to obtain a guarantor and serve his sentence outside of prison if he is seriously ill and it is necessary for him to seek medical treatment outside of prison (except for an offender whose crime is heinous), or if he is fifty-five years of age or more or is physically disabled, if his term of imprisonment is five years or less, and if he has lost the capacity to endanger society. The period served outside of prison is counted as within his term of imprisonment. From this it can be seen that obtaining a guarantor and serving sentence outside of prison is only applicable to offenders whose physiological conditions are not suited to their serving their sentences in prison because they are seriously ill, old, or physically disabled. When the conditions for obtaining a guarantor and serving sentence outside of prison no longer exist (for example, the illness is cured), although the offender has not committed a new crime during the period served outside of prison, he must return to prison to serve the remaining term of imprisonment. Conditional release, on the other hand, is the early release of a criminal on the basis of his having demonstrated repentance and reform. If a new crime is not committed during the period of conditional release, then the remaining term of imprisonment need not be executed.

. . . But how much of the term of punishment should be executed before conditional release may be applied? In a Joint Reply to the Former Department of Justice in East China Relating to Questions of Reduction of Sentence, Conditional Release, Restoration of Rights and Appeal for Counterrevolutionary Offenders, the Central Ministry of Justice pointed out in December 1950: "A counterrevolutionary offender may be conditionally released. But if his sentence is life imprisonment, fifteen years or more of the sentence must be executed, and if his sentence is imprisonment for a fixed term, two thirds or more of the term of imprisonment must be executed . . ." In practice, conditional release for criminals sentenced to life imprisonment is rarely used. This is because even

4. The authors of the *Lectures* have appended this footnote: "The term conditional release was introduced from Japan. Although it is not sufficiently precise or common, it has been used in our country for a long time. Therefore we might as well use this phrase."

if a criminal was sentenced to life imprisonment in 1949, up to now the executed term of imprisonment would still not exceed eight years. Thus we still lack experience in this area. As for putting conditional release into effect for criminals who have been sentenced to imprisonment for a fixed term, although the practice is not entirely consistent, generally one half or more of the term of imprisonment must be executed. We believe that this is appropriate. The question of how much of the term of life imprisonment must be executed before conditional release may be put into effect is worth study. On the basis of the possibility of reforming criminals and on the basis of the spirit of the policy of leniency which is at present in effect, we believe that with respect to criminals (including counter-revolutionary and other criminals) who have been sentenced to life imprison-ment, it would be even more appropriate [than the fifteen-year standard of the Joint Reply] if conditional release were put into effect after ten years or more of their term of imprisonment had been executed. Of course, before the instructions of the Central Ministry of Justice are changed or replaced by other new laws or decrees, we still should deal with the question of conditional release for counter-revolutionary criminals sentenced to life imprisonment on the basis of those in-structions.

.     .     .     .     .

On the whole, the prerequisites for conditional release are that the criminal demonstrate sincere repentance and reform and prove that his ideology has really been reformed so as to convince the people's court that he will no longer endanger society. These are the most essential prerequisites.

Some people advocate not applying conditional release to counterrevolution-ary and other major criminals. We do not agree with this point of view. The people's courts apply punishment to ordinary criminals in order to punish and reform them and to prevent crime. It is the same for counterrevolutionary criminals. We encourage ordinary criminals to reform themselves, and at the same time we should also encourage counterrevolutionary and other major criminals to reform themselves. Moreover, if a counterrevolutionary criminal sentenced to imprisonment satisfies the prerequisites for conditional release while serving his sentence and he is conditionally released, this is advantageous to splitting and disintegrating the enemy, and it conforms to the interests of the state and people.

A characteristic of conditional release is that the state does not completely lose the possibility of continuing to execute the unexecuted [portion of the] punishment against the criminal who has been conditionally released. If he commits a new crime, the execution of the punishment should be continued. Thus, if the period is not prescribed, the criminal who has been conditionally released will be kept in a perpetual state [of anxiety] over the possibility that the execution of the punishment may be continued. At the same time, if the criminal has not committed a new crime within a given period, this shows that he has been reformed and there is no longer any need to continue the execution of the punishment. Therefore, it is completely necessary to make appropriate regulations for the period of conditional release. But how should the appropriate period of conditional release be determined? The law still has no express provisions about this. In practice, the unexecuted portion of the punishment is generally taken as the period of conditional release. For instance, a certain person was sentenced to ten years of imprisonment, and after six years of the sentence had been executed he was conditionally released. The period of his conditional release is thus four years. We believe that this practice is appropriate and reasonable. As for life imprisonment, there is, of course, no way to determine the remaining period. But no matter what the period of conditional release, it cannot be unlimited. In accordance with what has previously been said, in cases of life imprisonment, ten years or more [of the sentence] should be executed before conditional release may be put into effect. We believe that the period of conditional release in this case may also be fixed at ten years. Because the social danger of criminals who have been sentenced to life imprisonment is relatively great and their wickedness relatively deep, it is rather appropriate to decide upon a ten-year test period.

.    .    .    .

With regard to the question of supervising an offender who has been conditionally released, we believe that during the period of conditional release he may be treated in the same way as an offender whose sentence has been declared suspended and that the methods of examination in cases of suspension of sentence may be applied.

As for the question of whether or not an offender who has been conditionally released has political rights during the period of conditional release, the Central Ministry of Justice on May 20, 1950, in the Explanation Relating to the Questions of Conditional Release, Suspension of Sentence and Deprivation of Rights of Citizens, pointed out that this question should be decided by judgment of the court. If the original judgment deprived the offender of his political rights, then he does not have political rights during the period of conditional release. If the original judgment did not deprive him of his political rights, then he has political rights during the period of conditional release. It cannot be considered that an offender who has been conditionally released automatically does not have political rights. When an offender who has been conditionally released has been deprived of his political rights, the period of deprivation is to be calculated from the day conditional release begins. When conditional release is granted to an offender who was sentenced to life imprisonment and deprived of his political rights, the court that decided upon the conditional release should at the same time decide upon the [length of the] period during which he is to be deprived of his political rights.

The period of conditional release is to be calculated from the day conditional release begins.

.    .    .    .

## ITEM 306

["High People's Court of the Province Grants Early Release to a Number of Women Offenders," *Shan-hsi jih-pao* (Shensi daily), Sept. 11, 1956]

In response to the request of the department of reform through labor, the people's court of Shensi province, after conducting a review, ordered the conditional release of women offenders who have really demonstrated their repentance and reform during the period of reform through labor. The court released some of them on August 6. The reform through labor organ gave the released offenders funds for travel and living expenses corresponding to the respective distances to their homes.

Some of the released women offenders, because of dissatisfaction with marriages arranged under the old society's system and because of insufficient awareness, had committed adultery and, in collusion with their lovers, murdered their husbands. Others had consistently despised labor, lived in a degenerate way, and engaged in stealing. Still others had become counterrevolutionaries after being lured by counterrevolutionaries into *I Kuan Tao* [a secret society] and actively engaging in its activities. However, during the period of their reform through labor, they admitted their errors and the evils which they had committed, affirmatively recognized their crimes, obeyed the law, actively engaged in labor, observed discipline, and conscientiously reformed themselves. For instance, those offenders who did not know how to labor have learned certain labor skills and those who did not have the labor habit have been educated to have the labor habit. After examining their behavior in labor and in observance of law, the prison believes that the conditional release of these criminals cannot endanger the society again. The order of the high people's court of the province provided that if during the period of conditional release these offenders commit no new crimes, their sentence will be deemed to have been served.

When those criminals heard the news of their early release, they were very grateful for the government's lenient handling and said that after returning to their homes, they would do their labor properly and contribute their strength to the socialist construction of their mother country.

## 2. Special Amnesty

### ITEM 307

[CONSTITUTION OF THE PRC (Sept. 20, 1954), pp. 12, 14–15]

Article 27. The National People's Congress shall exercise the following powers:
(12) To decide on general amnesties . . .
Article 31. The Standing Committee of the National People's Congress shall exercise the following powers:
(15) To decide on special amnesties . . .

### ITEM 308

[SPECIAL AMNESTY ORDER OF THE CHAIRMAN OF THE PRC (promulgated, Sept. 17, 1959), *FKHP*, 10:60–61]

Under the brilliant leadership of the Chinese Communist Party, the Central People's Government and Chairman Mao Tse-tung, great leader of the people of the various nationality groups in our country, after ten years of heroic struggle our country's socialist revolution and socialist construction have already won a great victory. Our mother country moves happily toward glory, production and construction are developing luxuriantly, and the lives of the people are improving every day. The regime of the people's democratic dictatorship is unprecedentedly consolidated and strong. The political awareness and degree of organization of the people of the entire country have been raised to unprecedented heights. The political and economic circumstances of the country are excellent. The Chinese Communist Party and the people's government, having put into effect the policy of combining the punishment of counterrevolutionaries and other criminals with leniency and combining their reform through labor with ideological education, have already had great success. A majority of the various kinds of criminals in custody have already attained different degrees of reform, and quite a few have already really reformed from evil into good persons. To celebrate the tenth anniversary of the establishment of the great People's Republic of China, to celebrate the victory of the Chinese Communist Party's general line for socialist construction, and to celebrate the brilliant accomplishments of the great leap forward and the people's commune movement, on the basis of the decision of the ninth meeting of the Standing Committee of the second session of the National People's Congress, a special amnesty shall be put into effect for war criminals of the Chiang Kai-shek group and of the counterfeit [puppet] state of Manchuria, counterrevolutionary criminals and ordinary criminals who have really reformed from evil into good persons.

1. War criminals of the Chiang Kai-shek group and of the counterfeit state of Manchuria who have already been held in custody for ten years and who have really reformed from evil into good persons shall be released.

2. Counterrevolutionary criminals who have been sentenced to five years or less (including those who have been sentenced to five years) of imprisonment, who have already served one half or more of their term of imprisonment and who have really reformed from evil into good persons, and counterrevolutionary criminals who have been sentenced to more than five years of imprisonment, who have already served two thirds or more of their term of imprisonment and who have really reformed from evil into good persons, shall be released.

3. Ordinary criminals who have been sentenced to five years or less (including those who have been sentenced to five years), who have already served one third or more of their term of imprisonment and who have really reformed from evil into good persons, and ordinary criminals who have been sentenced to more than five years, who have already served one half or more of their term of imprisonment and who have really reformed from evil into good persons, shall be released.

4. Criminals who have been sentenced to death with execution of sentence suspended for a two-year period, if one year of the period of suspension has already expired and if they have really demonstrated that they have reformed from evil into good persons, may have their sentences reduced to life imprisonment or to fifteen years or more of imprisonment.

5. Criminals who have been sentenced to life imprisonment, who have already

served seven years of their term of imprisonment and who have really demonstrated that they have reformed from evil into good persons, may have their sentences reduced to ten years or more of imprisonment.

This order shall be executed by the Supreme People's Court and high people's courts.

Chairman of the People's Republic of China    Liu Shao-ch'i

## ITEM 309

["Supreme People's Court Grants Amnesty to an Initial Group of War Criminals Who Have Changed into Good Persons," *JMJP,* Dec. 5, 1959]

In accordance with the amnesty decree of the Chairman of the People's Republic of China the Supreme People's Court today granted amnesty to an initial group of war criminals.

After promulgation of the amnesty decree of September 17, the organ of the people's government that handles war criminals carried out a comprehensive and thorough review of the war criminals in confinement. Finally, after approval by the Supreme People's Court, it was decided to release under the amnesty an initial group of thirty-three persons.

Similar procedure was followed for the amnesty of counterrevolutionary and ordinary criminals. In Shanghai, for example, the public security organs reviewed the cases of those in confinement, and release or reduction of sentence was granted upon approval of the high court of the city.[5]

## ITEM 310

The following excerpt is typical of those found on this subject in the work reports of high courts.

[Wang Kuang-li, "Report on High Level Court Work in Honan Province, Communist China," *Ho-nan jih-pao* (Honan daily), March 1, 1960; translated in *JPRS,* 6082: 3–4 (Oct. 13, 1960)]

2. In accordance with the special amnesty order of the chairman of the Chinese People's Republic at the time of the nation's 10th anniversary celebrations, we coordinated with the public security and investigatory organs in examining those criminals of the province who had conditions suitable for pardoning [amnesty]. Those who deserved special pardon [special amnesty] and release were accordingly granted special pardon and set free, and for those meriting special reduction in sentence, the procedure was followed for granting special reduction in sentence. In the whole province, 4263 persons were granted special pardon and released, and 294 were granted special reduction in sentence. In carrying out the special amnesty work, the various levels of people's courts everywhere did ideological education work, explained the policy, and indicated the future to labor reform offenders. Many criminals were deeply moved and expressed their desire to repent. The productivity of many

5. "Shanghai High Court Grants Amnesty to a Group of Criminals," *Wen-hui pao* (Literary news, Shanghai) [December ?], 1959, p. 1.

labor reform units rose greatly. For example, the small furnace and hoist shop set up by the provincial penal iron and steel factory completed in only two days' time what was planned to take four days. The offenders who underwent labor reform and received special pardons not only reformed their reactionary ideology, but also learned productive skills, and now can provide for themselves. All the offenders receiving special pardons were moved by the great revolutionary humanitarianism showed them by the party and the people's government; they compared the new society to a "reborn father and mother" and themselves to "reborn new men." Those offenders not yet pardoned also were deeply affected upon studying the amnesty order. They expressed their desire to obey the law always and to strive to become good citizens of the country soon. Also, the families of quite a few of the pardoned offenders have written to the government, expressing their desire to prove by actual deeds that the pardoned relatives have reformed and forsaken their evil ways and returned to righteousness. The special pardon work once again points out the way to antirevolutionists and other criminals; if they just confess their crimes, reform through labor, leave the evil and follow the good, they will be forgiven by the people and this is the only way. This shrewd measure is the application and development, under the country's new historical conditions, of the Party policy of combining punishment with leniency, combining labor reform with ideological education. It fully shows that our country's government and economic conditions are excellent, that the democratic dictatorship of the people is solid and strong, and the socialist system is one unexcelled.

## ITEM 311

[Ku Fang-p'ing, "The Great Victory of the Policy of Reforming Criminals," *CFYC*, 6:35–36 (1959)]

.    .    .    .    .

Our special amnesty is essentially different from the amnesties of past governments of old China and of contemporary bourgeois states, which protect the rule of the exploiter classes and ameliorate class contradictions when actually these contradictions definitely cannot be eliminated. Our special amnesty is for the purpose of reforming society and reforming people. It is not directed at specially prescribed persons or crimes but takes as its most fundamental criterion whether or not the various kinds of criminals have really changed from evil into good persons politically, ideologically, and in their actual conduct. By so doing, our special amnesty first of all points out the opportunity for these various kinds of criminals and the direction for their efforts. For a brilliant future they only have to admit their guilt, obey the law, and change from evil into good persons. Doing this is beneficial to further self-reform on the part of criminals who receive special amnesty. It also plays a major educational role with respect to criminals who have not received special amnesty and is beneficial to their continuing reform. At the same time, it also can play an educational, divisive, and disruptive role with respect to remnant counterrevolutionary and other bad elements still concealed in society, thereby even further benefiting the liquidation and reform of these counterrevolutionary and other bad elements. Next, since only those who have really changed from evil into good persons can receive special amnesty and those who have not changed cannot receive it, those who have not yet reformed are prevented from being released and continuing to endanger society. This embodies the strict attitude of the Party and government toward responsibility to the people and toward reform of criminals. If we do not take as the major criterion whether or not they have changed from evil into good persons but vaguely take a given term of imprisonment or a given crime as the condition for special amnesty, then we cannot avoid releasing some criminals who still have not reformed, and obviously this will be extremely disadvantageous to the stability of the social order, to the socialist revolution, and to socialist construction.

Our special amnesty must prescribe that the completion of a given term of imprisonment be taken as one of the conditions for applying special amnesty. We know that the various kinds of criminals, especially counterrevolutionary criminals, have lived for a long time in the position of oppressors and exploiters. Not only do they have in their minds a deeply rooted reactionary world outlook and personal philosophy, but they have also been penetrated by the bad habits of a rotten, parasitic life. To reform these persons so that they become new persons requires a process of reform. Without a certain period of reform through labor, this goal cannot be attained. From another point of view, without a certain period of examination it is also hard to determine whether or not these criminals genuinely admit their guilt, obey the law, and have changed from evil into good persons.

Since the crimes committed by the various kinds of criminals differ in nature, since the degree of their evil differs, and since their behavior during the actual process of reform usually differs, some of them require a relatively long period for reform, while others do not require so long a period. Generally speaking, nonhabitual offenders are easy to reform while major habitual offenders and [other] recidivists are relatively hard to reform; accomplices are easy to reform while principal offenders are relatively hard to reform; criminals who originate from the laboring people are easy to reform while criminals who originate from the exploiter classes are relatively hard to reform. From the point of view of the effect of the crime on society, if those criminals, particularly counterrevolutionary criminals, who commit serious crimes and are sentenced in accordance with law to relatively long terms of imprisonment, do not serve a rather long period of their term, then not only do they in fact not reform, but their early release also creates resentment among the laboring people. Therefore, in individually prescribing, on the basis of the nature of the crime and the length of the original term of imprisonment, differences in the term of imprisonment to be served [as a prerequisite] for the release of different kinds of criminals, the special amnesty order reflects the actual circumstances of reforming criminals and embodies the spirit of serious and careful differential treatment.

## E. POSTRELEASE PROBLEMS

### 1. Voluntary and Involuntary Retention

#### ITEM 312

[ACT OF THE PRC FOR REFORM THROUGH LABOR (Sept. 7, 1954), p. 40]

Section 6. Release

Article 61. Offenders shall be released on the basis of the following circumstances:

(1) Their term of imprisonment has expired;

(2) Investigation or adjudication organs notify the organs of reform through labor that they [the offenders] should be released;

(3) Conditional release [is ordered].

Offenders who should be released shall be given a certificate of release by organs of reform through labor and shall be released on time. Before their release an evaluation shall be made, and the conclusion shall be recorded in the certificate of release. Organs of reform through labor shall give released offenders funds for travel expenses for their return home. Members of families of those who have fallen seriously ill shall be notified in advance to come to meet them.

Article 62. All offenders, when their terms of imprisonment have expired and they are about to be released, may voluntarily remain in their group and get work, or if they have no home to which to return and no employment to get or if it is possible to place them in sparsely inhabited districts, organs of reform through labor shall then organize them for labor and get them employment. Methods for this shall be covered by separately issued provisions.

#### ITEM 313

[PROVISIONAL MEASURES OF THE PRC FOR DEALING WITH THE RELEASE OF REFORM THROUGH LABOR CRIMINALS AT THE EXPIRATION OF THEIR TERM OF IMPRISONMENT AND FOR PLACING THEM AND GETTING THEM EMPLOYMENT (approved at the 222d meeting of the Government Administration Council, Aug. 26, 1954; promulgated by the Government Administration Council, Sept. 7, 1954), FLHP 1954, pp. 44–45]

Article 1. These measures are adopted on the basis of the provisions of Article 62 of the Act of the People's Republic of China for Reform Through Labor in order to implement the policy of reform through labor, consolidate the security of society, and resolve the offenders' problem of getting employment after expiration of their term of imprisonment.

Article 2. Organs of reform through labor may retain, place, and get employment for offenders whose term of imprisonment has already expired and who are in any one of the following circumstances:

(1) They themselves desire to remain in the group and get employment, and they are needed for reform through labor production;

(2) They have no home to which to return and no employment to get;

(3) They are criminals who have undergone reform through labor in

sparsely inhabited districts and, after expiration of their term of imprisonment, they are needed to stay with settlers, have a family, and have an occupation there.

Article 3. Organs of reform through labor shall, three months before expiration of the term of imprisonment of an offender who meets any one of the conditions prescribed in Article 2 (2)–(3) of these Measures, submit their opinion to the people's public security organ in charge for review and approval in order to facilitate retaining, placing, and getting him employment after expiration of his term of imprisonment.

Article 4. For all persons who are retained and placed and who have obtained employment, on the day of expiration of their term of imprisonment, release procedures shall be carried out, their release announced and, in accordance with the original judgment, they shall have their political rights restored or shall continue to be deprived of them.

Article 5. Methods for placing and getting employment for offenders who are released upon expiration of their term of imprisonment:

(1) Those whose reform through labor was relatively good, who have production skills, and are needed by enterprises and departments for social production, may be encouraged to get their own employment or, under conditions where it is possible, may be introduced to employment by organs of reform through labor and departments of labor;

(2) Offenders may be placed and may get employment within reform through labor discipline groups, and their salary may be fixed in accordance with their labor conditions and skills;

(3) Some land on or near a reform through labor farm may be set aside for organizing collective production and establishing new villages.

Article 6. The establishment of new villages shall be jointly planned by provincial organs of reform through labor and civil affairs departments of the same level.

Article 7. When all those whose term of imprisonment has expired are placed and have obtained employment in sparsely inhabited districts, and they are able to support themselves through production, civil affairs departments may use settlement measures to assist them in receiving members of their families, having a family, and having an occupation there.

Article 8. In reform through labor units in factories, mines, enterprises, construction groups, and units with relatively small-scale production, with the exception of cases that are dealt with by those units in accordance with measures prescribed by Article 5 (1)–(2), if after the term of imprisonment of offenders has expired there is no way of dealing with them, provincial, city, or central organs of reform through labor shall transfer them to other assigned reform through labor production units or new villages for placement.

## ITEM 314

["High People's Court of the Province Grants Early Release to a Number of Women Offenders" (Sept. 11, 1956)]

·　　·　　·　　·　　·

Some of those criminals who have been released early are homeless and thus have asked repeatedly to stay in the department of reform through labor to continue to contribute to the undertaking of building the mother country. In order to enable them to obtain protection of their livelihood, the reform through labor organ has decided to retain them. However, it will not treat them as criminals but will pay them according to the principle of to each according to his labor.

## ITEM 315

[Interview]

Tiao, a married man, had been sentenced to eighteen months of reform through labor for having committed adultery with the fiancée of a member of the People's Liberation Army [see Item 131]. He was assigned to a labor battalion that was building a railroad through an undeveloped area of his district. Because Tiao had a rather high cultural level for a worker, he had proved valuable in helping with the battalion's office work. Before the expiration of his eighteen months there, through intensive and repeated persuasion labor battalion cadres attempted to "mobilize" him to stay on and continue to work with them after his sentence had been served. Tiao did not disagree with these cadres because he feared that it might adversely affect his release. Instead in a letter to friends in the public security bureau he managed to convey word of his plight. His friends then persuaded the bureau chief to instruct the labor battalion to release Tiao on time, on the ground that he was needed to support his girl friend and the child he had fathered, who in his absence had been living on the charity of friends. The battalion complied with this instruction.

## ITEM 316

[Snow, *The Other Side of the River* (1962), pp. 367–368]

.      .      .      .      .

Beside a round-roofed pergola in one corner of a compound near the [prison] clinic, half a dozen women were eating rice with their chopsticks, laughing and chattering. They didn't seem to belong.

"They are ex-prisoners," Wang explained. "Two of them work in the clinic, another is in charge of the laundry, one works in the office."

I stopped to take some pictures, to which they made no objection; one or two gave embarrassed smiles. They confirmed that they had stayed on voluntarily after their sentences expired and were working for wages. They felt "at home" here. One was a married woman who lived nearby; her husband worked in a neighborhood factory. I had no time to pursue what might have been a fascinating study of the psychology behind their choice of a place to work — if it was their choice. (Miss Mills [Harriet Mills, an American expert on Chinese thought reform techniques] later told me that she was prepared to believe it *was* voluntary.)

ITEM 317

*[Lectures* (September 1957), p. 14]

The capitalists need a large amount of subservient and cheap labor power for their exploitation, and the criminal punishment of deprivation of freedom is a method of instilling discipline in the hired laborers. Marx made a remarkable statement about the essence of such punishment. He said that under this system "[t]he capitalist philanthropist has an advantage in that an ex-convict becomes a subservient sheep; he works for the capitalist in the factories, the fields, the mines, and on the railways and waterways; he helps the capitalist make profits, but he dares not pick up even one small potato when he passes through a potato field with an empty stomach. Under these circumstances, as far as the philanthropist is concerned, for him [the ex-convict] to live this way is much better than to be beheaded."

## 2. Revocation of Conditional Release and Related Problems

ITEM 318

*[Lectures* (September 1957), p. 258]

.    .    .    .    .

If a criminal who has been released commits a new crime during the period of conditional release, he demonstrates that he has not sincerely repented and reformed. His conditional release should therefore be revoked and execution of the unexecuted [portion of his] punishment continued. Otherwise, it would violate the purpose of the system of conditional release which was originally established on the basis of the offender's demonstration of repentance and reform and of his not again endangering society. When conditional release is revoked, the period of conditional release should not be included in the term to be executed; in that case, we should take the punishment for his new crime and the unexecuted [portion of the] punishment for his previous crime and, in accordance with the principles of combined punishment for several crimes, decide upon the punishment which should be executed. From this it can be seen that the condition for revocation of conditional release is the commission of a new crime within the period of conditional release. There are many different opinions on this question. For example, some people make the criterion [for revoking conditional release] the quality of the offender's behavior during the period of conditional release. Others make the criterion the intentional or negligent nature of the [new] crime. Still others advocate making the criterion the seriousness of the crime (for example, conditional release should be revoked if the new crime is punishable by imprisonment for a fixed term or a more severe punishment or by imprisonment for not less than three years). We cannot agree with the above suggestions.

## ITEM 319

[Interview]

Hsiao was convicted of counterrevolutionary activity in 1952 and was sentenced to fifteen years of imprisonment. While undergoing reform through labor he denounced a number of others as being counterrevolutionaries, and the information which he provided proved to be accurate and valuable. As a reward Hsiao's sentence was reduced to five years of imprisonment. One year before this reduced sentence was to expire he was given a conditional release and returned to work in the agricultural producers' cooperative of his village. Shortly thereafter, during the "high tide" of agricultural cooperativization, he complained in front of a group of cadres that the cooperative of the advanced type failed to provide adequate compensation to its members for the land that they contributed to it. This was reported to the public security bureau's special agent at the district level, who in turn informed the bureau. The bureau decided not to treat the utterance as a separate crime, since it was not voiced at a public meeting and was not overheard by a large number of people. But on the basis of this remark it decided to revoke Hsiao's conditional release, and a militiaman was sent to escort him to the bureau and then back to the reform through labor camp to complete the remaining year of his sentence.

Recall Articles 6 and 7 of the Provisional Measures of the PRC for Control of Counterrevolutionaries, Item 100.

## ITEM 320

[*Lectures* (September 1957), pp. 245, 247]

.    .    .    .    .

Undoubtedly, correct regulation of the conditions for revoking suspended sentences is of great significance to correct application of suspension of sentence. But there are various points of view with respect to this question. For example, some advocate the revocation of a suspended sentence only when one [whose sentence has been suspended] intentionally commits a crime during the term of the suspended sentence. Some advocate that it should be revoked only when he commits a new crime for which the sentence is also detention or a more severe punishment. Others advocate revocation only when he commits a new crime more serious than the previous one. Still others advocate revocation only if his behavior is not good during the term of the suspended sentence. We believe that, although all of these opinions have a certain reasonableness, they also have shortcomings.

.    .    .    .    .

Therefore, we believe that a suspended sentence should be revoked if the criminal whose sentence has been declared suspended commits a new crime during the term of the suspended sentence, whether this crime is committed intentionally or negligently, is serious or minor, or is similar to the previous crime or not.

With respect to a criminal whose suspended sentence has been revoked, we should take the punishments to which he has been sentenced for his previous crime and for his new crime and decide the punishment to be executed in accordance with the principles of combined punishment for several crimes.

## ITEM 321

[Interview]

Hsia was a married man who was convicted of committing adultery with Kao, a married woman. He was sentenced to eighteen months of imprisonment. Execution of the sentence was suspended on condition that he and Kao separate, which they agreed to do. [See Item 93 and Item 239.]

Hsia and Kao subsequently both applied for divorce. While the divorce actions were pending, in checking on household registration one day the patrolman assigned to their brigade discovered that Hsia and Kao were still living in the same house, together with Hsia's children. He was furious with them, but was somewhat placated when they told him that they had initiated divorce proceedings, and he became amused when they claimed that they actually lived in separate rooms of the house. The patrolman felt sympathy for Kao, an attactive girl who had had a hard life and who had found it difficult to adjust to the strenuous routine of the sanction which the police had imposed upon her, rehabilitation through labor in a local unit. He knew that if the police reported their continuing cohabitation to the court Hsia might be sent to reform through labor, Kao's life would become miserable again, and Hsia's children would lose their principal means of support. Therefore the patrolman recommended that no report be made to the court, and the chief of his public security station agreed.

Recall Item 230.

# PART III BIBLIOGRAPHY GLOSSARY

# Bibliography

Act for Mediating Civil and Criminal Cases in the Border Regions in [the provinces of] Shensi, Kansu and Ninghsia; in Office of the Shen-Kan-Ning Border Region Government, ed., *Shan Kan Ning pien-ch'ü cheng-ts'e t'iao-li hui-pien*[1] (Collection of policies and acts for the border regions in Shensi, Kansu and Ninghsia, second series; n.p., 1944), pp. 266–270.

Act [of the PRC] for the Organization of City Residents' Committees (passed at the 4th meeting of the Standing Committee of the NPC, Dec. 31, 1954; promulgated by the Chairman of the PRC, Dec. 31, 1954), *FKHP*, 1:173–175 (September 1954–June 1955).

Act [of the PRC] for the Organization of City Street Offices (passed at the 4th meeting of the Standing Committee of the NPC, Dec. 31, 1954; promulgated by the Chairman of the PRC, Dec. 31, 1954), *FKHP*, 1:171–172 (September 1954–June 1955).

Act [of the PRC] for the Organization of Public Security Stations (passed at the 4th meeting of the Standing Committee of the NPC, Dec. 31, 1954; promulgated by the Chairman of the PRC, Dec. 31, 1954), *FKHP*, 1:243–244 (September 1954–June 1955).

Act of the PRC for Punishment of Corruption (approved at the 14th session of the Central People's Government Council, April 18, 1952; promulgated by the Chairman of the PRC, April 21, 1952), *FLHP* 1952, pp. 25–28.

Act of the PRC for Punishment of Counterrevolution (approved at the 11th meeting of the Central People's Government Council, Feb. 20, 1951; promulgated by the Chairman of the PRC, Feb. 21, 1951), *FLHP* 1951, 1:3–5.

Act of the PRC for Reform Through Labor (passed at the 222d meeting of the Government Administration Council, Aug. 26, 1954; promulgated by the Government Administration Council, Sept. 7, 1954), *FLHP* 1954, pp. 33–42.

1965 Amendment to RSFSR Statute on Comrades' Courts, art. 15(5), *Vedomosti Verkhovnovo Soveta RSFSR* (Gazette of the Supreme Soviet of the RSFSR), 4:81 (1965).

Anderson, Raymond H., "Courts' Freedom Urged in Soviet," *New York Times,* July 3, 1966, p. 14.

"Anhwei [Province] Corrects Erroneously Decided Cases in Accordance with the Spirit of Chairman Mao's Speech," *Wen-hui pao* (Literary news, Shanghai), May 13, 1957, p. 1.

Anonymous Legalists, 3d century B.C.; translated in J. J. L. Duyvendak, *The Book of Lord Shang* (Chicago: University of Chicago Press, 1963), 346 pp.

"Answering Questions from Readers: On Trial Procedure in Criminal Cases," *Kuang-ming jih-pao* (Enlightenment daily), March 11, 1955, p. 3.

"Answers of the Ministry of Supervision of the PRC to Some Questions of the

Provisional Regulations Relating to Rewards and Punishments for Personnel of State Administrative Organs" (June 12, 1958), *FKHP*, 7:218–220 (January–June 1958).

"Are All Crimes to Be Counted as Contradictions Between the Enemy and Us? Are They All To Be Regarded as Objects of Dictatorship?" *CFYC*, 3:73–81 (1958).

Arrest and Detention Act of the PRC (passed at the 3d meeting of the Standing Committee of the NPC, Dec. 20, 1954; promulgated by the Chairman of the PRC, Dec. 20, 1954), *FKHP*, 1:239–242 (September 1954–June 1955).

"At the Request of the Reform Through Labor Department of the Public Security Bureau, the Tientsin City High Court Granted Conditional Release or Reduction of Sentence to Criminals Who Demonstrated Their Repentance and Reform," *Hsin wan pao* (New evening news, Tientsin), Aug. 5, 1956.

"At Yangtan Commune Headquarters," *Peking Review*, 11:18–22 (March 11, 1966).

Barnett, A. Doak, *China on the Eve of Communist Takeover* (New York: Frederick A. Praeger, Inc., and London: Thames & Hudson, 1963) 371 pp.

—— *Communist China: The Early Years, 1949–55* (New York and Washington, D.C.: Frederick A. Praeger, Inc., and London: Pall Mall Press Ltd., 1964), 336 pp.

Benedek, Jeno, "Chinese System of Administering Justice," *Tarsadlmi szemle* (Budapest), February 1960; translated in *JPRS*, no. 3121 (April 1, 1960), 15 pp.

Berman, H. J., *Justice in the U.S.S.R.*, rev. ed. (New York: Alfred A. Knopf, Inc. and Random House, 1963), 431 pp. Reprinted by arrangement with Harvard University Press.

Berman, H. J. and J. W. Spindler, "Soviet Comrades' Courts," *Washington Law Review*, 38:842–910 (1963).

—— *Soviet Criminal Law and Procedure, The RSFSR Codes* (Cambridge, Mass.: Harvard University Press, 1966), 501 pp.

Blaustein, A. P., ed., *Fundamental Legal Documents of Communist China* (South Hackensack, N.J., 1962), 603 pp.

Bodde, Derk, "Basic Concepts of Chinese Law: The Genesis and Evolution of Legal Thought in Traditional China," *American Philosophical Society, Proceedings*, 107.5:375–398 (October 1963).

Brandt, Conrad et al., *A Documentary History of Chinese Communism* (Cambridge, Mass., 1959), 552 pp.

Bünger, Karl, "The Punishment of Lunatics and Negligents According to Classical Chinese Law," *Studia Serica*, pt. 2, IX (1950), 1–16.

Buxbaum, David C., "Preliminary Trends in the Development of the Legal Institutions of Communist China and the Nature of the Criminal Law," *International and Comparative Law Quarterly*, 11:1–30 (January 1962).

—— "Horizontal and Vertical Influences Upon the Substantive Criminal Law in China: Some Preliminary Observations," *Osteuropa-Recht*, 10:31–51 (March 1964).

Canton Military Region Committee of the CCP, "Regulations for Improving the Methods of Supervisory Education in Army Units," *Kung-tso t'ung-hsün* (Bulletin of activities), 7:23–28 (Feb. 1, 1961).

"Canton's Political-Legal Departments Experiment with Cooperation in Case Handling," *Nan-fang jih-pao* (Southern daily, Canton), March 30, 1958.

Chang Chien, "The System of Rehabilitation Through Labor in Our Country," *CFYC*, 6:42–46 (1959).

Chang Hsin, "American Justice as Depicted in 'the Unjust Court,'" *CFYC*, 4:45–49 (1962).

Chang Hui et al., "These Are Not the Basic Principles of Our Country's Criminal Litigation," *CFYC*, 4:76–80 (1958).

Chang Ting-ch'eng, "Work Report of the Supreme People's Procuracy," *JMJP*, Jan. 1, 1965, p. 3.

Chang Tzu-p'ei, "Censure the Bourgeois Principle of 'the Judge's Free Evaluation of the Evidence,'" *CFYC*, 2:42–48 (1958).

———— "Several Problems Relating to the Use of Evidence To Determine the Facts of a Case in Criminal Litigation," *CFYC*, 4:11–18 (1962).

Chang Wu-yün, "Smash Permanent Rules, Go 1,000 *Li* in One Day," *CFYC*, 5:58–61 (1958).

"Chao Feng-hsiang, Principal Criminal in the Murder of Li Kung-pu, Is Executed," *JMJP*, March 26, 1959, p. 6.

Chao Yuan, "Report on a Year's Work of the People's Court of Fukien Province," *Fu-chien jih-pao* (Fukien daily), Feb. 13, 1959; translated in *JPRS*, no. 1077-D (Dec. 17, 1959), 12 pp.

Ch'en Ho-feng, "Refute Rightist Chuang Hui-ch'en's Reactionary Fallacy Regarding Legal Relations Among the Public Security, Procuratorial and Adjudication Organs," *CFYC*, 2:64–66 (1958).

Ch'en Huai-ning, "People's Policewomen Who Closely Rely on the Masses," *JMJP*, March 4, 1959, p. 6.

Ch'en Kuo-liang, "Wu-ling Cooperative Strictly Controls the Enemy," *T'ung-ch'uan jih-pao* (T'ung-ch'uan daily), April 17, 1958.

Ch'en Mei-ying, "How I Fight for Freedom of Marriage," *Chung-kuo fu-nü* (Women of China), 10:18–19 (Oct. 1, 1963).

Ch'en, Theodore Hsi-en, *Thought Reform of the Chinese Intellectuals* (Hong Kong, 1960), 247 pp.

Cheng, F. T., "A Sketch of the History, Philosophy, and Reform of Chinese Law," in *Washington Foreign Law Society* (Studies in the law of the Far East and Southeast Asia; n.p., 1956), pp. 29–45.

Cheng, J. Chester, *The Politics of the Chinese Red Army* (Stanford, 1966), 776 pp.

Cheng Wen-chung, cartoon, in *Ch'üan-kuo nung-yeh fa-chan kang-yao* (*ts'ao-an*) *t'u-chieh*² (National agricultural development outline [draft] illustrated; Peking, 1957), p. 9.

Ch'i Wen, "We Must Thoroughly Liquidate the Bourgeois Ideological Influence of 'Independent Adjudication,'" *CFYC*, 2:52–58 (1960).

Chiang I-fan, "Western District Public Security Subbureau Handles a Batch of Traffic Violation and Accident Cases," *Kuang-chou jih-pao* (Canton daily), July 4, 1956.

Chiang Kai-shek, *China's Destiny*, ed. Philip Jaffe (New York: Roy Publishers, 1947), 347 pp.

Chiang Shih-min et al., "Correctly Handling Disputes Among the People," *CFYC*, 4:28–31 (1959).

China News Analysis, *Articles on Communist Chinese Law from CNA, 1953–1959* (Hong Kong, 1960).

Chome, Jules, "Two Trials in the People's Republic of China," *Law in the Service of Peace*, new series, 4:102–108 (Brussels: International Association of Democratic Lawyers, June 1956).

Chou En-lai, "Report on the Work of the Government" (given at the 4th meeting of the 1st session of the NPC, June 26, 1957), *FKHP*, 6:61–108 (July–December 1957).

Chou K'e-yung, "The Great Achievement Made in Work of Reforming Criminals Through Labor," *Chiang-hsi jih-pao* (Kiangsi daily), Dec. 17, 1959; translated in *JPRS,* 3349:100–101 (June 3, 1960).

Ch'ü T'ung-tsu, *Law and Society in Traditional China* (Paris, 1961), 304 pp.

———— *Local Government in China under the Ch'ing* (Cambridge, Mass., 1962), 360 pp.

Chugunov, Vladimir E., *Ugolovnoye Sudoproizvodstvo Kitayskoy Narodnoy Respubliki* (Criminal court procedures in the People's Republic of China; Moscow, 1959), 286 pp.; translated in *JPRS,* no. 4595 (Washington, D.C.: U.S. Department of Commerce, Office of Technical Services, May 8, 1961), 241 pp.

Chung Yu, "My View [on the Legality of a Search]," *Hsin chung-kuo jih-pao* (New China daily, Nanking), Oct. 28, 1956.

Circulating Order of the Government Administration Council of the PRC Relating to the Strict Prohibition of Opium (passed at the 21st meeting of the Government Administration Council, Feb. 24, 1950; issued, Feb. 24, 1950), *FLHP* 1949–1950, 1:173–174.

"The City Intermediate People's Court Yesterday Publicly Tried the Case of Fu Ken-lin and Decided to Annul the Judgment of the Pei-t'a District People's Court," *Hsin Su-chou pao* (New Soochow news), July 8, 1956.

Cohen, A. A., *The Communism of Mao Tse-tung* (Chicago and London, 1964), 210 pp.

Cohen, Jerome Alan, review of A. P. Blaustein, ed., *Fundamental Legal Documents of Communist China,* in *Yale Law Journal,* 72:838–843 (March 1963).

———— "The Criminal Process in the People's Republic of China: An Introduction," *Harvard Law Review,* 79.3:469–533 (January 1966).

———— "Chinese Mediation on the Eve of Modernization," *California Law Review,* 54.3:1201–1226 (August 1966).

———— "Interviewing Chinese Refugees: Indispensable Aid to Legal Research on China," *Journal of Legal Education,* 20.1:33 (October 1967).

Cohen, Ronald E., "Colonial Era Throwback: Side-Judges Part of Vermont Courts," *Boston Globe,* Oct. 16, 1964, p. 13.

Commission Internationale Contre Le Régime Concentrationnaire, *White Book on Forced Labour and Concentration Camps in the People's Republic of China,* 2 vols. (Paris, 1957–1958).

Common Program of the CPPCC (passed at the 1st plenary session of the CPPCC, Sept. 29, 1949), *FLHP* 1949–1950, 1:16–25.

"Comrade Lo Jui-ch'ing's Inspection Report on the Conditions of Army Units in Several Areas," *Kung-tso t'ung-hsün* (Bulletin of activities), 11:2–18 (March 2, 1961).

Concerning the Extension of Restrictions in the Application of Fines Levied Administratively (Decree of June 21, 1961), *Vedomosti Verkhovnovo Soveta SSSR* (Gazette of the Supreme Soviet of the U.S.S.R.), 35:837–843 (1961).

Confucius, *Analects,* II, 3, and XII, 13; translated in Derk Bodde, "Basic Concepts of Chinese Law: The Genesis and Evolution of Legal Thought in Traditional China," *American Philosophical Society, Proceedings,* 107.5:384 (October 1963).

Constitution of the CCP (adopted by the 8th National Congress of the CCP, Sept. 26, 1956), *Jen-min shou-ts'e, 1957* (People's handbook, 1957), pp. 49–55.

Constitution (Fundamental Law) of the Union of Soviet Socialist Republics (Moscow, 1960), 127 pp.

Constitution of the Communist Youth League of China (passed at the 9th National

Congress of the CYL, June 29, 1964), *JMJP*, July 8, 1964; translated in *CB*, 738: 23–30 (July 30, 1964).

Constitution of the CYL of the PRC (passed at the 9th National Congress of the CYL, June 29, 1964), *JMJP*, July 8, 1964, p. 3.

Constitution of the PRC (passed at the 1st meeting of the 1st session of the NPC, Sept. 20, 1954; promulgated by the Presidium, Sept. 20, 1954), *FKHP*, 1:4–31 (September 1954–June 1955).

Criminal Code of the Republic of China; in Chang Chih-pen,[3] ed., *Tsui-hsin liu-fa ch'üan-shu*[4] (Newest book of the complete six laws [of the Republic of China]; Taipei, 1959), pp. 233–250.

The Criminal Code of the RSFSR, Oct. 27, 1960, art. 27; translated in H. J. Berman and J. W. Spindler, *Soviet Criminal Law and Procedure, The RSFSR Codes* (Cambridge, Mass.: Harvard University Press, 1966), pp. 156–157.

"Criminal Judgment of the Nanchang City People's Court," *Chiang-hsi jih-pao* (Kiangsi daily), June 29, 1955.

Decision of the CCPCC and the State Council of the PRC Relating to the Problem of Dealing With Rightists Who Really Demonstrate that They Have Reformed (passed at the 92d plenary meeting of the State Council, Sept. 16, 1959; issued, Sept. 16, 1959), *FKHP*, 10:61–62 (July–December 1959).

Decision of the Standing Committee of the NPC [of the PRC] Relating to Cases the Hearing of Which Is To Be Conducted Nonpublicly (passed at the 39th meeting of the Standing Committee of the NPC, May 8, 1956), *FKHP*, 3:178 (January–June 1956).

Decision of the Standing Committee of the NPC of the PRC Relating to Control of Counterrevolutionaries in All Cases Being Decided Upon by Judgment of a People's Court (passed at the 51st meeting of the Standing Committee of the NPC, Nov. 16, 1956), *FKHP*, 4:246 (July–December 1956).

Decision of the Standing Committee of the NPC of the PRC Relating to Dealing Leniently With and Placing Remnant City Counterrevolutionaries (passed at the 51st meeting of the Standing Committee of the NPC, Nov. 16, 1956), *FKHP*, 4:243–245 (July–December 1956).

Decision of the Standing Committee of the NPC [of the PRC] Relating to Inspection of Work by Deputies of the NPC and Deputies of People's Congresses of Provinces, Autonomous Regions, and Cities Directly Under the Central Authority (passed at the 20th meeting of the Standing Committee of the NPC, Aug. 6, 1955), *FKHP*, 2:66–67 (July–December 1955).

Decision of the Standing Committee of the NPC of the PRC Relating to the Problem of Appointment and Removal of Assistant Judges of the Supreme People's Court and Local People's Courts of the Various Levels (passed at the 12th meeting of the Standing Committee of the 2d session of the NPC, Jan. 21, 1960; promulgated by the Chairman of the PRC, Jan. 21, 1960), *FKHP*, 11:120 (January–July 1960).

Decision of the Standing Committee of the NPC [of the PRC] Relating to the Problem of Whether Presidents of Local People's Courts of the Various Levels and Chief Procurators of Local People's Procuracies of the Various Levels May Concurrently Serve as Constituent Officers of People's Councils of the Various Levels (passed at the 26th meeting of the Standing Committee of the NPC, Nov. 10, 1955), *FKHP*, 2:71 (July–December 1955).

Decision of the Standing Committee of the NPC [of the PRC] Relating to Whether Persons Who Have Been Deprived of Political Rights May Serve as Defenders (passed at the 39th meeting of the Standing Committee of the NPC, May 8, 1956), *FKHP*, 3:179 (January–June 1956).

Decision of the State Council [of the PRC] on Abolishing Railroad and Water Transportation Courts (passed at the 56th plenary meeting of the State Council, Aug. 9, 1957; issued, Sept. 7, 1957), *FKHP*, 6:297–298 (July–December 1957).

Decision of the State Council [of the PRC] Relating to Problems of Rehabilitation Through Labor (approved at the 78th meeting of the Standing Committee of the NPC, Aug. 1, 1957; promulgated by the State Council, Aug. 3, 1957), *FKHP*, 6:243–244 (July–December 1957).

Decree of the Presidium of the Russian Republic Supreme Soviet, "On Amendments to the May 4, 1961, Decree of the Presidium of the Russian Republic Supreme Soviet 'On Intensifying the Struggle Against Persons Who Avoid Socially Useful Work and Lead an Antisocial, Parasitic Way of Life,'" *Vedomosti Verkhovnovo Soveta RSFSR*, 38(364):737–739 (Sept. 23, 1965); translated in *CDSP*, 17.44:13 (Nov. 24, 1965).

Decree of the Presidium of the Russian Republic Supreme Soviet, "On Intensifying the Struggle Against Persons Who Avoid Socially Useful Work and Lead an Antisocial, Parasitic Way of Life," *Sovetskaya Rossia*, May 5, 1961; translated in *CDSP*, 13.17:8–9 (May 24, 1961).

Dekkers, René, *Lettres de Chine* (Letters from China; Brussels: Editions de la Librairie Encyclopédique, S.P.R.L., 1956), 139 pp.

Deposition of Father André Bonnichon before the Committee on Criminal Law of the International Congress of Jurists, in André Bonnichon, *Law in Communist China* (The Hague: International Commission of Jurists, 1956), pp. 26–32.

Douglas, Sir Robert K., *Society in China* (London: A. D. Innes & Co., 1895), 434 pp.

Editorial, "Do People's Mediation Work Well, Strengthen the Unity of the People, Impel Production and Construction," *JMJP*, March 23, 1954, p. 1.

———— "Why Should Rehabilitation Through Labor Be Carried Out?" *JMJP*, Aug. 4, 1957.

Escarra, Jean, *Chinese Law: Conception and Evolution, Legislative and Judicial Institutions, Science and Teaching*, trans. Gertrude R. Browne (for Works Progress Administration, W.P. 2799, University of Washington, Seattle; Peking, 1936) (Cambridge, Mass.: Harvard Law School, 1961), 696 pp.

Fainsod, Merle, *How Russia Is Ruled*, rev. ed. (Cambridge, Mass., 1963), 684 pp.

Fairbank, John K. et al., *East Asia, The Modern Transformation* (A history of East Asian civilization, Vol. II; Boston, 1965), 955 pp.

Fan Ming, "Some Opinions about *Lectures on the General Principles of Criminal Law of the PRC*," *CFYC*, 4:72–75 (1958).

Feng Jo-ch'üan, "Refute Chia Ch'ien's Anti-Party Fallacy of 'Independent Adjudication,'" *CFYC*, 1:18–23 (1958).

"Fifth Group of People's Assessors Elected in Kwangtung," *Nan-fang jih-pao* (Southern daily, Canton), Nov. 19, 1963.

Fire Prevention Supervision Act [of the PRC] (approved at the 86th meeting of the Standing Committee of the NPC, Nov. 29, 1957; promulgated by the State Council, Nov. 30, 1957), *FKHP*, 6:261–263 (July–December 1957).

Fu Weng, "Talk on the History of Adjudication of Cases" *Kuang-ming jih-pao* (Enlightenment daily), March 20, 1962, p. 4.

Fukushima Masao, "Chinese Legal Affairs (Second Discussion)," in *Chūgoku no hō to shakai*[5] (Chinese law and society; Tokyo: Shindoku Shosha, 1960), pp. 39–50.

———— "Some Legal Problems Relating to the People's Commune," *Tōyō bunka* (Oriental culture), 32:1–26 (May 1962).

Fuller, Lawrence J. and Henry A. Fisher, Jr., trans., *The Code of Criminal Procedure of the Republic of China, bilingual* ed. (Sino-American legal series; Taipei, 1960), 141 pp.

Fuller, Lon, *The Morality of Law* (New Haven: Yale University Press, 1964), 202 pp.

Gittings, John, "China's Militia," *China Quarterly*, 18:100–117 (April–June 1964).

Goldstein, Joseph, "Police Discretion Not To Invoke the Criminal Process: Low Visibility Decisions in the Administration of Justice," *Yale Law Journal*, 69:543–594 (1960).

"The Good Eighth Company of the Public Security Front," *JMJP*, Jan. 25, 1964, p. 1.

Gower, L. C. B., "Looking at Chinese Justice: A Diary of Three Weeks Behind the Iron Curtain" (unpub. manuscript, n.d.), 177 pp.

Greene, Felix, *Awakened China* (New York: Doubleday & Co., Inc., 1961), 425 pp.

"A Group of Unlawful Elements are Sentenced to Control by the Ku-yüan County Circuit Tribunal," *Ku-yüan jih-pao* (Ku-yüan daily, Kansu province), Jan. 10, 1958.

Gudoshnikov, L. M., *Sudebnye Organy Kitayskoy Narodnoy Respubliki* (Legal organs of the People's Republic of China; Moscow, 1957), pp. 2–135; translated in *JPRS*, no. 1698N (Washington, D.C., June 30, 1959), 138 pp.

Harbin Office of Legal Advisors No. 3, "Arrest and Detention," *Hei-lung-chiang jih-pao* (Heilungkiang daily), Feb. 23, 1957.

Hart, H. M., Jr., "The Aims of the Criminal Law," *Law and Contemporary Problems*, 23:401–441 (1958).

Haruo Abe, "The Accused and Society: Therapeutic and Preventive Aspects of Criminal Justice in Japan," in A. T. von Mehren, *Law in Japan* (Cambridge, Mass.: Harvard University Press, 1963), pp. 324–363.

Hayward, Max, ed., *On Trial: The Soviet State versus "Abram Tertz" and "Nikolai Arzhak,"* (New York, Evanston, and London, 1966), 183 pp.

Hazard, John N., *Settling Disputes in Soviet Society* (New York: Columbia University Press, 1960), 534 pp.

———— "Unity and Diversity in Socialist Law," *Law and Contemporary Problems*, 30:270–290 (Spring 1965).

"He Should Be Punitively Restrained by Law," *JMJP*, July 18, 1956, p. 4.

"Hearing of the Szu-ming-t'ang Case Concluded," *Chieh-fang jih-pao* (Liberation daily, Shanghai), Aug. 31, 1957.

"Hearing of the Szu-ming-t'ang Medicated Liquor Store Case," *Hsin-wen jih-pao* (Daily news, Shanghai), June 4, 1957.

"High Court's Antirightist Struggle Gains Great Victory," *JMJP*, Dec. 12, 1957, p. 4.

"High People's Court of the Province Grants Early Release to a Number of Women Offenders," *Shan-hsi jih-pao* (Shensi daily), Sept. 11, 1956.

Ho Shuang-lu, "Several Problems Relating to Evidence in Criminal Litigation," *CFYC*, 2:31–37 (1963).

"How the Chuangtzup'ing (Kansu) Cooperative Carries Out Experiment in Labor Custody [Rehabilitation Through Labor]," *Kan-su jih-pao* (Kansu daily), July 20, 1958; translated in SCMP, 1862:6–8 (Sept. 26, 1958).

Hsia Tao-tai, "Communist China's First Decade: Justice and the Law," *New Leader*, 42:18–21 (June 22, 1959).

Hsia, T. A., *A Terminological Study of the Hsia-Fang Movement* (Studies in Chinese Communist Terminology, no. 10; Berkeley, 1963), 68 pp.

Hsiao Ch'ang-lun, "A Preliminary Approach to Problems of Control," *CFYC,* 2:9–12 (1957).

Hsiao, Gene T., "Communist China: Legal Institutions," *Problems of Communism,* 14:112–121 (March–April 1965).

Hsiao, K. C., *Rural China* (Seattle: University of Washington Press, 1960), 783 pp.

Hsiao Yung-ch'ing, "A Preliminary Approach to the Study of the History of the Chinese Legal System," *CFYC,* 3:25–35 (1963).

Hsieh Chia-lin et al., "The Role of the Socialist Patriotic Pact," *CFYC,* 1:52–53 (1959).

Hsieh Chüeh-ts'ai, "Report on the Work of the Supreme People's Court," *JMJP,* Jan. 1, 1965, p. 3.

Hsien Heng-han, "How Successfully To Conduct Supervisory Education in Army Units," *Kung-tso t'ung-hsun* (Bulletin of activities), 18:12–20 (April 30, 1961).

Hsü Yu-shan, "The Work of Reforming Bad Persons Is Actively Being Done Well," *Kuang-ming jih-pao* (Enlightenment daily), July 4, 1958, p. 3.

Huang Yüan,[6] *Wo-kuo jen-min lü-shih chih-tu*[7] (Our country's system of people's lawyers; Canton, December 1956), 18 pp.

Hucker, Charles O., *The Traditional Chinese State in Ming Times (1368–1644)* (Tucson: University of Arizona Press, 1961), 85 pp.

Hulsewé, A. F. P., *Remnants of Han Law* (Introductory studies and an annotated translation of chapters 22 and 23 of the History of the Former Han Dynasty, vol. I; Sinica Leidensia, no. 9; Leiden, 1955), 455 pp.

"In Response to the Demands of the People, the Canton Intermediate People's Court in Accordance with Law Resentences Hooligan Chief Ch'en Fu-pi to Four Years of Imprisonment," *Nan-fang jih-pao* (Southern daily, Canton), March 13, 1955.

Instructions of the CCPCC and the State Council [of the PRC] Relating to Checking the Blind Outflow of People from Rural Villages (Dec. 18, 1957), *FKHP,* 6:229–232 (July–December 1957).

Instructions of the CCPCC Relating to Abolishing the Complete Six Laws of the Kuomintang and Establishing Judicial Principles for the Liberated Areas (February 1949); quoted in the *Lectures,* pp. 20–21.

Instructions of the Ministry of Interior of the PRC Relating to the Work of Placement and Reform of City Vagrants (July 11, 1956), *FKHP,* 4:212–217 (July–December 1956).

Instructions of the Ministry of Justice of the PRC Relating to the Number, Term of Office and Methods of Selection of People's Assessors (July 21, 1956), *FKHP,* 4:239–241 (June–December 1956).

"Introducing the Soviet Union's Comrades' Courts for Enterprises," *JMJP,* Oct. 17, 1953, p. 3.

"Is it Right for the Public Security Organ To Do This?" *Hsin-hua jih-pao* (New China daily, Nanking), Oct. 28, 1956.

"Is a Ten-Year Sentence Appropriate for Hooligan Demeanor?" *Hsin-wen jih-pao* (Daily news, Shanghai), May 5, 1957.

Ishijima Yasushi, "A Pickpocket Case in Peking, Actualities of a Criminal Trial in China," in *Chūgoku no hō to shakai*[5] (Chinese law and society; Tokyo, 1960), pp. 64–71.

Jen Chen-to and Ho En-t'ao, "How to Establish China's New System of Criminal Litigation," *Chi-lin ta-hsüeh jen-wen k'o-hsüeh hsüeh-pao* (Kirin University journal of humanistic sciences), 2:121–126 (1959).

*JMJP,* Aug. 6, 1958; translated in Robert R. Bowie and John K. Fairbank, ed.,

*Communist China 1955–1959, Policy Documents with Analysis* (Cambridge, Mass.: Harvard University Press, 1962), p. 23.

Jones, F. Elwyn, "Justice in Modern China," *Listener*, 56:78–79 (July 1956).

Kao K'o-lin, "Crimes of Treason by Reactionary Groups in Tibet Are Something the Law of the State Does Not Tolerate" (address to the 1st meeting of the 2d session of the NPC, April 24, 1959), *Hsin-hua pan-yüeh-k'an* (New China semi-monthly), 9:64–66 (1959).

Kawasaki Mitsunari, "The Attorney System"; in *Chūgoku no hō to shakai*[5] (Chinese law and society; Tokyo: Shindoku Shosha, 1960), pp. 79–85.

Kawashima Takeyoshi, "Dispute Resolution in Contemporary Japan"; in A. T. von Mehren, *Law in Japan* (Cambridge, Mass.: Harvard University Press, 1963), pp. 41–72.

Khrushchev, N. S., "Problems of Theory" (report to the 21st extraordinary congress of the Communist Party of the Soviet Union, Jan. 27, 1959), *Pravda*, Jan. 28, 1959; translated in John N. Hazard and Isaac Shapiro, *The Soviet Legal System* (Dobbs Ferry, N.Y.: Oceana Publications, Inc., 1962), 174 pp.

Ko I, "A Group of Counterrevolutionaries Seized Because of a Letter — About Kuan Kuan-hui, an Advanced Mass Security Worker," *Kuang-chou jih-pao* (Canton daily), Feb. 26, 1955.

Ku Ang-jan, "Why Must Control of Counterrevolutionaries Be Decided Upon by Judgment of a People's Court?" *Shih-shih shou-ts'e* (Current events handbook), 23:35–36 (Dec. 10, 1956).

Ku Fang-p'ing, "The Great Victory of the Policy of Reforming Criminals," *CFYC*, 6:35–37 (1959).

"The Ku-lou Court of Foochow Accepts the Opinion of the Masses, Corrects the Situation of Too Lenient Sentences and Resentences Two Criminals Who Had Sexual Relations with Young Girls," *Fu-chien jih-pao* (Fukien daily), Nov. 29, 1957.

Kuan Feng, "Cannot the Criticized Comrades Have a Chance To Explain?" *Hsüeh-hsi* (Study), 102:6–7 (Dec. 2, 1956).

Kudryavtsev, V., "Pressing Problems of Soviet Criminology," *Sovetskaya Yustitsia*, 20:6–9 (October 1965); translated in *CDSP*, 17.48:12–13 (Dec. 22, 1965).

"Kwangtung Province Deals with Eight U.S.-Chiang Secret Agents, Four Are Not Prosecuted, Four Are Sentenced to Prison," *Ta Kung Pao* (Great public daily, Hong Kong), Feb. 12, 1964, p. 1.

Law for the Punishment of Police Offenses of the Republic of China, art. 28; in Chang Chih-pen,[3] ed., *Tsui-hsin liu-fa ch'üan-shu*[4] (Newest book of the complete six laws [of the Republic of China]; Taipei, 1959), p. 355.

Law for the Punishment of Police Offenses of the Republic of China; translated in Law Revision Planning Group, Council on United States Aid, the Executive Yuan, the Republic of China, comp., *Laws of the Republic of China* (First series — major laws; Taipei, December 1961), pp. 997–1025.

Law of the PRC for the Organization of Local People's Congresses and Local People's Councils of the Various Levels (passed at the 1st meeting of the 1st session of the NPC, Sept. 21, 1954; promulgated by the Chairman of the PRC, Sept. 28, 1954), *FKHP*, 1:139–150 (September 1954–June 1955).

Law of the PRC for the Organization of People's Courts (passed at the 1st meeting of the 1st session of the NPC, Sept. 21, 1954; promulgated by the Chairman of the PRC, Sept. 28, 1954), *FKHP*, 1:123–132 (September 1954–June 1955).

Law of the PRC for the Organization of People's Procuracies (passed at the 1st meeting of the 1st session of the NPC, Sept. 21, 1954; promulgated by the Chairman of the PRC, Sept. 28, 1954), *FKHP*, 1:133–138 (September 1954–June 1955).

Law Revision Planning Group, Council on United States Aid, the Executive Yuan, the Republic of China, trans. and comp., *Laws of the Republic of China*, 2 vols. (Taipei, 1961–1962).

Lee, Luke T. C., "Chinese Communist Law: Its Background and Development," *Michigan Law Review*, 60:439–472 (February 1962).

Leng Shao-chuan, "The Lawyer in Communist China," *Journal of the International Commission of Jurists*, 4.1:33–49 (Summer 1962).

────── "Post-Constitutional Development of 'People's Justice' in China," *Journal of the International Commission of Jurists*, 6.1:103–128 (Summer 1965).

Lethbridge, Henry J., *China's Urban Communes* (Hong Kong, 1961), 74 pp.

Li Hao-p'ei, "Condemn American Fascist Legislation and Adjudication, Support the Righteous Struggle of the American Communists," *CFYC*, 1:3–11 (1962).

Li Lo, "A Talk on Problems of Defending Socialist Construction in the Rural Villages," *CFYC*, 1:46–49 (1958).

Li Mu-an, "Censure Independent Adjudication That Proceeds from Concepts of the Old Law," *CFYC*, 1:24–27 (1958).

Liang, Lone, "Modern Law in China," in *Washington Foreign Law Society* (Studies in the law of the Far East and Southeast Asia; n.p., 1956), pp. 46–69.

Lifton, Robert Jay, *Thought Reform and the Psychology of Totalism, A Study of "Brainwashing" in China* (New York, 1961), 510 pp.

Lin Fu-shun, "Communist China's Emerging Fundamentals of Criminal Law," *American Journal of Comparative Law*, 13:80–93 (Winter 1964).

Ling Hung-chin, "Why Public Trial Should be Put into Effect," *Pao-t'ou jih-pao* (Paotow daily), Oct. 13, 1957.

Lipson, Leon, "Crime and Punishment; Execution: Hallmark of 'Socialist Legality,' " *Problems of Communism*, 11.5:21–26 (September–October 1962).

────── "Hosts and Pests: The Fight Against Parasites," *Problems of Communism*, 14.3:72–82 (March–April 1965).

Liu Hui-chen Wang, *The Traditional Chinese Clan Rules* (Monographs of the Association for Asian Studies, no. 7; Locust Valley, N.Y., 1959), 264 pp.

Liu Tse-chün, "Realizations from My Adjudication Work," *CFYC*, 1:48–51 (1959).

Lo Jui-ch'ing, "Explanation of the Draft Security Administration Punishment Act of the PRC," *FKHP*, 6:254–261 (July–December 1957).

────── "Public Security Work Must Further Implement the Mass Line," *CFYC*, 3:23–27 (1958).

────── "The Struggle of the Revolution against Counterrevolution in the Past Ten Years," *JMJP*, Sept. 28, 1959, p. 3.

Lunev, A. E., "Local Organs of People's Rule in China," *Sovety Deputatov Trudyaschikhsya*, no. 6 (December 1957); translated in JPRS, no. 375 (Nov. 18, 1958), 8 pp.

────── "Forms of the Participation of the Masses in the Activity of the State Organs of the PRC," *Sovetskoe Gosudarstvo i Pravo*, no. 1 (January 1958); translated in *JPRS*, no. 374 (Nov. 18, 1958), 13 pp.

McAleavy, Henry, "The People's Courts in Communist China," *American Journal of Comparative Law*, 11:52–65 (Winter 1962).

MacFarquhar, Roderick, ed., *The Hundred Flowers Campaign and the Chinese Intellectuals* (London: Stevens & Sons, Ltd., 1960), 324 pp.

"A Majority of Landlord and Rich Peasant Elements in the Administrative Village of Chang-ch'ing Change Their Status," *Shan-hsi jih-pao* (Shansi daily), Nov. 23, 1956.

Mannheim, Hermann, *Criminal Justice and Social Reconstruction* (London: Routledge & Kegan Paul, Ltd., 1946), 290 pp.

Mao Tse-tung, "On the People's Democratic Dictatorship" (address in commemoration of the 28th anniversary of the CCP), *JMJP*, July 1, 1949.

Mao Tse-tung, "Report of an Investigation into the Peasant Movement in Hunan (1927)"; translated in *Selected Works of Mao Tse-tung*, I (London: Lawrence & Wishart, Ltd., 1954), 21–59.

Mao Tse-tung, "Problems Relating to the Correct Handling of Contradictions Among the People" (address at the 11th enlarged meeting of the Supreme State Conference, Feb. 27, 1957), *FKHP*, 5:1–34 (January–June 1957).

Mao Tse-tung, "Problems Relating to the Correct Handling of Contradictions Among the People" (Feb. 27, 1957); translated in part in the *New York Times*, June 13, 1957, p. 8.

Marriage Law of the PRC (passed at the 7th meeting of the Central People's Government Council, April 13, 1950; promulgated by the Chairman of the PRC, May 1, 1950), *FLHP* 1949–1950, 1:32–36.

"The Masses Cleverly Recognize a Bandit; the People and Police Cooperate in Seizing a Criminal," *JMJP*, Feb. 25, 1959, p. 6.

Meijer, Marinus Johan, *The Introduction of Modern Criminal Law in China* (Sinica Indonesiana, no. 2; Batavia, 1950), 214 pp.

Meng Chao-liang, "The Basic Situation in Reform Through Labor Work in the Last Nine Years," *CFYC*, 5:66–70 (1958).

———— "Preliminary Accomplishments of the Work of Rehabilitation Through Labor," *CFYC*, 3:47–49 (1959).

Michael, Franz, "The Role of Law in Traditional, Nationalist, and Communist China," *China Quarterly*, 9:124–148 (January–March 1962).

"The Militia Plays an Enormous Role in Consolidating National Defense and Defending Socialist Construction," *Hsin-hua t'ung-hsün-she* (New China news agency, Peking), Sept. 26, 1964; translated in *SCMP*, 3314:8–9 (Oct. 8, 1964).

Mills, Harriet C., "Thought Reform: Ideological Remolding in China," *Atlantic Monthly*, 204:71–77 (December 1959).

Moraes, Frank, *Report on Mao's China* (New York, 1953), 212 pp.

Morse, H. B., *The International Relations of the Chinese Empire* [vol I]: *The Period of Conflict, 1834–1860* (London, New York, Bombay, and Calcutta: Longmans, Green, and Co., 1910), 727 pp.

Mou Min, "Enemy Property Concealed by Ma Po-sheng Confiscated in Accordance with Law," *Ta-chung jih-pao* (Masses' daily), Aug. 10, 1957.

Mu Fu-sheng (pseud.), *The Wilting of the Hundred Flowers; The Chinese Intelligensia under Mao* (Praeger publications in Russian history and world communism, no. 122) New York: Frederick A. Praeger, Inc., and London: William Heinemann, Ltd., 1963, 324 pp.

National Agricultural Development Outline [of the PRC] for 1956–1967 (revised draft, Oct. 25, 1957), *FKHP*, 6:37–58 (July–December 1957).

"A New Form of Self-Government by the Masses" (a report of an inspection team of the political-legal department of the Shensi provincial government), *Shan-hsi jih-pao* (Shensi daily), May 8, 1958, in *Chung-kuo kuo-fang ts'ung-shu*[8] (Collection of reprinted articles concerning China's national defense; Peking, 1958), 2:80–85.

"Notification of the State Council [of the PRC] Transmitting the Report of the Ministry of Public Security Relating to the Work of Preparing the Establishment of Houses of Discipline for Juvenile Offenders" (March 3, 1958), *FKHP,* 7:216–217 (January–June 1958).

O'Connor, Dennis, "Soviet People's Guards: An Experiment with Civic Police," *New York University Law Review,* 39:579–614 (1964).

Packer, Herbert L., "Two Models of the Criminal Process," *University of Pennsylvania Law Review,* 113:1–68 (1964).

"Party's Supervision Organs Dispose of Cases of Party Members Violating Party Discipline in Grain Collection," *Chi-lin jih-pao* (Kirin daily, Changchun), Feb. 28, 1958.

P'eng Chen, "Explanation of the Draft Act of the PRC for Punishment of Corruption," *Hsin-hua yüeh-pao* (New China monthly), 31:23–26 (May 1952).

People's Police Act of the PRC (passed at the 76th meeting of the Standing Committee of the NPC, June 25, 1957; promulgated by the Chairman of the PRC, June 25, 1957), *FKHP,* 5:113–116 (January–June 1957).

"People's Tribunal Protects the Rights of the Person. Wang Shao-ch'ing To Serve Imprisonment for Hitting Others," *Chung-ching jih-pao* (Chungking daily), April 23, 1957.

Piettre, A., "The People's Republic of China," *World Justice,* 3:450–460 (June 1962).

"Poor Peasant Girl, T'ang Yu-lien, Bravely Struggles Against Theft of Collective Property," *Chung-kuo ch'ing-nien pao* (China youth news, Peking), Nov. 24, 1964, p. 1.

"The Principal Criminal Who Persecuted the White-Haired Girl of I-pin Is Executed," *Szu-ch'uan jih-pao* (Szechuan daily), Jan. 15, 1959.

"A Procuracy's Bill of Prosecution . . ." *Hsin-wen jih-pao,* (Daily news, Shanghai), June 4, 1957.

Provisional Act of the PRC for the Organization of Security Defense Committees (approved by the Government Administration Council, June 27, 1952; promulgated by the Ministry of Public Security, Aug. 11, 1952), *FLHP* 1952, pp. 56–58.

Provisional Act of the PRC for Punishment of Crimes that Endanger State Currency (promulgated by the Government Administration Council, April 19, 1951), *FLHP* 1951, 1:149–150.

Provisional General Rules of the PRC for the Organization of People's Mediation Committees (passed at the 206th meeting on government administration by the Government Administration Council, Feb. 25, 1954; promulgated by the Government Administration Council, March 22, 1954), *FLHP* 1954, pp. 47–48.

Provisional Measures of the PRC for Control of Counterrevolutionaries (approved by the Government Administration Council, June 27, 1952; promulgated by the Ministry of Public Security, July 17, 1952), *FLHP* 1952, pp. 53–55.

Provisional Measures of the PRC for Dealing with the Release of Reform Through Labor Criminals at the Expiration of Their Term of Imprisonment and for Placing Them and Getting Them Employment (approved at the 222d meeting of the Government Administration Council, Aug. 26, 1954; promulgated by the Government Administration Council, Sept. 7, 1954), *FLHP* 1954, pp. 44–45.

Provisional Measures of the PRC for Receipt of Fees by Lawyers (approved at the 29th plenary meeting of the State Council, May 25, 1956; promulgated by the Ministry of Justice, July 20, 1956), *FKHP,* 4:235–238 (July–December 1956).

Provisional Regulations of the State Council [of the PRC] Relating to Rewards and

Punishments for Personnel of State Administrative Organs (approved at the 82d meeting of the Standing Committee of the NPC, Oct. 23, 1957; promulgated by the State Council, Oct. 26, 1957), *FKHP*, 6:197–202 (July–December 1957).

Reischauer, Edwin O. and John K. Fairbank, *East Asia, The Great Tradition* (A history of East Asian civilization, Vol I; Boston, 1958), 739 pp.

Reply of the Standing Committee of the NPC [of the PRC] to the Supreme People's Court Relating to Problems of How to Execute the Resolution that Death Penalty Cases Shall Be Decided by Judgment of or Approved by the Supreme People's Court (Sept. 26, 1957), *FKHP*, 6:297 (July–December 1957).

Resolution of the First Meeting of the Second Session of the NPC of the PRC Relating to Abolition of the Ministry of Justice and the Ministry of Supervision (passed, April 28, 1959), *FKHP*, 9:108–109 (January–July 1959).

"Revolutionary Theory Is Guide to Action: On the Dictatorship of the Proletariat," *Izvestia*, May 17, 1964, pp. 3–4; translated in *CDSP*, 16.21:3–8 (June 17, 1964).

Rickett, Allyn and Adele Rickett, *Prisoners of Liberation* (New York: Cameron Associates, Inc., 1957), 288 pp.

RSFSR Code of Criminal Procedure, art. 97; translated in H. J. Berman and J. W. Spindler, *Soviet Criminal Law and Procedure, The RSFSR Codes* (Cambridge, Mass.: Harvard University Press, 1966), p. 288.

1961 RSFSR Statute on Comrades' Courts, art. 15(5), *Vedomosti Verkhovnovo Soveta RSFSR* (Gazette of the Supreme Soviet of the RSFSR), 26:401; translated in *CDSP*, 13.33:9 (Sept. 13, 1961).

Rules [of the PRC] for Regulation of Explosive Articles (approved at the 63d plenary meeting of the State Council, Nov. 29, 1957; issued by the Ministry of Public Security, Dec. 9, 1957), *FKHP*, 6:267–270 (July–December 1957).

Schapiro, Leonard, "Prospects for the Rule of Law," *Problems of Communism*, 14.3:2–7 (March–April 1965).

Schram, Stuart R., *The Political Thought of Mao Tse-tung* (New York, Washington, D.C., and London, 1963), 319 pp.

Schurmann, Franz, *Ideology and Organization in Communist China* (Berkeley, Los Angeles, and London, 1966), 540 pp.

Schwartz, Benjamin, *Chinese Communism and the Rise of Mao* (Cambridge, Mass., 1951), 258 pp.

———— "On Attitudes toward Law in China," in Milton Katz, *Government under Law and the Individual* (Washington, D.C.: American Council of Learned Societies, 1957), pp. 27–39.

Security Administration Punishment Act of the PRC (passed at the 81st meeting of the Standing Committee of the NPC, Oct. 22, 1957; promulgated by the Chairman of the PRC, Oct. 22, 1957), *FKHP*, 6:245–254 (July–December 1957).

"Security Defense Organizations Have Developed Their Role in All Factories and Mines in the City of Pen-hsi," *Hsin-hua t'ung-hsün-she* (New China news agency), March 8, 1955.

"Severely Punish Wandering Thieves, Safeguard Security and Order in Society," *Ta-nan-shan jih-pao* (Ta-nan-shan daily, Kwangtung province), Dec. 11, 1959.

Shang Yin-pin, "Fully Develop the Militant Role of the Basic Level Security Defense Organizations," *CFYC*, 5:71–72 (1958).

"Shanghai High Court Grants Amnesty to a Group of Criminals," *Wen-hui pao* (Literary news, Shanghai) [December ?], 1959, p. 1.

Shen Ch'i-szu, "Censure 'the Principle of Debate' in the Criminal Litigation of the Bourgeoisie," *CFYC*, 1:30–34 (1960).

Shu-hsiang, "Letter of Protest to Tzu-ch'an (Prime Minister of the State of Cheng) Who in 536 B.C. Had Ordered 'Books of Punishment' to be Inscribed on a Set of Bronze Tripod Vessels"; translated in Derk Bodde, "Basic Concepts of Chinese Law: The Genesis and Evolution of Legal Thought in Traditional China," *American Philosophical Society, Proceedings,* 107.5:381–382 (October 1963).

Skolnick, Jerome H., *Justice without Trial* (New York, London and Sydney: John Wiley & Sons, Inc., 1966), 279 pp.

Snow, Edgar, *The Other Side of the River, Red China Today* (New York: Random House, 1962, and London: Victor Gollancz, Ltd., 1963), 810 pp.

Special Amnesty Order of the Chairman of the PRC (promulgated, Sept. 17, 1959), *FKHP,* 10:60–61 (July–December 1959).

Staunton, G. T., trans., *Ta Tsing Leu Lee; being the Fundamental Laws, and a selection from the Supplementary Statutes, of the Penal Code of China* (London, 1810), 581 pp.

Su I, "Should a Defender Attack Crime or Protect Crime?" *CFYC,* 2:76–77 (1958).

Sun Chia-hsing, "Realizations from Participating in Production and Defending Production," *JMJP,* May 13, 1959.

"The Supreme Court Wins a Great Victory in the Struggle against the Rightists," *JMJP,* Dec. 12, 1957, p. 4.

"Supreme People's Court Grants Amnesty to an Initial Group of War Criminals Who Have Changed into Good Persons," *JMJP,* Dec. 5, 1959.

Tadasuke Torio, "Chinese Lawyers," in *Horitsuka no mita Chūgoku*[9] (China as seen by lawyers; Tokyo, 1965), pp. 216–217.

T'an Cheng-wen, "Absorb Experience and Teaching, Impel a Great Leap Forward in Procuratorial Work," *CFYC,* 3:34–35 (1958).

Tang, Peter S. H., *Communist China Today* (Domestic and foreign policies, vol. I), 2d ed. (Research Institute on the Sino-Soviet Bloc No. 1; Washington, D.C., 1961), 745 pp.

Tao Lung-sheng, "The Criminal Law of Communist China," *Cornell Law Quarterly,* 51.1:43–68 (Fall 1966).

Teaching and Research Office for Criminal Law of the Central Political-Legal Cadres' School, ed., *Chung-hua jen-min kung-ho-kuo hsing-fa tsung-tse chiang-yi*[10] (Lectures on the general principles of criminal law of the People's Republic of China; Peking, Sept. 1957), 266 pp.

Teng Hsiao-p'ing, "Report Relating to the Rectification Movement" (at the 3d enlarged plenary meeting of the 8th session of the CCPCC, Sept. 23, 1957), *FKHP,* 6:5–36 (July–December 1957).

"This Year There Are Over 3,000 Lawyers Serving the Masses," *Kuang-ming jih-pao* (Enlightenment daily), Jan. 14, 1957.

Topping, Audrey R., "Through Darkest Red China," *New York Times Magazine,* Aug. 28, 1966, pp. 26–27, 89–92.

Ts'ui Ch'eng-hsüan, "How We Defended the Safety of Hsing-fu People's Commune," *CFYC,* 6:61–63 (1958).

Tu Chi-yüan, "Report on Improving the Work of Residents' Committees in Shanghai" (speech at the 75th administrative meeting of the Shanghai Municipal People's Government), *Chieh-fang jih-pao* (Liberation daily, Shanghai), Dec. 17, 1954.

Tung Ching-chih et al., "A Discussion of Bigamy and Adultery," *Fa hsüeh* (Legal Science), 4:36–39 (1957).

Tung Pi-wu, "Congratulations on the Founding of the Periodical *Political-Legal Research,*" *CFYC,* 1:1–2 (1954).

Tung Pi-wu, "Adjudication Work of the People's Courts in the Preceding Year," *Hsin-hua pan-yüch-k'an* (New China semi-monthly), 15:9–11 (1956).

Uniform Code of Military Justice of the United States, arts. 133–134; in *United States Code,* title 10, sects. 933–934 (1965).

Van der Sprenkel, Sybille, *Legal Institutions in Manchu China, a Sociological Analysis* (London School of Economics, Monographs on Social Anthropology, no. 24; London: Athlone Press, 1962), 178 pp.

Van der Valk, M. H., trans., *Interpretations of the Supreme Court at Peking, Years 1915 and 1916* (Sinica Indonesiana, vol. I, Batavia, 1949), 382 pp.

Van Gulik, Robert, *T'ang-yin-pi-shih, Parallel Cases from under the Pear-tree, a 13th-century manual of jurisprudence and detection* (Sinica Leidensia series, vol. X; Leiden, 1956), 198 pp.

Walker, Richard L., *China Under Communism: The First Five Years* (New Haven, 1955), 403 pp.

Wang Chao-sheng, "Refute the Principle of 'Not Making the Position of the Defendant Unfavorable in a Criminal Appeal,'" *Hsi-pei ta-hsüeh hsüeh-pao (jen-wen k'o-hsüeh)* (Northwestern Univ. Journal [humanistic sciences], 1:65–70 (July 1958).

Wang Hsin et al., "Several Problems Relating to the Procedure of Adjudication Supervision," *CFYC,* 2:71–75 (1958).

Wang Huai-ming, "Chinese and American Criminal Law: Some Comparisons," *Journal of Criminal Law, Criminology and Police Science,* 46:796–832 (March–April 1956).

Wang Ju-ch'i, "How the Enterprise Comrades' Courts Were Established in K'ai-luan Coal Mine," *JMJP,* April 19, 1954, p. 3.

Wang Kuang-li, "How Judicial Work in Honan Province Serves the Central Work," *CFYC,* 6:46–52 (1958).

Wang Kuang-li, "Report on High Level Court Work in Honan Province, Communist China," *Ho-nan jih-pao* (Honan daily), March 1, 1960; translated in *JPRS,* no. 6082 (Oct. 13, 1960), 10 pp.

Wang Min, "The Great Significance of People's Adjustment Work in Resolving Contradictions Among the People," *CFYC,* 2:27–32 (1960).

Wang Yü-feng, "Realizations from My Experience as a Secretary of a CYL Branch," *Chung-kuo ch'ing-nien* (China youth), 22:2–4 (Nov. 16, 1963).

Wang Yü-nan, "Important Measures For Strengthening State Discipline," *CFYC,* 1:51–53 (1958).

Wang Yün-sheng, "How Adjudication Work Implements the Mass Line," *CFYC,* 6:38–41 (1959).

"We Must Create Conditions to [Let a Hundred Schools] Contend in Legal Studies," *Kuang-ming jih-pao* (Enlightenment daily), June 12, 1957, p. 3; translated in Roderick MacFarquhar, ed., *The Hundred Flowers Campaign and the Chinese Intellectuals* (London: Stevens & Sons, Ltd., 1960), p. 116.

Weber, M., *Law in Economy and Society,* trans. E. A. Shils and M. Rheinstein, IV (Cambridge, Mass., 1954), 264–265; quoted in Sybille Van der Sprenkel, *Legal Institutions in Manchu China, a Sociological Analysis* (London: Athlone Press, 1962), p. 128.

Wei, Wen-ch'i (Henry), *Courts and Police in Communist China to 1952* (HRRI project: Chinese documents, Research Memorandum No. 44; Lackland Air Force Base, Texas, 1955), 63 pp.

"What Is One To Do If One Disagrees with the People's Procuracy?" *Kung-jen jih-pao* (Workers' daily, Peking), Feb. 21, 1957.

"What Is 'the System of the Court of Second Instance as the Court of Last Instance'?" *Kung-jen jih-pao* (Workers' daily, Peking), Jan. 26, 1957.

"What Shortcomings Are There in the Work of the Supreme People's Court?" *JMJP*, May 21, 1957, p. 2.

Williams, G., "The Definition of Crime," in George W. Keeton and Georg Schwarzenberger, ed., *Current Legal Problems*, VIII (London: Stevens & Sons, Ltd., 1955), 102–130.

Wills, Morris R. (as told to J. Robert Moskin), "Why I Chose China," *Look Magazine*, Feb. 8, 1966, pp. 75–84.

Wittfogel, Karl A., "Forced Labor in Communist China," *Problems of Communism*, 5.4:34–42 (July–Aug. 1956).

Wu Lei, "An Examination of the Article 'A Study of the Position of the Defender in Our Country's Criminal Litigation,'" *CFYC*, 2:78–81 (1958).

Wu Lei, "We Must Thoroughly Clean Out Old Legal Concepts and Rightwing Thinking in Our Teaching of 'Criminal Litigation,'" *Chiao-hsüeh yü yen-chiu* (Teaching and research), 4:1–3 (1958).

Wu Lei et al., "A Few Realizations from the Study of Our Country's Guiding Principles of Evidence in Litigation," *CFYC*, 1:21–25 (1963).

Wu Te-feng, "Struggle in Order to Defend the Socialist Legal System" (a speech broadcast Jan. 19, 1958, on the Central People's Broadcasting Station), *CFYC*, 1:10–16 (1958).

Wu Yü-su, "Censure the Bourgeois Principle of 'Presumption of Innocence,'" *CFYC*, 2:37–41 (1958).

Yang, C. K., *A Chinese Village in Early Communist Transition* (Cambridge, Mass.: The M.I.T. Press, 1959), 284 pp.

Yang Kuang-teh, "Neighbourhood Committee," *China Reconstructs*, July 1955, pp. 22–24.

Yang Lien-sheng, *Studies in Chinese Institutional History* (Harvard-Yenching Institute studies, no. 20; Cambridge, Mass., 1961), 229 pp.

Yang, Martin C., *A Chinese Village* (London, 1947), 275 pp.

Yang P'eng and Lin Ch'ih-chung, "Investigate Deeply, Handle Cases Conscientiously," *Fu-chien jih-pao* (Fukien daily), Aug. 14, 1956.

Yee, Frank S. H., "Chinese Communist Police and Courts," *Journal of Criminal Law, Criminology and Police Science*, 48:83–92 (May–June 1957).

## NOTES TO BIBLIOGRAPHY

1. 陝甘寧邊區懲治條
   例彙編
2. 全國農業發展綱要
   （草案）圖解
3. 張知本
4. 最新六法全書
5. 中國の法と社會
6. 黄遠
7. 我國人民律師制度
8. 中國國防叢書
9. 法律家の見た中國
10. 中華人民共和國刑
    法總則講義

abolish, abolition; fei ch'u 廢除

abortion; to t'ai 墮胎

abuse [in the sense of "corrupt practice"]; wu pi 舞弊

accept [a decision, etc.]; fu ts'ung 服從

accept [a petition, etc.]; shou li 受理

accept a bribe; shou hui 受賄, shou shou hui lo 收受賄賂

accept punishment [for a crime]; fu tsui 服罪

accidental homicide; wu shang jen ming 誤傷人命

accomplice; ts'ung fan 從犯

accountant, accounting; k'uai chi 會計

accumulated cases; chi an 積案

accusation meeting; chien chü hui 檢舉會

accuse, make an accusation, accusation; chien chü 檢舉, kao kao 告, kao fa 告發, k'ung su 控訴

accused; pei kao jen 被告人

accuser; chien chü che 檢舉者, k'ung su jen 控訴人

acquit; p'an wu tsui 判無罪

act [legislative, etc.]; t'iao li 條例

act indecently with women; t'iao hsi fu nü 調戲婦女

act obscenely; wei hsieh 猥褻

address [residential]; chu chih 住址

adjourn the court; hsiu t'ing 休庭

adjudge; p'an chüeh 判決

adjudicate, adjudication; shen p'an 審判

adjudicate a case, adjudication of a case; p'an an 判案

adjudicate at a higher level, adjudication at a higher level; t'i shen 提審

adjudication committee; shen p'an wei yüan hui 審判委員會

adjudication division; shen p'an t'ing 審判庭

adjudication officer [judge or assessor]; shen p'an jen yüan 審判人員

adjudication supervision, supervise adjudication; shen p'an chien tu 審判監督

adjustment committee; t'iao ch'u wei yüan hui 調處委員會

administer; administration; kuan li 管理

administer the law; szu fa 司法

administration, administrative; hsing cheng 行政

administrative area; hsing cheng ch'ü 行政區, hsing cheng ch'ü yü 行政區域

administrative law; hsing cheng fa
行 政 法

administrative village; hsiang 鄉,
hsing cheng ts'un 行 政 村

admit [a fact], admission; ch'eng jen
承 認, kung jen 供 認

admit one's error [wrongdoing],
admission of one's error [wrong-
doing]; jen shih ts'o wu 認 識 錯
誤, jen ts'o 認 錯

admit one's guilt, admission of one's
guilt; jen tsui 認 罪

admonish, admonition; ch'üan tao
勸 導

adopt [legislation, etc.]; chih ting
制 定, chih ting 制 訂

adopted children; yang tzu nü
養 子 女

adult offender; ch'eng nien fan
成 年 犯

adultery; t'ung chien 通 奸

affirm the original judgment; wei
ch'ih yüan p'an 維 持 原 判

aggregate sentence; tsung ho hsing
總 合 刑

aggression, aggressive; ch'in lüeh
侵 略

agitate, agitation; ku tung 鼓 動
shan huo 煽 惑, shan tung 煽 動

agree, agreement; hsieh i 協 議

agreement [in the sense of "a
contract"]; ho t'ung 合 同

aid the enemy; tzu ti 資 敵

alias; yu ming 又 名

alien; wai kuo jen 外 國 人

alimony; shan yang fei 贍 養 費

analogize [for purposes of applying
criminal punishment], analogy;
lei t'ui 類 推

anarchy, anarchical; wu cheng fu 無 政 府

announce; hsüan pu 宣 布

annul the original judgment, annul
the judgment; ch'e hsiao yüan p'an
撤 消 原 判

appeal (n.), appeal (v.); shang su
上 訴

appeal [written]; shang su chuang
上 訴 狀

appear in court; ch'u hsi fa t'ing
出 席 法 庭, ch'u t'ing 出 庭

appellant; shang su jen
上 訴 人

appellate court; shang su shen fa
yüan 上 訴 審 法 院

appellate division; shang su t'ing
上 訴 庭

application [in writing]; shen
ch'ing shu 申 請 書

application for security detention;
chih an chü liu shen ch'ing piao
治 安 拘 留 申 請 表

apply; shen ch'ing 申 請

appoint; jen ming 任 命

appoint and remove, appointment and
removal; jen mien 任 免

apprehend [a person]; chen ch'i 偵 緝

approve, approval; ho chun 核准,
  p'i chun 批准

approve and transmit; p'i chuan
  批轉

arbitrary; jen i 任意

arbitrary decision; shan tuan 擅斷

arbitrator; chung ts'ai jen 仲裁人

area of jurisdiction; kuan hsia ch'ü
  yü 管轄區域

argue [a case, etc.]; pien lun 辯論

armed fighting; chieh tou 械鬥

armed unit; pu tui 部隊

arms, armed; wu chuang 武裝

army; chün tui 軍隊

arranged marriage; pao pan te hun
  yin 包辦的婚姻

arrest (n.), arrest (v.), make an
  arrest; pu 捕, pu huo 捕獲,
  pu ya 捕押, tai pu 逮捕

arrest and take to [the authorities,
  etc.]; pu sung 捕送

arrest warrant; tai pu cheng
  逮捕証

arson; fang huo 放火, tsung huo
  縱火

assessor [people's]; p'ei shen yüan
  陪審員

assets; tzu ts'ai 資財

assistant judge; chu li shen p'an yüan
  助理審判員

atone for one's crime; shu tsui
  贖罪

attack; hsi chi 襲擊, ta chi 打擊

attack in retaliation, attack and retaliate;
  ta chi pao fu 打擊報復

attempt [to commit a crime], attempted
  [crime]; wei sui 未遂

attempt, try; ch'i t'u 企圖

attempt to commit a crime; fan tsui
  wei sui 犯罪未遂

attempted theft; hsing ch'ieh wei sui
  行竊未遂

attend [a meeting, etc., as an ob-
  server]; lieh hsi 列席

attend [a meeting, etc., as a
  participant]; ch'u hsi 出席

authority; ch'üan 權 ch'üan hsien
  權限 ch'üan li 權利

authorize; shou ch'üan 授權,
  wei t'o 委托

auto accident; ch'e huo 車禍

autonomous chou; tzu chih chou
  自治州

autonomous county; tzu chih hsien
  自治縣

backbone element; ku kan fen tzu
  骨幹分子

backward element; lo hou fen tzu
  落後分子

bad element; huai fen tzu 壞分子

bad person; huai jen 壞人

bandit; fei 匪, fei t'u 匪徒,
  tao fei 盜匪, t'u fei 土匪

banditry; tao fei tsui 盜匪罪

bankrupt, bankruptcy; p'o ch'an 破產

basic level people's court; chi ts'eng jen min fa yüan 基層人民法院

basic militia [lit., backbone militia]; ku kan min ping 骨幹民兵

beat [in the sense of "hit"], beat up; ou ta 毆打, ta 打

beat and injure; ta shang 打傷

become legally effective; fa sheng fa lü hsiao li 發生法律效力

beg; ch'i t'ao 乞討

beg for food; ch'i shih 乞食

behavior; piao hsien 表現

believe a coerced statement; pi kung hsin 逼供信

betray; pei p'an 背叛

bigamy; ch'ung hun 重婚

bill of prosecution; ch'i su shu 起訴書

blame (v.); tse pei 責備

blood-letting; liu hsieh 流血

bombardment; h'ung chi 轟擊

bonus system; fen hung chih 分紅制

borrow; chieh yung 借用

bourgeoisie; tzu ch'an chieh chi 資產階級

branch court; fen yüan 分院

branch tribunal; p'ai ch'u t'ing 派出庭

break a case; p'o an 破案, p'o huo an chien 破獲案件

break the law, law-breaking; fan fa 犯法

bribe, bribery; hsing hui 行賄, hsing shih hui lo 行使賄賂, hui lo 賄賂

bring a complaint; k'ung kao 控告

bring suit; ch'i su 起訴

bring to court and handle according to law; kuei an fa pan 歸案法辦

bring up for hearing; t'i shen 提審

bureaucrat; kuan liao 官僚

burn fields; shao huang 燒荒

burn hillsides; shao shan 燒山

cadre; kan pu 幹部

candidate [member]; hou pu 候補

capital punishment; chi hsing 極刑

case; an chien 案件, an tzu 案子

case involving the spreading of poison; t'ou tu an chien 投毒案件

case of an application for approval of arrest; p'i pu an chien 批捕案件

case of first instance; ti i shen p'an an chien 第一審判案件

case the result of which is unjust; yüan an 寃案

case that is being litigated; she sung an chien 涉訟案件

cause delay in one's work; i wu kung tso 貽誤工作

cell [of a prison]; chien 監

censure (n., v.); p'i p'an 批判

center for discipline; kuan chiao ch'ang 管教場

center for rehabilitation of children; erh t'ung chiao yang so 兒童教養所

Central People's Government; chung yang jen min cheng fu 中央人民政府

Central People's Government Council; chung yang jen min cheng fu wei yüan hui 中央人民政府委員會

certificate; cheng chao 証照, cheng chien 証件, cheng ming hsin chien 証明信件, cheng ming shu 証明書

chairman; chu hsi 主席

chairman of a committee [or a council or a commission]; wei yüan chang 委員長

change a judgment; kai p'an 改判

change unlawfully; ts'uan kai 篡改

chastise; ch'eng fa 懲罰

cheat; ch'i p'ien 欺騙

cheat one's organization; ch'i p'ien tsu chih 欺騙組織

check [facts, etc.]; ch'a shih 查實, ch'a tui 查對, ho tui 核對

check [in the sense of "restrain"]; chih chih 制止

check the evidence; tui cheng 對証

chief judge [of a division]; t'ing chang 庭長

chief procurator; chien ch'a chang 檢察長

child betrothal; t'ung yang hsi 童養媳

child criminal; fan tsui te erh t'ung 犯罪的兒童

Chinese traitor; han chien 漢奸

choke to death; ch'ia szu 掐死

chou [an administrative unit]; chou 州

circuit tribunal; hsün hui fa t'ing 巡迴法庭

circumstances of a case; an ch'ing 案情, ch'ing chieh 情節

circumstantial evidence; p'ang cheng 旁証

citizen; kung min 公民

city; ch'eng shih 城市, shih 市

city-administered district; shih hsia ch'ü 市轄區

city directly under the central authority [government]; chih hsia shih 直轄市

civil affairs department; min cheng pu men 民政部門

civil affairs section; min cheng k'o 民政科

civil compensation; min shih p'ei ch'ang 民事賠償

civil dispute; min shih chiu fen 民事糾紛

clarify, clear up; ch'a ch'ing 查清, ch'a ming 查明

clerk; pan shih yüan 辦事員

close a case; chieh an 結案

clue; hsien so 綫索

coastal defense public security representative; hai fang kung an yüan
海防公安員

coerce, coercion; ch'iang chih 强制, ch'iang p'o 强迫, hsieh p'o 脅迫

coercively command; ch'iang p'o ming ling 强迫命令

collaborate; ho huo 合伙, kou chieh 勾結

collegial panel; ho i t'ing 合議庭

collegial system; ho i chih 合議制

collude, collusion; ch'uan t'ung 串通

collude [collusion] with others regarding statements to be made; ch'uan kung 串供

combat banditry; chiao fei 剿匪

combine punishments, combined punishments; ping fa 并罰

combined; ho ping 合并

command (v.) [in the sense of "order"]; ming ling 命令

command [armed forces, etc.], commander; chih hui 指揮

commend, commendation; piao yang 表揚

commit arson; fang huo 放火, tsung huo 縱火

commit a crime; fan tsui 犯罪, tso an 作案

commit a deadly act; hsing hsiung 行兇

commit [an offense, etc.] repeatedly and fail to change; lü fan pu kai 屢犯不改

commit [an offense, etc.] repeatedly despite repeated warnings; lü chieh lü fan 屢戒屢犯

commit suicide; tzu sha 自殺

commit theft; hsing ch'ieh 行竊

commit to custody, commitment to custody; shou ya 收押

commodity exchange; chiao i so 交易所

companion in the commission of a crime; t'ung huo fan 同伙犯

compensate, compensation, pay compensation; p'ei ch'ang 賠償

compensate for damage; p'ei ch'ang sun hai 賠償損害

complainant; k'ung kao jen 控告人, yüan kao 原告, yüan kao jen 原告人

complaint, make a complaint; kao kao 告, kao chuang 告狀, kao fa 告發

comply with a punishment; fu hsing 服刑

comrades' court [lit., "comrades' adjudication committee"]; t'ung chih shen p'an hui 同志審判會

conceal; pao pi 包庇, ts'ang ni 藏匿, yin man 隱瞞, yin ts'ang 隱藏

conceal bad persons; pao pi huai jen 包庇壞人

conclude [a contract, etc.]; ting ch'u 定出, ting li 訂立

conclude adjudication; shen chieh 審結

conclusion of an expert witness; chien ting chieh lun 鑒定結論

concubinage; na ch'ieh 納妾

concurrently to hold office, concurrent office; chien chih 兼職

condemn, condemnation; ch'ien tse 譴責

conditional release; chia shih 假釋

confer; shang t'ung 商同

confess, confession; t'an pai 坦白, t'an pai chiao tai 坦白交待

confine in custody, confinement in custody; chi ya 羈押

confine to quarters, confinement to quarters; chin pi 禁閉

confinement; chien chin 監禁

confiscate, confiscation; mo shou 沒收

conspire, conspiracy; yin mou 陰謀

constitution [national]; hsien fa 憲法

constitution [of a party, etc.]; chang 章, chang ch'eng 章程

contraband article; wei chin p'in 違禁品, wei chin wu p'in 違禁物品

contract; ch'i yüeh 契約

control [a criminal sanction]; kuan chih 管制

control [one's acts, etc.]; k'ung chih 控制

control production, controlled production; kuan chih sheng ch'an 管制生產

convene the court, convene the tribunal, court session, in court; k'ai t'ing 開庭

convict (v.), conviction; p'an tsui 判罪, ting tsui 定罪

corporal punishment; jou hsing 肉刑, t'i fa 體罰

corrupt, corruption; t'an tsang 貪贓, t'an wu 貪污, wu pi 舞弊

corrupt in a way which involves the intentional misapplication of law; t'an tsang wang fa 貪贓枉法

corrupt scheming; ying szu wu pi 營私舞弊

corruptly accept a bribe; t'an wu shou hui 貪污受賄

corruptly steal state property; t'an wu tao ch'ieh kuo chia ts'ai ch'an 貪污盜竊國家財產

counterrevolution; fan ko ming 反革命

counterrevolutionary, counterrevolutionary element; fan ko
ming fen tzu 反革命分子

counterrevolutionary activity; fan ko
ming huo tung 反革命活動

counterrevolutionary criminal;
fan ko ming fan 反革命犯

counterrevolutionary movement;
fan ko ming yün tung 反革命
運動

country; kuo chia 國家

county; hsien 縣

county seat; hsien ch'eng 縣城

court; fa t'ing 法庭, fa yüan 法院

court-affiliated doctor; fa i 法醫

court of first instance; ti i shen fa
yüan 第一審法院

court which originally adjudicated;
yüan shen fa yüan 原審法院

create havoc; tao luan 搗亂

creditor; chai ch'üan jen 債權人

crime; fan tsui 犯罪, tsui, 罪
tsui hsing 罪行

crime against the internal security
of the state; nei luan tsui 內亂罪

crime against the security of the
state committed in conjunction
with a foreign power; wai huan
tsui 外患罪

crime and punishment; tsui hsing
罪刑

crime of concealing an offender or
destroying evidence; ts'ang ni jen

fan chi yin mo cheng chü tsui 藏匿
人犯及湮没証据罪

crime of corruption and misconduct
in office; t'an wu tu chih tsui
貪污瀆職罪

crime of creating public danger;
kung kung wei hsien tsui 公共
危險罪

crime of defamation; fei pang tsui
誹謗罪

crime of escaping from custody;
t'ao t'o tsui 逃脫罪

crime of falsifying weights or
measures; wei tsao tu liang heng
tsui 偽造度量衡罪

crime of forging an official document
or seal; wei tsao kung wen yin hsin
tsui 偽造公文印信罪

crime of hooliganism; liu mang tsui
流氓罪

crime of inflicting bodily injury;
shang hai tsui 傷害罪

crime of inflicting serious bodily
injury, infliction of serious bodily
injury; chung shang tsui 重傷罪

crime of interfering with agricultural
or industrial policy; fang hai nung
kung cheng ts'e tsui 妨害農工
政策罪

crime of interfering with elections;
fang hai hsüan chü tsui 妨害選
舉罪

crime of interfering with public affairs;

fang hai kung wu tsui 妨害公務罪

crime of interfering with water utilization; fang hai shui li tsui 妨害水利罪

crime of kidnapping for ransom; lu jen le shu tsui 擄人勒贖罪

crime of misconduct in office; tu chih tsui 瀆職罪

crime of sabotaging transportation or communication facilities; p'o huai chiao t'ung tsui 破壞交通罪

crime of undermining the currency or valuable securities; p'o huai huo pi chi yu chia cheng ch'üan tsui 破壞貨幣及有價証券罪

crime of undermining social order; p'o huai she hui chih hsü tsui 破壞社會秩序罪

crime of violating government laws and decrees; wei fan cheng fu fa ling tsui 違反政府法令罪

crime of which one is accused; pei k'ung tsui hsing 被控罪行

crime relating to one's duties in office; chih wu shang te fan tsui 職務上的犯罪

criminal; fan 犯, fan tsui che 犯罪者, fan tsui fen tzu 犯罪分子, tsui fan 罪犯

criminal act; tsui hsing 罪行

criminal articles; fan tsui wu p'in 犯罪物品

criminal case; hsing shih an chien 刑事案件

criminal code; hsing fa 刑法 hsing fa tien 刑法典

criminal element; fan tsui fen tzu 犯罪分子

criminal law; hsing fa 刑法

criminal law scholar; hsing fa hsüeh che 刑法學者

criminal offender; hsing shih fan 刑事犯

criminal record; ch'ien k'o 前科

criminal responsibility; tsui tse 罪責

criminal who is undergoing reform through labor; lao kai fan 勞改犯

criticize, criticism; p'i p'ing 批評

criticism-education; p'i p'ing chiao yü 批評教育

criticism meeting; p'i p'ing hui 批評會

current counterrevolution; hsien hsing fan ko ming 現行反革命

custody; tsai ya 在押

damage the prestige of state organs; sun hai kuo chia chi kuan wei hsin 損害國家機關威信

damage public property; sun hai kung kung ts'ai wu 損害公共財物

deadly weapon; hsiung ch'i 兇器

deal with [a case, etc.]; ch'u li 處理

deal with according to law; fa pan 法辦

death penalty, death sentence, sentence to death; szu hsing 死刑

debauch; wu ju 污辱

debt; chai wu 債務

deceased [person]; szu che 死者

deceitful; nung hsü tso chia 弄虛作假

deceive, deception; ch'i p'ien 欺騙

decide, decision; chüeh ting 決定, p'an ting 判定, ts'ai chüeh 裁決, ts'ai ting 裁定

decide by judgment; p'an chüeh 判決

decide a case; ting an 定案

decide upon punishment; liang hsing 量刑

declaration [written]; sheng ming shu 聲明書

declare; hsüan kao 宣告

deface; wu sun 污損

defend [a defendant, etc.], defense; pien hu 辯護

defendant; pei kao jen 被告人

defender; pien hu jen 辯護人

deficit; pu tsu pu fen 不足部分

delegate (v.); wei p'ai 委派

deliberate, deliberation; p'ing i 評議

delinquent conduct; pu liang hsing wei 不良行為

delinquent element; pu liang fen tzu 不良分子

demerit, give a demerit; chi kuo 記過

demotion in grade; chiang chi 降級

demotion in office; chiang chih 降職

denounce, denunciation; chien chü 檢舉

denouncer; chien chü che 檢舉者

deny; fou jen 否認

deny having committed a crime; fou jen tsui hsing 否認罪行

dependent; i lai ch'i sheng huo te jen 依賴其生活的人

deprive [of rights, etc.], deprivation; po to 剝奪

derelict in one's duty, dereliction of duty; shih chih 失職

desert [a child, spouse, etc.], desertion; i ch'i 遺棄

despot [local]; o pa 惡霸

destroy, destruction; p'o huai 破壞

destroy evidence of the crime; yin mieh tsui cheng 湮滅罪証

destroy unity; p'o huai t'uan chieh 破壞團結

detailed rules; hsi tse 細則

detain, detention; chü i 拘役, chü liu 拘留

detention house; k'an shou so
看守所

detention house guard; k'an shou so
yüan 看守所員

detention warrant; chü liu cheng
拘留証

dictatorship, dictatorial; chuan cheng
專政, tu ts'ai 獨裁

diminish guilt; che tsui 折罪

direct evidence; chih chieh cheng
chü 直接証据

discipline [in the sense of "order"];
chi lü 紀律

discipline (n.) [in the sense of
"corrective training"], discipline
(v.); kuan chiao 管教

discipline (v.) [in the sense of "to
punish"]; ch'eng chieh 懲戒

discriminate against; ch'i shih 歧視

discuss, discussion [in the sense of
"negotiation"]; hsieh shang 協商

disobey resolutions and orders of
higher levels; pu fu ts'ung shang
chi chüeh i, ming ling 不服從
上級決議, 命令

dispute; cheng lun 爭論, chiu fen
糾紛

dispute among the people; min chien
chiu fen 民間糾紛

disrupt; jao luan 擾亂

disrupt discipline, disruption of
discipline; luan chi 亂紀

dissuade, dissuasion; ch'üan tsu
勸阻

district public security assistant;
ch'ü kung an chu li yüan 區公安
助理員

district under the jurisdiction of;
hsia ch'ü 轄區

districted city; she ch'ü te shih
設區的市

disturb and damage; jao hai 擾害

divorce; li hun 離婚

divulge state secrets; hsieh lou kuo
chia chi mi 泄露國家機密

document for the partitioning of
property; fen tan 分單

documentary evidence; shu cheng
書証

domination; t'ung chih 統治

draft [of an act, etc.]; ts'ao an
草案

draw lots; ch'ou ch'ien 抽籤

drifting; liu lang 流浪

drifting and begging; liu lang ch'i
t'ao 流浪乞討

drown a baby; ni ying 溺嬰

due to an irresistible cause; yu
yü pu neng k'ang chü te yüan yin
由于不能抗拒的原因

duties [official]; chih shou 職守,
chih wu 職務

embassies and consulates; shih ling
kuan 使領館

embezzle; ch'in t'un 侵吞

employee; jen yüan 人員

encroach, encroachment; ch'in hai
侵害

endanger; wei hai 危害

engage in prostitution; mai yin
賣淫

enslavement; nu i 奴役

enterprise; ch'i yeh 企業

entice; kou yin 勾引

entrust; wei t'o 委託

equal rights; ch'üan li p'ing teng
權利平等

erroneous judgment; ts'o p'an
錯判

erroneously decided case; ts'o an
錯案, ts'o p'an an chien 錯
判案件

error; ts'o wu 錯誤

escape; t'ao 逃, t'ao i 逃逸,
t'ao p'ao 逃跑, t'ao t'o 逃脫

escape from prison; yüeh yü ch'ien
t'ao 越獄潛逃

escort [a person] in custody; ya
chieh 押解

espionage; chien tieh 間諜

establish a lottery; she ts'ai 設彩

establish one's merit; li kung 立
功, li yu kung chi 立有功績

evade [the law, etc.]; t'ao pi 逃避

evade taxes; lou shui 漏稅, t'ou
shui 偷稅, t'ou t'ao shui shou
偷逃稅收

evaluation committee; p'ing shen
wei yüan hui 評審委員會

evidence; cheng chü 証據, cheng
wu 証物

evidence of a crime; tsui cheng
罪証

evil, evil act, evil crime; tsui o
罪惡

examine, examination; chien ch'a
檢查, chien yen 檢驗
k'ao ch'a 考察, p'an ch'a
盤查, shen ch'a 審查,
tiao ch'a 調查

examine a corpse; yen shih 驗尸

examine evidence, examination
of evidence; ch'a cheng 查証

examine for approval, examination
and approval; shen p'i 審批

excesses; kuo huo hsing wei 過
火行為

ex-convict; ch'u yü che 出獄者

execute [a law, etc.], execution;
chih hsing 執行

exempted from punishment; mien
hsing 免刑, mien yü ch'u hsing
免予處刑

expel [from a country, etc.]; ch'ü
chu 驅逐

expel [from office, etc.--an administrative sanction], expulsion;
k'ai ch'u 開除

expenditure; k'ai chih 開支

expense; ching fei 經費

expert medical opinion; i liao chien
ting 醫療鑒定

expert opinion [opinion of an expert
witness]; chien ting 鑒定

expert witness, expert; chien ting jen 鑒定人

expose; chieh fa 揭發

extort, practice extortion; ch'iao cha 敲詐, le so 勒索, so ch'ü 索取

extort by force; ch'iang so 强索

eye-witness; chien cheng jen 見証人, ch'in yen k'an chien te jen 親眼看見的人, tsai ch'ang ch'in yen k'an chien te 在塲親眼看見的

fabricate evidence; wei cheng 偽証, wei tsao cheng chü 偽造証據

facts of a case; an ch'ing 案情

false evidence; wei cheng 偽証

false statement; hsü wei k'ou kung 虛偽口供

family members, members of a family; chia shu 家屬

fault; kuo shih 過失

favoritism, practice favoritism; hsün szu 徇私

felony [used with reference to U.S. crime statistics]; chung tsui 重罪

fight (n.), fight (v.); ou ta 毆打, ou tou 毆斗, szu ta 撕打, ta chia 打架, tou ou 斗毆

finance, financial; chin jung 金融

fine (n.), fine (v.); fa chin 罰金, fa k'uan 罰欵

fingerprint; chih wen 指紋

fire prevention; hsiao fang 消防

fix punishment; ting hsing 定刑

food ration coupon; liang p'iao 糧票

footprint; chiao yin 脚印, tsu chi 足迹

forbid; fei chih 廢止

force a person to commit suicide; pi szu jen 逼死人

forced to commit suicide; ch'iang p'o tzu sha 强迫自殺

forge a check; wei tsao chih p'iao 偽造支票

foster relationship [in child rearing]; fu yang kuan hsi 扶養關係

fraud, fraudulent; cha p'ien 詐騙

free evaluation of the evidence; tzu yu hsin cheng 自由心証

freedom; tzu yu 自由

freedom of assembly; chi hui tzu yu 集會自由

freedom of association; chieh she tzu yu 結社自由

freedom of correspondence; t'ung hsin tzu yu 通信自由, t'ung hsün tzu yu 通訊自由

freedom of demonstration; shih wei tzu yu 示威自由

freedom of movement of one's household; ch'ien hsi tzu yu 遷徙自由, ch'ien i tzu yu 遷移自由

freedom of procession; yu hsing tzu yu 遊行自由

freedom of publication; ch'u pan tzu
yu 出版自由

freedom of religious belief; tsung
chiao hsin yang tzu yu 宗教
信仰自由

freedom of [choice of] residence; chü
chu tzu yu 居住自由

freedom of speech; yen lun tzu yu
言論自由

fruits of crime; fan tsui so te chih wu
犯罪所得之物

fugitive; t'ung ch'i tsai t'ao te
通緝在逃的

function [official]; chih neng 職能

fund-raising, raise funds;
ch'ou k'uan 籌款

funds; fei hsiang 費項

funds to cover the maintenance expenses of family members; chia shu
shan yang fei 家屬贍養費

gamble, gambling; tu po 賭博

gamble in groups; chü tu 聚賭

gang; chieh huo 結伙

gang fighting; chieh huo ta chia
結伙打架

general amnesty; ta she 大赦

general protection; i pan yü fang
一般預防

general rules; t'ung tse 通則

genuinely enforceable; ch'ieh shih k'o
hsing te 切實可行的

give to another for care; chi yang
寄養

go insane; ching shen ts'o luan
精神錯亂

government; cheng fu 政府

Government Administration Council;
cheng wu yüan 政務院

government order; cheng ling
政令

grain levy; cheng liang 徵糧

guarantee (n.), guarantee (v.);
pao chang 保障, pao cheng
保証

guarantee money; pao cheng chin
保証金

guarantor; pao cheng jen 保証人,
pao jen 保人

guard (v.); chieh pei 戒備, ching
chieh 警戒, ching wei 警衛

guardian; chien hu jen 監護人

guideline; fang chen 方針

guilt, guilty; tsui hsing 罪行,
yu tsui 有罪

habitual loafer; i kuan yu shou hao
hsien 一慣游手好閒

habitual offender; kuan fan 慣犯

habitual robber; kuan tao 慣盜

habitual thief; kuan ch'ieh 慣竊

handle according to law; fa pan
法辦

handle a case; pan an 辦案

handwriting; pi chi 筆迹

harbor [a criminal etc.]; wo ts'ang
窩藏, yin ts'ang 隱藏

harbor resentment; hsia hsien

挾嫌

harm; wei hai 危害

have sexual relations with a woman

  secretly engaged in prostitution;

  chien su an ch'ang 奸宿暗娼

head of a family; chia chang 家長

hear [a case], hearing; shen li

審理

high people's court; kao chi jen min

  fa yüan 高級人民法院

hit; ta 打

hold [in confinement]; chien kuan

監管

hold in custody; kuan ya 關押

homicide; sha jen 殺人

homicide case; sha jen an

殺人案

hoodlum; a fei 阿飛

hooligan; liu mang 流氓

hostile element; ti tui fen tzu

敵對分子

house of discipline; kuan chiao so

管教所

household registration [lit.,

  "household"]; hu k'ou 戶口

household registration booklet;

  hu k'ou pen 戶口本

identify; chih jen 指認

idleness [used in Republic of China's

  Law for the Punishment of Police

  Offenses]; lan to 懶惰

ignore a summons; k'ang ch'uan

  pu tao 抗傳不到

illegal appropriation; ch'in chan

侵占

illegally obtained goods; tsang wu

贓物

illegally obtained money; tsang

  k'uan 贓款

illicit sexual relations; pu cheng

  tang te nan nü kuan hsi 不正

當的男女關係

impersonate; ting t'i 頂替

impose [a fine, etc.]; ch'u i 處

以 , k'o ch'u 科處

imprisoned; tso pan fang 坐班房

imprisonment; t'u hsing 徒刑

imprisonment for a fixed term;

  yu ch'i t'u hsing 有期徒刑

improper act; pu cheng tang hsing

  wei 不正當行為

inalienable; pu k'o fen li 不可

分離

incarcerate, incarceration; chü chin

拘禁

incite, incitement; chiao so 教唆,

  fa tung 發動, shan huo 煽惑,

  shan tung 煽動, so shih 唆使,

  so yin 唆引, ts'e tung 策動

incorrigible; hu o pu ch'üan

怙惡不悛

increase in severity, increased

  severity; chia chung 加重

indirect evidence; chien chieh cheng chü 間接証據

infiltrate; ch'ien ju 潛入

infliction of bodily injury; shang 傷, shang hai 傷害

informal discussion meeting; tso t'an hui 座談會

infringe; ch'in fan 侵犯

infringe the interests of the masses of people; ch'in fan jen min ch'ün chung li i 侵犯人民群眾利益

inherit; chi ch'eng 繼承

initiate prosecution; ch'i su 起訴, t'i ch'i kung su 提起公訴

injure; shang 傷, shang hai 傷害

injured as a result of being beaten up; pei ta ch'eng shang 被打成傷

injury; sun shang 損傷

innocent, not guilty, not a crime; wu tsui 無罪

inquire, inquiry; kuo wen 過問

inspect, inspection; chien ch'a 檢查, shih ch'a 視察

instruction; chih shih 指示

instrument of crime; fan tsui kung chü 犯罪工具

instrument of restraint; chieh chü 戒具

insulting and cursing others; ju ma t'a jen 辱罵他人

insurrection; pien t'ien 變天,

p'an pien 叛變

intelligence; ch'ing pao 情報

intentional homicide; yu i sha jen 有意殺人

intentionally misapply the law; wang fa 枉法

interfere, interference; fang hai 妨害

intermediate people's court; chung chi jen min fa yüan 中級人民法院

interrogate, interrogation; hsün wen 訊問, shen hsün 審訊

intoxication; chiu tsui 酒醉

investigate, investigation; chen ch'a 偵查, chien ch'a 檢查, chui chiu 追究, chui ch'a 追查, ch'a chiu 查究, mo ti 摸底, tiao ch'a 調查

investigate and solve; ch'a p'o 查破

investigator; chen ch'a yüan 偵察員

inviolable; pu shou ch'in fan 不受侵犯

irresistible cause; pu neng k'ang chü te yüan yin 不能抗拒的原因

irresistible influence; pu k'o k'ang li te ying hsiang 不可抗力的影響

issue [an order, etc.]; fa pu 發佈

itemized account; chang mu 帳目

joint offender; kung fan 共犯

judge (n.); fa kuan 法官, shen p'an yüan 審判員, t'ui shih 推事

judge (v.), judgment, make a judgment; p'an chüeh 判決, p'an tuan 判斷, ts'ai p'an 裁判

judgment [in writing], written judgment; p'an chüeh shu 判決書

judgment which erroneously convicts an innocent person; ts'o p'an 錯判

judgment which permits evasion of justice; tsung p'an 縱判

judgment which unjustifiably acquits a criminal; lou p'an 漏判

judicial; szu fa 司法

judicial sections and divisions; szu fa k'o ch'u 司法科處

jurisdiction; kuan hsia 管轄

jurist; fa hsüeh chia 法學家

juvenile; shao nien 少年

juvenile delinquent; pu liang shao nien 不良少年

juvenile offender; shao nien fan 少年犯

keep in custody; kuan ya 管押

kickback; hui k'ou 回扣

kidnap for ransom; lu jen le shu 擄人勒贖

kill; sha 殺, sha hai 殺害, sha szu 殺死

kill deliberately; hsü i sha szu 蓄意殺死

kill a person, killing; sha jen 殺人

labor bureau; lao tung chü 勞動局

labor service; lao i 勞役

land reform; t'u ti kai ko 土地改革

large character poster; ta tzu pao 大字報

large demerit, give a large demerit; chi ta kuo 記大過

last instance [final adjudication]; chung shen 終審

law; fa 法, fa ling 法令, fa lü 法律

law and discipline; fa chi 法紀

law enforcement; fa lü te shih shih 法律的實施

Law for the Punishment of Police Offenses [Republic of China]; wei ching fa fa 違警罰法

lawful, legal; ho fa 合法

lawful interest; ho fa li i 合法利益

laws and decrees; fa ling 法令

laws and regulations; fa kuei 法規

lawyer; lü shih 律師

Lawyers' Association; lü shih hsieh hui 律師協會

leader of the military units used in an insurrection; shuai tui p'an pien che 率隊叛變者

legal system; fa chih 法制

legality; fa chih 法治

legally effective; fa lü hsiao li 法律效力

legally prescribed; fa ting 法定

legislation; li fa 立法

legitimate; cheng tang 正當

leniently [punish, etc.]; ts'ung k'uan 從寬

Liberation Army [People's]; chieh fang chün 解放軍

license; chih chao 執照

life imprisonment; wu ch'i t'u hsing 無期徒刑

light criminal punishment, light punishment; ch'ing hsing 輕刑

lightly [punish, etc.]; ts'ung ch'ing 從輕

liquidate; su ch'ing 肅清

liquidate counterrevolution; su fan 肅反

litigation; su sung 訴訟

loafer; erh liu tzu 二流子

look for fights and make trouble; hsün hsin tzu shih 尋釁滋事

lose one's standpoint; sang shih li ch'ang 喪失立場

loss; sun shih 損失

major crime; chung tsui 重罪

make light of one's duties; wan hu chih shou 玩忽職守

make trouble; ch'ü nao 取鬧, sheng shih 生事

maliciously false accusation, make a maliciously false accusation; wu hsien 誣陷, wu kao 誣告

marriage; hun yin 婚姻

marry; chieh hun 結婚

mass armed uprising; ch'ih hsieh chü chung p'an luan 持械聚眾叛亂

measure; pan fa 辦法

mediate, mediation, settle through mediation; t'iao chieh 調解

mediation committee; t'iao chieh wei yüan hui 調解委員會

mediator, mediation personnel; t'iao chieh yüan 調解員

mental abnormality; shen ching pu cheng ch'ang 神經不正常

mental illness, mentally ill; ching shen ping 精神病

mentally ill person; ching shen ping jen 精神病人

merit mark, give a merit mark; chi kung 記功

military court; chün shih fa t'ing 軍事法庭

military government committee; chün cheng wei yüan hui 軍政委員會

military service, to do military service; fu ping i 服兵役

military unit; pu tui 部隊

militia, militiaman; min ping 民兵

Ministry of Interior; nei wu pu 內務部

Ministry of Justice; szu fa pu 司法部

Ministry of Public Security; kung an pu 公安部

Ministry of Supervision; chien ch'a pu 監察部

minor [lit., "not an adult"]; wei ch'eng nien jen 未成年人

minor crime; ch'ing wei te fan tsui 輕微的犯罪

minor criminal case; ch'ing wei hsing shih an chien 輕微刑事案件

minor unlawful act; ch'ing wei te wei fa hsing wei 輕微的違法行為

misappropriate, misappropriation; no yung 挪用

miscellaneous public expenses; kung tsa fei 公雜費

misconduct; kuo ts'o 過錯

missing child; mi shih te erh t'ung 迷失的兒童

mistake; ts'o wu 錯誤

mistake of fact; shih shih ts'o wu 事實錯誤

mistreat, mistreatment; nüeh tai 虐待

misuse; lan yung 濫用

misuse one's powers; lan yung chih shou 濫用職守

monetary compensation for labor; lao tung pao ch'ou fei 勞動報酬費

money and property; ch'ien ts'ai 錢財

monogamy; i fu i ch'i 一夫一妻

murder (n.); ku i sha jen tsui 故意殺人罪 , sha jen tsui 殺人罪

murder (v.); hsiung sha 兇殺 mou sha 謀殺, sha hai 殺害 , sha jen 殺人, t'a sha 他殺, yin mou sha jen 陰謀殺人

murderer; hsiung sha fan 兇殺犯 , sha jen fan 殺人犯

murderer-arsonist; sha jen fang huo fan 殺人放火犯

national bourgeoisie; min tsu tzu ch'an chieh chi 民族資產階級

National People's Congress; ch'üan kuo jen min tai piao ta hui 全國人民代表大會

nationalize; shou kuei kuo yu 收歸國有

negligent; kuo shih 過失

negligent homicide; kuo shih chih jen szu wang 過失至人死亡

negligently destroy by fire; shih huo
shao hui 失火燒毀

negotiable instrument; p'iao cheng
票証 , p'iao chü 票據

negotiate; hsieh shang 協商

noncurrent counterrevolution; fei
hsien hsing fan ko ming 非現
行反革命

nonhabitual offender; ou fan 偶犯

not engage in legitimate employment;
pu wu cheng yeh 不務正業

notify, notification, give notification; t'ung chih 通知

obey; fu ts'ung 服從

obey the law; fu fa 服法 , fu ts'ung
fa lü 服從法律

obliged, obligation; i wu 義務

obscene; wei hsieh 猥褻 , yin
hui 淫穢

observe the law, observance of the
law; shou fa 守法 , tsun shou
fa lü 遵守法律

obtain a guarantor; ch'ü pao 取保

obtain a guarantor and serve the
sentence outside of prison;
ch'ü pao chien wai chih hsing
取保監外執行

obtain a guarantor pending trial;
ch'ü pao hou shen 取保候審

obtain by force; tao ch'ü 盜取

obtain by illegal speculation;
t'ao ch'ü 套取

obtain by theft; t'ou te 偷得

obtain unreasonably large profits;
mou ch'ü pao li 牟取暴利

obtain wrongfully [in the name of
another], wrongful receipt;
mao ling 冒領

occupy illegally; ch'in lüeh
侵略

offender; fan 犯, fan jen 犯人,
jen fan 人犯

offender whose case has already
been adjudged; i chüeh fan
已決犯

offender whose case has not been
adjudged; wei chüeh fan
未決犯

offense; tsui 罪

Office of Legal Advisers; fa lü
ku wen ch'u 法律顧問處

officer; jen yüan 人員

officer in charge of the preparatory
investigation[i.e., the public
security organ's interrogator];
yü shen yüan 預審員

officer [judge] in charge of the
preparatory examination;
yü shen yüan 預審員

official document; kung wen 公文

official seal; kung chang 公章

offset guilt by merit; chiang kung
che tsui 將功折罪

old and crude rule; ch'en kuei
lou chü 陳規陋矩

old [KMT] army and government;
chiu chün cheng 舊軍政

on schedule; an ch'i 按期

on-the-spot adjudication, on-the-spot trial; chiu shen 就審

on-the-spot examination; k'an yen 勘驗

on-the-spot investigation; k'an ch'a 勘查

one who commits a crime of corruption; t'an wu fan 貪污犯

one who commits homicide; sha jen fan 殺人犯

one who is fleeing from arrest; pei chui pu te 被追捕的

one who is wanted for arrest; t'ung ch'i tsai an te 通緝在案的

one whose two or more related acts constitute different crimes; ch'ien lien fan 牽連犯

opium crime; yen tu tsui 烟毒罪

opium offender; yen fan 烟犯, yen tu fan 烟毒犯

opium trade; fan tu 販毒

oppose; fan tui 反對

oppress, oppression; ya chih 壓制, ya p'o 壓迫

order (n.), order (v.); ming 命, ming ling 命令, p'an ling 判令, tse ling 責令, ts'ai ting 裁定

order to repent; tse ling hui kuo 責令悔過

order to stop; chih chih 制止

organ of self-government; tzu chih chi kuan 自治機關

organ which deliberates on punishment; i ch'u chi kuan 議處機關

organize, organization; tsu chih 組織

original judgment; yüan p'an 原判

original owner; yüan chu 原主

originate from [in the sense "to be born of"], origin; ch'u shen 出身

overthrow; t'ui fan 推翻

ownership, ownership system; so yu chih 所有制

ownership of the means of production; sheng ch'an tzu liao so yu chih 生產資料所有制

pact; kung yüeh 公約

participation in a killing; ts'an yü sha jen 參與殺人

party [to a case], both parties; tang shih jen 當事人, shuang fang tang shih jen 雙方當事人

Party committee; tang wei 黨委

pass [an act, etc.]; t'ung kuo 通過

patriotic pact; ai kuo kung yüeh 愛國公約

patrolman [lit., "household registration policeman"]; hu chi ching 戶籍警

pay [a fine, etc.]; chiao na 交納

pay back [a debt]; ch'ing ch'ang 清償, ch'ing li ch'ang huan 清理償還

pay unpaid tax; pu shui 補税

payment for child-care expense;
fu yü fei 撫育費

peasant class; nung min chieh chi
農民階級

penal system; hsing fa t'i hsi
刑罰體系

penalize, penalty; ch'eng chu 懲處

pending judgment; p'an chüeh hai wei
ch'üeh ting 判決還未確定

pending trial; hou shen 候審

people's commune; jen min kung she
人民公社

people's congress; jen min tai piao
ta hui 人民代表大會

people's council; jen min wei yüan hui
人民委員會

People's Government; jen min cheng
fu 人民政府

People's Republic of China; chung
hua jen min kung ho kuo 中華人
民共和國

period of limitation for prosecution;
chui su shih hsiao te ch'i chien
追訴時效的期間

perjury; wei cheng tsui 偽証罪

persecute, persecution; p'o hai
迫害

person who prosecutes as a private
individual; tzu su jen 自訴人

person whose whereabouts is unknown;
hsia lo pu ming te jen 下落不
明的人

personnel; jen yüan 人員

persuade, persuasion; ch'üan t'an
勸談, shuo ch'üan 説勸,
shuo fu 説服

persuasion meeting; shuo fu hui
説服會

petition, petition for review (n.),
petition for review (v.); shen su
申訴

petty bourgeoisie; hsiao tzu ch'an
chieh chi 小資産階級

petty thief; hsiao t'ou 小偷

place where shelter is provided;
shou jung so 收容所

plan (v.); ch'i t'u 企圖

pleading; su chuang 訴狀

plot; kuei chi 詭計, ts'e mou
策謀 yin mou 陰謀

police; ching ch'a 警察

police bureau; ching ch'a chü
警察局

policy; cheng ts'e 政策

policy of confession; chiao tai
cheng ts'e 交待政策

political appearance; cheng chih
mien mao 政治面貌

Political Consultative Conference;
cheng chih hsieh shang hui i,
政治協商會議
cheng hsieh 政協

political-legal Party group; cheng
fa tang tsu 政法黨組

political power; cheng ch'üan 政權

political right; cheng chih ch'üan li
政治權利

position [official], post; chih wei
職位

power; ch'üan li 權力

power [official]; chih ch'üan 職權

power of adjudication; shen p'an
ch'üan 審判權

preliminary arrest; yü hsien tai pu
預先逮捕

preparatory examination; yü shen
預審

preparatory examination session; yü
shen t'ing 預審庭

preparatory investigation; yü shen
預審

preparatory investigation record;
yü shen pi lu 預審筆錄

preparatory investigation section;
yü shen k'o 預審科

prescribe; kuei ting 規定

prescribed by law; fa ting 法定

president of a court; fa yüan chang
法院長

presiding judge; shen p'an chang
審判長

presidium; chu hsi t'uan 主席團

presumption of innocence; wu tsui
t'ui ting lun 無罪推定論

prevent arson; fang huo 防火

prevent banditry; fang fei 防匪

prevent espionage; fang tieh 防諜

prevent [the activities of] secret
agents; fang t'e 防特

prevent theft; fang tao 防盜

prevent treason; fang chien 防奸

principal element; shou yao fen tzu
首要分子

principal offender; chu fan 主犯

principal punishment; chu hsing
主刑

principle of officiality; chih ch'üan
yüan tse 職權原則

prison; chien 監, chien so 監所,
chien yü 監獄

prison break; yüeh yü 越獄

prison cell; chien fang 監房

prison raid; chieh yü 劫獄

prison rule; chien kuei 監規

probation [within the CCP], place
on probation [within the CCP];
liu tang ch'a k'an 留黨察看

probationary expulsion [from office,
etc.]; k'ai ch'u liu yung ch'a k'an
開除留用察看

procedure; ch'eng hsü 程序,
shou hsü 手續

proclaim; hsüan pu 宣佈

procuracy; chien ch'a yüan
檢察院

procurator; chien ch'a kuan 檢察
官, chien ch'a yüan 檢察員

procuratorial committee; chien ch'a
wei yüan hui 檢察委員會

procuratorial office; chien ch'a shu 檢查署

procuratorial power; chien ch'a ch'üan 檢察權

profit; li jun 利潤

profit-making; ch'ü li 取利

prohibit, prohibited; chin chih 禁止

proletariat; wu ch'an chieh chi 無產階級

promulgate; kung pu 公布, pan hsing 頒行, pan pu 頒布

pronounce; hsüan kao 宣告

pronounce judgment, pronouncement of judgment; hsüan p'an 宣判

pronounce sentence, pronouncement of sentence; hsüan p'an 宣判

property; ts'ai ch'an 財產, ts'ai wu 財物

property status; ts'ai ch'an chuang k'uang 財產狀況

prosecute, prosecution; chui su 追訴, kung su 公訴

prosecutor, public prosecutor; kung su jen 公訴人

prostitute; ch'ang chi 娼妓

protect; pao hu 保護

protest (n.), protest (v.); k'ang i 抗議

prove, proof, probative; cheng ming 証明, cheng shih 証實

provide shelter; shou jung 收容

province; sheng 省

provision; kuei ting 規定, t'iao wen 條文

provoke, provocation; t'iao po 挑撥

provoke dissension; t'iao po li chien 挑撥離間

public employee; kung chih jen yüan 公職人員

public morality; kung kung tao te 公共道德

public order; kung kung chih hsü 公共秩序

public security; kung an 公安

public security bureau; kung an chü 公安局

public security department; kung an t'ing 公安廳

public security division; kung an ch'u 公安處

public security household registration list section; kung an hu chi tuan 公安戶籍段

public security special agent; kung an t'e p'ai yüan 公安特派員

public security station; kung an p'ai ch'u so 公安派出所, p'ai ch'u so 派出所

public trial session; kung p'an t'ing 公判庭

punish; chih tsui 治罪, ch'eng chih 懲治, ch'eng ch'u 懲處, ch'eng fa 懲罰, ch'eng pan 懲辦, ch'u ch'u 處, ch'u fa 處罰, ch'u hsing 處刑, lun ch'u 論處

punishment; hsing fa 刑罰

punitive restraint, restrain punitively;
chih ts'ai 制裁

purchase stolen property; shou mai
tsang wu 收買贓物

pursue [in the sense of "prosecute"];
chui chiu 追究

pursue for criminal responsibility;
chui chiu hsing shih tse jen
追究刑事責任

pursue in order to arrest; chui pu
追捕

put into effect on an experimental
basis; shih hsing 試行

put up for rent; ch'u tsu 出租

put up for sale; ch'u shou 出售

question (v.); chih wen 質問 , hsün
wen 訊問, shen hsün 審訊,
shen wen 審問

rank; chi pieh 級別

rape; ch'iang chien 強奸

rape-murder; ch'iang chien sha jen
強奸殺人

reactionary, reactionary element;
fan tung fen tzu 反動分子

readjudicate, readjudication; keng
shen 更審, tsai shen 再審

real evidence; wu cheng 物証

rebuttal evidence; fan cheng 反証

recall and replace [an official, etc.];
ch'e huan 撤換

recant; fan kung 翻供

receive [a case, etc.]; shou li 受理

recidivist; lei fan 累犯

recognize; ch'eng jen 承認

recommendation to arrest; li chieh
tai pu 理結逮捕

reconciliation agreement; t'iao chieh
hsieh i 調解協議

reconsider, reconsideration; fu i
覆議

record (n.), record (v.); chi lu
記錄

recover [stolen property, etc.];
chui chiao 追繳

recover sobriety; chiu hsing 酒醒

rectification movement; cheng feng
yün tung 整風運動

redeem oneself from punishment;
shu hsing 贖刑

reduce sentence, reduction of
sentence; chien hsing 減刑

reexamine, reexamination, reinvestigate, reinvestigation;
fu ch'a 覆查

reform-education; kai tsao chiao yü
改造教育

reform oneself, self-reform; tzu hsin
自新

reform through education; chiao yü
kai tsao 教育改造

reform through labor; lao tung kai
tsao 勞動改造

reform through labor camp; lao
tung kai tsao ch'ang 勞動改
造場

reform through labor service; lao i

kai tsao 勞役改造

reform through labor unit; lao tung

kai tsao tui 勞動改造隊

regime; cheng ch'üan 政權

regulate, regulation; kuan li 管理

regulation; chang 章, chang ch'eng

章程, kuei ting 規定

rehabilitation through labor; lao tung

chiao yang 勞動教養

release (n.), release (v.); shih fang

釋放

release early, early release; t'i

ch'ien shih fang 提前釋放

remit [punishment]; mien ch'u

免除

remove from office [or position],

removal from office; ch'e chih 撤

職, ch'e hsiao chih wu 撤銷

職務

reorganization; cheng tun 整頓

repeated education fails to change;

lü chiao pu kai 屢教不改

repeated punishment fails to change;

lü ching ch'u fa pu kai 屢經處

罰不改

repent, repentance; hui kuo 悔過

repent and reform, repentance and

reform; hui kai 悔改

replace in a regular election; kai

hsüan 改選

replace in a special election;

pu hsüan 補選

report (n.), report (v.), make a

report; pao kao 報告

repress; ch'ü ti 取締

reseize, reseizure; tao suan 倒算

resentence; kai p'an 改判

reserve fund; ch'u pei chin

儲備金

residence; chu ch'u 住處

residential surveillance; chien shih

chü chu 監視居住

residents' committee; chü min wei

yüan hui 居民委員會

resist, resistance, offer resistance;

fan k'ang 反抗, wei k'ang

違抗

resist arrest; k'ang chü tai pu

抗拒逮捕

resolution; chüeh i 決議

respondent [appellee]; pei shang su

jen 被上訴人

responsibility [official]; chih tse

職責

restoration [of an old regime];

fu pi 復辟

restoration of rights; fu ch'üan

復權

restrain; yüeh shu 約束

retaliate, retaliation; pao fu 報復

retroactivity; su chi hsiao li 溯及

效力, su chi li 溯及力

retry, retrial; keng shen 更審,

tsai shen 再審

return [a stolen article, etc.]; chui

huan 追還

reverse the decision of a case;
fan an 翻案

review (n.), review (v.); fu ho
覆核

revolution; ko ming 革命

reward; chiang li 獎勵

right; ch'üan 權, ch'üan li 權利

right to speak out; fa piao yen lun
ch'üan 發表言論權, fa yen
ch'üan 發言權

righteously revolt, righteous
revolt; ch'i i 起義

rights and interests; ch'üan i 權益

rights of citizens, rights as citizens;
kung ch'üan 公權, kung min
ch'üan li 公民權利

rights of the person; jen ch'üan
人權, jen shen ch'üan li
人身權利

ringleader; chu mou che 主謀者

riot (n.), riot (v.), rioting; pao
luan 暴亂, pao tung 暴動

rob, robbery; ch'iang chieh 搶劫,
hsing ch'iang 行搶, tsa ch'iang
砸搶

robbery on the roads; lu chieh
路劫

rotten and decadent; fu hua to luo
腐化墮落

rule (n.); kuei chang 規章, kuei
ch'eng 規程, kuei tse 規則

rule (n.), rule (v.); t'ung chih
統治

rule by law; fa chih 法治

sabotage; p'o huai 破壞

sanction; ch'u fen 處分

sane; ching shen cheng ch'ang
精神正常

scene [of an incident, etc.]; hsien
ch'ang 現場

scene of a crime; hsien ch'ang 現
場, hsing shih an chien te hsien
ch'ang 刑事案件的現場

scrutiny; shen i 審議

seal [indicating that the place to
which the seal is attached has
been closed]; feng yin 封印

search (n.), search (v.); sou ch'a
搜查

search warrant; sou ch'a cheng
搜查証

secondary punishment; ts'ung hsing
從刑

secret agent; t'e wu 特務

secretary-general; mi shu chang
秘書長

secretary of a Party branch; tang chih
shu 黨支書

secretly cross the borders of the
state; t'ou yüeh kuo ching
偷越國境

security [bond, note, etc.]; cheng
ch'üan 証券

security [in the sense of "safety"];
an ch'üan 安全, chih an 治安

security adjustment committee;

chih an t'iao ch'u wei yüan hui
治安調處委員會
security administration; chih an kuan
li 治安管理
security administration punishment;
chih an kuan li ch'u fa
治安管理處罰
security defense committee; chih an
pao wei wei yüan hui 治安保衛
委員會, chih pao hui 治保會
security detention; chih an chü liu
治安拘留
security detention warrant; chih an
chü liu cheng 治安拘留証
security of society; she hui chih an
社會治安
security section [of public security
bureau]; chih an k'o 治安科
seduce, seduction; yu chien 誘奸
seize and take to [the authorities,
etc.]; niu sung 扭送
seize forcibly; ch'iang to 搶奪
seizure; chü t'i 拘提
self-criticism; tzu wo p'i p'ing
自我批評
self-education; tzu wo chiao yü
自我教育
self-examination; chien t'ao 檢討
sentence (n.), sentence (v.), give a
sentence; ch'u 處, p'an 判, p'an
ch'u 判處, p'an hsing 判刑
sentence lightly; ch'ing p'an 輕判
sentence to criminal punishment;

p'an hsing 判刑
sentence to imprisonment; p'an
t'u hsing 判徒刑
sentence to imprisonment but pronounce the sentence suspended,
give a suspended sentence of
imprisonment; p'an t'u hsing
hsüan kao huan hsing 判徒
刑宣告緩刑
serve concurrently; chien jen
兼任
serve one's sentence; fu hsing
服刑
serve one's sentence in prison;
tsai chien fu hsing 在監服刑
serve the term of imprisonment; fu
hsing hsing ch'i 服刑刑期
settler; i min 移民
severely; ts'ung chung 從重
sexual intercourse; hsing hsing wei
性行為
shift the blame to another person;
chia huo yü jen 嫁禍于人
smuggle, smuggling; tsou szu
走私
solicit [funds]; ch'ou mu 籌募
solicit donations; mu chüan 募捐
solitary confinement [after sentence];
tan tu chien chin 單獨監禁
solitary confinement [before
sentence]; tan tu chi ya 單獨
羈押
solve a case; p'o an 破案,

p'o huo an chien 破獲案件

sovereignty; chu ch'üan 主權

speak reason struggle; shuo li tou cheng 說理鬥爭

special amnesty; t'e she 特赦

special compensatory allowance; yu fu 優撫

special district; chuan ch'ü 專區

special prevention; t'e shu yü fang 特殊預防

special privilege; t'e ch'üan 特權

speculation; tao pa 倒把, t'ou chi 投機, t'ou chi tao pa 投機倒把

speeding [in a vehicle]; ch'ao su 超速

spouse; p'ei ou 配偶

spread germs; san po ping chün 散播病菌

spread poison; t'ou fang tu wu 投放毒物, t'ou tu 投毒

spread rumors; san pu yao yen 散佈謠言, tsao yao 造謠

spy (n.), spying; chien tieh 間諜, chen tieh 偵諜

standard rule; chun tse 准則

standing committee; ch'ang wei hui 常委會, ch'ang wu wei yüan hui 常務委員會

state; kuo chia 國家

State Council; kuo wu yüan 國務院

state secret; kuo chia chi mi 國家機密

state security; kuo chia chih an 國家治安

stateless person; wu kuo chi jen 無國籍人

statement; k'ou kung 口供, kung tz'u 供詞

statement of confession; t'an pai shu 坦白書

statement of guarantee; pao cheng shu 保証書

statement of repentance; hui kuo shu 悔過書

status [social]; ch'eng fen 成份

status identification booklet; shen fen pu 身分簿

stay of execution; yen ch'i chih hsing 延期執行

stay of execution of punishment; hsing fa te yen ch'i chih hsing 刑罰的延期執行

steal; ch'ieh ch'ü 竊取, tao ch'ieh 盜竊, t'ou ch'ieh 偷竊, t'ou tao 偷盜

steal and use; ch'ieh yung 竊用, t'ou yung 偷用

stir up dissension; po nung shih fei 撥弄是非

stockholder; ku tung 股東

strangle; chiao shou 絞首

street office; chieh tao pan shih ch'u 街道辦事處

strike [a person, etc.]; ou ta 毆打

strike [with a vehicle] and injure;
ch'uang shang 撞傷

strike a case from the record;
chu hsiao an chien 注消案件

struggle (n.), struggle (v.);
tou cheng 鬥爭

struggle meeting; tou cheng hui
鬥爭會

subagency; p'ai ch'u chi kuan
派出機關

subbureau; fen chü 分局

submit to the law; fu fa 服法

subsidy for living expenses; sheng
huo pu chu fei 生活補助費

subvert, subversion; tien fu 顛覆

suicide; tzu sha 自殺

summon; ch'uan 傳, ch'uan huan
傳喚

summon and interrogate; ch'uan wen
傳問

summons; ch'uan huan cheng
傳喚証

supervise, supervision; chien tu
監督

supervise labor, supervised labor;
chien tu lao tung 監督勞動

supervise production, supervised
production; chien tu sheng ch'an
監督生產

Supervision Commission [of the
CCP]; chien ch'a wei yüan hui
監察委員會

supplementary civil compensation;
fu tai min shih p'ei ch'ang
附帶民事賠償

supplementary investigation; pu
ch'ung chen ch'a 補充偵查,
pu ch'ung chien ch'a 補充
檢察

supplementary punishment; fu chia
hsing 附加刑

support (children, etc.); fu yang
扶養

suppress, suppression; chen ya 鎮
壓, ch'eng chih 懲治, ya
chih 壓制

suppress counterrevolution,
suppression of counterrevolution;
chen fan 鎮反

suppress criticism; ya chih p'i p'ing
壓制批評

Supreme People's Court; tsui kao
jen min fa yüan 最高人民法院

surprise attack interrogation; t'u
chi hsün wen 突擊訊問

surrender voluntarily, voluntary
surrender; t'ou an 投案, tzu
shou 自首, tzu shou t'ou an
自首投案

surveillance; chien shih 監視

survivor benefits; fu hsü chin
撫恤金

suspect; hsien i fen tzu 嫌疑
分子, hsien i jen 嫌疑人

suspend from office; t'ing chih

chih wu 停止職務

suspend sentence, suspension of
sentence, suspended sentence,
suspension; huan ch'i 緩期,
huan hsing 緩刑

suspend temporarily; chan huan
暫緩

suspended death [sentence]; szu huan
死緩

swindle; cha p'ien 詐騙 chao yao
ch'uang p'ien 招搖撞騙,
ch'i cha 欺詐, kuai p'ien 拐騙

swindler; cha p'ien fan 詐騙犯
p'ien tzu 騙子

system of the court of second
instance as the court of last
instance; liang shen chung shen
chih 兩審終審制

take away by force; chieh to 刼奪

take an offender into custody; ya fan
押犯

take by force; pa chan 霸占

take into custody; k'ou ya 扣押,
sung ya 送押

take the lead in raising an uproar;
tai t'ou ch'i hung 帶頭起哄

tax-exemption slip; mien shui tan
免稅單

tax laws and regulations; shui wu fa
kuei 稅務法規

tax levy; cheng shui 徵稅

tempt, temptation; yin yu 引誘,
yu huo 誘惑

term of imprisonment, term of
punishment; hsing ch'i 刑期

term of office; jen ch'i 任期

term of punishment has expired;
hsing man 刑滿

territory; ling yü 領域

terror, terrorism; k'ung pu 恐怖

testify; tso cheng 作証

testimony; cheng yen 証言

theft; ch'ieh ch'ü 竊取, ch'ieh tao
竊盜 , hsing ch'ieh 行竊,
tao ch'ieh 盜竊 , t'ou ch'ieh
偷竊, t'ou tao 偷盜

theft and use; ch'ieh yung 竊用,
t'ou yung 偷用

theory of favoring the defendant;
yu li pei kao lun 有利被告論

thief; tao ch'ieh fan 盜竊犯

thought reform; szu hsiang kai tsao
思想改造

threaten, threat; wei hsieh 威脅

to each according to his labor;
an lao ch'ü ch'ou 按勞取酬

trace (v.); chui ch'a 追查

trace [of a crime, etc.]; hen chi
痕迹

trace of a crime; tsui chi 罪跡

traffic accident; chiao t'ung shih ku
交通事故

traffic regulation [in the sense of
"regulation of traffic"]; chiao
t'ung kuan li 交通管理

traffic violation; chiao t'ung wei chang
交通違章

692

traitor; mai kuo tsei 賣國賊

transaction; chiao i 交易

transform unlawfully; ts'uan kai 篡改

treason; p'an kuo 叛國

treason [to China]; han chien tsui 漢奸罪

tribunal; fa t'ing 法庭

tribunal for the protection of economic construction; ching chi chien she pao hu t'ing 經濟建設保護庭

try [a defendant], trial; shen p'an 審判

type of crime, type of offense; tsui ming 罪名

unauthorized reduction; k'o k'ou 尅扣

undermine; p'o huai 破壞

understand the nature of [one's acts, etc.]; pien jen 辨認

undistricted city; pu she ch'ü te shih 不設區的市

unfit to discharge one's duties; pu ch'eng chih 不稱職

unified purchasing and marketing [state]; t'ung kou t'ung hsiao 統購統銷

unjust enrichment; pu tang te li 不當得利

unjust judgment; wang p'an 枉判

unlawful; fan fa 犯法, fei fa 非法,

pu fa 不法, wei fa 違法

unlawful gain; wei fa so te 違法所得

unlawful operation of a business; pu fa ching ying 不法經營

uprising; p'an luan 叛亂

usurp; ch'ieh chü 竊據

utilize public resources for private gain; chia kung chi szu 假公濟私

vagrancy [used in Republic of China's Law for the Punishment of Police Offenses]; yu tang 游蕩

vagrant; yu min 游民

vehicular operation; ch'e liang hsing shih 車輛行駛

verify, verification; cheng shih 証實, yin cheng 印証

vice-president of a court; fa yüan fu yüan chang 法院副院長

viciously beat to death; tu ta chih szu 毒打致死

victim; pei hai jen 被害人

village public security representative; ts'un kung an yüan 村公安員

violate, in violation of; ch'u fan 觸犯, wei fan 違反, wei pei 違背

violate democratic centralism; wei fan min chu chi chung chih 違反民主集中制

violate the law, violation of law;
i shen shih fa 以身試法,
wei fa 違法

violate the law and be derelict in
one's duty; wei fa shih chih
違法失職

violate sexually; chien yin 奸淫

violator; wei chang che 違章者

violence; pao hsing 暴行

violent resistance; pao li k'ang chü
暴力抗拒

vote; hsüan chü 選舉

war criminal; chan cheng tsui fan
戰爭罪犯

warden; chien yü chang 監獄長

warn, warning; ching chieh 警戒,
ching kao 警告

warrant for commitment to custody;
ya p'iao 押票

waste state assets; lang fei kuo chia
tzu ts'ai 浪費國家資財

watch [in the sense of "keep under
surveillance"]; chien shih 監視

weapon used to commit a deadly
act; hsiung ch'i 兇器

widow; kua fu 寡婦

will [for disposition of property
at death]; i chu 遺囑

willful; jen i 任意

withdraw [from a case, etc.];
hui pi 迴避

witness; cheng jen 証人, jen
cheng 人証

worker class; kung jen chieh chi
工人階級

workers' union; kung hui 工會

wound (v.); shang 傷, shang hai
傷害, ta shang 打傷

wound with a knife; tao shang
刀傷

written decision; ts'ai chüeh shu
裁決書

written order; ts'ai ting shu
裁定書

written order for execution [of
sentence]; chih hsing shu
執行書

written petition for review; shen
su shu 申訴書

wrong, wrongdoing, wrongful;
ts'o wu 錯誤

wrong (v.), be wronged; yüan
wang 冤枉

Youth League; ch'ing nien t'uan
青年團

# Index

## DATE DUE